Advance Praise for *Head First PMP*

"This looks like too much fun to be a PMP study guide! Behind the quirky humor and nutty graphics lies an excellent explanation of the project management processes. Not only will this book make it easier to pass the exam, you'll learn a lot of good stuff to use on the job too."

— Carol Steuer, PMP
***PMBOK® Guide*, Third Edition Leadership Team**

"This is the best thing to happen to PMP since, well, ever. You'll laugh, learn, pass the exam, and become a better project manager all at the same time."

— Scott Berkun, author of *The Art of Project Management* and *The Myths of Innovation*

"Original, fresh, and fun... this is truly the perfect study companion for anyone aiming for PMP certification"

— Teresa Simmermacher, PMP and Project Manager at Avanade

I love this format! Head First PMP covers everything you need to know to pass your PMP exam. The sound-bite format combined with the whimsical images turns a dry subject into entertainment. The organization starts with the basics then drills into the details. The in-depth coverage of complex topics like Earned Value and Quality Control are presented in an easy to understand format with descriptions, pictures, and examples. This book will not only help you pass the PMP, it should be used as an daily reference for practicing project managers. I sure wish I had this when I was studying for the exam."

— Mike Jenkins, PMP, MBA

"I think that under the fonts and formalized goofiness, the book has a good heart (intending to cover basic principles in an honest way rather than just to pass the test). Head First PMP attempts to educate potential project managers instead of being a mere "how to pass the PMP exam" book filled with test taking tips. This is truly something which sets it apart from the other PMP certification exam books."

— Jack Dahlgren, Project Management Consultant

"Head First PMP is a great tool to help make sense of the Project Management Body of Knowledge for the everyday Project Manager."

—Mark Poinelli, PMP

Praise for other *HEAD FIRST* books

"This book's admirable clarity, humor and substantial doses of clever make it the sort of book that helps even non-programmers think well about problem-solving."

— Cory Doctorow, co-editor of Boing Boing
Author, *Down and Out in the Magic Kingdom*
and *Someone Comes to Town, Someone Leaves Town*

"I just finished reading HF OOA&D and I loved it! The thing I liked most about this book was its focus on why we do OOA&D—to write great software!"

— Kyle Brown, Distinguished Engineer, IBM

"One of the funniest and smartest books on software design I've ever read."

— Aaron LaBerge, VP Technology, ESPN.com

"If you thought Ajax was rocket science, this book is for you. Head Rush Ajax puts dynamic, compelling experiences within reach for every web developer."

—Jesse James Garrett, Adaptive Path

"I received the book yesterday and started to read it...and I couldn't stop. This is definitely très 'cool.' It is fun, but they cover a lot of ground and they are right to the point. I'm really impressed."

— Erich Gamma, IBM Distinguished Engineer, and co-author of Design Patterns

"*Head First Design Patterns* managed to mix fun, belly-laughs, insight, technical depth and great practical advice in one entertaining and thought provoking read. Whether you are new to design patterns, or have been using them for years, you are sure to get something from visiting Objectville."

— Richard Helm, co-author of *Design Patterns*

I *heart* *Head First HTML with CSS & XHTML*—it teaches you everything you need to learn in a 'fun coated' format!"

— Sally Applin, UI Designer and Fine Artist, *http://sally.com*

Praise for the *Head First* Approach

"It's fast, irreverant, fun, and engaging. Be careful—you might actually learn something!"

— Ken Arnold, former Senior Engineer at Sun Microsystems
Co-author (with James Gosling of Java),
The Java Programming Language

"I feel like a thousand pounds of books have just been lifted off of my head."

— Ward Cunningham, inventor of the Wiki
and founder of the Hillside Group

"This book is close to perfect, because of the way it combines expertise and readability. It speaks with authority and it reads beautifully."

— David Gelernter, Professor of Computer Science, Yale University

"Just the right tone for the geeked-out, casual-cool guru coder in all of us. The right reference for practical development strategies--gets my brain going without having to slog through a bunch of tired, stale professor-speak."

— Travis Kalanick, Founder of Scour and Red Swoosh Member of the MIT TR100

"The combination of humour, pictures, asides, sidebars, and redundancy with a logical approach to introducing the basic tags and substantial examples of how to use them will hopefully have the readers hooked in such a way that they don't even realize they are learning because they are having so much fun."

— Stephen Chapman, Fellgall.com

"This stuff is brain candy; I can't get enough of it."

— Pauline McNamara, Center for New Technologies and Education, Fribourg University, Switzerland

"I laughed, I cried, it moved me."

— Daniel Steinberg, Editor-in-Chief, java.net

"I literally love this book. In fact, I kissed this book in front of my wife."

— Satish Kumar

Other related books from O'Reilly

Applied Software Project Management

Art of Project Management

Practical Development Environments

Process Improvement Essentials

Time Management for System Administrators

How to Keep Your Boss From Sinking Your Project (Digital Short Cut)

Other books in O'Reilly's *Head First* series

Head First Object-Oriented Analysis and Design (OOA&D)

Head Rush Ajax

Head First HTML with CSS and XHTML

Head First Design Patterns

Head First Servlets and JSP

Head First EJB

Head First SQL (2007)

Head First Algebra (2007)

Head First Software Development (2007)

Head First PMP

Jennifer Greene, PMP
Andrew Stellman, PMP

Beijing • Cambridge • Köln • Paris • Sebastopol • Taipei • Tokyo

Head First PMP

by Jennifer Greene, PMP and Andrew Stellman, PMP

Printed in the United States of America.

Published by O'Reilly Media, Inc., 1005 Gravenstein Highway North, Sebastopol, CA 95472.

O'Reilly Media books may be purchased for educational, business, or sales promotional use. Online editions are also available for most titles (*safari.oreilly.com*). For more information, contact our corporate/institutional sales department: (800) 998-9938 or *corporate@oreilly.com*.

Series Creators: Kathy Sierra, Bert Bates

Series Editor: Brett D. McLaughlin

Acquisitions Editor: Mary O'Brien

Design Editor: Louise Barr

Cover Designers: Louise Barr, Steve Fehler

Production Editor: Sanders Kleinfeld

Indexer: Julie Hawks

Page Viewers: Quentin the whippet and Tequila the pomeranian

Printing History:

March 2007: First Edition.

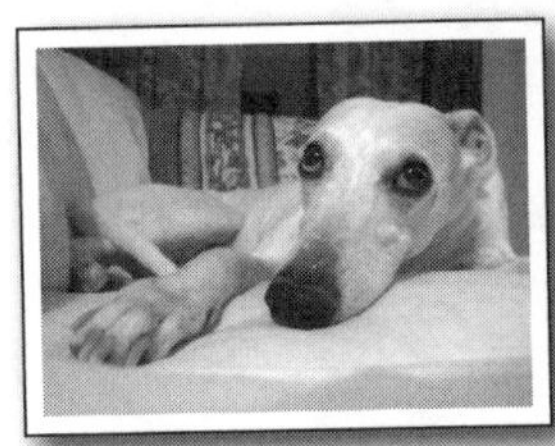

No dogs, rabbits, or bears were harmed in the making of this book. Okay, maybe one bear… but he'll get over it.

ISBN-10: 0-596-10234-8

ISBN-13: 978-0-596-10234-0

[M]

To our friends and family, and the people who make us laugh
(you know who you are)

Jennifer Greene studied philosophy in college but, like everyone else in the field, couldn't find a job doing it. Luckily, she's a great software tester, so she started out doing it at an online service, and that's the first time she really got a good sense of what project management was.

She moved to New York in 1998 to test software at a financial software company. She managed a team of testers at a really cool startup that did artificial intelligence and natural language processing.

Since then, she's managed large teams of programmers, testers, designers, architects, and other engineers on lots of projects, and she's done a whole bunch of procurement management (you'll learn all about procurement in Chapter 12!).

She loves traveling, watching Bollywood movies, drinking carloads of carbonated beverages, and owning a whippet.

Jenny and Andrew have been managing projects and writing about project management together since they first met in 1998. Their first book, Applied Software Project Management, was published by O'Reilly in 2005 and received widespread praise from both working project managers and academic researchers.

They founded Stellman & Greene Consulting in 2003, providing project management services and training to both companies and individuals. Andrew and Jenny regularly contribute to the project management body of knowledge, writing articles, presenting at conferences, and giving back to the project management community any time they have the opportunity to do so.

Andrew Stellman, despite being raised a New Yorker, has lived in Pittsburgh *twice*. The first time was when he graduated from Carnegie Mellon's School of Computer Science, and then again when he and Jenny were starting their consulting business and writing their first project management book for O'Reilly.

When he moved back to his hometown, his first job after college was as a programmer at EMI-Capitol Records—which actually made sense, since he went to LaGuardia High School of Music and Art and the Performing Arts to study cello and jazz bass guitar. He and Jenny first worked together at that same financial software company, where he was managing a team of programmers. He's since managed various teams of software engineers, requirements analysts, and led process improvement efforts.

Andrew keeps himself busy eating an enormous amount of string cheese and Middle Eastern desserts, playing music (but video games even more), studying taiji and aikido, having a girlfriend named Lisa, and owning a pomeranian.

Table of Contents (Summary)

	Intro xxiii	
1	Introduction: *Why Get Certified?*	1
2	Projects, Processes and Projects: *How You Do the Job*	19
3	The Process Framework: *It All Fits Together*	43
4	Integration Management: *Getting the Job Done*	69
5	Scope Management: *Doing the Right Stuff*	139
6	Time Management: *Getting it Done on Time*	211
7	Cost Management: *Watching the Bottom Line*	299
8	Quality Management: *Getting it Right*	365
9	Human Resource Management: *Getting the Team Together*	417
10	Communications Management: *Getting the Word Out*	461
11	Risk Management: *Planning for the Unknown*	507
12	Procurement Management: *Getting Some Help*	567
13	Professional Responsibility: *Making Good Choices*	617
14	A Little Last-Minute Review: *Check Your Knowledge*	631

Table of Contents (the real thing)

Intro

Your brain on PMP. Here *you* are trying to *learn* something, while here your *brain* is doing you a favor by making sure the learning doesn't *stick.* Your brain's thinking, "Better leave room for more important things, like which wild animals to avoid and whether naked snowboarding is a bad idea." So how *do* you trick your brain into thinking that your life depends on knowing enough to get through the PMP exam?

Who is this book for?	xxiv
We know what you're thinking	xxv
Metacognition	xxvii
Bend your brain into submission	xxix
Read me	xxx
The technical review team	xxxii
Acknowledgments	xxxiii

Introduction

1 Why get certified?

Tired of facing the same old problems? If you've worked on a lot of projects, you know that you face the same problems, over and over again. It's time to learn some common solutions to those problems. There's a whole lot that project managers have learned over the years, and passing the PMP exam is your ticket to putting that wisdom into practice. Get ready to change the way you manage your projects forever.

Do these problems seem familiar?	2
Projects don't have to be this way	4
Your problems... already solved	5
Let's start with the areas of responsibility	12
A PMP certification is more than just passing a test	16
Here's what happens to a certified PM	17

Organizations, processes, and projects

2 (Keeping) In good company

If you want something done right... better hope you're in the right kind of organization. All projects are about teamwork—but how your team works depends a lot on the type of organization you're in. In this chapter, you'll learn about the different types of organizations around—and which type you should look for the next time you need a new job.

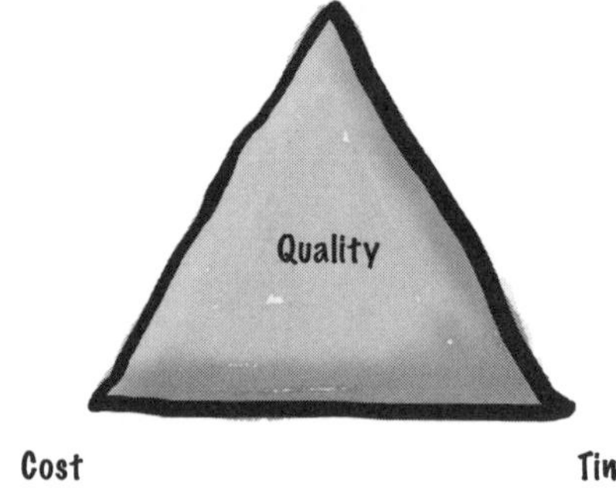

A day in Kate's life	20
Kate wants a new job	21
Three types of organizations	24
Kate takes a new job	29
What a project IS...	30
Back to Kate's maintenance nightmare	32
Managing cost, quality, scope, and schedule	34
Kate makes some changes…	38

3 The process framework

It All Fits Together

All of the work you do on a project is made up of processes. Once you know how all the processes in your project fit together, it's easy to remember everything you need to know for the PMP exam. **There's a pattern** to all of the work that gets done on your project. First you plan it, then you get to work. While you are doing the work, you are always comparing your project to your original plan. When things start to get off-plan, it's your job to make corrections and put everything back on track. And the **process framework**—the process groups and knowledge areas—is the key to all of this happening smoothly.

Cooking up a project	44
Projects are like recipes	46
Break it down	48
Anatomy of a process	51
Combine processes to complete your project	54
Knowledge areas organize the processes	55
The benefits of successful project management	61
Exam Questions	63
Exam Answers	65

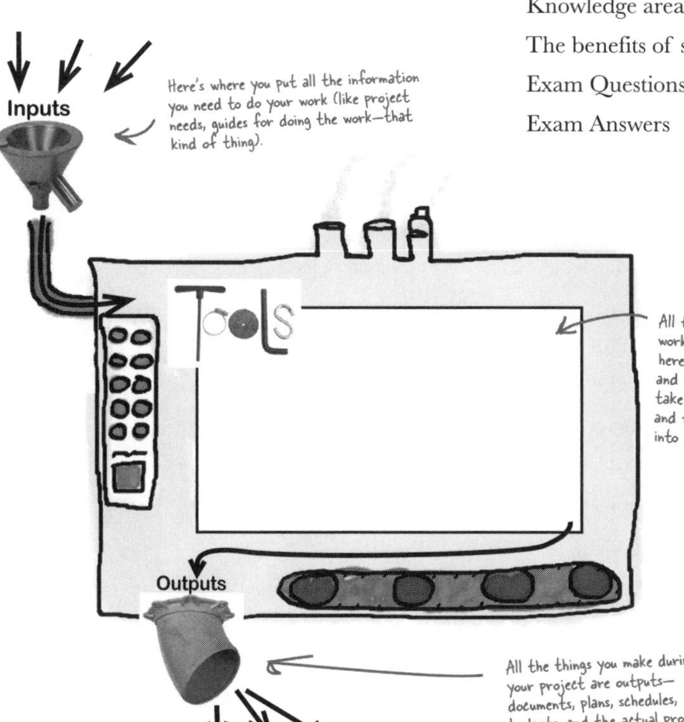

4 Integration management

Getting the Job Done

Want to make success look easy?

It's not as hard as you think. In this chapter, you'll learn about **a few processes** you can use in your projects every day. Put these into place, and your **sponsors** and **stakeholders** will be happier than ever. Get ready for **Integration Management**.

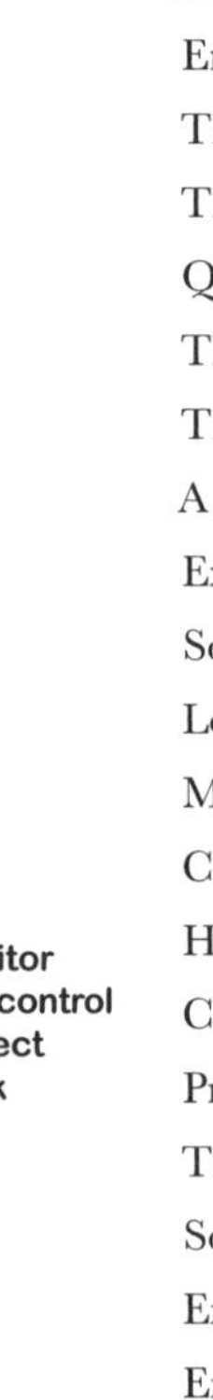

Time to book a trip	70
These clients are definitely not satisfied	72
The day-to-day work of a project manager	73
The seven Integration Management processes	74
Start your project with the Initiating processes	77
Integration management and the process groups	78
The Develop Project Charter process	80
Choose your project with project selection methods	82
A closer look at the project charter	84
Enterprise Environmental Factors and Organizational Process Assets	87
The "Develop Preliminary Scope Statement" process	91
The preliminary scope statement: a closer look	93
Question clinic: The "Just-The-Facts-Ma'am" Question	94
The Develop Project Management Plan process	96
The project management plan lets you plan ahead for problems	97
A quick look at all those subsidiary plans	99
Executing the project includes repairing defects	104
Sometimes you need to change your plans	107
Look for changes and deal with them	108
Make only the changes that are right for your project	109
Changes, defects, and corrections	110
How the processes interact with each other	111
Control your changes: use change control	112
Preventing or correcting problems	114
The Close Project process	116
So why INTEGRATION management?	118
Exam Questions	128
Exam Answers	134

scope management

5 Doing the Right Stuff

Confused about exactly what you should be working on?

Once you have a good idea of what needs to be done, you need to **track your scope** as the project work is happening. As each goal is accomplished, you confirm that all of the work has been done and make sure that the people who asked for it are **satisfied with the result**. In this chapter, you'll learn the tools that help your project team **set its goals** and keep everybody on track.

Out of the frying pan...	140
It looks like we have a scope problem	145
The five Scope Management processes	149
The Scope Planning process	151
Inside the scope management plan	153
Define the scope of the project	154
Build on the preliminary scope	155
How do you define the scope?	156
The scope isn't preliminary anymore	158
Question Clinic: The "Which-is-BEST" Question	162
The Create WBS process	164
Breaking down the work	166
Decompose deliverables into work packages	168
Templates are a useful shortcut	169
Inside the work package	174
The baseline is a snapshot of the plan	176
The outputs of the Create WBS process	178
Why scope changes	181
The Scope Control process	183
Anatomy of a change	184
A closer look at the Change Control System	186
More Scope Control tools & techniques	187
The Scope Verification process	191
The stakeholders decide when the project is done	192
Exam Questions	199
Exam Answers	204

Updates

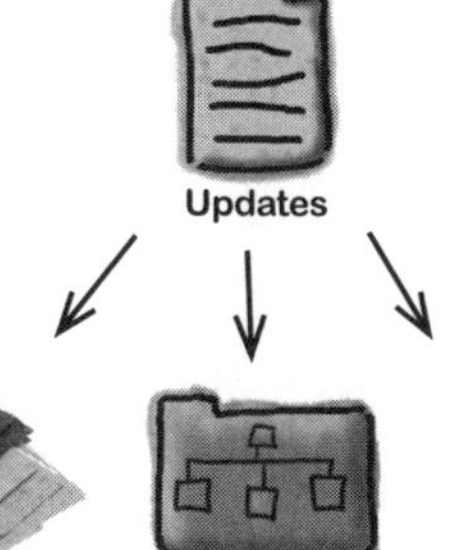

Project Scope Statement

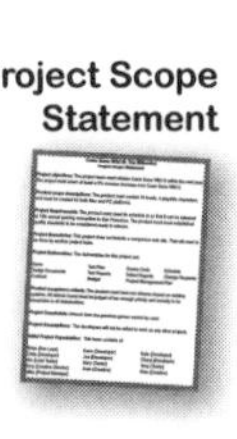

time management

6 Getting it Done on Time

Time management is what most people think of when they think of project managers. It's where the deadline is set and met. It starts with figuring out the work you need to do, how you will do it, what resources you'll use, and how long it will take. From there, it's all about developing and controlling that schedule.

Resource Calendar

Network Diagram

If the caterers come too early, the food will sit around under heat lamps! But too late and the band won't have time to play. I just don't see how we'll ever work this all out!

Activity List

Activity Duration Estimates

Activity Resource Requirements

Activity Attributes

Reality sets in for the happy couple	212
Time management helps with aggressive time lines	214
The Time Management processes *[time magnets solution]*	216
The Activity Definition process	219
Rolling wave planning lets you plan as you go	220
Activity Definition Outputs	223
The Activity Sequencing process	225
Diagram the relationship between activities	226
More tools for sequencing	230
Leads and lags	231
Create the network diagram	233
Rob and Rebecca have resource problems	234
The Activity Resource Estimation process	235
Estimating the resources	236
Figuring out how long the project will take	238
Estimation tools and techiques	241
The Activity Duration Estimating process	242
The Schedule Development process	244
Question Clinic: The "Which-Comes-Next" Question	246
Use the Critical Path method to avoid big problems	249
How to find the critical path: Using the Critical Path Method	250
Crash the schedule	266
Fast-tracking the project	267
Influence the factors that cause change	274
The Schedule Control process	275
Measuring and Reporting Performance	277
Exam Questions	289
Exam Answers	294

cost management

7 Watching the Bottom Line

Every project boils down to money. If you had a bigger budget, you could probably get more people to do your project more quickly and deliver more. That's why no project plan is complete until you come up with a budget. But no matter whether your project is big or small, and no matter how many resources and activities are in it, the process for figuring out the bottom line is always the same!

Time to expand the Head First Lounge 300
Introducing the Cost Management processes 303
The Cost Estimation process 304
Tools and techniques used only in Cost Estimation 307
Let's talk numbers 308
The Cost Budgeting process 310
What you need to build your budget 311
Cost Budgeting: How to build a budget 312
The Cost Control process 318
A few new tools and techniques 321
Question Clinic: The Red Herring 322
Earned value tells you how you're doing 324
Look at your schedule to figure out your budget 325
How to calculate planned value (PV) 326
How to calculate earned value (EV) 328
Put yourself in someone else's shoes 330
Is your project behind or ahead of schedule? (SV and SPI) 332
Are you over budget? (CV and CPI) 334
The Performance Measurement Analysis formulas 335
Interpret CPI and SPI numbers to gauge your project 338
Forecast what your project will look like when it's done 340
Once you've got an estimate, you can calculate a variance! (EAC, ETC and VAC) 341
Finding Missing Information 344
Exam Questions 354
Exam Answers 359

quality management

8 Getting It Right

It's not enough to make sure you get it done on time and under budget. You need to be sure you make the right product to suit your stakeholders' needs. Quality means making sure that you build what you said you would and that you do it as efficiently as you can. That means trying not to make too many mistakes and always keeping your project working toward the goal of creating the right product!

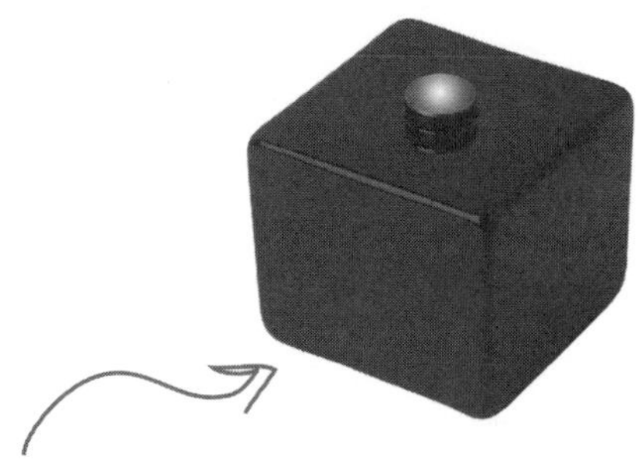

The Black Box 3000™.

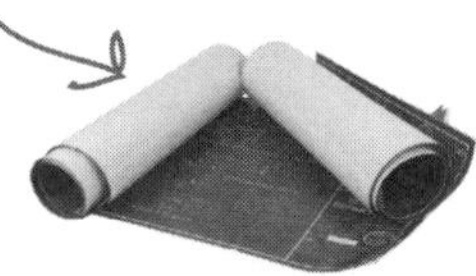

Lisa also inspected the blue prints for the black box when they were designed.

She looked for defects in the parts as they were being made too.

BB3K™ PARTS

What is quality? 366

You need more than just tests to figure out quality 367

Once you know what the product is supposed to do, it's easy to tell which tests pass and which fail 368

Quality up close 369

"An ounce of prevention..." 372

The Quality Planning process 375

How to plan for quality 376

The quality management plan gives you what you need to manage quality 378

The Perform Quality Control process 381

Use the planning outputs for Perform Quality Control 382

The seven basic tools of quality 383

Pareto charts, flowcharts and histograms 384

Run charts and scatter charts 385

Question Clinic: The "Which-One" Question 390

Quality control means finding and correcting defects 392

Trouble at the Black Box 3000™ factory 395

The Perform Quality Assurance process 396

A closer look at some tools and techniques 397

More ideas behind quality assurance 398

Exam Questions 408

Exam Answers 412

human resource management

9 Getting the Team Together

Behind every successful project is a great team. So how do you make sure that you get—and keep—the best possible team for your project? You need to plan carefully, set up a good working environment, and negotiate for the best people you can find. But it's not enough to put a good team together... If you want your project to go well, you've got to keep the team motivated and deal with any conflicts that happen along the way. Human resource management gives you the tools you need to get the best team for the job and lead them through a successful project.

Mike needs a new team 418
The Human Resource Management processes 420
The Human Resoucre Planning process 422
The staffing management plan 426
The Acquire Project Team process 428
The Develop Project Team process 432
Develop the team with your management skills 433
Lead the team with your management skills 434
Motivate your team *[theories of motivation]* 436
How's the team doing? 438
The Manage Project Team process 440
Conflict management up close 441
How to resolve a conflict 442
Question Clinic: The "Have-a-Meeting" Question 448
Exam Questions 454
Exam Answers 458

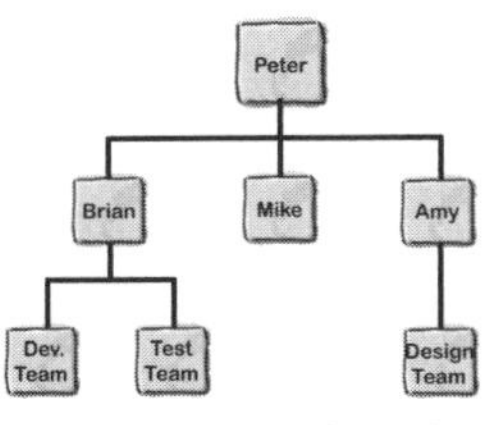

Organization Charts

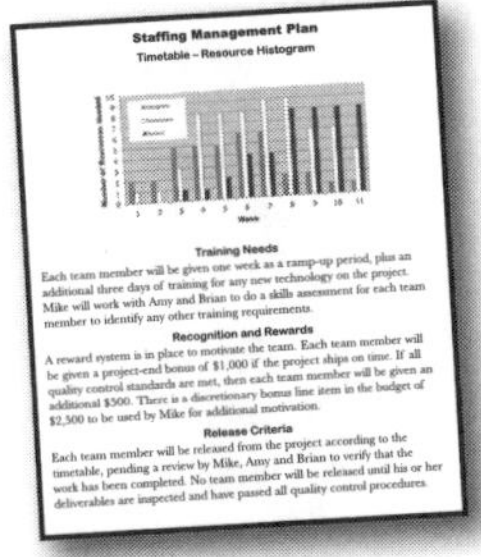

Staffing Management Plan

RACI Matrix		Role			
		Mike	Amy	Brian	Peter
Work Package	Project Management	R	I	I	I
	Design	C	R	C	I
	Construction	C	C	R	I
	Testing	C	C	R	I

R = Responsible A = Accountable C = Consult I = Inform

Roles and Responsibilities

10 communications management

Getting the Word Out

Communications management is about keeping everybody in the loop. Have you ever tried talking to someone in a really loud, crowded room? That's what running a project is like if you don't do get a handle on communications. Luckily, there's Communications Management, which is how to get everyone talking about the work that's being done, so that they all stay on the same page. That way everyone has the information they need to resolve any issues and keep the project moving forward.

Party at the Head First Lounge!	462
Anatomy of a phone call	464
The Communications Management processes	466
The Communications Planning process *[exercise solutions]*	470
The Information Distribution process	472
Get the message?	474
More information distribution tools	476
The Performance Reporting process	479
Take a close look at the work being done	480
Now you can get the word out	483
People aren't talking	485
The Manage Stakeholders process *[exercise solutions]*	488
Count the lines of communication	490
Question Clinic: The Calculation Question	494
Exam Questions	500
Exam Answers	503

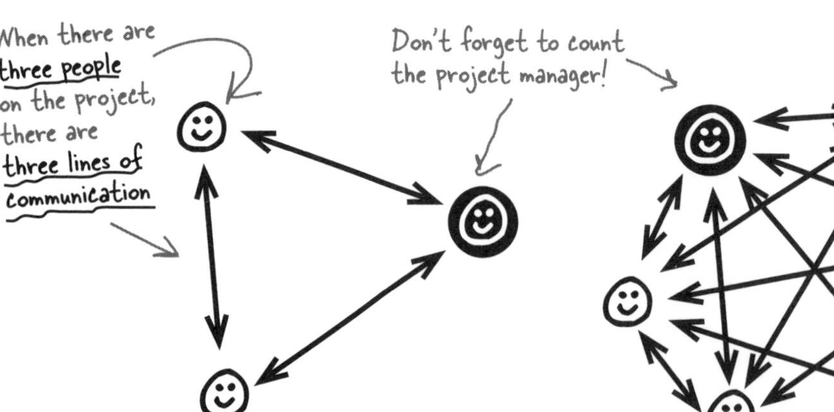

11 risk management

Planning for the Unknown

Even the most carefully planned project can run into trouble.

No matter how well you plan, your project can always run into unexpected problems. Team members get sick or quit, resources that you were depending on turn out to be unavailable—even the weather can throw you for a loop. So does that mean that you're helpless against unknown problems? No! You can use ***risk planning*** to identify potential problems that could cause trouble for your project, analyze how likely they'll be to occur, take action to prevent the risks you can avoid, and minimize the ones that you can't.

What's a risk? 508
How you deal with risk 509
The Risk Management Planning process 510
Use a risk breakdown structure to categorize risks 512
Anatomy of a Risk *[the Risk Management processes]* 514
The Risk Identification process 516
Information gathering techniques for Risk Identification 517
More risk identification techniques 518
Where to look for risks 520
Now put it in the risk register 521
The Qualitative Risk Analysis process 522
Examine each risk in the risk register 523
Qualitative vs. quantitative analysis 528
The Quantitative Risk Analysis process 529
First gather the data... then analyze it 530
Calculate the Expected Monetary Value of your risks (EMV) 532
Decsion tree analysis uses EMV to help you make choices 534
Update the risk register based on your quantitative analysis results 536
The Risk Response Planning process 538
You can't plan for every risk at the start of the project 543
The Risk Monitoring and Controlling process 546
Question Clinic" The "Which-os-NOT" Question 552
Exam Questions 557
Exam Answers 562

12 procurement management

Getting Some Help

Some jobs are just too big for your company to do on its own.

Even when the job isn't too big, it may just be that you don't have the expertise or equipment to do it. When that happens, you need to use Procurement Management to find another company to do the work for you. If you find the right seller, choose the right kind of relationship, and make sure that the goals of the contract are met, you'll get the job done and your project will be a success.

Contract

Closed Contracts

Victim of her own success	568
Calling in the cavalry	569
The Procurement Management processes	574
The Plan Purchases and Acquisitions process	575
The decision is made	581
Types of contracts	582
More about contracts	585
The Plan Contracting process	586
Figure out how you'll sort out potential sellers	588
The Request Seller Responses process	590
The Select Sellers process	592
Two months later...	598
The Contract Administration process	599
Stay on top of the seller	600
Close the contract when the work is done	604
Question Clinic: BYO Questions	607
Exam Questions	611
Exam Answers	614

13 professional responsibility

Making Good Choices

It's not enough to just know your stuff. You need to make good choices to be good at your job. Everyone who has the PMP credential agrees to follow the PMP Code of Professional Conduct, too. The Code helps you with ethical decisions that aren't really covered in the body of knowledge—and it's a big part of the exam. Most of what you need to know is really straightforward, and with a little review, you'll do well.

Doing the right thing 618
Keep the cash? 620
Fly business? 621
New software 622
Shortcuts 623
A good price or a clean river? 624
We're not all angels 625
Exam Questions 626
Exam Answers 628

a little last-minute review

14 Check Your Knowledge

Wow, you sure covered a lot of ground in the last 13 chapters! Now it's time to take a look back and drill in some of the most important stuff that you learned. So let's go back and cover some of the hardest stuff in the book. That'll keep it all fresh, and give your brain a final workout for exam day!

Process Magnets	632
Processcross	634
Exercise	636
Sharpen Your Pencil	637
Great job! It looks like you're almost ready.	638

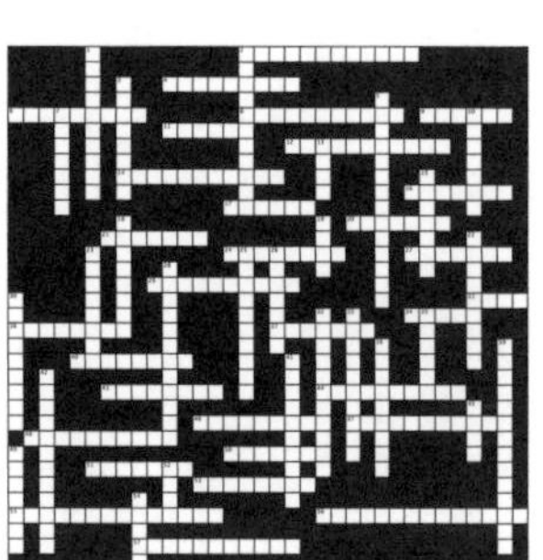

Pretty soon, this will be YOU!

Intro

In this section, we answer the burning question:
"So why DID they put that in a PMP exam prep book?"

Who is this book for?

If you can answer "yes" to all of these:

You can also use this book to help you study for the CAPM exam—a lot of the concepts are really similar.

1. Are you a **project manager**?

2. Do you want to **learn**, **understand**, **remember**, and ***apply*** important project management concepts so that you can prepare for **the PMP exam**, and learn to be a better project manager in the process?

3. Do you prefer **stimulating dinner party conversation** to **dry**, **dull**, **academic lectures**?

We'll help you study for the PMP exam in a way that will definitely make it easier for you to pass

this book is for you.

Who should probably back away from this book?

If you can answer "yes" to any of these:

1. Are you **completely new** to project management?

   (To qualify to take the PMP exam, you need to show a certain number of hours of experience as a professional project manager.)

But even if you don't have quite enough hours yet, this book can still help you study now, so you can be ready when you've got those hours under your belt! Plus, the ideas will help you on your job immediately..

2. Are you already PMP certified and looking for a ***reference* book** on project management?

3. Are you **afraid to try something different**? Would you rather have a root canal than mix stripes with plaid? Do you believe that a technical book can't be serious if project management concepts are anthropomorphized?

this book is not for you.

[Note from marketing: this book is for anyone with a credit card.]

We know what you're thinking.

How can *this* be a serious project management book?"

What's with all the graphics?"

Can I actually *learn* it this way?"

Your brain thinks THIS is important.

And we know what your *brain* is thinking.

Your brain craves novelty. It's always searching, scanning, *waiting* for something unusual. It was built that way, and it helps you stay alive.

So what does your brain do with all the routine, ordinary, normal things you encounter? Everything it *can* to stop them from interfering with the brain's *real* job—recording things that *matter*. It doesn't bother saving the boring things; they never make it past the "this is obviously not important" filter.

How does your brain *know* what's important? Suppose you're out for a day hike and a tiger jumps in front of you, what happens inside your head and body?

Neurons fire. Emotions crank up. *Chemicals surge.*

And that's how your brain knows...

This must be important! Don't forget it!

But imagine you're at home, or in a library. It's a safe, warm, tiger-free zone. You're studying. Getting ready for an exam. Or trying to learn some tough technical topic your boss thinks will take a week, ten days at the most.

Just one problem. Your brain's trying to do you a big favor. It's trying to make sure that this *obviously* non-important content doesn't clutter up scarce resources. Resources that are better spent storing the really *big* things. Like tigers. Like the danger of fire. Like how you should never again snowboard in shorts.

And there's no simple way to tell your brain, "Hey brain, thank you very much, but no matter how dull this book is, and how little I'm registering on the emotional Richter scale right now, I really *do* want you to keep this stuff around."

We think of a "Head First" reader as a learner.

So what does it take to *learn* something? First, you have to *get* it, then make sure you don't *forget* it. It's not about pushing facts into your head. Based on the latest research in cognitive science, neurobiology, and educational psychology, *learning* takes a lot more than text on a page. We know what turns your brain on.

Some of the Head First learning principles:

You could pound in a nail with a screwdriver, but a hammer is more fit for the job.

Make it visual. Images are far more memorable than words alone, and make learning much more effective (up to 89% improvement in recall and transfer studies). It also makes things more understandable. **Put the words within or near the graphics** they relate to, rather than on the bottom or on another page, and learners will be up to *twice* as likely to solve problems related to the content.

Use a conversational and personalized style. In recent studies, students performed up to 40% better on post-learning tests if the content spoke directly to the reader, using a first-person, conversational style rather than taking a formal tone. Tell stories instead of lecturing. Use casual language. Don't take yourself too seriously. Which would *you* pay more attention to: a stimulating dinner party companion, or a lecture?

Get the learner to think more deeply. In other words, unless you actively flex your neurons, nothing much happens in your head. A reader has to be motivated, engaged, curious, and inspired to solve problems, draw conclusions, and generate new knowledge. And for that, you need challenges, exercises, and thought-provoking questions, and activities that involve both sides of the brain and multiple senses.

Get—and keep—the reader's attention. We've all had the "I really want to learn this but I can't stay awake past page one" experience. Your brain pays attention to things that are out of the ordinary, interesting, strange, eye-catching, unexpected. Learning a new, tough, technical topic doesn't have to be boring. Your brain will learn much more quickly if it's not.

This sucks... they lost Frank's luggage, and I got my wallet stolen!

Touch their emotions. We now know that your ability to remember something is largely dependent on its emotional content. You remember what you care about. You remember when you *feel* something. No, we're not talking heart-wrenching stories about a boy and his dog. We're talking emotions like surprise, curiosity, fun, "what the...?", and the feeling of "I Rule!" that comes when you solve a puzzle, learn something everybody else thinks is hard, or realize you know something that "I'm more technical than thou" Bob from engineering *doesn't*.

Metacognition: thinking about thinking

If you really want to learn, and you want to learn more quickly and more deeply, pay attention to how you pay attention. Think about how you think. Learn how you learn.

Most of us did not take courses on metacognition or learning theory when we were growing up. We were *expected* to learn, but rarely *taught* to learn.

But we assume that if you're holding this book, you really want to learn about project management. And you probably don't want to spend a lot of time. And since you're going to take an exam on it, you need to *remember* what you read. And for that, you've got to *understand* it. To get the most from this book, or *any* book or learning experience, take responsibility for your brain. Your brain on *this* content.

The trick is to get your brain to see the new material you're learning as Really Important. Crucial to your well-being. As important as a tiger. Otherwise, you're in for a constant battle, with your brain doing its best to keep the new content from sticking.

So just how *DO* you get your brain to think that the stuff on the PMP exam is a hungry tiger?

There's the slow, tedious way, or the faster, more effective way. The slow way is about sheer repetition. You obviously know that you *are* able to learn and remember even the dullest of topics if you keep pounding the same thing into your brain. With enough repetition, your brain says, "This doesn't *feel* important to him, but he keeps looking at the same thing *over* and *over* and *over*, so I suppose it must be."

The faster way is to do ***anything that increases brain activity,*** especially different *types* of brain activity. The things on the previous page are a big part of the solution, and they're all things that have been proven to help your brain work in your favor. For example, studies show that putting words *within* the pictures they describe (as opposed to somewhere else in the page, like a caption or in the body text) causes your brain to try to makes sense of how the words and picture relate, and this causes more neurons to fire. More neurons firing = more chances for your brain to *get* that this is something worth paying attention to, and possibly recording.

A conversational style helps because people tend to pay more attention when they perceive that they're in a conversation, since they're expected to follow along and hold up their end. The amazing thing is, your brain doesn't necessarily *care* that the "conversation" is between you and a book! On the other hand, if the writing style is formal and dry, your brain perceives it the same way you experience being lectured to while sitting in a roomful of passive attendees. No need to stay awake.

But pictures and conversational style are just the beginning.

Here's what WE did:

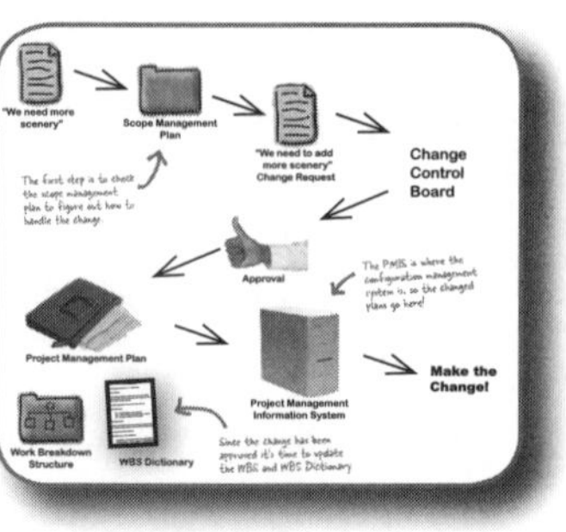

We used ***pictures***, because your brain is tuned for visuals, not text. As far as your brain's concerned, a picture really *is* worth a thousand words. And when text and pictures work together, we embedded the text *in* the pictures because your brain works more effectively when the text is *within* the thing the text refers to, as opposed to in a caption or buried in the text somewhere.

We used ***redundancy***, saying the same thing in *different* ways and with different media types, and *multiple senses*, to increase the chance that the content gets coded into more than one area of your brain.

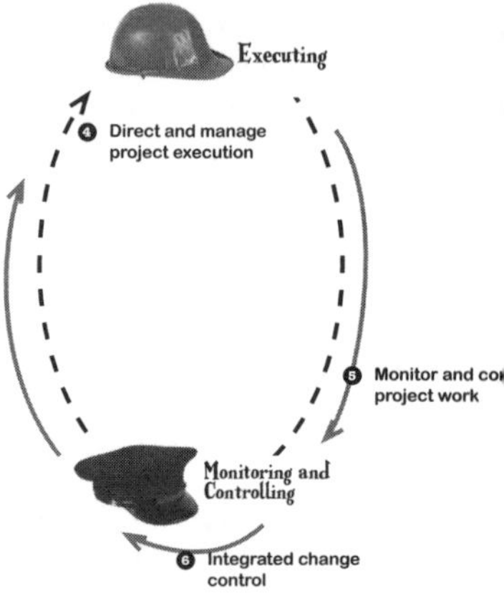

We used concepts and pictures in ***unexpected*** ways because your brain is tuned for novelty, and we used pictures and ideas with at least *some **emotional** content*, because your brain is tuned to pay attention to the biochemistry of emotions. That which causes you to *feel* something is more likely to be remembered, even if that feeling is nothing more than a little ***humor***, ***surprise***, or ***interest.***

We used a personalized, ***conversational style***, because your brain is tuned to pay more attention when it believes you're in a conversation than if it thinks you're passively listening to a presentation. Your brain does this even when you're *reading*.

We included more than 80 ***activities***, because your brain is tuned to learn and remember more when you ***do*** things than when you *read* about things. And we made the exercises challenging-yet-do-able, because that's what most people prefer.

We used ***multiple learning styles***, because *you* might prefer step-by-step procedures, while someone else wants to understand the big picture first, and someone else just wants to see an example. But regardless of your own learning preference, *everyone* benefits from seeing the same content represented in multiple ways.

We include content for ***both sides of your brain***, because the more of your brain you engage, the more likely you are to learn and remember, and the longer you can stay focused. Since working one side of the brain often means giving the other side a chance to rest, you can be more productive at learning for a longer period of time.

And we included ***stories*** and exercises that present ***more than one point of view,*** because your brain is tuned to learn more deeply when it's forced to make evaluations and judgments.

We included ***challenges***, with exercises, and by asking ***questions*** that don't always have a straight answer, because your brain is tuned to learn and remember when it has to *work* at something. Think about it—you can't get your *body* in shape just by *watching* people at the gym. But we did our best to make sure that when you're working hard, it's on the *right* things. That ***you're not spending one extra dendrite*** processing a hard-to-understand example, or parsing difficult, jargon-laden, or overly terse text.

We used ***people***. In stories, examples, pictures, etc., because, well, because *you're* a person. And your brain pays more attention to *people* than it does to *things*.

Here's what YOU can do to bend your brain into submission

So, we did our part. The rest is up to you. These tips are a starting point; listen to your brain and figure out what works for you and what doesn't. Try new things.

cut this out and stick it on your refrigerator.

1. **Slow down. The more you understand, the less you have to memorize.**

   Don't just *read*. Stop and think. When the book asks you a question, don't just skip to the answer. Imagine that someone really *is* asking the question. The more deeply you force your brain to think, the better chance you have of learning and remembering.

2. **Do the exercises. Write your own notes.**

   We put them in, but if we did them for you, that would be like having someone else do your workouts for you. And don't just *look* at the exercises. **Use a pencil.** There's plenty of evidence that physical activity *while* learning can increase the learning.

3. **Read the "There are No Dumb Questions"**

   That means all of them. They're not optional sidebars—***they're part of the core content!*** Don't skip them.

4. **Make this the last thing you read before bed. Or at least the last challenging thing.**

   Part of the learning (especially the transfer to long-term memory) happens *after* you put the book down. Your brain needs time on its own, to do more processing. If you put in something new during that processing time, some of what you just learned will be lost.

5. **Drink water. Lots of it.**

   Your brain works best in a nice bath of fluid. Dehydration (which can happen before you ever feel thirsty) decreases cognitive function.

6. **Talk about it. Out loud.**

   Speaking activates a different part of the brain. If you're trying to understand something, or increase your chance of remembering it later, say it out loud. Better still, try to explain it out loud to someone else. You'll learn more quickly, and you might uncover ideas you hadn't known were there when you were reading about it.

7. **Listen to your brain.**

   Pay attention to whether your brain is getting overloaded. If you find yourself starting to skim the surface or forget what you just read, it's time for a break. Once you go past a certain point, you won't learn faster by trying to shove more in, and you might even hurt the process.

8. **Feel something!**

   Your brain needs to know that this *matters*. Get involved with the stories. Make up your own captions for the photos. Groaning over a bad joke is *still* better than feeling nothing at all.

9. **Create something!**

   Apply this to your daily work; use what you are learning to make decisions on your projects. Just do something to get some experience beyond the exercises and activities in this book. All you need is a pencil and a problem to solve…a problem that might benefit from using the tools and techniques you're studying for the exam.

Read me

This is a learning experience, not a reference book. We deliberately stripped out everything that might get in the way of learning whatever it is we're working on at that point in the book—although we didn't take anything out that you might see on the PMP exam. And the first time through, you need to begin at the beginning, because the book makes assumptions about what you've already seen and learned.

The chapters are ordered the same way as the PMBOK® Guide

We did this because it makes sense… The PMP exam focuses on your understanding of the Guide and the inputs, outputs, tools, and techniques it references. It's a good idea for you to understand the material the way the test organizes it. If you are cross-referencing this book with the PMBOK® Guide, it will really help you that the structure has been pretty much maintained throughout this book, too.

We encourage you to use the PMBOK® Guide with this book.

This book talks about the practical applications of a lot of the ideas in the PMBOK® Guide, but you should have a pretty good idea of how the guide talks about the material, too. There's some information that's on the test that isn't in the guide, so we haven't limited this book to a retread of what's in the PMBOK® Guide at all. But it's a great reference, and you should be cross-referencing the two books as you go. That will help you understand all of the terminology better and make sure that there are no surprises on exam day.

The activities are NOT optional.

The exercises and activities are not add-ons; they're part of the core content of the book. Some of them are to help with memory, some are for understanding, and some will help you apply what you've learned. ***Don't skip the exercises.*** Even crossword puzzles are important—they'll help get concepts into your brain the way you'll see them on the PMP exam. But more importantly, they're good for giving your brain a chance to think about the words and terms you've been learning in a different context.

The redundancy is intentional and important.

One distinct difference in a Head First book is that we want you to *really* get it. And we want you to finish the book remembering what you've learned. Most reference books don't have retention and recall as a goal, but this book is about *learning*, so you'll see some of the same concepts come up more than once.

The Brain Power exercises don't have answers.

For some of them, there is no right answer, and for others, part of the learning experience of the Brain Power activities is for you to decide if and when your answers are right. In some of the Brain Power exercises, you will find hints to point you in the right direction.

We want you to get involved.

Part of being a PMP-certified project manager is getting involved in the community and helping others out. An easy way to start doing this is to head over to the Head First web site where you'll be able to submit your own Head Libs and see what other people have come up with, too:

http://www.headfirstlabs.com/books/pmp/

The technical review team

Technical Reviewers:

When we wrote this book, it had a bunch of mistakes, issues, problems, typos, and terrible arithmetic errors. Okay, it wasn't quite that bad. But we're still really grateful for the work that our technical reviewers did for the book. We would have gone to press with errors (including one or two big ones) had it not been for the most kick-ass review team EVER. They did a fantastic job of getting the bugs out of this book. When you read about inspection in the Quality Management chapter, take a few seconds to think about these guys:

Dennis Bolles led the project core team for the PMBOK® Guide Third Edition, which the PMP exam is based on. He brought an enormous amount of knowledge and experience to this project, and we're deeply indebted to him for his guidance and encouragement.

Carol Steuer was a member of the leadership team for the PMBOK® Guide Third Edition. She was one of our most prolific reviewers, and this book would not be what it is without her valuable contribution.

After helping enormously with our first book, **Lisa Kellner** returns to our review team, and we couldn't be happier. Lisa made this book much more readable, and helped us catch problems which would have been pretty embarrassing had we gone to press with them. Thanks, Lisa!

We're really happy that **David W. Robinson** and **Rashmi Upadhyay** were very helpful in making sure the book made sense from a test-taker's perspective.

Mark C. Poinelli is currently working at a top-tier financial services firm in the Big Apple. His detailed review of the math in Chapter 7 indubitably kept us from publishing egregious errors.

Acknowledgments

Our editors:

First of all, we want to thank our editor, **Brett McLaughlin**, for flying out to New York and spending days giving us a Head First boot camp. Brett was more than an editor—he was a combination sounding board and sherpa. There's absolutely no way this book would have been written without his guidance, constant support, and interest. He really got his hands dirty on this one, and he gave us a whole lot of advice, hints, and more than a little coaching throughout this whole process. Thanks, Brett!

Brett McLaughlin

This is the second time we've had the pleasure of writing the following sentence: "Special thanks to **Mary O'Brien** for guiding us from the first draft to the completed version that you're holding." Wow, Mary, you've been amazingly supportive and really cool through two books. This whole thing wouldn't have happened without you. You came to us with this project, you made the connection for us, you and Brett gave us this amazing opportunity, and you made this whole thing happen. And we really can't thank you enough. You rock!

Mary O'Brien

The O'Reilly team:

Lou Barr is an amazing graphic designer who went above and beyond on this one, putting in unbelievable hours and coming up with some pretty amazing visuals. If you see anything in this book that looks fantastic, you can thank her (and her mad InDesign skillz) for it. Thanks so much, Lou!

But we would have gone to press with a whole lot of errors had it not been for the technical review process, and **Catherine Nolan**, our editor in charge of reviews, managed it like a pro. She told us, "Head First is really more of a marathon than a sprint," and she was right on the money with that. And **Sanders Kleinfeld** did a great job as production editor, getting this book ready for press and basically working magic. Finally, we want to give a warm thanks to our many friends at O'Reilly, especially **Kathryn Barrett** (the most fabulous publicist EVER), and **Mike Hendrickson** and **Andrew Odewahn** for giving us our start at O'Reilly.

Lou Barr

1 Introduction

Why get certified?

Tired of facing the same old problems? If you've worked on a lot of projects, you know that you face the same problems, over and over again. It's time to learn some common solutions to those problems. There's a whole lot that project managers have learned over the years, and passing the PMP exam is your ticket to putting that wisdom into practice. Get ready to change the way you manage your projects forever.

Do these problems seem familiar?

Kate's boss promised a delivery date that she couldn't possibly meet.

S M T W T F S
The Boss's delivery date
When the project will actually be done

Kate

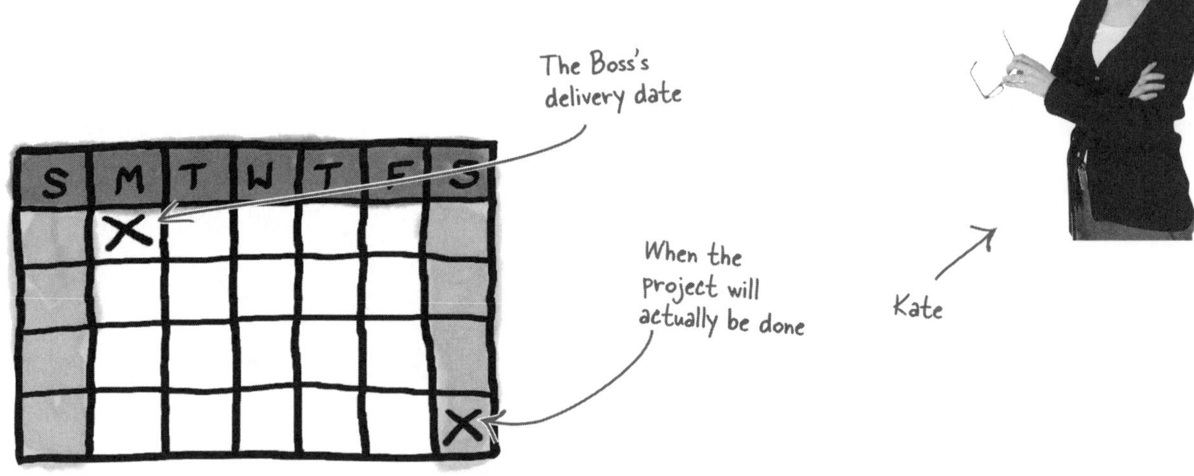

Then, when the project was halfway done, the customer demanded a big change.

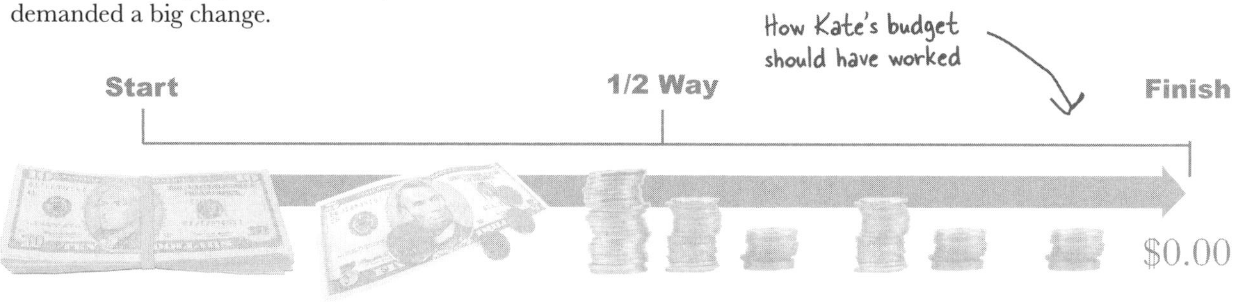

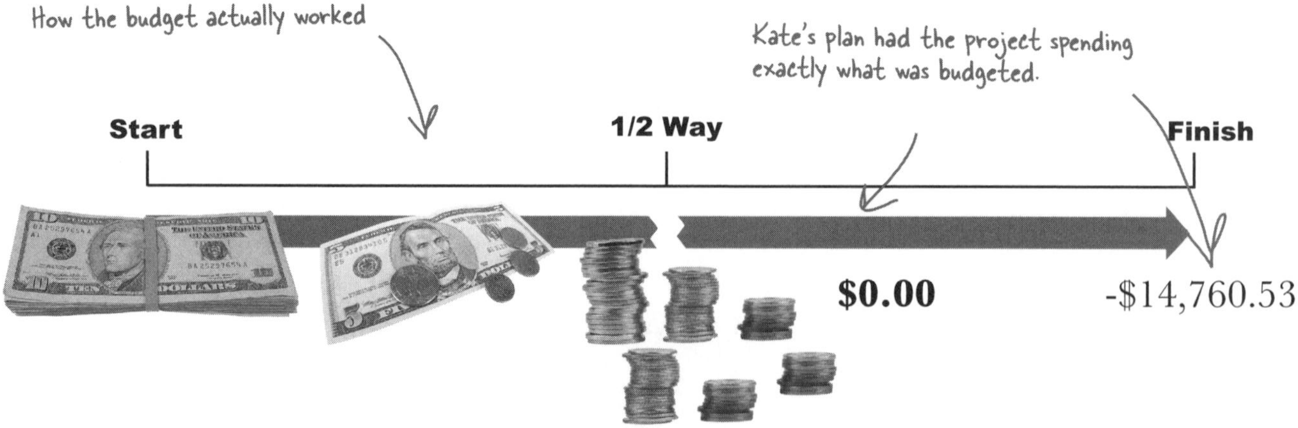

How Kate's budget should have worked
Start
1/2 Way
Finish
$0.00

How the budget actually worked
Kate's plan had the project spending exactly what was budgeted.
Start
1/2 Way
Finish
$0.00
-$14,760.53

Then, just as the project was about to be completed, someone noticed a typo, and 10,000 leaflets had to be reprinted.

Projects don't have to be this way

It may seem like all projects have these types of problems, but there are proven solutions to them… and someone else has already done a lot of the work for you! Realizing that all projects have common problems with solutions, The PMBOK® Guide is put together to pass those solutions on to you.

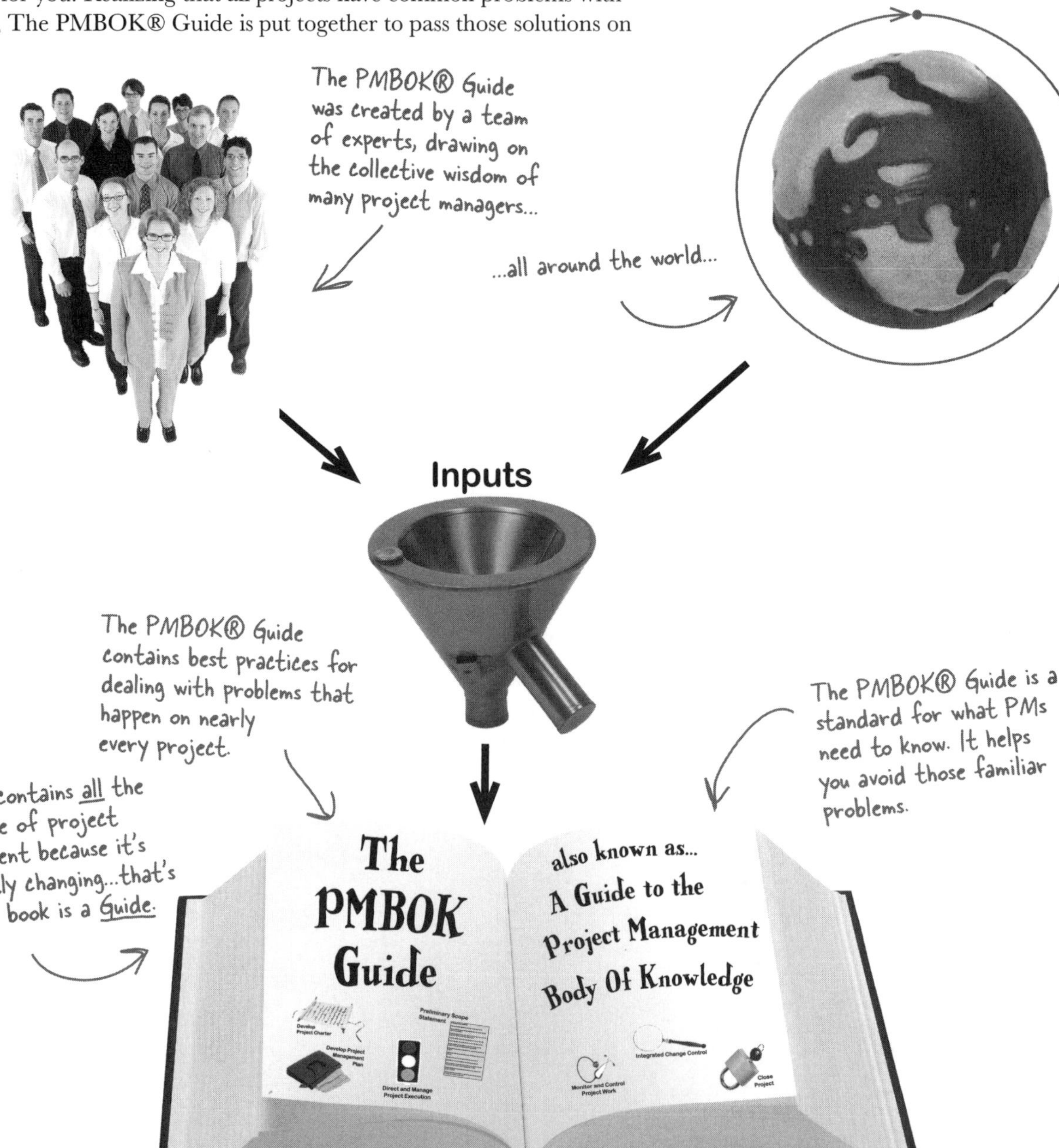

Your problems... already solved

Every project eventually runs into the same kinds of issues. But a project manager with good training can spot them and quickly figure out the best solutions. The PMBOK® Guide will help you:

✓ Learn from past projects that have run into similar problems to avoid running into them again.

✓ Plan and execute your projects to avoid common pitfalls.

Common pitfalls: better avoid these.

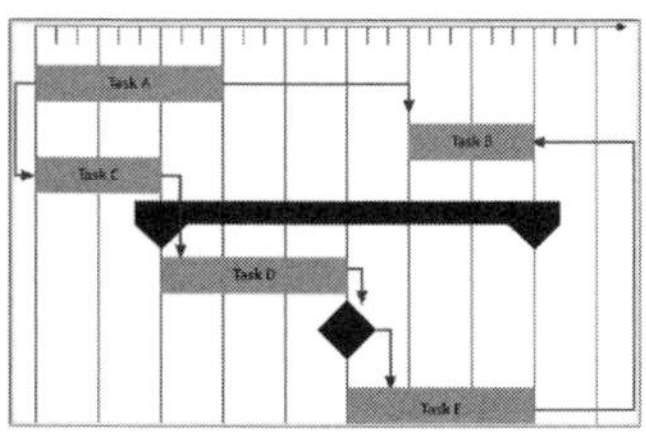

The PMBOK® Guide has great ideas on how to estimate your tasks and put them in the right sequence to get your projects done as quickly and efficiently as possible.

It outlines techniques for planning and tracking your costs.

It helps you learn how to plan for and protect against defects in your project.

The PMBOK® Guide is really just a collection of things that you probably already know a lot about. It defines four major **areas of responsibility** for a project manager. We've listed these four areas below; your job is to write down what you think each area of responsibility means.

1. Identify the requirements for the project

....

....

....

....

....

2. Establish objectives that can be achieved

....

....

....

....

....

3. Balance scope, time, and cost

....

....

....

....

....

4. Satisfy everyone's needs

....

....

....

....

....

Process Group Magnets

In addition to the four areas of responsibility, the PMBOK® Guide divides up the generally recognized good project management practices into **44 processes** that fall into **5 process groups**. See if you can match the process group magnets below into the right blanks, in the right order.

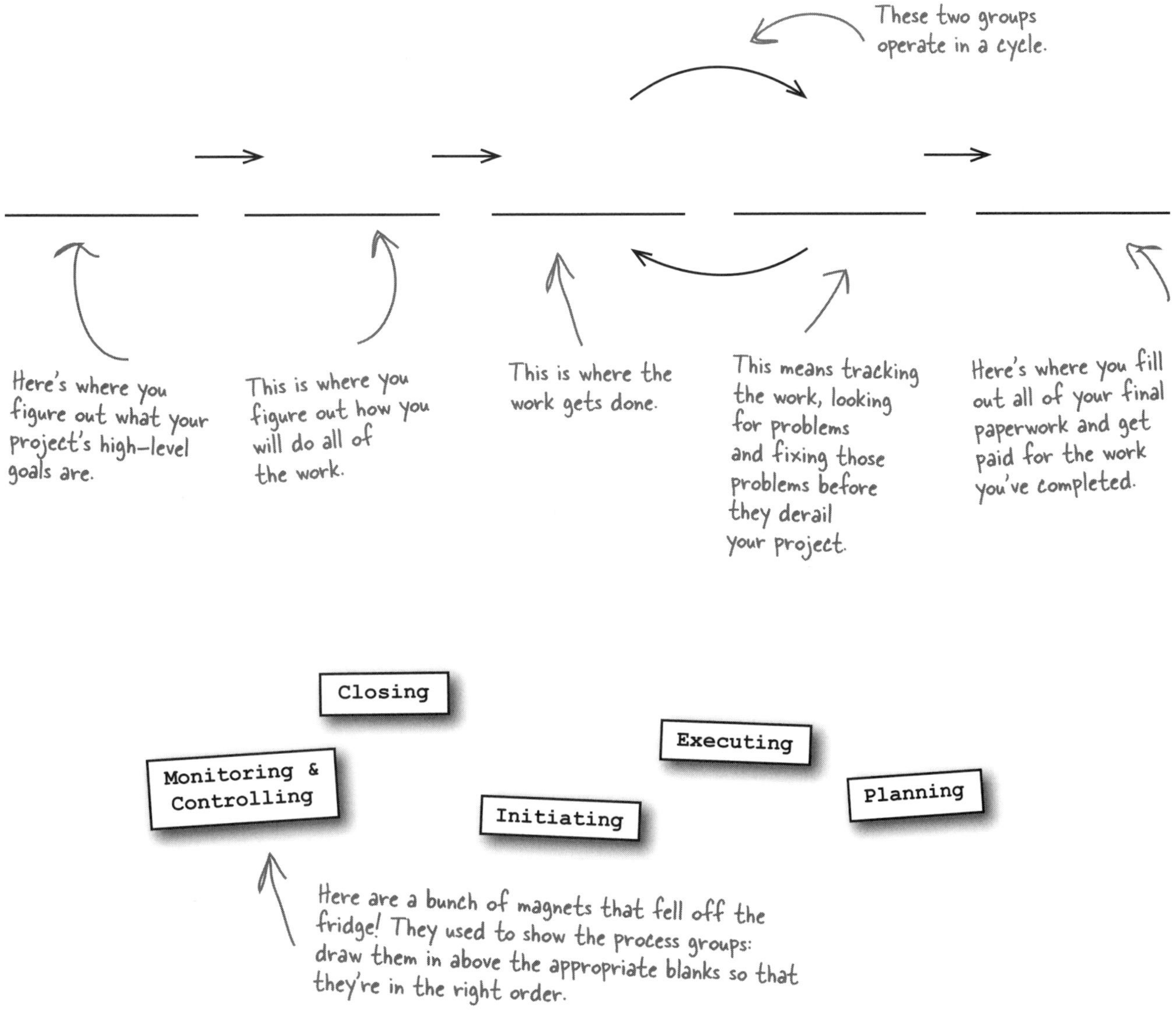

These two groups operate in a cycle.

______ → ______ → ______ ______ → ______

Here's where you figure out what your project's high-level goals are.

This is where you figure out how you will do all of the work.

This is where the work gets done.

This means tracking the work, looking for problems and fixing those problems before they derail your project.

Here's where you fill out all of your final paperwork and get paid for the work you've completed.

Closing

Executing

Monitoring & Controlling

Planning

Initiating

Here are a bunch of magnets that fell off the fridge! They used to show the process groups: draw them in above the appropriate blanks so that they're in the right order.

The PMBOK® Guide is really just a collection of things that you probably already know a lot about. It defines four major **areas of responsibility** for a project manager. We've listed these four areas below; your job is to write down what you think each area of responsibility means.

1. Identify the requirements for the project

Figure out what it will take to make the project a success.

This is where you ask what the project is all about.

Don't worry if your answers aren't exactly the same as ours. There are lots of ways to describe these responsibilities.

2. Establish objectives that can be achieved

Plan out the goals that your team will work toward and the way you'll achieve them.

Everyone needs to agree on the goals so they make decisions that help each other succeed.

3. Balance scope, time, and cost

Keep track of how your project is doing compared to its planned schedule, budget, and quality requirements. Any time you make a change that affects one of those three, the other ones are affected, too. So, you always need to manage them together.

You DO have to manage all three. For a project to be a success, you need to deliver what you said you would on time and within budget.

4. Satisfy everyone's needs

Communicate with everybody who is affected by your project.

A lot of a PM's job is about communication.

Process Group Magnets Solutions

In addition to the four areas of responsibility, the PMBOK® Guide divides up the generally recognized good project management practices into **44 processes** that fall into **5 process groups**. See if you can match the process group magnets below into the right blanks, in the right order.

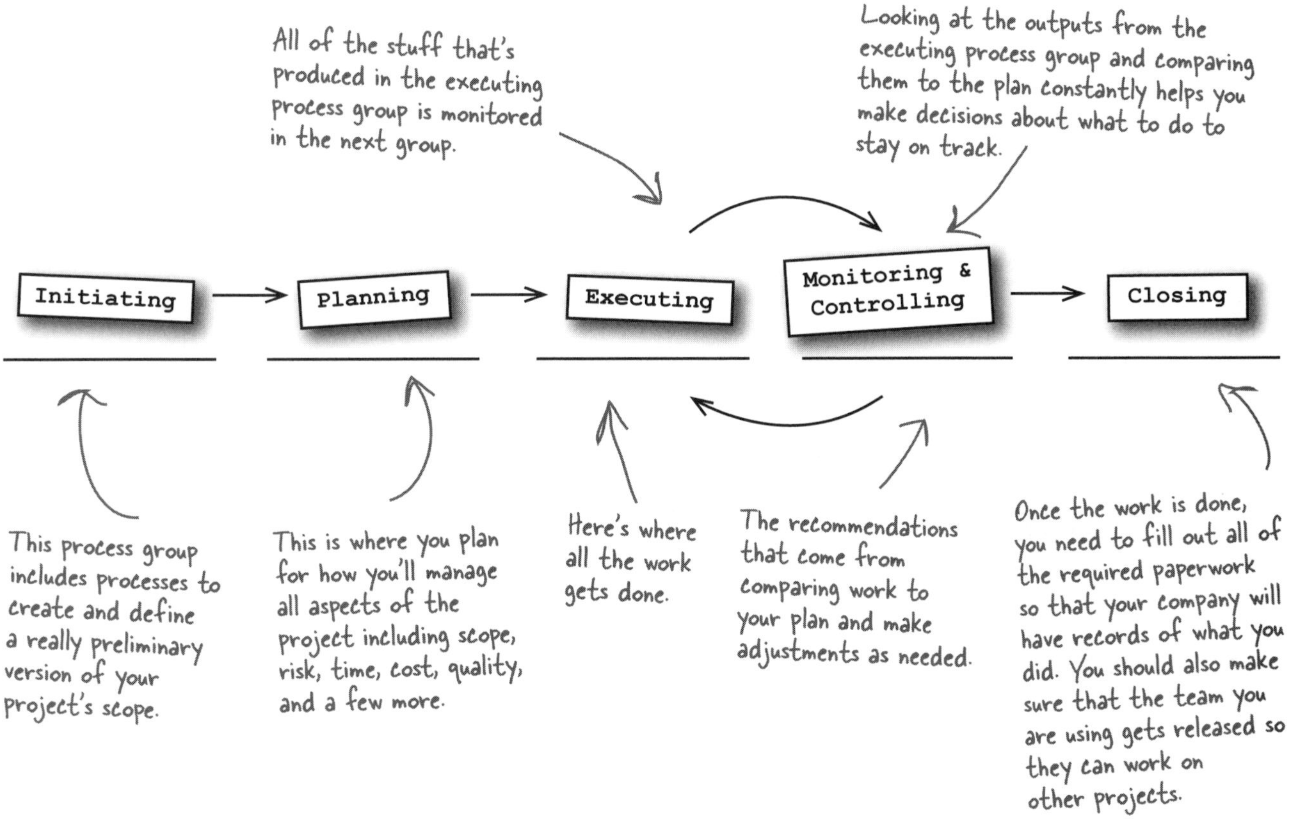

All of the stuff that's produced in the executing process group is monitored in the next group.

Looking at the outputs from the executing process group and comparing them to the plan constantly helps you make decisions about what to do to stay on track.

Initiating → Planning → Executing → Monitoring & Controlling → Closing

This process group includes processes to create and define a really preliminary version of your project's scope.

This is where you plan for how you'll manage all aspects of the project including scope, risk, time, cost, quality, and a few more.

Here's where all the work gets done.

The recommendations that come from comparing work to your plan and make adjustments as needed.

Once the work is done, you need to fill out all of the required paperwork so that your company will have records of what you did. You should also make sure that the team you are using gets released so they can work on other projects.

Relax

You're going to cover all of this information in a lot more depth soon, so for now, just sit back and relax!

You'll understand a lot more about project management if you're not worrying about getting it all this minute. Using this book together with the PMBOK® Guide, you're going to do much more than just learn this stuff by rote for the exam—you're going to understand these concepts.

Across all of the process groups, there are **9 knowledge areas** that span all of the different kinds of information you'll need to keep up with to manage your project. Match the knowledge area, on the left, to the description of what that knowledge area focuses on.

Risk	Defining contracts and choosing a contractor to do work on your project.
Quality	Keeping everybody working toward the same goal and dealing with changes.
Scope	Budgeting your project and tracking the money you are spending.
Procurement	Getting the people who will do the work and keeping them motivated.
Communication	Planning for things that could happen (positive or negative) and dealing with them when they do.
Time	Making sure that you build the right product and that you do it as efficiently as possible.
Integration	Figuring out who should talk to whom to keep everybody in the loop on your project.
Cost	Estimating the time it will take to complete your project and making sure you meet the deadlines you set.
Human Resources	Defining the tasks that will (and won't) be done on the project.

Answers on page 18.

Areas of responsibility... processes...process groups... knowledge areas...what does any of this have to do with ***my*** project?

All of these terms are ways of organizing your project, and solving common problems.

Remember, The PMBOK® Guide is the collective wisdom of a lot of people, so you can use it to learn from their experience rather than having to learn it ~~the hard way~~ on your own for yourself.

Let's start with the areas of responsibility

One of the ways that the PMBOK® Guide organizes information is into four areas of responsibility:

1 **Identify the requirements for the project**

If you do this before you begin, your project starts on the right track.

This means writing down what everyone needs from the project. Figure out your cost and scope, schedule, and the overall requirements for your project.

2 **Establish objectives that can be achieved**

When everyone understands the goal, it's much easier to keep them all on the right path.

Make sure you set up goals that everyone agrees on to avoid team conflicts later on.

3 **Balance scope, time, and cost**

Project managers need to balance these three to succeed.

Keep track of how your project is doing compared to its planned schedule (time), budget, and scope requirements. Any time you make a change that affects one of these three items, the other ones are affected as well. They always need to be managed together.

4 **Satisfy everyone's needs**

Understanding the needs of everyone affected by the project means that the end result of your project is far more likely to satisfy your stakeholders.

This means all of your team members, the people who are financing the project, the customers, or anyone else who is affected by what's going on...including the project team.

Not paying attention to these areas of responsibility is sure to give your project problems. Which of the four areas of responsibility was neglected in the failed projects listed below? Sometimes, more than one area of responsibility will apply; just pick the one that makes the most sense to you.

Your project was delivered early but it didn't have all of the features that the customers asked for.

Neglected area of responsibility:

....

The project created a great product but it was still considered a failure because there was a constraint that it needed to be delivered in March to be of any use to the company. It was delivered in May—so nobody could use it.

Neglected area of responsibility:

....

The project manager thought his job was to meet the deadline above all else. So he demanded that the product be released on the date it was due regardless of quality.

Neglected area of responsibility:

....

The project team had so many conflicts about the project that they couldn't work together. They made decisions that undercut each other, and in the end they couldn't deliver anything at all.

Neglected area of responsibility:

....

The project was late because the tasks weren't planned to occur in a sequence that would get it done on time.

Neglected area of responsibility:

....

The project manager spent all of his time holding status meetings with his team and didn't plan how to deal with all of the 9 knowledge areas. When the product was delivered, it turned out there was a stakeholder he hadn't identified, and the project didn't meet their needs.

Neglected area of responsibility:

....

Not paying attention to these areas of responsibility is sure to give your project problems. Which of the four areas of responsibility was neglected in the failed projects listed below? Sometimes, more than one area of responsibility will apply; just pick the one that makes the most sense to you.

The project was delivered early but it didn't have all of the features the customers asked for.

You might also have written "Manage cost, and quality." These project problems can be the result of more than one of the areas of responsibility being neglected.

Neglected area of responsibility:

Identify the requirements for the project

This is known as a project constraint.

The project created a great product, but it was still considered a failure because there was a constraint that it needed to be delivered in March to be of any use to the company. It was delivered in May -- so nobody could use it.

Since the constraint came from outside the project, it should've been known from the beginning.

Neglected area of responsibility:

Identify the requirements for the project

The project manager thought his job was to meet the deadline above all else. So he demanded that the product be released on the date it was due regardless of quality.

It's never a good idea to choose schedule over cost, scope, and quality. PMs need to balance all of them to deliver successful products.

Neglected area of responsibility:

Balance scope, time, and cost

The project team had so many conflicts about the project that they couldn't work together. They made decisions that undercut each other and in the end they couldn't deliver anything at all.

If the objectives were clear throughout the project, it would be easy to keep the team unified.

Neglected area of responsibility:

Establish objectives that can be achieved

The project was late because the tasks weren't planned to occur in a sequence that would get it done on time.

Neglected area of responsibility:

Establish objectives that can be achieved

The project manager spent all of his time holding status meetings with his team and didn't plan how to deal with all of the knowledge areas. When the product was delivered, it turned out there was a stakeholder he hadn't identified, and the project didn't make that stakeholder happy.

It's important that a PM identify and manage all of the stakeholder relationships.

Neglected area of responsibility:

Satisfy everyone's needs

there are no Dumb Questions

Q: How can the PMBOK® Guide claim to be the entire body of knowledge for project management?

A: Actually, it doesn't claim that at all. That's why the PMBOK® Guide is called "A ***Guide*** to the Project Management Body of Knowledge." It's a reference book that organizes a lot of information about how project managers do their jobs—but it doesn't claim to have all the information itself. Instead, it provides you a framework for managing projects and tells you what information you need to know.

A lot of people are surprised to find out that there are a bunch of things on the PMP exam that are never explicitly mentioned in the PMBOK® Guide. (Don't worry: we'll cover that stuff in the rest of this book.) There's a whole lot of information that modern project managers should know about risk management or time management or cost or quality... And you're expected to learn more about the knowledge areas as you move forward in your career. That's why you should never limit your study to just what's in the PMBOK® Guide. It's meant just as a guide to all of the knowledge areas that project managers use on the job.

Q: What if I don't do all of this stuff in my job?

A: Then you should start doing it! Seriously, it's the best way to learn. You might find that your projects go better after you start using a new concept you are learning while you study.

Q: I've heard that there are a whole bunch of formulas you have to memorize for the PMP exam. Will I have to do that?

A: Yes, but it won't be that bad. The formulas are actually really useful. They help you understand how your project is doing and make better decisions. When you read about them later in the book, you'll focus on how to use them and why. Once you know that, it's not about memorizing a bunch of useless junk. The formulas will actually make sense, and you'll find them intuitive and helpful in your day-to-day work.

Q: Aren't certification exams just an excuse that consultants use so that they can charge their clients more money?

A: Some consultants charge more money because they are certified, but that's not the only reason to get certified. The best reason to get PMP certification is because it helps you understand all of the project management concepts available to help you do your job better. If you learn these tools and apply them to your job, you will be a better Project Manager. Hey, if it turns out you can make more money too, that's great.

The PMBOK® Guide is just a guide, but if you understand all the material in it, then you'll ultimately be a better project manager.

A PMP certification is more than just passing a test

Getting your PMP certification means that you have the knowledge to solve most common project problems.

It proves that you know your stuff.

Once you're certified, your projects are more likely to succeed because:

You have the skills and knowledge to make them successful.

Meet a real-life PMP-certified project manager

PMs have demonstrated that they understand the tools it takes to be successful at leading projects. They know what it means to juggle their project priorities and still have their projects come out on top. Being certified doesn't mean you won't have problems on your projects anymore, but it does mean that you'll have the wisdom of many experienced and smart project managers behind you when you make decisions about how to solve these problems.

This could be YOU!

Across all of the process groups, there are nine knowledge areas that span all of the different kinds of information a PM needs to juggle to do the job right. Match the knowledge area to the description of what it does.

Knowledge area	Description
Risk	Defining contracts and choosing a contractor to do work for the project.
Quality	Keeping everybody working toward the same goal and dealing with changes.
Scope	Budgeting your project and tracking the money you are spending.
Procurement	Getting the people who will do the work and keeping them motivated.
Communication	Planning for things that could happen (positive or negative) and dealing with them when they do.
Time	Making sure that you build the right product and that you do it as efficiently as possible.
Integration	Figuring out who should talk to whom to keep everybody in the loop about your project.
Cost	Estimating how long you need to do your project and making sure you get it done by your deadline.
Human Resources	Defining the work that will (and won't) be done on the project.

2 Organizations, processes, and projects

(Keeping) In good company

If you want something done right... better hope you're in the right kind of organization. All projects are about teamwork—but how your team works depends a lot on the type of organization you're in. In this chapter, you'll learn about the different types of organizations around—and which type you should look for the next time you need a new job.

A day in Kate's life

Morning

We just finished testing, and the product should be ready to go to test on schedule.

Lunch time

We're halfway done updating the user manual.

Afternoon

The web site needs new graphics.

This is Kate's job—writing status reports.

Status Report

Programming

"We just finished testing, and the product should be ready to go to test on schedule."

Tech Writing

"We're halfway done updating the user manual."

Information Systems

"The web site needs new graphics."

All Kate does all day is document what people say in status meetings.

Kate wants a new job

Now that's she's working on getting her PMP certification, Kate's learning a whole load of new skills. And she's even started to look for a new job—one where she does more than write down what other people say all day…

All I do all day is collect status. Even if I have ideas about how to improve the project, it's not like I have the power to actually change anything.

Kate's not responsible for the success or failure of her project. She just keeps everybody informed of its progress.

Kate is a <u>project expeditor</u> right now.

Kate's job is to document what's happening on a project, but she doesn't have the authority to make decisions on it. She may work on projects, but she's certainly not managing anything.

When Kate surfs over to Monster.com, what types of things do you think she should look for in a new organization?

Kate spilled a hot cup of Starbuzz half caff nonfat latte on her job hunting checklist. Can you match the notes she scribbled at the bottom of the page to what's covered up by coffee stains?

Answers on page 40.

What would **you** look for in your perfect job? Does your wish list look anything like Kate's?

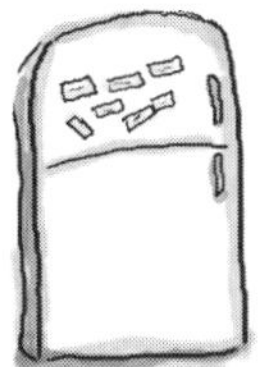

Organization Magnets

In a **functional organization**, which is what Kate works in, project managers don't have the authority to make major decisions on projects. **Projectized organizations** give all of the authority to the PM.

Can you work out which description goes with which organization type?

In this kind of company, the team reports to the project manager, who has a lot more authority.

In a functional organization, the teams working on the project don't report directly to the PM. Instead, the teams are in departments, and the project manager needs to "borrow" them for the project.

Functional Organization

1. ....

2. ....

3. ....

Projectized Organization

1. ....

2. ....

3. ....

Teams are organized around projects.

Project managers estimate and track budget and schedule.

PMs don't set the budget.

Project managers choose the team members, and release them when the project is over.

PMs spend half their time doing admin tasks.

Project managers need to clear major decisions with department managers.

Answers on page 41.

Three types of organizations

Kate's got three major options when looking at the kinds of organizations she can work for. **Functional organizations** are set up to give authority to functional managers, **projectized organizations** give it to the PM, and **matrix organizations** share responsibility and authority between the two.

Functional

- Project management decisions need to be cleared with functional managers.
- Project managers are assistants to the functional managers in getting the work done.
- Project managers spend a lot of time doing administrative tasks and often only work as PMs part of the time.

All of the project work typically happens within a particular department, and that department's manager is completely in charge of everything.

WEAK MATRIX

- PMs have some authority but they aren't in charge of the resources on a project.
- Major decisions still need to be made with the functional manager's cooperation or approval.
- Project expeditors can work in weak matrix organizations.

Project coordinators are like expeditors, except that coordinators typically report to higher-level managers and have some decision-making ability. Expeditors have no authority at all.

BALANCED MATRIX

Matrix Organizations

- Project managers share authority with the functional managers.
- PMs run their people-management decisions by the functional manager, but the functional manager runs his project decisions by the PM, too.

Folks who work in a balanced matrix organization report to a PM AND a functional manager equally.

The Project Manager has the most authority and power in a projectized organization.

STRONG MATRIX

For the PMP exam, most questions, assume that you work in a matrix organization unless they say otherwise.

- Project managers have more authority than functional managers, but the team still reports to both managers.
- The team might be judged based on performance on their projects, as well as on their functional expertise. In a strong matrix, delivery of the project is most important.

Projectized

If you've worked with a contractor or consulting company, they are usually organized like this.

- Teams are organized around projects. When a project is done, the team is released, and the team members move to another project.
- The project manager makes all of the decisions about a project's budget, schedule, quality, and resources.
- The PM is responsible for the success or failure of their project.

Wait a second. Not all companies will fit into one of these five categories, will they?

This is just one way to think about it.

Most importantly, it's the way that appears on the exam, so you're going to need to know it.

there are no Dumb Questions

Q: I'm still not clear on the difference between a project *coordinator* and a project *expeditor*.

A: They're actually pretty similar. A project expeditor is somebody who keeps track of status but has no decision-making authority on a project at all. A project coordinator is someone who does pretty much the same thing, but does get to make some of the minor decisions on the project without having to run them by the functional manager. Coordinators usually report to somebody who is pretty high up in the organization, while expeditors are more like assistants to the functional manager. Both of them usually exist in weak-matrix organizations.

Q: What's the difference between the way teams are run in a functional organization and a projectized one?

A: Think of a major bookkeeping project being run by the Admin department. Usually the head of Admin is the one who is ultimately responsible for what happens to it. If a project manager is called in to help out, she's just there to keep things straight for the Admin department manager. The team is made up of people who already report to the Admin manager, so nobody questions his authority. That's an example of a functional organization.

Contrast that with the way the bookkeeping project would be run if a consulting company that specialized in bookkeeping were contracted to do it. They would assemble a team of bookkeepers and assign a project manager to lead them. When the project was over, the team would dissolve, and the team members would go join other teams working for other project managers. That's how a projectized organization works. The team is organized around a project and not around a job function.

Q: Can I be an effective PM in a functional organization?

A: Since project managers don't have much authority in a functional organization, it's hard to have as much impact in a functional organization as you would in a matrixed or projectized one.

Of course, you can be good at your job in any kind of organization. But, for your company to really get the most out of having project managers on staff, it really pays for them to look into changing the way they balance power. The project managers who are accountable for project success or failure should also have the chance to influence the team, budget, and schedule for those projects.

Q: Does the PMP exam favor any kind of organization?

A: When you're taking the PMP exam, if you see a question that mentions a PM, then you should assume that the question is asking about a matrix or projectized organization if it doesn't say up front which kind of organization is being described. Functional organizations are usually painted in a negative light because they tend to give less authority to project managers.

BULLET POINTS: AIMING FOR THE EXAM

- Functional managers have all the power in a functional organization, Project managers have the power in a projectized organization.

  If a question on the exam doesn't state an organization type, assume it's referring to a matrix organization. That means the PM is responsible for making budgets, assigning tasks to resources, and resolving conflicts.

- Project coordinators and expeditors don't exist in a projectized organization.
- A project expeditor keeps track of project status only. A project coordinator has some authority, and usually reports to someone higher up in the company. Neither role has as much power or authority as a real project manager, even though an expeditor or coordinator may have "Project Manager" written on their business cards.

Here are a few excerpts from some of Kate's job interviews. Can you figure out what kind of organization each interviewer is representing?

Interviewer #1: We'relooking for someone who can work with our development manager to deliver our products on time. We have a good programming team; they just need a little encouragement to meet their deadlines. You'll be expected to keep really good status meeting notes. If you run into any trouble with the team, just kick it back to the Dev Manager, and she'll address the problem.

☐ Functional ☐ Matrix ☐ Projectized

Interviewer #2: Weneed someone who can manage the whole effort, start to finish. You'll need to work with the client to establish goals, choose the team, estimate time and cost, manage and track all of your decisions, and make sure you keep everybody in the loop on what's going on. We expect the project to last six months.

☐ Functional ☐ Matrix ☐ Projectized

Interviewer #3: Wehave a project coming up that's needed by our customer service team. The project is a real technical challenge for us, so we've assembled a team of top-notch programmers to come up with a good solution. We need a project manager to work with the programming manager on this one. You would be responsible for the schedule, the budget, and managing the deliverables. The programming manager would have the personnel responsibilities.

☐ Functional ☐ Matrix ☐ Projectized

Interviewer #4: Mostof the work you'll be doing is contract work. You'll put together three different teams of software engineers, and you'll need to make sure that they build everything our customer needs. And don't forget: you've got to stay within budget, and it's got to be done on time! It's a big job, and it's your neck on the line if things go wrong. Can you handle that?

☐ Functional ☐ Matrix ☐ Projectized

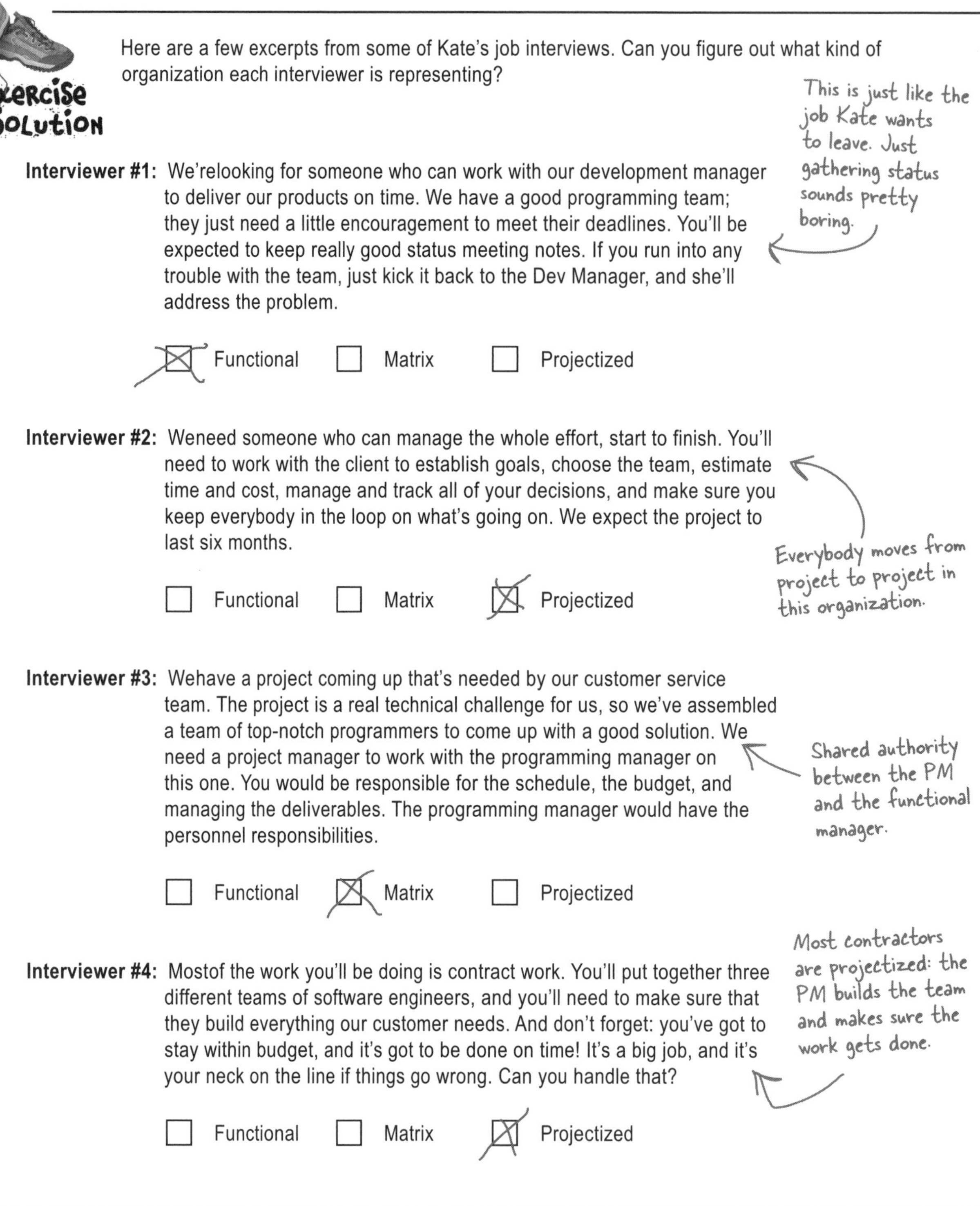

Here are a few excerpts from some of Kate's job interviews. Can you figure out what kind of organization each interviewer is representing?

Interviewer #1: We're looking for someone who can work with our development manager to deliver our products on time. We have a good programming team; they just need a little encouragement to meet their deadlines. You'll be expected to keep really good status meeting notes. If you run into any trouble with the team, just kick it back to the Dev Manager, and she'll address the problem.

This is just like the job Kate wants to leave. Just gathering status sounds pretty boring.

☒ Functional ☐ Matrix ☐ Projectized

Interviewer #2: We need someone who can manage the whole effort, start to finish. You'll need to work with the client to establish goals, choose the team, estimate time and cost, manage and track all of your decisions, and make sure you keep everybody in the loop on what's going on. We expect the project to last six months.

Everybody moves from project to project in this organization.

☐ Functional ☐ Matrix ☒ Projectized

Interviewer #3: We have a project coming up that's needed by our customer service team. The project is a real technical challenge for us, so we've assembled a team of top-notch programmers to come up with a good solution. We need a project manager to work with the programming manager on this one. You would be responsible for the schedule, the budget, and managing the deliverables. The programming manager would have the personnel responsibilities.

Shared authority between the PM and the functional manager.

☐ Functional ☒ Matrix ☐ Projectized

Interviewer #4: Most of the work you'll be doing is contract work. You'll put together three different teams of software engineers, and you'll need to make sure that they build everything our customer needs. And don't forget: you've got to stay within budget, and it's got to be done on time! It's a big job, and it's your neck on the line if things go wrong. Can you handle that?

Most contractors are projectized: the PM builds the team and makes sure the work gets done.

☐ Functional ☐ Matrix ☒ Projectized

Kate takes a new job

Welcome aboard, Kate! I'm Ben, the programming manager.

Kate: Hi, Ben. I'm excited to be here.

Ben: We're excited too, since you'll be taking care of our main software development project. It's in maintenance mode right now.

Kate: Sounds great. How do we handle that here?

Ben: Well, we're constantly getting business reports from the field, and when people think of new ideas, we just add them to the project.

Kate: Umm… So how do you know when you're done?

Ben: We're never really done; we try to release new versions as often as possible.

Why do you think Kate is suddenly nervous about her new job?

What a project IS...

Temporary

Projects always have a **start** and a **finish**. They start when you decide what you are going to do, and they end when you create the product or service you set out to create. Sometimes they end because you decide to stop doing the project. But they are never

Processes are ongoing. If you're building cars on an assembly line, that's a process. If you're designing and building a prototype of a specific car model, that's a project.

Creating a unique result

When you create the product of your project, it is **measurable**. If you start a project to create a piece of software or build a building, you can tell that software or that building from any other one that has been produced.

Progressively elaborated

You learn more and more about a project as it goes on. When you start, you have goals and a plan but there is always new information to deal with as your project goes on and you are always having to make decisions to keep it on track. While you do your best to plan for everything that will happen, you know that you will keep learning more about your project as you go.

... and what a project is NOT

Projects are NOT: always strategic or critical

Projects are NOT: ongoing processes

Kate's "project" is really a process. It has no definite end.

Projects are NOT: always successful

Sharpen your pencil

Which of these scenarios is a process, and which is a project?

1. Building an extension on a house

☐ Process ☐ Project

2. Shelving books at the library

☐ Process ☐ Project

3. Baking a wedding cake

☐ Process ☐ Project

4. Stapling programs for a play

☐ Process ☐ Project

5. Watering your plants twice a week

☐ Process ☐ Project

6. Walking the dog every day

☐ Process ☐ Project

7. Knitting a scarf

☐ Process ☐ Project

8. Making a birdhouse

☐ Process ☐ Project

9. Changing your air filters every six months

☐ Process ☐ Project

10. Running an assembly line in a toy factory

☐ Process ☐ Project

11. Organizing a large conference

☐ Process ☐ Project

12. Going to the gym three times a week

☐ Process ☐ Project

→ Answers on page 42.

Back to Kate's maintenance nightmare

Let's figure out how things are working in Kate's new organization… and start to think about how we can improve things.

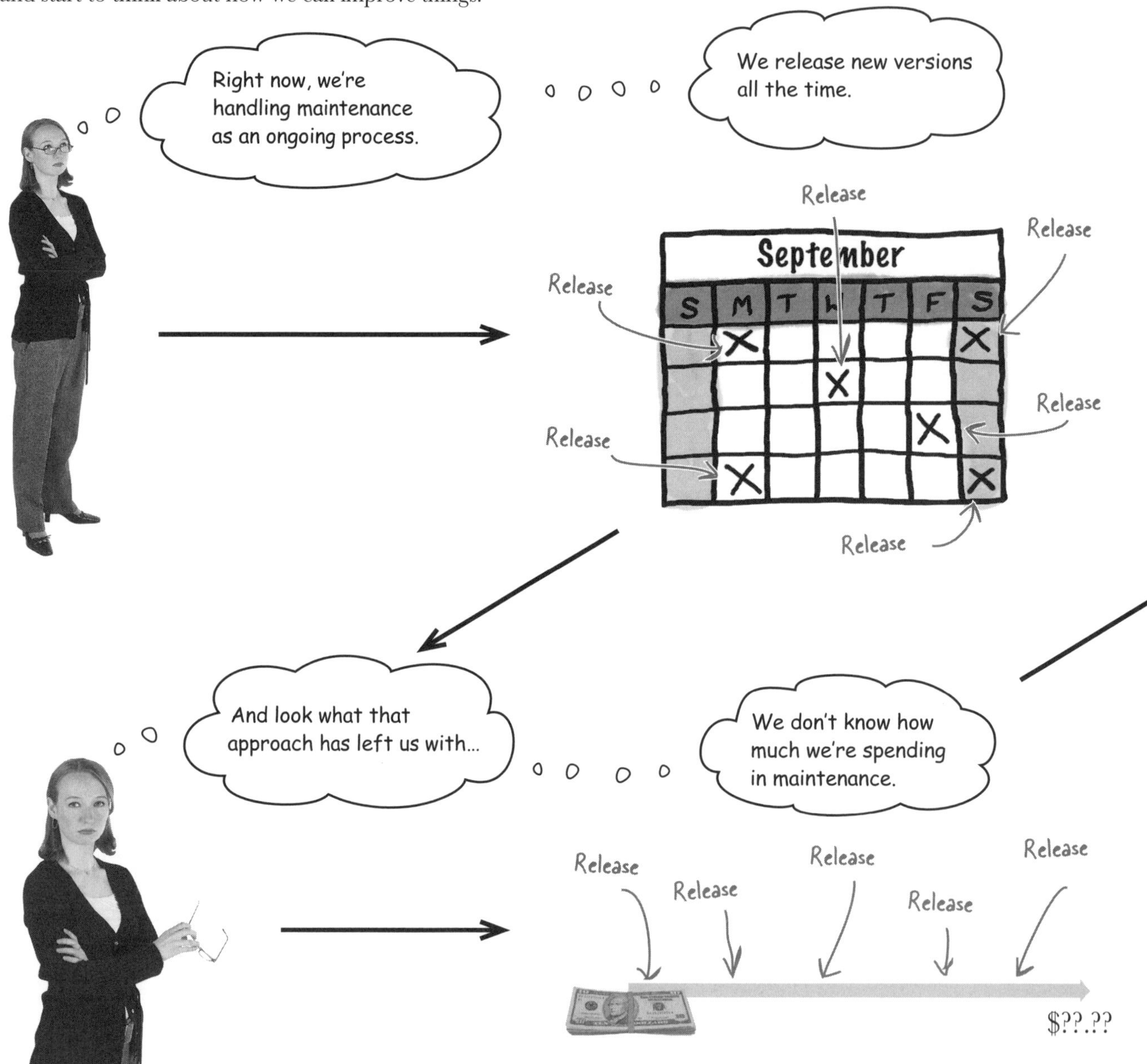

BRAIN POWER

What would you do to fix this problem?

Managing cost, quality, and schedule

When Kate thinks about solutions, she's going to have to deal with the project's time, its scope, and its budget. Every project, regardless of what is being produced or who is doing the work is affected by the **triple constraint** of time, scope, and cost. We refer to these three constraints as the **iron triangle** because doing something to deal with one of the constraints always has an effect on the other two constraints.

Any time your project changes, you'll need to know how that change affects all three constraints.

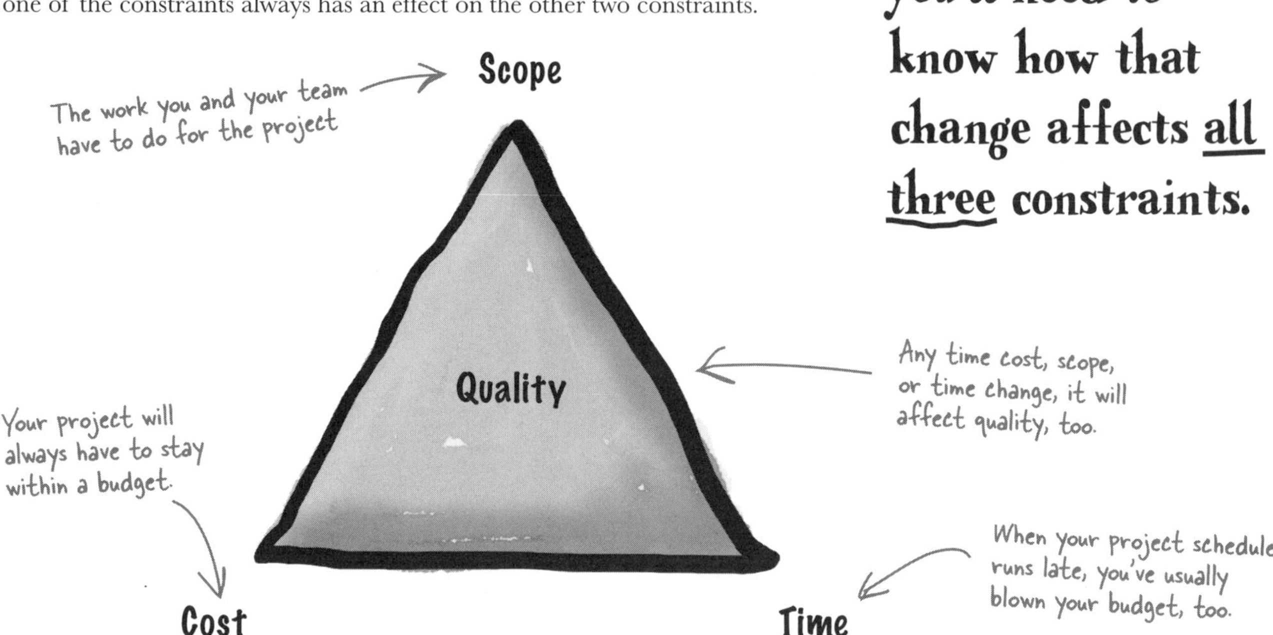

For Kate's project to succeed, she needs to think about the **triple constraint**. If she doesn't manage these three constraints at the same time, she'll find that her project is either late, overbudget, or unacceptable to her customers.

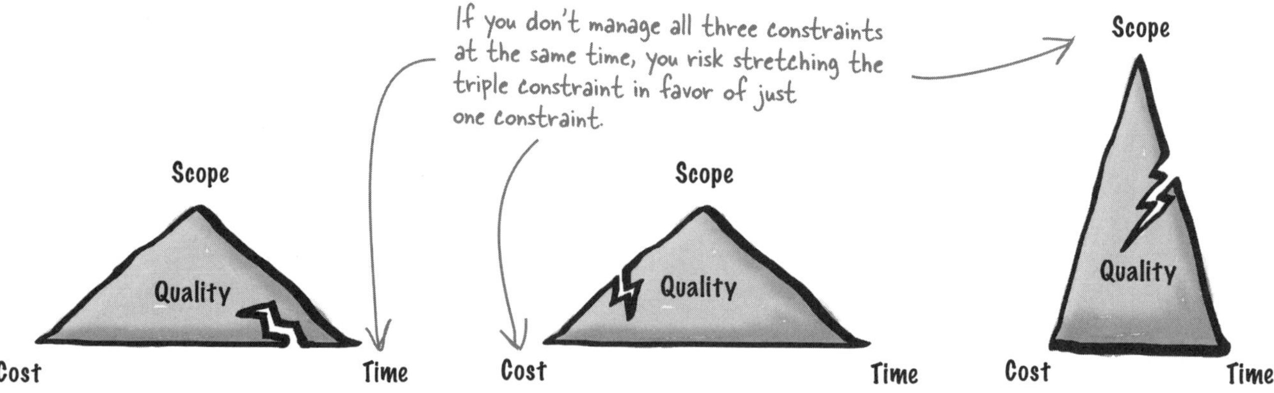

When you make a change to one of the triple constraints, the other two are also affected. Can you figure out which of the three constraints is going to be affected the most in each of these problematic situations? (Sometimes there's more than one good answer!)

The project was running late, so the PM decided to release it on time even though the work was incomplete.

Constraint affected:

....

The product isn't passing any of its quality inspections. The PM added more quality activities to try to head off bugs before they derailed the project.

Constraint affected:

....

The project's scope had ballooned out of control, and it looked like the project was never be completed. The project manager set up a meeting with stakeholders to decide what to do.

Constraint affected:

....

About halfway through the project, the PM realized that the money was running out faster than expected. She went through the schedule to try to find tasks that could be cut from the project to save money.

Constraint affected:

....

The company needed this project to be done by the end of the first quarter but it looked like it wouldn't be done until the *third* quarter. The PM told upper management what was going on and tried to negotiate a new deadline.

Constraint affected:

....

The company didn't have much money to invest in the project so they asked the PM to cut corners wherever possible to stay on budget.

Constraint affected:

....

When you make a change to one of the triple constraints, the other two are also affected. Can you figure out which of the three constraints is going to be affected the most in each of these problematic situations? (Sometimes there's more than one good answer!)

The project was running late, so the PM decided to release it on time even though the work was incomplete.

Constraint affected:

scope

The PM stuck to the original budget and schedule, but released a product that wasn't complete. That means the scope was affected, and the time and cost were left untouched.

The product isn't passing any of its quality inspections. The PM added more quality activities to try to head off bugs before they derailed the project.

Constraint affected:

cost and schedule

The PM added work to make sure the final product had good quality. But that work costs money and takes time.

The project's scope had ballooned out of control, and it looked like the project was never be completed. The project manager set up a meeting with stakeholders to decide what to do.

Constraint affected:

schedule

It looks like the project will blow its schedule, and now the PM is doing damage control.

About halfway through the project, the PM realized that the money was running out faster than expected. She went through the schedule to try to find tasks that could be cut from the project to save money.

Constraint affected:

schedule

The project schedule lists all of the tasks on the project, so when you cut some of them out, you're messing with the schedule! And those tasks were important, which means that not doing them will cause quality problems.

The company needed this project to be done by the end of the first quarter but it looked like it wouldn't be done until the *third* quarter. The PM told upper management what was going on and tried to negotiate a new deadline.

Constraint affected:

schedule

The PM decided to try to change the schedule—and that's probably a good idea, because it will protect quality, and it might even help with cost.

The company didn't have much money to invest in the project so they asked the PM to cut corners wherever possible to stay on budget.

Constraint affected:

scope

Cutting corners means that your team does less work. A good PM makes sure that the team does the work that they need to do for a quality product.

there are no Dumb Questions

Q: Why are these things in a triangle?

A: Because it makes it really easy to think about how they relate to each other. The whole idea here is that scope, cost, and time are all related. If you make a change to one of them, the other two also change.

Q: I've heard of an old saying: "Faster, cheaper, better—pick two," but doesn't that mean it's a *double* constraint?

A: No, that's an old (and somewhat cynical) project management saying. When a project manager says it to a customer or stakeholder, what he is saying is that there's no way to reduce cost, shorten the schedule, and increase quality all at the same time. At least one of those things absolutely has to give... but the saying is a little disingenuous! We already know that all three of the constraints are related to each other, and there's almost never an easy, obvious trade-off where you can sacrifice one to improve the other two.

Q: What if I know that a change will impact just scope, but not schedule or cost. Can I go ahead and make it?

A: Whenever you are making a change that affects the triple constraint, you need to be sure that the change is acceptable to **your stakeholders**. They're the people who will be impacted by your project. The term applies to your team, your customer, your sponsor, and anybody else who is affected by the change.

A lot of project management is about evaluating what a change is going to do to your triple constraint and using that impact analysis to help stakeholders make choices about what to do when changes come up. Sometimes a change that affects the quality of your product is completely unacceptable to your stakeholders, and they would rather delay the project than sacrifice the product's quality.

A stakeholder is anyone who is affected by the cost, time, or scope of your project.

Kate makes some changes...

1. She divides maintenance into releases, each with a well-defined start ***and*** a finish.

2. She works with stakeholders to set scope goals that each release must meet.

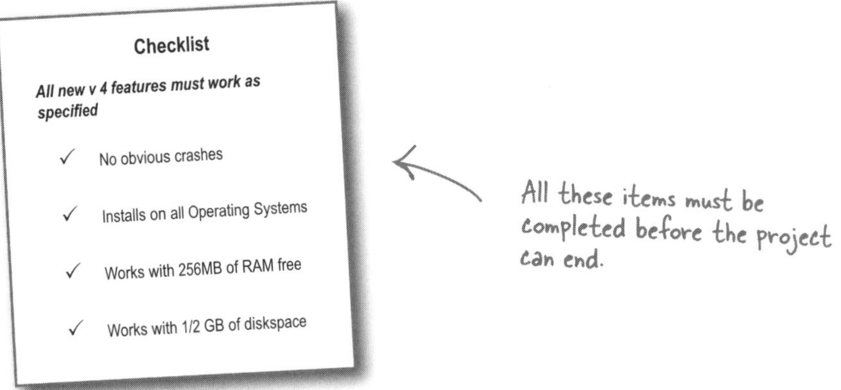

3. She manages the budget for each release and keeps the costs contained.

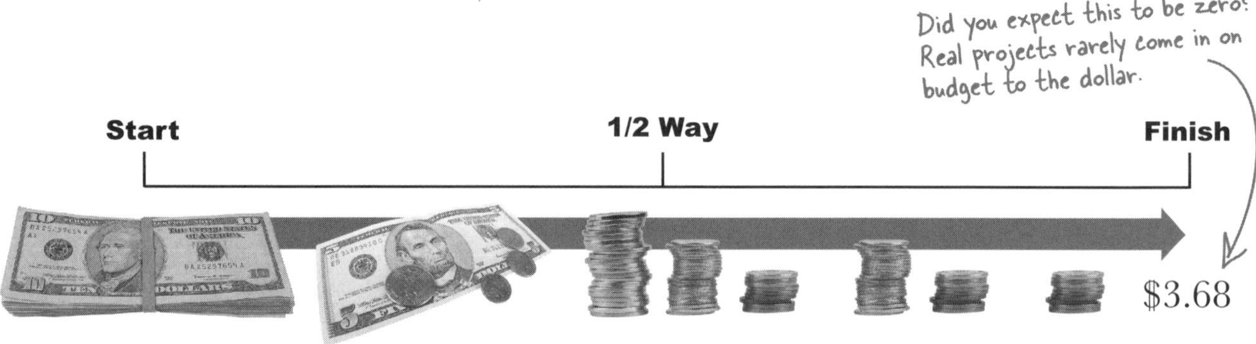

... and her project is a success!

Now the company knows when their products will be done, how much they will cost, and that the products will satisfy their customers…

...and that earns Kate and Ben big bonuses!

Kate spilled a hot cup of Starbuzz half caff nonfat latte on her job hunting checklist. Can you match the notes she scribbled at the bottom of the page to what's covered up by coffee stains?

Job Hunting Checklist

- I should have authority over my projects
- I am allowed to assign work to people on my project team
- I am in control of my project's budget
- I focus on managing projects, not irrelevant tasks
- I shouldn't spend my whole day filing stuff
- I can assign work to my project team without having to clear it with their bosses.

Organization Magnets Solutions

In a functional organization, which is what Kate works in, project managers don't have the authority to make major decisions on projects. Projectized organizations give all of the authority to the PM.

Can you work out which description goes with which organization type?

In a functional organization, the teams working on the project don't report directly to the PM. Instead, the teams are in departments, and the project manager needs to "borrow" them for the project.

In this kind of company, the team reports to the project manager, who has a lot more authority.

Functional Organization

1. Project managers need to clear major decisions with department managers.
2. PMs don't set the budget.
3. PMs spend half their time doing admin tasks.

Projectized Organization

1. Teams are organized around projects.
2. Project managers choose the team members, and release them when the project is over.
3. Project managers estimate and track budget and schedule.

Sharpen your pencil Solution

Which of these scenarios is a process, and which is a project?

1. Building an extension on a house
   - [ ] Process
   - [x] Project
2. Shelving books at the library
   - [x] Process
   - [ ] Project
3. Baking a wedding cake
   - [ ] Process
   - [x] Project
4. Stapling programs for a play
   - [ ] Process
   - [x] Project
5. Watering your plants twice a week
   - [x] Process
   - [ ] Project
6. Walking the dog every day
   - [x] Process
   - [ ] Project
7. Knitting a scarf
   - [ ] Process
   - [x] Project
8. Making a birdhouse
   - [ ] Process
   - [x] Project
9. Changing your air filters every six months
   - [x] Process
   - [ ] Project
10. Running an assembly line in a toy factory
    - [x] Process
    - [ ] Project
11. Organizing a large conference
    - [ ] Process
    - [x] Project
12. Going to the gym three times a week
    - [x] Process
    - [ ] Project

3 the process framework

It all fits together

All of the work you do on a project is made up of processes. Once you know how all the processes in your project fit together, it's easy to remember everything you need to know for the PMP exam. **There's a pattern** to all of the work that gets done on your project. First you plan it, then you get to work. While you are doing the work, you are always comparing your project to your original plan. When things start to get off-plan, it's your job to make corrections and put everything back on track. And the **process framework**—the **process groups** and **knowledge areas**—is the key to all of this happening smoothly.

Cooking up a project

When you cook something from a recipe for the first time, there are certain steps you always follow:

1. First figure out what you're going to make.

2. Then you make all your plans

3. Next, it's time to start cooking!

4. Finally, you can give the cookies to a loved one.

Projects are like recipes

All projects, no matter how big, or small, break down into process groups. **Process groups** are like the steps you use when following a recipe.

Needs

Initiating process group

Planning process group

This is where you figure out what it is you need: a huge product, or maybe just some homemade cookies.

Then you initiate your project—researching and deciding what you're going to build to fulfill the project's needs.

Next, you determine what "ingredients" you already have and which ones you still need. You'll figure out where to get those missing resources, and think about what they'll cost.

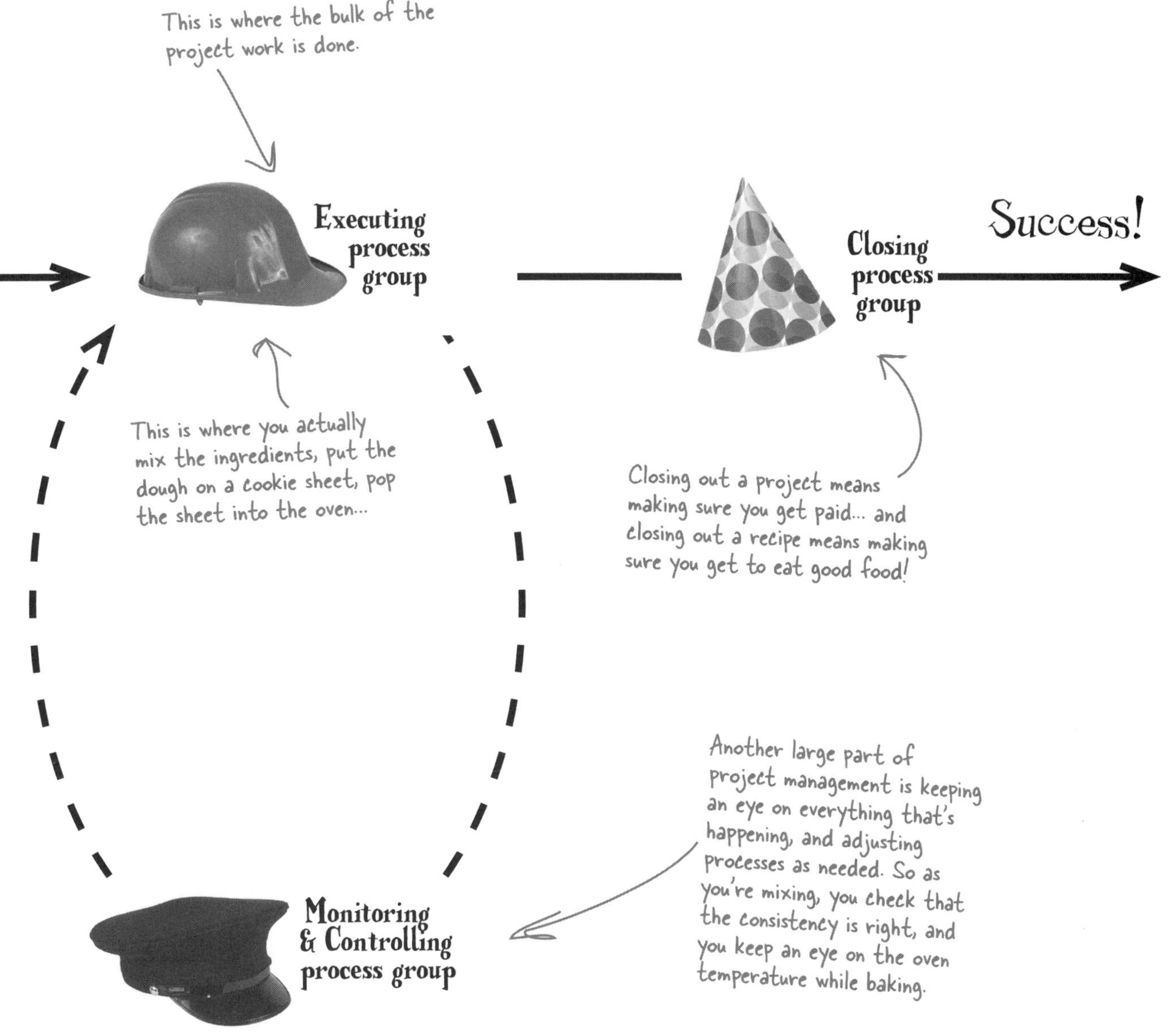
This is where the bulk of the project work is done.
Executing process group
This is where you actually mix the ingredients, put the dough on a cookie sheet, pop the sheet into the oven...
Closing process group
Success!
Closing out a project means making sure you get paid... and closing out a recipe means making sure you get to eat good food!
Monitoring & Controlling process group
Another large part of project management is keeping an eye on everything that's happening, and adjusting processes as needed. So as you're mixing, you check that the consistency is right, and you keep an eye on the oven temperature while baking.

Break it down

Within each process group are several individual **processes**, which is how you actually do the work on your project. The PMBOK® Guide breaks every project down into 44 processes—that sounds like a lot to know, but don't start looking for the panic button! In your day-to-day working life, you actually use most of them already… and by the time you've worked your way through this book, you'll know all of them.

Taking a vacation is simple, even though there are several steps.

Forty-four processes might seem like a lot to remember, but once you've been using them for a while, they'll be second nature—just like all the things you do without thinking when you go on a trip.

Stuff you do when you take a vacation

The PMBOK® Guide processes that those steps correspond to

Stuff you do when you take a vacation	The PMBOK® Guide processes
1. Figure out how much time you have off, how much money you can spend, and where you want to go.	1. Develop project charter
2. Find your flights and hotel information and put together an itinerary using a travel web site.	2. Develop project management plan
3. Take your flight, stay in the hotel, see the sights. Enjoy yourself.	3. Direct and manage project work
4. Make sure you get the seat you want on the plane, your hotel room is clean, and the sight-seeing tours are worth your money. If not, complain, correct any problems that come up, and try to get better service.	4. Monitor and control project work
5. Come home, pay all the bills, and write up your reviews of the trip for the hotel feedback web site.	5. Close project

Simultaneous (steps 3 and 4)

Don't worry about memorizing these process names now… you'll see a lot more of each of them throughout the book.

Process Magnets

Below are several of the 44 processes. Try and guess which process group each process belongs to just from the name. We've done the first two for you.

Initiating process group

Planning process group

Executing process group

Monitoring & Controlling process group

Closing process group

Planning process group: Develop Project Management Plan

Executing process group: Direct and Manage Project Work

Quality Planning

Monitor and Control Project Work

Scope Control

Develop Project Charter

Risk Identification

Schedule Control

Activity Duration Estimating

Information Distribution

Close Project

Process Magnets

Below are several of the 44 processes. Try and guess which process group each process belongs to just from the name!

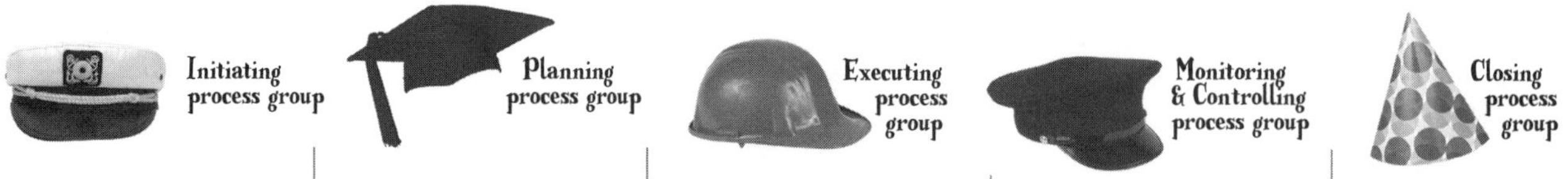

Initiating process group	Planning process group	Executing process group	Monitoring & Controlling process group	Closing process group
Develop Project Charter	Develop Project Management Plan	Direct and Manage Project Work	Scope Control	Close Project
	Risk Identification	Information Distribution	Monitor and Control Project Work	
	Quality Planning		Schedule Control	
	Activity Duration Estimating			

There are only two processes in the entire Initiating process group, and this is one of them.

This one was a little tricky, but if you keep in mind that the Executing process is where you do your work, it makes more sense.

When a process ends in "control" it's part of the Monitoring and Controlling group.

Some of these exercises are hard—and it's okay to get some answers wrong! Making mistakes actually helps you remember."

Anatomy of a process

You can think of each process as a little machine. It takes the **inputs**—information you use in your project—and turns them into **outputs**: documents, deliverables, and decisions. The outputs help your project come in on time, within budget, and with high quality. Every single process has inputs, **tools and techniques** that are used to do the work, and outputs.

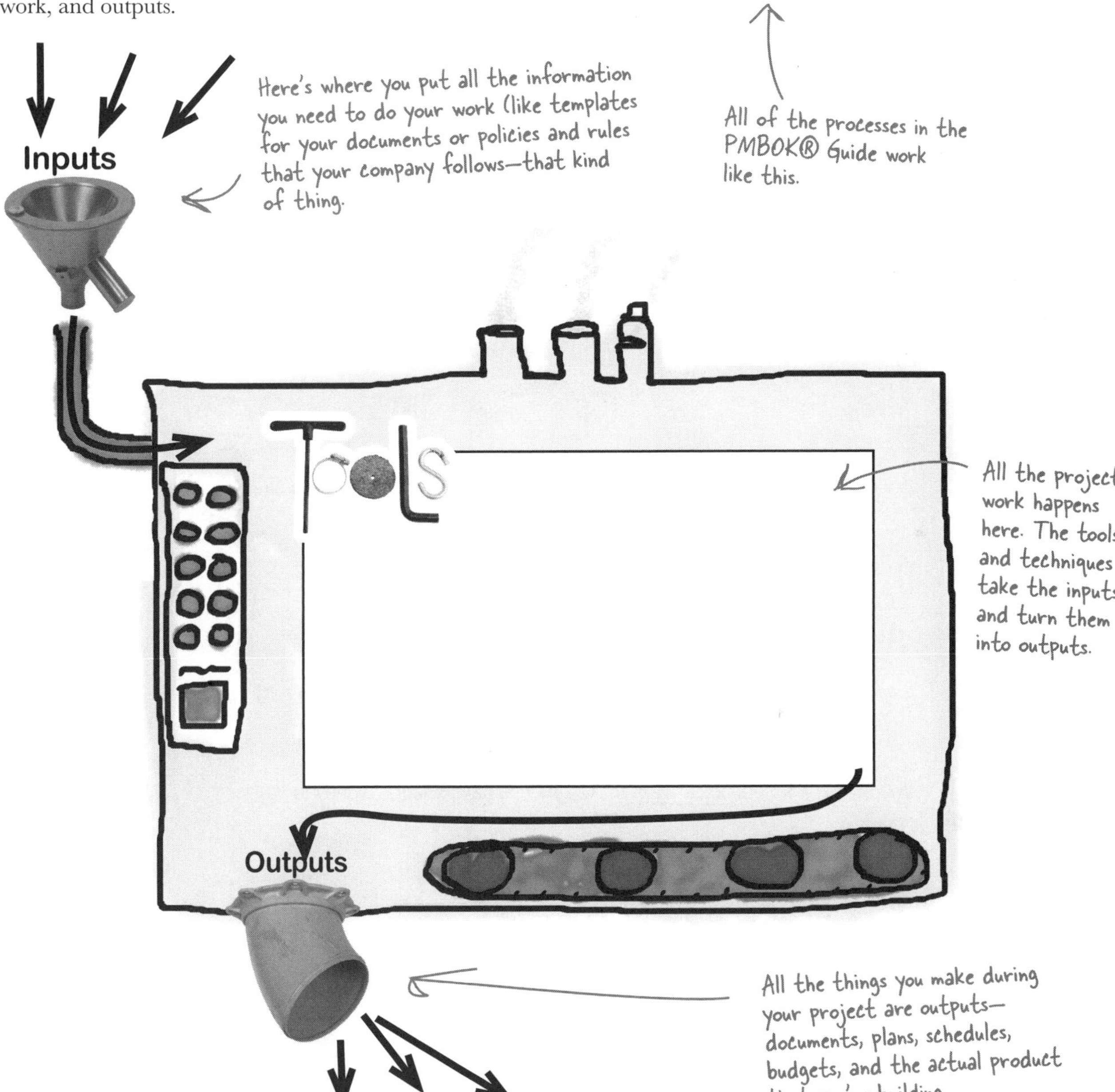

Sharpen your pencil

Think of the vacation we talked about on page 48 as a project, and each of its steps as a process. Here are some inputs, tools, and outputs that could be used in each of the vacation steps. Can you look at each of the underlined words and figure out if the words represent an input, tool, or output? (Here's a hint: some of them are an output from one process and an input for another.)

Look at each of these underlined things, and figure out if it's an input, output and/or tool.

1. You log in and check your company's vacation calendar to see how much vacation time you have for your trip.

   ☐ Input ☐ Tool ☐ Output

2. You create an itinerary on a travel web site. You'll use the itinerary when you board your flight.

   ☐ Input ☐ Tool ☐ Output

3. You have some hotel reservation documents you created on the travel web site, too. You'll use those when you check into your hotel.

   ☐ Input ☐ Tool ☐ Output

4. You use a travel web site to book the plane, hotel, and sights you'll see on your trip.

   ☐ Input ☐ Tool ☐ Output

5. You verify your bank account balance to make sure you have enough money to pay for everything.

   ☐ Input ☐ Tool ☐ Output

6. You use a hotel feedback web site to review your stay in the hotel once you get back home.

   ☐ Input ☐ Tool ☐ Output

→ Answers on page 62.

These processes are meant to work on any type of project.

The processes are there to help you organize how you do things. But they have to work on small, medium, and large projects. Sometimes that means a lot of processes—but it also ensures that what you're learning here will work on all your projects.

there are no Dumb Questions

Q: Can a process be part of more than one process group?

A: No, each of the processes belongs to only one process group. The best way to figure out which group a process belongs to is to remember what that process does. If the process is about defining high-level goals of the project, it's in Initiating. If it's about planning the work, it's in Planning. If you are actually doing the work, it's in Executing. If you're tracking the work and finding problems, it's in Monitoring & Controlling. And if you're finishing stuff off after you've delivered the product, that's Closing.

Q: Do you do all of the processes in every project?

A: Not always. Some of the processes only apply to projectized organizations or subcontracted work, so if your company doesn't do that kind of thing, then you won't need those processes. But if you want to make your projects come out well, then it *really does make sense* to use the processes. Even a small project can benefit from taking the time to plan out the way you'll handle all of the knowledge areas. If you do your homework and pay attention to all of the processes, you can avoid most of the big problems that cause projects to run into trouble!

Q: Can you use the same input in more than one process?

A: Yes. There are a lot of inputs that show up in multiple processes. For example, think about a schedule that you'd make for your project. You'll need to use that schedule to build a budget, but also to do the work! So that schedule is an input to at least two processes. That's why it's really important that you write down exactly how you use each process, so you know what its inputs and outputs are.

Your company has records of all of these process documents, and the stuff the PMs learned from doing their projects. We call these things "Organizational Process Assets," and you'll see a lot of them in the next chapter.

Combine processes to complete your project

Sometimes the output of one process becomes an input of the next process. In the cookie project, the raw ingredients from the store are the outputs of the planning process, but they become the inputs for the executing process, where you mix the ingredients together and bake them:

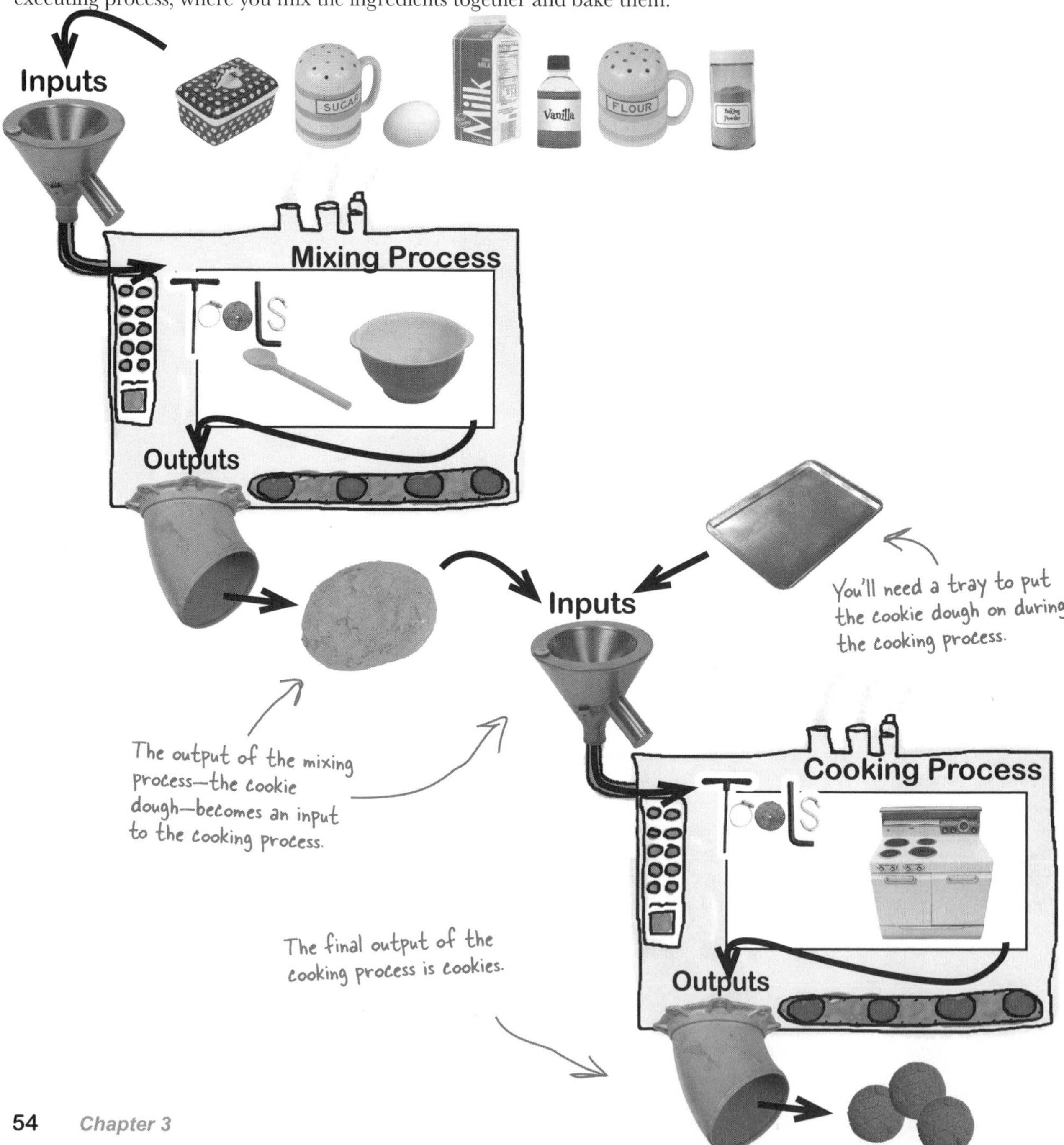

Knowledge areas organize the processes

The **process groups** help you organize the processes by the *kind of work* you do. The **knowledge areas** help you organize by the *subject matter* you're dealing with. The following nine elements of the cookie process are the PMBOK® Guide Knowledge ares.

The processes are organized in two ways—the process groups are about how you do the work, and the knowledge areas are there to help you orgranize them and help you learn.

Integration

Making sure all the right parts of the project come together in the right order, at the right time

Scope

Could you have decorated the cookies? Or made more batches?

Time

Preparation and cooking time

Cost

Budgeting for the cookie project

Quality

Checking that the cookies look and taste right

Human Resource

Making sure your schedule is clear and your honey is going to be home on time

Communications

Making sure you're not mixing metric and imperial measurements

Risk

Could you burn the cookies or yourself on the range? Are the eggs fresh?

Procurement

Selecting the right store to supply your ingredients

Knowledge Area Magnets

Match the knowledge areas to each description. We've done the first for you.

______	______	Time Management	______	______
Coordinating all of the work so that it happens correctly. Making sure changes are approved before they happen.	Figuring out what work needs to be done for your project. Making sure your end product has everything you said it would.	Figuring out the time it will take to do your work and the order you need to do it in. Tracking your schedule and making sure everything gets done on time.	Knowing how much you're able to invest in the project and making sure you spend your budget accordingly.	Making sure you work as efficiently as you can and don't add defects into the product.

Risk Management

Procurement Management

Human Resource Management

Quality Management

Communications Management

Getting the people to work on the team and helping them stay motivated. Rewarding them for a job well done and resolving conflicts that come up.

Making sure that everybody knows what they need to know to do their job right. Tracking how people talk to each other and dealing with misunderstandings or miscommunications if they happen.

Figuring out how to protect your project from anything that could happen to it. Dealing with the unexpected when it does happen.

Finding contractors to help you do the work. Setting the ground rules for their relationships with your company.

Scope Management

Integration Management

Cost Management

Knowledge Area Magnets Solutions

Match the knowledge areas to each description.

This knowledge area includes processes to direct and manage project work as well as monitor and control it.

Quality is about preventing defects and working efficiently

Integration Management

Coordinating all of the work so that it happens correctly. Making sure changes are approved before they happen.

Scope Management

Figuring out what work needs to be done for you project. Making sure your end product has everything you said it would.

Time Management

Figuring out the time it will take to do your work and the order you need to do it in. Tracking your schedule and making sure everything gets done on time.

Cost Management

Knowing how much you're able to invest in the project and making sure you spend it right.

Quality Management

Making sure you work as efficiently as you can and don't add defects into the product.

If you nail down your scope in the beginning, you have a much better chance of success in the end.

A lot of people think that this is all a project manager does, but it's only one of the nine knowledge areas!

How well you keep to your budget can be the difference between success and failure for your project.

Since the PMBOK® Guide covers projectized organizations, it talks about actually acquiring your team as a process, too. People in most organizations don't get a chance to do that. The team is often determined by the time you get assigned to it.

This one is another area that a lot of PMs don't have much experience with. It's all about selecting suppliers, contractors and vendors, and setting up contracts with them.

Human Resource Management

Getting the people to work on the team and helping them stay motivated. Rewarding them for a job well done and resolving conflicts that come up.

Communications Management

Making sure that everybody knows what they need to know to do the job right. Tracking how people talk to each other and dealing with gaps if they happen.

Risk Management

Figuring out how to protect your project from anything that could happen to it. Dealing with the unexpected when it does happen.

Procurement Management

Finding contractors to help you do the work. Setting the ground rules for their relationships with your company.

Communication is a really important part of the project manager's job.

Risk Management can also be about making sure that you are in the right position to take advantage of the opportunities that come your way.

there are no Dumb Questions

Q: So what's the difference between process groups and knowledge areas?

A: The process groups divide up the processes by function. The knowledge areas divide the same processes up by subject matter. Think of the process groups as being about the *actions* you take on your project, and the knowledge areas as the things you need to *understand*.

In other words, the knowledge areas are more about helping you understand the PMBOK® Guide material than about running your project. But that doesn't mean that every knowledge area has a process in every process group! For example, the Initiating process group only has two processes, and they both show up in the Integration Management knowledge area. The Risk Management knowledge area only has Planning and Monitoring & Controlling processes. So the process groups and the knowledge areas are two different ways to think about all of the processes, but they don't really overlap.

Q: Is every knowledge area in only one process group?

A: Every process belongs to exactly one process group, and every process is in exactly one knowledge area. But a knowledge area has lots of processes in it, and they can span some, or all, of the groups. Think of the processes as the core information in the PMBOK® Guide, and the process groups and knowledge areas as two different ways of grouping these processes.

Q: It seems like the Initiating and Planning process groups would be the same. How are they different?

A: Initiating is everything you do when you first start a project. You start by writing down (at a very high level) what the project is going to produce, who's in charge of it, and what tools they need to do the work. In a lot of companies, the project manager isn't even involved in a lot of this. Planning just means going into more detail about all of that as you learn more about it, and writing down specifically how you're going to do the work. The Planning processes are where the project manager is really in control and does most of the work.

Process groups and knowledge areas are two different ways to organize the processes... but they don't really overlap each other! Don't get caught up trying to make them fit together.

The benefits of successful project management

Take a moment to digest all this new knowledge because you're going to start putting it all into practice when we take a look at project integration management in Chapter 4.

Sharpen your pencil Solution

Think of the vacation we talked about on page 48 as a project, and each of its steps as a process. Here are some inputs, tools, and outputs that could be used in each of the vacation steps. Can you look at each of the underlined words and figure out if the words represent an input, tool, or output? (Here's a hint: some of them are an output from one process and an input for another.)

1. You log in and check your company's vacation calendar to see how much vacation time you have for your trip.

   ☒ Input ☐ Tool ☐ Output

2. You create an itinerary on a travel web site. You'll use the itinerary when you board your flight.

   ☒ Input ☐ Tool ☒ Output

   The itinerary was an output of the Develop Plan process but an input to the Direct and Manage Project Work process.

3. You have some hotel reservation documents you created on the travel web site, too. You'll use those when you check into your hotel.

   ☒ Input ☐ Tool ☒ Output

4. You use a travel web site to book the plane, hotel, and sights you'll see on your trip.

   ☐ Input ☒ Tool ☐ Output

   This one was the tool you used... to book your tickets and hotel reservations.

5. You verify your bank account balance to make sure you have enough money to pay for everything..

   ☒ Input ☐ Tool ☐ Output

   You had to know this to know how much you could spend on your trip. It's an input.

6. You use a hotel feedback web site to review your stay in the hotel once you get back home.

   ☐ Input ☒ Tool ☐ Output

   Here's the tool you used to give feedback about your hotel in the Close Project process.

Exam Questions

1. You're a project manager working on a software engineering project. The programmers have started building the software, and the testers have started to create the test environment. Which process group includes these activities?

A. Initiating

B. Planning

C. Executing

D. Closing

2. Which of the following is not a stakeholder?

A. The project manager who is responsible for building the project

B. A project team member who will work on the project

C. A customer who will use the final product

D. A competitor whose company will lose business because of the product

3. Which of the following is NOT a characteristic of a project?

A. A project is unique.

B. A project is temporary.

C. A project is progressively elaborated.

D. A project always critical to the company.

4. You're a project manager for a construction project. You don't control the project budget, the team doesn't report to you, and you routinely have to request their time from their manager. What kind of organization do you work in?

A. Functional

B. Weak matrix

C. Strong matrix

D. Projectized

5. Which process group contains the Develop Project Charter process and the Develop Preliminary Project Scope Statement process?

A. Initiating

B. Executing

C. Monitoring and Controlling

D. Closing

Exam Questions

6. Which of the following is NOT a project?

A. Repairing a car

B. Building a highway overpass

C. Running an IT support department

D. Filming a motion picture

7. Which of the following is NOT one of the triple constraints?

A. Time

B. Scope

C. Cost

D. Quality

8. Which of the following is NOT true about the triple constraint?

A. The project manager needs to pay attention to all three constraints.

B. You can increase quality by increasing scope.

C. A change in one of the three constraints often leads to a change in the other two.

D. Any change in time, cost, or scope can potentially affect quality.

9. You're the project manager for an industrial design project. Your team members report to you, and you're responsible for creating the budget, building the schedule, and assigning the tasks. When the project is complete, you release the team so they can work on other projects for the company. What kind of organization do you work in?

A. Functional

B. Weak Matrix

C. Strong Matrix

D. Projectized

10. You're a project manager working in a weak matrix organization. Which of the following is NOT true?

A. Your team members report to functional managers.

B. You are not in directly charge of resources.

C. Functional managers make decisions that can affect your projects.

D. You have sole responsibility for the success or failure of the project.

1. Answer: C

The Executing process group is the one where the team does all the work. You'll get a good feel for the process groups pretty quickly!

2. Answer: D

One of the hardest things that a project manager has to do on a project is figure out who all the stakeholders are. The project manager, the team, the sponsor (or client), the customers and people who will the software, the senior managers at the company—they're all stakeholders. Competitors aren't stakeholders, because even though they're affected by the project, they don't actually have any direct influence over it.

3. Answer: D

There are plenty of projects that aren't necessarily critical to the company, even if they're very important to the project manager, the team and the sponsor! There are plenty of research projects that are important to the team and the project manager, but which aren't mission-critical for the company.

4. Answer: A

In a functional organization, the project manager has very little power or influence. The project team members report to a separate functional manager who has discretion over the tasks to which they're assigned.

In a functional organization, PMs are basically just administrators.

5. Answer: A

The first things that are created on a project are the charter and the preliminary scope statement. You do those things when you're initiating the project.

Exam ~~Questions~~ Answers

6. Answer: C

The work of an IT support department doesn't have an end date—it's not temporary. That's why it's not a project. Now, if that support team had to work over the weekend to move the data center to a new location, then that would be a project!

7. Answer: D

The triple constraint consists of schedule, cost, and scope. And every decision that you make about the project will affect at least one of those constraints.

You can remember this because you always want to build the software Faster, Better, Cheaper.

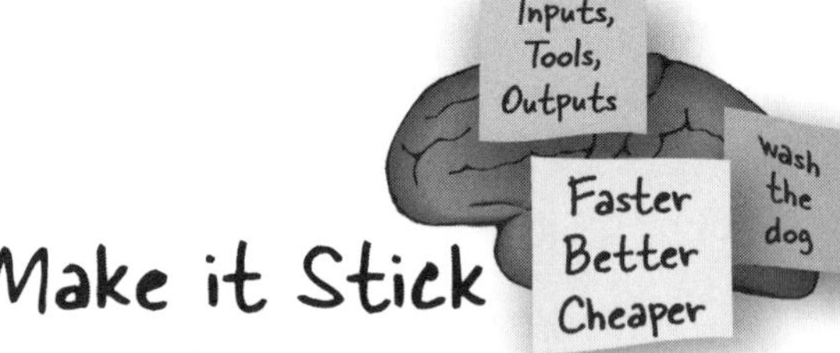

You want to do all three of these, but you need to strike a balance between them. Even if that expression isn't always true (see page 37), it's easy to remember.

Exam ~~Questions~~

8. Answer: B

This is a tough question because all four answers sound right. But think about what answer B really means. Let's say you're working on a weekend project to help your neighbor build a tree house for his kids. Think about what quality problems could come up… things like holes in the roof, an uneven floor, or a wall that's not stable. Now think of ways you'd add to the scope: say, building a rope swing or adding another window. How could that fix the quality problems? It wouldn't! That doesn't mean you can't find ways to increase the scope that will fix quality problems, or increase your product's quality. But you definitely can't **always** increase quality just by adding to the scope.

Sometimes you can think your way through some of the questions by imagining what would happen in a real project.

9. Answer: D

In a projectized organization, the project manager has the power to assign tasks, manage the budget, and release the team.

10. Answer: D

In a weak matrix, project managers have very limited authority. They have to share a lot of responsibility with functional managers, and those functional managers have a lot of leeway to make decisions about how the team members are managed. In an organization like that, the project manager isn't given a lot of responsibility.

That's why you're likely to find a project expeditor in a weak matrix.

4 Project integration management

Getting the Job Done

Want to make success look easy? It's not as hard as you think. In this chapter, you'll learn about **a few processes** you can use in your projects every day. Put these into place, and your **sponsors** and **stakeholders** will be happier than ever. Get ready for **Integration Management**.

Time to book a trip

Everyone in the Midwestern Teachers' Association has gotten together and planned a trip—a tour of Asia and Europe, starting with Mumbai, India.

We want to go in February, and we need to stay in budget. Can you get us a good deal? Gotta run, we've got classes in five.

Yes, I got that: you want window, not aisle...

Acme Travel Agency

Larry, the teachers' travel agent

Joanne and Tom were "volunteered" to organize the trip by the other eight teachers in the group.

Larry's cutting corners

Larry wants to dive into the project and make his clients happy. When he sees an opportunity to save them money, he takes it! But sometimes the cheapest way to do things isn't the way that will end up satisfying everyone.

Hmm... If I book their tickets in **June** instead of February, that'll reduce the fare. I'll bet that convinces them to change their plans. Who wouldn't love those savings?!

The teachers are thrilled... for now

Larry convinces the teachers to travel in June because of the great price he got on tickets. But he's not really planning for the results of that decision—and neither are the teachers.

One of the keys of project management is thinking a project through *before* starting the work, so problems that could arise down the line are anticipated ahead of time. That's why so much of project management is spent **planning**.

Larry may think this itinerary is a plan, but it doesn't detail any of the problems that could arise on the teachers' vacation.

Acme Travel

TRAVEL ITINERARY FOR MIDWESTERN TEACHERS ASSN.

Record Locator	HF184-Z	**Agent ID**	Larry
Trip ID	189435163		Acme Travel

Travel Details

Flight Information

Leg 1			
Airline	Econo Airlines	Departing	1:45PM
Flight	8614	Arriving	1:00AM
Origin	St. Paul, MN	Terminal	1
Destination	Mumbai, INDIA	Arriving	June 13
Est Time	17 hours 45 Minutes	Distance	7942mi

Larry changed the date to June, and now the project's coming in way under budget.

These clients are definitely not satisfied

When the clients arrived in Mumbai, they found out why the fare was so low: June is monsoon season in India! Larry may have saved them a bundle, but he also got them all wet.

Larry's been let go

From the minute they got off the plane, the clients were extremely unhappy. The senior managers at Acme Travel don't want to lose the teachers' business… so they've appointed YOU as the new travel agent.

It's your job to finish planning the trip, and make sure that the teachers leave their vacation satisfied.

The day-to-day work of a project manager

Project managers make projects run well. They plan for what's going to happen on the project. A big part of the job is watching closely to make sure the plan is followed, and when things go wrong they make sure they're fixed. And sometimes the plan itself turns out to be inadequate! Project managers look for those kinds of problems, and fix them too. That day-to-day work is what the **Integration Management** processes are all about.

A bird's-eye view of a project

Every project follows the same kind of pattern. First it gets initiated, then planned, then executed (and monitored), and finally closed. That's why the process groups are so useful—they're a good way to think about how you do the work.

For a large project, you'll often see this pattern repeated several times. Each major chunk of deliverables is treated as its own **sub-project** that goes through all of the process groups and processes on its own.

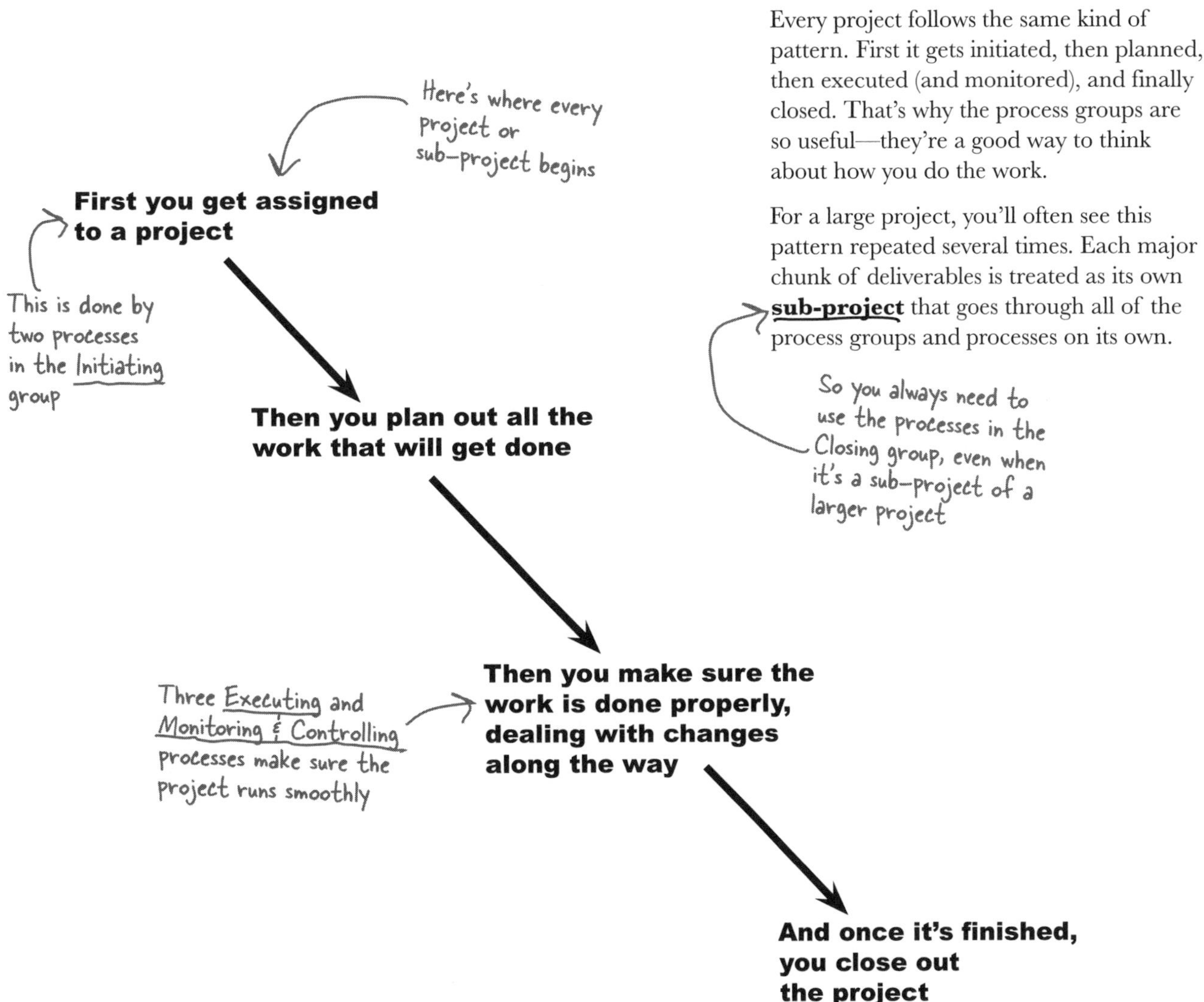

The seven Integration Management processes

The PMBOK® Guide divides Integration Management into seven processes that you need to understand for the exam. They're what people usually think of as a project manager's "core" responsibilities.

Without the Project Charter, you don't have the authority to tell your team what to do and when to do it.

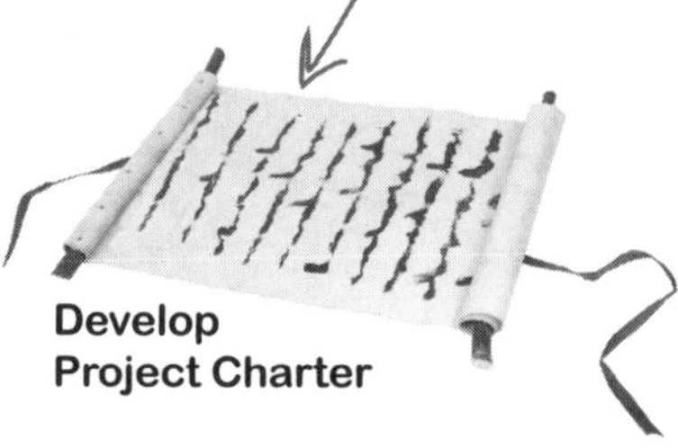

1 Develop Project Charter

The very first thing that's done on a new project is the development of the project charter. That's the document that authorizes you to do your work. But you're not always involved in making it—oftentimes it's handed to you by the sponsor.

The sponsor is the person who pays for the project

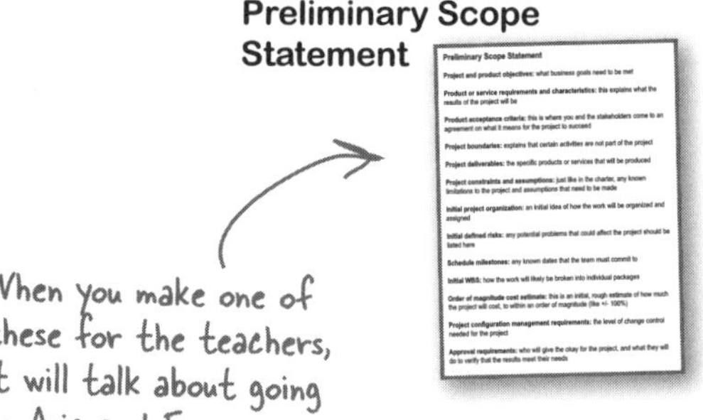

Preliminary Scope Statement

Project and product objectives: what business goals need to be met

Product or service requirements and characteristics: this explains what the results of the project will be

Product acceptance criteria: this is where you and the stakeholders come to an agreement on what it means for the project to succeed

Project boundaries: explains that certain activities are not part of the project

Project deliverables: the specific products or services that will be produced

Project constraints and assumptions: just like in the charter, any known limitations to the project and assumptions that need to be made

Initial project organization: an initial idea of how the work will be organized and assigned

Initial defined risks: any potential problems that could affect the project should be listed here

Schedule milestones: any known dates that the team must commit to

Initial WBS: how the work will likely be broken into individual packages

Order of magnitude cost estimate: this is an initial, rough estimate of how much the project will cost, to within an order of magnitude (like +/- 100%)

Project configuration management requirements: the level of change control needed for the project

Approval requirements: who will give the okay for the project, and what they will do to verify that the results meet their needs

2 Develop Preliminary Scope Statement

This is a document that lays out all of the goals of the project. You create it before you've started to plan the project—that's why it's preliminary. When you learn more details, you'll come up with a more detailed project scope.

Develop Project Management Plan

3 Develop Project Management Plan

The project management plan is the most important document in the entire PMBOK® Guide because it guides everything that happens on the project. It spans all of the knowledge areas.

A big part of the Project Management Plan is that it tells you how to handle changes when problems come up

4 Direct and Manage Project Execution

After you're done planning, it's time to do the work. Your job is to make sure that everybody is doing what they should be doing, and that the products or services your project creates meet the needs of the stakeholders.

Keep everyone satisfied by catching problems as early as possible

5 Monitor and Control Project Work

A good project manager is constantly monitoring every single thing that goes on in their project. Remember, the later you find a problem, the harder and more expensive it usually is to fix.

Once you catch problems, this is where you figure out how to fix them—or if they should be fixed at all.

6 Integrated Change Control

Once you've found problems on your project, you've got to work with your stakeholders and sponsors to figure out how to deal with those problems. You should also update your project management plan to reflect any extra steps you'll need to take to complete the project. Updating the project management plan also makes sure everyone working on the project stays on the same page.

Keep an eye out for potential changes. Part of your job is helping the people around you anticipate changes, and maybe even prevent them.

7 Close Project

The last thing you do on the project is close it out. Make sure you document everything... especially the lessons you and your team have learned along the way. You can never tell when these lessons may help you out on your *next* project.

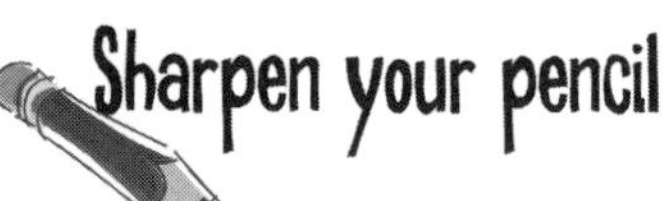

Here are a few of the things you might have to deal with in working on the teachers' vacation trip. Figure out which of the seven Integration Management processes you'd use in each situation, and write down the process name in the blank.

1. It turns out that one of the teachers is a vegetarian, so you need to change your plans to include vegetarian meals on the airlines and find restaurants that accommodate him.

   ____

2. You get one of the teachers on the phone and come up with a list of all of the places they want to go for the rest of the trip, and anything that may limit the tour.

   ____

3. You come up with a detailed description of everything that you plan to do to get the teachers where they want to be.

   ____

4. The CEO of Acme Travel sends you a document that assigns you to the project.

   ____

5. You check in with the teachers at each destination to make sure everything is going according to plan.

   ____

6. When the teachers get back, you write up everything you learned while handling the trip so other travel agents can learn from your experience.

   ____

7. You book the tickets and hotel accommodations.

   ____

Develop Project Charter

Develop Preliminary Scope Statement

Develop Project Management Plan

Direct and Manage Project Execution

Monitor and Control Project Work

Integrated Change Control

Close Project

Answers on page 123.

Start your project with the Initiating processes

These are the only two processes in the Initiating process group.

Initiating process group

All you need to get your project started are the only two processes in the Initiating process group.* First, the **Develop Project Charter** process tells everyone in the company why the project is needed, and gives you the authority you need to make it happen. Then you use the **Develop Preliminary Scope Statement** process to write down everything you need to know about the work that's going to be done. Once these things are done, the project is ready to begin!

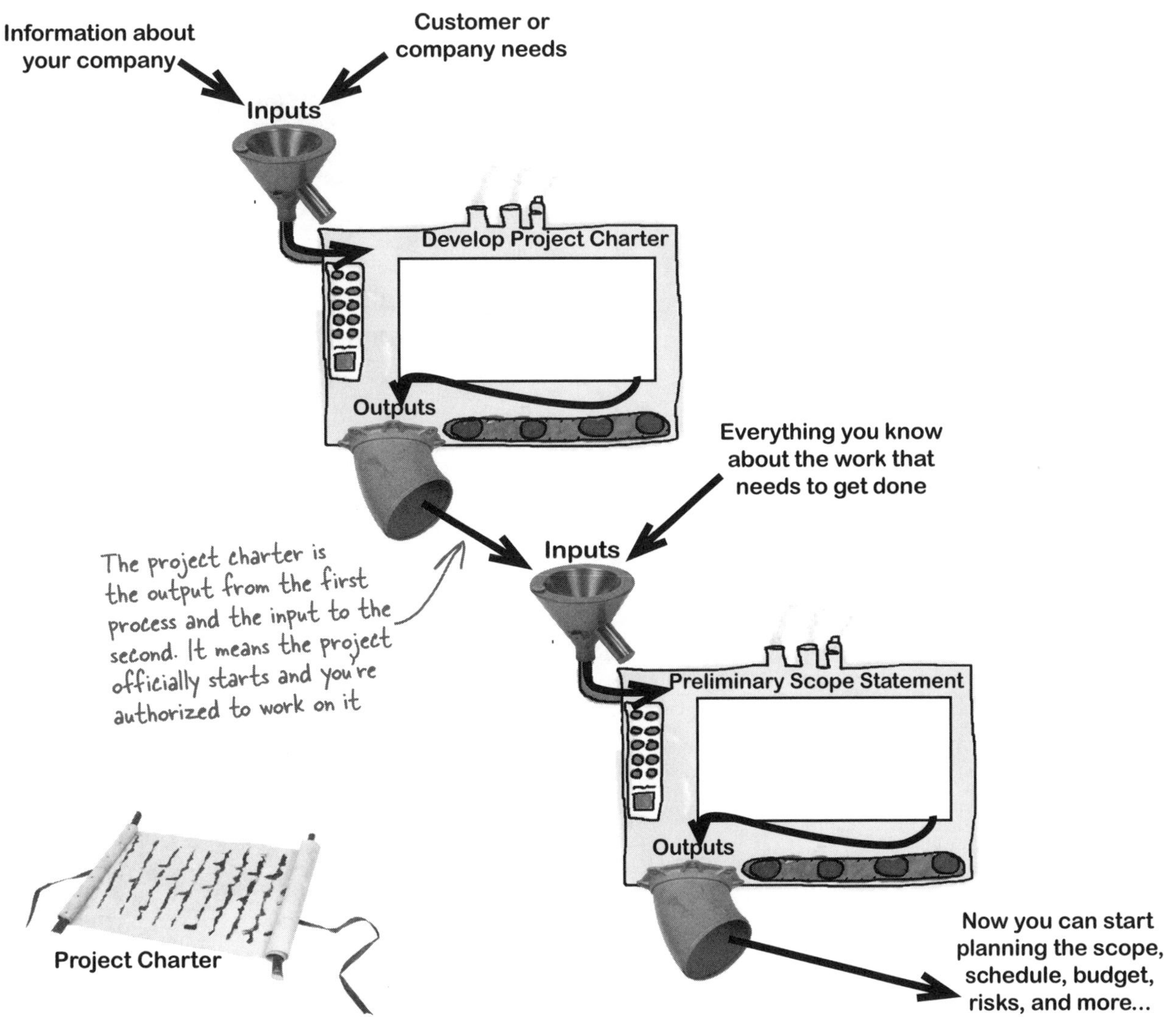

* flip the page to see how the Initiating processes fit into Integration Management.

Integration management and the process groups

Here is how the process groups all fit into this whole Integration Management thing. The process groups show you the order in which these things happen, and how the processes interact.

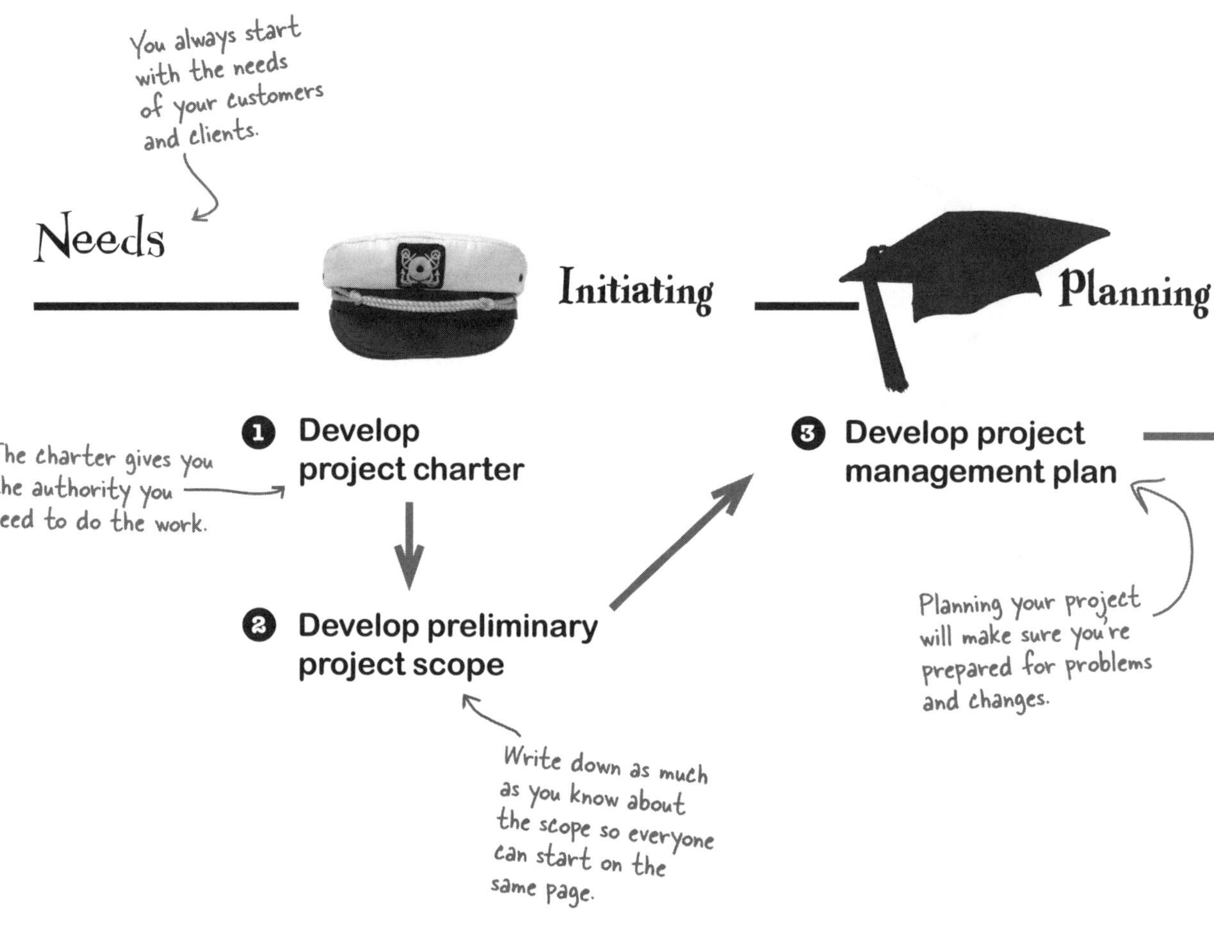

The goal of every project: you and your customers are satisfied with the result of the project.

Success!

Executing

Closing

4 Direct and manage project execution

Manage the work so it gets done efficiently.

7 Close project

Closing out the project makes sure you get paid—and more importantly, that you have a chance to write down all the lessons you learned along the way.

5 Monitor and control project work

This is where you constantly look for any problems in the project.

Monitoring and Controlling

6 Integrated change control

You need to make sure that you make ONLY those changes that are necessary and will help your project.

The "Develop Project Charter" process

If you work in a matrixed organization, then your team doesn't report to you. They report to functional managers, and might have other work to do. But when they're on your project, you're effectively their boss. So how do you make that happen? Well, you need some sort of **authorization**, and that's what the project charter is for. It says exactly what you're authorized to do on the project (like assign work to the team members and use the company's resources), and why you've been assigned to it. But the charter isn't just important for matrixed companies. In any kind of company, it's really important to know who's in charge, and what resources you have available to you when you manage a project.

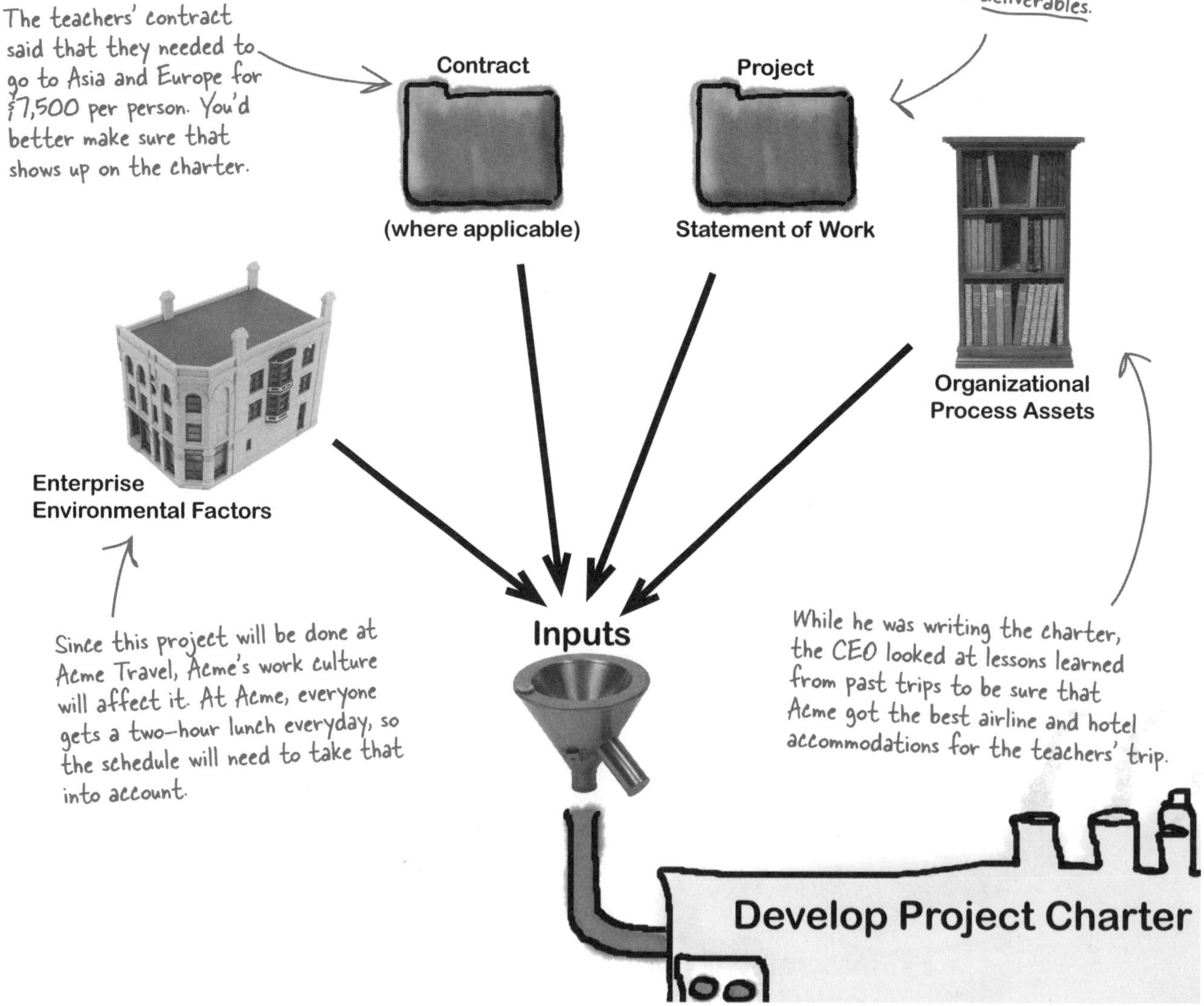

The teachers' contract said that they needed to go to Asia and Europe for $7,500 per person. You'd better make sure that shows up on the charter.

This is a list of all of the things that you need to create as part of the project. These are called deliverables.

Contract (where applicable)

Project Statement of Work

Organizational Process Assets

Enterprise Environmental Factors

Since this project will be done at Acme Travel, Acme's work culture will affect it. At Acme, everyone gets a two-hour lunch everyday, so the schedule will need to take that into account.

Inputs

While he was writing the charter, the CEO looked at lessons learned from past trips to be sure that Acme got the best airline and hotel accommodations for the teachers' trip.

Develop Project Charter

Project selection methods are ways you choose which projects your company works on. They're ways that you can objectively compare two potential projects, and figure out which one makes sense for your company to take on.

The project management information system (PMIS) is a computer tool to help project managers create schedules, calculate costs, and control changes that occur during a project's lifecycle.

You might already be familiar with a PMIS like Microsoft Project or OpenWorkbench. Don't worry—the exam doesn't test you on the details of how to use specific PMISes, you just need to know what they are.

Develop Project Charter process

Tools

Expert Judgment

You use expert judgment any time you bring in an expert from outside of your project to give you advice or lend his or her expertise.

Project Management Information System

PMBOK® Guide

Project Management Methodology

Project Selection Methods

Outputs

Project Charter

The PMBOK® Guide defines 44 different processes, but it doesn't tell you exactly how to apply each process to your own projects. That's what a Project Management Methodology is: how your company uses those processes—including which processes are used, and in what order.

We'll take a closer look at this one on the next page...

Choose your project with project selection methods

The Midwestern Teachers' Association contract wasn't the only one that Acme could have taken. They've got more work than they can handle right now, and occasionally they need to turn away a client. That's where **project selection methods** come in handy. If a project is too risky, won't make enough money, or isn't strategic, or isn't likely to succeed, then the senior managers at Acme could choose to pass on it.

But to figure all that out, you need an objective way to compare projects:

Project selection methods are part of the tools & techniques for Develop Project Charter

Benefit measurement models **are the most common models used to choose between projects. These models compare projects by figuring out how much each project benefits the company. These often involve simple calculations or scoring of different projects, based on factors like cost, risks, or even community goodwill.**

This is also called the **comparative approach** because it involves comparing the benefits and features of two or more projects.

A lot of companies use murder boards, meetings where people ask a lot of tough questions to try to "murder" the project

Mathematical models **are less common than benefit measurement models, and involve complex mathematical formulas that attempt to predict the success of a particular project before you start.**

These are often called constrained optimization. The exam uses that term sometimes, so be ready for it.

Don't worry, you won't need to do a lot of complex math for the exam—you'll just need to know the names of a few methods.

Here's a hint: any time you see "programming," it's usually a mathematical model!

The main difference between the two types of project selection methods is that mathematical models try to predict success rates using formulas, while benefit measurement models compare them based on features and benefits.

Here are a bunch of project selection methods. Try to figure out which ones are benefit measurement models and which ones are mathematical models.

1. Murder boards are meetings where people ask a bunch of questions about how the project can go wrong, and try and figure out if a project is really worth doing. Which model is a murder board?

A. Benefit measurement   B. Mathematical model

2. Linear programming involves predicting a project's success by optimizing a formula based on linear constraints.

A. Benefit measurement   B. Mathematical model

3. Benefit-to-cost ratios compare projects by evaluating the benefit of the project versus its projected costs.

A. Benefit measurement   B. Mathematical model

4. Peer review has people within the organization review the candidate projects and give their opinions on them. The opinions are compiled and compared.

A. Benefit measurement   B. Mathematical model

5. Dynamic programming maximizes the present value of a project by subjecting the investment to known constraints.

A. Benefit measurement   B. Mathematical model

Answers on page 124.

A closer look at the project charter

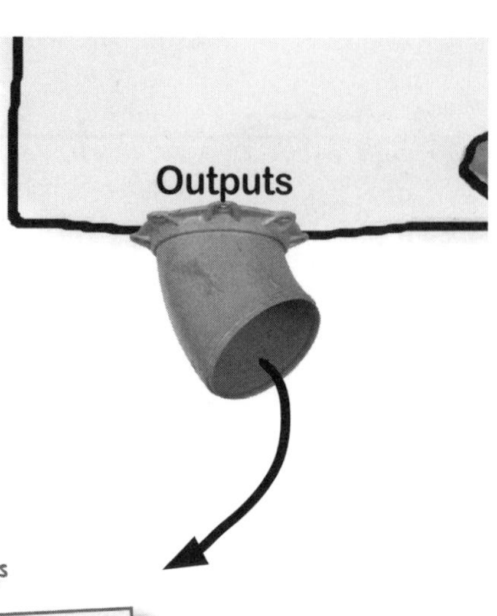

The charter is the **only output** of the Develop Project Charter process. We know that it makes sense to do the project—that's what we did with the project selection methods. And we know that it assigns authority so that you can do your job. But what else does a charter have in it?

The charter assigns you the authority to use resources, like people on your team, computers, office equipment, conference rooms—the things you need to get the job done.

Project Charter

Acme Travel

Project Description: World vacation in 4 weeks
A group of teachers from Minnesota want to take a trip around the world, starting with Mumbai, India, and ending somewhere in Europe. They have contracted Acme Travel Agency to make their dream a reality.

Larry should have paid attention to this information.

Project Requirements:
- Trip should be planned to coincide with good weather
- Need to see famous monuments at each point of destination
- Restaurant recommendations and nightlife information on request
- Need assistance for missed flights, lost luggage and other issues in transit

As the project charter officially assigns the PM, it can be written before the PM is even involved.

Assigned Project Manager and Authority Level:
You have the authority to use dedicated money and resources to accomplish this goal

Constraints are any known limitations, and assumptions are the things you are assuming to be true at the outset of the project.

Summary Milestone Schedule
June 13–20—Mumbai
June 24–29—Shanghai
July 5–8—Barcelona
June 20–23—Hong Kong
June 30–July 4—Rome
July 9–14—Paris

External Assumptions and Constraints:
Project budget cannot exceed $7,500 per person. We are assuming that group rates for accommodations in all cities will be available.

When you use project selection methods, you're really making a case to the business that one project should be chosen over another.

Business Case:
This project will be a sound investment for Acme. Provided it is planned and executed properly, we should receive around $700 per person in profit.

There will be two signatures here; it's OK if a project has more than one sponsor.

SIGNED,

CEO, Acme Travel

Acme VP of Asia Travel

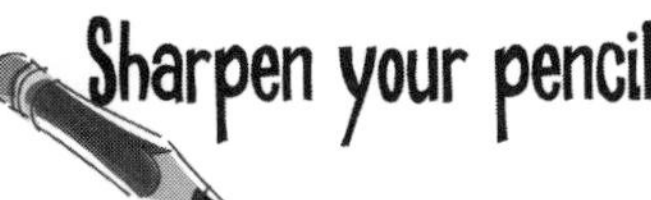

Take a look at the charter for the teachers' trip, and write down what you think each of the following sections of a typical project charter is used for.

Project Description:

Project Requirements:

Assigned Project Manager and Authority Level:

Summary Milestone Schedule:

External Assumptions and Constraints:

Business Case:

Sharpen your pencil Solution

Take a look at the charter for the teachers' trip, and write down what you think each of the following sections of a typical project charter is used for.

Project Description:

The purpose of the project

This is a high-level description of the goals of your project. It's usually a few sentences that describe the project's main purpose.

Project Requirements:

Describes the product your project has to make

Anything you know that the customer, stakeholder, or sponsor expects to get out of the project should go here.

Assigned Project Manager and Authority Level:

Who the project manager is and what he has to do

This is where you're assigned to the project. If it's known who is going to be the project manager, the name of that person is noted. Otherwise, you may just have a department listed that you know the PM will come from. This is also where any specific decision-making authority you might need can be described.

Summary Milestone Schedule:

A list of dates that your project needs to meet

These are any dates that your project must hit in order to be successful. This is usually a very high-level schedule—you haven't assigned resources or done any planning yet, so there's no way to know anything but really generic details when the charter is written.

External Assumptions and Constraints:

Any rules or judgments you're making about the project

A date given to you is only one kind of constraint. This charter had a $7,500 budget limit per person, which is a cost constraint. That project also had an assumption about group rates. When there isn't a definite answer to a critical issue, it's often necessary to make assumptions—and you'll need to write those assumptions down so you can remember them, or in case they turn out to be false.

Business Case:

Why your company has decided to do this project

This section lists the reasons why it makes sense for your business to do this project. You might note the return on investment, building infrastructure, goodwill with clients, or anything else that will help people understand why this project is important.

Two things you'll see over and over and over...

There are two inputs that you'll see repeatedly for a bunch of different processes throughout the rest of the book. **Enterprise Environmental Factors** are anything that you need to know about how your company does business. And **Organizational Process Assets** have information about your projects: how people in your company are supposed to perform them, and how past projects have gone.

Enterprise Environmental Factors

Enterprise Environmental Factors tell you about how your company does business.

There's a lot of information about your company that will be really useful to you when you're planning your project. You need to know how each of the different departments operates, the market conditions you're working in, the company's overall strategy, any policies you need to work with, your company's culture, and all about the people who work at the company.

One of the Enterprise Environmental Factors you'll use in the Integration Management processes is **the work authorization system**, which determines how your company assigns work to people and ensures that tasks are done properly and in the right order.

Organizational Process Assets

Organizational Process Assets tell you about how your company normally runs its projects.

Every company has standards for how to run the projects. There are guidelines and instructions for managing projects, procedures you need to follow, categories for various things you need to keep track of, and templates for all of the various documents that you need to create. These things are usually stored in some sort of library.

One of the most important organizational process assets is called **lessons learned**. At the end of every project, you sit down with the project team and write down everything you learned about the project. This includes both positive and negative things. That way, when you or another project manager in your company plans the next project, you can take advantage of the lessons you learned on this one.

Can you think of how these would be useful for starting and planning your project?

there are no Dumb Questions

Q: I've never had a project charter. Is it really necessary?

A: Yes, definitely. Have you ever been on a project where you didn't feel like you had enough authority to do your job? The project charter gives you the authority to manage your project. Every project should have a charter, and writing the charter is the first thing that should happen on any project.

Q: Wait a minute! How can I be the one writing the charter, when it's what gives me all of my authority and I might not even be assigned to the project yet?

A: Right, you're not usually going to write a charter. The charter is usually handed to you. The project sponsor usually writes the charter. And it's always easy to tell who the project sponsor is: the sponsor is the person who pays for the project, and comes up with the project's overall goals.

Q: I don't get some of these terms on the charter. What's a business case, constraint, or assumption?

A: The business case is a description of what your company is trying to get out of the project—like how much money you're planning on making from the project, how it will benefit parts of your organization, and future business you might gain from the project.

A constraint is any sort of limitation that comes from outside of your project. For example, you could be required to work within a certain budget. You might need to work with certain vendors. Or you could have a contract that requires you to be done by a certain date.

An assumption is a temporary decision that you make to compensate for information you don't have yet. Here's an example: Let's say you don't know whether the teachers prefer to spend the extra money for a nonstop flight. You need to know this in order to book the tickets, so you might assume that they want the cheaper fare... but as Larry learned when he booked the trip in June, some assumptions can be wrong!

All three of these things need to be in the charter because you should know them all before you begin the project.

Q: I'm still not clear on who the sponsor is. How's that different than the customer?

A: The sponsor is the person (or people) paying for the project. The customer is the person who uses the product of the project. Sometimes the customer is the same person as a sponsor. This is often true in consulting companies. For the teachers' project, the two sponsors are the CEO and VP of Asia Travel, and the customers are the teachers. But it's possible that in another travel agency, the teachers themselves would be the sponsors. This happens a lot in contracted work.

For the exam, you'll need to be careful about this. Sometimes you'll see the word "customer" in a question that's asking you about the sponsor. You might even see the word "client"—a word that only appears in the PMBOK® Guide twice! (It's usually used when you're talking about procurement.) When you see this, you should assume that the question is asking you about a consulting situation, where the sponsor, customer, and client are all the same person.

The sponsor of a project is responsible for creating the project charter.

The sponsor of a project <u>pays</u> for the project. The PM <u>manages</u> the project.

BULLET POINTS: AIMING FOR THE EXAM

- The **project charter** officially sanctions the project. Without a charter, the project cannot begin.
- The **sponsor** is the person (or people) responsible for paying for the project and is part of all important project decisions.
- **Develop Project Charter** is the very first process performed in a project.
- The project charter gives the project manager authority to **do the project work**, and to **assign work** or take control of project resources for the duration of the project. It also gives the project manager authority to **spend money** and **use other company resources**.
- The charter documents project assumptions. An **assumption** is any decision that you make **temporarily** in order to compensate for things that are unknown about the project.
- The project charter does not include details about what will be produced or how. Instead, it contains the **business case**, **constraints**, and **assumptions**.
- Two inputs to Develop Project Charter are the **contract** and the **statement of work**. The contract is what you agreed to do, although not all projects have a contract. The statement of work lists all of the **deliverables** that you and your team need to produce.

In matrixed organizations, your team doesn't report to you, so the charter gives you the authority to put them to work.

The project charter shouldn't be too detailed. You shouldn't have to update the charter every time you change something about your project for it to stay accurate.

At Acme, the CEO and VP of Asia Travel were the sponsors. But at another travel agency, Frank and Joanne could just as easily sponsor the project, since they're the customers.

Watch it!

When you're taking the PMP exam, be careful when you see a question that asks you about the customer or client.

There's a good chance that the question is asking you about a consulting or procurement situation where the customer or client is also the sponsor.

Scope: what needs to get DONE

You're in charge of the project (thanks to the project charter). So what's next? You need to figure out what your clients need and write a **preliminary scope statement**. Time to talk to the teachers...

We want to go to Paris, we don't want any more monsoons, and I **hate** overpaying for those expensive hotels.

This time, you asked the teachers what they wanted, rather than making assumptions.

Since this is a **preliminary** scope statement, we can just get the big picture, right? So the teachers want a trip to Paris, but we'll probably figure out exactly what restaurants they'll eat at a little further along.

The preliminary scope statement is PRELIMINARY.

At this stage, the project hasn't even started. Focus on the major details of the project, and you'll fill in all the other stuff as you get deeper into the project.

The "Develop Preliminary Scope Statement" process

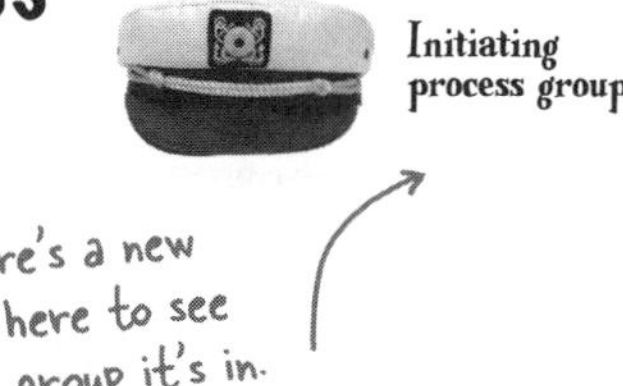

Now that you know what the preliminary scope statement is, let's look at what it takes to put it together. A lot of this should look familiar—most of these are the same inputs you've already used to develop the project charter. The only new input is the charter itself:

Any time there's a new process, look here to see what process group it's in.

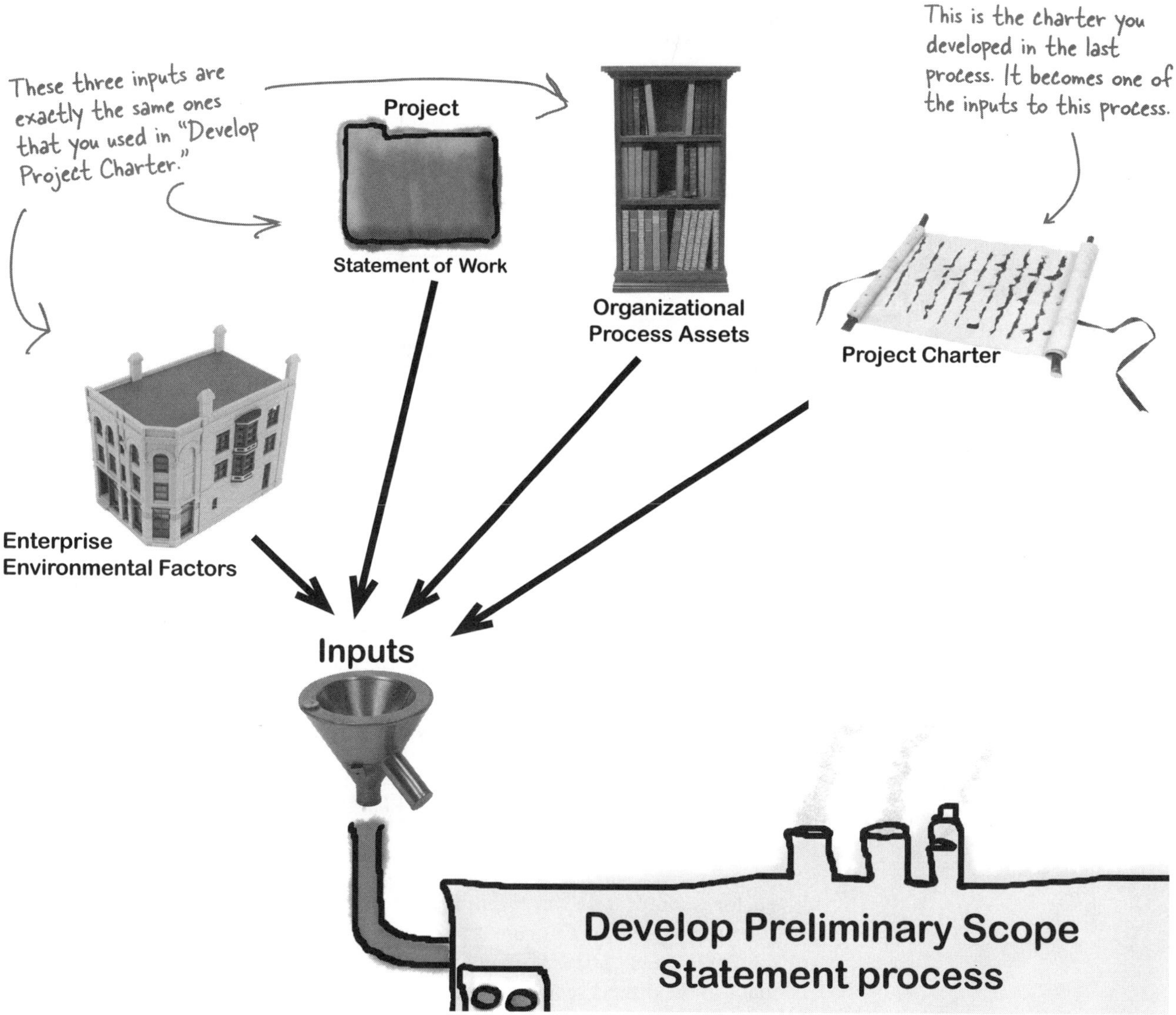

This is the charter you developed in the last process. It becomes one of the inputs to this process.

These three inputs are exactly the same ones that you used in "Develop Project Charter."

Project Statement of Work

Organizational Process Assets

Project Charter

Enterprise Environmental Factors

Inputs

Develop Preliminary Scope Statement process

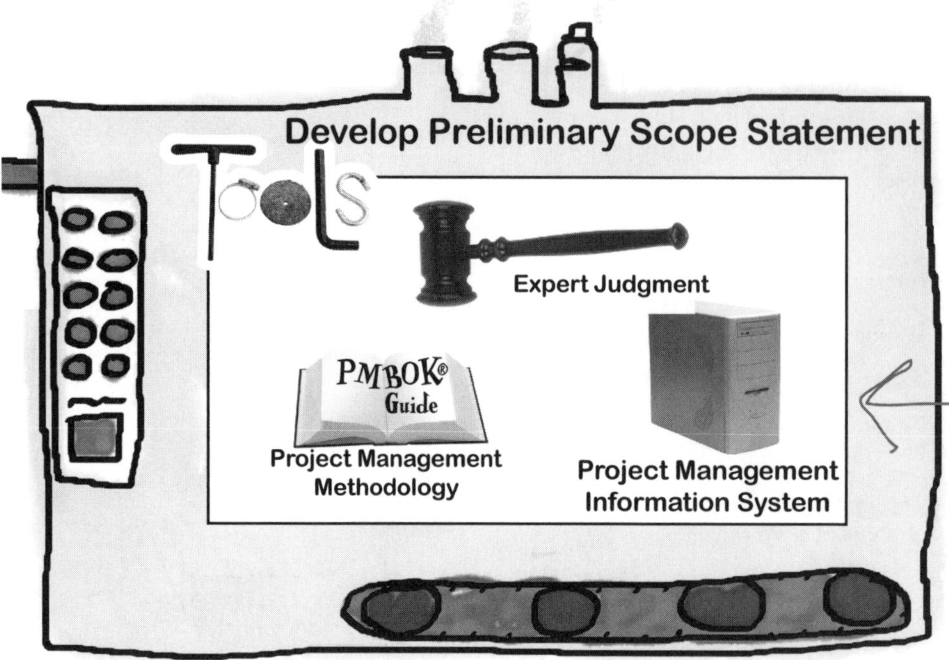

You saw these same three tools in Develop Project Charter.

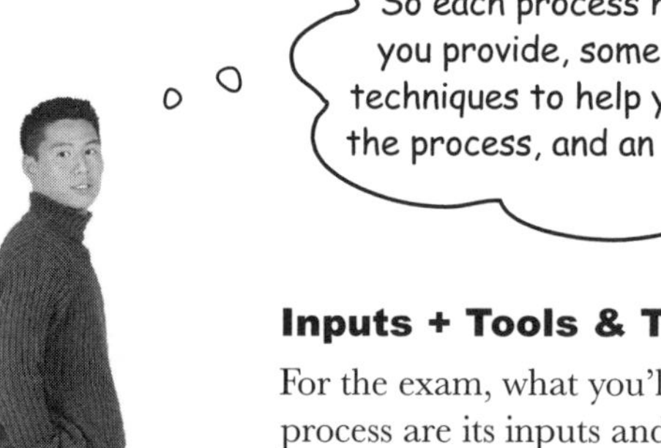

Remember this from the last chapter?

Inputs + Tools & Techniques = Output

For the exam, what you'll need to know about any process are its inputs and outputs, what processes came before it and after it, and what the tools and techniques are that help you work through that process.

So, for example, take the preliminary scope statement. You need to know that it comes after the project charter, that it contains a *preliminary* version of the information that's in the project scope statement (which you'll learn about next chapter), and that it's created within the Initiating process group.

The preliminary scope statement: a closer look

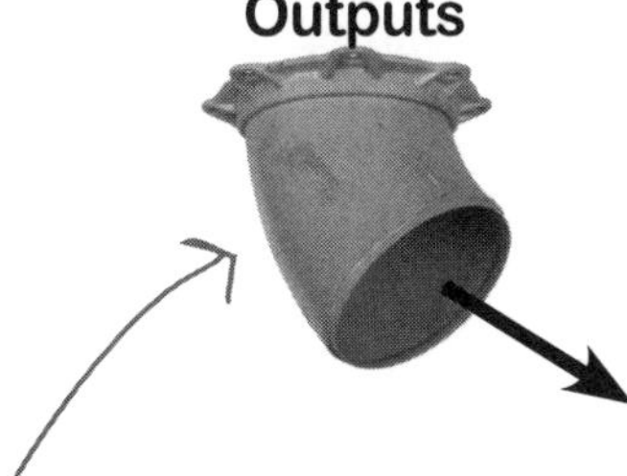

The preliminary scope statement is the ONLY output of Develop Preliminary Scope Statement.

Preliminary Scope Statement

Project and product objectives: what business goals need to be met

Product or service requirements and characteristics: this explains what the results of the project will be

Product acceptance criteria: this is where you and the stakeholders come to an agreement on what it means for the project to succeed

Project boundaries: explains that certain activities are not part of the project

Project deliverables: the specific products or services that will be produced

Project constraints and assumptions: just like in the charter, any known limitations to the project and assumptions that need to be made

Initial project organization: an initial idea of how the work will be organized and assigned

Initial defined risks: a list of potential problems that could affect the project

Schedule milestones: any known dates that the team must commit to

Order of magnitude cost estimate: this is an initial, rough estimate of how much the project will cost

Project configuration management requirements: the level of change control needed for the project

Approval requirements: who will give the okay for the project, and what they will do to verify that the results meet their needs

Not all of this information will be available before some projects start—which means that not all of these sections will appear on every preliminary scope statement.

Don't worry about memorizing all of this. We'll cover it in more detail later, so just use this to get a basic idea of what the scope statement looks like.

Not all preliminary scope statements have all of the information that's shown here. For the teachers' trip to Asia, which sections would make sense to fill out? Would all of those sections be helpful for this particular project?

Question Clinic: The "Just-The-Facts-Ma'am" Question

A great way to prepare for the exam is to learn about the different kinds of questions, and then try writing your own. Each of these Question Clinics will look at a different type of question, and give you practice writing one yourself.

Take a little time out of the chapter for this Question Clinic. It's here to give your brain a break and think about something different.

A lot of questions on the exam are pretty straightforward—but it's the answers to those questions that can really hang you up. Here, take a look:

27. Which of the following can be found in the Preliminary Scope Statement?

A. Project Selection Methods

Some answers will clearly be wrong. Project Selection Methods is one of the tools and techniques from Develop Project Charter.

B. Project Management Methodology

Some answers are a little misleading! This is part of the Develop Preliminary Scope Statement process—but it's from the tools and techniques, not a part of the Preliminary Scope Statement itself.

C. Authorization for the project manager

This is something you'll find in the Charter, not the Preliminary Scope Statement

D. Schedule Milestones

Here's the right answer. Milestones should be included as part of the Preliminary Scope Statement.

When you see a "Just-The-Facts-Ma'am" question, read the question really carefully! If you don't, it's easy for a wrong answer to look right.

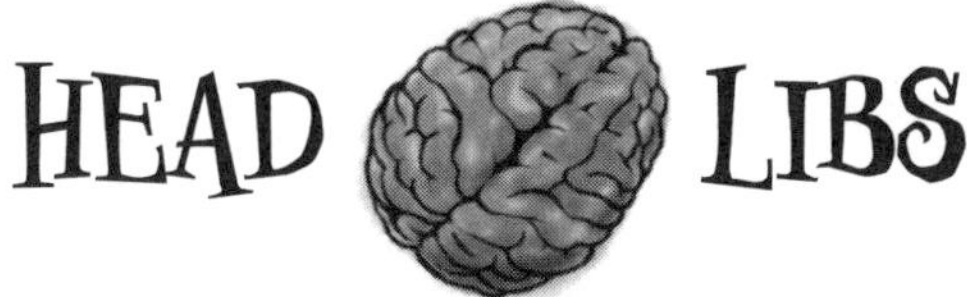

Fill in the blanks to come up with your own "Just-The-Facts-Ma'am" question.

You are managing a ____________ project. You are using
(an industry)
____________ and ____________
(an input) (an input)
to create a ____________. What process are you performing?
(an output)

A. ____________
(the name of the wrong process)

B. ____________
(the name of the right process)

C. ____________
(a made-up process that sounds like a real process)

D. ____________
(the name of a tool and technique from the right process)

Ladies and Gentlemen, We Now Return You To Chapter Four

Plan your project!

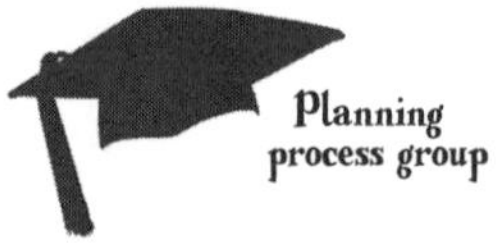

Planning process group

Planning the project is when you really take control. You write a plan that says exactly how you're going to handle everything that goes on in the project. The **Develop Project Management Plan** process is where you organize all of the information about your project into one place, so everyone knows exactly what needs to happen when they do the project work—no matter what their jobs are.

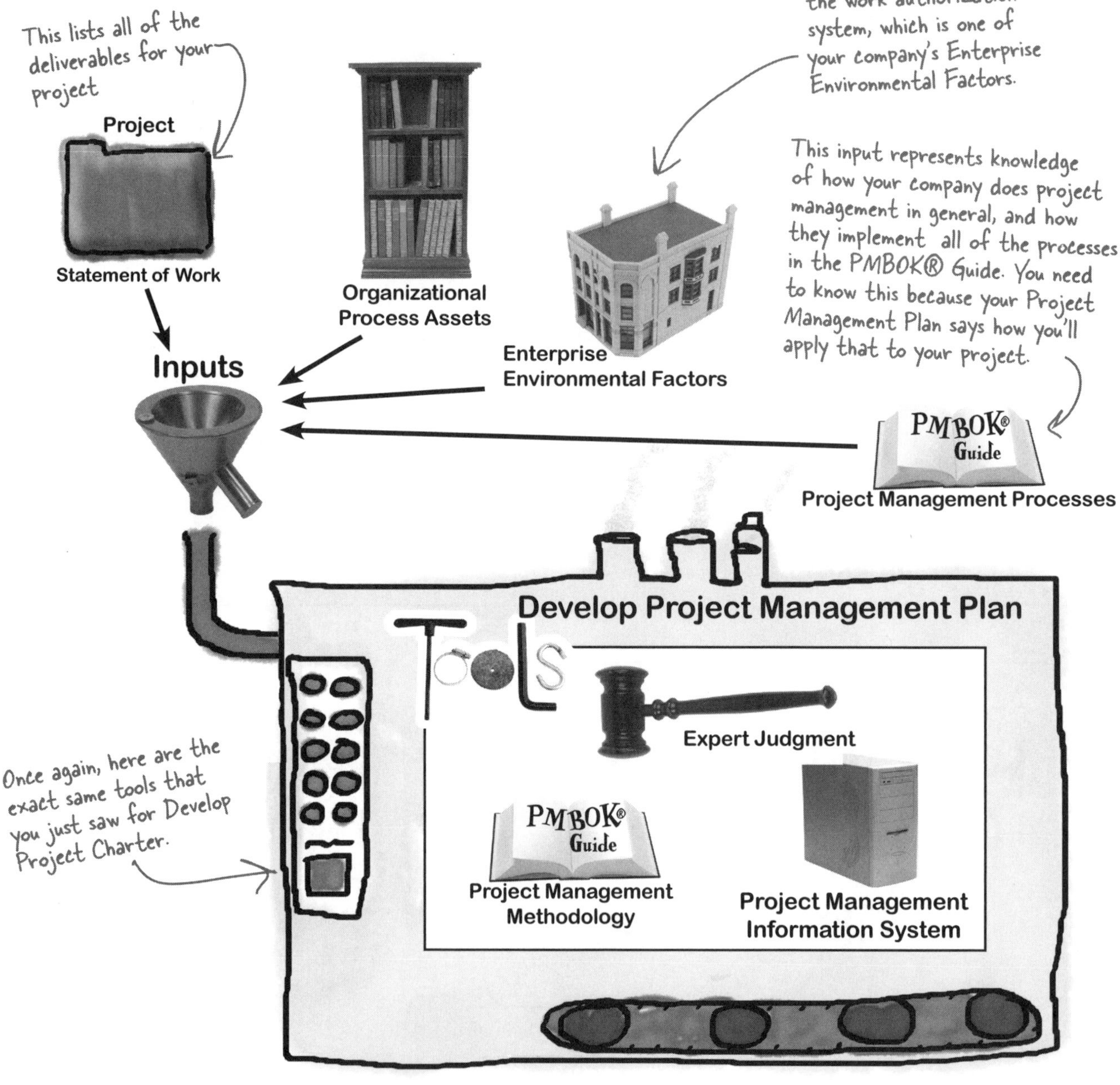

This lists all of the deliverables for your project

Project Statement of Work

Organizational Process Assets

This is where you use the work authorization system, which is one of your company's Enterprise Environmental Factors.

Enterprise Environmental Factors

This input represents knowledge of how your company does project management in general, and how they implement all of the processes in the PMBOK® Guide. You need to know this because your Project Management Plan says how you'll apply that to your project.

PMBOK® Guide

Project Management Processes

Inputs

Develop Project Management Plan

Tools

Expert Judgment

PMBOK® Guide

Project Management Methodology

Project Management Information System

Once again, here are the exact same tools that you just saw for Develop Project Charter.

The project management plan lets you plan ahead for problems

The **Planning** process group is where you figure out how you're going to do the project—because you need to come up with a plan before you bring the team in to do the work. This is where you think about everything that will happen on your project, and try to plot a course to completing it with as few errors as possible.

And it's where you figure out how you'll handle changes—because every project has plenty of problems, but not all of those problems mean that you need to change course. If you plan well, your project will make only the right changes.

Outputs

The project management plan is the only output of the Develop Project Management Plan process.

The project management plan is a collection of other plans

The project management plan is a single document, but it's broken into a bunch of pieces called **subsidiary plans**. There's one subsidiary plan for each of most of the knowledge areas: **scope management**, **time management, cost management, quality management**, **human resource management**, **communications management**, **risk management**, and **procurement**.

The project management plan is actually a whole bunch of documents called "subsidiary plans," each dedicated to a knowledge area and the problems that could happen related to that area.

The project management plan is all about planning for problems, and having the information you need to correct those problems when they occur.

Communications Management is another knowledge area. In that plan, we've got important numbers for the trip, like the U.S. Embassy... and we can help Frank get his passport replaced.

Project Management Plan

If you take over a project that's already under way, but there isn't a project management plan or it's out of date, the first thing you need to do is get a current, accurate plan written up.

There's a sub-plan for Risk Management. We used it when we took out traveler's insurance for the teachers' trip. That means if bags or cash are stolen, we'll have a plan for dealing with it.

Isn't a project plan just something I get out of Microsoft Project?

No. The project management plan is not the same thing as a project schedule.

You'll use a tool like Microsoft Project when you're doing Time Management to build the project schedule. (It's also useful for other knowledge areas as well.) But you'll use your project management plan as a guide to help you develop that schedule. It will tell you what tools to use when you develop it, and how changes will be handled.

Don't worry about memorizing all of the subsidiary plans.

You're going to learn about all of the knowledge areas throughout the book, so don't worry about memorizing all of these subsidiary plans right now. Just know that the project management plan has plans within it that map to each of the knowledge areas.

A quick look at all those subsidiary plans

You'll be learning about each of the knowledge areas throughout this book, and you'll learn all about the subsidiary plan that goes with each area. But let's take a quick look at what each subsidiary plan focuses on.

Project Management Plan—Subsidiary Plans

The **project scope management plan** describes how scope changes are handled—like what to do when someone needs to add or remove a feature to a service or product your project produces.

The **schedule management plan** shows you how to deal with changes to the schedule, like updated deadlines or milestones.

The **cost management plan** tells you how you'll create the budget, and what to do when your project runs into money problems.

The **quality management plan** deals with problems that could arise when a product doesn't live up to the customer or client's standards.

You use the **staffing management plan** to deal with changes in your staff, and to identify and handle any additional staffing needs and constraints you might have in your specific project.

The **communications management plan** lists all of the ways that you communicate with your project's team, stakeholders, sponsors, and important contacts related to the project.

The **risk management plan** is about detailing all the bad things that might happen and coming up with a plan to address each risk when and if it occurs.

The **procurement management plan** focuses on dealing with vendors outside of your company.

The project management plan is the core of Integration Management. It's your main tool for running a project.

Below is a whole crop of problems that the teachers are running into. Write down which subsidiary plan you'd look in to get some help. If you're not sure, just reread the descriptions of each subsidiary plan on the last page, and take your best guess.

1. Theteachers want to go Bali, but Acme Travel doesn't book flights there so you need to subcontract one leg of the travel to another travel agency.

   ____

2. Theteachers are having so much fun that they want to stay at a better hotel. They tell you to increase their budget by 15% to do that.

   ____

3. Justas you're about to mail off the teachers' tickets, you notice they've been printed incorrectly.

   ____

4. The teachers might run into more bad weather, and you've got to figure out what contingencies you can put into place if that happens.

   ____

5. The teachers are concerned that they won't be able to get in touch with you when they're away.

   ____

6. Oneof the teachers realizes that he needs to come back earlier, and you want to make sure the budget reflects his lessened costs.

   ____

7. You find out that you need to get the tickets out earlier than expected, because the teachers' contract requires that all trips be preapproved by the superintendent of their school district.

   ____

→ Answers on page 125.

there are no Dumb Questions

Q: How far should I go when trying to anticipate every possible problem and list it in the project management plan?

A: It's really important to think about everything that could go wrong on your project, so that you can have plans for what to do when problems crop up. An unexpected change can sometimes derail a project, and doing some planning up front can keep issues like that to a minimum. Planning can help you avoid problems in the first place, which is a lot better for everyone than reacting to them when they happen. So think of everything you can; the extra time you spend planning could be what keeps your project a success.

Q: Does the project manager create the project management plan all by himself?

A: No, it should be a group effort between the PM and the stakeholders. Everyone on the project team and all of the stakeholders need to agree that the plan is acceptable.

Q: What about things that I don't think about? And sometimes, I know there could be problems in a certain area, but I'm not sure what they'll be until the project gets going.

A: You're never going to think of everything that could go wrong. To help keep your plan flexible, you should add an Open Issues section to the plan. You can write down any open issues or concerns in this section, and deal with them as they come up down the line. However, you have to have all your project requirements complete before starting the project—you should *never* have any requirements in your Open Issues section.

Q: I still don't get what Enterprise Environmental Factors are.

A: Your company's Enterprise Environmental Factors are all of the information you have about its policies, processes, departments and people. You need to know how your company does business in order to do a project. For example, you need to know about the different departments in your company if you're managing a project that will be used by people in them.

BULLET POINTS: AIMING FOR THE EXAM

- Remember that the project management plan is **formal**—which means that it's **written down** and **distributed** to your team.
- You may get a question on the exam that asks what to do when you encounter a change. You ***always*** begin dealing with change by **consulting the project management plan**.
- The **work authorization system** is a part of your company's Enterprise Environmental Factors, and it's generally part of any change control system. It defines how **work is assigned to people**.

The Direct and Manage Execution process

Once you have a project management plan, your project is ready to begin. And as the project unfolds, it's your job to direct and manage each activity on the project, every step of the way. That's what happens in the **Direct and Manage Execution** process: you simply follow the plan you've put together and handle any problems that come up.

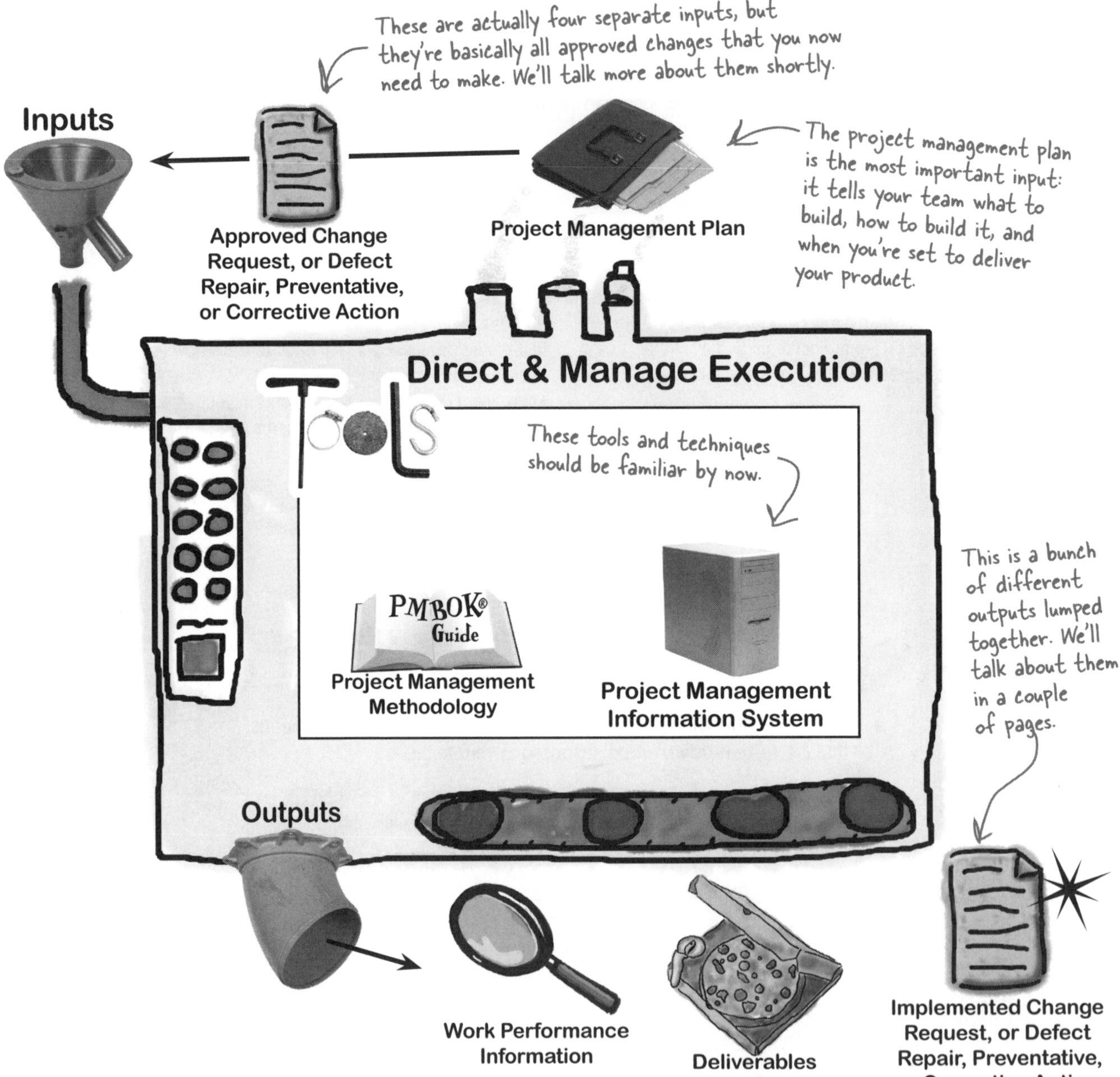

The project team creates deliverables

The work you're doing on the teachers' project creates lots of things: airline reservations, hotel reservations, invoices, defect reports, and customer comments (to name a few). These things are all your **deliverables**, and they are one of the two outputs of the **Direct and Manage Execution** process.

The other output is **work performance information**, and that's what we call the reports Acme's running on the project. These reports track how many negative versus positive customer comments the project gets, and how well the project is doing at meeting its cost estimates. In fact, a project manager should figure out a way to measure how well the processes from each knowledge area are being performed.

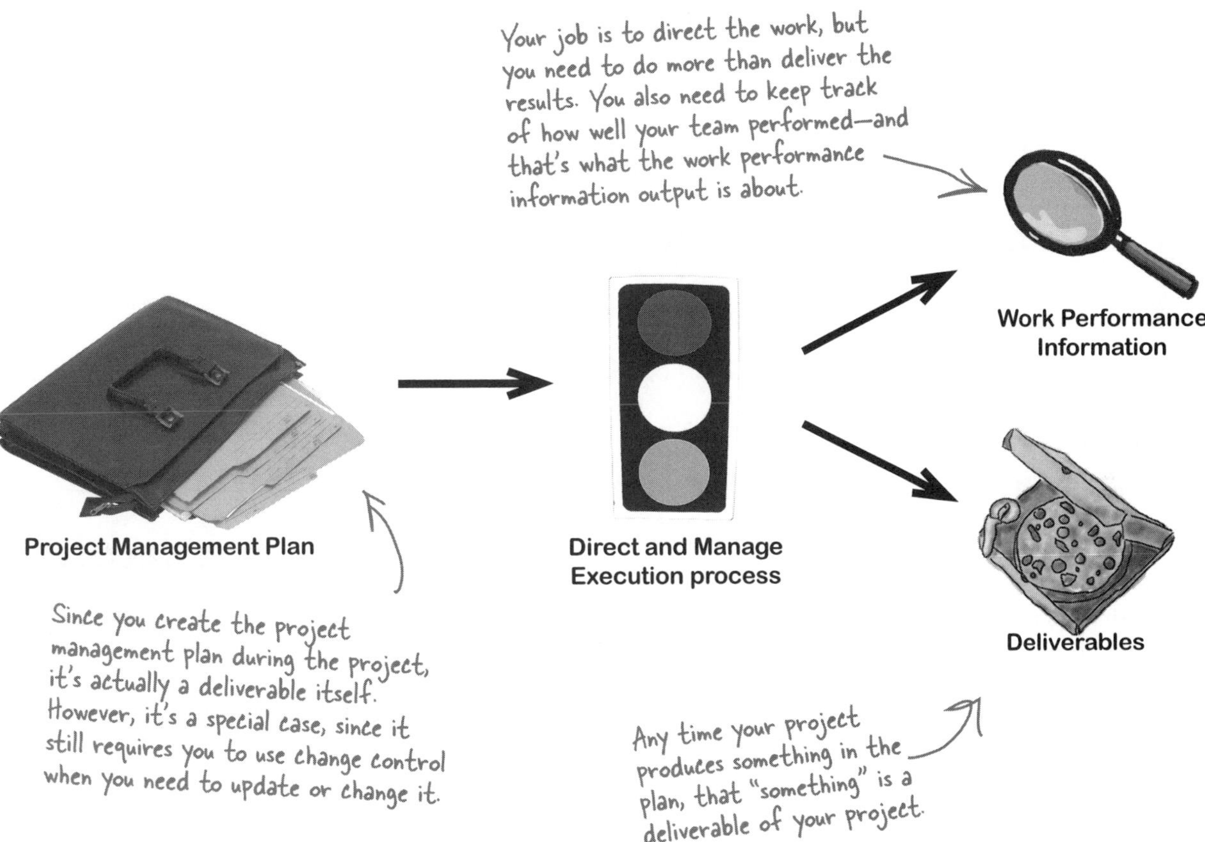

You create work performance information by measuring how well the processes from each knowledge area are being performed.

Executing the project includes repairing defects

The Direct and Manage Execution process has a bunch of inputs and outputs—but most of them have to do with implementing changes, repairs, and corrective action. If there's a defect repair that's been approved, this is where it happens. Once the defect is repaired, the result is an **implemented defect repair.** The same is true for changes and corrective actions; once they're approved, they become process inputs, and then they can be implemented and become process outputs.

Any time you have to correct a mistake or make a repair in a deliverable, you're fixing a defect.

The three components of the Direct and Manage Execution process:

1. Use the plan to create deliverables
2. Repair defects in deliverables
3. Make approved changes and corrections to deliverables

Deliverables are anything you produce in the course of doing your project activities.

Your Quality Management plan focuses on catching defects as you go, so you can repair them as soon as possible.

Deliverables include everything that you and your team produce for the project

The word **deliverable** is pretty self-explanatory. It means anything that your project **delivers**. The deliverables for your project include all of the products or services that you and your team are performing for the client, customer, or sponsor.

But deliverables include more than that. They also include every single document, plan, schedule, budget, blueprint, and anything else that gets made along the way... including all of the project management documents that you put together.

Deliverables

The Direct and Manage Execution Process is where you and your team actually does the project work to produce the deliverables.

Sharpen your pencil

Here's a list of things produced by some typical projects. Some of them are deliverables, and others are work performance information produced by running reports. There's also a list of changes, some of which affect the project management plan, and some of which just affect the project deliverables. It's up to you to figure out which is which.

1. The software project team builds software.

☐ Deliverable ☐ Work performance information

2. A builder hangs a door.

☐ Deliverable ☐ Work performance information

3. A wedding photographer sends the photo proofs to the client.

☐ Deliverable ☐ Work performance information

4. The cable repair technicians takes an average of four hours per job.

☐ Deliverable ☐ Work performance information

Sometimes something that looks like a defect in a deliverable is really a change that you need to make to the plan.

5. The construction crew worked 46 hours of overtime in March.

☐ Deliverable ☐ Work performance information

6. The construction crew built the six houses required by the plan.

☐ Deliverable ☐ Work performance information

7. A software test team finds bugs in the software.

☐ Defect in deliverable ☐ Change to project management plan

8. A bride asks the photographer to stop asking her mother for permission to make changes.

☐ Defect in deliverable ☐ Change to project management plan

9. A construction crew used the wrong kind of lumber in a house.

☐ Defect in deliverable ☐ Change to project management plan

10. A photographer's prints are grainy.

☐ Defect in deliverable ☐ Change to project management plan

Answers on page 126.

Eventually, things WILL go wrong...

Even if you work through all the processes you've seen so far, things can still go wrong on your project. In fact, the teachers are already letting you know about some issues they're having:

This sucks... they lost Frank's luggage, and I got my wallet stolen!

I can't find my passport. What am I going to do?

... but if you keep an eye out for problems, you can stay on top of them!

Sometimes you need to change your plans

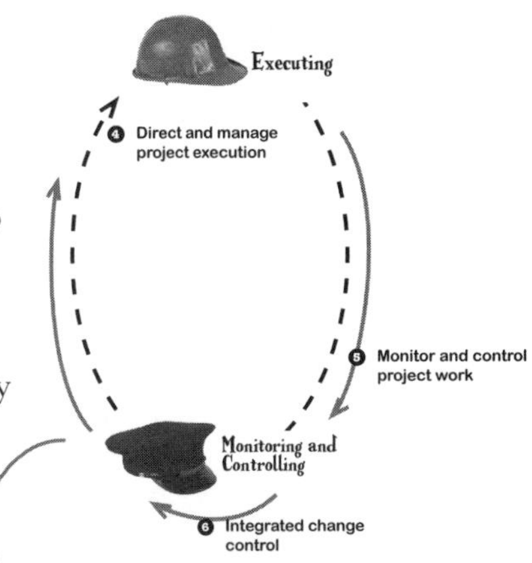

Take a minute and flip back to page 79. Notice how there's a loop between the Executing and the Monitoring & Controlling processes? That's because when your team is executing the plan and working on the deliverables, you need to keep a constant lookout for any potential problems. That's what the **Monitor and Control Project Work** process is for. When you find a problem, you can't just make a change... because what if it's too expensive, or will take too long? You need to look at how it affects the triple constraint—time, cost, scope, and how they impact quality—and figure out if it's worth making the change. That's what you do in the **Integrated Change Control** process.

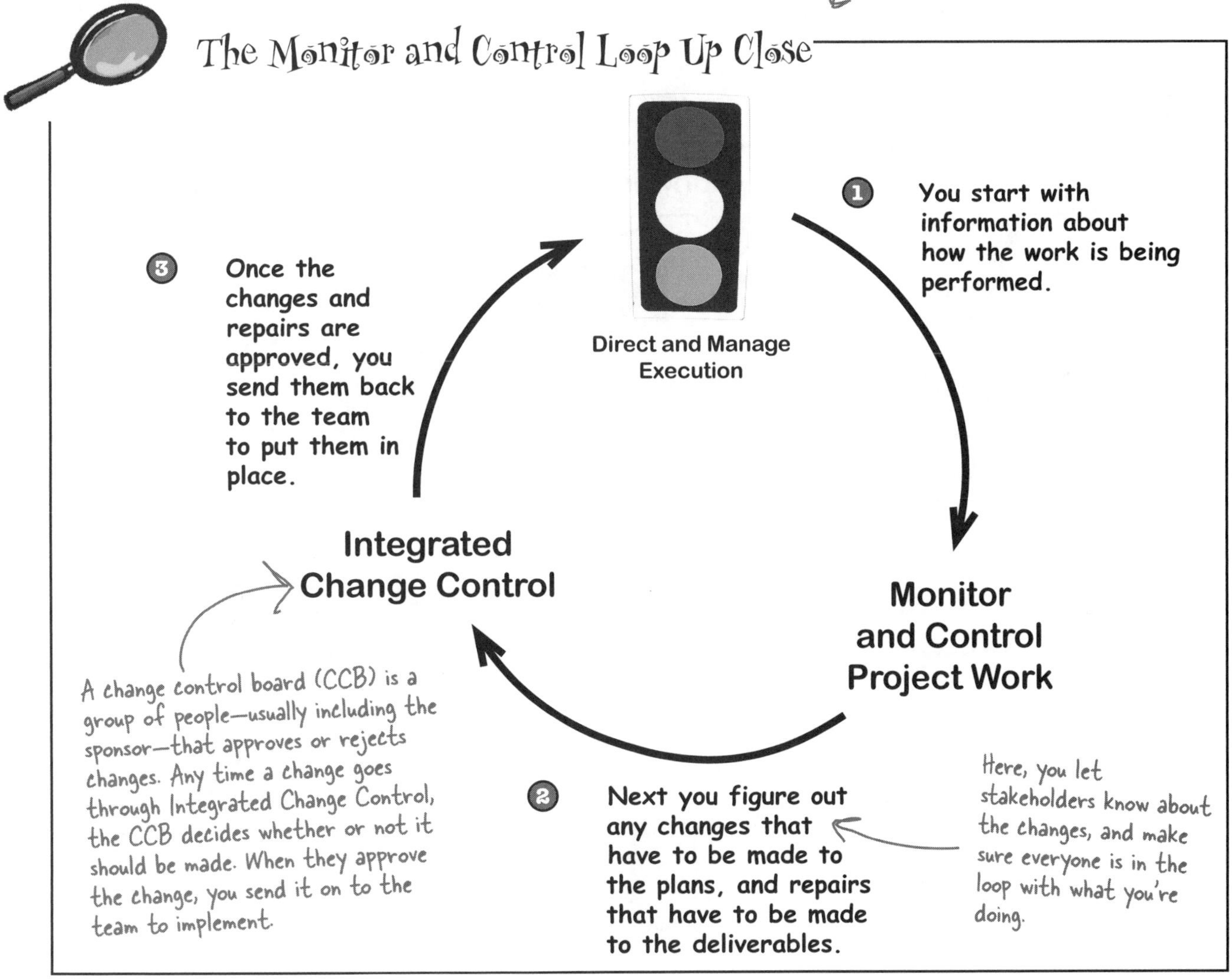

The Monitor and Control Loop Up Close

Direct and Manage Execution

1. You start with information about how the work is being performed.

Monitor and Control Project Work

2. Next you figure out any changes that have to be made to the plans, and repairs that have to be made to the deliverables.

Here, you let stakeholders know about the changes, and make sure everyone is in the loop with what you're doing.

Integrated Change Control

A change control board (CCB) is a group of people—usually including the sponsor—that approves or rejects changes. Any time a change goes through Integrated Change Control, the CCB decides whether or not it should be made. When they approve the change, you send it on to the team to implement.

3. Once the changes and repairs are approved, you send them back to the team to put them in place.

Look for changes and deal with them

Monitoring & Controlling process group

You need to stay on top of any possible changes that happen throughout your project, and that's what the **Monitor and Control Project Work** process is for. Usually the work is progressing just fine. But sometimes you find out that you need to change something, and that's when you use the **Integrated Change Control** process to see if the change is worth the impact it will have on your project.

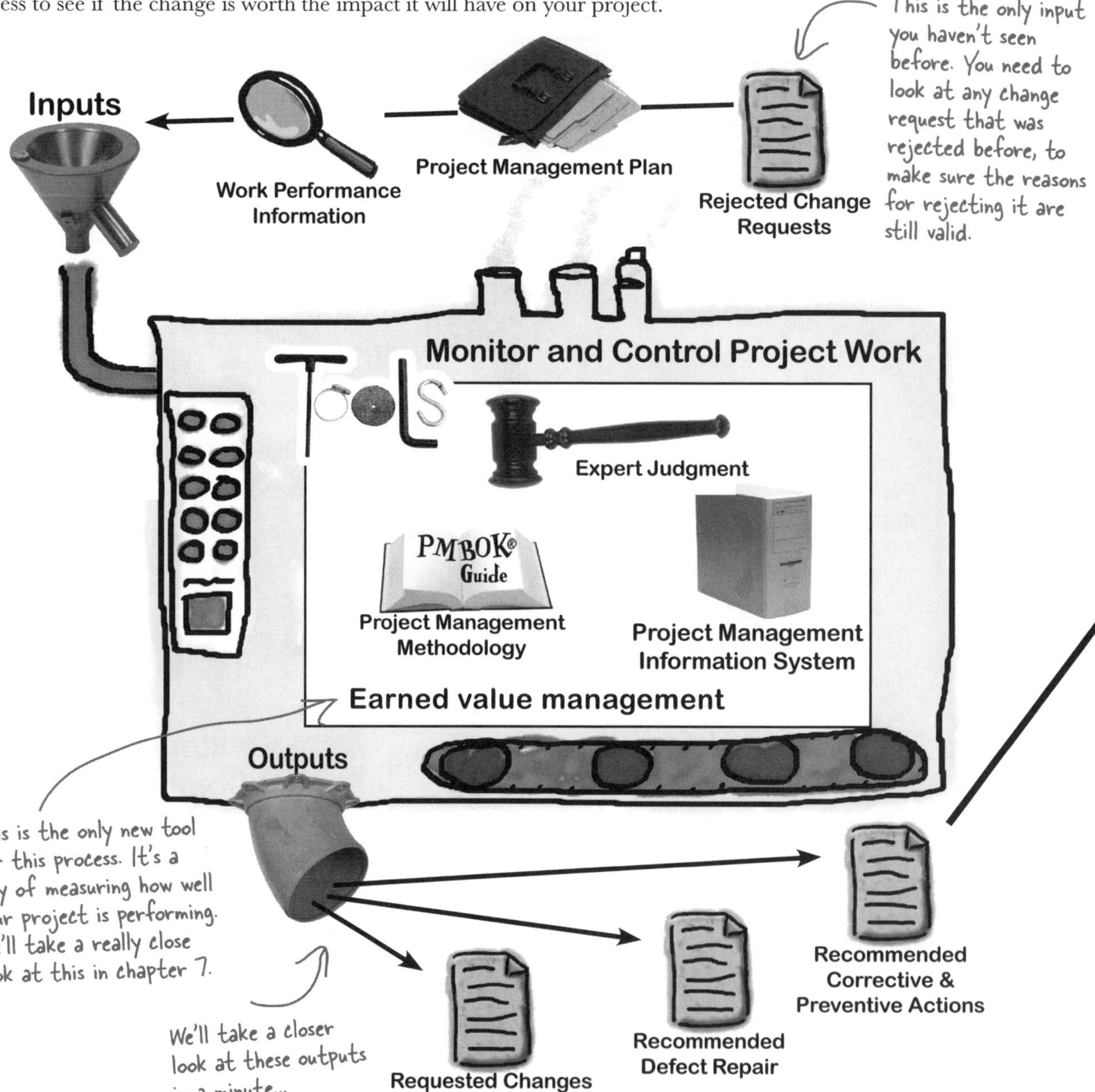

Make only the changes that are right for your project

The Monitor and Control Project Work process is where you find the changes that you may want to make. The **Integrated Change Control** process is where you decide whether or not to make them. But you're not the one actually making that decision – a big part of Integrated Change Control is that you **need to get your changes approved by the Change Control Board**.

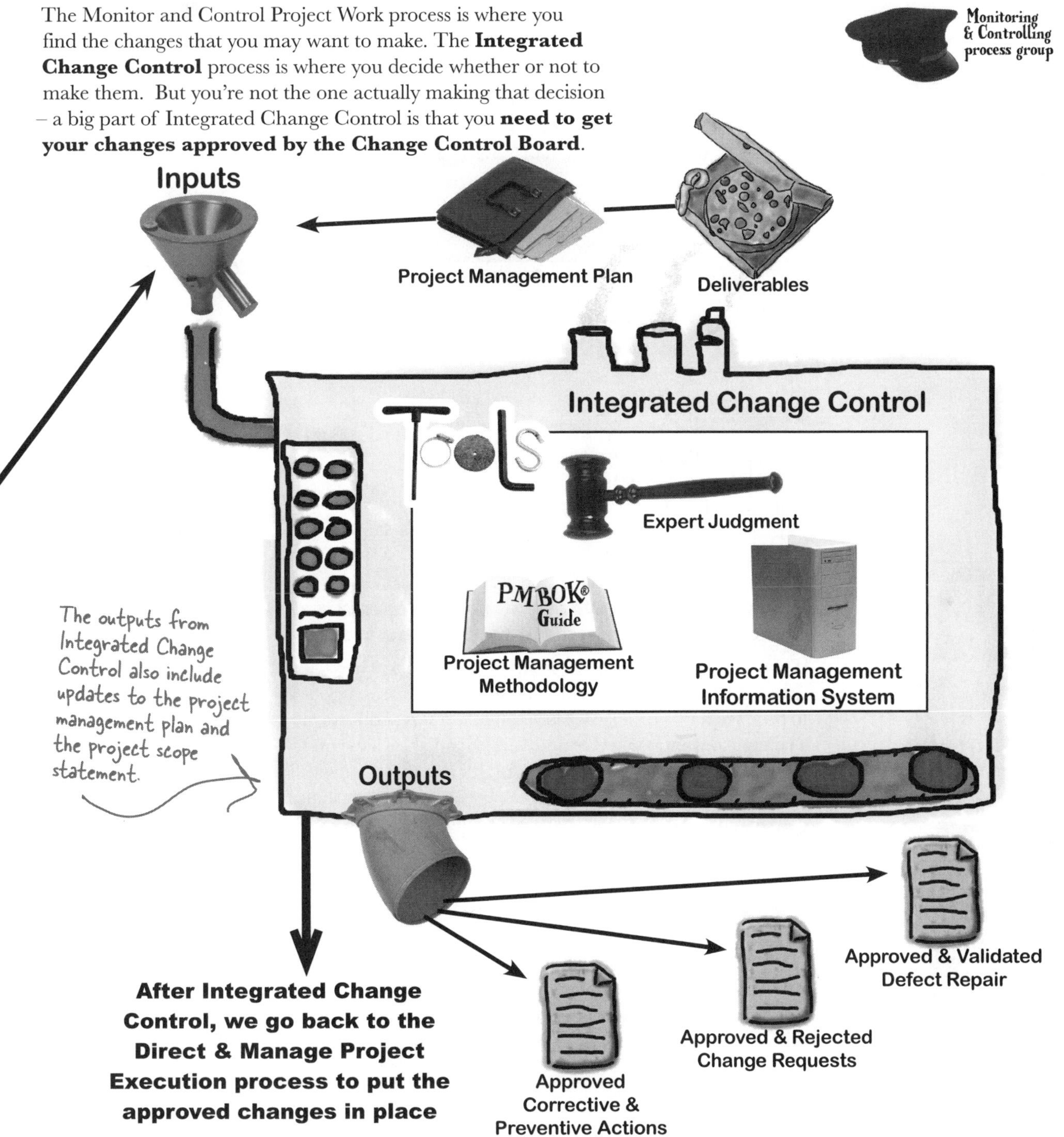

Changes, defects, and corrections

When the team is repairing defects to deliverables, they still need to go through change control.

You've already seen how a project can change as it goes along. When the teachers asked for their hotel to be upgraded, you took the request through the **change control** process at Acme, and when the change control board approved the change, you directed the agents to make the booking for the group.

But sometimes, things go wrong with what you intended to have happen in the first place. When your quality department told you that you had booked the teachers on the flight to Rome without putting them in the same row, you quickly fixed the reservation. But you intended the teachers to sit together in the first place, so that's not a change, its a **defect**.

In the process, you realized that your team wasn't reading your documentation carefully, which is why they screwed up the airline reservations. To fix the way your team is working, you need to take **corrective action**. That's when you need to change the way you're doing the work on your project. Got all that?

Whoa... repairing defects, making changes, and taking corrective action all sound like the same thing to me.

Defects relate to what you produce, and corrective actions relate to how you work.

When the trip you planned doesn't include one teacher's ticket, you've found a **defect**. The service you were supposed to produce had a problem. But fixing the reservations wasn't a change to what you were producing—you always meant to book the ticket, but you found a mistake. But the change still needs to go through change control, because the team should only repair the defects that make sense to fix. (There may be defects that are acceptable but that would be too expensive to repair.)

A defect relates to a problem with your work product—what your project produces.

Corrective actions deal with how you work, rather than what you actually produce.

If you're finding that your team isn't reading all your plans, then you've got to change the way they work. That's **corrective action**, and involves changing what you do and how you do it, not what your project creates. Corrective actions and preventive actions both need to go through change control—that's what turns them from **recommended** actions into **approved** ones.

How the processes interact with each other

While monitoring the teachers' trip, you notice that they all ask for nonsmoking rooms every time they check into a hotel. But some hotels don't have enough nonsmoking rooms available, and the teachers aren't too thrilled about that.

After talking it over with the teachers it's clear that it's worth splitting up the group over multiple hotels to make sure they all are in non-smoking rooms—and some hotels are more expensive than you'd planned. The cost change will put you over budget, so the cost management plan needs to be updated. Time to take the request to change control:

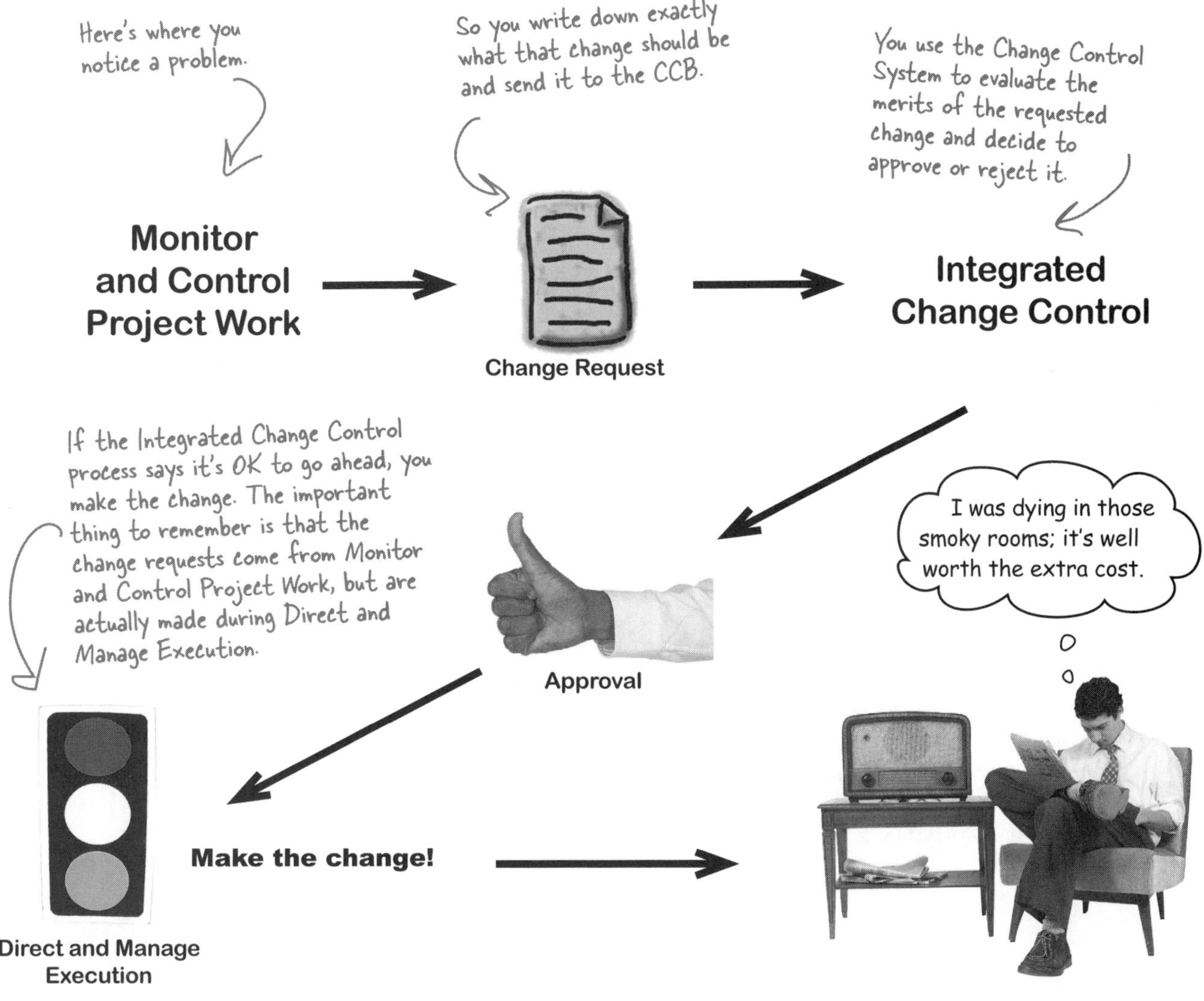

Control your changes; use change control

There's a beautiful hotel across the street, and we want to transfer. Increase the budget by 15%, and book us there.

Project Management Plan

Your project management plan should detail how you deal with changes that happen during your project.

Any time you need to make a change to your plan, you need to start with a **change request**. This is a document that either you or the person making the change needs to create. Any change to your project needs to be documented so you can figure out what needs to be done. Once you have a change request, that then kicks off your project's set of change control procedures.

The key here is PROCEDURE—change control is about how your company handles changes. You may use a computer system to monitor and document changes, but that's just one part of your change control system.

This means you need to write down exactly what needs to be changed and put it in something called a change request. That's a form that you fill out to send a change through change control.

Change control is how you deal with changes to your project management plan.

A change control system is the set of procedures that let you make those changes in an organized way.

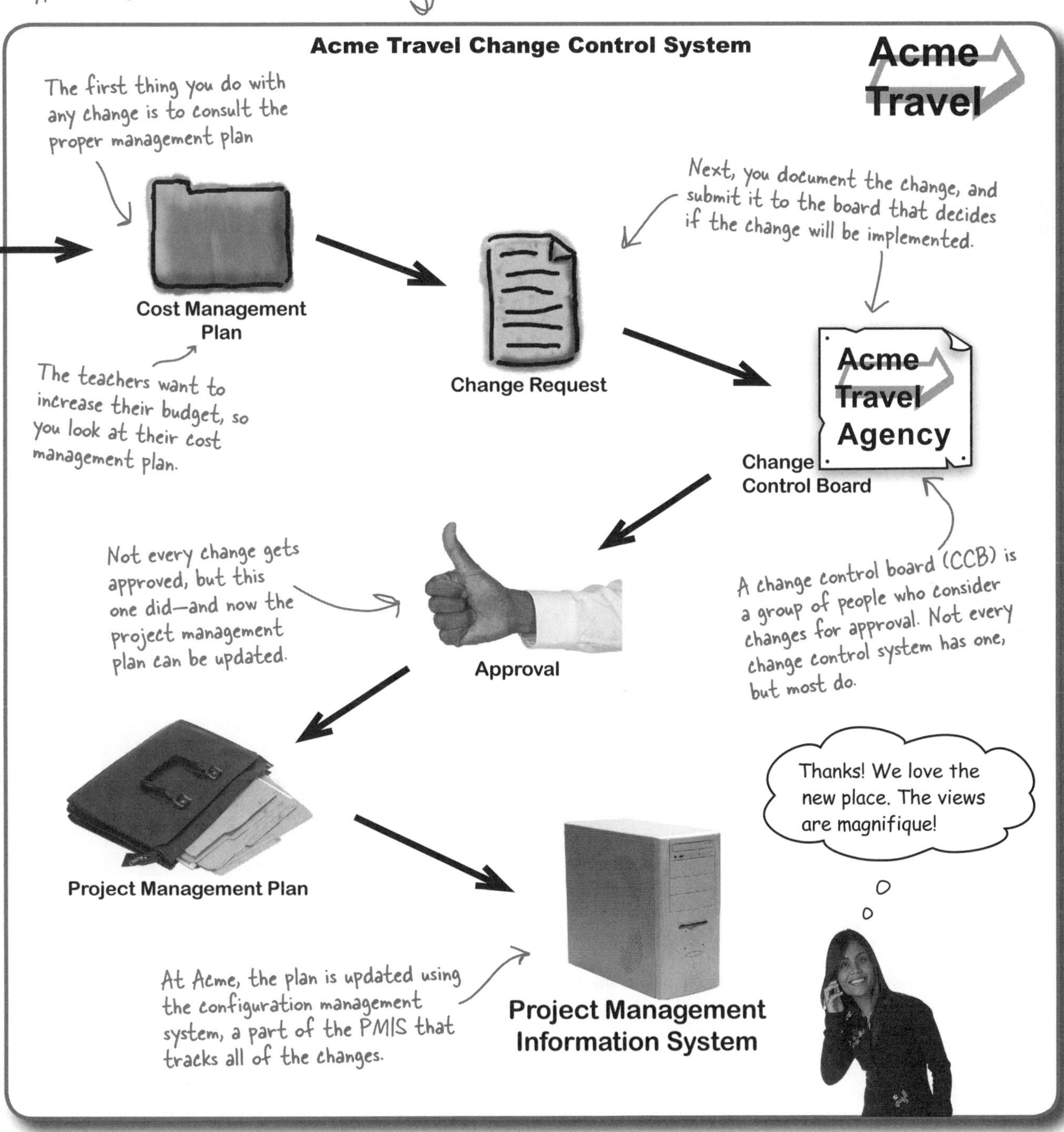
This is Acme's change control system. It's specific to their company, but it contains all of the steps you'd see in a typical change control system.
Acme Travel Change Control System
Acme Travel
The first thing you do with any change is to consult the proper management plan
Cost Management Plan
The teachers want to increase their budget, so you look at their cost management plan.
Next, you document the change, and submit it to the board that decides if the change will be implemented.
Change Request
Acme Travel Agency
Change Control Board
A change control board (CCB) is a group of people who consider changes for approval. Not every change control system has one, but most do.
Not every change gets approved, but this one did—and now the project management plan can be updated.
Approval
Project Management Plan
Thanks! We love the new place. The views are magnifique!
At Acme, the plan is updated using the configuration management system, a part of the PMIS that tracks all of the changes.
Project Management Information System

Preventing or correcting problems

When you monitor your project, you might be checking the actual time it's taking you to do scheduled work versus the amount of time you planned, or you might be gathering information on the number of defects you have found versus the number you expected. In both cases, it's possible that you might find problems. If you do, you have to change the way you do your work and keep your project from being dragged down. When you make a course change on your project, that's taking **corrective action**.

It's also possible that you might see problems that are going to occur even though they haven't happened yet. If you do, you will want to take **preventive action**, or steps that you take to avoid potential problems.

When people predict problems on projects before they happen, it's called a **forecast**. A forecast can be a good reason to make a change too!

In both corrective and preventive action, you always need to submit your proposed change and put it through the Monitor and Control Project Work process—and only if it is approved will you implement it. If your recommended action makes it through, you need to change the plan and any of your baselines to include it.

Here is a list of actions that are recommended by a project manager. Which are preventive and which are corrective?

1. A software project is running late, so a software project manager looks to find slack time and reassign resources to get things done more quickly.

☐ Preventive action ☐ Corrective action

2. A caterer notices that the crudités are all gone and assigns a chef to make more.

☐ Preventive action ☐ Corrective action

3. A photographer brings an extra camera body to a shoot, in case one breaks down.

☐ Preventive action ☐ Corrective action

4. A consulting company assigns extra resources to a project to compensate for possible attrition.

☐ Preventive action ☐ Corrective action

Answers on page 124.

there are no Dumb Questions

Q: Sometimes my team members come to me and tell me that the project could have problems later. What do I do with that?

A: For some project managers, it seems natural to dismiss these "negative Nellies" who seem concerned with problems that could go wrong in the future. But this is one of the best ways you can satisfy your stakeholders.

When someone makes an estimate or prediction of a future condition that could lead to trouble, it's called a **forecast**, and that's very valuable information. You should distribute it along with your work performance information, and try to think of ways to avoid the problem—which is what preventive action is all about.

A big part of your job as a project manager is to figure out how to prevent changes. This might seem a little weird—how can you prevent changes before the project is implemented? One way to do this is plan as well as possible, because a lot of changes happen because of a lack of planning. But it also means talking to stakeholders throughout the project and keeping an eye out for potential problems. When you take the PMP exam, if you see the phrase "**Influencing factors that cause change**," this is what it's referring to.

Q: Who approves changes?

A: Usually there's a **change control board (CCB)** that approves changes. That's a group of people, most often including the stakeholders and sponsor, who look at the benefits of a change and figure out if it's worth the cost. If there's a CCB, your change control system will include a procedure that mentions it. But not every company has a CCB, and there is no requirement in the PMBOK® Guide that you have one.

Q: What if there's a problem outside my project, and I'm not sure that it affects me?

A: You should still consider its potential impact when you're monitoring your project's work. It's important that you're always on the lookout for potential problems. If you're not sure whether something could impact your project, it's your responsibility as a project manager to bring it to the attention of your stakeholders. And if you can make a change on your own that doesn't impact scope, cost, schedule, or quality, then **it's completely within your rights as a project manager to do it**.

Q: Once a change is approved, what do I do with it?

A: You change your project management plan to incorporate the change. This can mean that you create a new baseline with the new project management plan. For example, say you forgot to add a stakeholder to the change control board, so your project plan now describes the wrong process for making changes. You'll need to fix that, and you'll need to go through change control to do it.

Q: What about changes that don't affect schedule, cost, scope or quality?

A: If you evaluate the impact of a change and find that it won't have an impact on the project's triple constraint, then you can make the change without going through change control. Sometimes you need to change resources or move tasks around, and you can make those changes without affecting the bottom line or the end product. In these cases, change control wastes time and resources, rather than helping your project.

You always have the authority to make changes to your project if they don't affect cost, schedule, or quality.

Finish the work, close the project

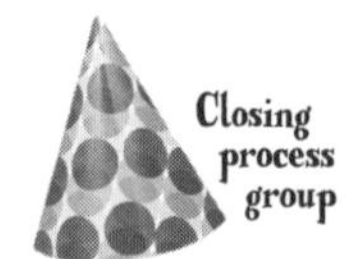

You can't finish the project until you get paid! Most projects start with contracts, and when they do you need to make sure the terms are met. Acme signed a contract with the Midwestern Teachers' Association when the project started, and now it's time to make sure all of the parts of that contract are met.

And that's part of what you do in the **Close Project** process. But an even more important part of this process is that you create the **lessons learned** and add them to your company's Organizational Process Assets. That way you and other project managers can learn from the project in the future.

The **inputs** to the Close Project process include the project management plan, organizational process assets, enterprise environmental factors, work performance information, and deliverables, along with any contract you have for the work (if there is one). And you use the same familiar **tools and techniques** you've seen all chapter: project management methodology, the PMIS, and expert judgment.

Outputs

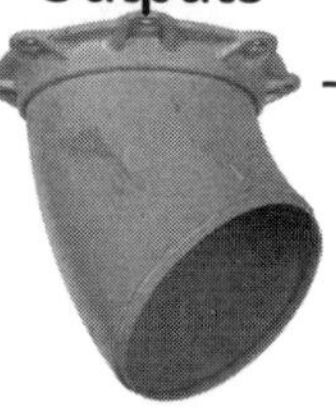

You've seen the Organizational Process Assets input a bunch of times now. But where does it really come from? It turns out that it comes from other project managers just like you. Every time a project is closed, you update those assets so that you can use them later. And new project managers will be able to learn from everything that's happened on your project.

During the teachers' trip you collected documentation that showed they actually checked into every hotel along the way. This proves you delivered everything in the scope.

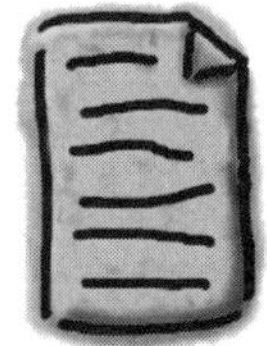

Project Closure Documents

Project Files

This is every piece of paper or computer file you made along the way: reservations, itineraries, copies of tickets, notes, etc.

Organizational Process Assets

These are the lessons learned, so that future projects can take advantage of them. This comes from the work performance information that you and your team gathered throughout the project.

This is a written document that shows the sponsors and stakeholders agree that you've done what you said you would.

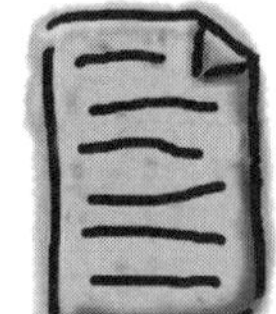

Formal Acceptance Documentation

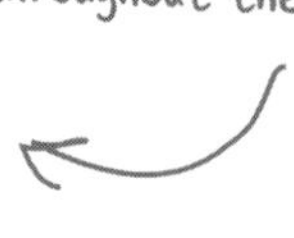

Historical Information

You don't have to go home, but you can't stay here

The teachers have gone through their entire itinerary. They're now on their way to Paris, which is the final leg of their tour. They've had a great time, and now it's time for you to finish up.

Every project needs to end, and that's what the Close Project process is all about. You want other travel agents at Acme to learn from anything new you've discovered. Remember how you had to scramble with the nonsmoking room request? Maybe your friends at Acme can learn from that, and ask new clients up front what they want! That's why you write down your lessons learned, and that's a big part of closing the project.

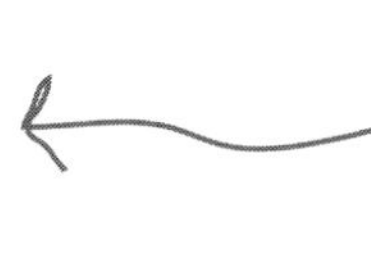

Lessons learned are finished in Close Process, but written down throughout the entire project. And it's not just by the project manager — the whole team writes down lessons learned.

You always need to close out the project and write down lessons learned, even when the project terminates early—like if a client pulled the plug on the project.

Anyone who cares about the project going well needs to be satisfied with the results.

Using the Administrative Closure Procedure

Administrative closure is about doing everything that Acme needs you to do in order to end the project.

The whole point of the project is that you need to deliver what you promised. By making sure that you delivered everything you said you would, you made sure that all of the stakeholders were satisfied. Once that happens, your project can finish.

Think about a major project you've heard of that did not end well, like one that was shut down before the work was done. What lessons could have been learned from that project?

How can the project manager use the Close Project process to make sure that something good comes out of early termination?

So why INTEGRATION management?

The Integration Management knowledge area has all of the processes that you do in your day-to-day work as a project manager. So why are they called "Integrated Management" processes? Because when your team is estimating how long it will take to do the work, they may need information or to consult with experts elsewhere in your company, and it's your job to get that for them.

And when they need to work with consultants, your job is to procure the services for the team. And you need to plan for all of it at the beginning—which is when you **integrate** all of these things together into a single plan. It's your job to make sure that every one of the 44 processes in the PMBOK® Guide is addressed in the plan, even if you're not going to use it (like if you don't need contractors, you won't use Procurement processes).

Integration Management means making sure that all of the processes work together seamlessly to make your project successful.

I get it! When I'm putting together my project management plan, I need to look at every single process and figure out how it's integrated into my project. So that's what "Integration Management" means.

What else is there?

Huh... It seems like we covered the whole project, right? You got authorized to do the work, you planned the project, you executed it, you corrected problems along the way, and you closed it out. Isn't that everything?

Well, of course not! There's a whole lot more planning that you have to do, and many skills that you need to have. Luckily, we've got the PMBOK® Guide to help us figure out exactly what we need to know to manage projects effectively.

That's what the rest of the book is about.

Project Integration Management Magnets

These inputs, outputs and processes are all scrambled up on the fridge. Can you reconstruct them so that they work?

Initiating	Planning	Executing	Monitoring and Controlling	Closing

INPUTS / OUTPUTS	Tools

Work Performance Information

Direct and Manage Execution

Contract

Develop Preliminary Scope Statement

Project Management Information System

Develop Project Charter

Close Project

Organizational Process Assets

Approved Corrective Action

Develop Project Management Plan

Expert Judgment

Monitor and Control Project Work

Earned Value Technique

Project Management Processes

Integrated Change Control

Project Integration Management Magnets Solution

These inputs, outputs and processes are all scrambled up on the fridge. Can you reconstruct them so that they work?

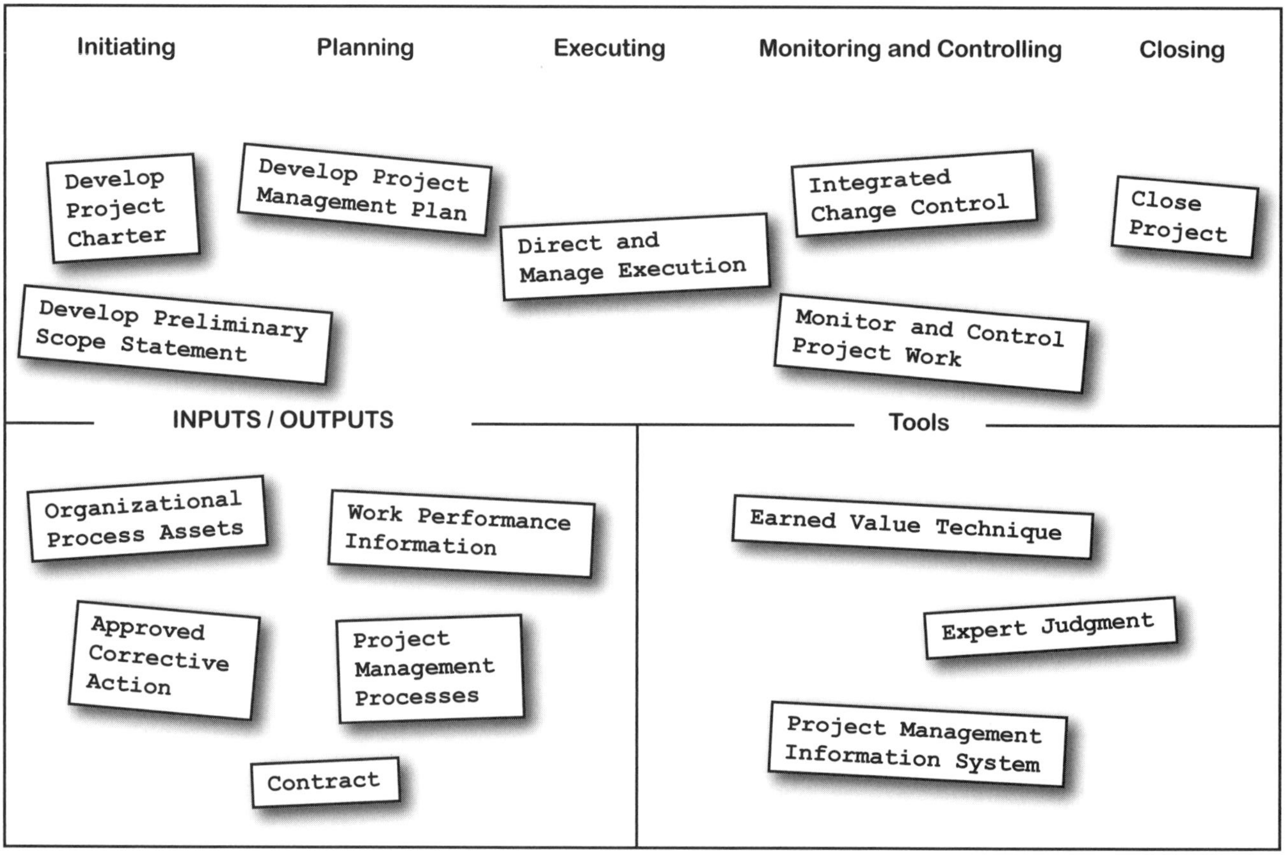

Initiating	Planning	Executing	Monitoring and Controlling	Closing
Develop Project Charter Develop Preliminary Scope Statement	Develop Project Management Plan	Direct and Manage Execution	Integrated Change Control Monitor and Control Project Work	Close Project

INPUTS / OUTPUTS	Tools
Organizational Process Assets Work Performance Information Approved Corrective Action Project Management Processes Contract	Earned Value Technique Expert Judgment Project Management Information System

Integration Management kept your project on track, and the teachers satisfied

By using all of the Integration Management processes, you kept the project on track. You handled all of the problems that came up, made some important changes in the process, and the teachers got to all of their destinations on time and on budget.

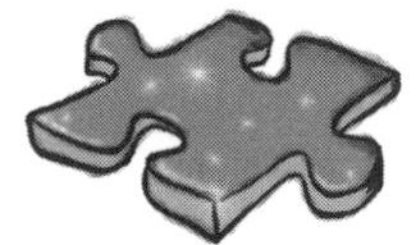

Integrationcross

Take some time to sit back and give your right brain something to do. It's your standard crossword; all of the solution words are from this chapter.

Across

1. The things your project produces.

3. A temporary decision you make to compensate for information you don't know.

5. Fixing problems that have already happened is called ______________ action.

7. The Project Management Plan is a collection of ____________ plans.

8. Work culture and company policies are called Enterprise _______________ Factors.

10. The Project __________ is a document that gives the project manager authority over the team.

11. When you watch what's happening in your project to look for changes, corrective and preventive actions you are in the ___________ and Control Project Work process.

Down

2. When you ask someone who has experience to help you figure something out you are using the __________ Judgement tool and technique.

4. A problem in a deliverable that shows that it does not do what you meant for it to do.

6. The ______________ Process Group contains the processes that help you start your project.

9. A record of all of the decisions you have made and their consequences that you write when you close your project is called ___________ learned.

Answers on page 127.

Here are a few of the things you might have to deal with in working on the teachers' vacation trip. Figure out which of the seven Integration Management processes you'd use in each situation, and write down the process name in the blank.

1. It turns out that one of the teachers is a vegetarian, so you need to change your plans to include vegetarian meals on the airlines and find restaurants that accommodate him.

   Integrated Change Control

2. You get one of the teachers on the phone and come up with a list of all of the places they want to go for the rest of the trip, and anything that may limit the tour.

   Develop Preliminary Scope Statement

3. You come up with a detailed description of everything that you plan to do to get the teachers where they want to be.

   Develop Project Management Plan

4. The CEO of Acme Travel sends you a document that assigns you to the project.

   Develop Project Charter

5. You check in with the teachers at each destination to make sure everything is going according to plan.

   Monitor and Control Project Work

6. When the teachers get back, you write up everything you learned while handling the trip so other travel agents can learn from your experience.

   Close Project

7. You book the tickets and hotel accommodations.

   Direct and Manage Project Execution

Develop Project charter

Develop Preliminary Scope Statement

Develop Project Management Plan

Direct and Manage Project Execution

Monitor and Control Project Work

Integrated Change Control

Close Project

Here are a bunch of project selection methods. Try to figure out which ones are benefit measurement models and which ones are mathematical models!

1. A. Benefit measurement (circled) — B. Mathematical model
2. A. Benefit measurement — B. Mathematical model (circled)
3. A. Benefit measurement (circled) — B. Mathematical model
4. A. Benefit measurement (circled) — B. Mathematical model
5. A. Benefit measurement — B. Mathematical model (circled)

Here is a list of actions that are recommended by a project manager. Which are preventive and which are corrective?

1. A software project is running late, so a software project manager looks to find slack time and reassign resources to get things done more quickly.

☐ Preventive action ☑ Corrective action

2. A caterer notices that the crudités are all gone and assigns a chef to make more.

☐ Preventive action ☑ Corrective action

3. A photographer brings an extra camera body to a shoot, in case one breaks down.

☑ Preventive action ☐ Corrective action

4. A consulting company assigns extra resources to a project to compensate for possible attrition.

☑ Preventive action ☐ Corrective action

Below is a whole crop of problems that the teachers are running into. Write down which subsidiary plan you'd look in to get some help. If you're not sure, just reread the descriptions of each subsidiary plan on the last page, and take your best guess.

1. Theteachers want to go Bali, but Acme Travel doesn't book flights there so you need to subcontract one leg of the travel to another travel agency.

   Procurement management plan

2. Theteachers are having so much fun that they want to stay at a better hotel. They tell you to increase their budget by 15% to do that.

   Cost management plan

3. Justas you're about to mail off the teachers' tickets, you notice they've been printed incorrectly.

   Quality management plan

4. The teachers might run into more bad weather, and you've got to figure out what contingencies you can put into place if that happens.

   Risk management plan

5. The teachers are concerned that they won't be able to get in touch with you when they're away.

   Communications management plan

6. Oneof the teachers realizes that he needs to come back earlier, and you want to make sure the budget reflects his lessened costs.

   Cost management plan

7. You find out that you need to get the tickets out earlier than expected, because the teachers' contract requires that all trips be preapproved by the superintendent of their school district.

   Schedule management plan

Sharpen your pencil Solution

Here's a list of things produced by some typical projects. Some of them are deliverables, and others are work performance information produced by running reports. There's also a list of changes, some of which affect the project management plan, and some of which just affect the project deliverables. It's up to you to figure out which is which.

1. The software project team builds software.

- [x] Deliverable
- [ ] Work performance information

2. A builder hangs a door.

- [x] Deliverable
- [ ] Work performance information

3. A wedding photographer sends the photo proofs to the client.

- [x] Deliverable
- [ ] Work performance information

4. The cable repair technicians takes an average of four hours per job.

- [ ] Deliverable
- [x] Work performance information

5. The construction crew worked 46 hours of overtime in March.

- [ ] Deliverable
- [x] Work performance information

6. The construction crew built the six houses required by the plan.

- [x] Deliverable
- [ ] Work performance information

7. A software test team finds bugs in the software.

- [x] Defect in deliverable
- [ ] Change to project management plan

8. A bride asks the photographer to stop asking her mother for permission to make changes.

- [ ] Defect in deliverable
- [x] Change to project management plan

9. A construction crew used the wrong kind of lumber in a house.

- [x] Defect in deliverable
- [ ] Change to project management plan

10. A photographer's prints are grainy.

- [x] Defect in deliverable
- [ ] Change to project management plan

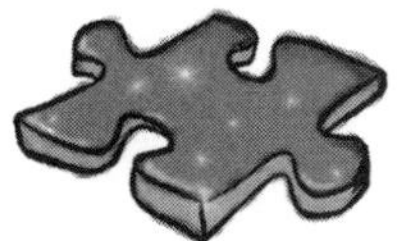

Integrationcross Solution

Take some time to sit back and give your right brain something to do. It's your standard crossword; all of the solution words are from this chapter.

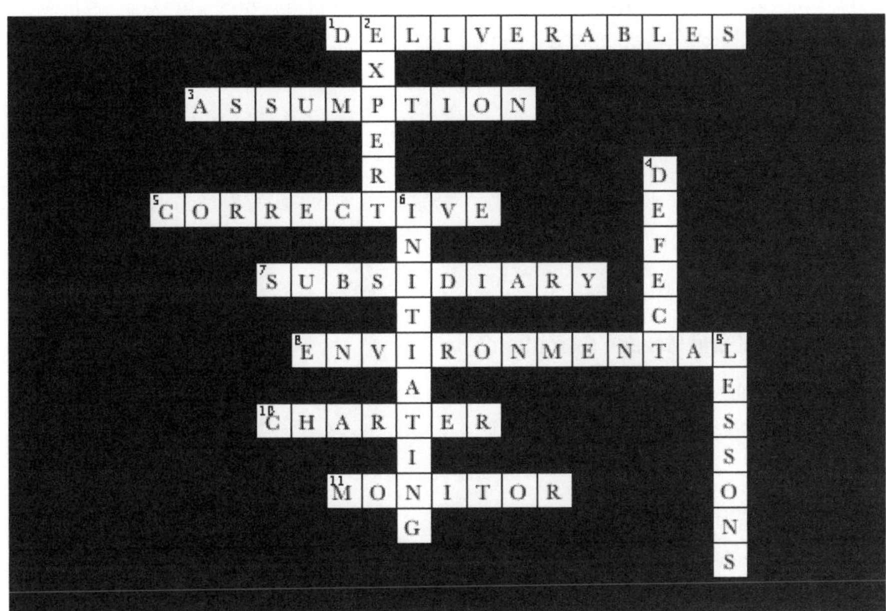

Exam Questions

1. You've just received a change request. This means:

A. The project charter is complete, but the work cannot begin yet because you need to make a change to the preliminary scope statement.

B. You are in the Direct and Manage Execution process, and you can implement the change now.

C. The change needs to be approved before it can be implemented.

D. There is a defect in a deliverable that must be repaired.

2. Which of these is not an input to Develop Project Charter?

A. Enterprise environmental factors

B. Preliminary scope statement

C. Contract

D. Project statement of work

3. What is the output of Direct and Manage Execution?

A. Approved change requests

B. Project management processes

C. Deliverables

D. Work performance information

4. You're managing a graphic design project. One of your team members reports that there is a serious problem, and you realize that it will cause a delay that could harm the business of the stakeholders. Even worse, it will take another two days for you to fully assess the impact—until then, you won't have the whole story. What is the BEST way to handle this situation?

A. Create a change request document and submit it to the change control board

B. Pull out the project charter and show them that you have authority to make decisions

C. Meet with the stakeholders and tell them that there's a problem, but you need two more days to get them the information they need

D. Update the lessons learned and add it to your organizational process assets

5. You're a project manager on a construction project. The electrician has started laying out the wiring, when the client comes to you with a change request. He needs additional outlets, and you think that will increase the cost of the electrical work. What is the first thing you do?

A. Refuse to make the change because it will increase the cost of the project and blow your budget

B. Refer to the project management plan to see how the change should be handled

C. Consult the contract to see if there is a clause

D. Make the change, since the client requested it

Exam Questions

6. The work authorization system:

A. Ensures that every work package is performed at the right time and in the proper sequence

B. Authorizes the project manager to spend money on work

C. Is a set of processes and tools that aids project manager in effectively guiding the project to completion

D. Is a formalized, written description of how to carry out an activity

7. You're the project manager at a telecommunications company. You recently had stakeholders approach you with changes. You figured out that the changes would cost additional time and money. The stakeholders agreed, you were given additional time and budget, and the changes were approved. Now you have to incorporate the changes into the project. What do you do next?

A. Modify the preliminary scope statement to include the changes

B. Use the work authorization system to make sure the work is performed

C. Make sure to track your changes against the project's baseline so you know how much they eventually cost

D. Incorporate the changes into the baseline so you can track the project properly

8. You are a project manager on a software project. When you planned the project, your Enterprise Environmental Factors included a policy that all changes that cost over 2% of the budget need to be approved by the CFO, but smaller changes could be paid for by a management contingency fund. One of your stakeholders submitted a change request that requires a 3% increase in the budget. Your company has an outsourcing effort, and you believe that a small change to the way that the change is requested could allow you to take advantage of it and cut your costs in half. What is the BEST way to handle this situation?

A. Work with the stakeholder to figure out how to reduce the cost of the change by a third

B. Request approval from the CFO

C. Refuse the change because it is over 2% of the budget

D. Document the change request, since all changes must be documented

9. You're on the project selection committee. A potential project is being presented by its sponsor. Everyone else in the room is asking questions intended to discover its potential value, its likelihood of success and to expose weaknesses and flaws in the project. What BEST describes this meeting?

A. Constrained optimization

B. Murder board

C. Benefit measurement method

D. Linear programming

Exam Questions

10. One of your team members has discovered a defect in a deliverable and has recommended that it be repaired. Which of the following is NOT true:

A. The project charter has authorized you to perform the work

B. Your project is in Monitor and Control Project Execution

C. The defect repair must be approved before the deliverable can be repaired

D. You must update the project management plan to document the defect

11. You are holding a formal, approved document that defines how the project is executed, monitored and controlled. You are holding:

A. The project management plan

B. The preliminary scope statement

C. The project charter

D. The work breakdown structure

12. You are the project manager for a software project, when the sponsor pulls the plug and cancels the project. What do you do?

A. Give the team the day off to recuperate from the bad news

B. Create a budget summary for the remaining unspent budget

C. Create the closure procedures and update the organizational process assets

D. Find new assignments for any people previously assigned to your project

13. You are managing a software project, when you find out that a programming team who you were supposed to have access to has been reassigned to another project. What is the first thing that you should do?

A. Figure out the impact that this will have on your project

B. Bring a copy of your project's charter to the other manager, and explain that you need that team for your own project

C. Go to your sponsor and demand the team

D. Figure out a way to compress the project schedule so that you can work with the team if they become available

14. You are a project manager on a software project. There are several changes that need to be made, and you need to decide how to apply project resources in order to implement them. What do you do?

A. Decide the priority of the changes and announce them to the team

B. You should call a team meeting and invite the stakeholders, so that everyone can reach a consensus on the priority

C. Deny the changes because they will delay the project

D. Consult the Change Prioritization Plan for guidance on prioritizing new changes

Exam Questions

15. You're a project manager on a software project. Your team is busy executing the project and creating the deliverables, but there have been several changes requested by stakeholders over the past few weeks. Each time you got one of these changes, you called a meeting with your team and the stakeholders to discuss it. Why did you do this?

A. Every change needs to be evaluated by a change control board

B. You're delegating the work of evaluating changes

C. You do not have a good change control system in place

D. You are using a work authorization system to assign the work

16. You are the project manager on a construction project, and you have just received a change request. You consulted the project management plan, and followed the procedures laid out in the Change Control System. You are in the process of reviewing the change and documenting its impact. Your manager asks you why you are doing this. What are you doing by reviewing the change and documenting its impact?

A. Integrated Change Control

B. Monitor and Control Project Work

C. Manage Requested Changes

D. Direct and Manage Execution

17. Which of the following is NOT true about the project charter?

A. The project charter defines the requirements that satisfy customer needs

B. The project charter defines the work authorization system

C. The project charter makes the business case that justifies the project

D. The project charter includes the summary budget

18. You have just verified that all of the work on your project is completed. Which of these things is NOT part of the Closing process?

A. Update historical information by documenting lessons learned

B. Document the work performance information to show the deliverables that have been completed and record the lessons learned

C. Verify that all of the work has been completed correctly

D. Follow the administrative closure procedure

19. Which of the following is NOT true about the preliminary scope statement?

A. The preliminary scope statement is refined into a more detailed scope statement later on in the project

B. The preliminary scope statement will serve as the basis for directing the project work

C. The preliminary scope statement contains the project and product objectives

D. The preliminary scope statement is used to develop the project management plan

Exam Questions

20. Which of the following is NOT an output of Direct and Manage Project Execution?

A. Work performance information

B. Deliverables

C. Implemented change requests

D. Forecasts

21. You are a project manager starting a new project. Your manager warns you that previous projects ran into trouble. Which of the following would be BEST for you to rely on to help plan your project:

A. Our project management expertise

B. Historical information

C. The change control system

D. Forecasts

22. Which is NOT true about the project charter:

A. The project manager must be consulted before the charter is finalized

B. The charter is issued by the project sponsor

C. The project manager's authority to manage the project is granted by the charter

D. The charter describes how stakeholders influence the project

23. Which of the following is NOT an example of a project selection method?

A. A murder board

B. A mathematical model for predicting project success

C. Expert judgment

D. Cost-benefit analysis

24. You are the project manager on a network engineering project. Two weeks ago, your team began executing the project. The work has been going well, and you are now a day ahead of schedule. Two stakeholders just approached you to tell you that they have an important change that needs to be made. That change will put you behind schedule. What do you do?

A. Implement the change because you're ahead of schedule

B. Refuse to make the change because the stakeholders did not take it to the change control board

C. Refuse to make the change until the stakeholders document it in a change request

D. Make sure the stakeholders know that you're open to change, and tell them to talk to the project sponsor

Exam Questions

25. Which of the following is NOT an output of Integrated Change Control?

A. Approved change requests

B. Rejected change requests

C. Validated defect repair

D. Recommended change requests

Start thinking about the kinds of questions you're seeing. Some have extraneous details—we call them "red herrings". Others are about inputs and outputs. That will definitely make the exam more familiar and easier.

Oh, I see. Sometimes the details of the question don't matter. They're just there to throw you off track.

Exactly, watch out for those red herrings.

Take some time to go over the answers to these questions and if they did throw you off track, reread the question to understand why.

Just remember... if you get something wrong now, that means you're actually MORE likely to remember it on the exam! That's why practice exams are so useful.

Exam ~~Questions~~ Answers

1. Answer: C

This is really a question about inputs and outputs. There's only one process that takes "requested changes" as an input, and that's Integrated Change Control. That's where your changes get approved. The other answers all refer to other processes: A is about Develop Preliminary Scope Statement, while B and D are both about Direct and Manage Execution.

2. Answer: B

This is a "which-is-not" question. When you see a question asking you to choose which input or output is not associated with a process, one good strategy is to try to think of what it is that process does.

The preliminary scope statement is created in the Develop Preliminary Scope Statement process, which happens after Develop Project Charter. Develop Project Charter is the very first process on any project, and the inputs in answers A, C and D exist before the project started. The preliminary scope statement is created during the project.

3. Answer: C

The whole reason for the Direct and Manage Execution process is to actually do the project work, and the deliverables are the products or services that are created by the project. Don't get fooled by answer D—even though the work is performed in "Direct and Manage Execution", the information about how that work is performed is collected in "Monitor and Control Project Work".

That makes sense. You need to monitor the work to figure out how well it's being performed.

4. Answer: C

When you get a question about communication, look for the answer that provides the most complete, honest, and up-front information, even if that information won't necessarily solve the problem or make everyone happy.

5. Answer: B

All changes must be handled using the change control system, which is a set of procedures that is contained in the project management plan. There is no way to tell from the question what specific steps will be in that change control system—answers A, C and D are all possible ways to deal with changes, depending on the situation. The only way to know for sure what to do is to follow the change control procedures in the project management plan.

Exam Questions

6. Answer: A

This is a "just the facts" question, and answer A is the actual definition of the work authorization system from the PMBOK® Guide. After you're done with these questions, look it up—it's on page 379. Underline or highlight it, and then read it out loud. Once you've read about it in the chapter, answered this question about it, and then looked up the definition, you'll never forget it!

7. Answer: D

The first thing you do after a change is approved is to update the baseline. If you chose answer C, don't feel bad—it's easy to get a little mixed up about what a baseline is used for. The whole purpose of the baseline is to figure out whether your project has deviated from the plan. But a change isn't a deviation from the plan! A deviation is accidental, while a change is done on purpose. That's why it's so important to get the change approved: that way, everyone knows about it, which means that you can plan for it. And updating the baseline is how you do that planning.

You use the baseline to protect yourself from nasty surprises... and an approved change is not a surprise.

8. Answer: B

When your company has a policy, you need to follow it and not try to work around it. Also, don't get fooled by answer D—the question said that a change request was submitted, so it's already documented. The exam could contain tricks like that!

The important stuff in this question is all in the first sentence. The outsourcing detail is a red herring.

9. Answer: B

This is a murder board—a group of people asking tough questions in order to try to figure out whether a project is likely to succeed. Answer C is also true, but it's not the BEST answer because B is more specific.

There will be questions on the exam where there are two valid answers but only one BEST answer.

10. Answer: D

Defects do not need to be documented in the project management plan. Take a look at the other answers—do you understand why they are correct? Answer A is simply the definition of the project charter; it doesn't have anything to do with the defect, but it's still true. "Recommended defect repair" is an output of the Monitor and Control Project Work process, so answer B is true as well. And as far as answer C goes, that's the whole purpose of the Integrated Change Control process: to approve defect repairs, changes, and preventive and corrective actions!

Exam ~~Questions~~ Answers

11. Answer: A

This is the definition of the project management plan!

12. Answer: C

Even when a project is terminated, you still need to close it out. And what are the outputs of the Close Project process? They're the administrative and contract closure procedures, and updates to the organizational process assets.

A question like this needs you to actually think about what you'd do—it's not just about applying a rule that you've learned.

13. Answer: A

If a resource is not available to you, it doesn't matter what's in your project charter or what your sponsors and stakeholders want. You need to figure out how to move forward from here, and the first step in doing that is evaluating the impact that this new problem will have on your project.

There's no such thing as a Change Prioritization Plan! Keep an eye out for fake artifacts and processes.

14. Answer: A

The project manager must decide the priority of the changes. If the changes need to be made, that means that they were approved. So you can't simply deny them. And you can't call the team in for a meeting, because they need to do the work. Some people may think that the stakeholders need to be involved—but since the change was already approved, you've gotten their buy-in. Now it's up to you to decide the order in which they're implemented.

This is NOT a good change control board because a CCB doesn't usually include the whole team!

15. Answer: C

When you get a change request, you need to consult the project management plan and follow the procedures defined in the change control system. It is generally not a good idea to involve the entire team in evaluating each change that comes in—there may be many changes, and if you pull your team off the job for each one, they'll never get their job done!

Doesn't C seem like the right answer? Too bad it's not a real process!

16. Answer: A

Once a change is requested, all of the work that you do with it falls under Integrated Change Control, right up until it's approved and you can implement it.

17. Answer: B

The work authorization system is defined by the company, and it's external to the project. You can think about it as the rules that you are told to follow in order to assign work in your company. They are part of the Enterprise Environmental Factors, an input to Develop Project Charter.

18. Answer: B

The work performance information is documented as part of Direct and Manage Execution. By the time the project closes, it's too late to use the work performance information! That's why it's an input to Monitor and Control Project Work—so you can take corrective action if the work is not being performed well.

Remember that lessons learned are documented throughout the project, not just at the end! That's why they're part of Work Performance Information.

19. Answer: B

By the time the project work is occurring during Direct and Manage Execution, the preliminary scope statement has already been refined into the a more detailed scope statement.

We'll learn about Scope Management in the next chapter.

20. Answer: D

Forecasts are created in Monitor and Control Project Work. The forecasts are important because they are used to help predict whether the project will come in on time and within budget. If not, preventive or corrective actions will be needed!

21. Answer: B

Historical information is an important input into Develop Project Charter, which is the first process that you perform when you start a new project. Historical information is very important, because it's how you learn about past projects' successes and failures. It's not actually listed as its own input. It's a part of Organizational Process Assets—and it really is a huge asset to any organization!

It seems like historical information is an important concept. I'll bet there will a question or two about it on the exam.

Exam ~~Questions~~ Answers

22. Answer: A

The project manager may be consulted when the project charter is created, but that's not always the case. It's possible that the project manager for a project is not even known when the charter is created!

23. Answer: C

While you may employ good judgment in determining the benefit of various projects, Expert Judgment is not a project selection method. It's an input into various processes.

24. Answer: C

The first step in handling any change is to document it. That's why "Requested Change" is the input to Integrated Change Control: the change control process cannot begin until the change is written down!

25. Answer: D ← Didn't D look like a good answer?

If you're having trouble remembering what the inputs and outputs are for Monitor and Control Execution and Integrated Change Control, one way to think about it is that change control is all about deciding whether or not to do something. Monitor and Control Execution is where you spot the problems—that's why all of the RECOMMENDED actions and changes are outputs of it, and inputs into Integrated Change Control. ICC is where those recommendations get evaluated turned into APPROVED actions and changes. The ones that are not approved are REJECTED. Then they go back to Direct and Manage Execution, where they are IMPLEMENTED, because that's project work and all project work happens in that process.

Remember, this is how you handle changes: Find it... evaluate it... fix it.

So how did you do?

5 Scope management

Doing the Right Stuff

Confused about exactly what you should be working on?

Once you have a good idea of what needs to be done, you need to **track your scope** as the project work is happening. As each goal is accomplished, you confirm that all of the work has been done and make sure that the people who asked for it are **satisfied with the result**. In this chapter, you'll learn the tools that help your project team **set its goals** and keep everybody on track.

Out of the frying pan...

The people at Ranch Hand Games have been working hard for a over a year on the sequel to their most successful title, *Cows Gone Wild*. It seemed like the project would never end…

... and right back into the fire

Since it took so long to get this version out, it's already time to start working on the next version. But nobody wants to see that project spin out of control the way it did last time.

The Cows Gone Wild II team ran into a lot of changes throughout the project. Could they have done something to avoid that problem?

Cubicle conversation

Brian: The project rocked in the beginning. We brought in some really talented programmers so that we could handle all of the technical challenges that might come up. We spent all that time whiteboarding and working our way through the technical issues in design. It really felt like this game was going to be amazing and fun to build. What went wrong?

Amy: We got sidetracked all over the place. Remember what happened with the web site? We spent months making that site look just like the game. It got to the point where it actually looked a lot better than the game did.

Brian: Yeah, you're right. And there were all these changes along the way—the story got updated like a thousand times. It was nuts.

Amy: I remember that. What a mess.

Brian: Totally. Oh man, and that time we realized you had to redraw all the artwork for the Haymaker level? We all slept in the office for like a week!

Amy: Right... Um, so what's gonna keep that from happening this time?

Maybe the Cows Gone Wild II project would have gone better if they'd had a project manager on board...

How would you solve these problems that happened in Cows Gone Wild II so they don't cause the same kind of trouble on CGW III?

Just write down a short sentence for each of these.

1. The web site got larger and larger and took almost as much time to build as the game itself.

....

The team had to rework a bunch of artwork because the game story changed.

2. Last minute story changes. ....

....

3. Artwork changes that caused rewrites at the last minute. ....

....

4. The game was over a year late. ....

....

Here are some answers that are good for dealing with these scenarios.

1. The web site got larger and larger and took almost as much time to build as the game itself.

Keep the team from doing unnecessary work.

You can't depend on the team to figure out what to do along the way. You need to scope out the work from the very beginning.

Luckily, if you nail down the scope up front, your team won't waste time doing unnecessary work later.

2. Last minute story changes. **Plan ahead and avoid late-breaking changes.**

Writing down all of the work and the effort required to do it will help everyone understand the impact of their changes

If the creative team figured out earlier that they'd need to make changes, the programmers could have worked on parts that weren't going to change. That would have been a lot more efficient.

3. Artwork changes that caused rewrites at the last minute.

Get started on the artwork changes sooner.

It's easier to figure out what's going to have to change if everyone is in sync on the scope.

Sounds like this game was late because the scope kept changing. Better planning could have fixed this.

4. The game was over a year late. **Start planning sooner. Figure out what the team is going to do before they start.**

Knowing what you're going to build up BEFORE you build it means you can do a better job predicting how long it will take.

Doing more planning at the start of the project helps you prioritize so that the most important work gets done efficiently.

It looks like we have a scope problem

All of the major problems on Cows Gone Wild II were **scope problems**. The web site was bloated with features that were added on late in the project. The creative team kept realizing that they had to do a lot more work. These are classic scope problems.

The product scope is all about the final product—its features, components, pieces.

When people talk about scoping out their projects, a lot of times they're talking about figuring out the features of the product, not the work that goes into it.

Product scope means the features and functions of the product or service that you and your team are building.

For the test, you should know that scope management is NOT concerned with product scope! Your job is about how the product is built, not deciding what goes into it and what stays out.

When we talk about scoping out a project, we mean figuring out all of the work that needs to be done to make the product.

Project scope is all of the work that needs to be done to make the product.

THIS is what the project manager is concerned with... the work the team has to do.

For the exam, you should ALWAYS remember that you're dealing with the PROJECT scope, not the product scope.

This means changes that just went in without anyone bothering to figure out what effect they'd have on the project's schedule, cost, or scope.

Scope creep means uncontrolled changes that cause the team to do extra work.

For the exam, think of scope as the work you do to complete the project

Sharpen your pencil

Here are some attributes of Cows Gone Wild III. Which are project scope and which are product scope?

1. Programming

☐ Project Scope ☐ Product Scope

2. 34 levels in the game

☐ Project Scope ☐ Product Scope

3. Graphic design

☐ Project Scope ☐ Product Scope

4. Four playable characters

☐ Project Scope ☐ Product Scope

5. Great graphics

☐ Project Scope ☐ Product Scope

6. Testing

☐ Project Scope ☐ Product Scope

7. Mac and PC compatible

☐ Project Scope ☐ Product Scope

8. A "boss battle" milk fight level at the end

☐ Project Scope ☐ Product Scope

Answers on page 196.

there are no Dumb Questions

Q: Does the scope include all of the stuff that I make, like a project schedule or a budget? What about things that are used to build the product but not actually delivered to the people who use it?

A: Yes, the project scope includes every single thing made by you and the team, and that includes the project plan and other project management documents. There are plenty of things on a project that are deliverables, but which the people who use the product will never see... like a project schedule, specifications, blueprints, and budgets. And while some of these things are made by the project manager, there are a lot of them that aren't, and it's not your job to figure out what goes into them. You just need to make sure they get done.

Q: Won't the team care more about what they are making than how they are making it?

A: Yes, definitely. It's your job as project manager to worry about all of the work the team does to build the product, so that they can focus on actually building it. But that doesn't mean you don't need their cooperation to make sure you've written down all of the work, and nothing else.

Q: Does that mean the project manager doesn't care about the product scope at all, just the project scope?

A: No, you still need to think about your project's final product. You can never ignore product scope, because most projects have changes to the product scope along the way. You'll have to change your product scope to include the work that's caused by product scope changes. Changes like that will probably have an impact on time and cost, too.

Here's an example: If somebody asks for a new feature in Cows Gone Wild III, the first thing the team needs to do is understand how much work is involved to accommodate it, and what that scope change will do to the cost and schedule.

As a project manager, your main concern is understanding that impact, and making sure everyone is OK with it before the change gets made. It's not your job to decide which is the best feature for the product, just to help everybody involved keep their priorities in mind and do what's best for the project.

You've got to know what (and how) you will build before you build it

You always want to know exactly what work has to be done to finish your project BEFORE you start it. You've got a bunch of team members, and you need to know exactly what they're going to do to build your product. So how do you write down the scope?

That's the goal of the **five scope planning processes**. They're about figuring out how you will identify all of the work your team will do during the project, coming up with a way to make sure that you've written down what work will be done (and nothing else!) and making sure that when things change on your project, you keep its scope up to date so that your team is always building the right product.

Scope management means figuring out what's OUT OF scope, not just what's part of it

Scope Management Plan

You need to write down exactly how you're going to do all of those things in the scope management plan.

Can't I just have my team spend a day brainstorming a list of every possible thing they might have to do?

That's a good idea. But what happens if they miss something?

It often seems like you should just be able to get everyone in the same room when the project starts and just hash all this stuff out. But it's really easy to miss something, and it's even easier for a team to get sidetracked.

It's way too easy for people to go off track and start doing things that don't really contribute to the project—like building the web site for a video game instead of building the game itself.

This is why the scope management plan needs to say how you're going to keep unnecessary work out of the project.

The scope management plan describes how you write down the scope, make sure it's right, and keep it up to date.

The power of scope management

When you take control of your project's scope, you're doing more than just planning. It turns out that when projects have scope problems, the results are actually pretty predictable. Take a look at these problems that the Ranch Hand team ran into. Do any of these sound familiar to you? Many project managers run into similar problems on their own projects.

1. **The team had trouble getting the project off the ground.** Everyone on the team was good at their individual jobs, but it seemed like nobody knew how to get the project started.

They'd sit around in meetings talking about what they wanted to build, but it seemed like weeks before anything started getting done.

2. **There were a lot of false starts.** Just when they thought they were getting the project under way, it seemed like something would shift and they'd be back to square one.

3. **The sponsor and stakeholders were unpredictable.** There were three different times that Amy and Brian thought they were done. But each time, a stakeholder found a problem that sent them back to the drawing board.

The worst part about this was that there was no way to know when they were done with the project without asking for the sponsor's opinion... and it seemed like that opinion was always changing.

4. **There were a whole lot of changes.** They were always scrambling to keep up with shifting priorities and ideas, and they never knew for sure what they'd be working on each week.

The team was tempted to lay down the law and forbid any changes... but a lot of those changes were necessary, and good ideas.

The five Scope Management processes

Each of the Scope Management processes was designed to help you avoid the kinds of scope problems that cause a lot of projects to go offtrack. One of the best ways to remember these processes for the exam is to understand why they're useful, and how they solve the kinds of problems that you've seen on your own projects.

Scope Management Plan

Scope Planning

You can get the project moving quickly with the **scope management plan**. It contains processes that guide you through defining all of the work that will be done by the team to complete the project. That way, the team doesn't waste time figuring out what needs to be done.

ProjectScope Statement

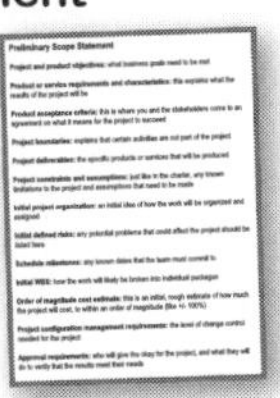

Scope Definition

By developing a project scope statement, you figure out exactly what your stakeholders need, and turn those needs into exactly what work the team will do to give them a great product.

When you do this right, the stakeholders are never unpredictable because you already understand their needs.

Work Breakdown Structure

Create WBS

The work breakdown structure (or WBS) organizes all of your team's work into work packages—or discrete pieces of work that team members do—so that you can keep the momentum of the project going from the start.

Pay attention to the WBS—there will be a lot of questions about it on the exam.

Scope Control

Scope Control

We already know how important it is to control changes on your project. When scope changes aren't controlled, it leads to the most frustrating sort of project problems. Luckily, you already know about change control, and now you can use it to manage your project's scope.

Remember Integrated Change Control from the last chapter? Now you'll see it in action.

Scope Verification

Once the work is complete, you need to make sure that what you're delivering matches what you wrote down in the scope statement. That way, the team never delivers the wrong product to the customer.

On the exam, "customer" can mean the same thing as "client" and "sponsor."

Accepted Deliverables

Cubicle conversation

Meet Mike, the new project manager at Ranch Hand Games

It looks like I got here just in time.

Brian: So we finally hired a project manager. Welcome aboard!

Amy: I'm glad they brought you in to help fix this mess.

Brian: So what are you gonna do to help us? Because I don't see what you can really change.

Mike: Thanks for the vote of confidence. Look, I might not be able to fix everything, but we should be able to keep this scope under control.

Brian: Sure, you say that now. But we all thought the last project would go fine too, and that one was a real pain!

Mike: Well, did you plan out the scope for your last project?

Amy: No, but we've built video games before and we knew basically what we needed to do when we started out.

Mike: It sounds like that wasn't enough.

What's the first thing Mike should do to make sure that Cows Gone Wild III goes well?

The Scope Planning process

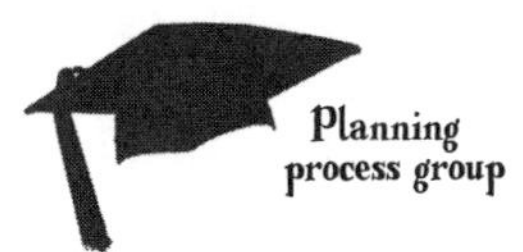

The **Scope Planning** process is where you build the scope management plan. It's in the Planning process group, so its inputs are really similar to ones you saw in the last chapter, because they're the same ones you used in the Integration Management planning process. The rest are things that you created earlier in the project.

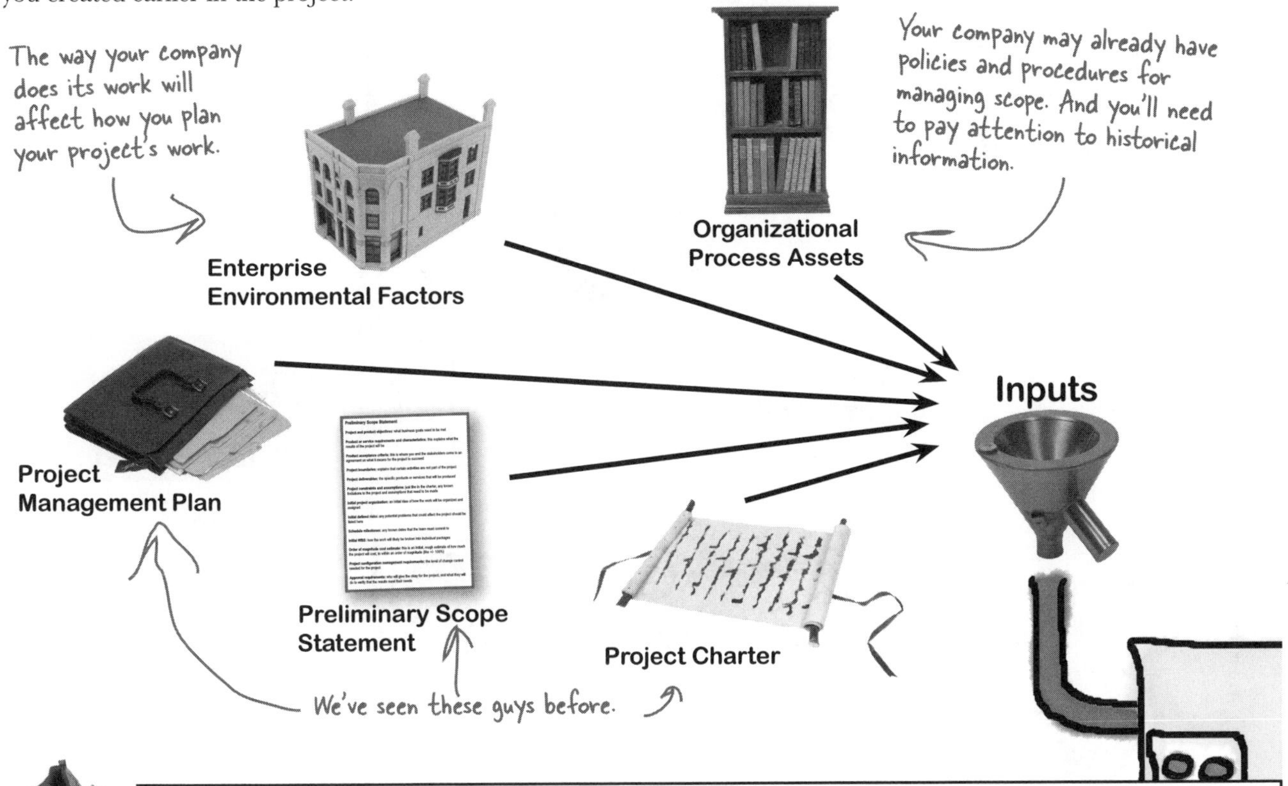

The way your company does its work will affect how you plan your project's work.

Enterprise Environmental Factors

Organizational Process Assets

Your company may already have policies and procedures for managing scope. And you'll need to pay attention to historical information.

Inputs

Project Management Plan

Preliminary Scope Statement

Project Charter

We've seen these guys before.

Exercise

Three of these inputs were outputs of Integration Management processes. Write down which process created each of them, and which process group it was in.

1. Project Charter: ....

2. Preliminary Scope Statement: ....

3. Project Management Plan: ....

Answers on page 196.

More on the scope planning process

The **Scope Planning** process is the very first thing you do to manage your scope. The idea behind scope planning is that first you figure out what you need to do to create and manage the scope, and then you write it down in the project's Scope Management Plan.

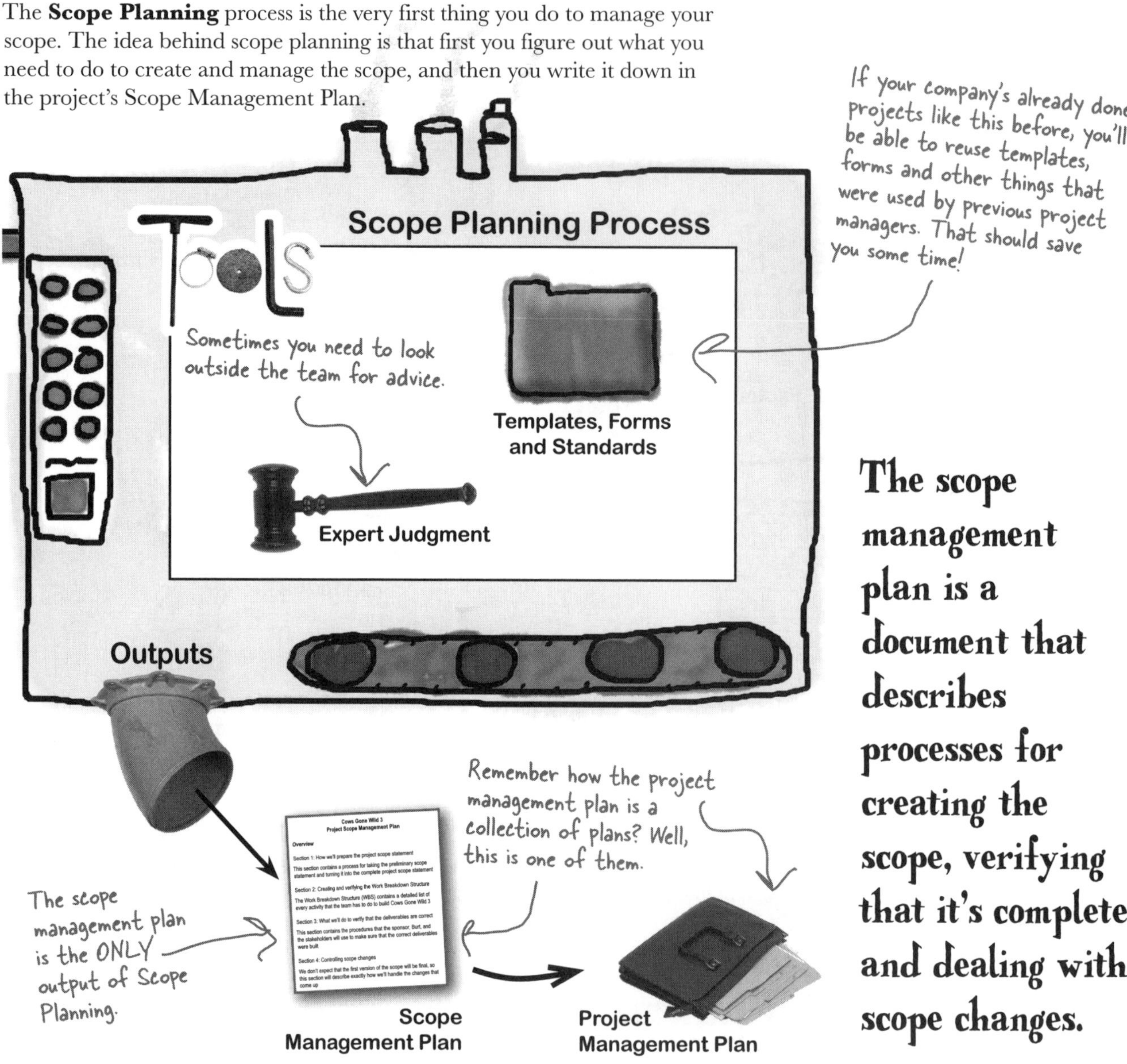

The scope management plan is a document that describes processes for creating the scope, verifying that it's complete, and dealing with scope changes.

The Scope Management Plan is the only output of Scope Planning. You use it to guide how the scope will be defined, how you'll verify that it contains all of the work required for the project, how you'll make sure the work done by the team actually created the right deliverables, and how requests for changes to the scope will be handled.

Inside the scope management plan

When you create the scope management plan, you'll write down processes that will help you manage the scope. The whole idea here is that when you start the project, you need to have a clear picture of all of the work that needs to happen on the project, with no extraneous or unnecessary work. And as the project progresses, you need to keep that scope up to date. The scope management plan is your tool to make sure that happens.

Project managers use the scope statement and work breakdown structure to keep track of the project scope.

There's a separate Scope Management process for each of these sections.

Remember how every piece of the project management plan tells you how to handle changes? Here's where you define that.

Cows Gone Wild III
Scope Management Plan

Overview

Section 1: How we'll prepare the project scope statement

This section contains a process for taking the preliminary scope statement and turning it into the complete project scope statement

Section 2: Creating and verifying the Work Breakdown Structure

The Work Breakdown Structure (WBS) shows all of the deliverables of the Cows Gone Wild III project, broken down into work packages that can be estimated and assigned to team members.

Section 3: What we'll do to verify that the deliverables are correct

This section contains the procedures that the sponsor and the stakeholders will use to make sure that the correct deliverables were built.

Section 4: Controlling scope changes

We don't expect that the first version of the scope will be final, so this section will describe exactly how to handle the changes that come up.

How will this scope management plan prevent the kinds of problems that affected the team's last project from happening on Cows Gone Wild III?

Define the scope of the project

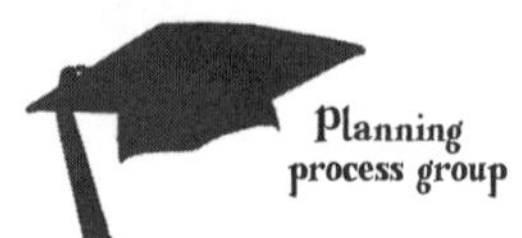

Now that the Ranch Hand team has a project manager, everything will go smoothly, right? Well, not exactly. Just assigning a project manager isn't enough to get the scope under control. That's why you need the **Scope Definition** process. Even the best project managers need to rely on things from the company and the people around them. That's why the inputs to Scope Definition are so important. They contain everything you need to know before you can begin to break the project down into the work that the team members will do.

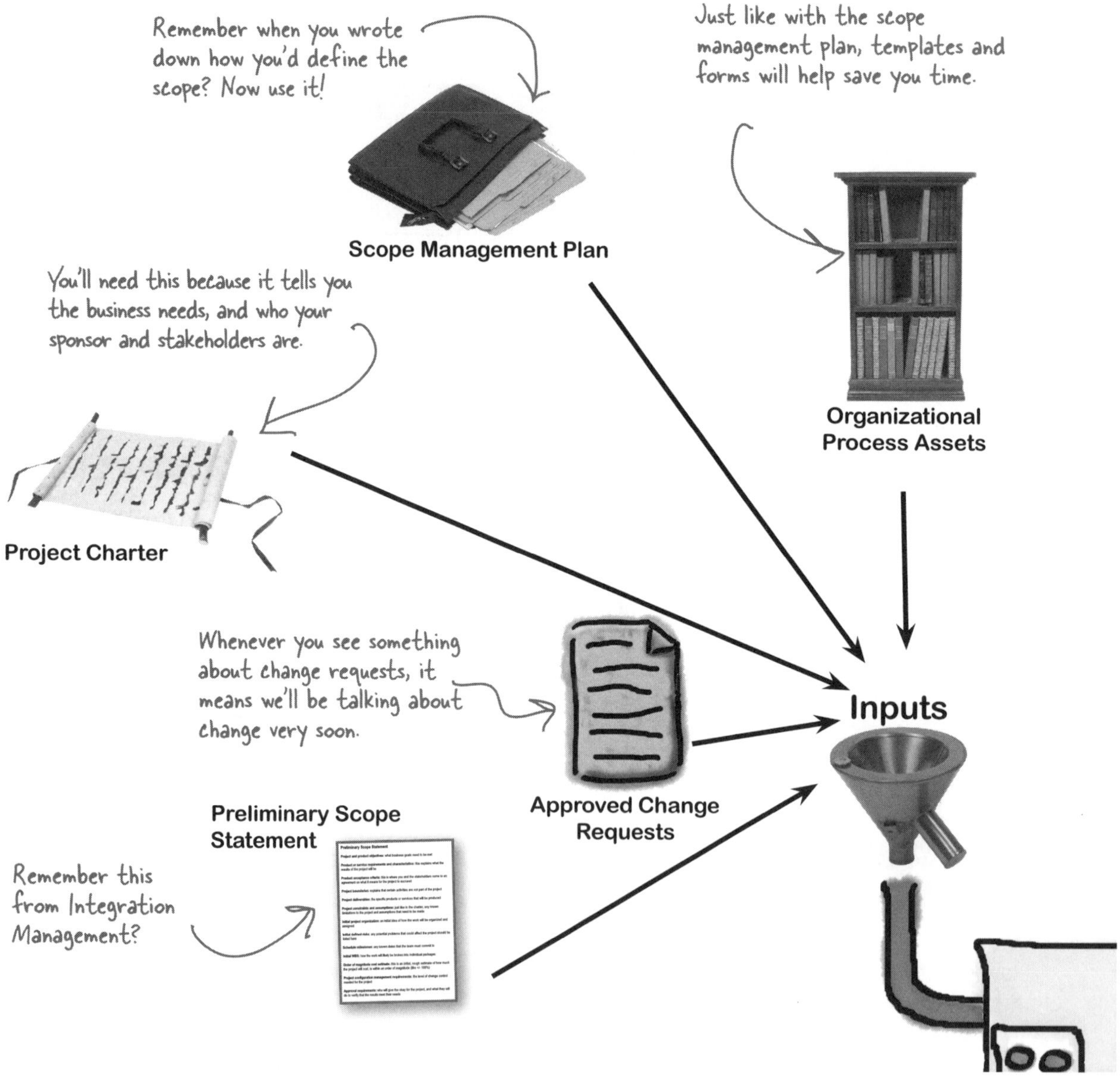

Remember when you wrote down how you'd define the scope? Now use it!

Scope Management Plan

Just like with the scope management plan, templates and forms will help save you time.

Organizational Process Assets

You'll need this because it tells you the business needs, and who your sponsor and stakeholders are.

Project Charter

Whenever you see something about change requests, it means we'll be talking about change very soon.

Approved Change Requests

Preliminary Scope Statement

Remember this from Integration Management?

Inputs

Build on the preliminary scope statement

Remember the preliminary scope statement? Well, now it's time to flesh it out so it's not preliminary any more. You're going to start with the preliminary scope statement, because it contains a lot of the information that you'll need to develop the project scope statement. The first thing you do on any project is sit down with the sponsor—in this case, that's the CEO—and the stakeholders to come up with a preliminary scope statement... and now you'll find out why you need it.

It's a good thing you already made this! Now you can use it to build the scope statement.

This won't be preliminary for long

Cows Gone Wild III: The Milkening
Preliminary Scope Statement

Objective: To create a sequel to *Cows Gone Wild II: Armoogeddon* that will outsell it and keep our loyal fan base

Requirements: Great graphics, 24 levels, four playable characters, big boss battle

Acceptance criteria: The game must pass our intensive testing process and our beta testers need to give the game play good reviews

Deliverables: Story, artwork, graphics, scenery, software, user manual, box packaging design, web site

Initial work breakdown structure: The work will be divided into phases: design, construction, testing, project management

Approval requirements: Cows Gone Wild III will ship after it has been approved by the project team, the CEO sponsor, and the Ranch Hand marketing department

This list of deliverables will come in handy, but Mike better check with the team to make sure he didn't leave any out

You'll need to know who's going to approve the final product, because they'll need to OK the scope statement, too.

BULLET POINTS: AIMING FOR THE EXAM

- **Product scope** means the features and functions of the product or service being built. **Project scope** means the work that's needed to build the product.
- The PMP exam **focuses only on the project scope**, not the product scope. That's why all of these processes focus on the **work the team will do**, not on features or components.
- **Scope management** is about figuring out all of the work that's going to be needed for the project, and making sure only that work is done—and nothing else.
- The **scope management plan** tells you how to develop the scope statement, create the WBS, verify that all of the work has been done, and control scope changes. It's the only output of the Scope Planning process.
- You'll need to know the **order of processes** for the exam. A good way to remember them is to understand how the output of one process is used as the input for another.

How do you define the scope?

You already got a head start on defining the project scope when you put together the Preliminary Scope Statement—that's why it's an input to Scope Planning. But now you need to go a lot further and write down all of the work that you and your team are going to do over the course of the project. Luckily, the **Scope Definition tools and techniques** are there to help guide you through creating the scope statement.

Stakeholder analysis

When you do stakeholder analysis, you talk to the stakeholders, figure out what they need, and write it all down. The reason you do this is because you need to make sure that what you're delivering really meets the needs of the stakeholders. This keeps the team from delivering a poor product.

An important part of stakeholder analysis is doing your best to set **quantifiable goals**. That means writing down specific project goals that you can measure, which makes it a lot easier for the team to plan for the work they have to do.

Product analysis

Remember product vs. project scope? People naturally think about the product they are making when they start to define the scope. This tool is all about turning those things into project work that needs to be done.

Once the work is complete, you're going have to make sure that what you're delivering matches what you put in the scope plan. The better your product analysis is at the start of the project, the happier your stakeholders will be with the product, and the less likely it is that you'll discover painful, last-minute problems at the end.

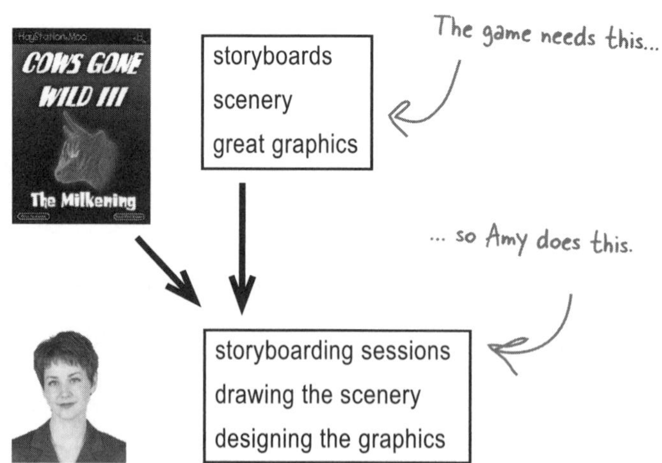

Alternatives identification

Think of other ways that you could do the work. Exploring different ways to do the work will help you find the one that is most efficient for the project. It's always possible that you might find a better way of doing things and need to change your original plan.

Designing the graphics: alternatives

A.  Hire a graphic designer

B.  Send the design work to an outside studio

C.  License artwork that already exists

Expert judgment

You've seen this one before! Bring in an expert to help you figure out what work needs to be done.

Expert Judgment

there are no Dumb Questions

Q: Is product analysis the same as requirements gathering?

A: Not exactly. When people gather requirements, they're trying to understand what needs the product should fill. Requirements are the contents of the product. When you use product analysis to define the scope of the work to be done, you're figuring out what deliverables the team needs to work on in order to build your scope statement. So product analysis is concerned with how the work will be done, not what's in it.

Q: What if there is only one way to do something? Do I still need to do alternatives identification?

A: There aren't too many things out there that can only be done one way, but if you happen across one, then you don't have to spend much time on alternative identification because there aren't any alternatives to identify.

Q: What if a stakeholder can't tell me how to measure his needs?

A: That can get kind of tricky. Sometimes stakeholders know that they want things to get better, but they don't know how to tell when they've succeeded. You need to work with them to find something that can be measured in their ideas about project success. Without a way to measure your success, you won't know whether or not you are accomplishing your goals.

The scope isn't preliminary anymore

After you have done your scope planning, figured out as much as you could using stakeholder and product analysis, and identified all of the possible ways of doing the work, you should be ready to add any new findings to the preliminary scope statement and make it a full-fledged scope statement.

Outputs

All the project objectives need to be measureable.

Even though you probably can't fit ALL of the requirements here, there should be enough detail to let you keep on planning and refer back to it later.

This means looking for all the work the project DOESN'T include.

The deliverables listed here are EVERYTHING the project creates, including project management stuff.

Constraints are known limitations. Assumptions are things you think are true.

Cows Gone Wild III: The Milkening
Project Scope Statement

Project objectives: The project team ~~must release~~ Cows Gone Wild III within the next year. The project must return at least a 5% revenue increase over Cows Gone Wild II.

Product scope descriptions: The product must contain 34 levels, 4 playable characters, and must be created for both Mac and PC platforms.

Project Requirements: The product must meet its schedule so that it can be released at the 14th annual gaming convention in San Francisco. The product must meet established quality standards to be considered ready to release.

Project Boundaries: This project does not include a companion web site. That will need to be done by another project team.

Project Deliverables: The deliverables for this project are:

Game
Design Documents
Contract
Test Plan
Test Reports
Budget
Source Code
Defect Reports
Project Management Plan
Schedule
Change Requests

Product acceptance criteria: The product must not have an adverse impact on existing systems. All defects found must be judged of low enough priority and severity to be acceptable to all stakeholders.

Project Constraints: Artwork from the previous games cannot be used.

Project Assumptions: The developers will not be asked to work on any other projects.

Initial Project Organization: This team will start with a project manager, five developers, four testers, and five creative staff members.

There are two more outputs of the process, and they both have to do with change control. We'll get to that when we talk about the Scope Control process.

Change Request

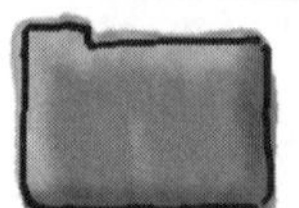

Scope Management Plan Updates

Here are a few things that Mike left out of the *CGW III* scope statement. Can you figure out where each of them should go?

1. The game must have fewer than 15 defects per 10,000 lines of code.

2. There will be four graphic designers reporting to the art director, and six programmers and four testers reporting to the development manager.

3. No more than 15 people can be allocated to work on the game at any time.

4. Scenery artwork

5. The product shall reduce tech support calls by 15%

6. The game needs to run on a machine with 1 GB of memory or less.

A. Project objectives

B. Project deliverables

C. Project constraints

D. Initial project organization

E. Project requirements

F. Product acceptance criteria

Answers on page 197.

The <u>project scope statement</u> tells what <u>work</u> you are—and are not—going to do to do in the project.

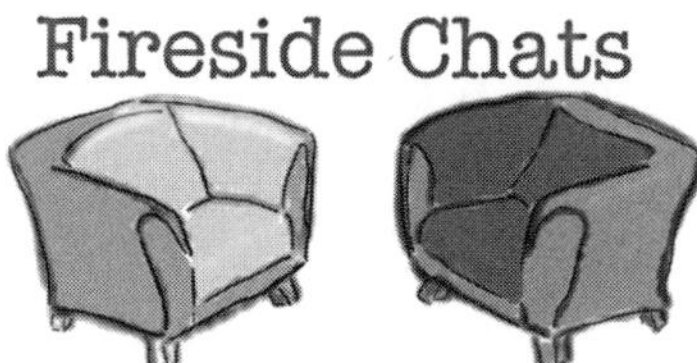

Tonight's talk: **Scope Management Plan and Project Scope Statement spar over what's important in scope management**

Scope Management Plan:

I'm glad we're finally getting a chance to chat in person.

Project Scope Statement:

Really? I never got the impression that you had much respect for me.

Scope Management Plan:

I wouldn't say that! It's just that, well, I think it's not hard to see why I'm such a critical part of scope management.

Project Scope Statement:

Typical. Everything's about you.

Scope Management Plan:

Well, it ought to be. I mean, you wouldn't even exist if it weren't for me.

Project Scope Statement:

How do you figure?

Scope Management Plan:

I tell the team how to create you, and let's face it, you're never exactly right when the project starts. The team needs me to figure out how to deal with all of the changes that they'll need to make to you.

Project Scope Statement:

Now wait a minute; that's just not fair. When the team creates me, there's no way for them to tell that I'm wrong. In fact, when they create me, I'm not wrong at all! I can't help that the project changes, and that the team needs to adjust me to deal with those changes.

Scope Management Plan:

But they still need me to tell them how to make sure you're up to date.

Project Scope Statement:

That may be true, but think about it for a minute. There are plenty of project teams that figure out the scope of the project and do the work, and don't even take the time to use you at all.

Scope Management Plan:

That's true. And it's no wonder that so many projects have problems. If everyone used me, their projects would be in much better shape.

Project Scope Statement:

Maybe so, but without me no project would be able to happen, because nobody would know what work would have to be done.

Scope Management Plan: Whoa, just a minute! A responsible project manager would have both of us in their project.

Project Scope Statement: That's exactly my point. We're both useful, but I'm the one everyone thinks of first when they think about managing scope.

Scope Management Plan: But you're always changing, and I need to step in to fix you.

Project Scope Statement: But you don't actually talk about any of the work that has to get done on the project. All you say is how to make sure that work happens.

Scope Management Plan: That seems like a pretty important job to me.

Project Scope Statement: I guess we're never going to see eye-to-eye on this.

You'll need to know the difference between scope planning and scope definition for the exam. Which of these things is part of the scope management plan, and which is part of the project scope statement?

1. The work required to create the graphics

☐ Scope Mgmt. Plan ☐ Scope Statement

2. How to handle scope changes

☐ Scope Mgmt. Plan ☐ Scope Statement

3. A list of programming deliverables

☐ Scope Mgmt. Plan ☐ Scope Statement

4. A process for evaluating change requests

☐ Scope Mgmt. Plan ☐ Scope Statement

5. A description of how the WBS is created

☐ Scope Mgmt. Plan ☐ Scope Statement

6. How the software will be tested

☐ Scope Mgmt. Plan ☐ Scope Statement

7. How the stakeholders will verify the deliverables

☐ Scope Mgmt. Plan ☐ Scope Statement

8. A list of all artwork that will be created

☐ Scope Mgmt. Plan ☐ Scope Statement

Answers: Numbers 1, 3, 6 and 8 are in the scope statement because they describe actual project deliverables or the work that will be done to create them. Numbers 2, 4, 5 and 7 are in the scope management plan because they are processes that guide scope management.

Question Clinic: The "Which-is-BEST" Question

When you're taking any sort of exam, the more familiar you are with it, the more relaxed you'll be. And one way to get familiar with the PMP exam is to get to know the different kinds of questions you'll see. One important sort is the "Which-is-BEST" question.

The Which-is-BEST question sometimes starts with a sentence or two talking about a particular situation.

This is one of those questions where "customer" is used in place of "sponsor."

Okay, now you have enough information to answer the question. What do you do when you find out that certain deliverables need to change?

36. You are the project manager for a building contracting project. You schedule a meeting with your customer and stakeholders to give them an update on the progress of the project. At that meeting, they tell you that certain deliverables need to be changed before they can be accepted. Which is the BEST way for you to proceed?

A. Inform the stakeholders that they have no authority to decide what deliverables are acceptable

B. Consult the project charter and use it to show the stakeholders that you are the authorized project manager

C. Figure out what needs to be fixed so that you can tell the team how to make the deliverables acceptable

D. Document the requested changes so that you can put them through change control

Some of the answers will simply be wrong. You should be able to eliminate them first.

This one sounds good... That's what the project charter is for, right? But wait a minute! What does the charter have to do with the scope of the work?

Okay, this actually seems right—you do need to do that. But is it really the BEST answer?

Aha! Here's the BEST answer! Even though C was technically correct, D is a much better description of how change control actually works.

The Which-is-BEST question may have more than one good answer, but it only has one ***BEST*** answer.

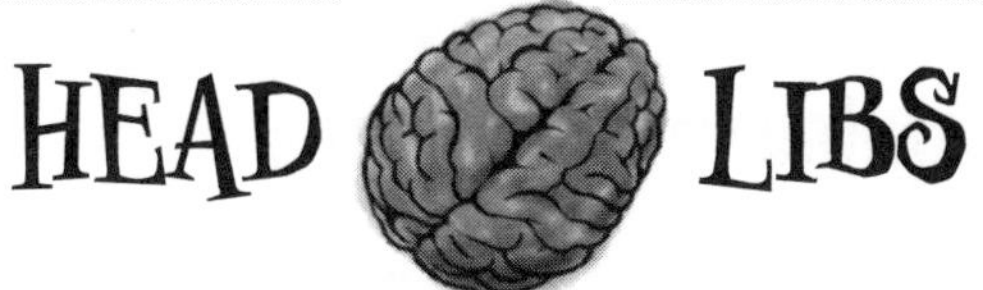

Fill in the blanks to come up with your own "Which-is-BEST" question.

You are the project manager for ______________ (an industry or the name of a project). At the end of ______________ (a Scope Management process), you ran into a problem. You find out that ______________ (a tool or technique that is part of that process) was not performed by ______________ (the team member or person who is supposed to do that tool or technique) correctly. Which is the BEST way for you to proceed?

A. ______________ (an obviously wrong answer where the person or project manager uses the tool or technique incorrectly)

B. ______________ (an answer that sounds correct, but isn't the BEST answer)

C. ______________ (the BEST answer that describes exactly how to use the process properly)

D. ______________ (an answer that says something that's true about an irrelevant process, like one from Chapter 4)

Join the Head First PMP community at **http://www.headfirstlabs.com/PMP** You can add your Head Libs answer, and see what Head Libs other project managers came up with!

Create the Work Breakdown Structure

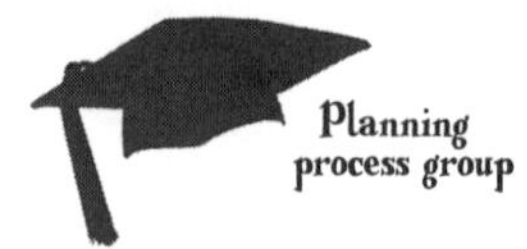

The **Create WBS** process is the most important process in the Scope Management knowledge area because it's where you actually figure out all the work you're going to do. It's where you create the **Work Breakdown Structure** (or WBS), which is the main Scope Management output. Every single thing that anyone on the project team—including you—will do is written down in the WBS somewhere.

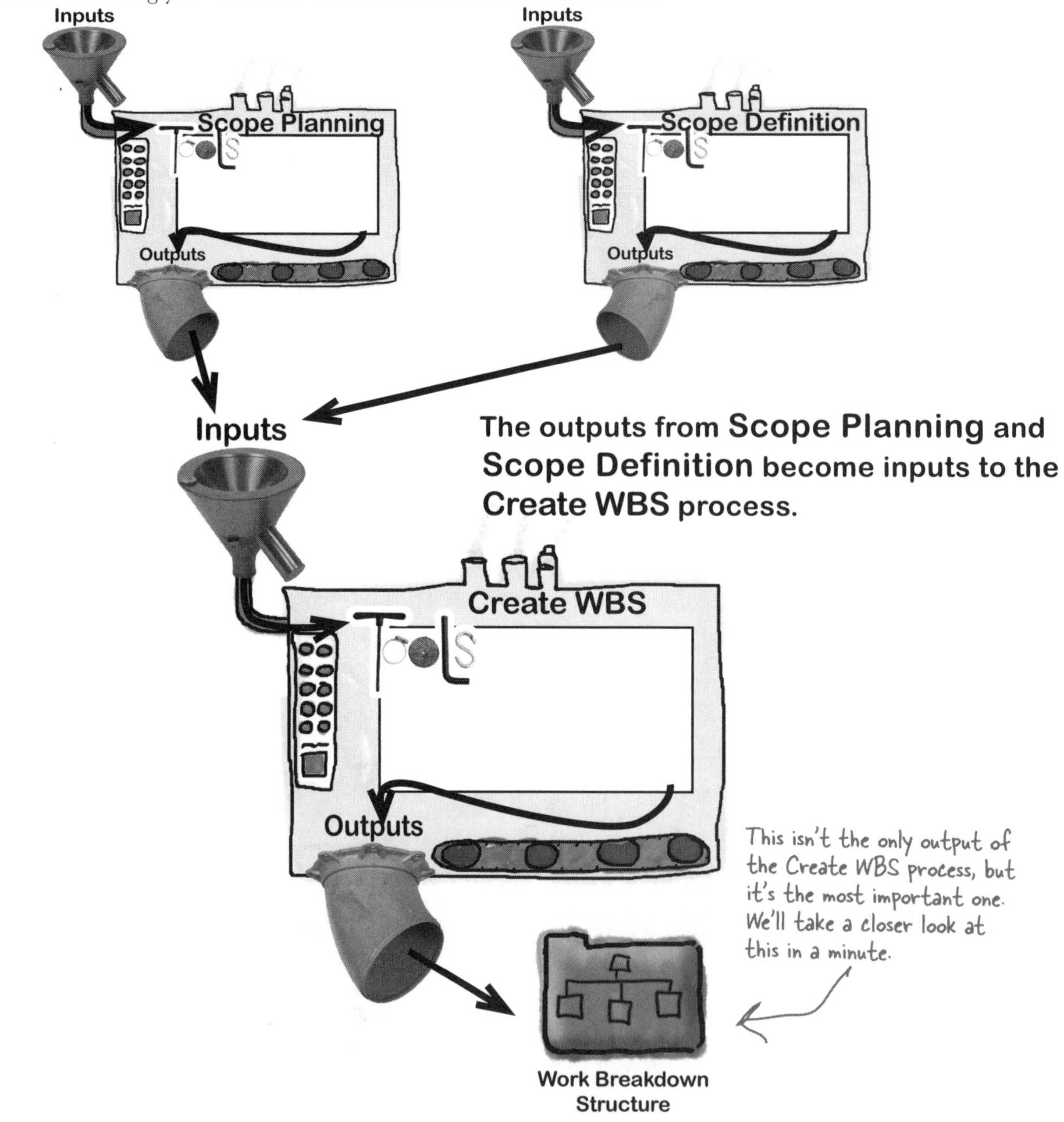

Inputs

Scope Planning

Tools

Outputs

Inputs

Scope Definition

Tools

Outputs

Inputs

The outputs from Scope Planning and Scope Definition become inputs to the Create WBS process.

Create WBS

Tools

Outputs

This isn't the only output of the Create WBS process, but it's the most important one. We'll take a closer look at this in a minute.

Work Breakdown Structure

The inputs for the WBS come from other processes

You've already seen all of the inputs that you need to create the WBS. It shouldn't be too surprising that you need the scope management plan, scope statement, and organizational process assets before you create the WBS. When you're developing these things, you're learning what you need to know in order to decompose the project work.

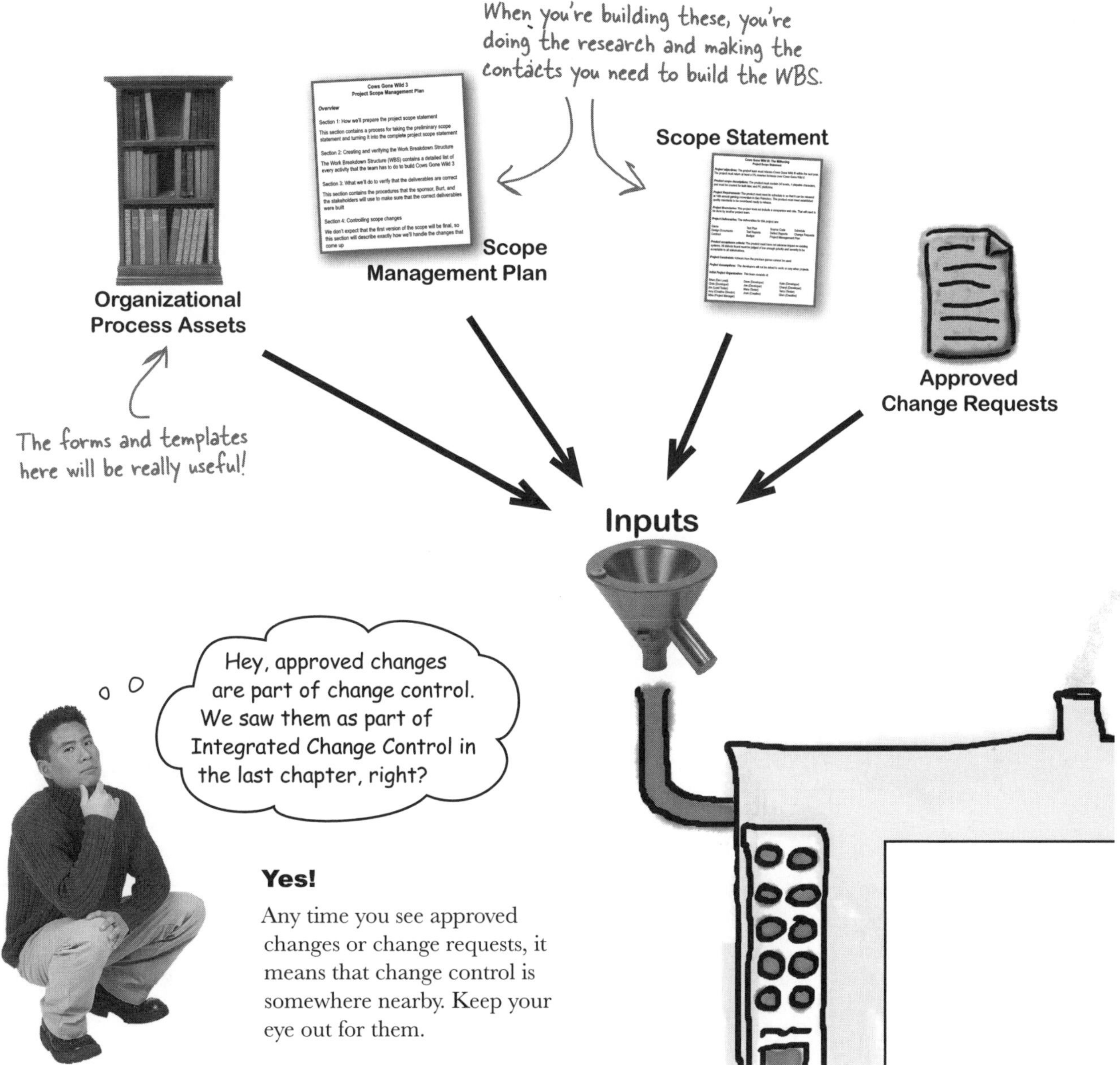

Yes!

Any time you see approved changes or change requests, it means that change control is somewhere nearby. Keep your eye out for them.

Breaking down the work

One way to get a clear picture of all of the work that needs to be done on a project is to create a work breakdown structure. The WBS doesn't show the order of the work packages or any dependencies between them. Its only goal is to show the work involved in creating the product.

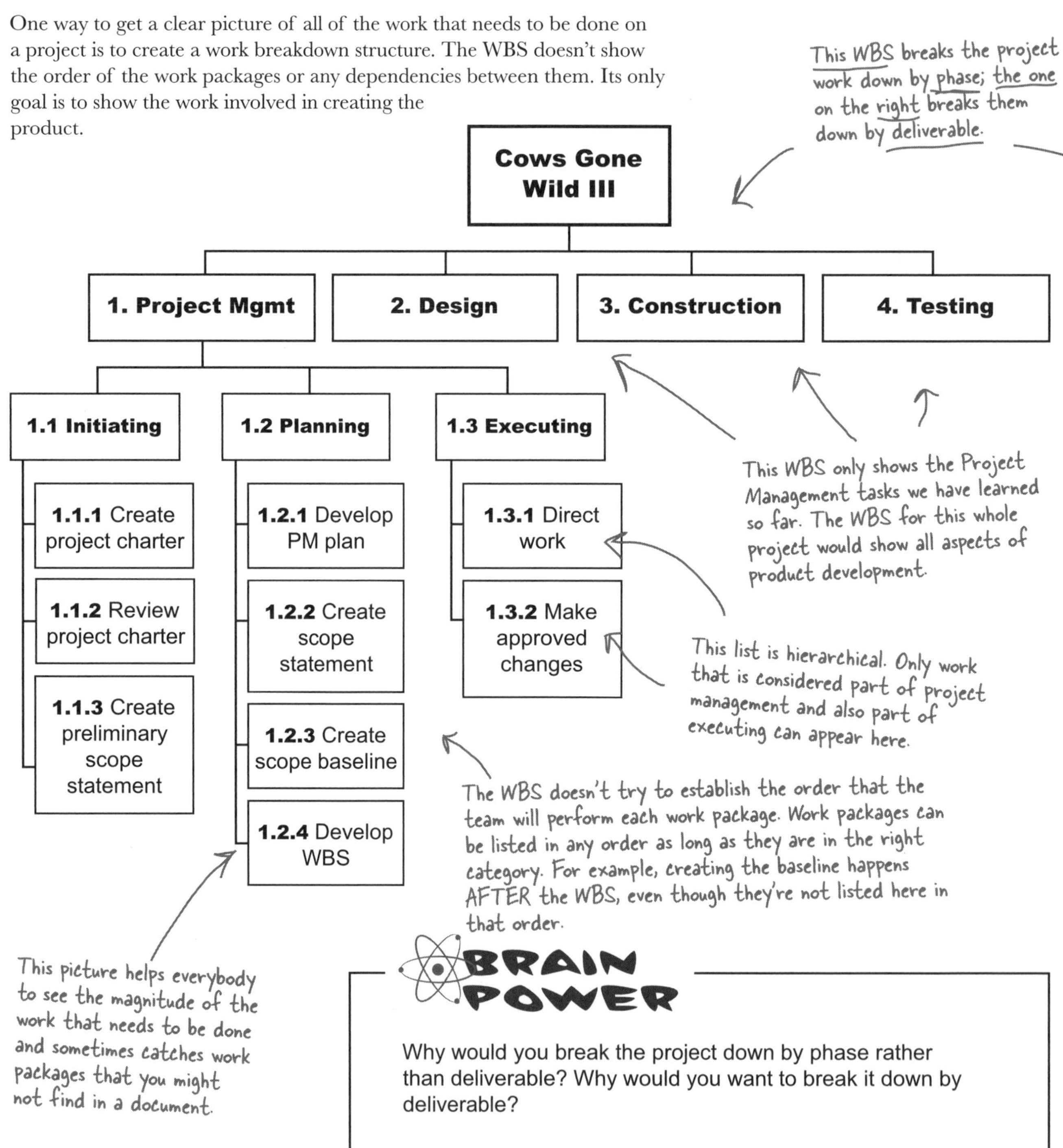

BRAIN POWER

Why would you break the project down by phase rather than deliverable? Why would you want to break it down by deliverable?

Break it down by project or phase

A WBS can be structured any way it makes the most sense to you and your project team. The two most common ways of visualizing the work are by deliverable or by phase. Breaking down the work makes it easier to manage because it means you are less likely to forget work packages that need to be included. This is the same project as the one on the left, but this time, it's broken down by deliverable.

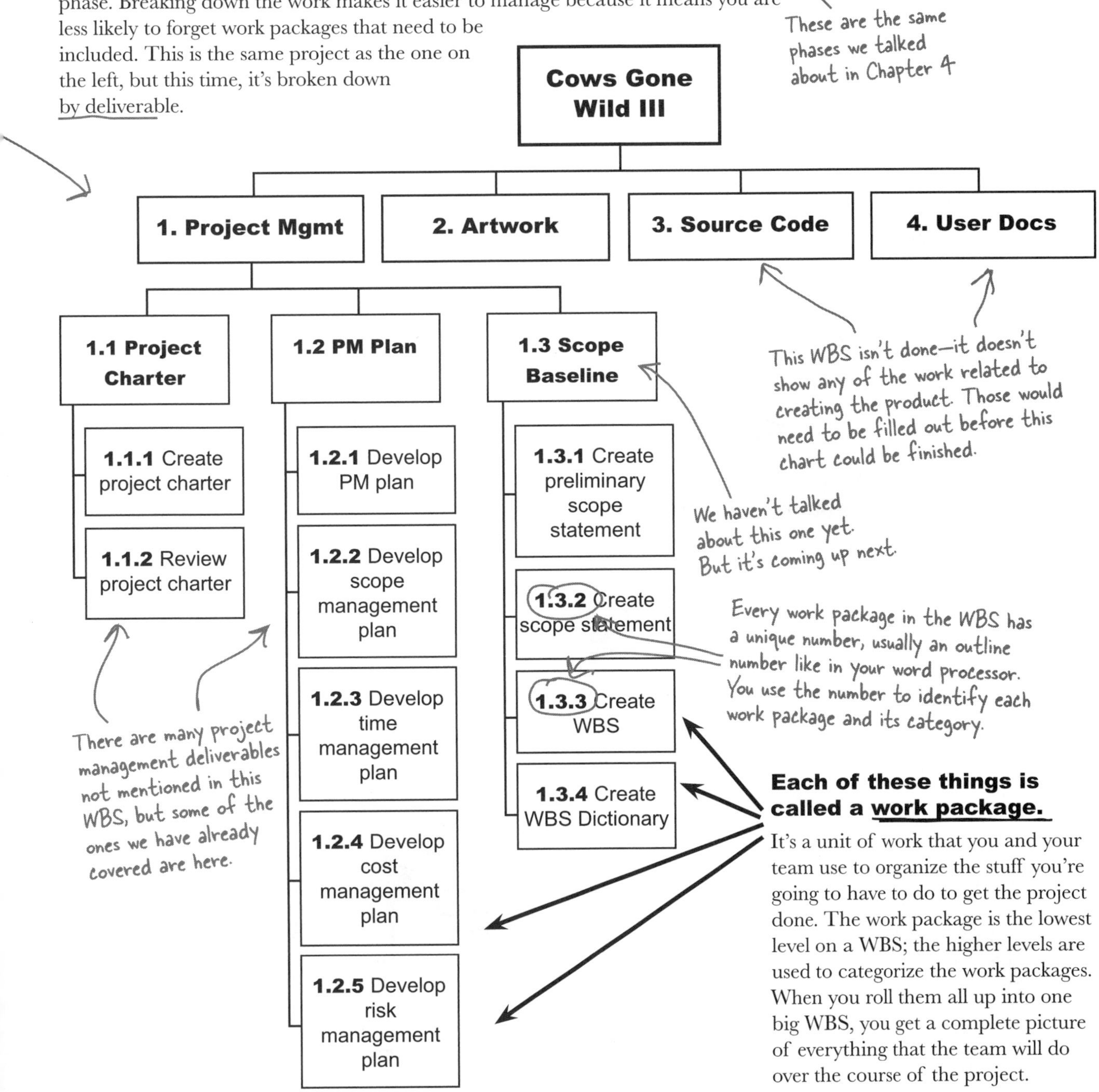

These are the same phases we talked about in Chapter 4

Cows Gone Wild III

1. Project Mgmt
2. Artwork
3. Source Code
4. User Docs

1.1 Project Charter
- 1.1.1 Create project charter
- 1.1.2 Review project charter

1.2 PM Plan
- 1.2.1 Develop PM plan
- 1.2.2 Develop scope management plan
- 1.2.3 Develop time management plan
- 1.2.4 Develop cost management plan
- 1.2.5 Develop risk management plan

1.3 Scope Baseline
- 1.3.1 Create preliminary scope statement
- 1.3.2 Create scope statement
- 1.3.3 Create WBS
- 1.3.4 Create WBS Dictionary

This WBS isn't done—it doesn't show any of the work related to creating the product. Those would need to be filled out before this chart could be finished.

We haven't talked about this one yet. But it's coming up next.

Every work package in the WBS has a unique number, usually an outline number like in your word processor. You use the number to identify each work package and its category.

There are many project management deliverables not mentioned in this WBS, but some of the ones we have already covered are here.

Each of these things is called a work package.

It's a unit of work that you and your team use to organize the stuff you're going to have to do to get the project done. The work package is the lowest level on a WBS; the higher levels are used to categorize the work packages. When you roll them all up into one big WBS, you get a complete picture of everything that the team will do over the course of the project.

Decompose deliverables into work packages

Creating the WBS is all about taking deliverables and coming up with work packages that will create them. When you do that, it's called **decomposition**, and it's the main tool you use to create a WBS.

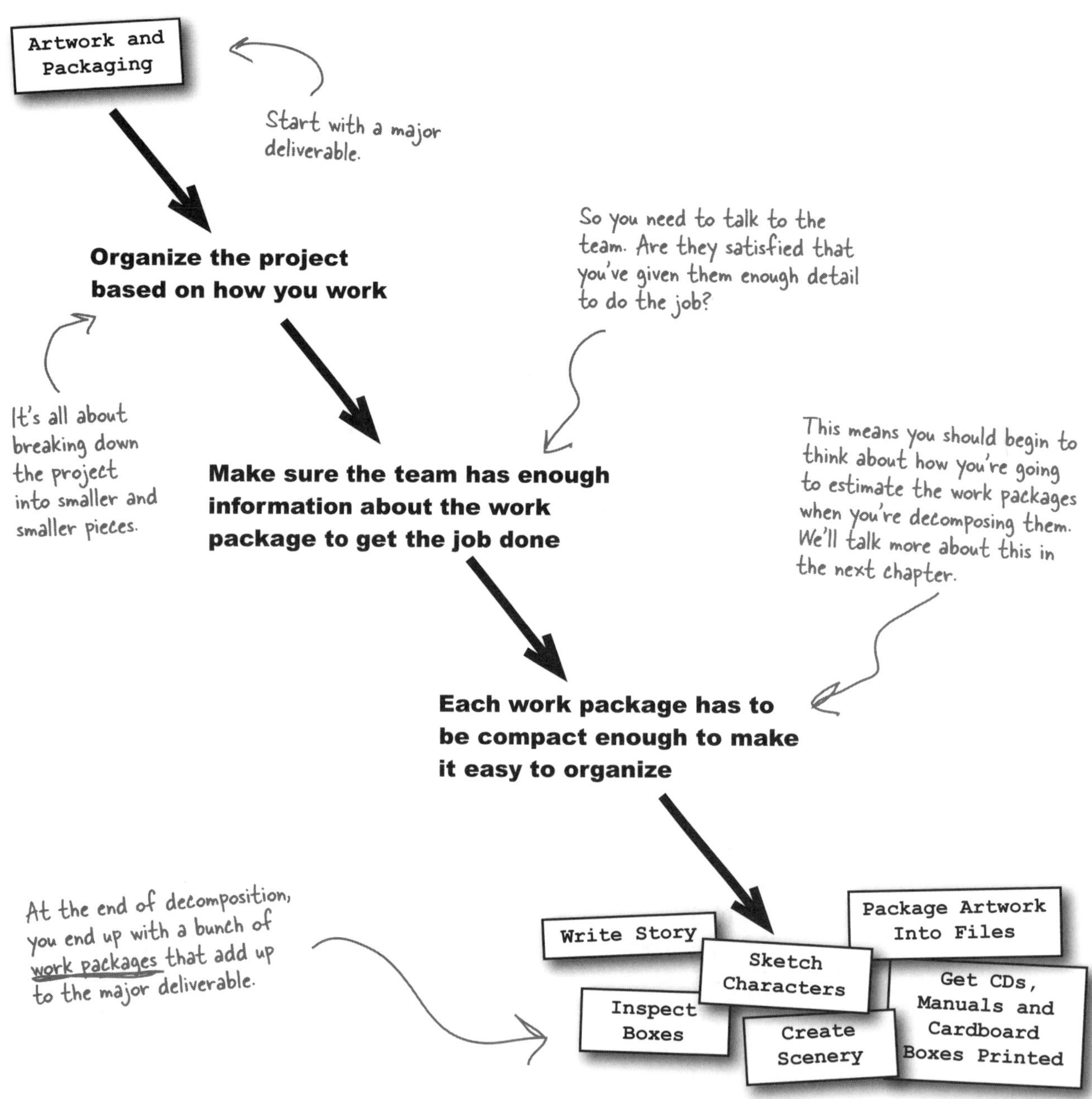

Templates are a useful shortcut

These are the only two tools & techniques of Create WBS—decomposition and templates

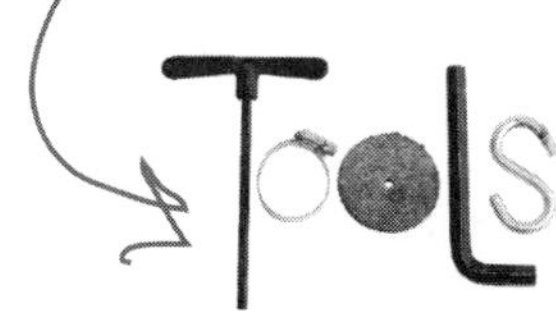

Decomposition is the most important tool in creating the WBS, but it's not the only one. You can also use **templates**, the other Create WBS tool, to help you with your WBS. The most common way to do this is to use a WBS from a similar project you've done in the past as a starting point for your current one.

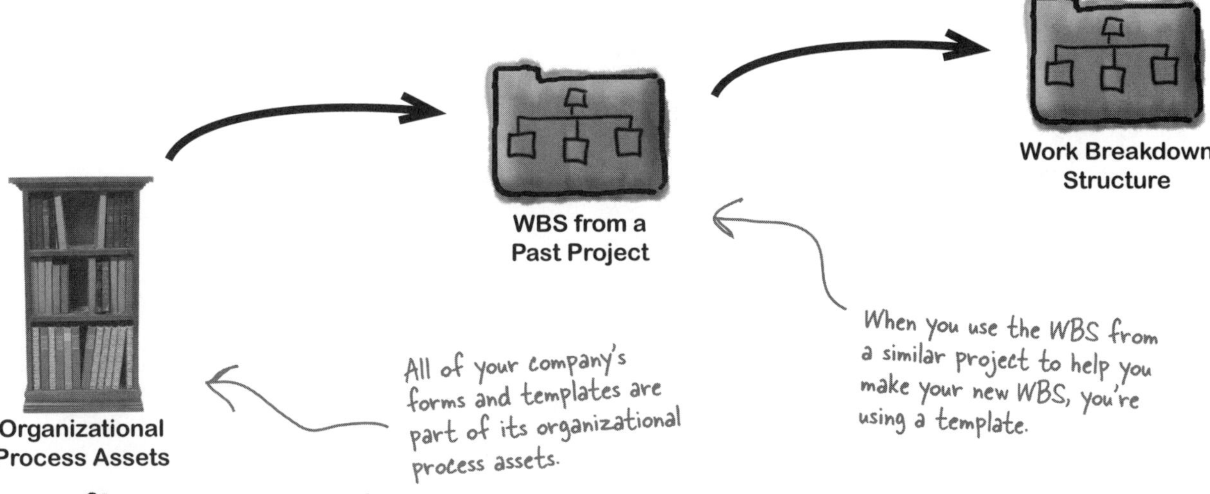

When you use the WBS from a similar project to help you make your new WBS, you're using a template.

All of your company's forms and templates are part of its organizational process assets.

Sharpen your pencil

You'll need to understand decomposition for the exam. Here are a few deliverables from *Cows Gone Wild III*. Based on what you've seen so far, decompose them into work packages. There are no right or wrong answers—this is practice for thinking about decomposition.

Software ....

....

....

Artwork ....

....

....

Marketing materials ....

....

....

Throwing a party for the team ....

....

....

Project Scope Management Magnets

Understanding how to build a work breakdown structure is very important for the exam—it's one of the most important parts of the Scope Management knowledge area. Here's your chance to create a WBS for *Cows Gone Wild III: The Milkening*. There are two ways you can break down the work. See if you can use decomposition to do it!

On this page, create a work breakdown structure broken down by project phase.

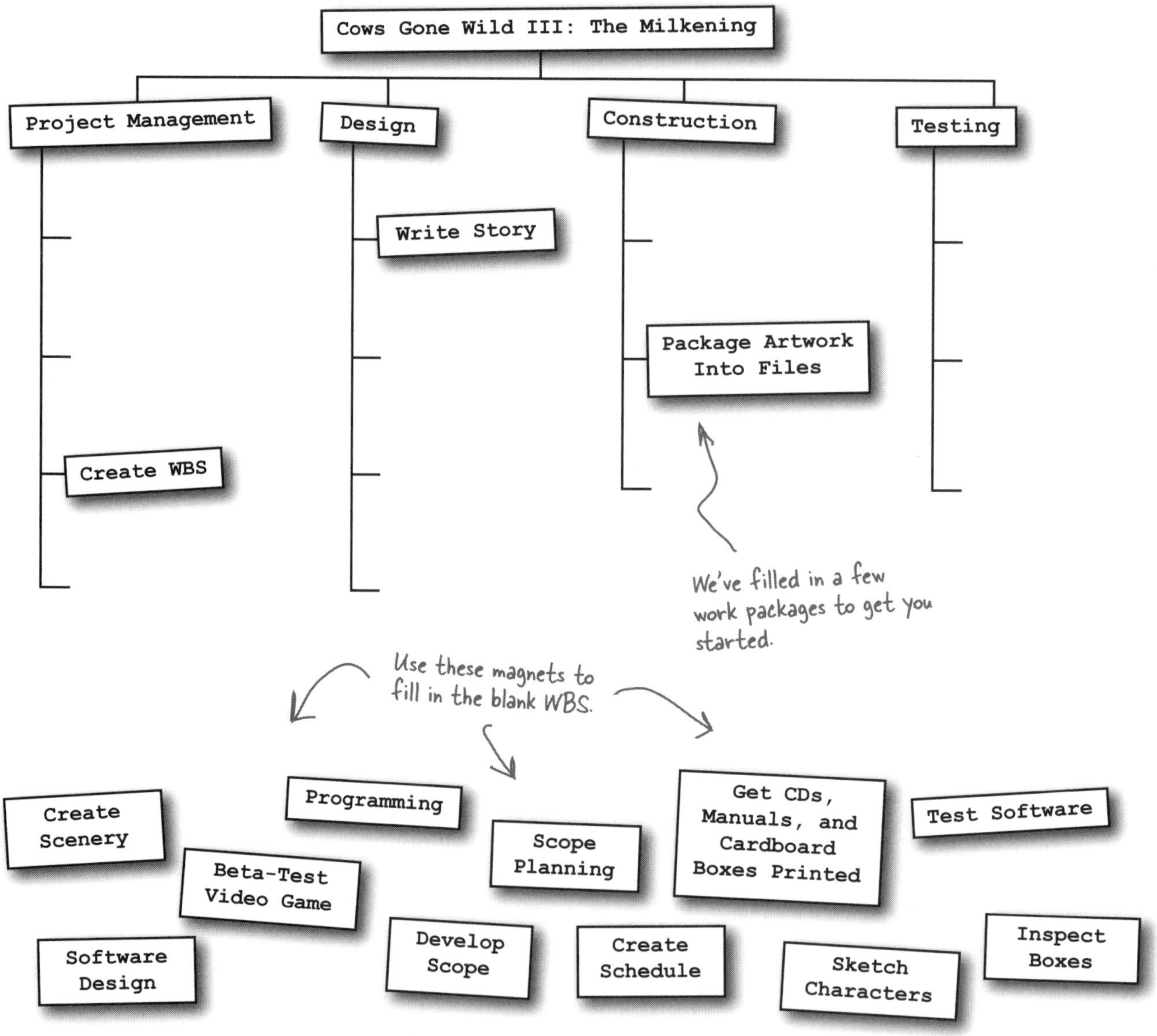

Cows Gone Wild III: The Milkening

- Project Management
  - Create WBS
- Design
  - Write Story
- Construction
  - Package Artwork Into Files
- Testing

We've filled in a few work packages to get you started.

Use these magnets to fill in the blank WBS.

Create Scenery

Programming

Scope Planning

Get CDs, Manuals, and Cardboard Boxes Printed

Test Software

Beta-Test Video Game

Software Design

Develop Scope

Create Schedule

Sketch Characters

Inspect Boxes

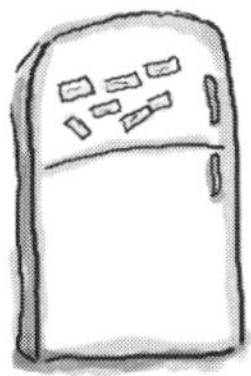

More Magnets

Oops! Looks like the magnets fell off the fridge. Here's your chance to practice breaking down the work to create a different WBS using the same magnets as before. But this time, instead of decomposing project phases into work packages, break the project down by deliverable.

On this page, create a work breakdown structure broken down by deliverable.

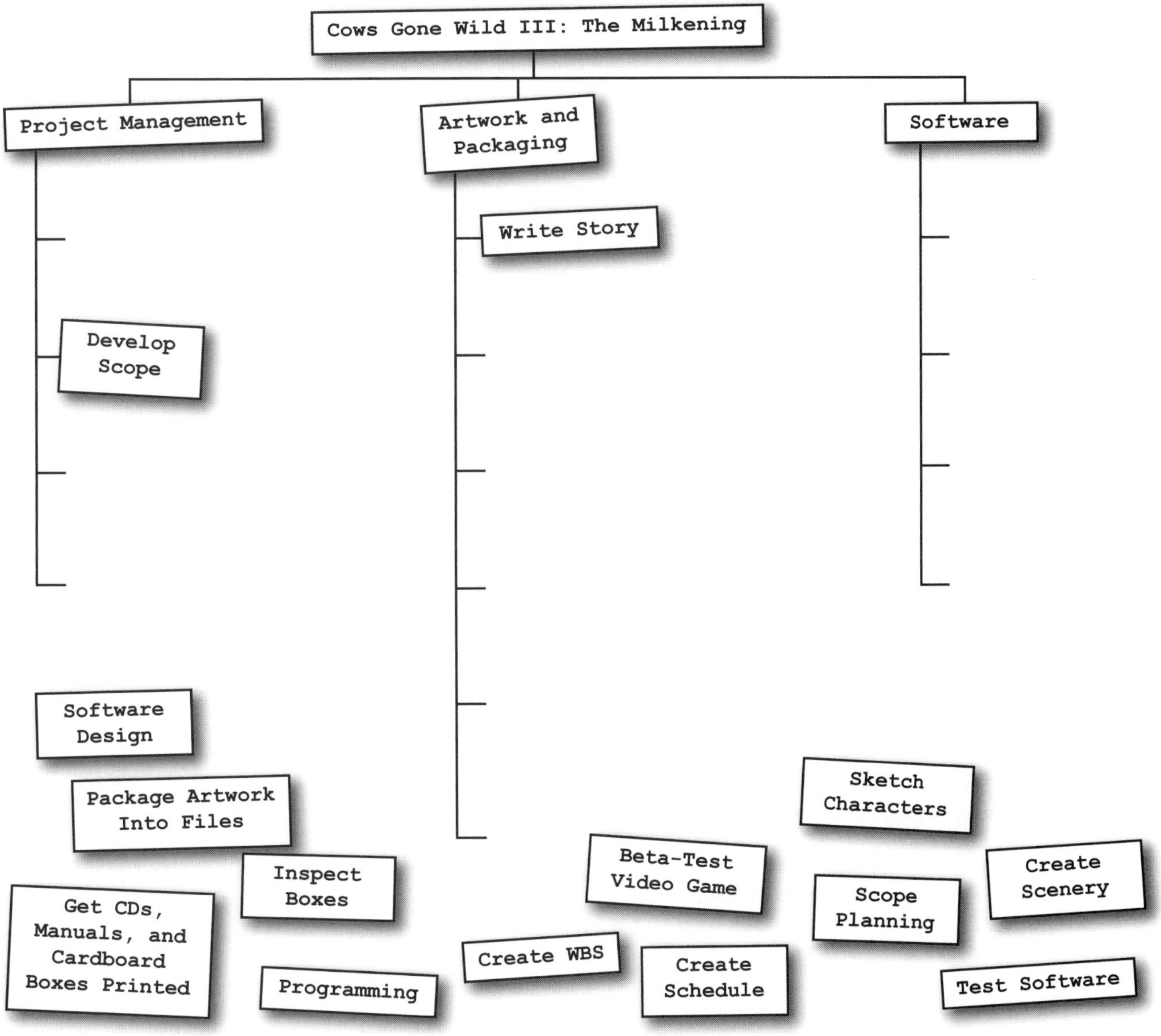

Cows Gone Wild III: The Milkening

Project Management

Artwork and Packaging

Software

Write Story

Develop Scope

Software Design

Package Artwork Into Files

Sketch Characters

Inspect Boxes

Beta-Test Video Game

Create Scenery

Scope Planning

Get CDs, Manuals, and Cardboard Boxes Printed

Create WBS

Create Schedule

Programming

Test Software

Project Scope Management Magnets Solutions

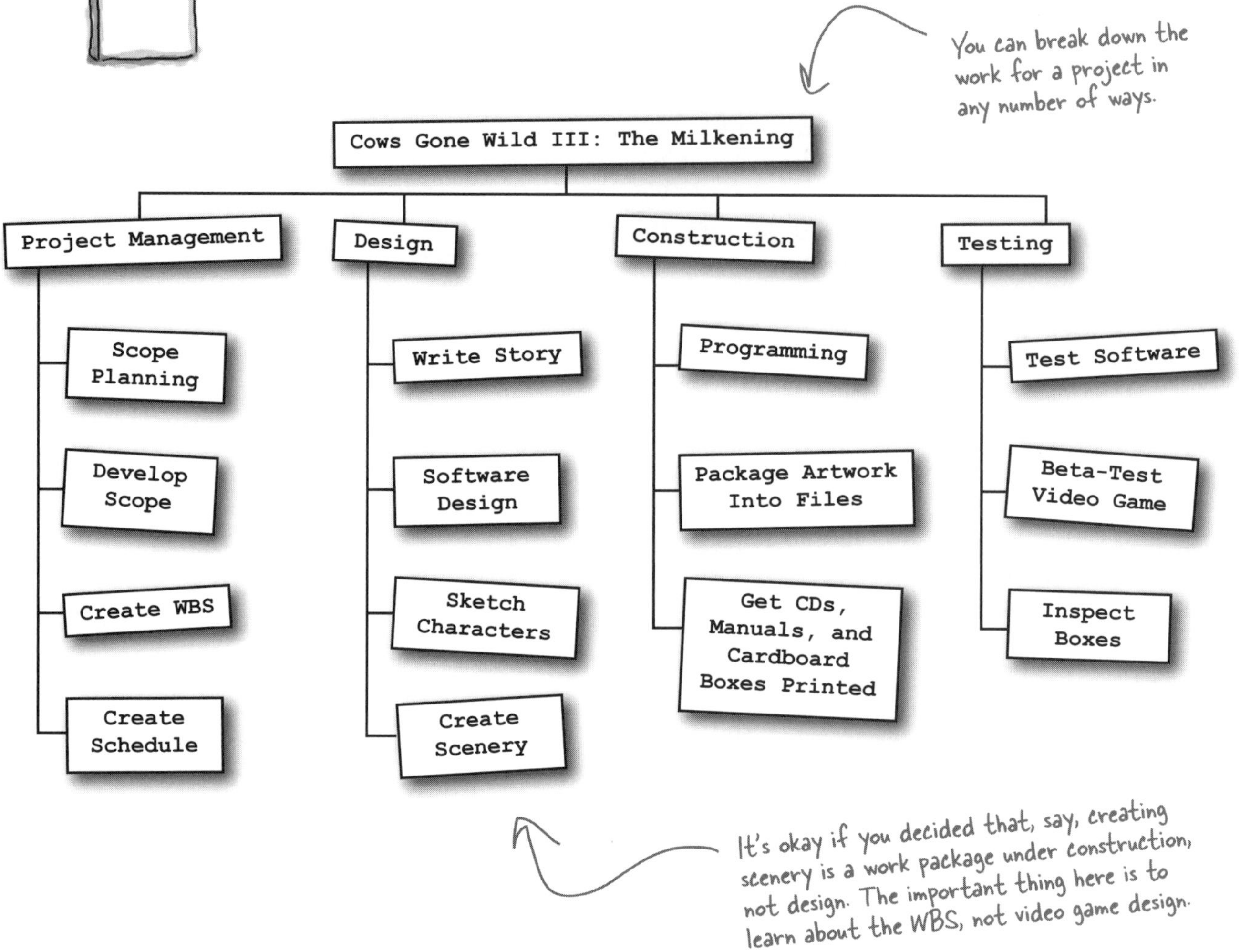

You can break down the work for a project in any number of ways.

- Cows Gone Wild III: The Milkening
  - Project Management
    - Scope Planning
    - Develop Scope
    - Create WBS
    - Create Schedule
  - Design
    - Write Story
    - Software Design
    - Sketch Characters
    - Create Scenery
  - Construction
    - Programming
    - Package Artwork Into Files
    - Get CDs, Manuals, and Cardboard Boxes Printed
  - Testing
    - Test Software
    - Beta-Test Video Game
    - Inspect Boxes

It's okay if you decided that, say, creating scenery is a work package under construction, not design. The important thing here is to learn about the WBS, not video game design.

Can you think of a reason that Mike would break Cows Gone Wild III work down by phase? Can you think of why he'd break it down by deliverable?

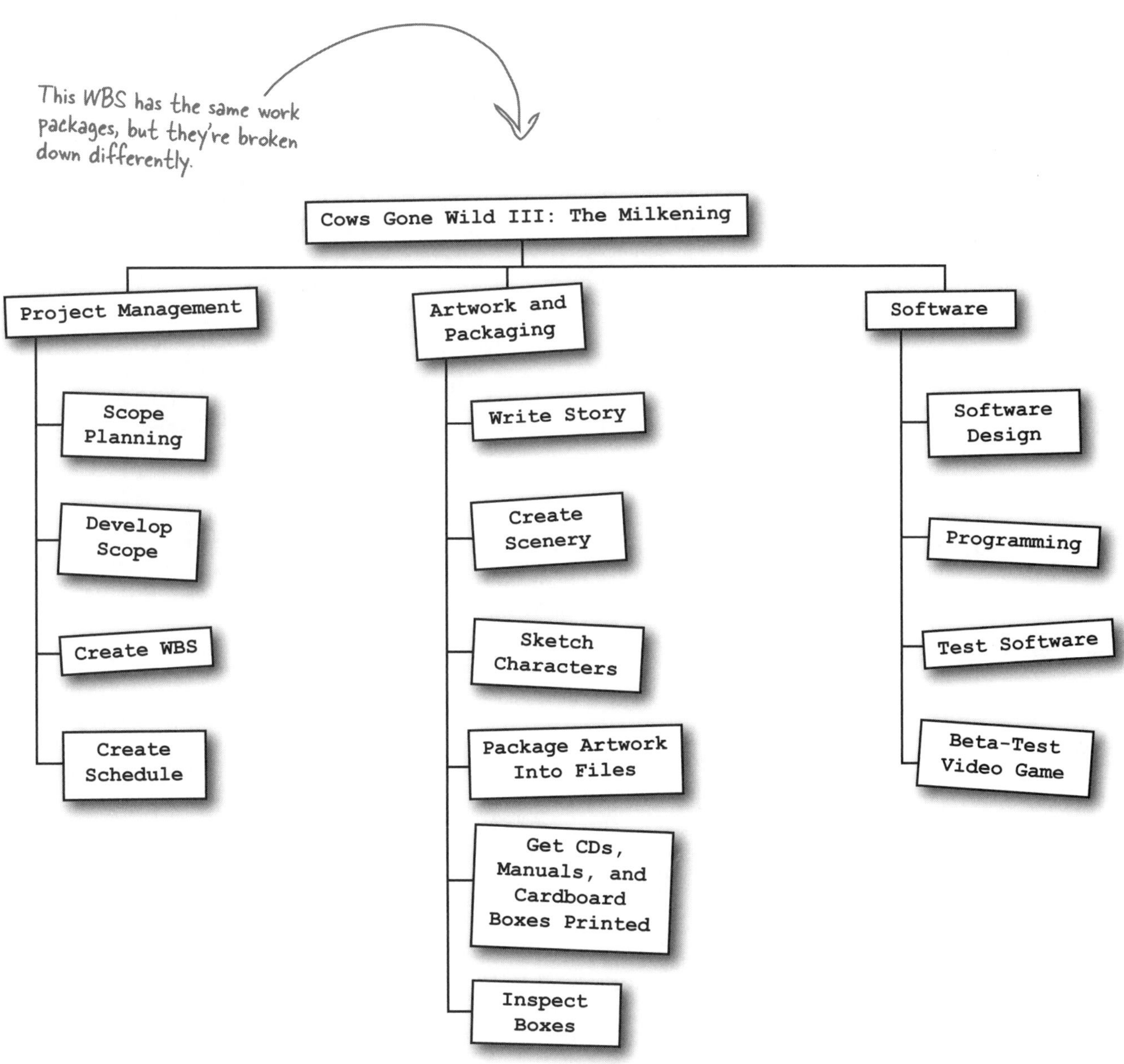

Did you notice how the project management work packages are the same in both WBSes? You could break them down into more detailed project management deliverables, and then you'd see a difference.

Inside the work package

You've probably noticed that the work breakdown structure only shows you the name of each work package. That's not enough to do the work! You and your team need to know a lot more about the work that has to be done. That's where the **WBS Dictionary** comes in handy. It brings along all of the details you need to do the project work. The WBS Dictionary is an important output of the Create WBS process—the WBS wouldn't be nearly as useful without it.

The WBS Dictionary contains the details of every work package. It's a separate output of the Create WBS process.

This is one of the WBS Dictionary entries for the Cows Gone Wild III project. It goes with the "Test Software" work package in the WBS.

Test Software
WBS Dictionary Entry

Work Package ID and Name: 3.2.4 – Test Software

Statement of Work:

The goal of software testing is to verify that the Cows Gone Wild III software implements all of the requirements. Each requirement will be fully tested by a team of quality engineers.

Responsible Organization: Ranch Hand Games QA Team

Schedule Milestones:

- 4/26 – Programming team delivers software
- 6/18 – Functional testing and graphics testing completed
- 8/10 – QA approves software for beta testing

Quality Requirements:

The software must meet the requirements defined by the Ranch Hand Games QA team's quality standards document ("RHG QA Standards.doc")

Code of Account Identifier: RHG-236

Required Resources and Cost Estimate:

- Test planning – One QA lead and two QA analysts ($8,500)
- Functional testing – 2 leads, 3 analysts, 11 testers ($36,000)
- Monitor beta testing – 2 leads, 1 analyst ($6,000)

Each work package has a name, and in many WBSes the work packages will also have ID numbers.

Here's what the WBS entry would look like with this ID number.

3.2.4 – Test Software

This is just a description of the work that needs to be done.

Each work package should be small enough to make cost and resource estimates.

*This account identifier is important—it's how you hook your WBS into your company's accounting system. That way you can make sure all of the work is paid for.

Don't forget that the WBS doesn't show dependencies among work packages.

Sharpen your pencil

It will help you on the exam to know why all of the outputs are important, and the WBS is one of the most important ones. Write down as many reasons for using a WBS as you can think of.

....

....

....

....

....

....

there are no Dumb Questions

Q: Does the work breakdown structure need to be graphical? It looks like a lot of work. Can't I just write out a list of tasks?

A: Yes, the WBS has to be graphical. The WBS needs to show all of the work packages, and how they decompose into phases or deliverables. When you look at a simple WBS, it might seem like you could manage your work packages just as efficiently using a simple list. But what if you have a large team with dozens, hundreds or even thousands of work packages? That's when you'll be really happy that you know how to decompose deliverables into a hierarchy.

Q: What if one work package depends on another one?

A: There are definitely dependencies among work packages. For example, the Ranch Hand QA team can't begin to test the software until the programming team has finished building it. But while this information is important, the WBS isn't where you figure out the dependencies.

The reason is that you need to figure out what work needs to be done before you start to figure out how the work packages depend on each other.

Q: What if I don't know enough to estimate the cost of a work package? What do I add to the WBS Dictionary?

A: The WBS Dictionary should only contain information that you can fill in when you create it. A lot of the time, you'll know all of the information that needs to go into it. If you have an estimate and know the resources that should be used, then put it in. But if all you have is a statement of work and an account code, then that's all the information you'll be able to add to the entry.

The baseline is a snapshot of the plan

As the project goes on, you will want to compare how you are doing to what you planned for. So, the **scope baseline** is there to compare against. It's made up of the scope statement, the WBS, and the WBS Dictionary. When work gets added to the scope through change control, you need to change the baseline to include the new work packages for that work, so you can always track yourself against the plan.

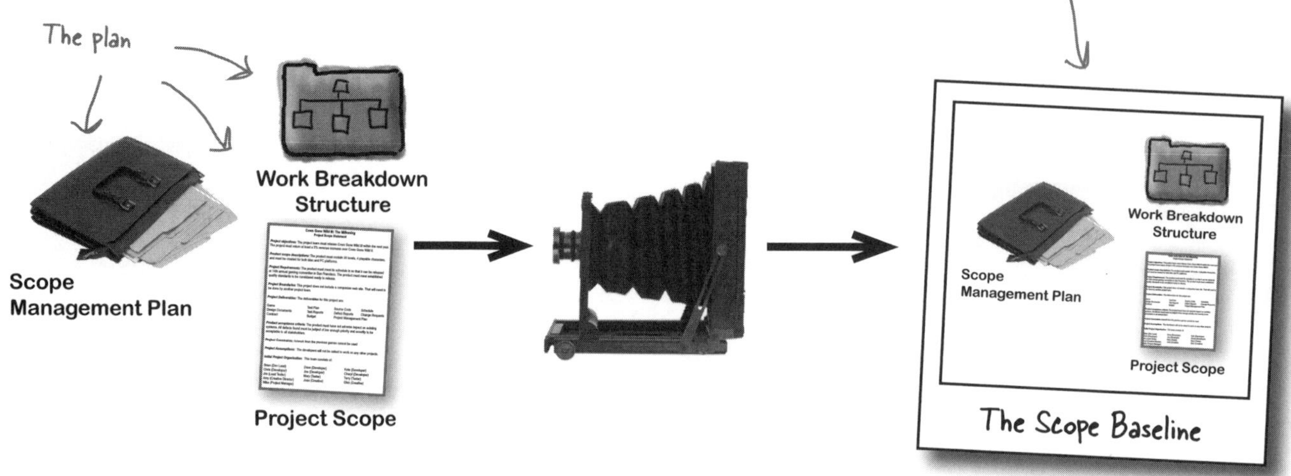

Yes. When there's a change you need to take a new snapshot.

Whenever a change is approved through change control, the baseline needs to be updated. Approved changes are changes to the scope management plan also, so it's important that you re-baseline your project when they are approved. That way, you'll always be comparing your performance to the most updated plan.

there are no Dumb Questions

Q: What happens if I need to change the scope?

A: You need to put it through change control – just like a change to the product scope. As you're building the product, it's always possible that some work will pop up in an unexpected place.

It could be that the initial technical design is inadequate or buggy. Or maybe you just think of a better way to do things while you're working. In either case, you have to determine the impact to the schedule, the budget, the scope, and the quality of the product and put the proposed change through change control. That's what it means to look at the triple constraint every time there's a change.

Once everyone understands the impact and approves the change, you need to go back and adjust your scope baseline to include the new work. If your budget or schedule are affected, you'll need to change those baselines too and integrate all of them into the project management plan. But we'll talk more about that in later chapters.

Q: Do I really need to create a baseline?

A: Yes. It might seem like a formality in the beginning, but the baseline is a really useful tool. As you are building your project, you will need to refer back to the baseline if you want to know how you are tracking against stakeholders' expectations.

Let's say you said it would take you 12 months to build Cows Gone Wild III, and a wrong technical decision creates a two-week delay. You can use the baseline to figure out the impact of that change to all of the different plans you have made, and then explain to everybody the impact of the change.

You can think of the baseline as a way of keeping track of the project team's understanding of their goals and how they are going to meet them. If the goals change, then the understanding of them needs to change too. By telling everyone who needs to approve the two-week delay about it, you make sure that the goals change for the team as well. Then you change the baseline, so you can measure your team against the new deadline of 12 and a half months.

Q: Wait a minute. Doesn't that mean I need to do change control and update the baseline every time I make any change to the document while I'm writing it? That's going to make it really hard to write the first version of anything!

A: Don't worry, you don't have to go through change control until the scope baseline is approved. And that goes for ANY document or deliverable. Once it's accepted and approved by all of the stakeholders, only then do the changes need to go through change control. Until it's approved, you can make any changes you want. That's the whole reason for change control—to make sure that once a deliverable is approved, you run all of the changes by a change control board to make sure that they don't cause an unacceptable impact to the schedule, scope, cost or quality.

Q: How can you know all of this up front?

A: You can't. Even the best planned projects have a few surprises. That's why the scope planning cycle is iterative. As you find out something new about your scope of work, you put it through change control. When it's approved, you need to add it to your scope management plan, your scope statement, your WBS, and your WBS Dictionary.

It's also possible that you might find new things that the team should do when you're making your WBS or your scope statement. So all of the scope planning documents are closely linked and need to be kept in sync with one another.

Q: What if I come up with new work for the team later on?

A: You use change control to update the scope baseline. Your project can change at any time, but before you make a change you need to figure out how it will affect the triple constraint—and make sure your sponsors and stakeholders are okay with that impact. That's what change control does for you.

Anytime you make a change, you need to get it approved, and then update the baseline

The outputs of the Create WBS process

The Create WBS process has three major outputs: the **Work Breakdown Structure**, the **WBS Dictionary** and the **Scope Baseline**. But there are others as well. When you create the WBS, you usually figure out that there are pieces of the scope that you missed, and you may realize that you need to change your plan. That's what the last three outputs are for.

Outputs

We've already seen the most important ones.

Work Breakdown Structure

Scope Baseline

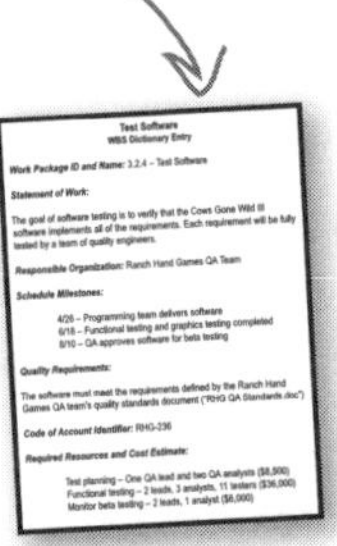

WBS Dictionary

When you're creating the WBS, you often discover missing pieces of the scope. You'll need to go back and plan for them. That kicks off the planning cycle again.

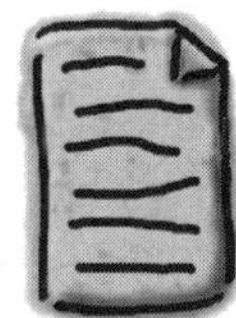

Updates to the Scope Statement

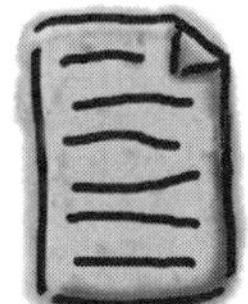

Updates to the Scope Management Plan

Change Requests

BULLET POINTS: AIMING FOR THE EXAM

- The **Create WBS** process is a really important process on the PMP exam.
- The WBS is created by **decomposing** large work products into **work packages**.
- The **WBS Dictionary** is a description of each work package listed in the WBS
- The inputs to WBS creation are the outputs to the Scope Planning and Definition processes, the Scope Management Plan, and the Scope Statement.
- As you decompose the work, you find new information that needs to be added to the Scope Management plan and the Scope Statement. That information is treated as a change and goes through change control. Once it's approved, it can be added into the document, and that kicks off the planning cycle again.

there are no Dumb Questions

Q: How do I know if I should use phases or deliverables for my WBS?

A: It really depends on the project. You want to present the information so that it allows the management in your organization the ability to visualize and control your project. So, if most people in your organization divide it by phases, then you should, too.

If people do it different ways from project to project where you work, then you might make your decision based on how people think about the work you are about to do.

The point behind the WBS is to help other people see the work that is necessary to get the project done, so if your management thinks of projects in terms of phases and understands them best that way, then it's better to divide your project work along those lines.

It could be that the work you are doing is anxiously awaited by a lot of people who will look at the WBS to understand the project, and, in that case, it probably makes sense to divide your work up by deliverable.

Q: How do I know when I have decomposed the work to a small enough work package?

A: The short answer is that you should decompose that work until it is manageable.

You need to be careful when you come up with the work packages for your WBS. If you decompose to the most granular level, you could end up wasting everybody's time trying to figure out exactly how much effort goes into, say, "writing up meeting minutes" for each and every meeting in your project.

So, you should break down the work to small enough packages that everybody can understand what's being done and describe it in the dictionary… and no further.

Q: I know how to make scope changes during planning. What do I do if I run into scope changes during execution?

A: Any time you run into a change to your scope, regardless of where you are in the process, you put it through change control. Only after examining the impact and having the change approved can you incorporate the change.

We've planned the scope and we've broken down the work for Cows Gone Wild III. Now we're ready to begin the project!

Cubicle conversation

Everything is great. The project is rolling along, and there are no problems with the scope… until something goes wrong.

Something's not right with the artwork...

Brian: At first I thought we could use the same five backgrounds over and over, but it's starting to look really stale.

Amy: Huh, I guess you're right. It looks like we need to create more scenery.

Mike: Why were we trying to limit the backgrounds in the first place?

Amy: I think they were worried about disk space.

Brian: Yeah, but that's not so much a concern right now.

Amy: Great! Let's just change the artwork, then.

This is work that was not planned for, and isn't in the WBS. That means it's a scope change.

Mike: Not so fast, Amy. There are a couple of things we need to do first...

What homework do you need to do before you make a change to the scope by adding or removing project work? Why?

Why scope changes

Sometimes something completely unexpected happens. Say, a really important customer asks for a new feature that nobody saw coming and demands it right away. Or, a design for a feature just isn't working, and you need to rethink it. Or, new stakeholders come on board and ask for changes.

The scope can change while you are working for a lot of reasons. Some changes are good for your project, while others will definitely reduce your chance of success. Change control is there to help you to see which is which.

Good change

A good change makes the product better with very little downside. It doesn't cost more time in the schedule or more money from the budget, and it doesn't destabilize the product or otherwise threaten its quality.

Good changes happen pretty rarely and nearly EVERY change has some impact that should be fully explored before you go forward.

Bad change

A bad change is one that might seem from the outside like a good idea but ends up making an impact on the triple constraint. Here are a couple of examples:

Scope Creep

This happens when you think you know the impact of a change so you go ahead, but it turns out that *that* change leads to another one, and since you are already making the first change, you go with the next. Then another change comes up, and another, and another, until it's hard to tell what the scope of the project is.

The way to avoid scope creep is to plan your changes completely.

Be on the lookout for examples of scope creep and gold plating on the exam. Both are considered very bad and should never be done.

Gold plating

Sometimes people think of a really great improvement to the product and go ahead and make it without even checking the impact. In software, this can happen pretty easily. A programmer thinks of a way to make a feature better, for example, and just implements it, without talking it over with anybody. This may sound good, but it's not—because now you have to pay for these features you never asked for.

Here's the WBS that you created for the Cows Gone Wild III project, and below that are some changes that the team has asked Mike to make since the work started. All of them are bad changes. Check either scope creep or gold plating for each one.

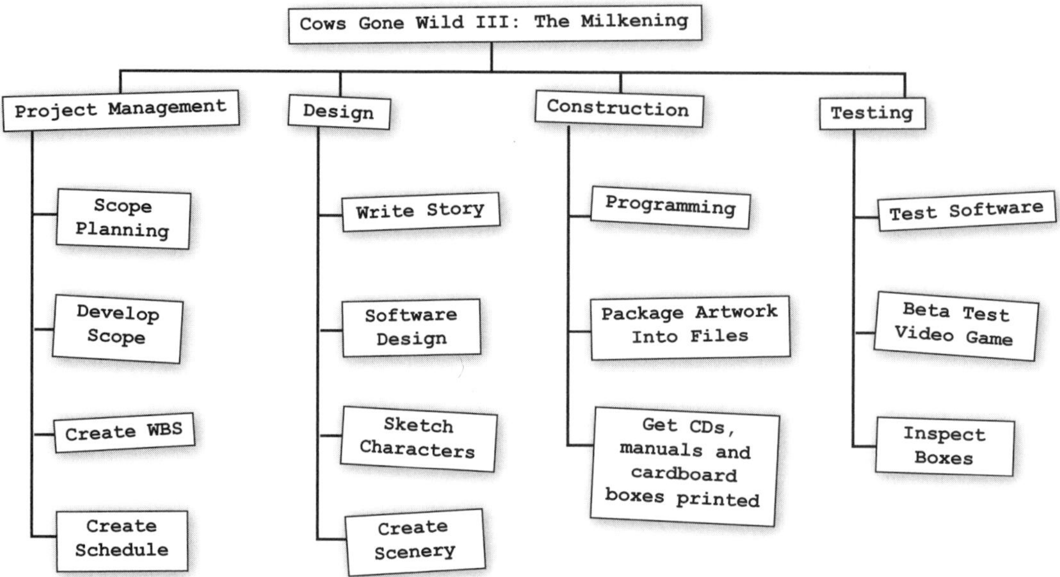

1. We need to create a screensaver to market the game. Let's kill two birds with one stone and test out a brand new graphics engine on it. Oh, and we'll need a story for the screensaver, so we should write that too. Of course we have to recruit some killer voice talent for the screensaver. Memorable names sell more games.

   ☐ Scope Creep ☐ Gold Plating

2. Testing the most recent build, I just noticed that if the player presses x–x–z–a–Shift–Shift–Space in that order, Bessie does the Charleston—it's really funny.

   ☐ Scope Creep ☐ Gold Plating

3. We should add a calculator for tracking gallons of milk collected in the game. It will be really easy. We could even release the calculator as a separate add-in, and we could probably make it full-featured enough for the folks developing the game down the hall to use it too.

   ☐ Scope Creep ☐ Gold Plating

4. The printer just told us that she could also do silk screen T-shirts for everybody as a ship gift. Let's get our design team to do some special artwork for them. We can have everybody's names written in cows!!! Then we could use the same artwork on posters that we put around the office—oh, and coffee mugs for new people, too

   ☐ Scope Creep ☐ Gold Plating

Answers: 1, 3, and 4 are Scope Creep. 2 is Gold Plating

The Scope Control process

Monitoring & Controlling process group

There's no way to predict every possible piece of work that you and your team are going to do in the project. Somewhere along the way, you or someone else will realize that a change needs to happen, and that change will affect the scope baseline. That's why you need the **Scope Control** process. It's how you make sure that you make only those changes to the scope that you need to make, and that everyone is clear on what the consequences of those changes are.

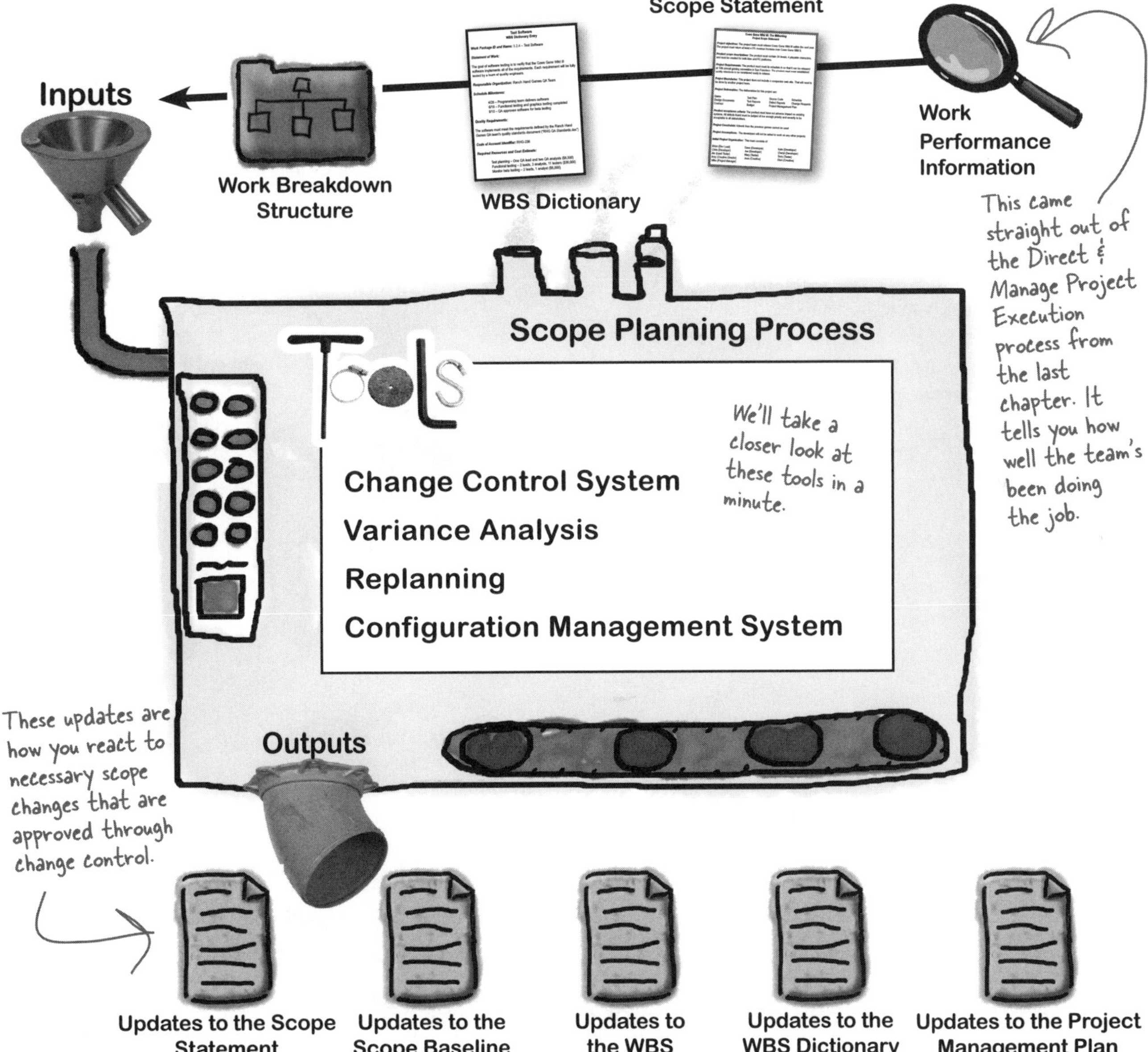

Anatomy of a change

Let's take a closer look at what happens when you need to make a change. You can't just go and change the project whenever you want—the whole reason that you have a baseline is so you can always know what work the team is supposed to do. If you make changes, then you need to change the baseline... which means you need to make sure that the change is ***really*** necessary. Luckily, you have some powerful tools to help you manage changes:

1 A change is needed

Every change starts the same way. Someone realizes that if the project sticks with the plan, then the outcome will lead to problems.

I know we're under pressure to get the game out the door, but we need to make a change. We only planned on making four meadows on level 3 and reusing them for level 6, but it's just not working for us. We've got to change this if we want the game to sell.

A change can come from anywhere – the project manager, a team member, even a stakeholder!

2 Create a change request

Before a change can be made, it needs to be approved. That means that it needs to be documented as a requested change. The only way to get a handle on a change is to write it down and make sure everyone understands it.

We'll write up a change request, and then put it through Integrated Change Control to get it approved.

3 Get the change approved

Remember Integrated Change Control from the last chapter? That's the process where the project manager takes a requested change and works with the sponsor and stakeholders to get approval to put it in place.

Think of Integrated Change Control as a kind of machine that converts requested changes into approved changes.

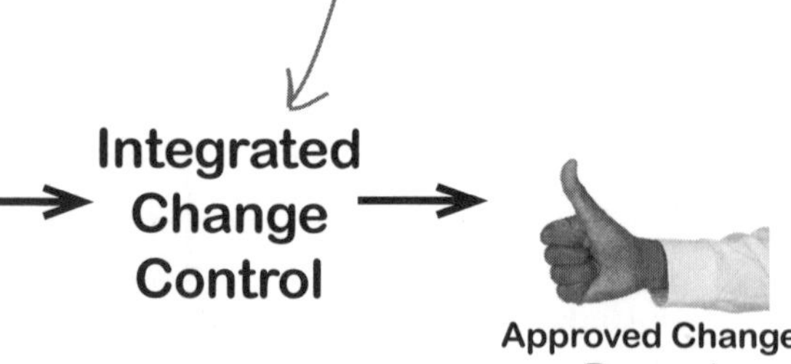

4 **Do variance analysis**

Take a look at the baseline and see how the change will affect it. This is where you decide whether you need to take some sort of corrective action. You compare the scope baseline against the change that you want to make, and figure out just how big the change really is.

5 **Replan the work**

Now it's time to go back to the scope documentation and update it to reflect the change.

6 **Create a new baseline**

Now that you've figured out that you need to change the scope, it's time to update the baseline. Go back to the scope statement, WBS, and WBS Dictionary, and update them so that they reflect the change that needs to be made.

The change is done!

Now you can move on with the project using the new baseline that you saved and distributed to the team.

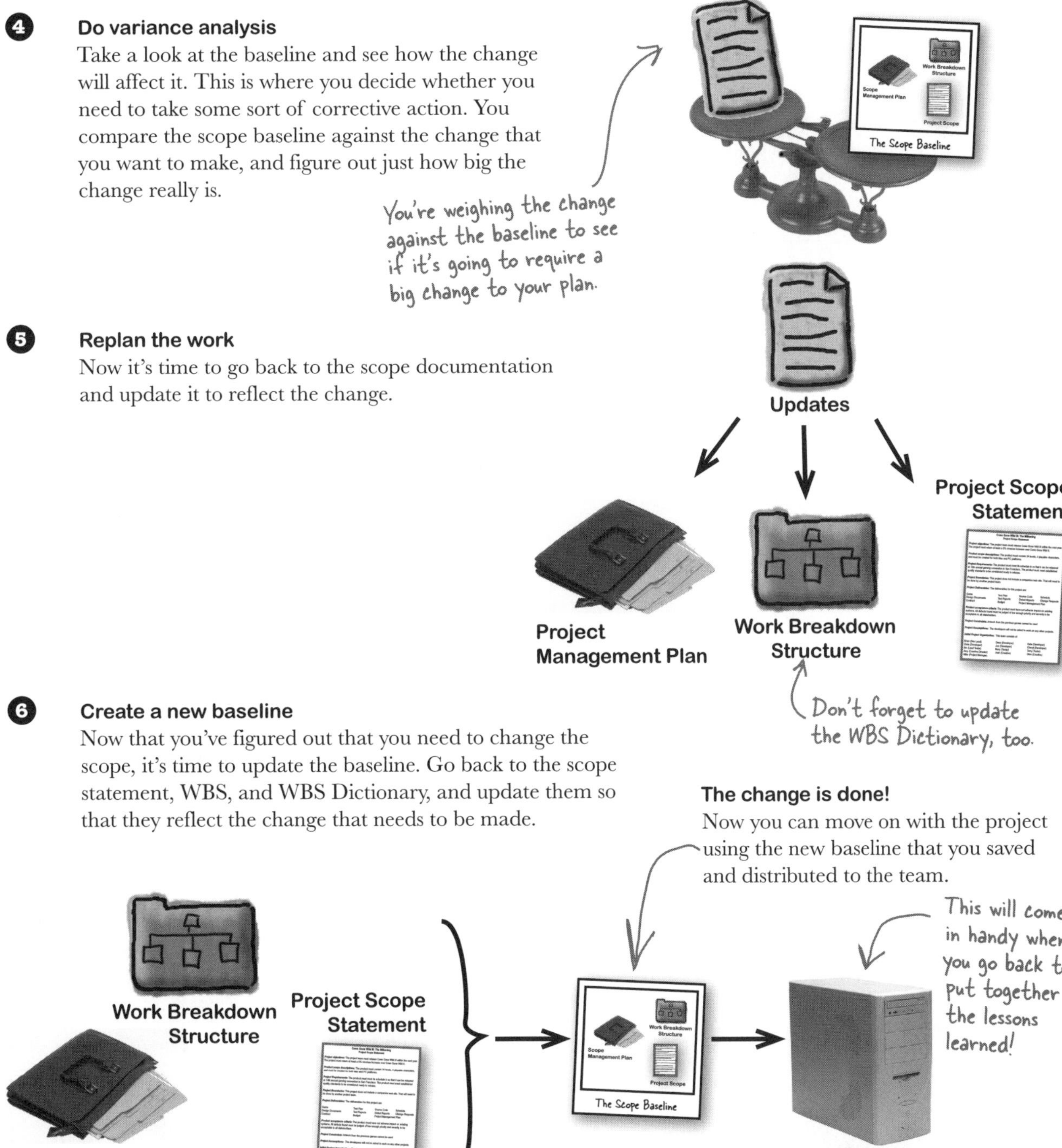

A closer look at the Change Control System

One of the most important tools in any Monitoring & Controlling process is the **Change Control System**. Let's take a closer look at how it works.

Since the folks at Ranch Hand need a change to add more scenery to *Cows Gone Wild III*, Mike takes a look at the scope management plan to understand the impact before forwarding it to the change control board. Once they approve the change, he updates the project management plan, checks it into the configuration management system, and changes the WBS and WBS Dictionary to include the new work packages.

Remember this from the last chapter? It's exactly the same change control system tool that we already learned about.

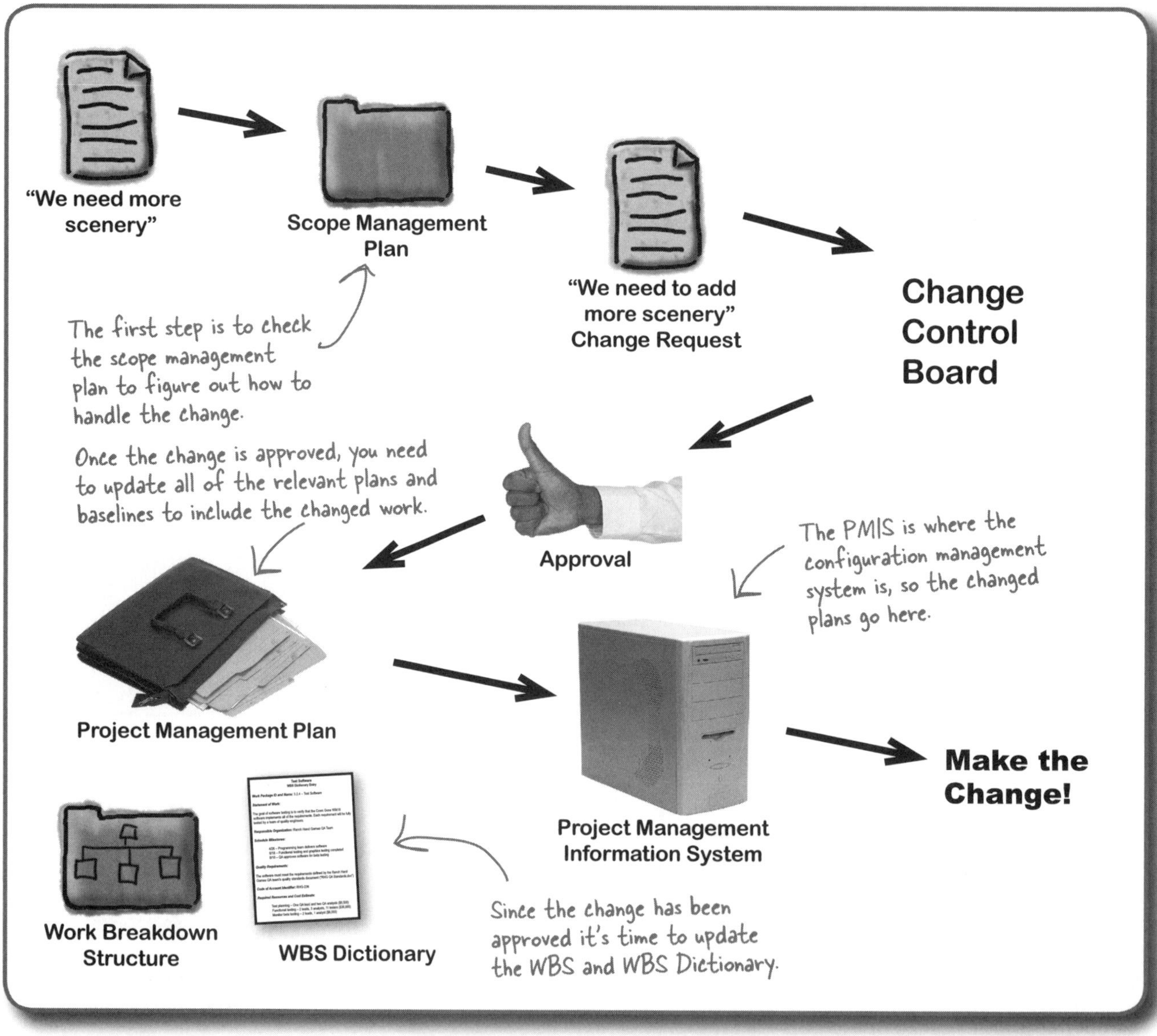

"We need more scenery"

Scope Management Plan

"We need to add more scenery" Change Request

Change Control Board

The first step is to check the scope management plan to figure out how to handle the change.

Once the change is approved, you need to update all of the relevant plans and baselines to include the changed work.

Approval

The PMIS is where the configuration management system is, so the changed plans go here.

Project Management Plan

Project Management Information System

Make the Change!

Work Breakdown Structure

WBS Dictionary

Since the change has been approved it's time to update the WBS and WBS Dictionary.

More Scope Control tools & techniques

There are three more tools and techniques in the Scope Control process. They're pretty intuitive: just take a minute and think of what you would need to do if you had to make a change to your project's scope. You'd need to figure out how big the change is, you'd need to update your plans, and then you'd need a way to keep track of that change in case you had to back it out. And that's exactly what these tools do.

Variance Analysis

This means comparing the data that can be collected about the work being done to the scope baseline. When there is a difference between the two, that's variance.

This tool of Scope Control is all about analyzing the difference between the baseline and the actual work to figure out if the plan needs to be corrected. If so, then you recommend a corrective action and put that recommendation through change control.

Replanning

When a change or approved corrective action comes out of the change control system, you need to revisit the plan and adjust it to include the new work. This usually means replanning all of the work to include the changes. That means updating the WBS, WBS Dictionary, Scope Statement, PM Plan, or Scope Baseline to include the new information

Configuration Management System

This is the place to look for information about the deliverables that have already been completed. All of your documents are kept here, so, when you incorporate a change to any plan, it needs to be versioned properly and kept here also.

The Configuration Management System is from the PMIS, Chapter 4. It's a set of applications that tracks your work and deliverables.

The goal of scope control is updating the scope, plan, baseline and WBS info.

there are no Dumb Questions

Q: Is scope control always about work and *project* scope? Can it ever be about deliverables and *product* scope?

A: No, scope control is **always about the work that the team does**, because the whole Scope Management knowledge area is about the project scope, not the product scope. In other words, as a project manager, you manage the work that the team is doing, not the things that they're making. Now, that doesn't mean you should never pay attention to deliverables. You still need to pay attention to the scope of the product, too, since the two are pretty closely related. For example, in the CGW III project, anytime somebody wants to add a new feature to the game, a programmer will need to program it, an artist will need to make new artwork, and a tester will have to test it. Any time you make changes to the project scope, it affects the product scope, and vice versa.

Q: What if a change is really small? Do I still have to go through all of this?

A: Yes. Sometimes what seems like a really small change to the scope—like just adding one tiny work package—turns out to be really complex when you take a closer look at it. It could have a whole lot of dependencies, or cause a lot of trouble in other work packages. If you don't give it careful consideration, you could find yourself watching your scope creep out of control. Each and every change needs to be evaluated in terms of impact. If there is any impact to the schedule, cost, or scope, you HAVE to put it through change control.

Q: How can you do variance analysis without knowing all of the changes are that are going to happen?

A: You do variance analysis as an ongoing thing. As information comes in about your project, you constantly compare it to how you planned. If you're running a month behind, that's a good indication that there are some work packages that took longer than your team estimated—or that you missed a few altogether. Either way, you need to take corrective action if you hope to meet your project objectives. Waiting until all possible changes are known will be too late for you to actually meet your goals. So you need to constantly check your actuals versus your baseline and correct where necessary (after putting your recommended actions through change control, of course!).

Q: I thought the configuration management system was part of the Project Management Information System from the Integration chapter. What does that have to do with change control?

A: When you write and modify documents throughout your project, you need to make sure that everybody is working with the same version of them. So you check them into a Configuration Management System, and that way everybody always knows where to go for the latest version.

Since you are checking all of your documents in, that's where you will keep your work performance information too. The most recent version of the schedule, any reports you have gathered on defects, and individual work performance should all be there, too. So, when you want to figure out what's going on in your project, you look there first. It follows that you would modify your documents and check them back into the CMS after any change has been approved too.

Every scope change goes through scope control.

Scope Control Magnets

Whenever you make a scope change, you need to go through all of the steps of change control. So what are those steps? Arrange the magnets to show the order that you handle changes to the scope.

1. ______________________
2. ______________________
3. ______________________
4. ______________________
5. ______________________
6. ______________________
7. ______________________
8. ______________________

Create a change request

Compare the change against the baseline

Store the updated baseline in the configuration management system

Go back and plan for the new work

Update the baseline

You figure out that you have to make a change

Now the team can change the way they do the work

Get approval to make the change

We put the finishing touches on the artwork...

... and construction and testing are done.

Good work!

Scope Control Magnets Solutions

Arrange all of the activities you do to control scope in the right order.

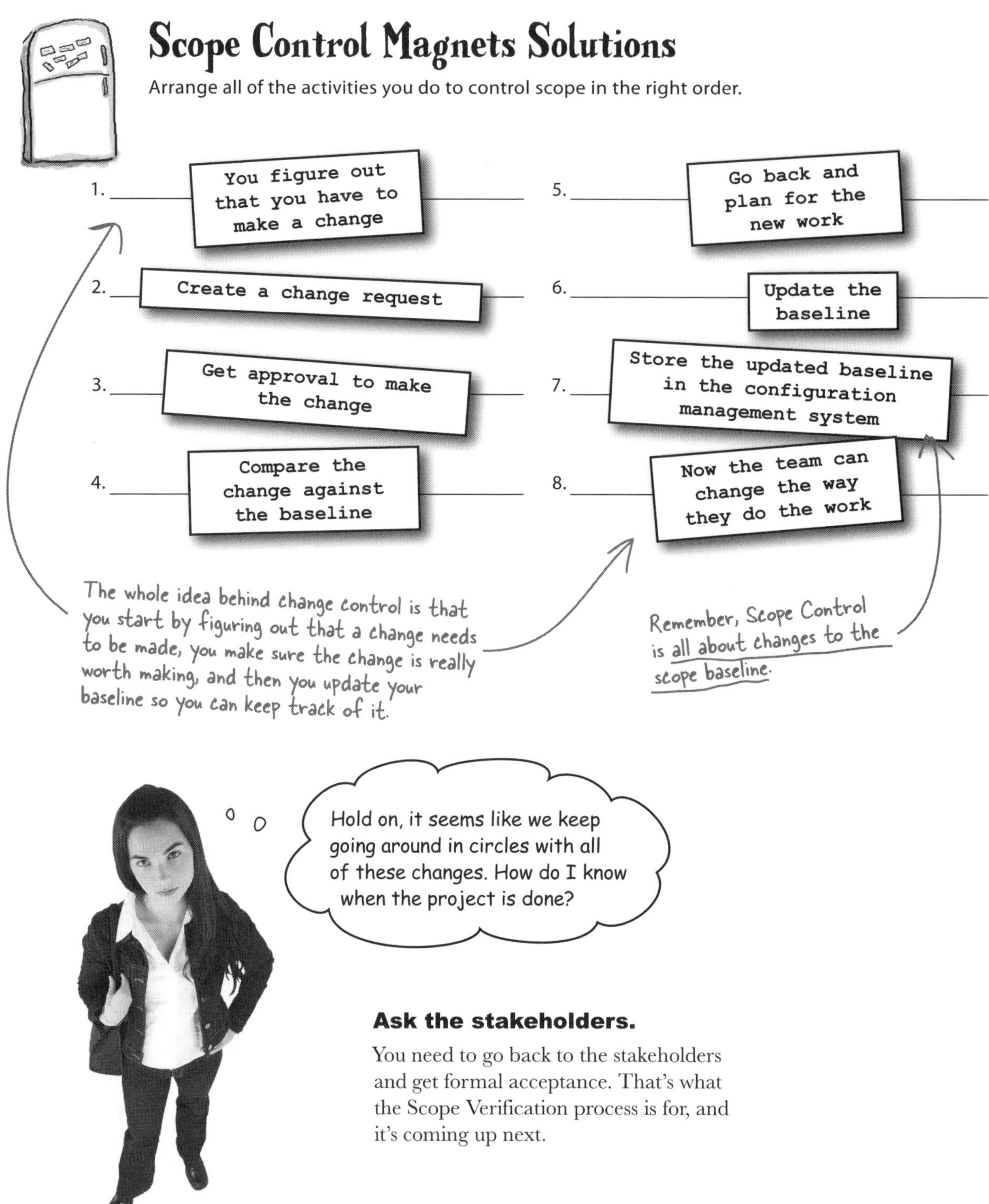

Ask the stakeholders.

You need to go back to the stakeholders and get formal acceptance. That's what the Scope Verification process is for, and it's coming up next.

Make sure the team delivered the right product

Monitoring
& Controlling
process group

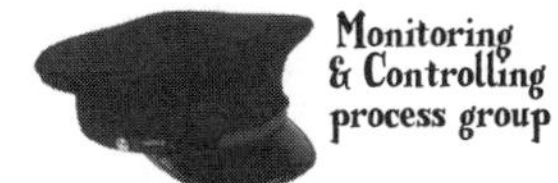

When the team is done, what happens? You still have one more thing you need to do before you can declare victory. You need to gather all the stakeholders together and have them make sure that all the work really was done. We call that the **Scope Verification** process.

Inputs
Scope Management Plan
WBS Dictionary
Project Scope Statement
Deliverables
Scope Verification Process
Tools
There's only one tool in the Scope Verification process: inspection. This is where the stakeholders actually look closely at the what the team did and make sure that every single piece of work was completed.
Inspection
Outputs
If the team did the work right, then the stakeholders will formally accept the deliverables (which means they do it in writing).
Accepted Deliverables
Requested changes
Recommended corrective actions
If they DON'T think that all the work was done, then you'll need to make some changes. Back to change control!

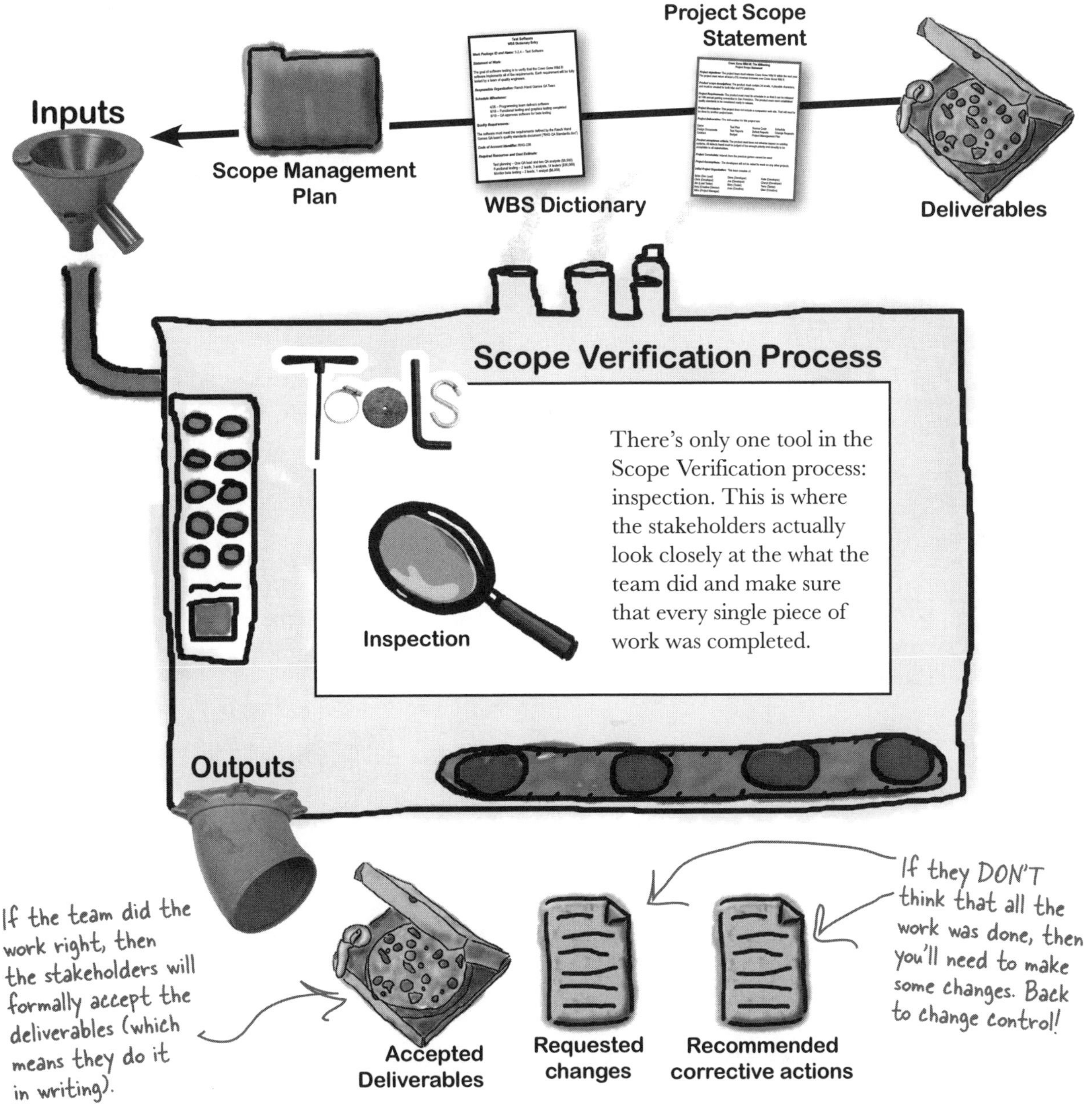

The stakeholders decide when the project is done

As you deliver the stuff in your scope statement, you need to make sure that each of the deliverables has everything in it that you listed in the scope statement. You inspect all of your deliverables versus the scope statement, the WBS, and the scope management plan. If your deliverables have everything in those documents, then they should be acceptable to stakeholders. When all of the deliverables in the scope are done to their satisfaction, *then* you're done.

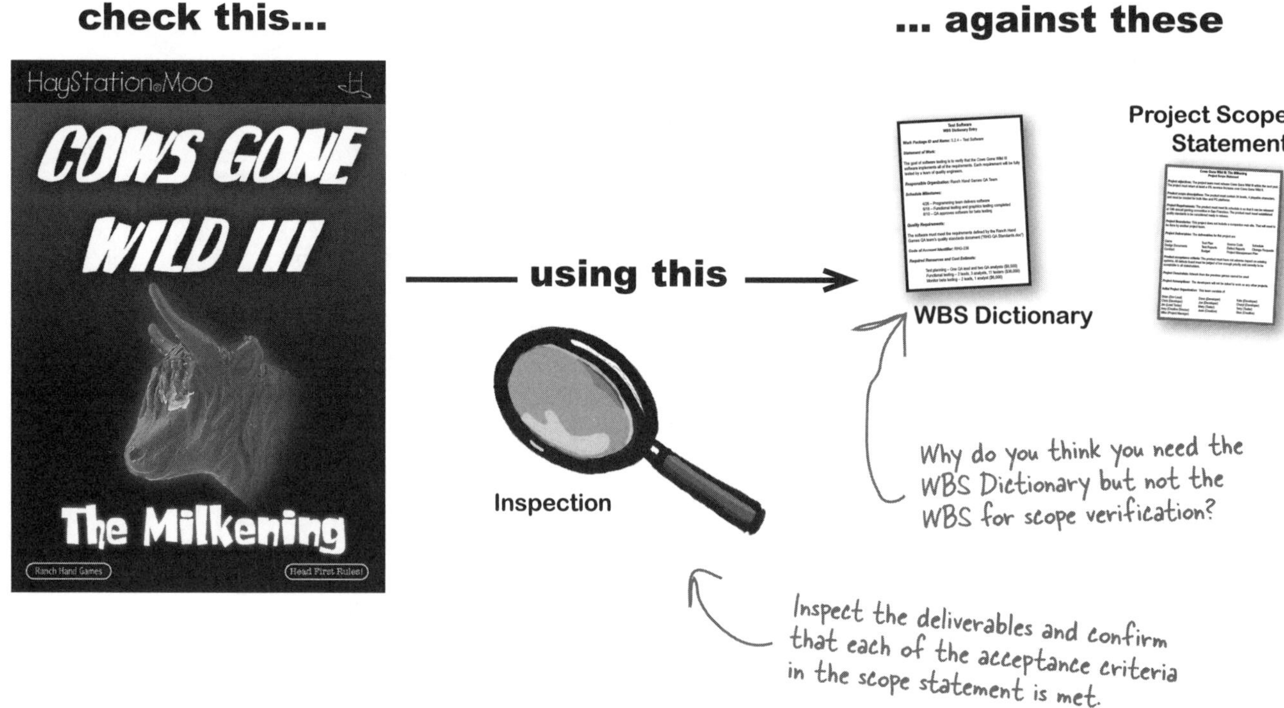

Formal acceptance means that you have written confirmation from all of the stakeholders that the deliverables match the requirements and the project management plan.

Is the project ready to go?

Once the deliverables are ready for prime time, you inspect them with the stakeholders to make sure that they meet acceptance criteria. The purpose of Scope Verification is to obtain formal, written acceptance of the work products. If they are found to be unsatisfactory, the specific changes requested by the stakeholders get sent to change control so that the right changes can be made.

Inspection just means sitting down with the stakeholders and looking at each deliverable to see if it's acceptable.

EVERY deliverable should be inspected, including all project management documents and everything produced by the team.

Inspection

If the deliverables are not acceptable, the project goes back to change control.

No

Yes

Change control

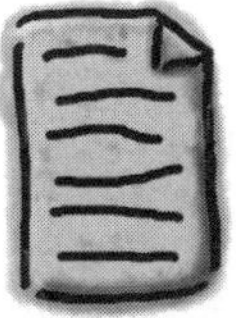

Requested Changes

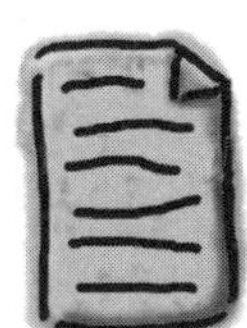

Recommended Corrective Actions

Here's a list of what wasn't acceptable about the product. Once these are addressed, we should be all set.

Ship it

YAY!

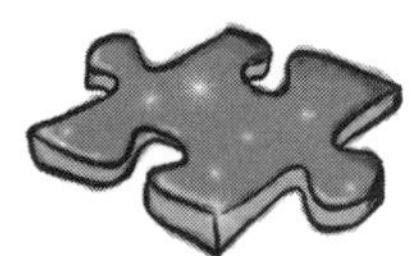

Scopecross

Take some time to sit back and give your right brain something to do. It's your standard crossword; all of the solution words are from this chapter.

Across

3. Looking closely at the product to see if you completed all of the work.

6. The process where you write the project scope statement is called Scope _________________.

7. When one change leads to another and another and another, it's called scope ________.

9. Getting work packages out of deliverables.

10. Exploring all of the ways that you can do the work so that you can find the best way to do the work in your project is called ______________ identification.

Down

1. Figuring out how big a change is by comparing it to the baseline is called _________analysis.

2. The details of every work package in the WBS are stored in the WBS _____________.

4. When you're making a WBS, you can break the work down by phase or ____________.

5. A version of the Scope Management Plan, Work Breakdown Structure, and Product Scope that you will compare your project to is called the scope ____________.

8. ____________ scope means the features or functions of the thing or service that you are building.

Answers on page 198.

The project is ready to ship!

There were a few unexpected changes to the scope along the way. But, for the most part, everything went according to plan. The stakeholders and the CEO got together with the team and went through everything they did—and it's ready to go. Great job, guys!

Sharpen your pencil Solution

Here are some attributes of Cows Gone Wild III. Which are project scope and which are product scope?

1. Programming

   - [x] Project Scope
   - [ ] Product Scope

2. 34 levels in the game

   - [ ] Project Scope
   - [x] Product Scope

3. Graphic design

   - [x] Project Scope
   - [ ] Product Scope

4. Four playable characters

   - [ ] Project Scope
   - [x] Product Scope

5. Great graphics

   - [ ] Project Scope
   - [x] Product Scope

6. Testing

   - [x] Project Scope
   - [ ] Product Scope

7. Mac and PC compatible

   - [ ] Project Scope
   - [x] Product Scope

8. A "boss battle" milk fight level at the end

   - [ ] Project Scope
   - [x] Product Scope

This will help you on the exam. Knowing that one process's output is another's input makes it a lot easier to remember the order of the processes.

Exercise Solution

Three of these inputs were outputs of Integration Management processes. Write down which process created each of them, and which process group it was in.

1. Project Charter: Develop Project Charter (Initiating group)

2. Preliminary Scope Statement: Develop Preliminary Scope Statement (Initiating group)

3. Project Management Plan: Develop Project Management Plan (Planning group)

Here are a few things that Mike left out of the *CGWIII* scope statement. Can you figure out where each of them should go?

1. The game must have fewer than 15 defects per 10,000 lines of code.

2. There will be four graphic designers reporting to the art director, and six programmers and four testers reporting to the development manager.

3. No more than 15 people can be allocated to work on the game at any time.

4. Scenery artwork

5. The product shall reduce tech support calls by 15%.

6. The game needs to run on a machine with 1 GB of memory or less.

A. Project objectives

B. Project deliverables

C. Project constraints

D. Initial project organization

E. Project requirements

F. Product acceptance criteria

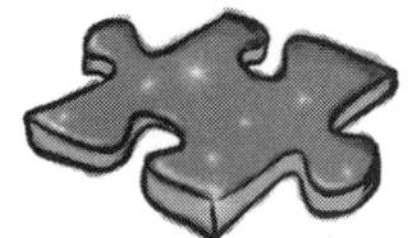

Scopecross

Take some time to sit back and give your right brain something to do. It's your standard crossword; all of the solution words are from this chapter.

Exam Questions

1. Which of the following is TRUE about a work breakdown structure?

A. It contains work packages that are described in a linear, unstructured list

B. Each item in the WBS represents a feature in the product scope

C. The WBS represents all of the work that must be done on the project

D. The WBS is created by the product sponsor and stakeholders

2. Which is NOT an output of a scope management process?

A. Preliminary scope statement

B. WBS Dictionary

C. Requested changes

D. Accepted deliverables

3. Which of the following is NOT TRUE about a work breakdown structure?

A. It describes processes to define the scope, verify work, and manage scope changes.

B. It contains a graphical, hierarchical list of all work to be performed

C. It can be broken down by project phase or deliverable

D. It is an important element of the scope baseline

4. What is the correct order of the scope management processes?

A. Scope Definition, Create WBS, Scope Planning, Scope Verification

B. Scope Planning, Scope Control, Create WBS, Scope Verification

C. Scope Planning, Scope Definition, Create WBS, Scope Verification

D. Scope Planning, Scope Baseline, Scope Definition, Scope Control

5. You are managing a software project. Your team has been working for eight weeks, and so far the project is on track. The lead programmer comes to you with a problem: there is a work package that is causing trouble. Nobody seems to know who is responsible for it, the accounting department does not know what cost center to bill it against, and it's not even clear exactly what work should be performed. Which of the following would BEST help this situation?

A. Alternatives Analysis

B. WBS Dictionary

C. Scope Management Plan

D. Scope Verification

Exam Questions

6. The goal of Scope Verification is:

A. To inspect the scope statement for defects so that it is correct

B. To gain formal acceptance of the project deliverables from the sponsor and stakeholders

C. To get everyone in the project working together towards a common goal

D. To verify that all PMBOK® Guide processes are complied with

7. Historical information and lessons learned are part of:

A. Organizational process assets

B. Enterprise environmental factors

C. Project management information system (PMIS)

D. Work performance information

8. You've taken over as a project manager on a highway construction project, and the execution is already underway. Your sponsor tells you that moving forward, all asphalt should be laid down with a 12" thickness. The scope statement and the WBS call for 9" thick asphalt. What is the BEST course of action?

A. Look for a cheaper supplier so the cost impact is minimized

B. Tell the sponsor that the work is already underway, so you can't accommodate his request

C. Refuse to alter the plans until the change control system has been used

D. Tell the team to accommodate the request immediately

9. Which of the following BEST describes the purpose of the project scope statement?

A. It describes the features of the product of the project

B. It is created before the scope management plan

C. It decomposes deliverables into work packages

D. It describes the objectives, requirements, and deliverables of the project, and the work needed to create them

10. It's the end of execution for a large highway construction project. The work has been done, and the workers are ready to pack up their equipment. The project manager and project sponsor have come by with specialists to check that each requirement has been met, and that all of the work in the WBS has been performed. What process is being done?

A. Scope Control

B. Scope Verification

C. Scope Testing

D. Scope Definition

Exam Questions

11. You have just been put in charge of a project that is already executing. While reviewing the project documentation, you discover that there is no WBS. You check the Scope Management Plan and discover that there should be one for this project. What is the BEST thing for you to do:

A. Immediately alert the sponsor and make sure the project work doesn't stop

B. Stop project work and create the WBS, and don't let work continue until it's created

C. Make sure you closely manage communications to ensure the team doesn't miss any undocumented work

D. Mark it down in the lessons learned so it doesn't happen on future projects

12. A project manager on an industrial design project finds that the sponsor wants to make a change to the scope after it has been added to the baseline. What document should he consult?

A. WBS

B. Scope management plan

C. Change request form template

D. Preliminary scope statement

13. You have just started work on the project scope statement. You are analyzing the expected deliverables, when you discover that one of them could be delivered in three different ways. You select the best method for creating that deliverable. What is the BEST way to describe what you are doing?

A. Alternatives analysis

B. Decomposition

C. Scope definition

D. Stakeholder analysis

14. You're the project manager on a software project. Your team has only completed half of the work, when the sponsor informs you that the project has been terminated. What is the BEST action for you to take?

A. Verify the deliverables produced by the team against the scope, and document any place they do not match

B. Call a team meeting to figure out how to spend the rest of the budget

C. Work with the sponsor to see if there is any way to bring the project back

D. Tell the team to stop working immediately

15. You are managing an industrial design project. One of your team members comes to you with a suggestion that will let you do more work while at the same time saving the project 15% of the budget. What is the BEST way for you to proceed?

A. Tell the team to make the change because it will deliver more work for less money

B. Refuse to make the change until it a change request is documented and change control is performed

C. Refuse to consider the change because it will affect the baseline

D. Do a cost-benefit analysis and then make sure to inform the sponsor that the project scope changed

Exam Questions

16. You are the project manager for a telecommunications project. You are working on the project scope statement. Which of the following is NOT included in this document?

A. Authorization for the project manager to work on the project

B. Requirements that the deliverables must meet

C. A description of the project objectives

D. The list of deliverables that must be created

17. Which of the following is NOT an input to scope control?

A. WBS Dictionary

B. Approved change requests

C. Requested changes

D. Project scope statement

18. Which of these processes is not a part of Scope Management?

A. Scope Identification

B. Scope Planning

C. Scope Control

D. Scope Verification

19. You are the project manager for a new project, and you want to save time creating the WBS. Which is the BEST way to do this?

A. Make decomposition go faster by cutting down the number of deliverables

B. Use a WBS from a previous project as a template

C. Don't create the WBS Dictionary

D. Ask the sponsor to provide the work packages for each deliverable

20. The project manager for a telecommunications project is using the Scope Definition process. Which BEST describes this?

A. Creating a document that lists all of the features of the product

B. Creating a plan for managing changes to the scope baseline

C. Creating a document that describes all of the work the team does to make the deliverables

D. Creating a graphical representation of how the phases or deliverables decompose into work packages

Exam Questions

21. You are the project manager for a construction project. You have completed project initiation activities, and you are now creating a document that describes processes to document the scope, decompose deliverables into work packages, verify that all work is complete, and manage changes to the baseline. What process are you performing?

A. Scope Planning

B. Scope Definition

C. Create WBS

D. Scope Verification

22. You are a project manager working on a project. Your sponsor wants to know who a certain work package is assigned to, what control account to bill it against, and what work is involved. What document do you refer her to?

A. Scope Management Plan

B. WBS

C. WBS Dictionary

D. Scope Statement

23. Which of the following BEST describes the change control system?

A. It describes processes that guide you in building the scope statement, breaking down the work, and verifying the scope

B. It describes all of the deliverables in the project decomposed into work packages

C. It contains historical information, lessons learned, templates and forms

D. It describes how specific approved changes are used to update the project documents

24. You are the project manager for a software project. One of the teams discovers that if they deviate from the plan, they can actually skip one of the deliverables because it's no longer necessary. They do the calculations, and realize they can save the customer 10% of the cost of the project without compromising the features in the product. They take this approach, and inform you the following week what they did during the status meeting. What is the BEST way to describe this situation?

A. The project team has taken initiative and saved the customer money

B. A dispute is resolved in favor of the customer

C. The team informed the project manager of the change, but they should have informed the customer too

D. The team did not follow the Scope Control process

Exam ~~Questions~~

1. Answer: C

The work breakdown structure is all about breaking down the work that your team needs to do. The WBS is graphical and hierarchical, not linear and unstructured. Did you notice that answer B was about product scope, not project scope?

2. Answer: A

There are two ways you can get to the right answer for this question. You can recognize that the WBS Dictionary, Requested Changes, and Accepted Deliverables are all Scope Management process outputs. (You'll see Requested Changes in every knowledge area!) But you can also recognize that the Preliminary Scope Statement was created by the Develop Preliminary Scope Statement, which is part of the Initiating process group.

3. Answer: A

Did you recognize that answer A was describing the scope management plan? Once you know what the WBS is used for and how to make one, questions like this make sense.

4. Answer: C

You'll need to know what order processes come in, and one good way to do that is to think about how the outputs of some processes are used as inputs for another. For example, you can't create the WBS until the scope is defined, which is why A is wrong. And you can't do change control until you have a baseline WBS, which is why B is wrong.

Be on the lookout for fake processes like "Scope Baseline." It sounds like a real process, but it's not.

5. Answer: B

An important tactic for a lot of exam questions is to be able to recognize a particular tool, technique, input or output from a description. What have you learned about that tells you who is responsible for a work package, what control account to associate with it, and describes the work associated with it? That's a good description of the WBS Dictionary.

6. Answer: B

Inspection isn't just done at the end of the project. You do Scope Verification on every single deliverable made by you and the team.

There are some questions where you'll just have to know what a process is all about, and this is one of them. That's why it's really helpful to know why Scope Verification is so helpful to you on a project. You use Scope Verification to check that all of the work packages were completed, and get the stakeholders and sponsor to formally accept the deliverables.

Exam Questions

7. Answer: A

It's easy to forget that Organizational Process Assets is more than just an input. It's a real thing that's part of your company. Take a second and think about what **assets** are in your **organization** that help you with carry out each **process**. Get it? Good! So what is historical information, anyway? It's stuff like reports and data that you or another project manager wrote down on a previous project and stored in a file cabinet or a database. That's an asset you can use now! What are lessons learned? Those are lessons you wrote down at the end of a previous project and stuck in a file cabinet or a database. And now those lessons are another asset you can use.

The PMBOK® Guide says this stuff is stored in a "corporate knowledge base", but that's just another word for a file cabinet or a folder on your network

These inputs and outputs make sense when I think about how I'd use them on a project. Organizational Process Assets are just things that my organization keeps track of to help me do my job, like information from old projects and procedures that help me do my job.

8. Answer: C

One thing to remember about change control is that if you want to make the sponsor and stakeholders happy with the project in the end, sometimes you have to tell them "no" right now. When you're doing Scope Control, the most important tool you use is the change control system. It tells you how to take an approved change and put it in place on a project, and there's no other way that you should ever make a change to any part of the baseline. That means that once everyone has approved the scope statement and WBS, if you want to make any change to them, then you need to get that change approved and put it through the change control system.

9. Answer: D

Some questions are just definition questions. When that definition is a "Which-is-BEST" question, there could be an answer that makes some sense, and it's tempting to stop with it. In this case, answer A sounds like it might be right. But if you read answer D, it's much more accurate.

Don't forget that the exam is always about the PROJECT scope, not the PRODUCT scope. Make sure you know the difference.

Exam Questions

10. Answer: B

When you're getting the sponsor and stakeholders to formally accept the results of the project, you're doing scope verification. There's only one tool for it: inspection. That means carefully checking the deliverables (in this case, what the workers built on the highway) to make sure they match the WBS.

Answer D is a good idea, but it's not as important as creating a new WBS.

11. Answer: B

This question is a little tricky. The most important thing about a WBS is that if your Scope Management Plan says it should be there, then your project absolutely cannot be done without it. And a general rule is that if you ever find that there is no WBS, you should always check the Scope Management Plan to find out why.

12. Answer: B

This is another question that is testing you on the definition of a specific document, in this case the scope management plan. Think about what you use a scope management plan for. It tells you how to define the scope, break down the work, verify the deliverables and **manage scope changes** – which is what this question is asking. All of the other answers have inputs and outputs that don't have anything to do with managing changes.

13. Answer: A

Here's another example of how there are two correct answers but only one BEST one. Answer C is true – you are doing scope definition. But is that really the best way to describe this situation? Alternatives analysis is part of scope definition, and it's a more accurate way to describe what's going on here.

When you look at a few ways to create a deliverable and then decide on the best one, that's variance analysis.

14. Answer: A

This question is an example of how you need to rely on more than just common sense to pass the PMP exam. All four of these answers could be good ways to handle a terminated project, but there's only one of those answers that corresponds to what the PMBOK® Guide says. When a project is terminated, you still need to complete the Scope Verification process. That way, you can document all of the work that has been completed, and the work that has not been completed.

That way, if I need to restart the project later or reuse some of its deliverables, I'll know exactly where my team left off when it ended.

15. Answer: B

Are you starting to get the hang of how this change control stuff works? The baseline isn't etched in stone, and you need to be able to change it, but you can't just go ahead and make changes whenever you want. You need to document the change request and then put that request through change control. If it's approved, then you can update the baseline so that it incorporates the change.

You definitely can't just make the change and inform the sponsor later. All changes need to be approved.

16. Answer: A

When a question asks you about what a particular document, input, or output contains, be on the lookout for answers that talk about a different document. What document do you know about that gives the project manager authorization to do the work? That's what the project charter is for.

17. Answer: C

Sometimes Scope Control is easiest to think about if you think of it as a kind of machine that turns approved changes into updates. It sucks in the approved changes and all of the other Scope Management stuff (the Scope Statement, WBS, and WBS Dictionary), does all the stuff that it needs to do to update those things, and then spits out updates. And sometimes it spits out new requested changes because when you're making changes to the WBS or Scope Statement you realize that you need to make even more changes.

18. Answer: A

Scope Identification is a made-up process. It didn't appear in this chapter, and even though it sounds real, it's wrong.

I think of Integrated Change Control as a machine that turns change requests into approved changes, and Scope Control as the machine that turns approved changes into updates to the scope baseline.

19. Answer: B

WBS templates are a great way to speed up creating the WBS, and the easiest way to create a template is to use one from a previous project. It is **not** a good idea to cut out deliverables, skip important outputs like the WBS Dictionary, or make the sponsor do your job for you.

You can also use a template for the scope management plan.

Exam Questions

20. Answer: C

This question asked you about the Scope Definition process, but all of the answers describe various outputs. Which of these outputs matches Scope Definition? Well, the main output of Scope Definition is the Scope Statement, and answer C is a good description of the scope statement.

21. Answer: A

Most of the processes that you have to learn for the exam have one key output, and a lot of questions will describe that output and ask you to figure out which process is being performed. What document is being described here? It's the Scope Management Plan, which you create in the Scope Planning process.

22. Answer: C

There's only one document you've seen that shows you details of individual work packages and contains a control account, a statement of work, and a resource assignment. It's the WBS Dictionary.

23. Answer: D

Here's another question where you need to know how to describe an important tool. In this case, you need to know what the change control system is used for. Luckily, answer D is a pretty good description.

Hey, I'll bet a good way to study for the exam is to look at answers A, B and C in question 23 and figure out what each of them is describing. It'll be great practice identifying an output from a description!

Exam ~~Questions~~

24. Answer: D

When you read the question, it looks like the team really helped the project, right? But think about what happened: the team abandoned the plan, and then they made a change to the project without getting approval from the sponsor or stakeholders. Maybe they discovered a useful shortcut. But isn't it possible that the shortcut the team found was already considered and rejected by the sponsor? That's why change control is so important.

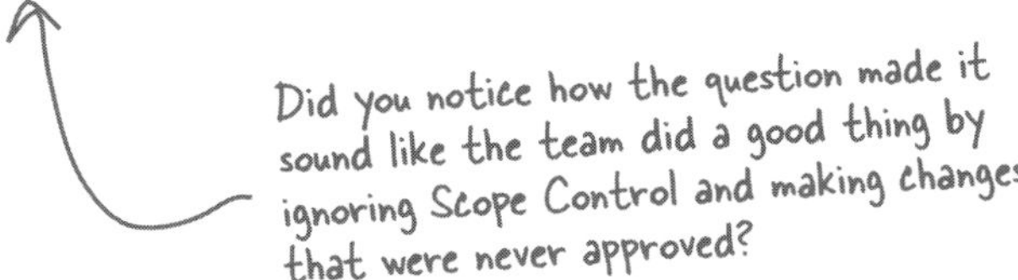

Keep an eye out for questions that describe an input or output and then ask you to name it. Look at each answer and think up own descriptions for them—one of them will match the question.

6 time management

Getting it Done on Time

Time management is what most people think of when they think of project managers. It's where the deadlines are set and met. It starts with **figuring out the work** you need to do, how you will do it, what **resources you'll use**, and how long it will take. From there, it's all about developing and controlling that **schedule**.

Reality sets in for the happy couple

Rob and Rebecca have decided to tie the knot, but they don't have much time to plan their wedding. They want the big day to be unforgettable. They want to invite a lot of people and show them all a great time.

But just thinking about all of the details involved is overwhelming. Somewhere around picking the paper for the invitations, the couple realize they need help…

They've always dreamed of a June wedding, but it's already January.

Everything has to be perfect! But it seems so huge. I don't know where to start.

Don't worry. My sister's wedding planner was great. Let me give her a call.

Meet the wedding planner

Rob: We want everything to be perfect.

Rebecca: There is so much to do! Invitations, food, guests, music…

Rob: Oh no, we haven't even booked the place.

Rebecca: And it's all got to be done right. We can't print the invitations until we have the menu planned. We can't do the seating arrangements until we have the RSVPs. We aren't sure what kind of band to get for the reception, or should it be a DJ? We're just overwhelmed.

Rob: My sister said you really saved her wedding. I know she gave you over a year to plan.

Rebecca: But I've always dreamed of a June wedding, and I'm not willing to give that up. I know it's late, but can you help us?

What should Kathleen do first to make sure they have time to get everything done?

Time management helps with aggressive time lines

Since there are so many different people involved in making the wedding go smoothly, it takes a lot of planning to make sure that all of the work happens in the right order, gets done by the right people and doesn't take too long. That's what the **Time Management** knowledge area is all about.

Initially, Kathleen was worried that she didn't have enough time to make sure everything was done properly. But she knew that she had some powerful time management tools on her side when she took the job, and they'll help her make sure that everything will work out fine.

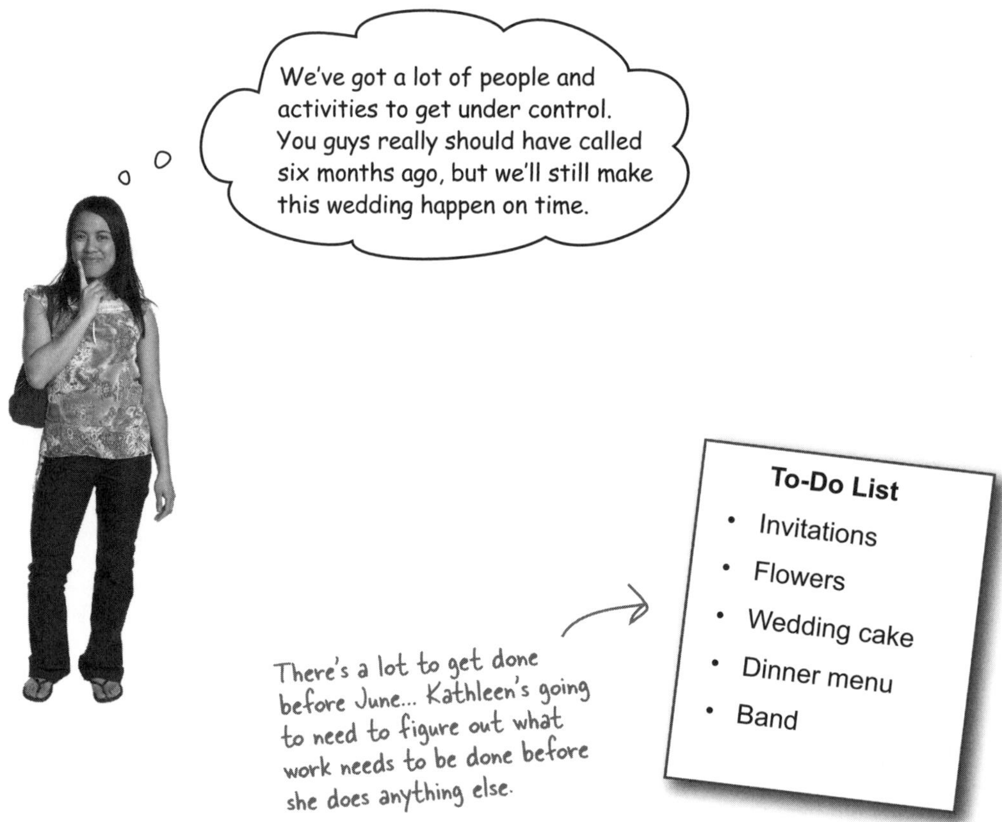

Time Management Magnets

You need to know the order of the time management processes for the exam. Luckily, they are pretty intuitive. Can you figure out the order?

1.

2.

3.

4.

5.

6.

Schedule Control

Activity Duration Estimating

Schedule Development

Activity Sequencing

Activity Definition

Activity Resource Estimating

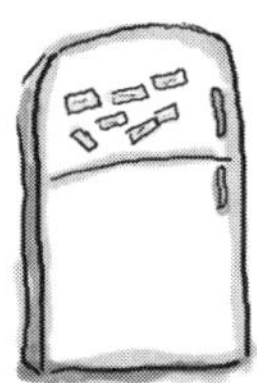

Time Management Magnets Solution

Here are the correct order and the main output for each of the time management processes.

1 Activity Definition

Activity List

First you come up with a list of all of the activities that will need to be completed.

The activity list is the basis for the network diagram that you create in the next process.

2 Activity Sequencing

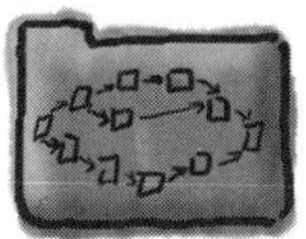

Network Diagram

Next, you figure out which activities need to come before others and put them in the right order. The main output here is a **network diagram**, a picture of how activities are related.

Knowing the stuff that needs to happen and the sequence is half the battle. Now you need to figure out who will do the work.

3 Activity Resource Estimating

Resource Requirements

Then you estimate the resources you need to do the job and create a list of them.

Once you have the network diagram, you can start to figure out who and what are needed to get the project done.

4 Activity Duration Estimating

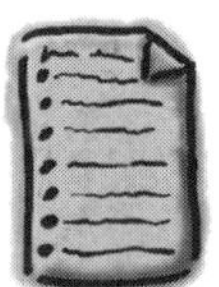

Activity Duration Estimates

And then the time it will take to do each activity.

You can use lots of different estimation techniques to determine how long the project will take.

5 Schedule Development

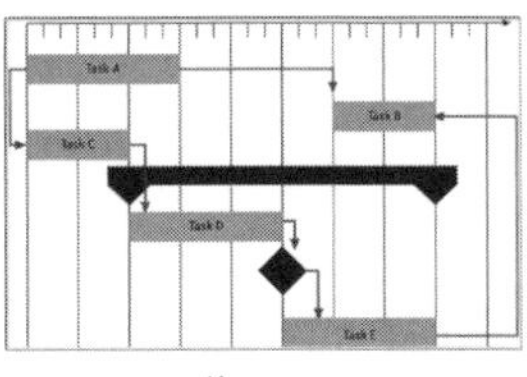

Then you build a schedule from all of the estimates, and the resource and activity information you've created.

The schedule pulls all of the information together to predict the project end date.

Schedule Control

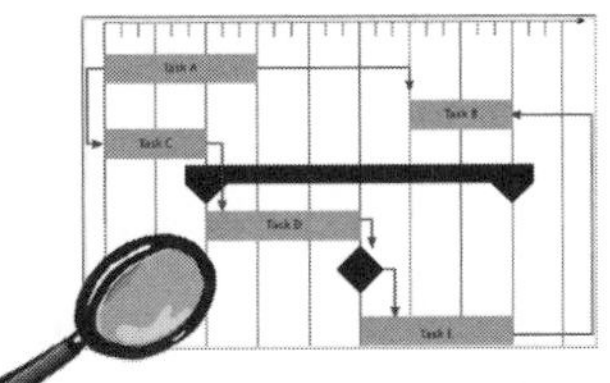

Finally, you monitor and control changes to the schedule to make sure that it is kept up to date.

Keeping track of the issues that require schedule changes and dealing with them is as important in Time Management as it was in Scope Management.

The first five Time Management processes are in the Planning process group because they're all about coming up with the schedule—and you need that before you can start executing your project.

The last process, Schedule Control, is in the Monitoring & Controlling process group.

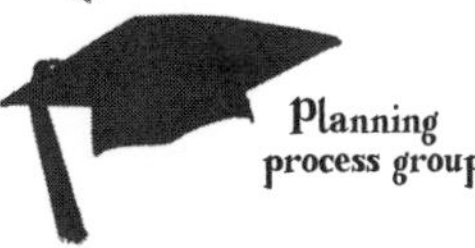

Time Management is all about breaking the work down into activities, so you can put them in order and come up with estimates for each of them.

What do you need to know before you can figure what activities are needed for a project?

Break down the work with Activity Definition

Activity definition uses everything we already know about the project to divide the work into activities that can be estimated. The inputs for this process all come from the processes in the Scope Management and Integration Management knowledge areas. The first step in time management is figuring out how the project work breaks down into activities—and that's what the **Activity Definition process** is for.

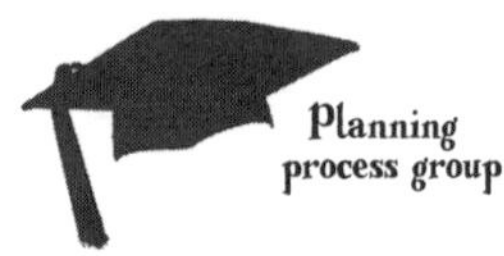

Inputs

Instead of drawing out the whole machine for each process, we'll just show you the "Inputs" funnel here.

The project management plan includes a plan on time management that talks about your process for getting the activity list defined.

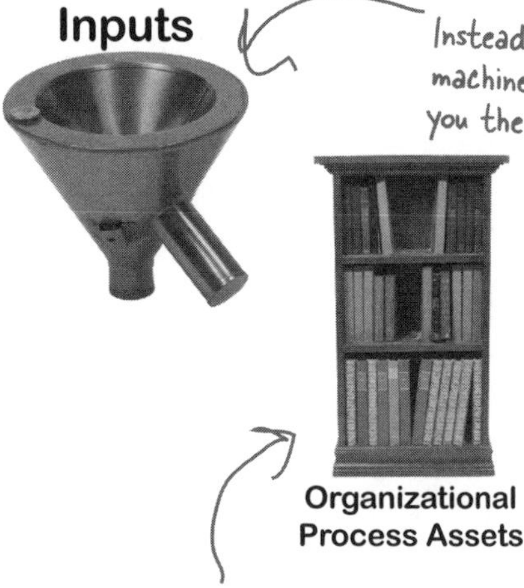

Organizational Process Assets

Enterprise Environmental Factors

Project Management Plan

You might want to look at all of the lessons from similar projects your company has done to get a good idea of what you need to do on the current one.

The project scope statement is still the main place to go to figure out what the project is supposed to produce.

Work Breakdown Structure

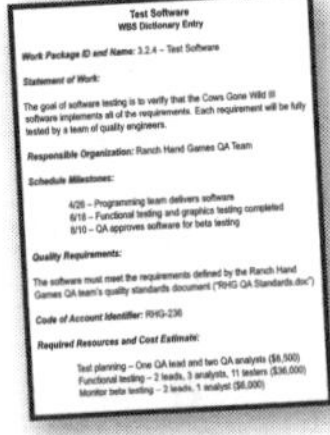

WBS Dictionary

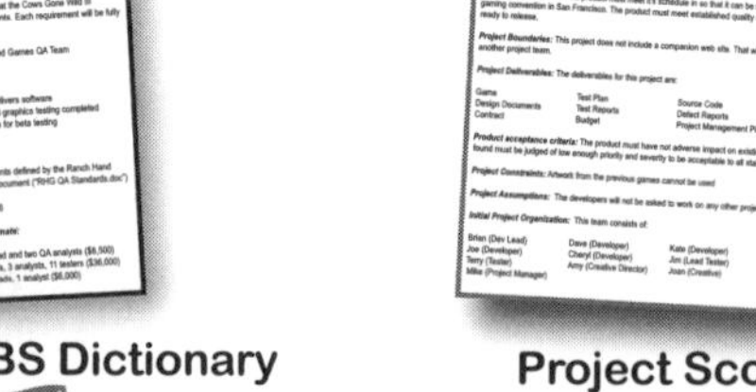

Project Scope Statement

The WBS and WBS Dictionary have the work explained to the work package level. That's more detailed than the scope statement, but still too high to estimate well.

Tools and techniques for the Activity Definition process

Kathleen sat down and wrote down everything she knew about the project. She used the Activity List from her last wedding as a guide and then thought about the things that Rob and Rebecca wanted that were different from her past projects. She broke those things down into activities and pulled everything together into an activity list.

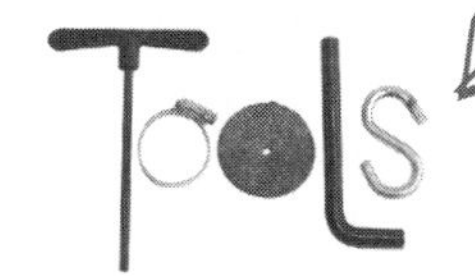

This "Tools" icon means we're showing you the tools and techniques for the process. Get the picture?

Decomposition

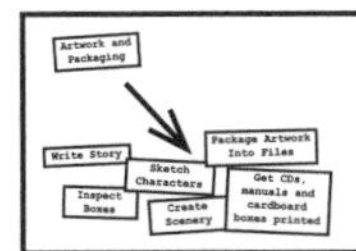

This means taking the work packages you defined in the scope management processes and breaking them down even further into activities that can be estimated.

Templates

If your organization has done other projects similar to this one, you can probably use a template to come up with many of the activities that are necessary.

Expert Judgment

Ask somebody who has done this before to give their opinion on what activities will be needed to get the job done.

Planning Component

When you don't know enough about a project to come up with a complete activity list, you can use a planning component as a placeholder until you know more. These are extra items put at high levels in the WBS to allow you to plan for the unknown. Two such components are the **control account** and the **planning package**.

Control Account

This placeholder is inserted at a level higher than a work package for accounting purposes. Anything written in the control account is tracked in a control account plan.

Planning Package

This is a placeholder that is put between the control account and an actual work package.

Rolling wave planning lets you plan as you go

Sometimes you start a project without knowing a lot about the work that you'll be doing later. Rolling wave planning lets you plan and schedule only the stuff that you know enough about to plan well.

If Kathleen were using rolling wave planning, she might write a schedule for only the tasks it takes to do the invitations and leave the planning for the menu and the seating up in the air until she knows who will RSVP.

Rob and Rebecca probably wouldn't be happy hearing that Kathleen was only going to plan for the invitations to be sent, though. They want to know that their wedding is going to happen on time. That's why rolling wave planning should only be used in cases where it's not possible to plan any other way.

there are no Dumb Questions

Q: How would you use experts to help you define tasks?

A: A wedding is something that a lot of people have experience with, but some projects are not as easy to get a handle on. If you were asked to manage a project in a new domain, you might want to ask an expert in that field to help you understand what activities were going to be involved.

Even in Kathleen's case, access to a catering expert might help her think of some activities that she wouldn't have planned for on her own.

It could be that you create an activity list and then have the expert review it and suggest changes. Or, you could involve the expert from the very beginning and ask to have an activity definition conversation with him before even making your first draft of the activity list.

Q: I still don't get planning packages and control accounts.

A: Planning packages are somewhere between control accounts and work packages in the WBS hierarchy. They are just placeholders that are used to plan against when you don't know much about certain areas of your project. By using a Planning package, you can add buffer time into your schedule and flag areas that are going to need further planning work in the future.

Control accounts are used for budgeting. They're accounting tools. You would use control accounts if you have a bunch of activities that you had to do in order to track your budget, and you need to track them separately from the rest of the project.

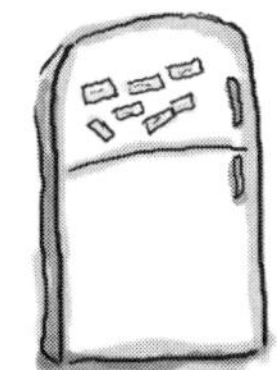

Activity Magnets

Here is part of a WBS. Arrange the activities underneath the WBS to show how the work items decompose into activities.

This is one work package from the wedding WBS. How does it decompose into activities?

This is part of the WBS that Kathleen made for the wedding project.

Wedding

Food	Invitations	Bridal
1.	1.	1. ....
2.	2.	2. ....
3.	3.	3. ....
	4.	4. ....

Shop for Shoes

Shop for Dress

Mail the Invitations

Finalize the Menu

Create the Guest List

Find Caterer

Print the Invitations

Tailoring and Fitting

Cater the Wedding

Choose Bouquet

Wait for the RSVPs

Activity Magnets Solution

Here is part of a WBS. Arrange the activities underneath the WBS to show how the work items decompose into activities.

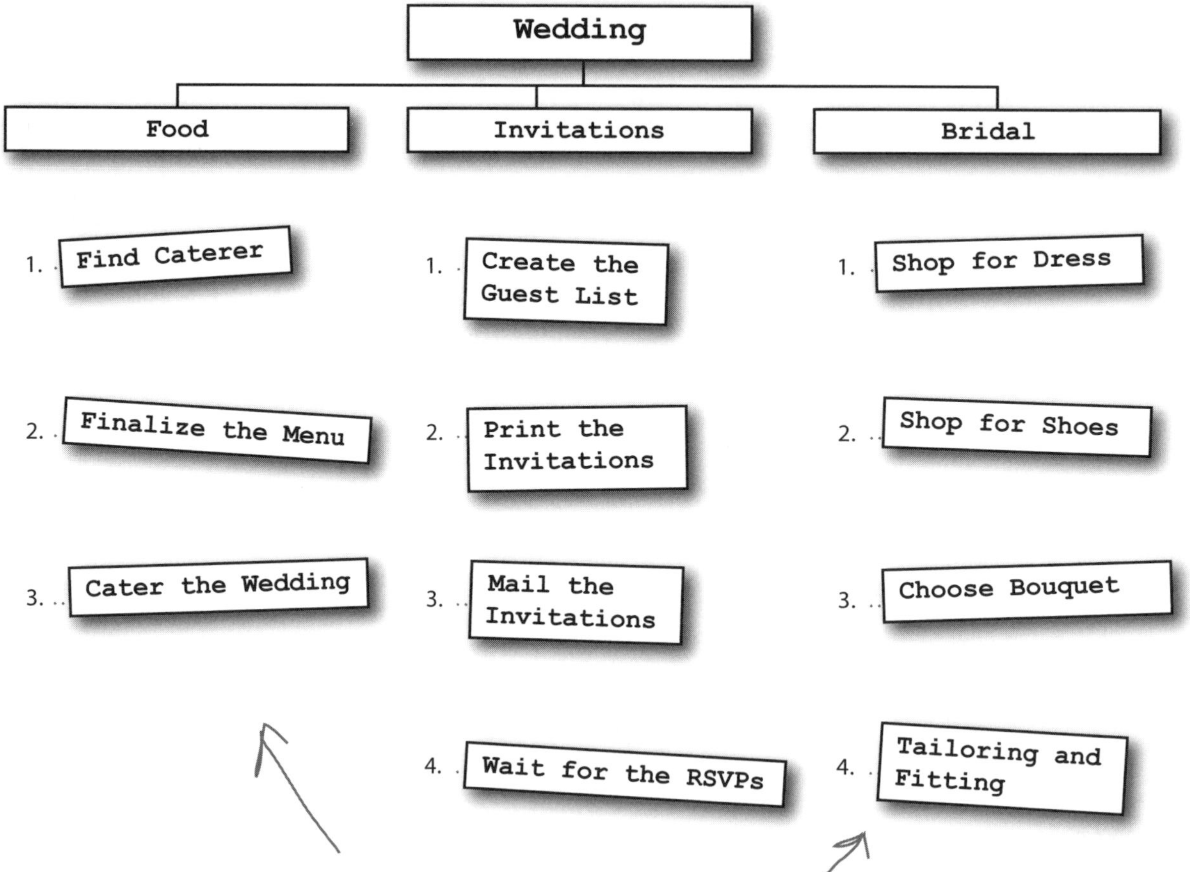

Wedding

Food	Invitations	Bridal
1. Find Caterer	1. Create the Guest List	1. Shop for Dress
2. Finalize the Menu	2. Print the Invitations	2. Shop for Shoes
3. Cater the Wedding	3. Mail the Invitations	3. Choose Bouquet
	4. Wait for the RSVPs	4. Tailoring and Fitting

There are lots of other activities that could be defined for the three work packages in Kathleen's WBS.

The important thing to remember about activities, though, is that they are broken down to the level at which they can be estimated accurately.

Activity Definition Outputs

The main output of this process is the **activity list**. It's the basis for all of the estimation and scheduling tasks you will do next. But there are a few others that go along with it and help to make the estimates more detailed and accurate.

Outputs

Activity List

This is a list of everything that needs to be done to complete your project. This list is lower-level than the WBS. It's all the activities that must be accomplished to deliver the work packages.

Activity List

Activity Attributes

Here's where the description of each activity is kept. All of the information you need to figure out the order of the work should be here, too. So any predecessor activities, successor activities or constraints should be listed in the attributes along with descriptions and any other information about resources or time that you need for planning.

Activity Attributes

Milestone Lists

All of the important checkpoints of your project are tracked as milestones. Some of them could be listed in your contract as requirements of successful completion; some could just be significant points in the project that you want to keep track of. The milestone list needs to let everybody know which are required and which are not.

Some milestones for the wedding:

* Invitations sent
* Menu finalized
* Church booked
* Bridesmaids' dresses fitted

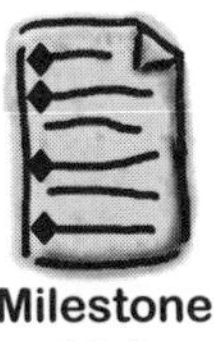

Milestone List

Requested Changes

As you figure out which activities will need to be done, you may realize that the scope needs to change. When that happens, you need to create a change request and send it through the change control system.

Change Request

Rob: The quartet cancelled. They had another wedding that day.

Rebecca: Aunt Laura is supposed to do the reading at the service, but after what happened at Uncle Stu's funeral, I think I want someone else to do it.

Rob: Should we really have a pan flute player? I'm beginning to think it might be overkill.

Rebecca: Maybe we should hold off printing the invitations until this stuff is worked out.

Kathleen: OK, let's think about exactly how we want to do this. I think we need to be sure about how we want the service to go before we do any more printing.

The Activity Sequencing process puts everything in order

Now that we know what we have to do to make the wedding a success, we need to focus on the order of the work. Kathleen sat down with all of the activities she had defined for the wedding and decided to figure out exactly how they needed to happen. That's where she used the **Activity Sequencing** process.

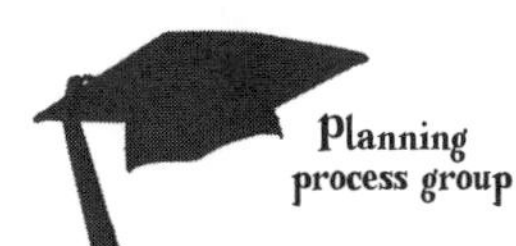

The **activity attribute list** she had created had most of the predecessors and successors necessary written in it. Her **milestone list** had major pieces of work written down and there were a couple of changes to the scope she had discovered along the way that were approved and ready to go.

Inputs

This includes information about each activity, including known predecessors and successors.

Activity List

Activity Attributes

Milestone List

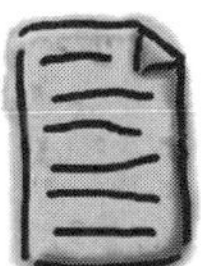

Change Request

When Kathleen realized Rob and Rebecca were going to need another limo to take the bridesmaids to the reception hall, she put that change through change control—including running everything by Rebecca's mother—and it was approved.

Rob and Rebecca had asked that the invitations be printed at least three months in advance to be sure that everyone had time to RSVP. That's a milestone on Kathleen's list.

Diagram the relationship between activities

One way to visualize the way activities relate is to create a network diagram. Kathleen created this one to show how the activities involved in producing the invitations depend on one other.

Showing the activities in rectangles and their relationships as arrows is called a **Precedence Diagramming Method (PDM)**.

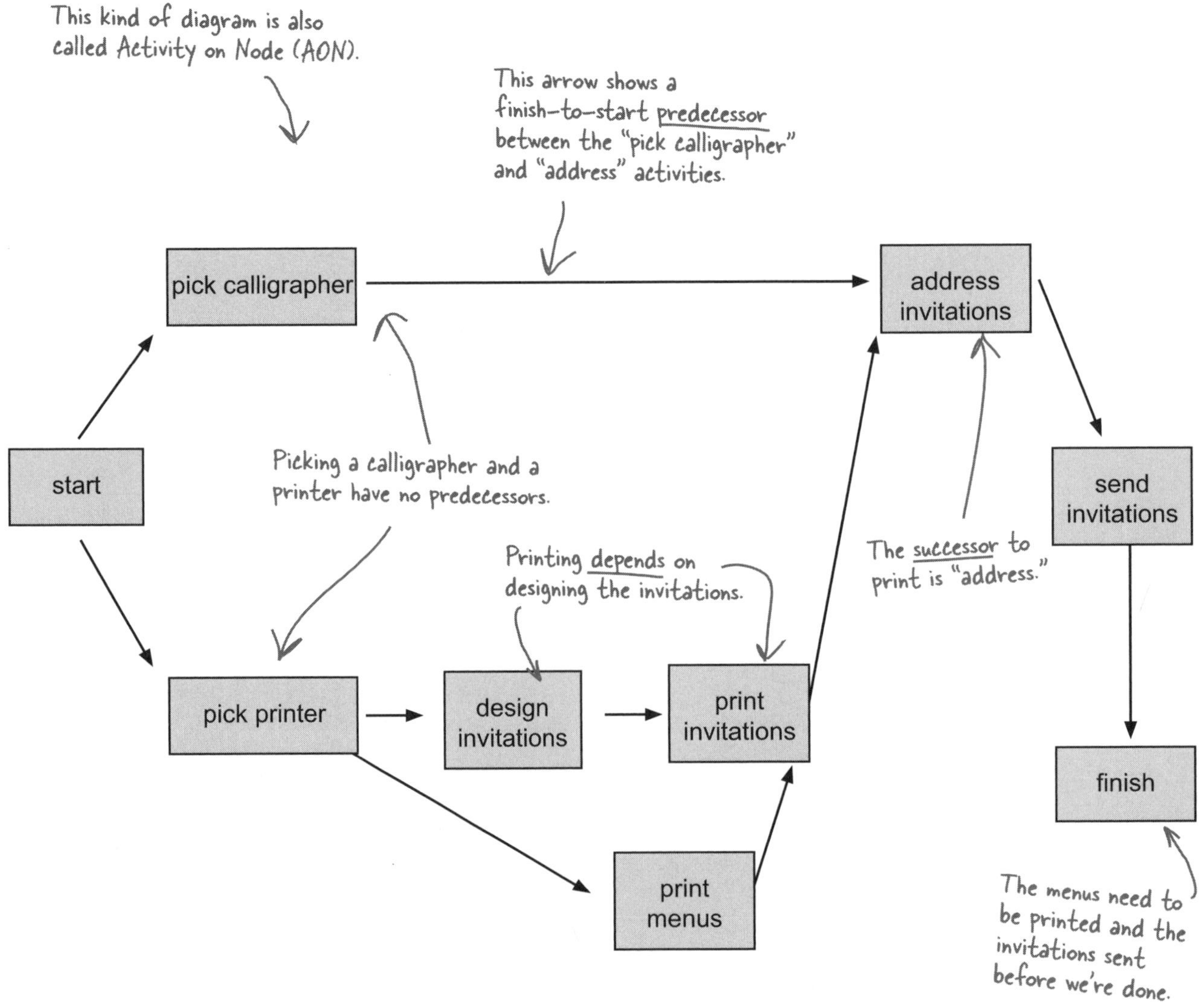

Another way to show how tasks relate

This is the same set of activities as on the previous page, but shown using the **Arrow Diagramming Method (ADM)**. The main difference is that the activities are written on arrows when you create this kind of diagram.

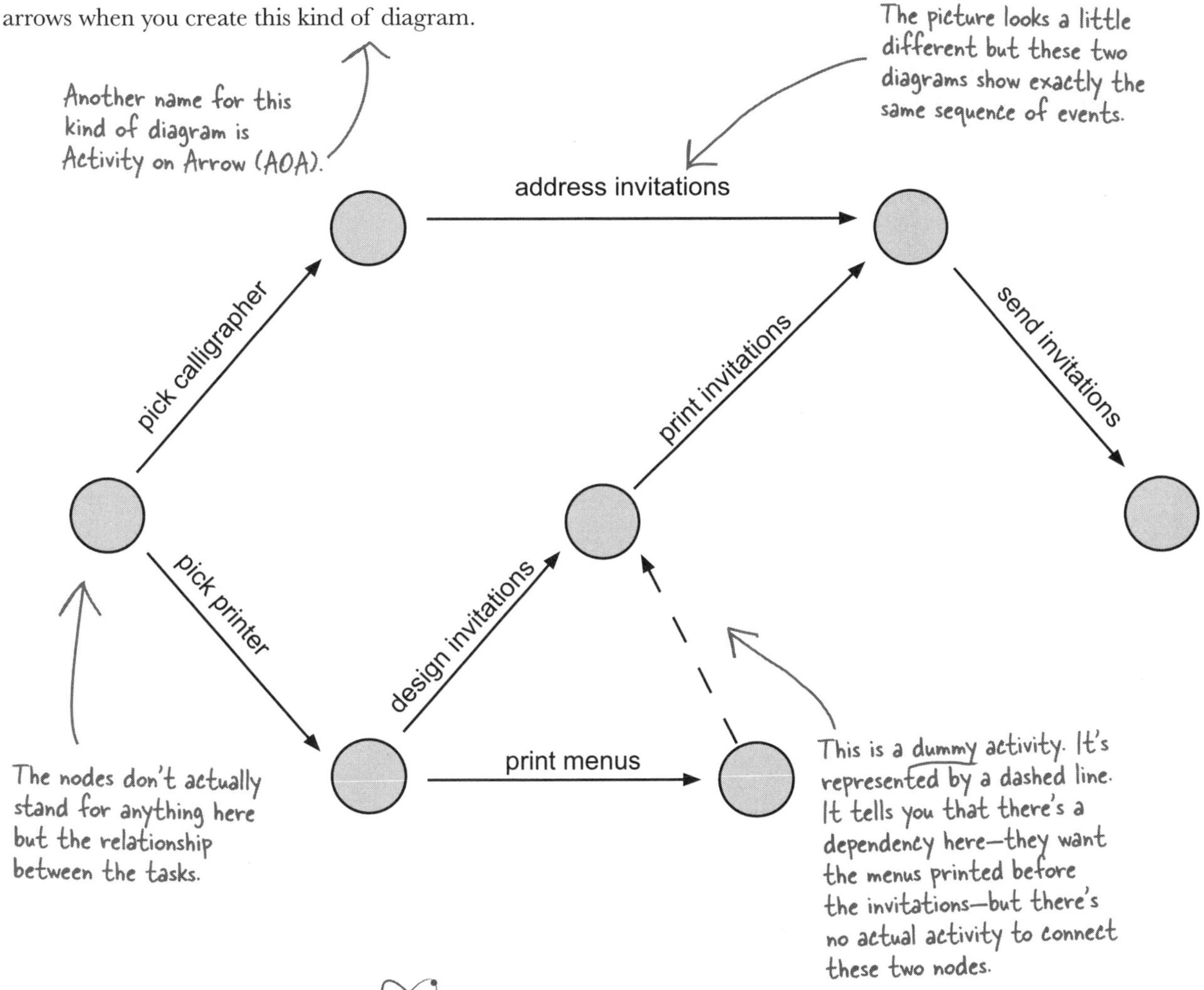

Another name for this kind of diagram is Activity on Arrow (AOA).

The picture looks a little different but these two diagrams show exactly the same sequence of events.

address invitations

pick calligrapher

print invitations

send invitations

pick printer

design invitations

print menus

The nodes don't actually stand for anything here but the relationship between the tasks.

This is a dummy activity. It's represented by a dashed line. It tells you that there's a dependency here—they want the menus printed before the invitations—but there's no actual activity to connect these two nodes.

BRAIN POWER

Can you see benefits to using an ADM diagram over a PDM diagram? When might you use one instead of the other?

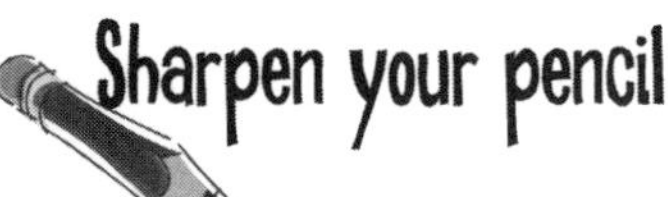

You'll need to know how to turn a table of nodes into a network diagram, so here's your chance to get some practice! Here's a list of nodes for a PDM network diagram. Try drawing the diagram based on it:

Name	Predecessor
Start	—
A	Start
B	A
C	B
D	Start
E	D
F	B
G	C
H	D
I	E, H
Finish	F, G, I

Now try an ADM network diagram! Here's a list of nodes for one:

Use a dashed line to show dummy activities—they show you dependencies between nodes that don't have activities between them.

Node	Dummy?
Start–1	No
1–2	No
2–3	Yes
Start–5	No
5–4	No
4–3	No
3–End	No
5–6	Yes
6–End	No

Answers on page 286.

More tools for sequencing

The most common kind of predecessor is the Finish to Start. It means that one task needs to be completed before another one can start. There are a few other kinds of predecessors, though. They can all be used in network diagrams to show the order of activities. The three main kinds of predecessor are **Finish to Start** (**FS**), **Start to Start** (**SS**) and **Finish to Finish** (**FF**).

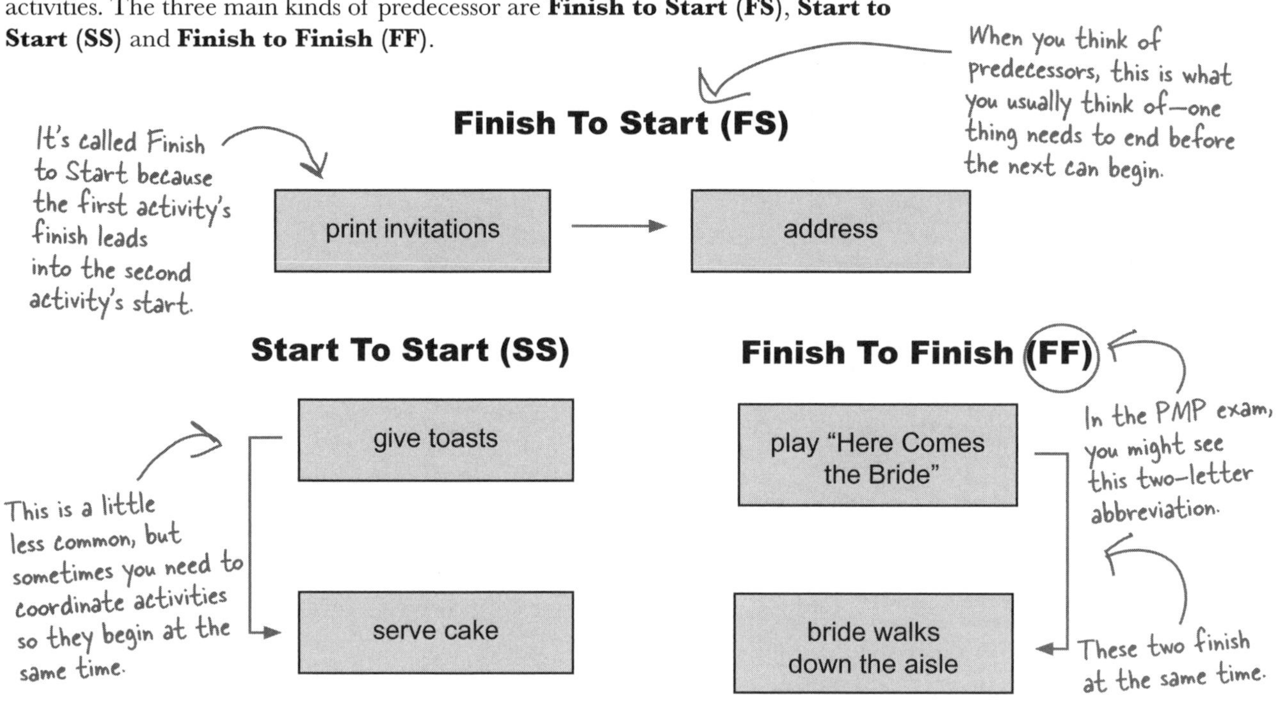

External predecessors

Sometimes your project will depend on things outside the work you are doing. For the wedding, we are depending on the wedding party before us to be out of the reception hall in time for us to decorate. The decoration of the reception hall then depends on that as an external predecessor.

Discretionary predecessors

Rob and Rebecca really want the bridesmaids to arrive at the reception before the couple. There's no necessity there—it's just a matter of preference. For the exam, know that you should set discretionary predecessors based on your knowledge of the best practices for getting the job done.

Mandatory predecessors

You can't address an invitation that hasn't been printed yet. So, printing invitations is a mandatory predecessor for addressing them. Mandatory predecessors are the kind that have to exist just because of the nature of the work.

Leads and lags

Sometimes you need to give some extra time between activities. **Lag time** is when you purposefully put a delay between the predecessor task and the successor. For example, when the bride and her father dance, everybody waits a while before they join them.

Lead time is when you give a successor task some time to get started before the predecessor finishes. So you might want the caterer preparing dessert an hour before everybody is eating dinner.

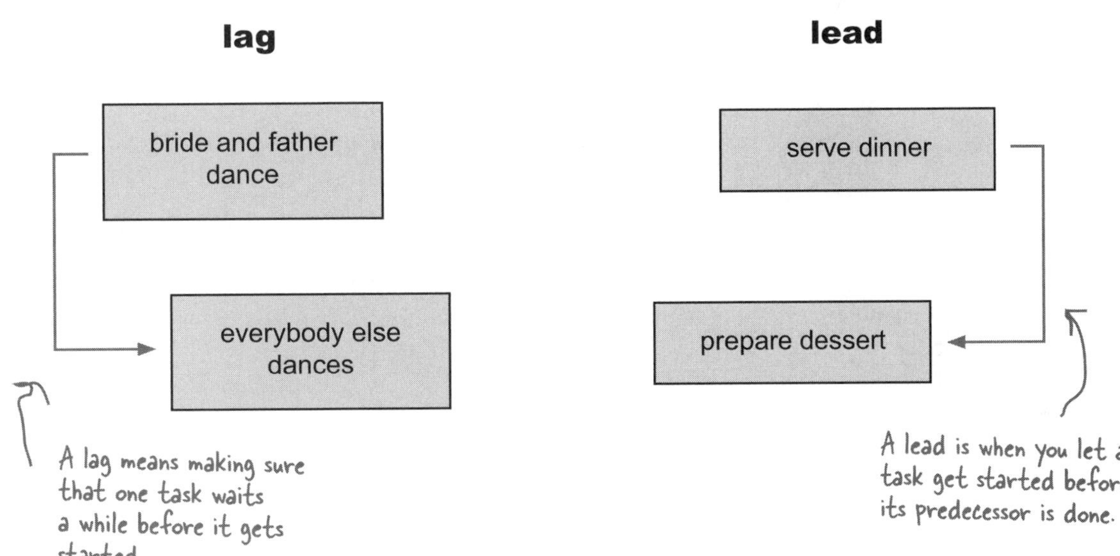

there are no Dumb Questions

Q: Where do you get the predecessor information to figure out your network diagram?

A: Your activity attribute list should list the predecessors and successors for each activity. As you build the network diagram you might discover new predecessors as well. Your project team will determine the predecessors necessary for each of the activities.

Q: What about Start to Finish predecessors?

A: It's possible for activities to require that a task has been started before it can finish. An example might be that singing couldn't start until after the music had started. But tasks like that are pretty rare and almost never show up in network diagrams.

Q: When do you use ADM and when do you use PDM diagrams?

A: Most often people use PDM diagrams these days. ADMs only represent Finish to Start relationships, so they can cause some problems if you have more complex relationships to show. Sometimes, it's necessary to put dummy tasks in an Arrow Diagram to show how tasks relate without using the other kinds of predecessors.

You should still think of things in sequence.

For the test, it's important to know the order of these processes. And, even though you might do it all at once, you probably spend some time thinking about each of these things.

What's the advantage of thinking about activity definition and sequencing separately?

Create the network diagram

As you sequence the activities, you will find new activities that need to be added and new attributes for activities that you didn't know about. So, while the main product of this process is the network diagram, you also produce changes to all of the activity definition documents.

Outputs

The network diagram can be either PDM or ADM.

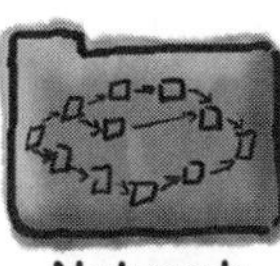

Sometimes sequencing will show that two tasks rely on each other. If you find new predecessors or successors, their attributes will need to be changed.

If you find a new activity while sequencing, updates need to be made to the activity list.

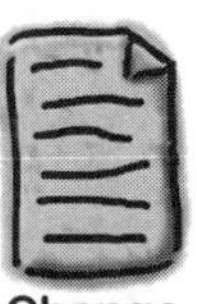

You could find additions to scope or changes to other management plans while creating your network diagram. Those are tracked as change requests and sent back to change control.

Rob and Rebecca have resource problems

Getting a handle on all of the tasks that have to be done is a great start. But it's not enough to know the tasks and the order they come in. Before you can put a schedule together, you need to know who is going to do each job, and the things they need available to them in order to do it! Those are **resources**, and getting a handle on them is a very important part of time management.

Resources are people, equipment, locations, or anything else that you need in order to do all of the activities that you planned for. Every activity in your activity list needs to have resources assigned to it.

What do you need to know about a project before you can assign resources?

What you need to estimate resources

Good news: you've already seen most of the inputs to the **Activity Resource Estimation process** already! Before you can assign resources to your project, you need to know which ones you're authorized to use on your project. That's an input, and it's called **Resource Availability**. You'll also need the activity list that you created earlier, and you'll need to know about how your organization typically handles resources. Once you've got a handle on these things, you're set for resource estimation.

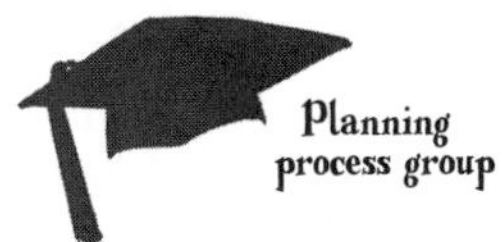

You need to know what the resources are going to do! That's what these are for—good thing you created them earlier in Activity Definition.

You probably already guessed that these three inputs would be here—they show up for most of these planning processes!

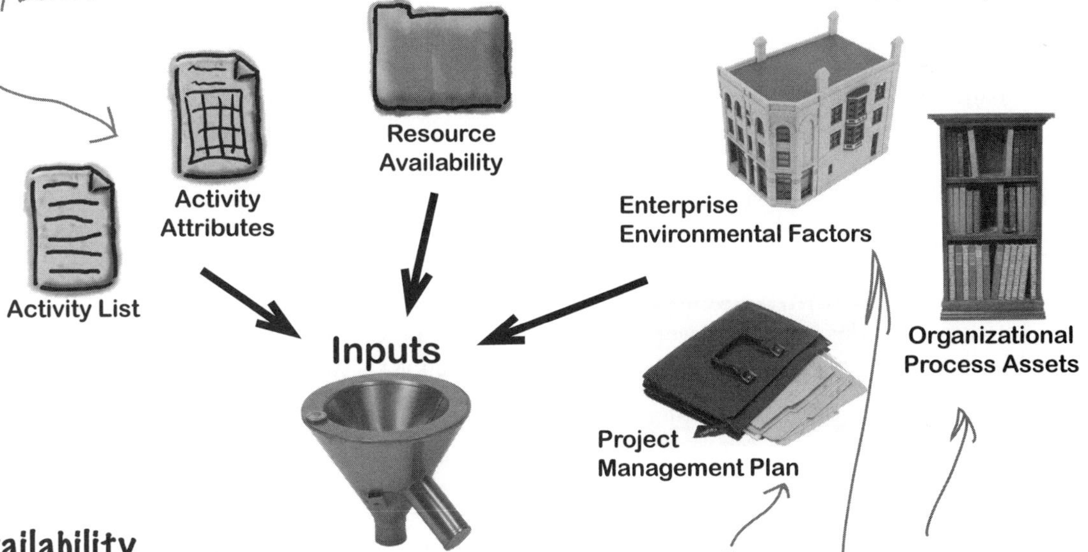

Activity List

Activity Attributes

Resource Availability

Enterprise Environmental Factors

Organizational Process Assets

Project Management Plan

Inputs

How could policies, lessons learned, and historical information help you assign resources to your project?

Resource Availability

Means information about what resources you can use on your project and when they're available to you. Don't forget that some resources like consultants or training rooms have to be scheduled in advance, and they might only be available at certain times. You'll need to know this before you can finish planning your project.

A June wedding is harder to plan than one in December, because the wedding halls are all booked up. That's a resource constraint!

Resource Availability is the only new input to the Activity Resource Estimation process. You've already seen the rest of the inputs.

Estimating the resources

The goal of **Activity Resource Estimating** is to assign resources to each activity in the activity list. There are **five tools and techniques** for the Activity Resource Estimating process. Some of them have technical-sounding names, but they're all actually pretty sensible when you think about it. They should all make sense to you when you think about what you have to do when you have to figure out what resources your project needs.

Expert Judgment means bringing in experts who have done this sort of work before and getting their opinions on what resources are needed.

Alternatives Analysis means considering several different options for how you assign resources. This includes varying the number of resources as well as the kind of resources you use.

Published Estimating Data is something that project managers in a lot of industries use to help them figure out how many resources they need. They rely on articles, books, journals, and periodicals that collect, analyze, and publish data from other people's projects.

Project Management Software like Microsoft Project will often have features designed to help project managers play around with resources and constraints and find the best combination of assignments for the project.

Bottom-Up Estimating is a technique that you may have used before without even knowing it! It means breaking down complex activities into pieces, and working out the resource assignments for each of those simpler pieces using the other four tools and techniques.

there are no Dumb Questions

Q: In my company, I'm given my resources—I don't get to assign them myself. How do these tools help me?

A: When you work in a functional organization or some matrixed organizations, you don't have as much freedom in selecting resources as you do in a projectized organization. But that doesn't mean these tools aren't important! Whoever is doing the resource selection and assignment should be using them. And they'll be on the PMP exam, so you need to understand them all.

Q: Is choosing a consultant, contractor, or vendor to do project work part of resource estimation?

A: When you're working with a resource outside your company, like a contractor or consultant, you consider that resource the same way you consider any other resource. But actually negotiating the contract and selecting the vendor is not part of the Activity Resource Estimation process. There's a whole other knowledge area for that—Procurement Management.

Q: What if I need a resource that isn't available when my project needs it?

A: This is one of the reasons that project management is a tough job! When you need a resource that isn't available, you need to negotiate for it. Think about it... your project depends on getting this resource, and without it your project won't get done. You need it, or you'll face delays! You have to do whatever you can to get that resource for your project.

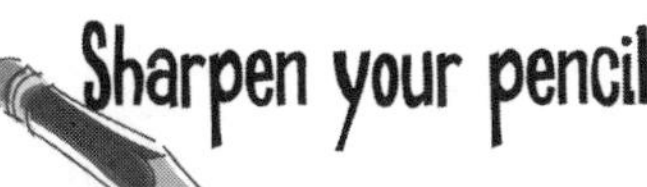

You'll need to understand the different Activity Resource Estimation tools and techniques for the exam. Look at each of these scenarios and write down which of the five Activity Resource Estimation tools and techniques is being used.

1. Kathleen has to figure out what to do for the music at Rob and Rebecca's wedding. She considers using a DJ, a rock band, or a string quartet.

2. The latest issue of Wedding Planner's Journal has an article on working with caterers. It includes a table that shows how many waiters work with various guest-list sizes.

3. There's a national wedding consultant who specializes in Caribbean themed weddings. Kathleen gets in touch with her to ask about menu options.

4. Kathleen downloads and fills out a specialized spreadsheet that a project manager developed to help with wedding planning.

5. There's so much work that has to be done to set up the reception hall that Kathleen has to break it down into five different activities in order to assign jobs.

6. Kathleen asks Rob and Rebecca to visit several different caterers and sample various potential items for the menu.

7. Kathleen calls up her friend who knows specifics of the various venues in their area for advice on which one would work best.

→ Answers on page 283.

Figuring out how long the project will take

Once you're done with Activity Resource Estimating, you've got everything you need to figure out how long each activity will take. That's done in a process called **Activity Duration Estimating**. This is where you look at each activity in the activity list, consider the scope and the resources, and estimate how long it will take to perform.

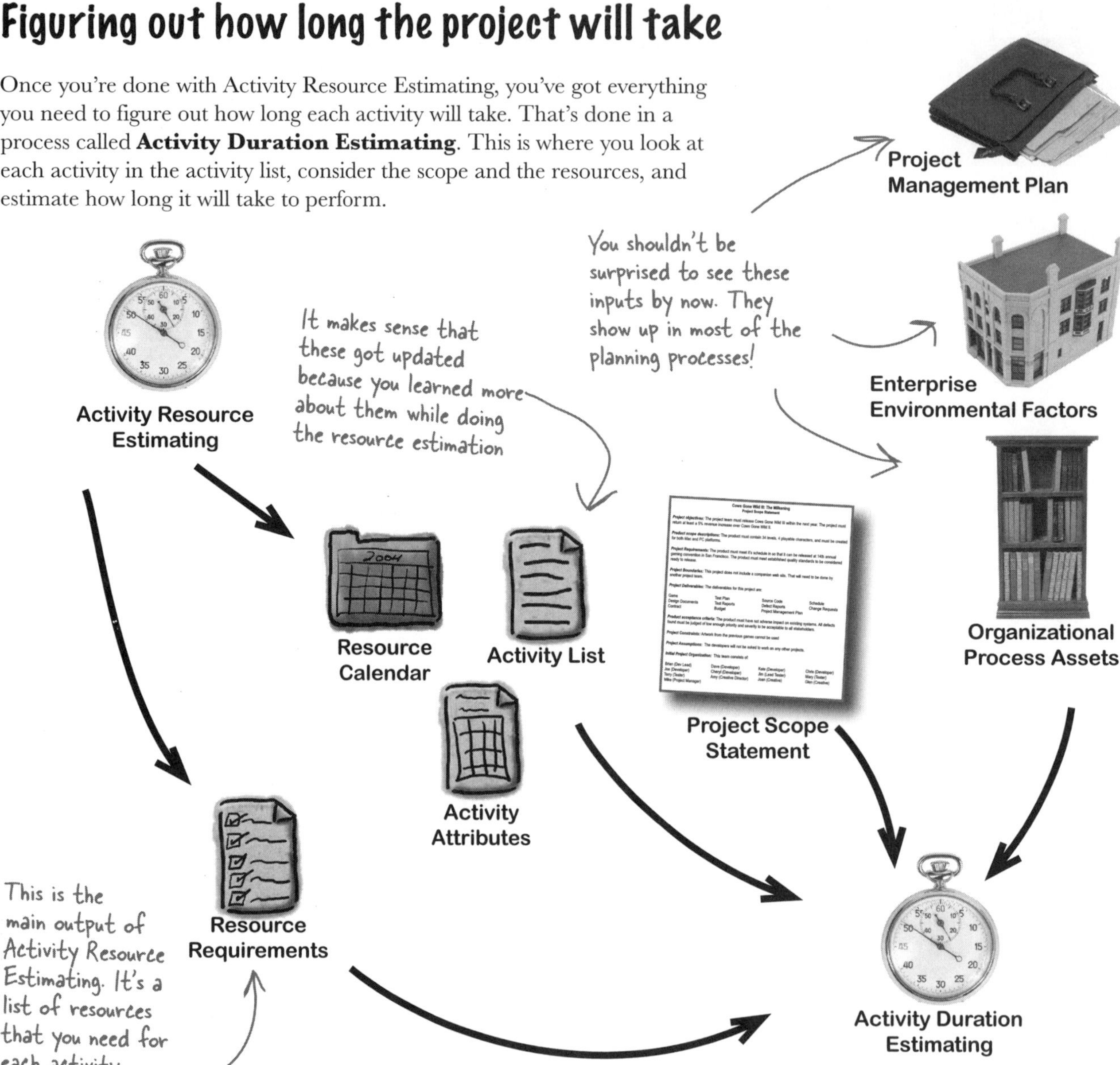

The outputs of Activity Resource Estimating are immediately used as inputs for Activity Duration Estimating, which is where your estimates come from.

You'll need to understand the various inputs and outputs for each process for the exam. Write down what you think each of the inputs to the Activity Duration Estimating process will be used for when you actually sit down and estimate how long each activity will take.

1. Activity List and Activity Attributes

2. Activity Resource Requirements

3. Resource Calendar

4. Project Management Plan

5. Project Scope Statement

6. Enterprise Environmental Factors

7. Organizational Process Assets

You'll need to understand the various inputs and outputs for each process for the exam. Write down what you think each of the inputs to the Activity Duration Estimating process will be used for when you actually sit down and estimate how long each activity will take.

You need these because the goal of this process is to estimate the duration of each activity.

1. Activity List and Activity Attributes

Contains information about the activities that are being estimated

The more resources you add to an activity, the less time it takes.

But sometimes adding people won't get the job done any faster! Remember, nine women can't have a baby in one month.

2. Activity Resource Requirements

Shows which resources are assigned to each activity

You need to know when the resources are available, because that's going to impact the final estimate for the activity.

3. Resource Calendar

Shows the availability, capabilities and skills of each human resource, or the quantity and availability of equipment and other resources

4. Project Management Plan

Gives the information about the rest of the project

The project management plan contains activity cost estimates, which will be very useful here. It also has the risk register, which you'll learn about in Chapter 11.

5. Project Scope Statement

Lists constraints and assumptions for each activity

You're probably not the first person in your company to do this sort of project. Information from people around you will be very valuable when you're creating estimates.

6. Enterprise Environmental Factors

Other people or databases in my company can help with estimation

This input is always about looking elsewhere in your organization for information.

7. Organizational Process Assets

Contains historical information and records from past projects

Any time you see this, think about historical information and project records!

The more you know about how past projects went, the more accurate your estimates will be.

Estimation tools and techniques

Estimating the duration of an activity means starting with the information you have about that activity and the resources that are assigned to it, and then working with the project team to come up with an estimate. Most of the time you'll start with a rough estimate and then refine it (maybe a few times!) to make it more accurate. You'll use these five tools and techniques to create the most accurate estimates.

Expert Judgement will come from your project team members who are familiar with the work that has to be done. If you don't get their opinion, then there's a huge risk that your estimates will be wrong!

Analogous Estimating is when you look at activities from previous projects that were similar to this one and look at how long it took to do similar work before. But this only works if the activities and the project team are similar!

Parametric Estimating means plugging data about your project into a formula, spreadsheet, database, or computer program that comes up with an estimate. The software or formula that you use for parametric estimating is built on a database of actual durations from past projects.

Three-Point Estimates are when you come up with three numbers: a **realistic** estimate that's most likely to occur, an **optimistic** one that represents the best-case scenario, and a **pessimistic** one that represents the worst-case scenario. The final estimate is the average.

Reserve Analysis means adding extra time to the schedule (called a contingency reserve or a buffer) to account for extra risk.

A contingency reserve (or buffer) is money you set aside to deal with stuff you haven't planned for.

Exercise

Each of these scenarios describes a different tool or technique from Activity Duration Estimating. Write down which tool or technique is being described.

1. Kathleen comes up with three estimates (one where everything goes wrong, one where some things go wrong, and one where nothing goes wrong) for printing invitations, and averages them together to come up with a final number. ....

2. There will be two different catering companies at the wedding. Kathleen asks the head chef at each of them to give her an estimate of how long it will take each of them to do the job. ....

3. There's a spreadsheet Kathleen always uses to figure out how long it takes guests to RSVP. She enters the number of guests and their ZIP codes, and it calculates an estimate for her. ....

4. Kathleen's done four weddings that are very similar to Rob and Rebecca's, and in all four of them it took exactly the same amount of time for the caterers to set up the reception hall. ....

Answers on page 283.

Create the duration estimate

You've got a list of activities, you know what resources are needed to actually do each activity, and you've got your estimation tools and techniques... now you have enough to create the estimates! That's the whole point of the **Activity Duration Estimating** process, and it's also the main output.

You don't always know exactly how long an activity will take, so you might end up using a range (like 3 weeks +/– 2 days)

Outputs

The **Activity Duration Estimates** are an estimate of how long each activity in the activity list will take. The estimate can be in hours, days, weeks... any work period is fine, and you'll use different work periods for different jobs. A small job (like booking a DJ) may just take a few hours; a bigger job (like catering—including deciding on a menu, ordering ingredients, cooking food, and serving guests on the big day) could take days.

The Activity Duration Estimate consists of estimates for each activity. It's the main output of the Activity Duration Estimating process.

You'll also learn more about the specific activities while you're estimating them. That's something that always happens—you have to really think through all of the aspects of a task in order to estimate it. So the other output of Activity Duration Estimating is **updates to the Activity Attributes**.

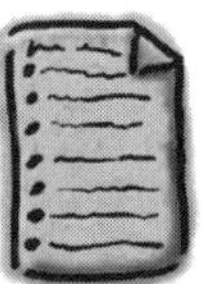
Activity Duration Estimates

Activity Attributes

there are no Dumb Questions

Q: When you use parametric estimation, how does the program or formula know how much to estimate?

A: When someone designs a system for parametric estimation, they collect a lot of data from past projects and condense it into a table or a database. And then they come up with a **heuristic** (like a rule of thumb) that lets you boil your estimation down into just a few parameters that you need to enter. Most successful parametric estimation systems need a lot of time to develop.

Q: Since reserve analysis lets me use buffers, why can't I just put everything I don't know about into the reserve?

A: The idea behind reserve analysis is that there are always unknowns on any project, but you can account for these unknowns by taking your best guess at what's going to go wrong and inserting a buffer. But you can't just make an enormous reserve, because then there's no reason to ever do any estimation! The entire project becomes one big unknown, and that's not particularly useful to anyone.

Q: What's the difference between a duration estimate and an effort estimate?

A: Duration is the amount of time that an activity takes, while effort is the total number of person-hours that are expended. If it takes two people six hours to carve the ice sculpture for the centerpiece of a wedding, the duration is six hours. But since two people worked on it for the whole time, it took twelve person-hours of effort to create!

Back to the wedding

Kathleen's really got a handle on how long things are going to take, but that's not enough to get the job done. She's still got some work to do before she's got the whole project under control.

Rob and Rebecca know where they want to get married, and they've got the place booked now.

But what about the caterer? They have no idea who's going to be providing the food.

And what about the band that they want? Will the timing with their schedule work out?

If the caterers come too early, the food will sit around under heat lamps! But too late, and the band won't have time to play. I just don't see how we'll ever work this all out.

It's not easy to plan for a lot of resources when they have tight time restrictions and overlapping constraints. How would you figure out a schedule that makes everything fit together?

Bringing it all together

The **Schedule Development process** is the core of time management. It's the process where you put it all together—where you take everything you've done so far and combine it into one final schedule for the whole project. A lot of project managers consider this the most important part of their job. The schedule is your most important tool for managing a project.

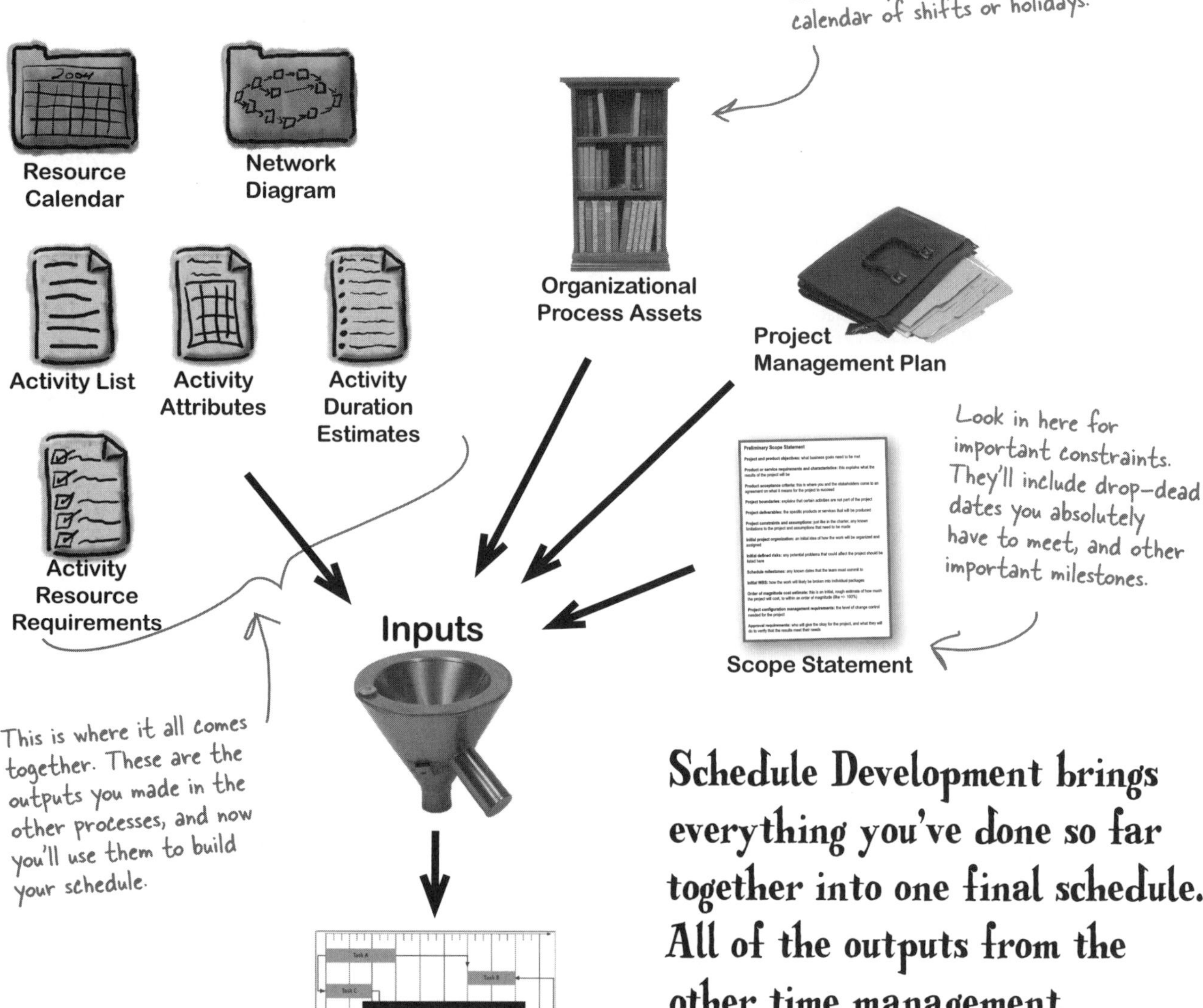

Schedule Development brings everything you've done so far together into one final schedule. All of the outputs from the other time management processes are inputs to Schedule Development.

Hold on! I don't really work like that all the time when I'm managing projects! I figure some things out, then I go back and make changes. Like what if I'm working on the schedule and I realize I need to change my resources? This says I should have figured that all out by now, right?

Don't worry, even though you're done with the Activity Resource Estimating process, you're not done with the resources.

You're never going to have the complete resource picture until you're done building the schedule. And the same goes for your activity list and duration estimates, too! It's only when you lay out the schedule that you'll figure out that some of your activities and durations didn't quite work.

That's why the processes have the word "Estimating" in their names! Because you're taking an educated guess, but you won't know for sure until you've actually developed the schedule.

Each of the processes allows updates to an output from a previous one, so when you discover changes, you can include them in the schedule.

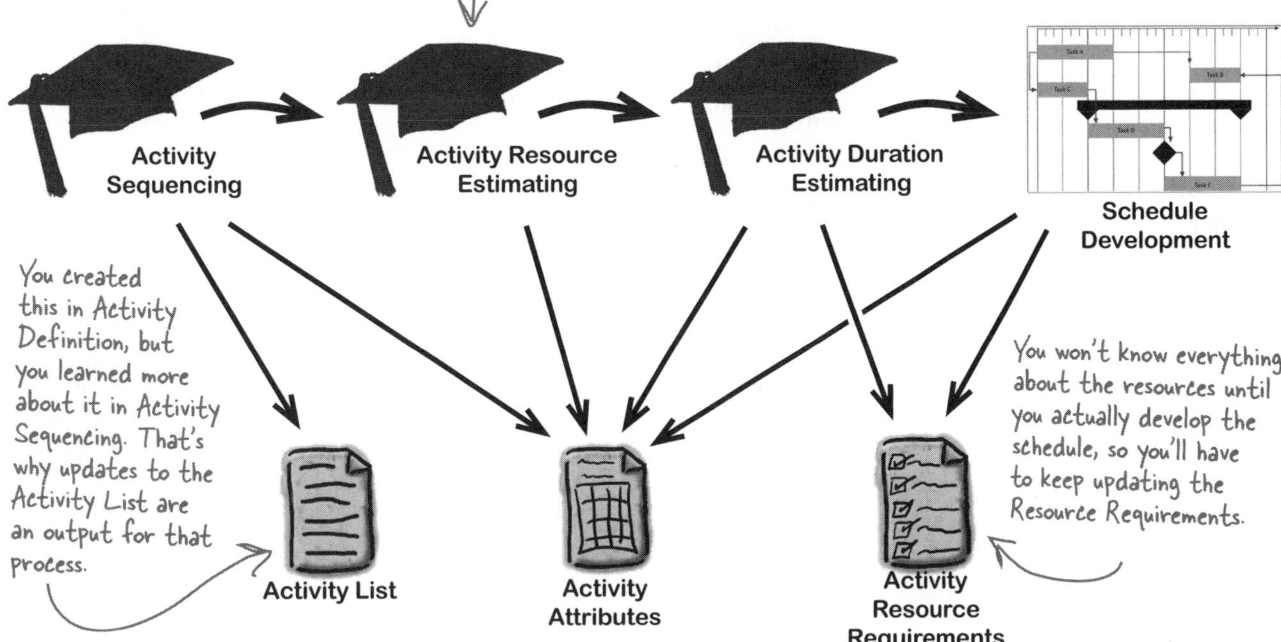

Question Clinic: The "Which-comes-next" Question

If you want to pass the PMP exam, you'll need to have a good feel for the order that the processes are performed in, because you'll be asked a lot of "Which-comes -next" questions! These are questions that quiz you on how the processes fit together into one big framework. These questions aren't hard, but they can be a little misleading.

Hold on – this question doesn't look like it's asking about the order of the processes! But a lot of Which-comes-next questions describe a situation and ask you what you'd do.

Don't be thrown if the question asks about an industry you don't know much about. All projects follow the same processes.

In other words, you've used decomposition and created an activity list. These are part of the Activity Definition process.

27. You're the project manager for a highway construction project. You've analyzed the work that has to be done and come up with a list of activities. You consulted with the project sponsor in order to find out any important milestones that you need to meet. What's the next thing that you do?

A. Create the project schedule

B. Perform the Activity Definition process

C. Consult your project management plan to figure out how to handle any schedule changes

D. Figure out the dependencies between activities and create a network diagram

The Milestone List is an input that you've seen before.

The Schedule Development process needs more than an activity list and resource availability.

The question described the Activity Definition process, so you've already performed it.

You only do this during Schedule Control, but since there's no schedule yet, there's nothing to control.

This answer describes Activity Sequencing, which happens after Activity Definition and takes the Activity List and Milestone List as inputs. That's the right answer.

The Which-comes-next question doesn't always look like it's asking about the order of the processes! Keep an eye out for questions that describe inputs, outputs, tools, or techniques and ask you what you're supposed to do next.

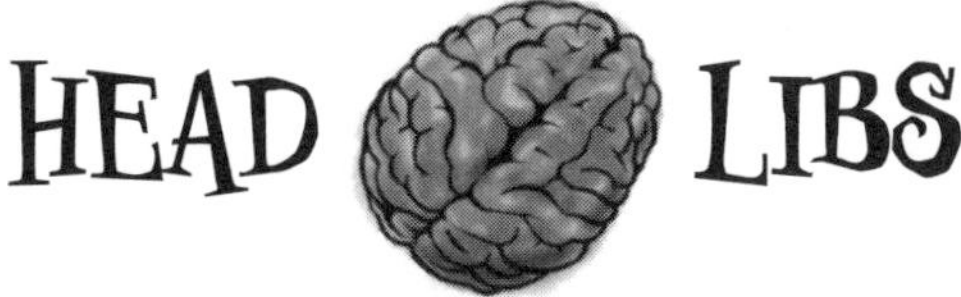

Fill in the blanks to come up with your own "Which-comes-next" question! Start by thinking of a process to be the correct answer, and then figure out which process came right before it—that's the one you'll describe in the question!

You are managing a ______________________ (an industry or the name of a project). You've finished creating the ______________________ (an output from the previous process), you've come up with ______________________ (another output from the previous process) and you've just finished ______________________ (a tool or technique from the previous process). What's the next thing you do?

A. ______________________ (the correct answer - a brief description of what happens during the process)

B. ______________________ (a description of a different process)

C. ______________________ (the name of a tool or technique that's part of a totally different process)

D. ______________________ (the name of an irrelevant process)

Join the Head First PMP community at **http://www.headfirstlabs.com/PMP** You can add your Head Libs answer, and see what Head Libs other project managers came up with!

One thing leads to another

Aunt Laura is a vegetarian. That won't be a problem, right?

Rob thought this was just a little problem...

Rebecca: Well, let's see. What menu did we give to the caterers?

Rob: We didn't give it to them yet, because we won't have the final menu until everyone RSVPs and lets us know which entrée they want.

Rebecca: But they can't RSVP because we haven't sent out the invitations! What's holding that up?

Rob: We're still waiting to get them back from the printer. We can't send them out if we don't have them yet!

Rebecca: Oh no! I still have to tell the printer what to print on the invitations, and what paper to use.

Rob: But you were waiting on that until we finished the guest list.

Rebecca: What a mess!

... but it turns out to be a lot bigger than either Rob or Rebecca realized at first! How'd a question about one guest's meal lead to such a huge mess?

Can you think of a situation where a delay in an activity early on in a project can lead to a problem in a later activity, which leads to another problem in another activity, leading to a cascade of problems that makes the project late?

Use the Critical Path Method to avoid big problems

The **Critical Path Method** is an important tool for keeping your projects on track. Every network diagram has something called the **critical path**. It's the string of activities that, if you add up all of the durations, is longer than any other path through the network. It usually starts with the first activity in the network and usually ends with the last one.

The reason that the critical path is, well, *critical*, is that every single activity on the path must finish on time in order for the project to come in on time. A ***delay in any one of the critical path activities*** will cause the **entire project to be delayed**.

The Critical Path is the string of activities that will delay the whole project if any one of them is delayed.

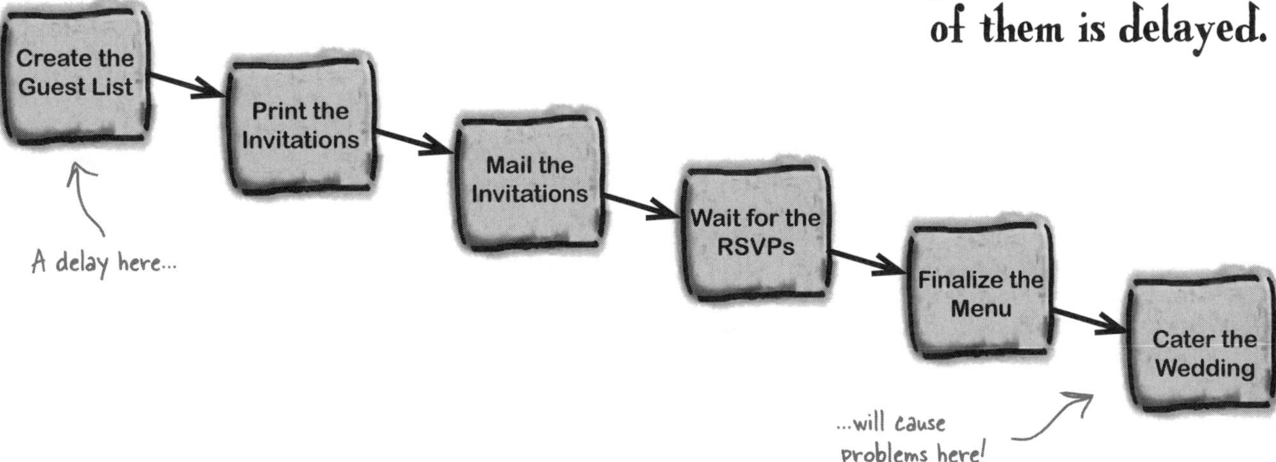

How does knowing your critical path help?

Knowing where your critical path is can give you a lot of freedom. If you know an activity is *not* on the critical path, then you know a delay in that activity may not *necessarily* delay the project.

This can really help you handle emergency situations. Even better, it means that if you need to bring your project in earlier, you know that adding resources to the critical path will be much more effective than adding them elsewhere.

How to find the critical path

It's easy to find the critical path in any project! With a little practice, you'll get the hang of it. Of course, on a large project with dozens or hundreds of tasks, you'll probably use software like Microsoft Project to find the critical path for you. But when it does, it's following the same exact steps that you'll follow here.

1 Start with an activity network diagram.

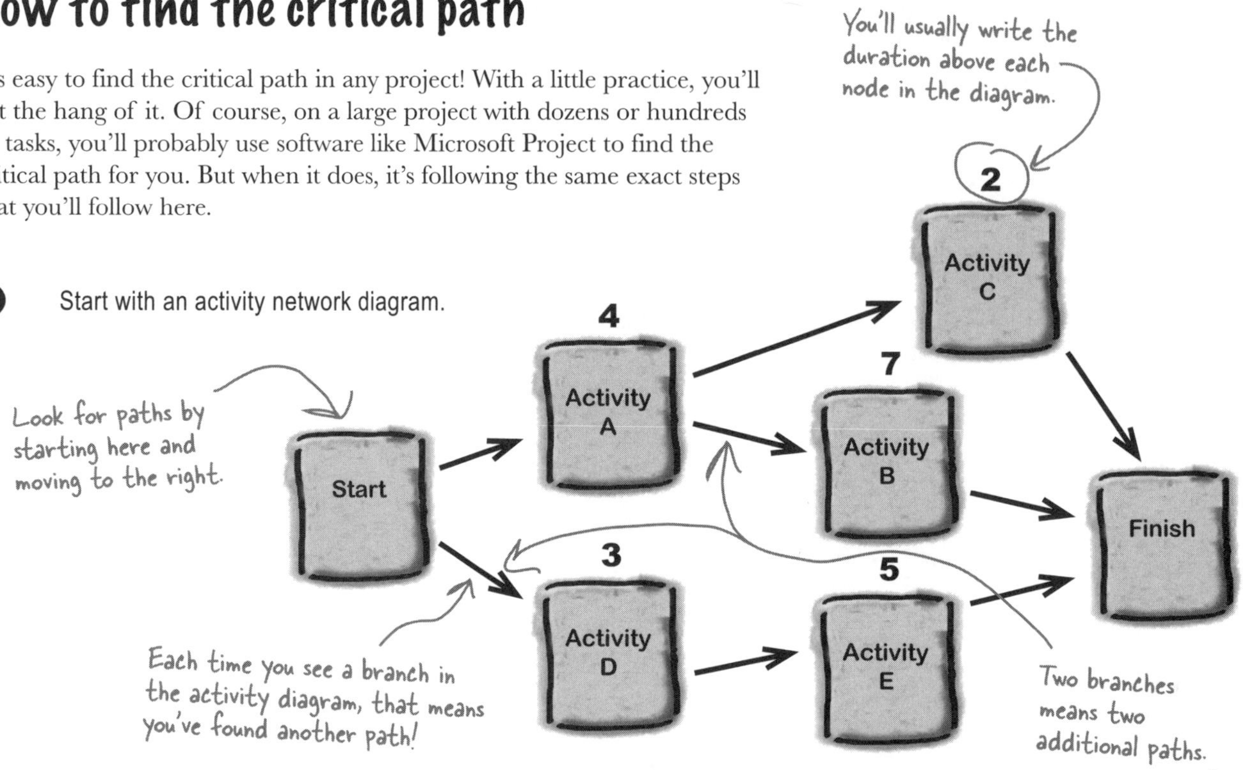

You'll usually write the duration above each node in the diagram.
2
Activity C
4
Activity A
7
Activity B
Start
Finish
3
Activity D
5
Activity E
Look for paths by starting here and moving to the right.
Each time you see a branch in the activity diagram, that means you've found another path!
Two branches means two additional paths.

2 Find all of the paths in the diagram. A path is any string of activities that goes from the start of the project to the end.

Start ⟶ Activity A ⟶ Activity B ⟶ Finish

Start ⟶ Activity A ⟶ Activity C ⟶ Finish

Start ⟶ Activity D ⟶ Activity E ⟶ Finish

3 Find the duration of each path by adding up the durations of each of the activities on the path.

Start ⟶ Activity A ⟶ Activity B ⟶ Finish = 4 + 2 = **6**

Start ⟶ Activity A ⟶ Activity C ⟶ Finish = 4 + 7 = **11**

Start ⟶ Activity D ⟶ Activity E ⟶ Finish = 3 + 5 = **8**

This path has a duration of 11, which is longer than the other two (6 and 8). So it's the critical path!

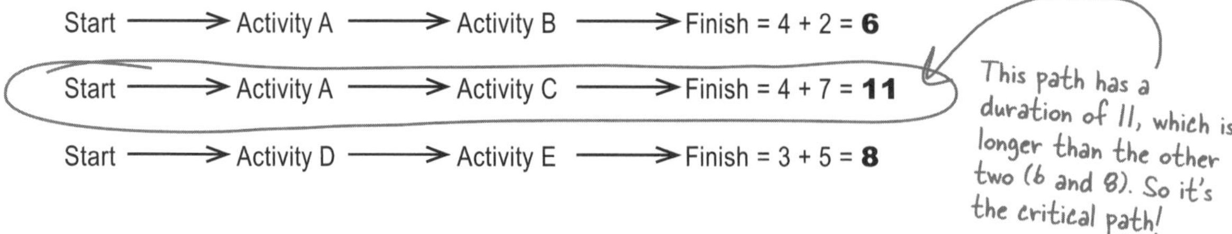

The critical path is the one with the longest duration!

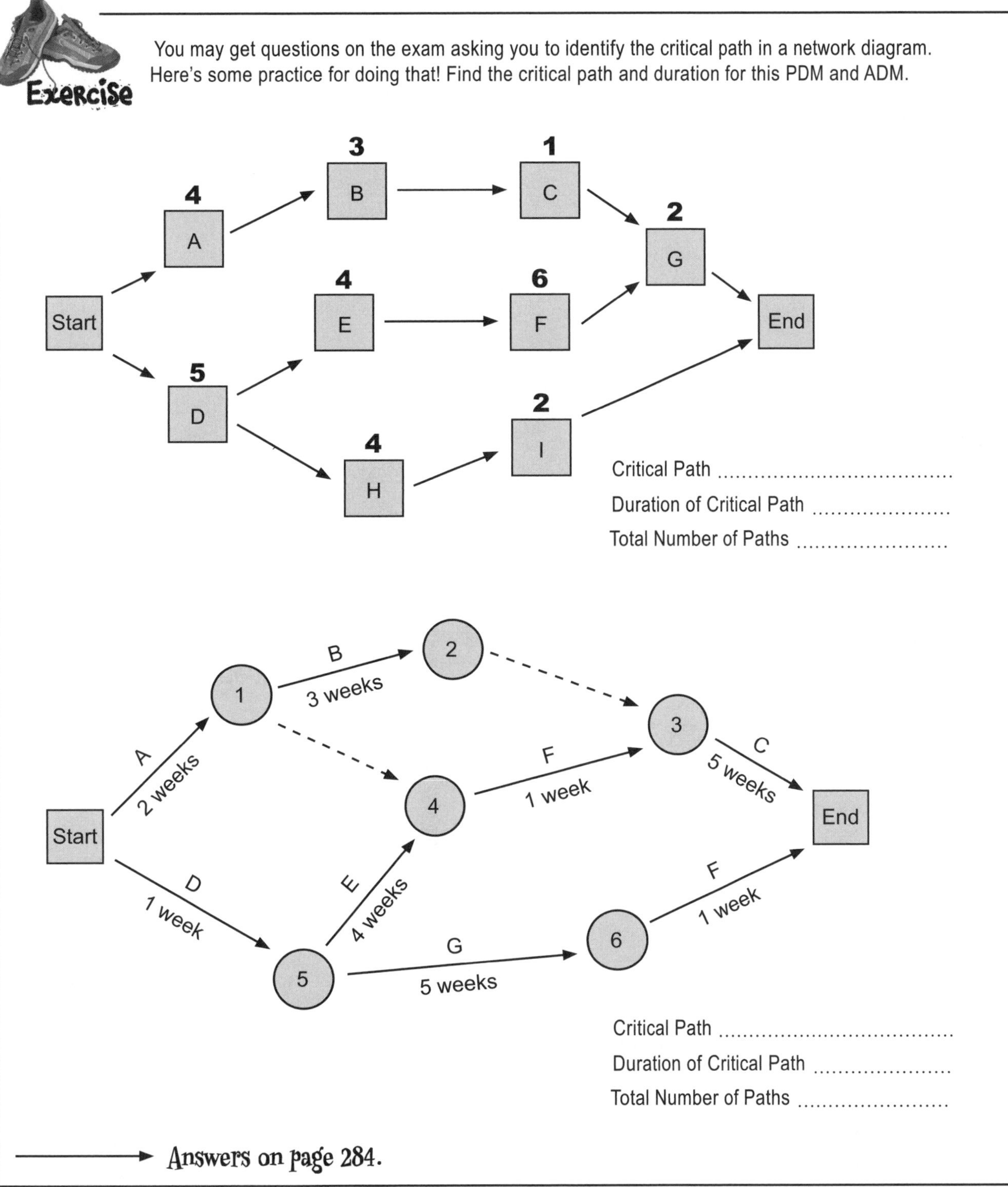

Answers on page 284.

Finding the float for any activity

The goal is to find the float for each activity. We're not really concerned with finding a total float for each path—we're looking at the activities independently.

Once you've figured out the critical path, there's all sorts of useful stuff you can do with it. One of the most useful things you can do is calculate the **float**. The float for any activity is the amount of time that it can slip before it causes your project to be delayed. You might also see the word "slack" – it's the same thing.

Luckily, it's not hard to figure out the float for any activity in a network diagram. First you write down the list of all of the paths in the diagram, and you identify the critical path. The float for every activity in the critical path is zero.

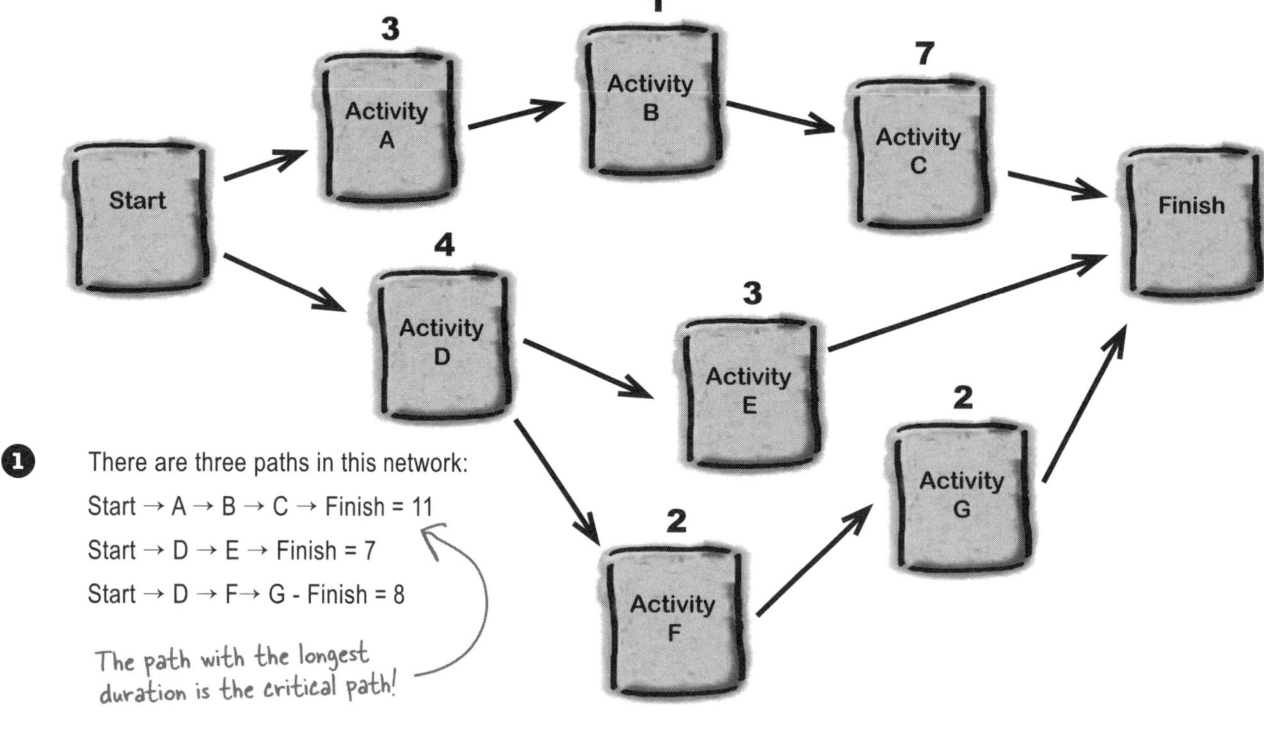

1. There are three paths in this network:
   Start → A → B → C → Finish = 11
   Start → D → E → Finish = 7
   Start → D → F→ G - Finish = 8

The path with the longest duration is the critical path!

2. The float for each of the activities on the critical path is zero.

Start
3
Activity A
Float=0
1
Activity B
Float=0
7
Activity C
Float=0
Finish

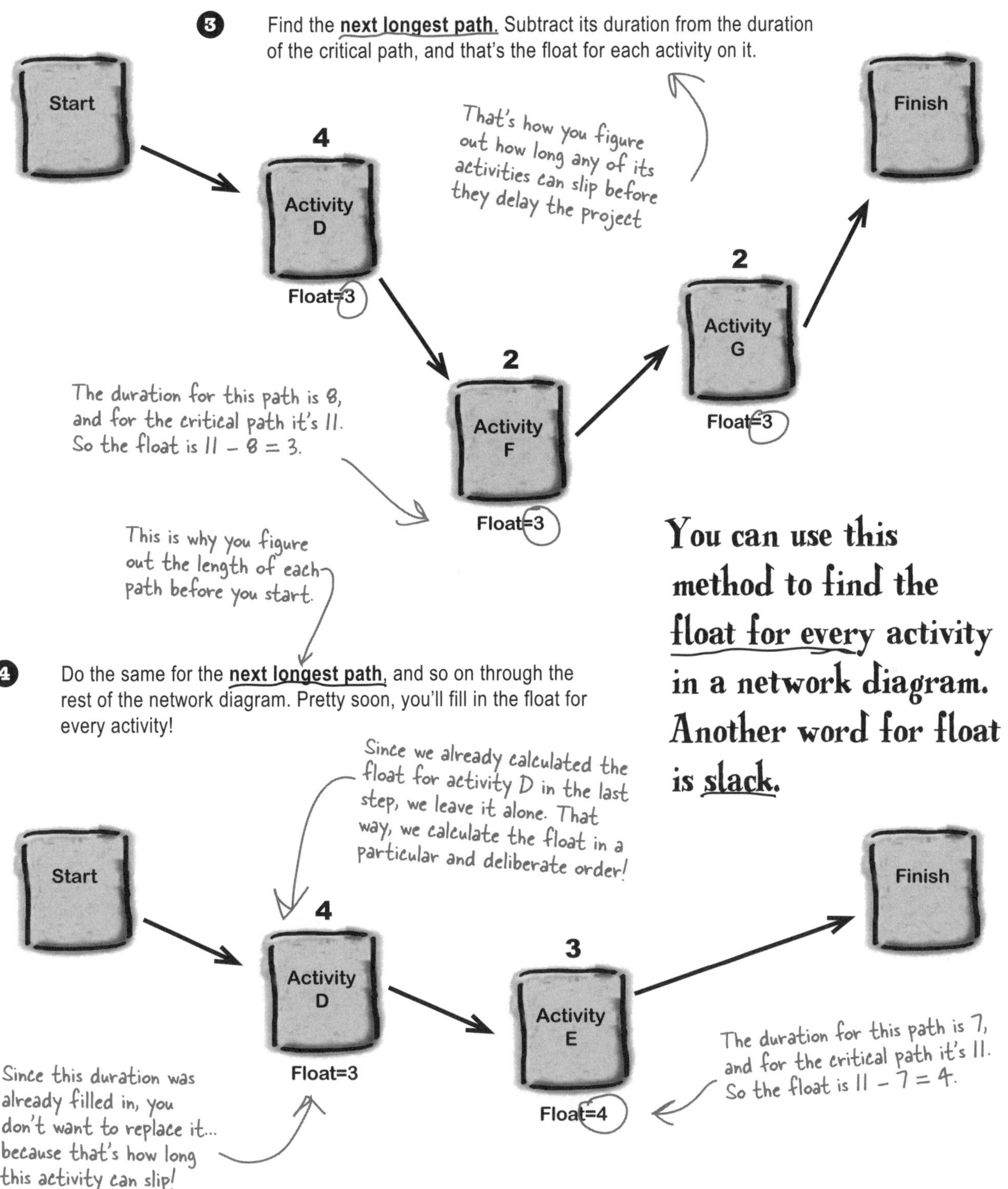

You can use this method to find the float for every activity in a network diagram. Another word for float is slack.

Float tells you how much extra time you have

Once you know the float, you know how much play you have in your schedule. If an activity has a float of 2 days, it can slip by that much without affecting the end date.

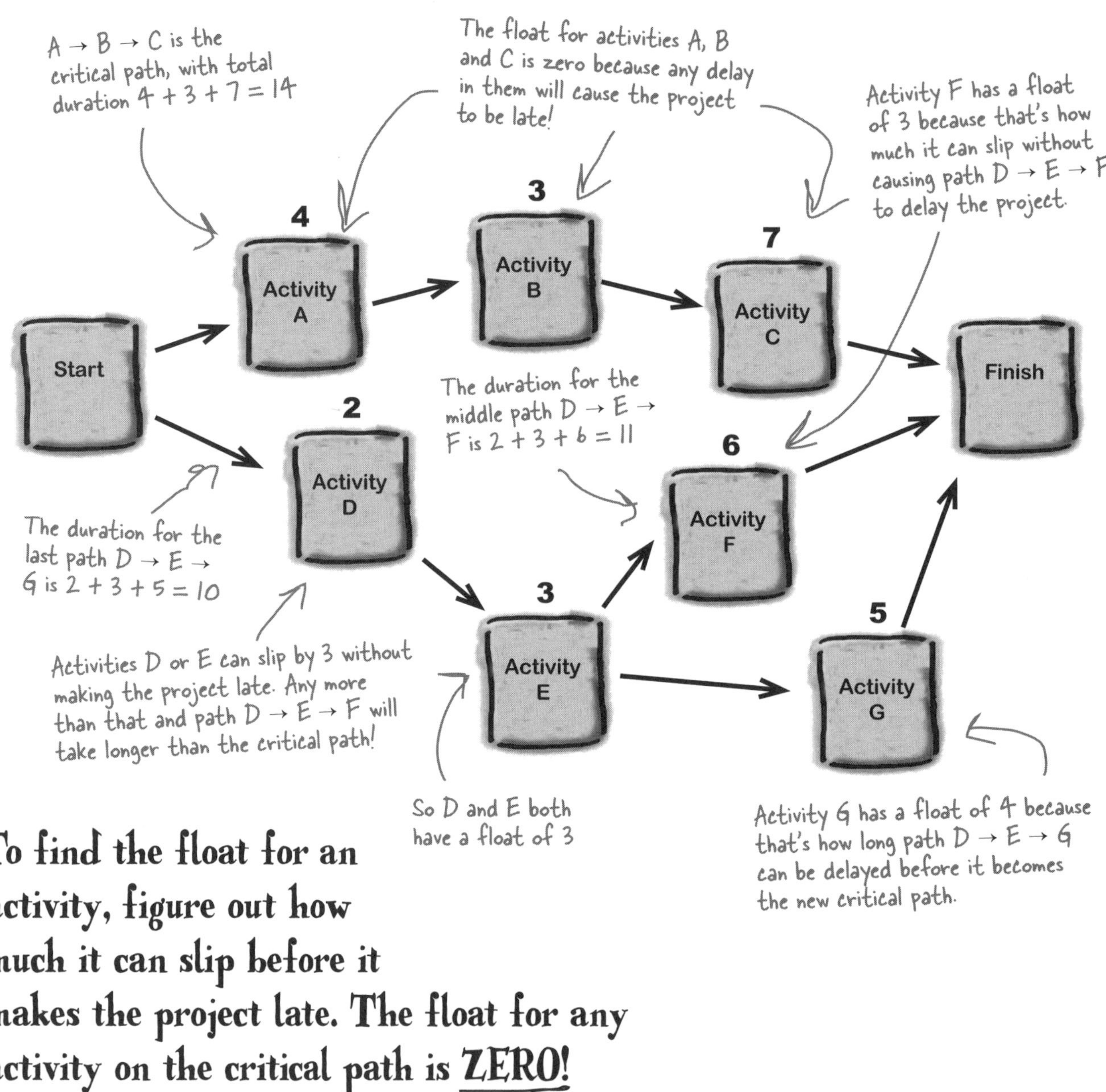

To find the float for an activity, figure out how much it can slip before it makes the project late. The float for any activity on the critical path is ZERO!

You'll need to be able to calculate the float of an activity in a network diagram for the exam. Take another look at this PDM from the last exercise. Can you calculate the float for each activity?

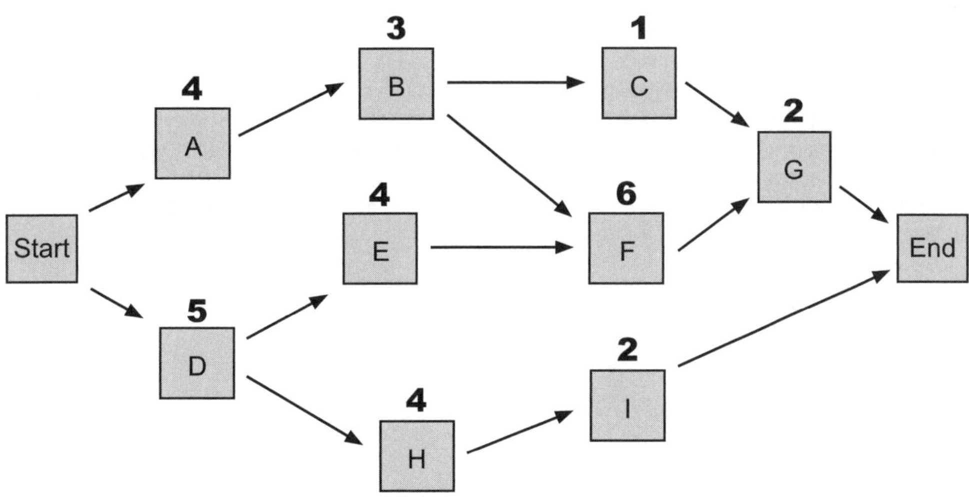

1. What is the float for each activity on the critical path?........

2. What is the total duration for path A → B → C → G?......

3. What is the total duration for path A → B → F → G?......

4. What is the total duration for path D → E → F → G?......

5. What is the total duration for path D → H → I?.......

6. Which path is the critical path?........ → .... → .... → ....

7. Write down the float for each activity:

A........ B........ C........ D........ E........

F........ G........ H........ I........

Hint: First fill in the float for the critical path activities. Then move on to the next-longest path, and then the next-longest one, filling in any float that hasn't been filled in yet.

Answers on page 285.

there are no Dumb Questions

Q: Where do the duration numbers come from on each activity?

A: A lot of people ask that question. It's easy to forget that everything you do in Activity Sequencing builds on the stuff you did in the other Time Management processes. Remember the estimates that you came up with Activity Duration Estimating? You used techniques like Three Point Estimates, Analogous Estimating, and Parametric Estimating to come up with an estimate for each activity. Those are the estimates that you use on your network diagrams!

Q: What if there's a path that's not critical, but where even a small slip in one activity would delay the project?

A: This is exactly why it's important to know the float for each of your activities. When you're managing your project, it's not enough to just pay attention to the activities on the critical path. You need to look for any activity with a low float. And don't forget that there may be some activities that aren't on the critical path but still have a float of zero! These are the ones where you really want to pay attention and watch out for potential resource problems.

I see—so when I created the network diagram in Activity Sequencing, I was building on what I did in Activity Definition. It all ties together!

All of the processes in Time Management tie together! When you develop your schedule, you're using the durations for your activities that you came up with in Activity Duration Estimating.

Figure out the early start and early finish

Coming up with the float for each activity is useful, but you can actually do better! When you have a long critical path, but the other paths in your network diagram are short, then you have a lot of freedom in when you can start and finish each of the activities that are not on the critical path. You can use **early start** and **early finish** to get a handle on exactly how much freedom you have in your schedule.

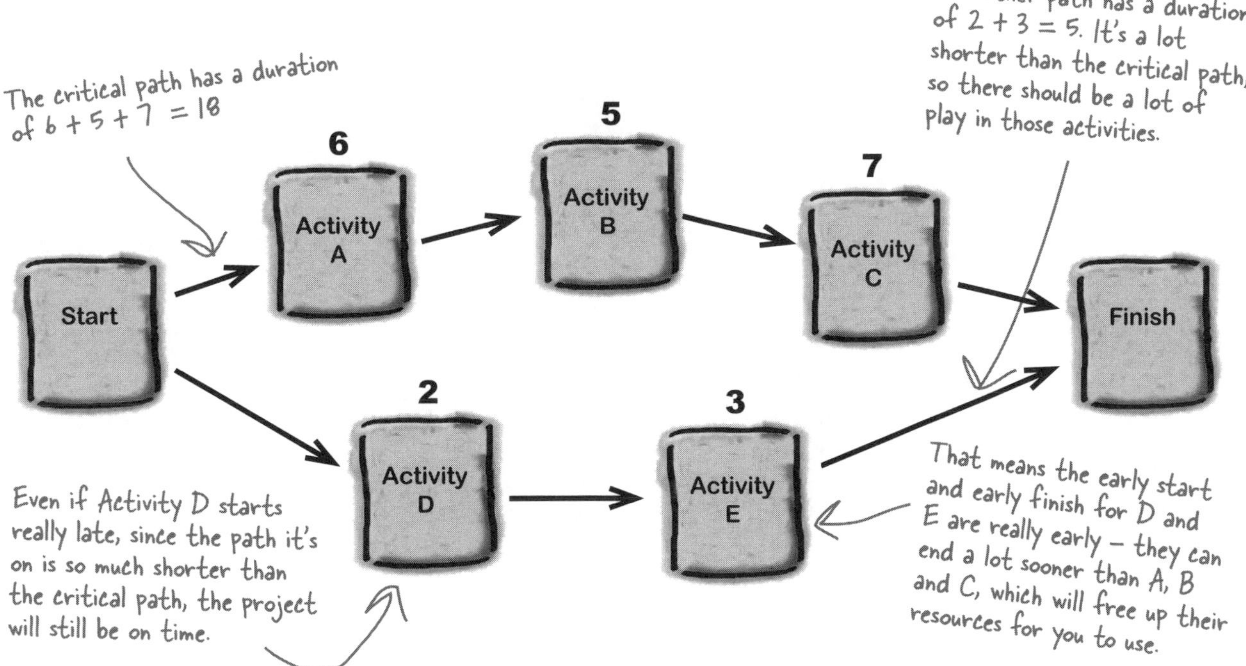

Early start

Is the earliest time that an activity can start. An activity near the end of the path will only start early if all of the previous activities in the path also started early. If one of the previous activities in the path slips, that will push it out.

Early finish

Is the earliest time that an activity can finish. It's the date that an activity will finish if all of the previous activities started early and none of them slipped.

When you find the early start and early finish for each task, you know exactly how much freedom you have to move the start dates for those activities around without causing problems.

Figure out the latest possible start and finish

It's also important to know how late any activity can run before it delays the project. That's what **late start** and **late finish** are for! They let you figure out how late you can start a certain task and how much it can slip before it delays your project.

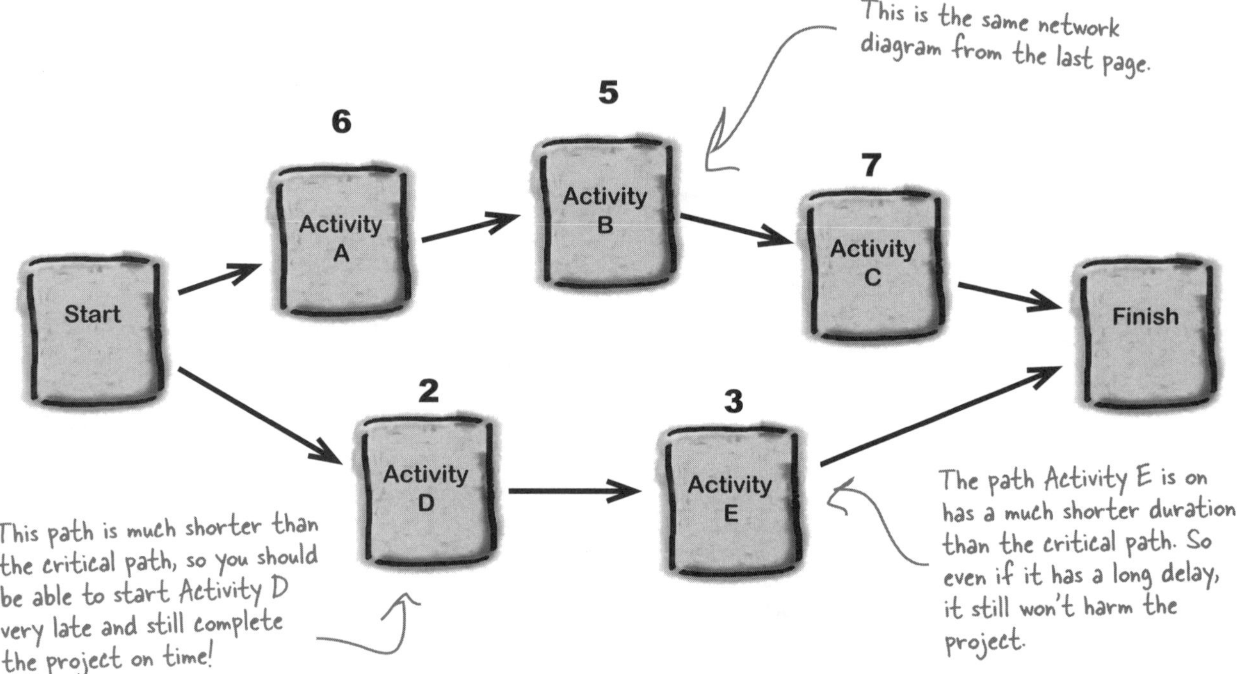

Late start

Is the latest time that an activity can start. If an activity is on a path that's much shorter than the critical path, then it can start very late without delaying the project – but those delays will add up quickly if other activities on its path also slip!

Late finish

Is the latest time that an activity can finish. If an activity is on a short path and all of the other activities on that path start and finish early, then it can finish very late without causing the project to be late.

Figuring out the late start and late finish will help you see how much "play" you have in your schedule. An activity with a large late start or late finish means you have more options.

Add early and late durations to your diagrams

You can use a method called **forward pass** to add the early start and finish to each path in your network diagram. Once you've done that, you can use **backward pass** to add the late start and finish. It makes your network diagrams look a little more complicated, but it gives you a lot of valuable information.

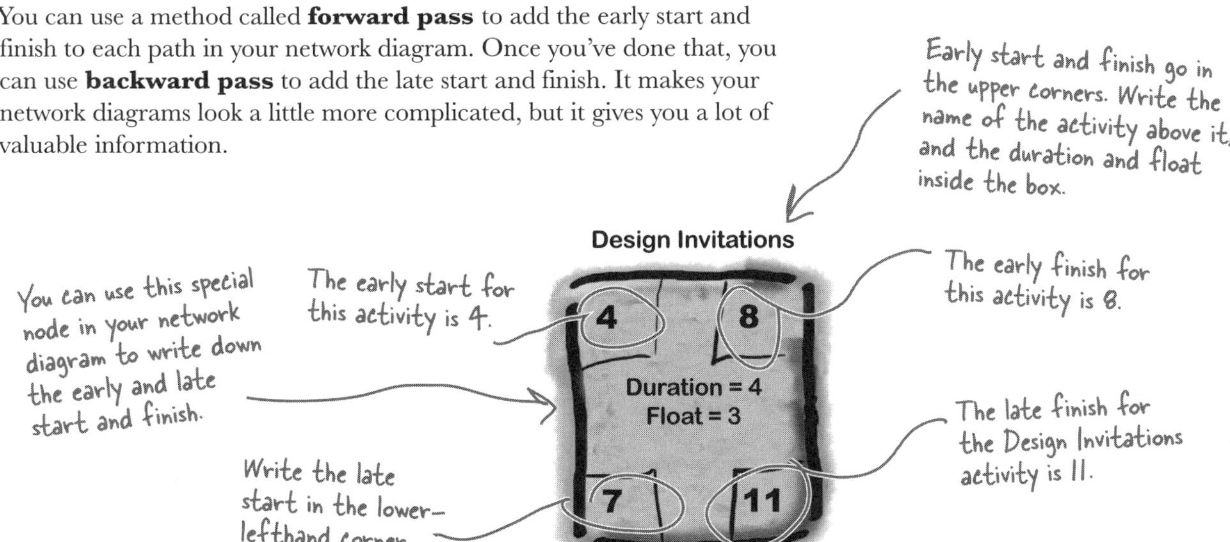

Take a forward pass through the network diagram.

Start at the beginning of the critical path and move forward through each activity. Follow these three steps to figure out the early start and early finish!

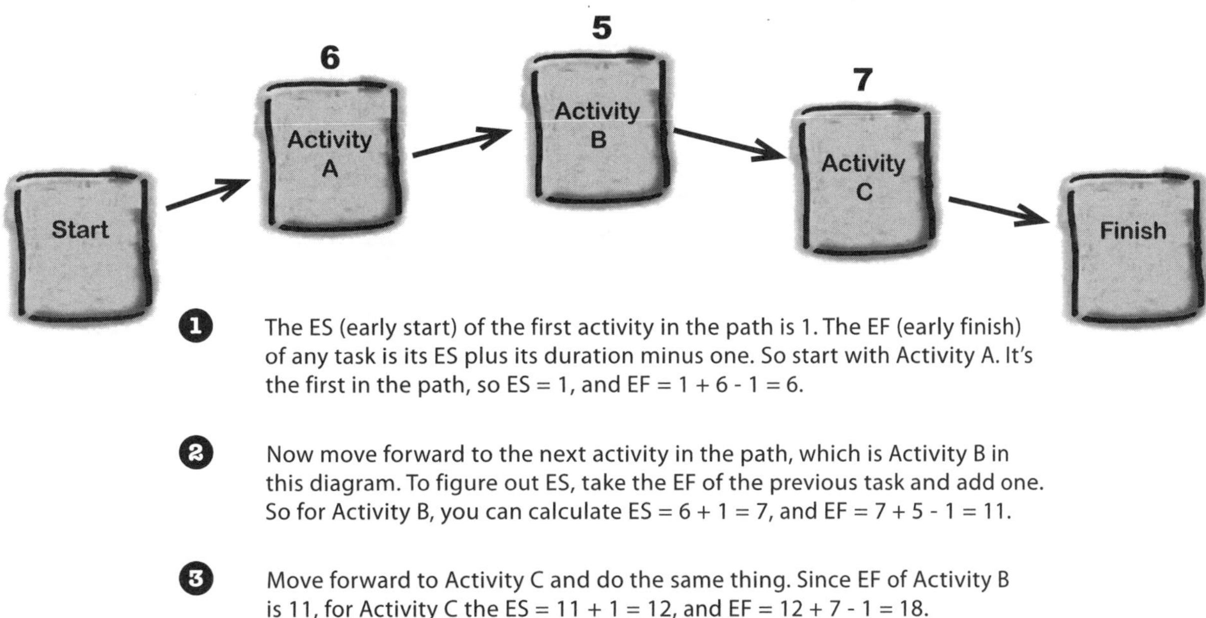

1. The ES (early start) of the first activity in the path is 1. The EF (early finish) of any task is its ES plus its duration minus one. So start with Activity A. It's the first in the path, so ES = 1, and EF = 1 + 6 - 1 = 6.

2. Now move forward to the next activity in the path, which is Activity B in this diagram. To figure out ES, take the EF of the previous task and add one. So for Activity B, you can calculate ES = 6 + 1 = 7, and EF = 7 + 5 - 1 = 11.

3. Move forward to Activity C and do the same thing. Since EF of Activity B is 11, for Activity C the ES = 11 + 1 = 12, and EF = 12 + 7 - 1 = 18.

Take a backward pass to find late start and finish

Now that you've figured out the early start and early finish for a path in your network diagram, you can turn around and do a **backward pass** to find the late start and late finish.

Now take a backward pass through the same network diagram.

The backward pass is just as easy as the forward pass. Start at the end of the path you just took a pass through and work your way backward to figure out the late start and finish.

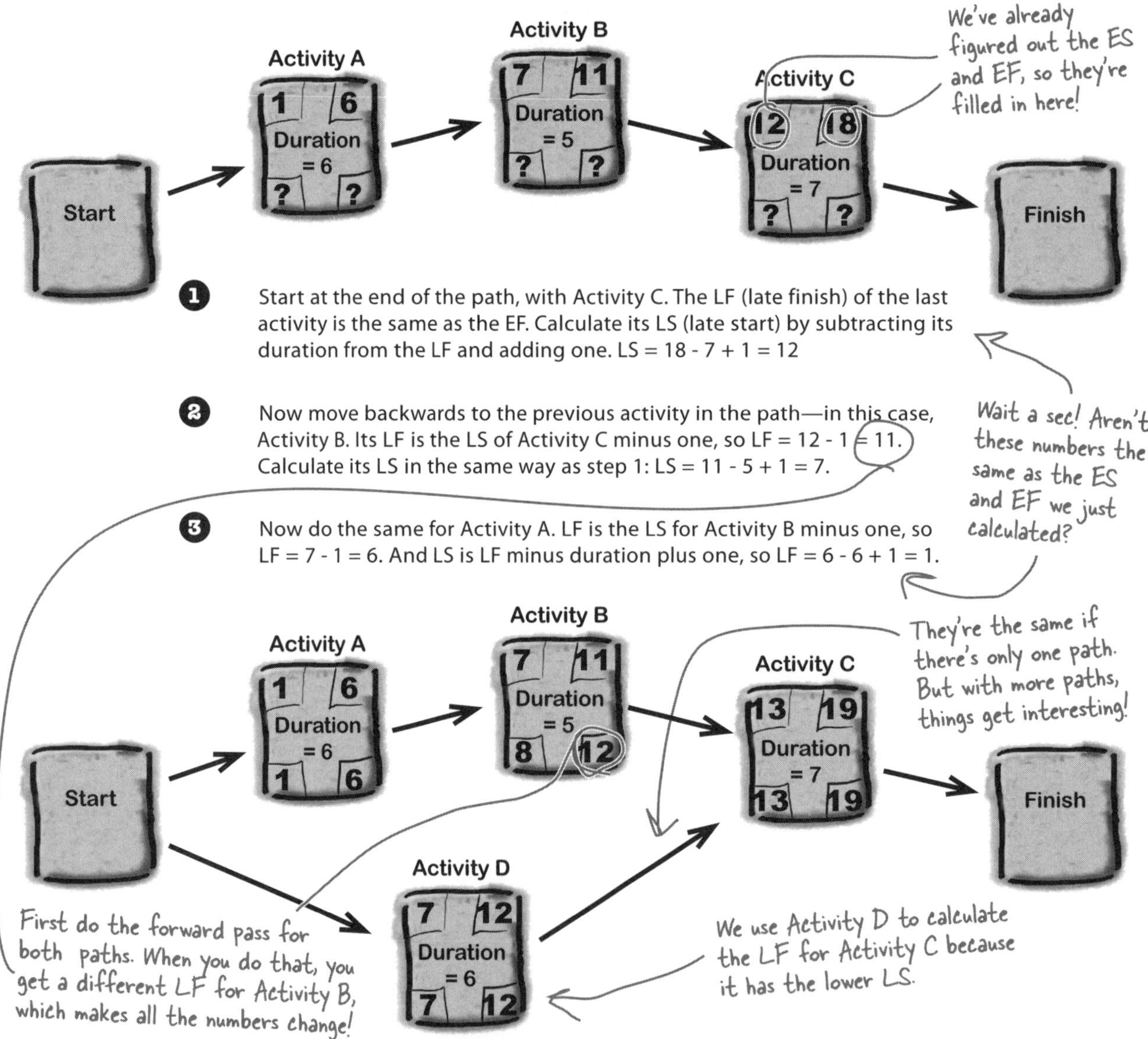

1. Start at the end of the path, with Activity C. The LF (late finish) of the last activity is the same as the EF. Calculate its LS (late start) by subtracting its duration from the LF and adding one. LS = 18 - 7 + 1 = 12

2. Now move backwards to the previous activity in the path—in this case, Activity B. Its LF is the LS of Activity C minus one, so LF = 12 - 1 = 11. Calculate its LS in the same way as step 1: LS = 11 - 5 + 1 = 7.

3. Now do the same for Activity A. LF is the LS for Activity B minus one, so LF = 7 - 1 = 6. And LS is LF minus duration plus one, so LF = 6 - 6 + 1 = 1.

Let's take some time out to walk through this!

All of this critical path stuff seems pretty serious, right? It's one of the toughest concepts on the exam. But don't sweat it, because it's actually not hard! It just takes a little practice. Once you do it yourself, you'll see that there's really nothing to worry about.

Calculating the ES, EF, LS, and LF may seem complicated, but it only takes a little practice to get the hang of it. Once you walk through it step by step, you'll see that it's actually pretty easy!

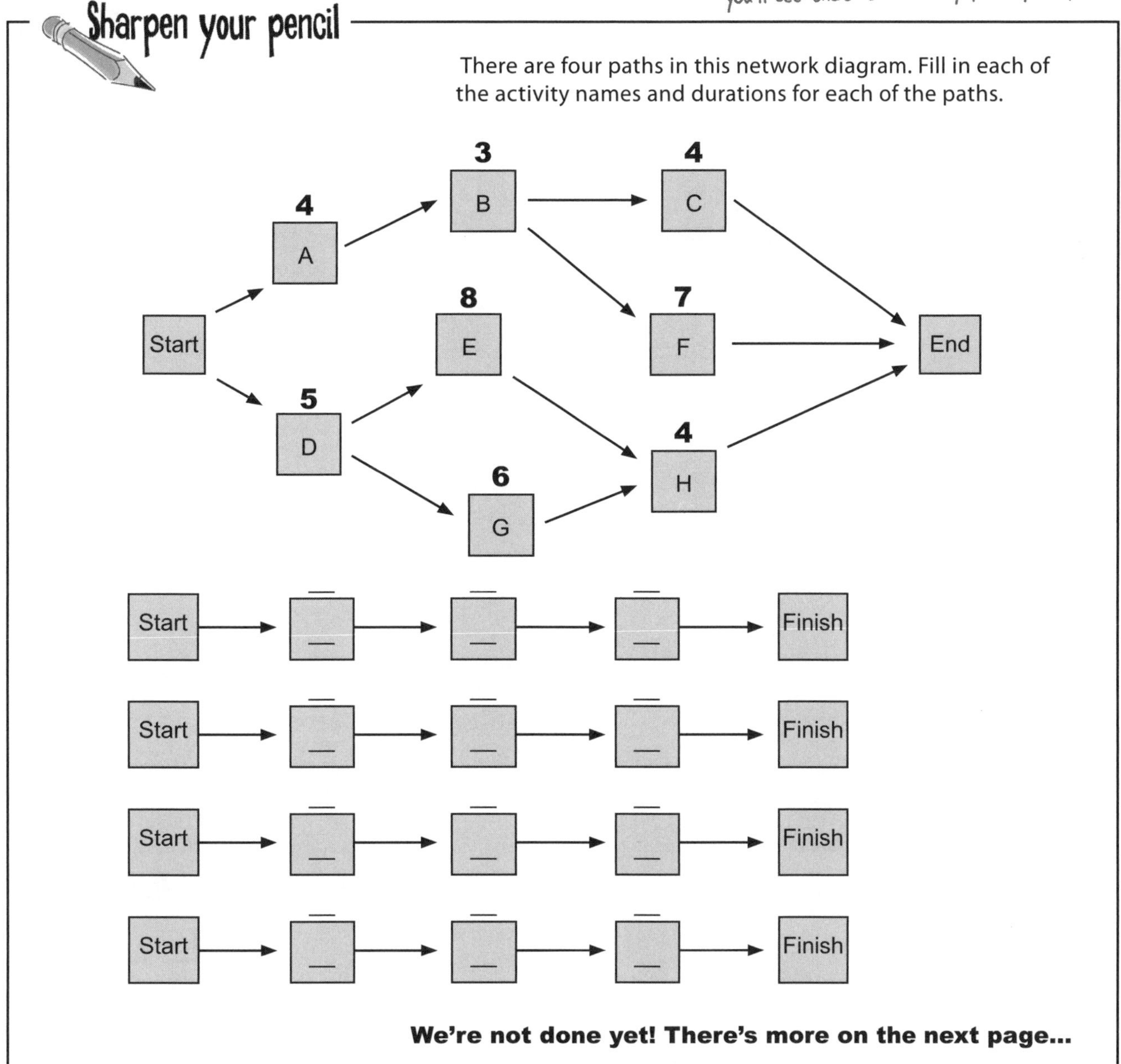

Sharpen your pencil

Take a forward pass through each of the four paths in the diagram and fill in the early starts and early finishes for each activity. Start with the first one.

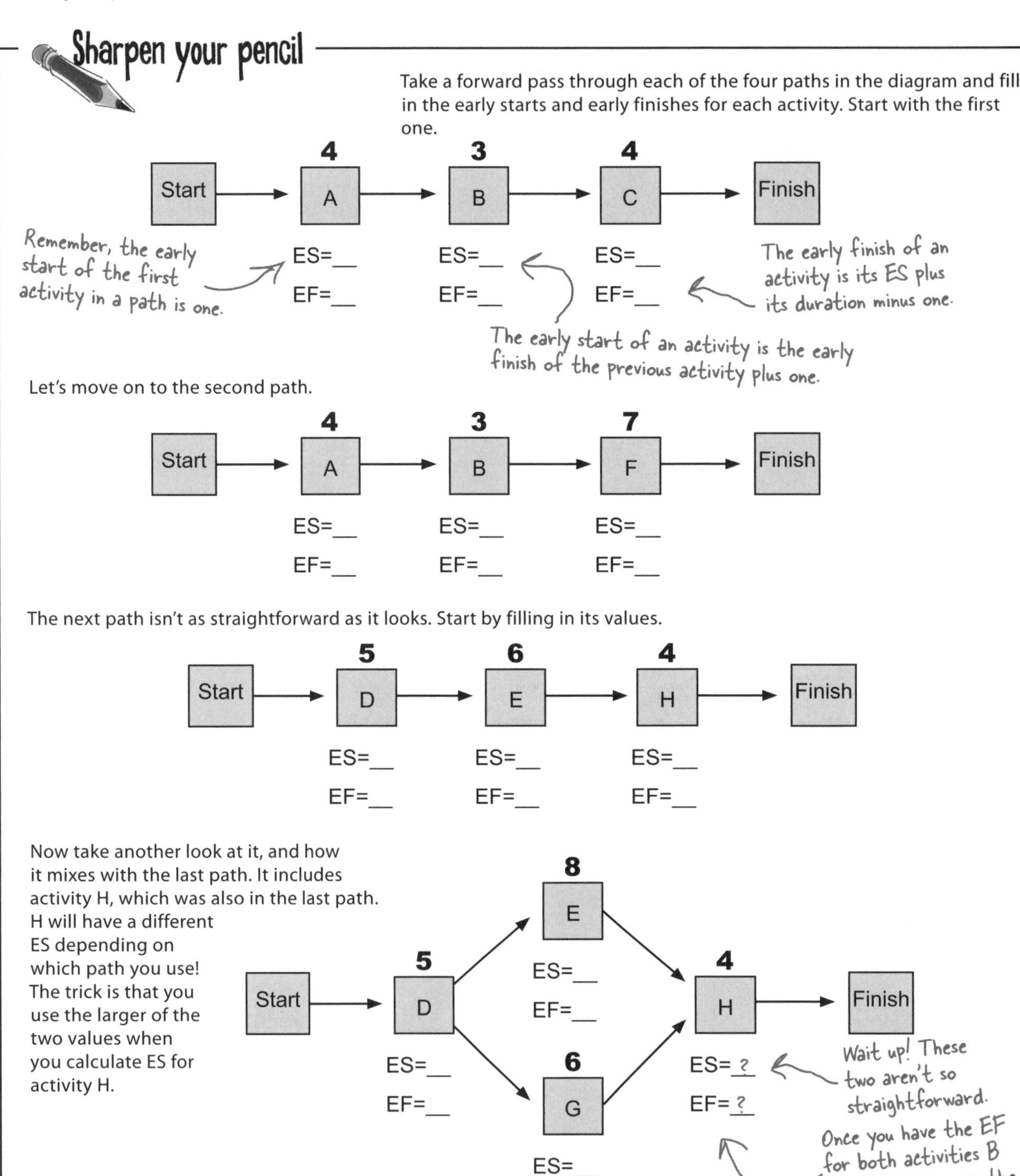

You've calculated the ES for each activity. Use that information and take a backward pass through the paths, starting with the first two paths.

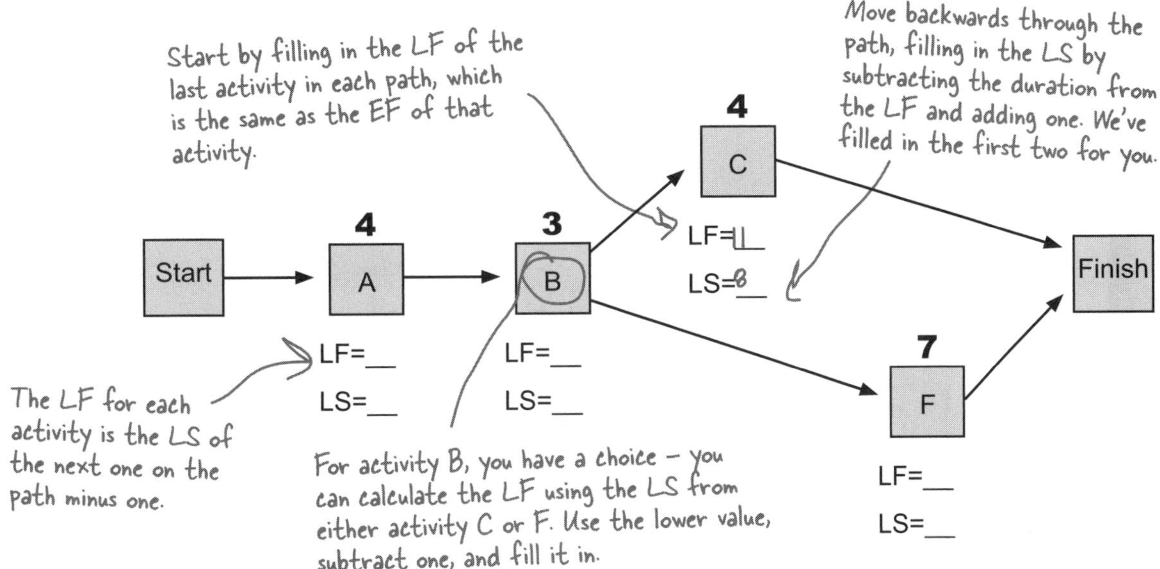

Finish up by calculating the LS and LF for the last two paths!

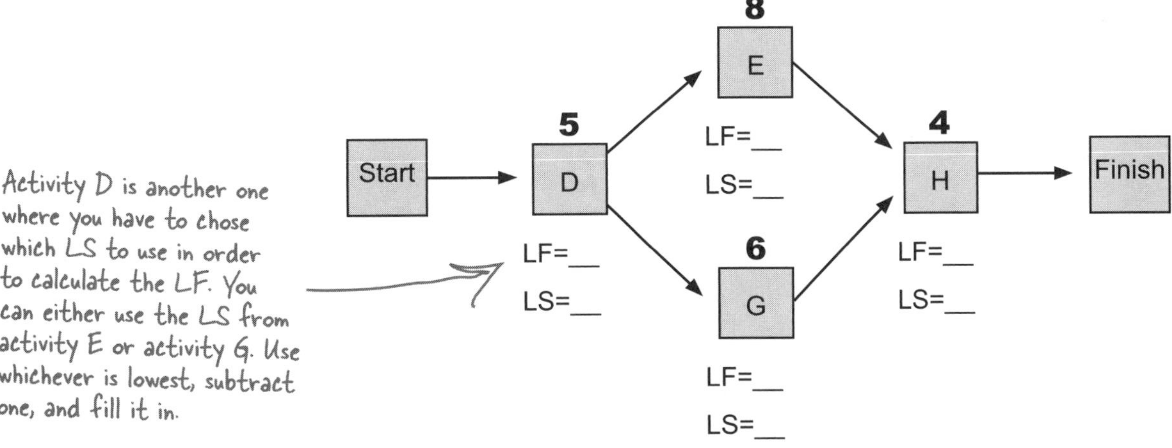

Sharpen your pencil Solution

For the exam, you'll only have to do one or two of these calculations, not a whole string of them like this. You'll definitely be able to handle the exam questions now!

If you got a few of these wrong, don't worry. It's easy to miss one calculation, and that leads to a problem on the whole path.

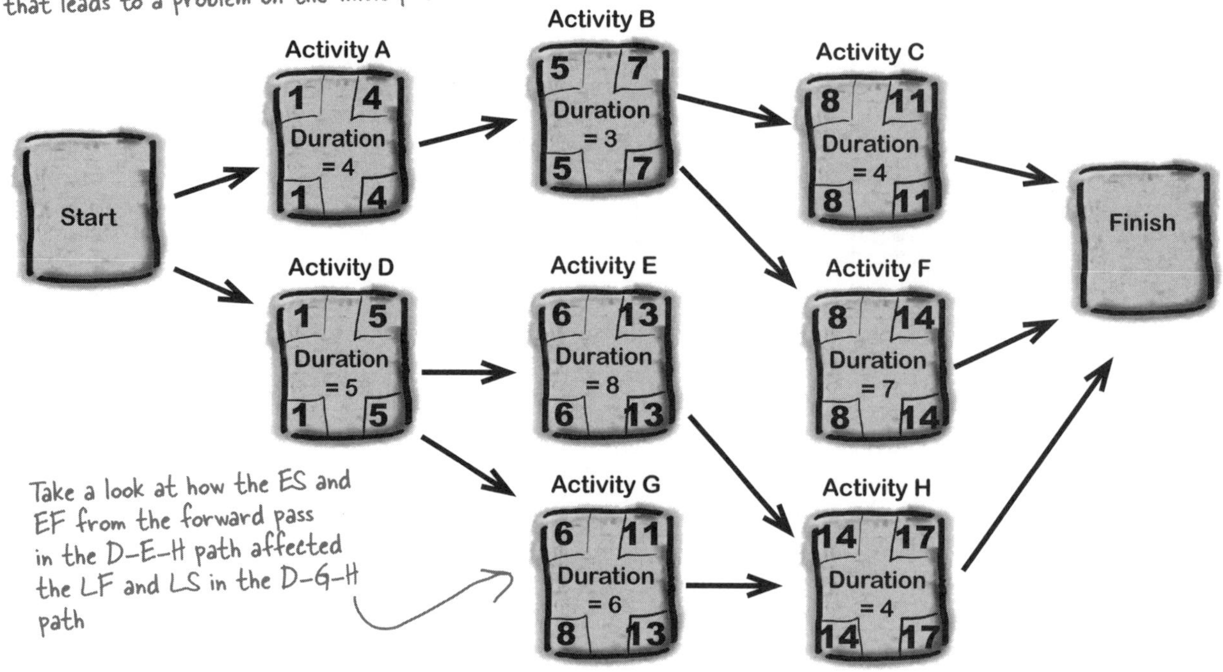

Activity	ES	EF	Duration	LS	LF
Activity A	1	4	4	1	4
Activity B	5	7	3	5	7
Activity C	8	11	4	8	11
Activity D	1	5	5	1	5
Activity E	6	13	8	6	13
Activity F	8	14	7	8	14
Activity G	6	11	6	8	13
Activity H	14	17	4	14	17

Start → A, Start → D; A → B; B → C, B → F; D → E, D → G; E → H; G → H; C → Finish, F → Finish, H → Finish

Take a look at how the ES and EF from the forward pass in the D–E–H path affected the LF and LS in the D–G–H path

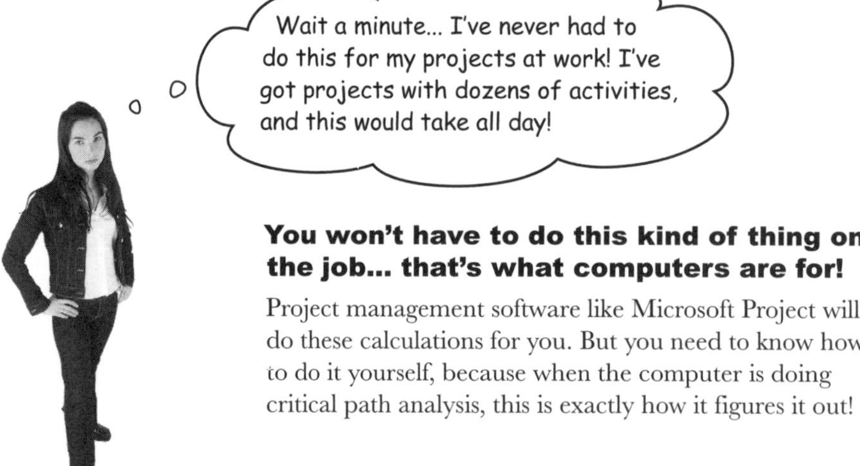

You won't have to do this kind of thing on the job... that's what computers are for!

Project management software like Microsoft Project will do these calculations for you. But you need to know how to do it yourself, because when the computer is doing critical path analysis, this is exactly how it figures it out!

there are no Dumb Questions

Q: Would I really use this critical path stuff in real life, or is it just something I need to memorize for the PMP exam?

A: Yes, critical path analysis really is important in real life! Sure, for a small project with a dozen or so activities, it's pretty easy to figure out which activities are critical and which can slip by a little bit. But what happens if you've got a project with dozens of team members and hundreds of activities? That's where critical path analysis can come in very handy. For a project like that, you'd probably be using project management software rather than calculating the critical path yourself, and the software will be able to highlight that path for you. Pay special attention to all of the activities that are on the critical path—those are the ones that could potentially delay the project.

Q: What about the other numbers? How do I use float, early start, late finish?

A: Float is a very powerful planning tool that you can use to figure out how well your project is going, and to predict where your trouble spots might be. Any activity with a low or zero float absolutely must come in on time, while the people performing an activity with a larger float have more freedom to slip without delaying the project. So you might want to assign your "superstar" resources to the low-float activities, and those people who need a little more mentoring to the ones with higher float.

Early and late start and finish numbers are also very useful. How many times have you been in a situation where you've been asked, "If we absolutely had to have this in two months, can we do it?" Or, "How late can this project realistically be?" Now you can use these numbers to give you real answers, with actual evidence to back them up.

Q: I can see how the critical path is useful on its own, but what does it have to do with the rest of time management?

A: If you start putting together your schedule but the activities are in the wrong order, that's really going to cause serious problems... and sometimes doing critical path analysis is the only way you'll really figure out that you've made that particular mistake. That's why you need to pay a lot of attention to the Activity Sequencing tools and techniques. If you've come up with an inefficient or inaccurate sequence, with too many or incorrect predecessors and dependencies, then your entire critical path analysis will be useless.

BULLET POINTS: AIMING FOR THE EXAM

- The **critical path** is the path that has the longest duration.
- You should be able to figure out the number of paths in a **network diagram**, and the duration of each path.
- The **float** for an activity is the amount that its duration can slip without causing the project to be delayed. The float for any activity on the critical path is zero.
- You'll need to know how to calculate the **early start**, **late start**, **early finish**, and **late finish** for an activity in a network diagram using the forward pass and backward pass. This is the core of critical path analysis.
- You may see a **PDM** (or **activity-on-node**) diagram with special nodes that have extra boxes in the corners for the ES, EF, LF and LS. You may see an ADM (or activity-on-arrow) diagram too, but that's much less common.
- Don't forget that when two paths intersect, you have to decide which ES or LF value to take for the calculation in the next node. For the **forward pass**, use the larger value; for the **backward pass**, use the smaller one.

Crash the schedule

When you absolutely have to meet the date and you are running behind, you can sometimes find ways to do activities more quickly by adding more resources to critical path tasks. That's called **crashing**.

Crashing the schedule means adding resources or moving them around to shorten it. Crashing ALWAYS costs more and doesn't always work!

Then you can't crash the schedule.

There's no way to crash a schedule without raising the overall cost of the project. So, if the budget is fixed and you don't have any extra money to spend, you can't use this technique.

Fast-tracking the project

Sometimes you've got two activities planned to occur in sequence, but you can actually do them at the same time. On a software project, you might do both your UAT testing and your functional testing at the same time, for example. This is pretty risky, though. There's a good chance you might need to redo some of the work you have done concurrently.

On the exam, if you see something about "overlapping activities," it's talking about fast-tracking.

We can save time by having the florist work on the reception hall flowers while we figure out the rest of the decorations.

If the decorations don't match the flowers well enough, we'll have to do some rework.

Crashing and fast-tracking are SCHEDULE COMPRESSION tools.

Exercise

Each of these scenarios describes a schedule compression technique. Pick which are examples of fast tracking and which are crashing.

1. Kathleen guesses that 70% of the invitees will RSVP. Instead of waiting for all of them to come in, she goes ahead and reserves the tables and chairs now.

   ☐ Fast-tracking ☐ Crashing

2. Rebecca is taking a really long time to choose the decorations so Kathleen brings in a professional decorator to help, even though it will cost more.

   ☐ Fast-tracking ☐ Crashing

3. Kathleen needs to get the invitations out quickly, so she hires two temps to come in and help her stuff envelopes for a few days.

   ☐ Fast-tracking ☐ Crashing

→ Answers on page 285.

What-if analysis

- It's always a good idea to think about all of the things that could go wrong on your project in advance.
- What if the limo breaks down?
- What if the florist cancels at the last minute?
- What if the dress doesn't fit?
- What if the band gets sick?
- What if the guests get food poisoning?
- What if there's a typo in the church address on the invitation?
- What if the bridesmaids don't show up?
- What if the cake tastes horrible?
- What if we lose the rings?

That way, you can plan a way to deal with any problems that might come your way. Sometimes there's no way to still meet your dates and deal with these scenarios. But, it always makes sense to try to understand the impact they will have on your schedule.

Monte Carlo Analysis

This is a specific kind of what-if analysis where you model uncertainty using a computer. There are some packages that will help to calculate risk using random numbers and Monte Carlo algorithms. While this is not a commonly used technique, there might be a question or two about it on the PMP exam, and you should know what it is.

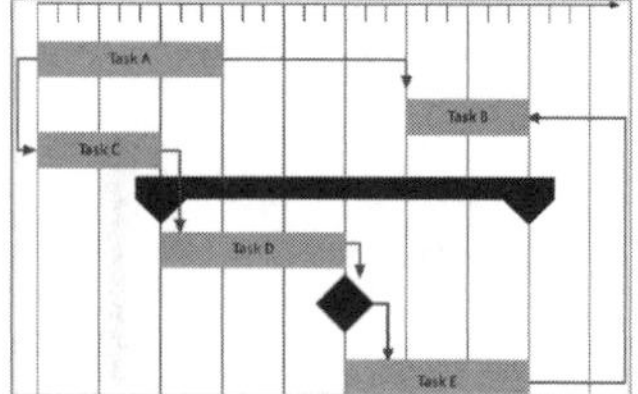

Schedule Model

Using a project management software package to create a model of the schedule and adjust various elements to see what might happen is another technique for analyzing network diagrams.

Other schedule network analysis techniques

There are just a few more tools for working with network diagrams that you should know.

Critical chain method

In this method, resource dependencies are used to determine the critical path. Then, buffers are added working backwards from the delivery date into the schedule at strategic points, and the project is managed so that each milestone is hit on time.

Resource leveling

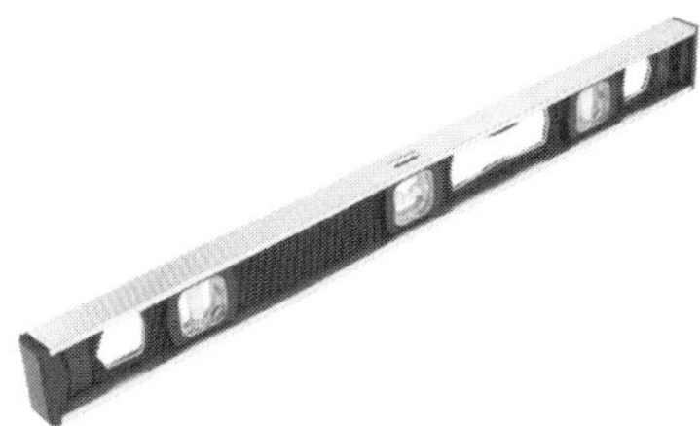

Sometimes only one resource can do a given activity. If that resource is busy doing another activity on the critical path, the path itself needs to change to include that dependency. That's the point of resource leveling. It evaluates all of the resources to see if the critical path needs to change to accommodate resource assignments.

Applying Calendars

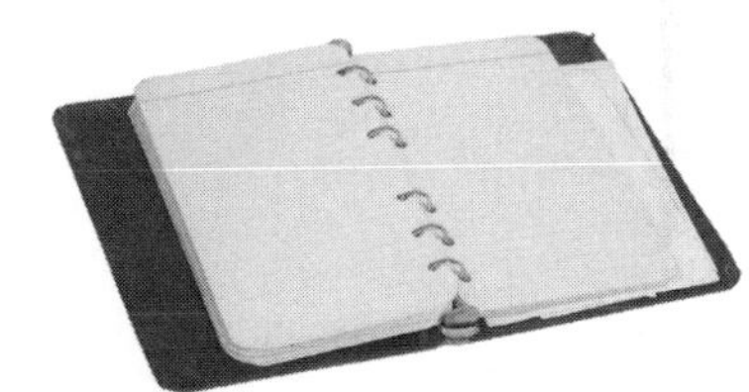

Sometimes there are calendar constraints that might affect the critical path. Like, if you are trying to schedule a skiing event, it would have to happen when the weather cooperated with your plans. There might also be external resource calendars if your resources are only available at specific times.

Adjusting leads and lags

If you made any mistakes in your leads and your lags, you might be able to adjust them to change the projected end date.

Outputs of schedule development

Of course the main product of schedule development is the schedule. But there are a few other supporting documents that help you understand how the work will get done as well.

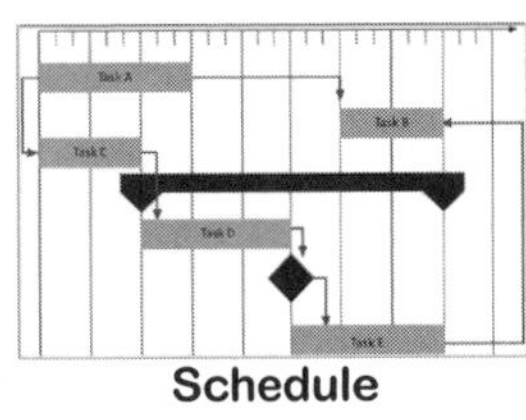

Schedule

Schedule

All of that analysis and modeling should produce a schedule that everyone can get behind. After thinking your way through everything that can go wrong and assigning resources you should have a pretty accurate prediction of the work required to complete the project.

The reason you go through all of that what-if analysis is to make sure everybody agrees that this schedule is achievable!

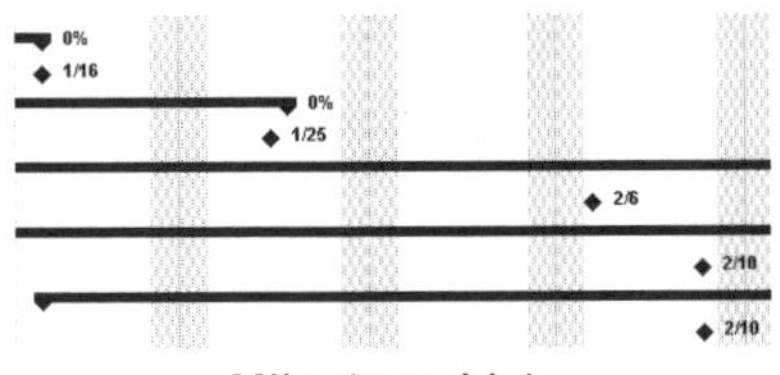

Milestone List

Milestone List

All of the major chunks of work can be marked with milestones to track their completion. Usually this list is published for other teams or stakeholders who are depending on parts of the work to be accomplished by a certain time.

The main thing to remember here is that milestones are usually used to track stuff that will be used by people outside the project.

Before you can do change control, you need requested changes. Once the change is approved, you can update the baseline!

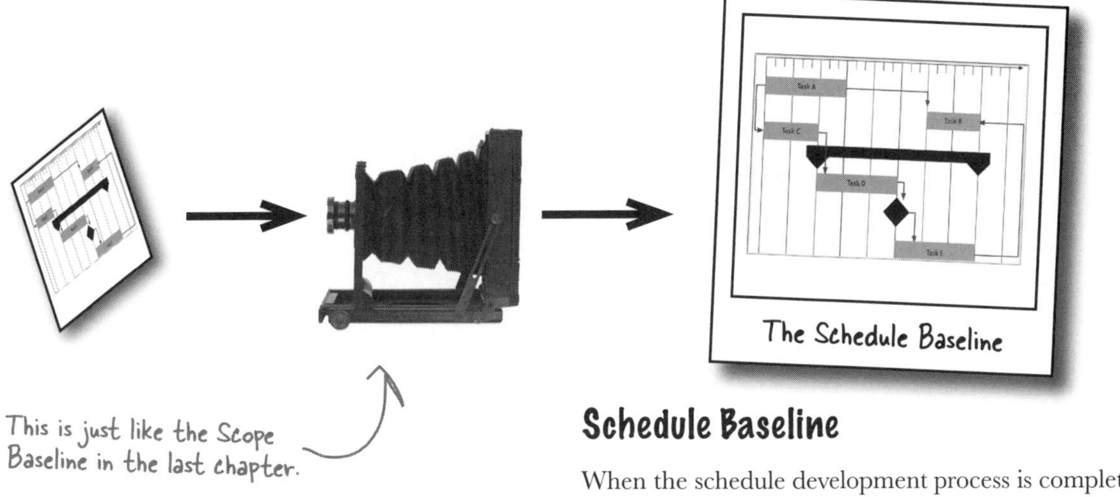

Schedule Baseline

When the schedule development process is complete, a baseline is created so that actual progress can be compared to the plan.

Resource Requirements Updates

Project Calendar Updates

Activity Attributes Updates

Project Management Plan Updates

Requested Changes

Updates and Requested Changes

In the course of developing the schedule, you will find changes to your resource requirements, activity attributes, and project calendars. Some changes may affect your overall plan for handling all other areas of project management. In that case, the Project Management Plan will need to be updated.

For the exam, you need to know schedule development outputs. Several outputs from the wedding's schedule development process are on the left match them to the correct description on the right.

A. Schedule

B. Milestone List

C. Schedule Baseline

D. Update to Resource Requirements

E. Update to Project Management Plan

1. Kathleen gives a list of dates to the caterer telling him when he will have his menu plans and when shopping for the ingredients needs to be complete for the Reception and Rehearsal Dinner.

2. Kathleen realizes that she needs to make a change to how she keeps track of the waiters' time, so she makes a change to the document that describes it.

3. While making the schedule, Kathleen realizes that she is going to need a lot more waiters.

4. Kathleen makes a copy of the schedule when it's done so that she can compare how she is doing to the original plan.

5. There's a big poster on the wall where Kathleen keeps track of who does what, and when.

Answers: A - 5; B - 1; C -4; D - 3; E - 2

there are no Dumb Questions

Q: Don't we need to go through change control before we update the resource requirements or the activity attributes?

A: No. You need to go through change control if you are requesting changes to, say, your cost management plan. But while you are working on creating your schedule, everything you have created as part of the Time Management knowledge area is fair game.

As you work your way through your network diagram and figure out new dependencies, you are going to find that you need more resources for some items or that the activity itself has changed. That's why this process gives you the freedom to refine your earlier idea and make all of the time management documents in sync with your new understanding.

The schedule development process is about taking all of the information you are able to think of up front and putting it into a schedule that is realistic. When you are done with this process, you should have a really good idea of what you are going to do, who will do it, and how long it will take.

Q: We always want to do our projects as quickly as we can. Why don't we always fast-track and crash our schedules?

A: Because crashing is expensive and fast tracking is risky. While it may look good on paper to add a lot of resources to a project that is running late, it often adds so much management overhead and training issues that the project just comes in later.

Even though it might seem like some predecessors are really unnecessary, you usually planned them for a reason. So when you break your dependencies to fast-track your project, you can significantly compromise the quality of the work that gets done. That means you might have to redo it altogether—which would probably take a lot of time.

While fast-tracking and crashing might work sometimes, they always add both risk and cost to your project.

Q: Do people really do Monte Carlo Analysis to figure out their schedules? I have never heard of that before.

A: No. Most people don't use this technique to figure out what might go wrong on their projects. This is just one of those things that is on the PMP exam, so you have to know what it is.

Q: Critical Chain sounds complicated. Do I need to know how to do it?

A: Not really. You need to know that it is a technique for developing schedules that takes resource assignment into account early on.

When project managers use Critical Chain techniques, they identify strategic points to put buffers in their schedule and then manage the size of the buffers so that each milestone in the schedule is met.

Don't worry, you won't be asked to create a schedule using this technique. You just need to know the definition.

Updates refine the outputs of previous processes so you don't have to go back and redo them.

Influence the factors that cause change

You might get a question on the PMP exam that asks you about this.

Kathleen doesn't just sit around and wait for schedule changes to happen...

Joe (on phone): Good Afternoon, Joe's Catering. Joe speaking. How can I help you?

Kathleen: Hello, Joe. This is Kathleen calling about Rob and Rebecca's wedding.

Joe: Oh, Hi! Everything's going fine with that wedding.

Kathleen: Are you sure? What about that big convention across town that's going to be happening at the same time? Won't it be tough to find waiters in June?

Joe: I didn't think of that; we'd better start figuring out how we'll handle it now.

By realizing that the convention across town will need waiters, too, Kathleen prevents a lot of changes before they cause schedule problems!

The project manager doesn't just wait for change to happen! She finds the things that cause change and influences them.

Schedule control inputs and outputs

As the project work is happening, you can always discover new information that makes you re-evaluate your plan, and use the **Schedule Control process** to make the changes. The inputs to Schedule Control cover the various ways you can discover that information. The outputs are the changes themselves.

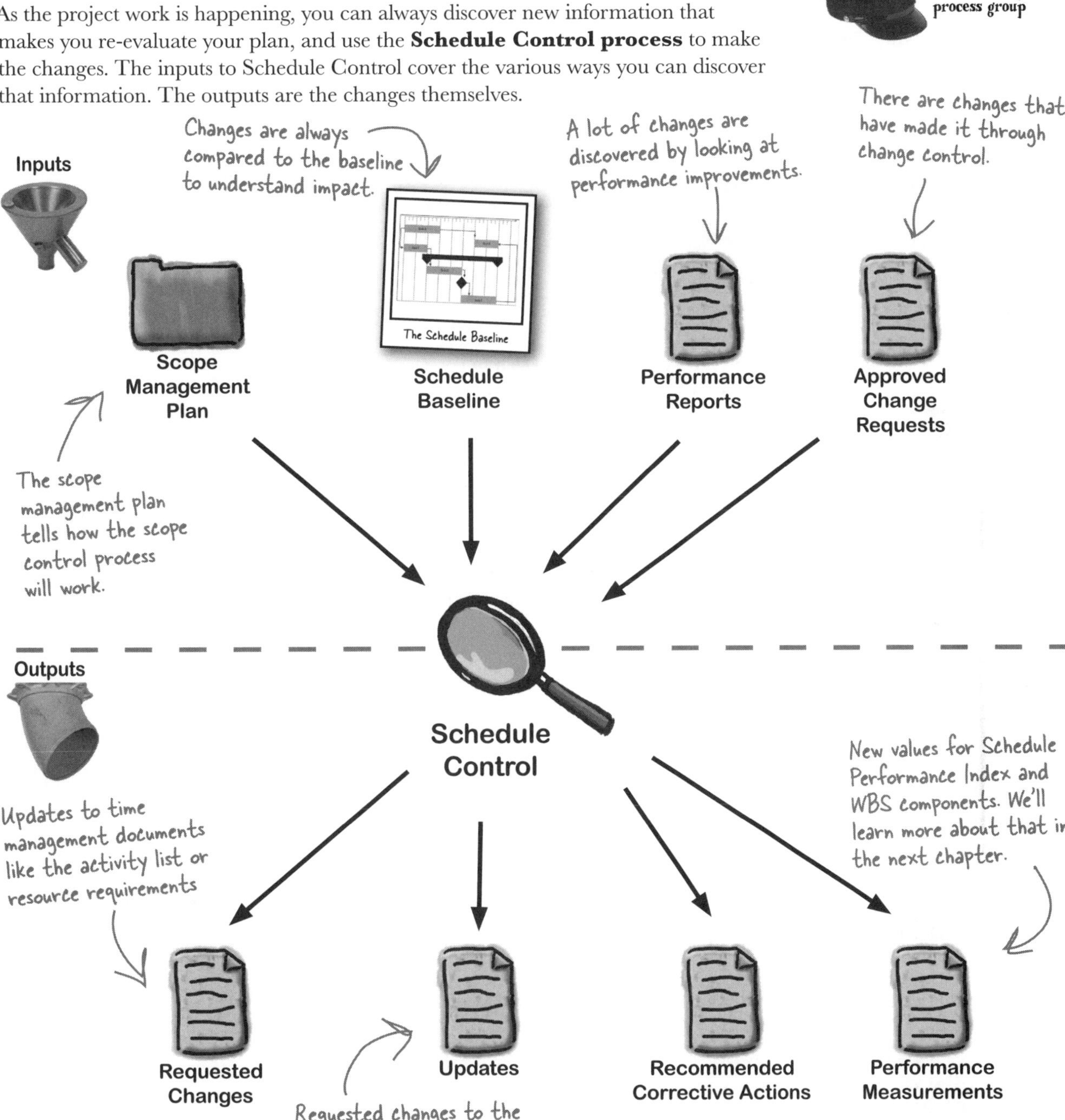

What schedule control updates

All of the stuff you made during the schedule development process gets updated using the schedule control process. Here's a closer look at what those updates mean.

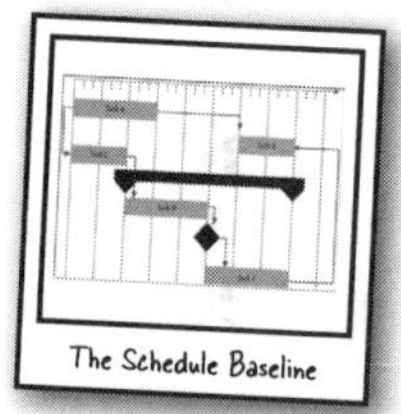

Schedule Baseline

Whenever a change is approved to your schedule, the baseline needs to be updated. That way, you will always be comparing your results to the right plan.

Organizational Process Assets

As you make changes to your project schedule, you should be tracking your lessons learned so that other projects can benefit from your experience. Sometimes you might find changes to templates that will help future projects, too

Activity List

Activity Attributes

If the work you need to do changes, then you need to update your activity list and attributes to match the new information.

Schedule Model Data

Some scenarios for what might go wrong on your project might show up when you are already doing the work. You need to update your schedule model accordingly.

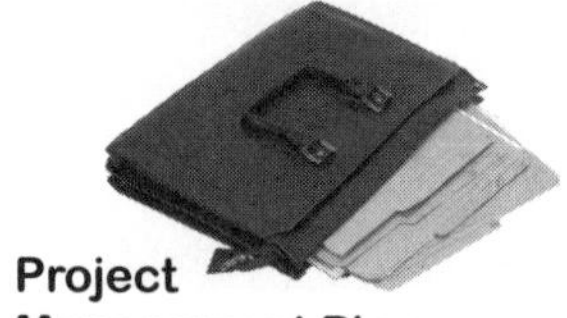

Project Management Plan

It could happen that the way you manage schedule control needs to change, and those changes would need to be updated in the **project management plan**.

Managing schedule change means keeping all of your schedule documents up to date.

Measuring and reporting performance

Most often, changes are identified through looking at performance data. It's just as important once you make a change to gather performance data as it was when you found the change in the first place. Here's how performance data feeds into the schedule control process.

When your schedule changes, you need to take performance measurements so you can keep your stakeholders up to date.

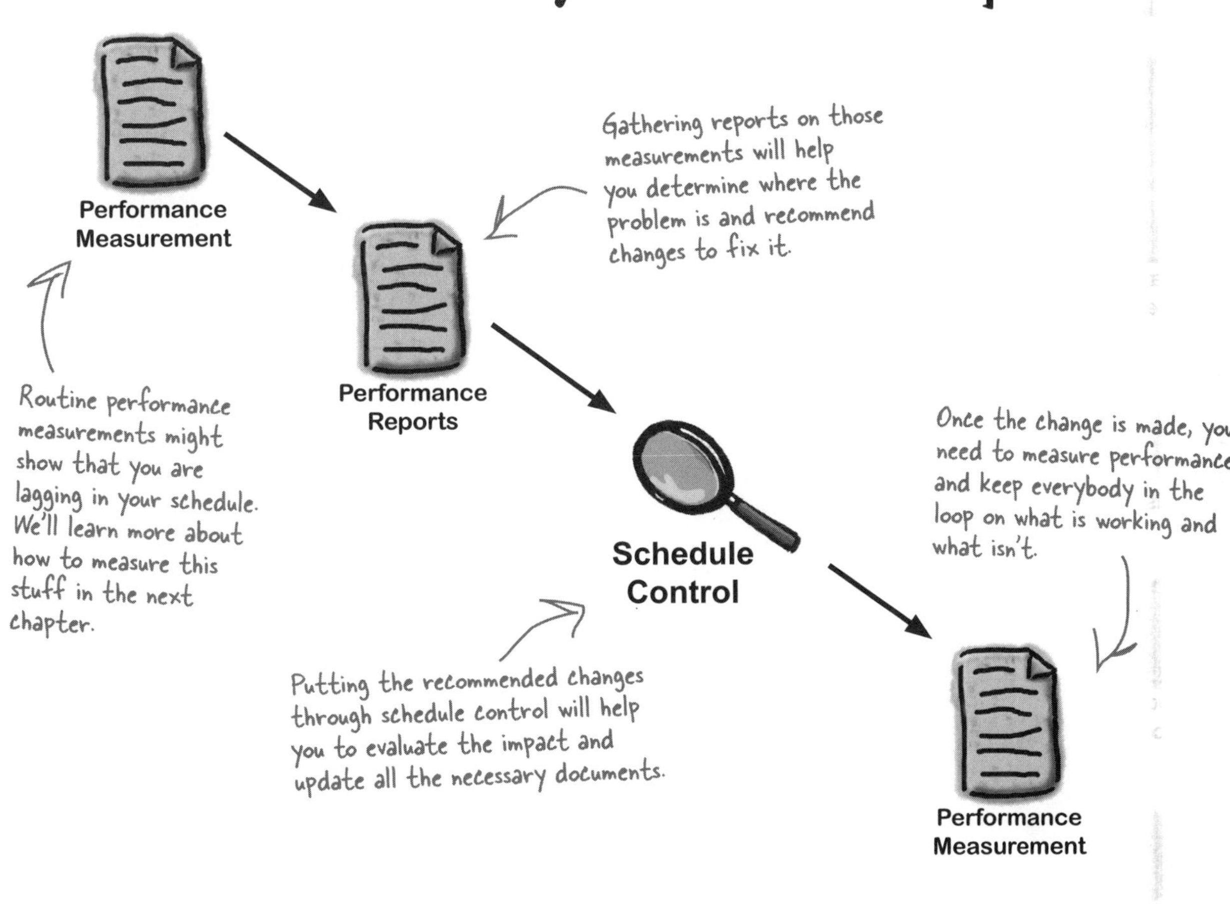

Schedule control tools and techniques

The tools and techniques for Schedule Control are all about figuring out where your project schedule stands. By comparing your actual project to the schedule you laid out in the baseline and looking at how people are performing, you can figure out how to handle every schedule change.

You did the same thing in scope control!

Variance Analysis

Use this to take stock of where your project is right now and compare that against what you'd planned to do in the baseline. If there's a big difference there, you know there's a problem!

Performance Measurement

There are two important calculations called Schedule Variance (SV) and Schedule Performance Index (SPI) that give you valuable information about how your project is doing. You'll learn all about them in the next chapter.

Schedule Comparison Bar Charts

This is like a normal bar chart, except that it shows you two bars for every activity: one for where you expected to be, and one for where you are right now.

These three tools and techniques are all about measuring how the project has done and comparing it to the baseline.

Progress Reporting

Most project managers have probably done a lot of progress reporting! It's one of those things that most people think of when they think of project management. It's when you create a report that says what the team has done, what milestones you've reached, and what's left to be done. You'll usually use a report template for this.

Project Management Software

This is software like Microsoft Project that helps you organize and analyze all of the information you need to evaluate the schedule of any project.

Schedule Change Control System

You already know how important a change control system is to any change control process! It includes all of the procedures that you need to follow in order to make sure that a change is properly analyzed and, if approved, done.

Here's something else you already know about from scope control.

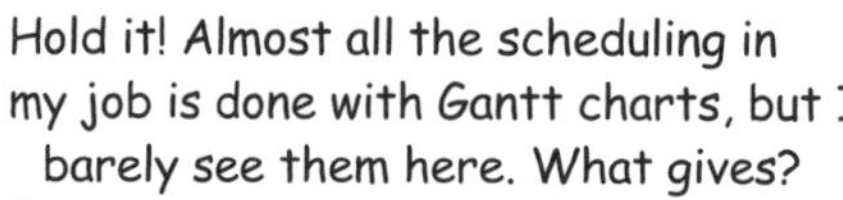

Remember, Gantt charts—the bar charts you make with MS Project—are just one tool for scheduling. You may use them a lot in your day-to-day work, but they're only one piece of time management. And remember, on the exam they're called **bar charts**, not Gantt charts!

there are no Dumb Questions

Q: When I create performance reports, who uses them?

A: The performance reports that you create are used by a lot of people. The team uses them to keep an eye on the project. If there's a schedule problem coming up, it alerts the team so that they can help you figure out how to avoid it.

Performance reports are also used by your project's sponsor and stakeholders, who are very interested in whether or not your project is on track. Those reports give them a good picture of how the project is doing... and that's especially important in schedule control, because most change control systems require that every change is approved by a Change Control Board that includes sponsor and stakeholders.

Q: What's schedule model data used for?

A: You use the schedule model data to build the schedule. It includes detailed information about things like resource requirements, alternate best-case and worst-case schedules, and contingency reserves.

When you put together your schedule, you should look at all of these things in order to create an accurate plan. The more information you have when you're building your schedule, the more likely it is that you'll catch those little problems that add up to big schedule slips.

Q: One of the tools is Project Management Software. Do I need to know how to use software in order to pass the exam?

A: No. The PMP exam does not require that you know how to use software like Microsoft Project. However, if you spend a lot of time using project management software, then you probably have become very familiar with a lot of the Time Management concepts. It's a good way to learn the basics of time management.

Q: How often am I supposed to update the project calendar?

A: The project calendar shows you the working days for your team, holidays, nonworking days, planned training, and the dates that could affect your project. Luckily, in most companies these dates don't change very often. You probably won't need to update it—and most project managers just use their company's existing project calendar.

When you're doing schedule development, you may discover that you need to make a change to the project calendar. That's why Updates to the Project Calendar is an output of Schedule Development.

Q: What do I do with the progress reports and performance measurements?

A: When you're planning your project, you'll often look to your company's past projects to see what went well and what could have been planned better. And where do you look? That information is in the Organizational Process Assets.
So where do you think that information comes from? It comes from project managers like you who added their progress reports and performance measurements.

Any time you generate data about your project, you should add it to your organizational process assets so you can use it for future projects.

Schedule Control Management Magnets

You'll see change control over and over again—every single knowledge area has its own change control process! Luckily, you'll start to see how similar they all are. But Schedule Control has its own quirks, and they're important for understanding Time Management.

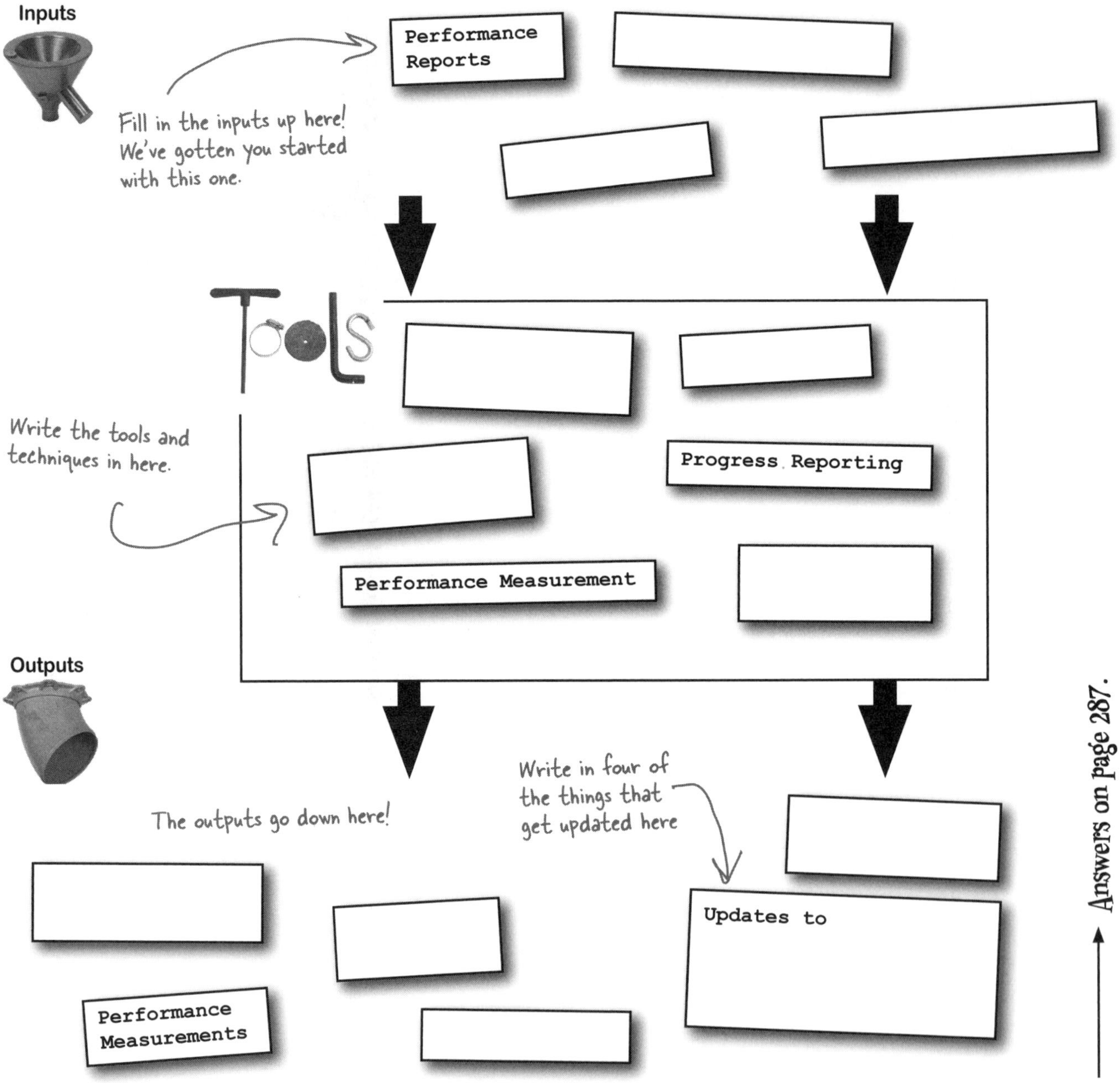

Inputs

Performance Reports

Fill in the inputs up here! We've gotten you started with this one.

Tools

Write the tools and techniques in here.

Progress Reporting

Performance Measurement

Outputs

The outputs go down here!

Write in four of the things that get updated here

Updates to

Performance Measurements

Answers on page 287.

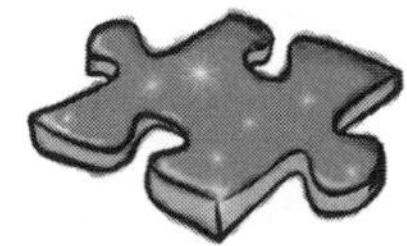

Timecross

Take some time to sit back and give your right brain something to do. It's your standard crossword; all of the solution words are from this chapter.

Across

2. Activity _____________ is the process where you put the activities in order.
5. Any delay in an activity on the __________ path will delay the entire project.
8. _____________ estimation is plugging in data about your project into a database of historical inforomation to get an estimate of how long it will take to do your the work.
9. How long an activity can slip before the whole project is delayed.

Down

1. Adding more resources to a project so that you can get it done faster is called ________ the schedule.
3. A dependency on soemthing outside your project is an ___________ dependency.
4. The kind of network diagram where the activity is written on the connections between nodes is called Activity on ___________.
6. Giving a successor task some time to start before a predecessor finishes.
7. A kind of predecessor that only appears in AOA network diagrams.

Another satisfied customer!

Rob and Rebecca had a beautiful wedding! Everything was perfect. The guests were served their meals, the band was just right, and everyone had a blast...

You'll need to understand the different Activity Resource Estimation tools and techniques for the exam. Look at each of these scenarios and write down which of the five Activity Resource Estimation tools and techniques is being used.

1. Kathleen has to figure out what to do for the music at Rob and Rebecca's wedding. She considers using a DJ, a rock band, or a string quartet. **Alternatives Analysis**

2. The latest issue of Wedding Planner's Journal has an article on working with caterers. It includes a table that shows how many waiters work with various guest-list sizes. **Published Estimating Data**

3. There's a national wedding consultant who specializes in Caribbean themed weddings. Kathleen gets in touch with her to ask about menu options. **Expert Judgment**

4. Kathleen downloads and fills out a specialized spreadsheet that a project manager developed to help with wedding planning. **Project Management software**

5. There's so much work that has to be done to set up the reception hall that Kathleen has to break it down into five different activities in order to assign jobs. **Bottom-Up Estimating**

6. Kathleen asks Rob and Rebecca to visit several different caterers and sample various potential items for the menu. **Alternatives Analysis**

7. Kathleen calls up her friend who knows specifics of the various venues in their area for advice on which one would work best. **Expert Judgment**

Each of these scenarios describes a different tool or technique from Activity Duration Estimating. Write down which tool or technique is being described.

1. Kathleen comes up with three estimates (one where everything goes wrong, one where some things go wrong, and one where nothing goes wrong) for printing invitations, and averages them together to come up with a final number. **Three-point estimate**

2. There will be two different catering companies at the wedding. Kathleen asks the head chef at each of them to give her an estimate of how long it will take each of them to do the job. **Expert judgment**

3. There's a spreadsheet Kathleen always uses to figure out how long it takes guests to RSVP. She enters the number of guests and their ZIP codes, and it calculates an estimate for her. **Parametric estimating**

4. Kathleen's done four weddings that are very similar to Rob and Rebecca's, and in all four of them it took exactly the same amount of time for the caterers to set up the reception hall. **Analogous estimating**

You may get questions on the exam asking you to identify the critical path in a network diagram. You had to practice that by finding the critical path and duration for this PDM and ADM.

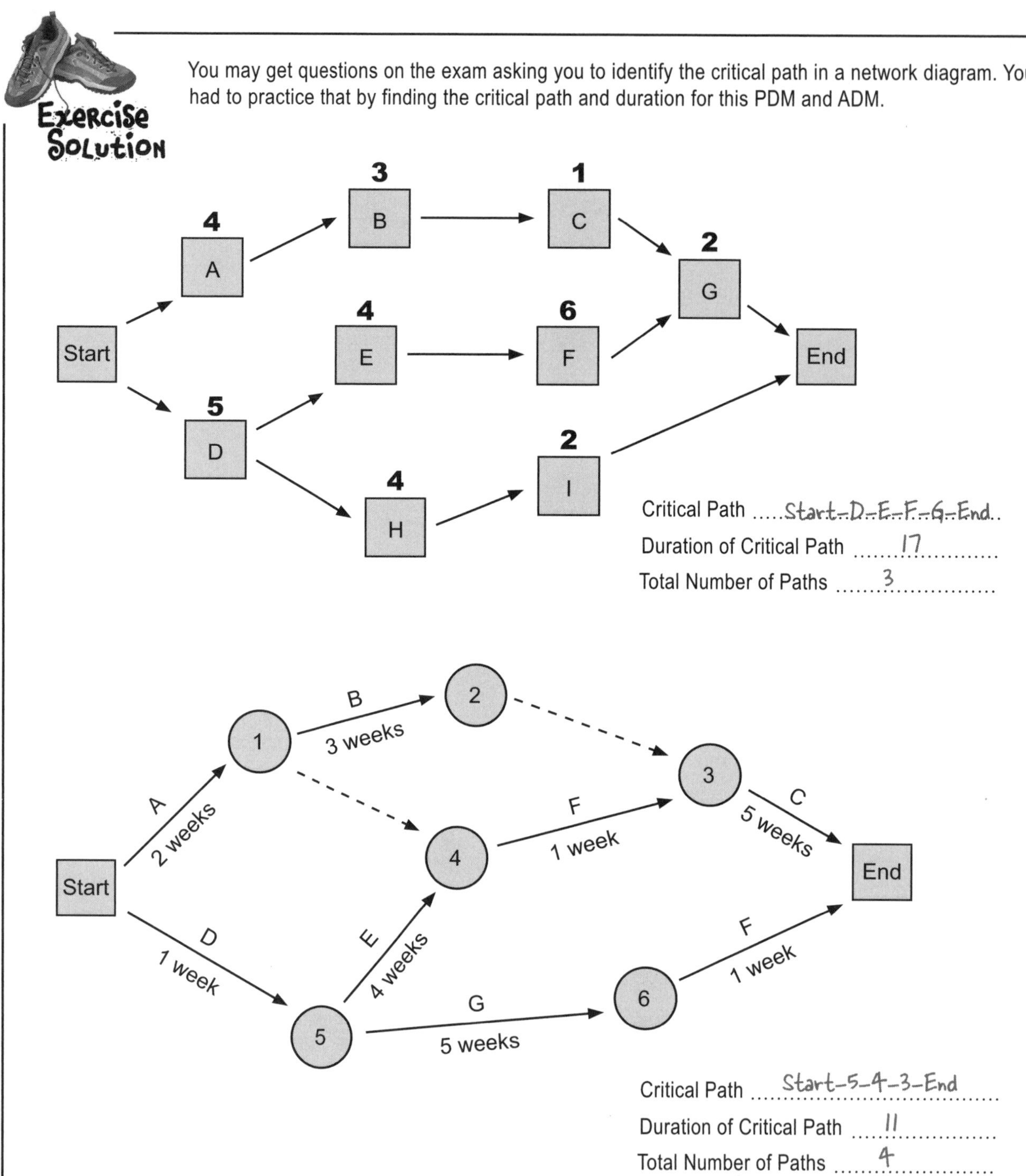

Exercise instructions should be repeated here.

1. What is the float for each activity on the critical path? 0
2. What is the total duration for path A – B – C – G? 10
3. What is the total duration for path A – B – F – G? 15
4. What is the total duration for path D – E – F – G? 17
5. What is the total duration for path D – H – I? 11
6. Which path is the critical path? D – E – F – G
7. Write down the float for each activity:

A 2 B 2 C 7 D 0 E 0

F 0 G 0 H 6 I 6

Each of these scenarios describes a schedule compression technique. Pick which are examples of fast-tracking and which are crashing.

1. Kathleen guesses that 70% of the invitees will RSVP. Instead of waiting for all of them to come in, she goes ahead and reserves the tables and chairs now.

   ☑ Fast-tracking ☐ Crashing

2. Rebecca is taking a really long time to choose the decorations so Kathleen brings in a professional decorator to help, even though it will cost more.

   ☐ Fast-tracking ☑ Crashing

3. Kathleen needs to get the invitations out quickly, so she hires two temps to come in and help her stuff envelopes for a few days.

   ☐ Fast-tracking ☑ Crashing

You'll need to know how to turn a table of nodes into a network diagram, so here's your chance to get some practice! Here's a list of nodes for a PDM network diagram. Try drawing the diagram based on it:

Name	Predecessor
Start	—
A	Start
B	A
C	B
D	Start
E	D
F	B
G	C
H	D
I	E, H
Finish	F, G, I

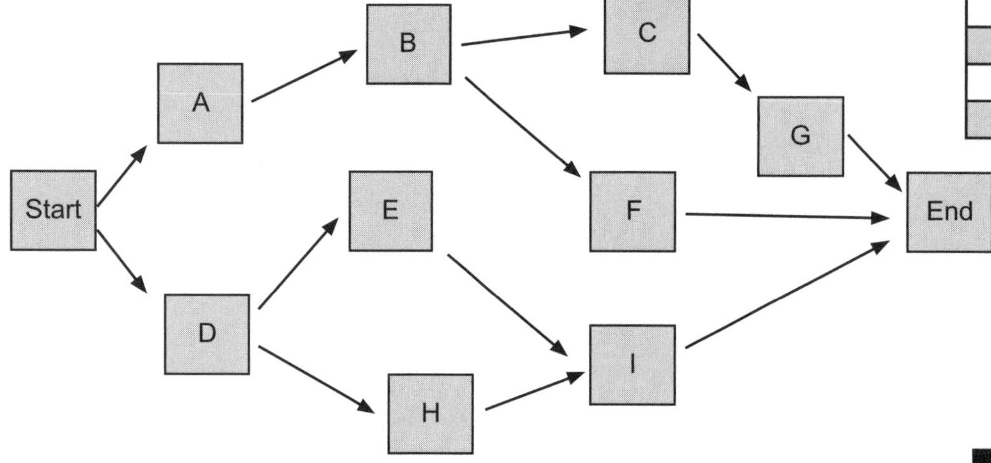

Now try an ADM network diagram! Here's a list of nodes for one:

Node	Dummy?
Start–1	No
1–2	No
2–3	Yes
Start–5	No
5–4	No
4–3	No
3–End	No
5–6	Yes
6–End	No

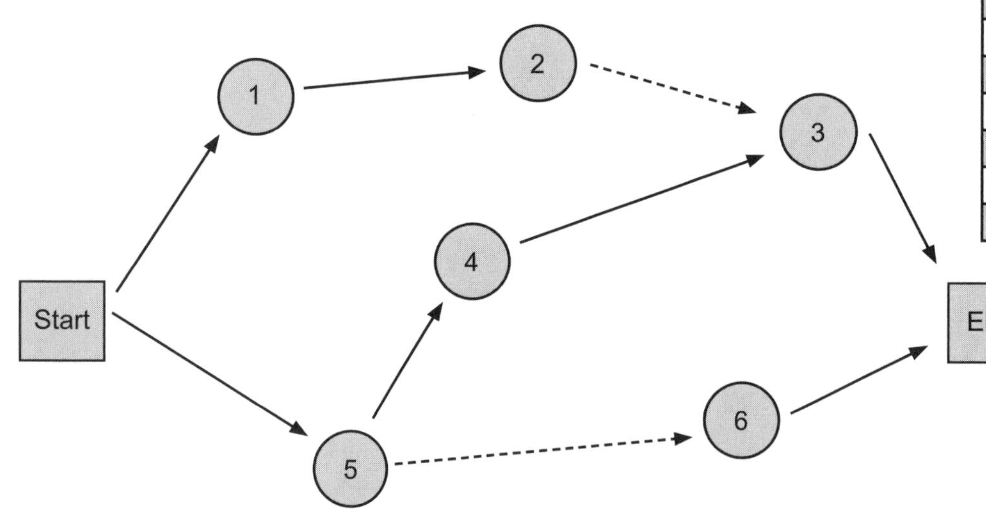

Schedule Control Magnets Answers

You'll see change control over and over again—every single knowledge area has its own change control process! Luckily, you'll start to see how similar they all are. But Schedule Control has its own quirks, and they're important for understanding Time Management.

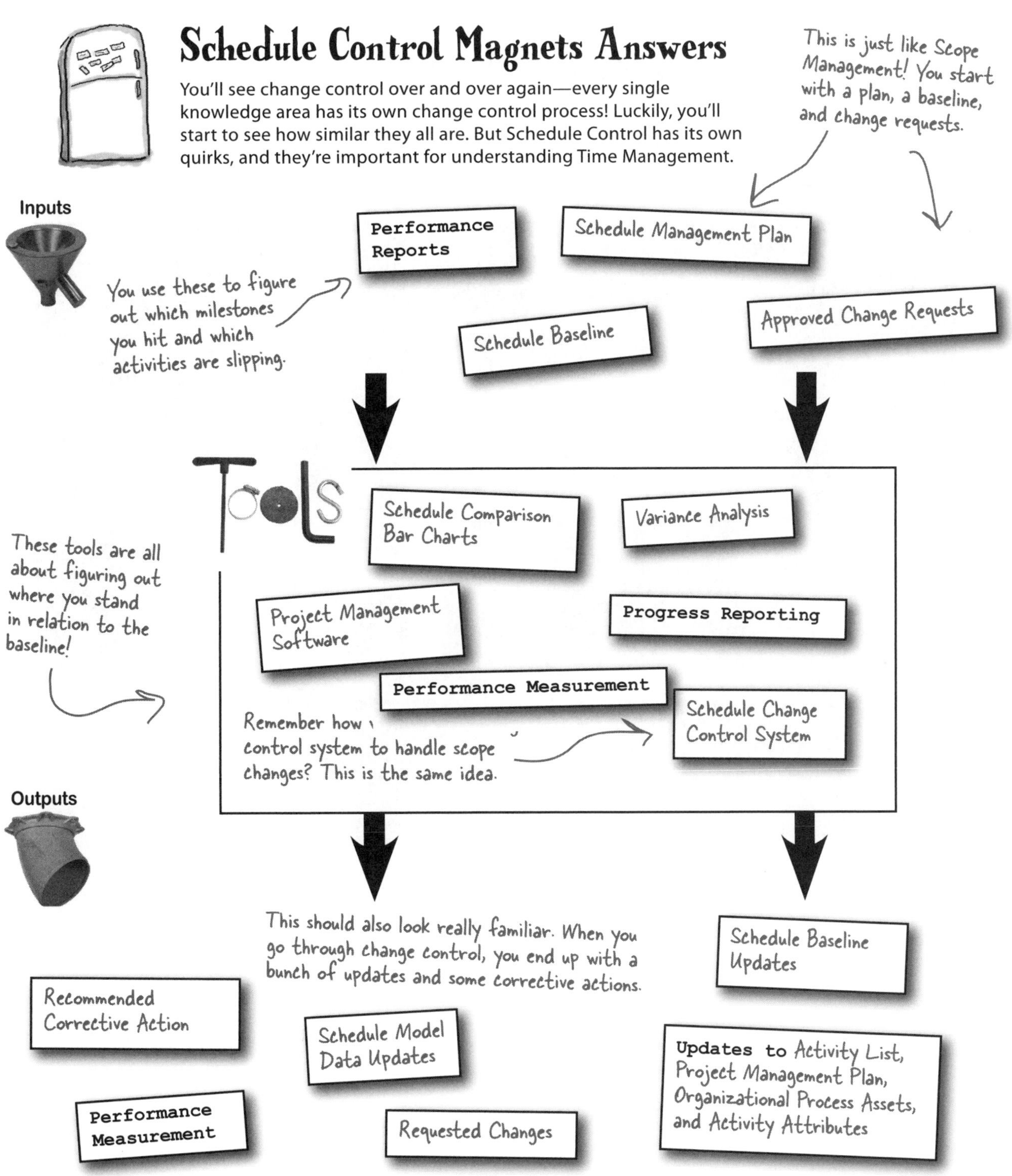

Timecross solution

Take some time to sit back and give your right brain something to do. It's your standard crossword; all of the solution words are from this chapter.

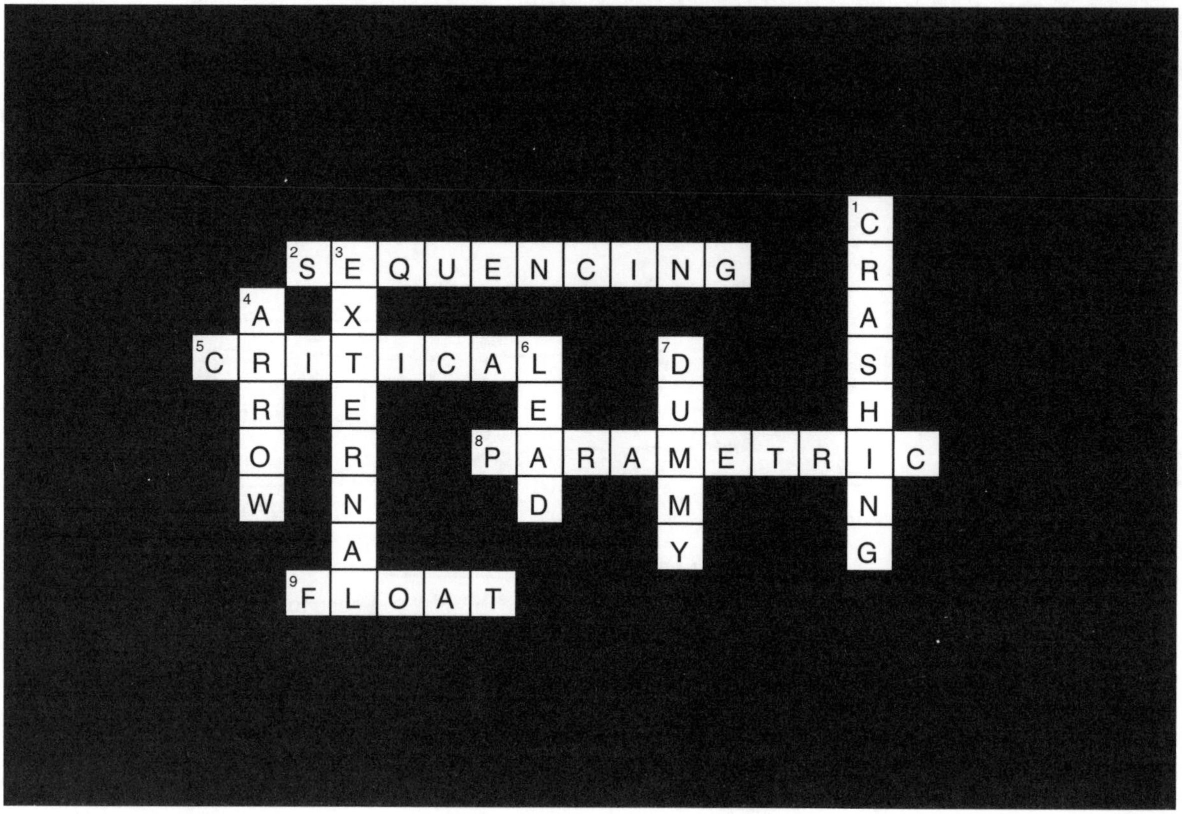

														1 C	
		2 S	3 E	Q	U	E	N	C	I	N	G			R	
	4 A		X											A	
5 C	R	I	T	I	C	A	6 L			7 D				S	
	R		E				E			U				H	
	O		R			8 P	A	R	A	M	E	T	R	I	C
	W		N				D			M				N	
			A							Y				G	
		9 F	L	O	A	T									

Exam Questions

1. You're managing a project, when your client tells you that an external problem happened, and now you have to meet an earlier deadline. Your supervisor heard that in a situation like this, you can use schedule compression by either crashing or fast-tracking the schedule, but he's not sure which is which. What do you tell him?

A. Crashing the project adds risk, while fast-tracking adds cost.

B. When you crash a project, it always shortens the total duration of the project.

C. Crashing the project adds cost, while fast-tracking adds risk.

D. When you fast-track a project, it always shortens the total duration of the project.

2. Given this portion of the network diagram to the right, what's the ES of activity F?

A. 9

B. 10

C. 12

D. 13

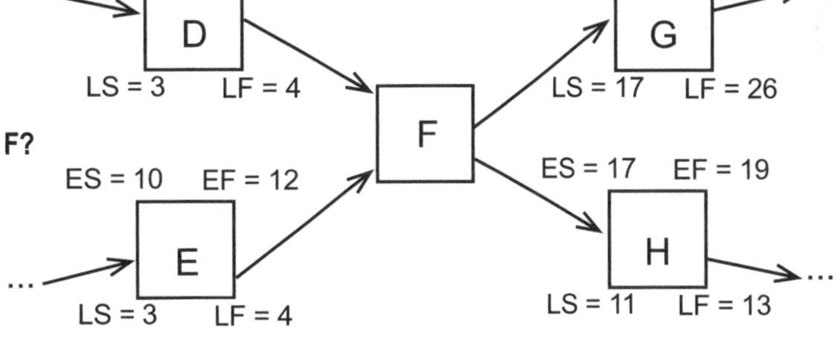

3. Given this portion of the network diagram to the right, what's the LF of activity F?

A. 10

B. 11

C. 16

D. 17

4. You are managing a software project. Your QA manager tells you that you need to plan to have her team start their test planing activity so that it finishes just before testing begins. But other than that, she says it can start as late in the project as necessary. What's the relationship between the test planning activity and the testing activity?

A. Start-to-Start (SS)

B. Start-to-finish (SF)

C. Finish-to-Start (FS)

D. Finish-to-Finish (FF)

5. You're managing an industrial design project. You've come up with the complete activity list, created network diagrams, assigned resources to each activity, and estimated their durations. What's the next thing that you do?

A. Use Rolling Wave Planning to compensate for the fact that you don't have complete information

B. Create the schedule

C. Consult the project scope statement and perform Activity Sequencing

D. Use fast-tracking to reduce the total duration

Exam Questions

6. Which of the following is NOT an input to Schedule Development?

A. Activity list

B. Project schedule network diagrams

C. Resource calendars

D. Schedule baseline

7. Three members of your project team want to pad their estimates because they believe there are certain risks that might materialize. What is the BEST way to handle this situation?

A. Estimate the activities honestly, and then use a contingency reserve to cover any unexpected costs

B. Allow more time for the work by adding a buffer to every activity in the schedule

C. Tell the team members not to worry about it, and if the schedule is wrong it's okay for the project to be late

D. Crash the schedule

8. Which of the following tools is used for adding buffers to a schedule?

A. Three-point estimates

B. Critical chain method

C. Expert judgment

D. Critical path analysis

Name	Predecessor	Duration
Start	—	—
A	Start	6
B	A	4
C	B	8
D	A	1
E	D	1
F	E	2
G	Start	3
H	G	3
I	H	2
J	B, I	3
Finish	F, J, C	—

9. What is the critical path in the activity list to the right?

A. Start-A-B-C-Finish

B. Start-A-D-E-F-Finish

C. Start-G-H-I-J-Finish

D. Start-A-B-J-Finish

10. What is the float for activity F in the activity list to the right?

A. 0

B. 7

C. 8

D. 10

11. You're managing an interior decoration project, when you've found out that you need to get it done earlier than originally planned. You decide to fast-track the project. This means:

A. Starting the project sooner and working overtime

B. Assigning more people to the tasks at a greater total cost, especially for activities on the critical path

C. Starting activities earlier and overlapping them more, which will cost more and could add risks

D. Shortening the durations of the activities and asking people to work overtime to accommodate that.

Exam Questions

12. Slack is a synonym for:

A. Float

B. Lag

C. Buffer

D. Reserve

13. You're managing a construction project. You've decomposed work packages into activities, and your client needs a duration estimate for each activity that you come up with. Which of the following will you use for this?

A. Milestone list

B. Activity list

C. Critical path analysis

D. Project schedule network diagram

14. What's the correct order of the Time Management planning processes?

A. Activity Sequencing, Activity Definition, Activity Resource Estimating, Activity Duration Estimating, Schedule Development

B. Activity Definition, Activity Sequencing, Schedule Development, Activity Resource Estimating, Activity Duration Estimating

C. Activity Definition, Activity Sequencing, Activity Resource Estimating, Activity Duration Estimating, Schedule Development

D. Schedule Development, Activity Definition, Activity Sequencing, Activity Resource Estimating, Activity Duration Estimating

15. Which of the following is NOT a tool or technique used in Activity Duration Estimating?

A. SWAG Estimation

B. Parametric Estimation

C. Analogous Estimation

D. Three-Point Estimation

16. You're working on a project schedule network diagram, and you need to decide on either the arrow diagramming method or precedence diagramming method. Which of the following is NOT true?

A. PDM has activities on arrows, while ADM has activities on nodes

B. ADM uses dummy activities with zero duration to add paths to the network

C. Both ADM and PDM diagrams can be used in critical path analysis

D. PDM can show different kinds of dependencies, while ADM can only show finish-to-start (FS) dependencies

Exam Questions

17. Given the network diagram below, what's the critical path?

A. Start-A-B-C-End

B. Start-A-E-F-C-End

C. Start-A-E-G-H-End

D. Start-D-G-H-End

18. For that same network diagram below, what's the float for activity F?

A. 0 weeks

B. 2 weeks

C. 4 weeks

D. 5 weeks

19. For that same network diagram below, what's the float for activity G?

A. 0 weeks

B. 2 weeks

C. 4 weeks

D. 5 weeks

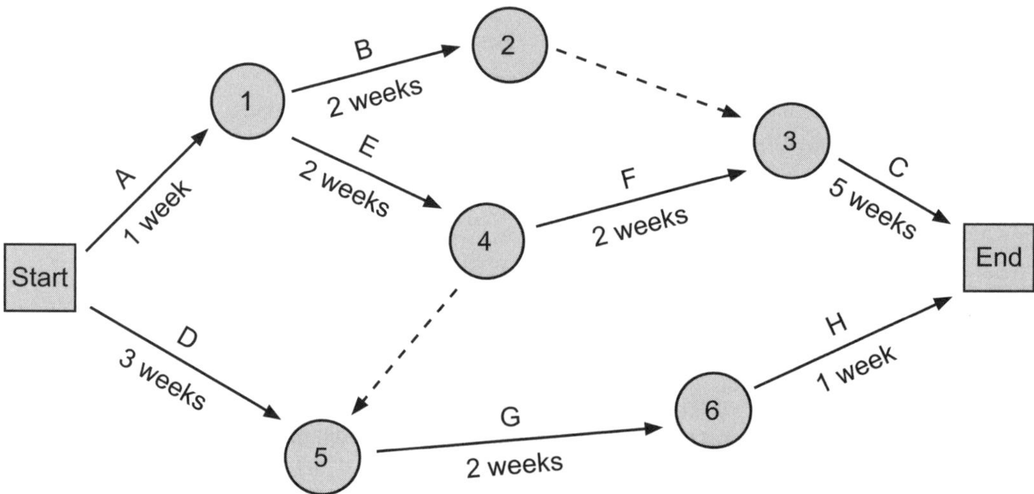

Exam Questions

20. You're managing a software project, when your customer informs you that a schedule change is necessary. Which is the BEST thing to do?

A. Consult the schedule management plan.

B. Notify the team and the sponsor that there's going to be a schedule change.

C. Influence the factors that cause change.

D. Refuse to make the change because there's already a schedule baseline.

21. Your company has previously run other projects similar to the one you're currently managing. What is the BEST way to use that information?

A. Check the organizational process assets for lessons learned and other information about the past projects.

B. Use parametric estimation to estimate your project based on past projects' performance.

C. Start from scratch because you don't want mistakes from past projects to influence you.

D. Reuse the project management plan from a past project.

22. You're planning the schedule for a highway construction project, but the final date you came up with will run into the next budget year. The state comes up with capital from a reserve fund, and now you can increase the budget for your resources. What's the BEST way to compress the schedule?

A. Go back to your three-point estimates and use the most optimistic ones

B. Use the extra budget to increase your contingency reserve

C. Hire more experts to use expert judgment so your estimates are more accurate.

D. Crash the schedule

23. You're managing a software project. You've created the schedule, and you need to figure out which activities absolutely cannot slip. You've done critical path analysis, identifying the critical path and calculating the early start and early finish for each activity. Which activities cannot slip without making the project late?

A. The ones with the biggest difference between ES and LF

B. The activities on the critical path

C. The activity with the most lag

D. The last activity in the project, because it has no float

24. You're managing a construction project. You've decomposed work packages into activities, and your client needs a duration estimate for each activity that you came up with. Which of he following will you use for this?

A. Activity sequencing

B. Resource calendar

C. Critical path analysis

D. Milestone list

Answers

Exam ~~Questions~~

1. Answer: C

You'll definitely get some questions that ask you about crashing and fast-tracking, and it's important to know the difference between them. When you crash the project, it means that you add resources to it, especially to the critical path. There's no real risk in doing that—in the worst-case scenario, the extra people just sit around!—but it does cost more. Fast-tracking means adjusting the schedule so that activities overlap. The same resources are doing the work, so it's not going to cost more, but it's definitely riskier, because now you've eliminated buffers and possibly broken some dependencies! And remember that crashing or fast-tracking won't always work to make the project go faster!

2. Answer: D

Calculating the early start (ES) of an activity isn't hard. All you need to do is look at the early finish (EF) of the previous activity and add one. If there's more than one predecessor, then you take the largest EF and add one. In this case, the predecessors to activity F are D, with an EF of 9, and E, with an EF of 12. So the ES of F is 12 + 1 = 13.

3. Answer: A

It's just as easy to calculate the late finish (LF). Look at the following activity, take its LS (late start), and subtract one. If there's more than one following activity, use the one with the lowest LS. So for activity F in the question, the following activities are G, with an LS of 17, and H, with an LS of 11. So the LF of F is 11 - 1 = 10.

4. Answer: C

Don't let the jargon fool you! You don't need to know anything about software testing to answer this question. When you have two activities, and the first activity has to be timed so that it finishes before the second one starts, then you've got a Finish-to-Start relationship, or FS.

5. Answer: B

Did answer A trick you? No need for rolling wave planning when you've got enough info to define all the activities!

This is a Which-is-next question that describes a project that's completed the Activity Definition, Activity Sequencing, Activity Resource Estimating, and Activity Duration Estimating processes. The next process in Time Management is Schedule Development, which means that the next thing you do is create the schedule!

Exam Questions Answers

6. Answer: D

The schedule baseline is an output of the Schedule Development process, not an input. You should definitely know what goes into the schedule baseline: it's a specific version of the schedule that you set aside and use for comparison later on, when you want to know if the project is running late.

I get it—we can use the schedule baseline the same way that we use the scope baseline! We take a snapshot of it and then save it, so we can compare the project's performance against it later!

7. Answer: A

You always want to be honest with your estimates. Every project has unknowns and risks, and there's no way to estimate any activity exactly! Luckily, we have tools to deal with this. You can use reserve analysis, a tool of Activity Duration Estimating, to come up with a contingency reserve that you can use to plan for these risks.

8. Answer: B

Critical chain method is a technique that's part of Schedule Development that lets you figure out how to handle the problems that come with having limited resources. You use it to shuffle both activities and resources on your critical path. One important aspect of the critical chain method is that you can use it to add buffers to the schedule to reduce the risk of certain activities.

9. Answer: A

When you draw out a network diagram for the activities in the table, you end up with four paths. And you definitely should draw out the activity diagram for a question like this! You're allowed to use scratch paper on the exam, and this is one place where you should definitely do it. Of the four paths, only one has the longest duration: Start-A-B-C-Finish, which has a duration of 6+ 4 + 8 = 18. That's the critical path.

Exam ~~Questions~~

10. Answer: C

Activity F is in the path Start-A-D-E-F-Finish. This path has a duration of 6 + 1 + 1 + 2 = 10. The float of an activity is the longest time it can slip before it affects the critical path. In this case, activity F can slip by 8 without causing the path that it's on to go beyond the critical path. But any more than that, and its path becomes the new critical path!

Did you notice answer A? Don't forget that the float of any activity in the critical path is zero!

11. Answer: C

This is the definition of fast tracking, and you're probably getting the hang of this one by now. You may get a question like this, but you'll almost certainly see fast tracking as an incorrect answer to several questions!

12. Answer: A

Remember that when you see "slack", it's the same thing as float. Either term could appear on the exam!

When a question asks what you'd use for a process, it's asking you to pick an input, tool or technique that's part of the process.

13. Answer: B

This question is asking about the Activity Duration Estimating process. Take a look at the answers—there's only one answer that's used in that process: you need to start with the activity list in order to do the estimates for the activities! The other answers are things that are inputs, tools or techniques for other processes.

14. Answer: C

It's not hard to remember the order in which the Time Management processes are performed. If you use a little common sense, you can reason your way through a question like this. You need to define your activities before you can sequence them, you need to know who's going to be doing an activity before you can estimate how long it's going to take, and you need to do all of that before you can build a schedule!

15. Answer: A

You'll have to know the different kinds of estimating techniques for the exam. You don't necessarily have to be good at doing them, but you should recognize which are which. Parametric estimating is when you plug values into a formula, program, or spreadsheet and get an estimate. Analogous estimating uses similar activities from past projects to calculate new estimates. Three-point estimating uses an optimistic, pessimistic, and realistic estimate.

Exam Questions

16. Answer: A

The precedence diagramming method, or PDM, is also known as activity-on-node. It's the most common kind of project schedule network diagram. Its activities are on the nodes, which are connected by arrows. Arrow diagramming method, or activity-on-arrow, has activities and durations on each arrow. It's less flexible than the PDM method because it can only use finish-to-start (FS) dependencies.

The answer to this kind of question can be a process, an input, or a tool or technique!

17. Answer: B

The path Start-A-E-F-C-End has a duration of 1 + 2 + 2 + 5 = 10 weeks, which is the longest total duration in the entire network.

18. Answer: A

Influencing the factors that cause change is a good idea, but by the time the change happens it's too late to do that!

Since activity F is on the critical path, its float is zero, because the float of any activity on the critical path is zero.

It looks like there will be a bunch of questions on the critical path method! It's a good thing I've got so much practice with it.

19. Answer: C

Activity G is on the path Start-D-G-H-End, which has a total duration of 3 + 2 + 1 = 6 weeks. Since the critical path is 10 weeks long, that means it could slip by four weeks before it delays the project.

20. Answer: A

The schedule management plan tells you how changes to the schedule are to be handled. Any time there's a change, the first thing you should do is consult the plan to see how it should be handled.

21. Answer: A

The organizational process assets contain historical information about past projects. When you write up your lessons learned, or create work performance information, you store it in your company's organizational process asset library! Also, did you notice that answer B was the wrong definition of parametric estimation?

22. Answer: D

Crashing the schedule is the form of schedule compression that increases cost. This is a difficult question because all of the answers sound good, and one or two are a little misleading! Don't fall into the trap of choosing an answer because you recognize a valid tool or technique in it. Reserve analysis and three-point estimates are very useful techniques, but they're not the answer to this question.

23. Answer: B

The critical path is the path in the network diagram where any delay will cause a delay in the schedule. These are the activities that cannot slip without making the project late!

24. Answer: B

Keep an eye out for questions that ask you what you'll use to do a certain project management task. This sort of question is usually describing a specific process, and the question asks you something about that process. What process comes after you decompose work packages into activities, and has you coming up with an estimate for each activity that you came up with? That's the Activity Duration Estimating process! And the only answer that's an input to Activity Duration Estimating is the resource calendar.

7 Cost Management

Watching the bottom line

Every project boils down to money. If you had a bigger **budget**, you could probably get more people to do your project more quickly and deliver more. That's why no project plan is complete until you come up with a budget. But no matter whether your project is big or small, and no matter how many **resources** and **activities** are in it, the process for figuring out the bottom line is *always the same*!

Time to expand the Head First Lounge

The Head First Lounge is doing so well that the guys are going to go ahead and open another Lounge near you. They're renting a basement bar and now all they need to do is renovate it.

The guys go overboard

When they start planning out what to buy, they want really expensive original retro stuff—the biggest bar they can find, and seventies textiles for the walls, floor, and upholstery, plus accessories—this is going to cost a lot of money…

Lounge conversation

Jeff: That bar is soooo cool! I can just imagine mixing up some crazy elixirs at parties!

Alice: Look. I know you want the new Lounge to look as good as the original, but you only have a little spare cash to spend on this. That means you have a limit of $10,000.

Charles: We should be able to get the new place looking so sweet with that!

Alice: Costs can creep up on you if you don't watch what you're doing. The best way to handle this is to create a budget and check your progress against it as you go.

Jeff: You always turn everything into a project, even mixing elixirs! Can't we just have fun with this?

Alice: Not if you don't want to go into debt.

Introducing the cost management processes

To make sure that they don't go over budget, Jeff, Charles, and Alice sit down and come up with detailed estimates of their costs. Once they have that, they add up the cost estimates into a budget and then they track the project according to that budget while the work is happening.

Cost Estimating process

This means figuring out exactly how much you expect each work activity you are doing to cost. So each activity is estimated for its time and materials cost, and any other known factors that can be figured in.

You need to have a good idea of the work you're going to do and how long it will take to do that work.

Cost Budgeting process

Here's where all of the estimates are added up and baselined. Once you have figured out the baseline, that's what all future expenditures are compared to.

This is just like the scope baseline from Chapter 5 or the schedule baseline from Chapter 6.

Cost Control process

This just means tracking the actual work according to the budget to see if any adjustments need to be made.

Controlling costs means always knowing how you are doing compared to how you thought you would do.

What Alice needs before she starts Cost Estimation

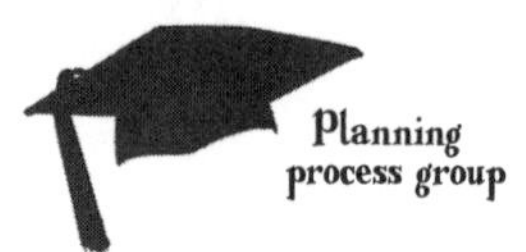

Alice wants to keep the Lounge project's costs under control, and that starts with the **Cost Estimation** process. Before Alice can estimate costs, she needs a Scope Statement, a Project Management Plan, and a WBS. Understanding cost estimates means knowing how much work will be done and when.

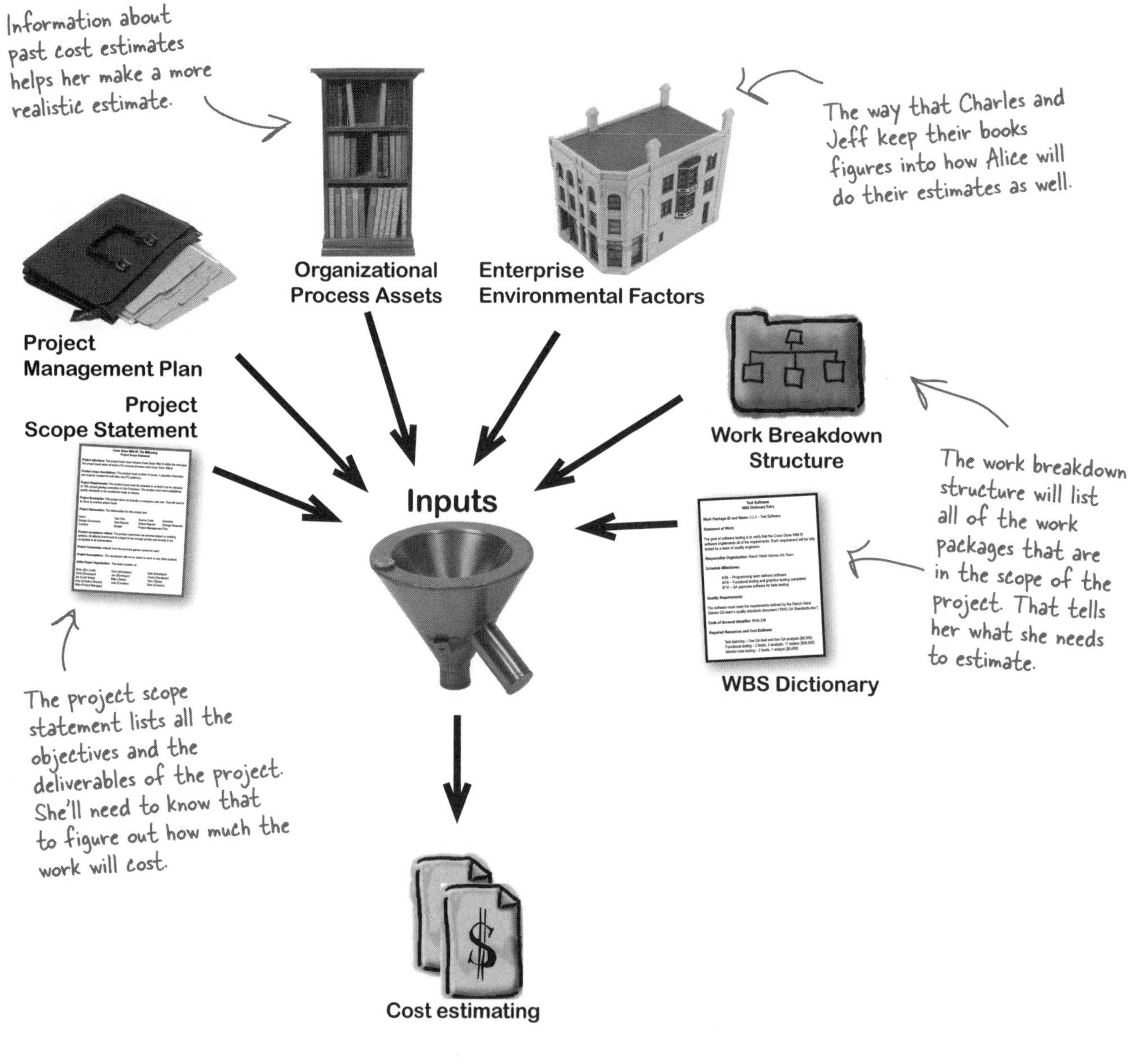

Information about past cost estimates helps her make a more realistic estimate.

The way that Charles and Jeff keep their books figures into how Alice will do their estimates as well.

Organizational Process Assets

Enterprise Environmental Factors

Project Management Plan

Project Scope Statement

Work Breakdown Structure

WBS Dictionary

Inputs

The work breakdown structure will list all of the work packages that are in the scope of the project. That tells her what she needs to estimate.

The project scope statement lists all the objectives and the deliverables of the project. She'll need to know that to figure out how much the work will cost.

Cost estimating

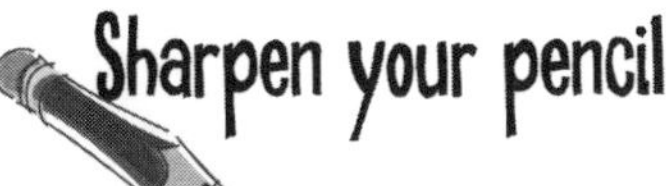

You've already seen four of the tools and techniques in Cost Estimation. Take a look at the list of tools, and try to figure out which one of them Alice is using when she estimates costs. Can you write down which tool is being used in each scenario?

A. Bottom-up estimating

B. Analogous estimating

C. Project management software

D. Parametric estimating

1. The Starbuzz across the street opened just a few months ago. Alice sits down with the contractor who did the work there and asks him to help her figure out how much it will cost. He takes a look at the equipment Charles and Jeff want to buy and the specs for the cabinets and seating and tells her what she can afford to do with the budget she has.

Tool: ....

2. Alice creates a spreadsheet with all of the historical information from similar remodeling projects that have happened on her block. She sits down and types in the guys' desired furnishings and the square footage of the room to generate an estimated cost.

Tool: ....

3. Once she has her schedule completed, Alice uses software to change resources around and play with some of the dates to try to find a mix that works best with the money they have to spend.

Tool: ....

4. Alice sits down and estimates each and every activity and resource that she is going to need. Then she adds up all of the estimates into "rolled-up" categories. From there she adds up the categories into an overall budget number.

Tool: ....

5. Jeff sets up an appointment with the same contractor his friend used for some remodelling work. The contractor comes to the house, takes a look at the room, and then gives an estimate for the work.

Tool: ....

6. Alice uses some software to play with all of the contractors' estimates they have gathered. She tries changing the cost of materials and the cost of labor to understand better how things are going to pan out for her project. She even takes a look at what it would take to implement contingency plans for some of the risks she has identified.

Tool: ....

Did you work out which estimating tool from Time Management Alice is using when she estimates costs in each of these scenarios?

1: **B. Analogous estimating.**
Since Alice is using the contractor's experience with a similar project to figure out how long her project will take, she is assuming that her project will go like the Starbuzz one did.

2: **D. Parametric estimating.**
In this one Alice is just applying some numbers particular to her project to some historical information she has gathered from other projects and generating an estimate from that.

3: **C. Project management software.**
Anytime a question talks about using software to analyze estimates, this is the tool they are talking about.

4: **A. Bottom-up estimating.**
Starting at the lowest level and rolling up estimates is bottom-up estimating. Alice started with the activities on her schedule and rolled them up to categories and finally to a budget number.

5: **B. Analogous estimating.**
This is another example of asking somebody who has direct experience with this kind of work to give an estimate.

6: **C. Project management software.**
Another example of using software to tweak estimates.

Good question.

Not all of the estimation techniques for cost are the same as the ones we used for time. Often, people only have a certain amount of time to devote to a project and a fixed amount of money too. So, it makes sense that some of the tools for estimating both would overlap. We'll learn a few new ones next.

Tools and techniques used only in cost estimation

A lot of times you come into a project and there is already an expectation of how much it will cost or how much time it will take. When you make an estimate really early in the project and you don't know much about it, that estimate is called a **Rough Order of Magnitude** estimate. (You'll also see it called a **ballpark estimate**.) It's expected that it will get more refined as time goes on and you learn more about the project. Here are some more tools and techniques used to estimate cost:

This estimate is REALLY rough! It's got a range of -50% to +100%, which means it can be anywhere from half to twice the actual cost! So you only use it at the very beginning of the project.

Determine Resource Cost Rates

People who will be working on the project all work at a specific rate. Any materials you will use to build the project (like wood or wiring) will be charged at a rate, too. This just means figuring out what the rate for labor and materials will be.

Vendor Bid Analysis

Sometimes you will need to work with an external contractor to get your project done. You might even have more than one contractor bid on the job. This tool is all about evaluating those bids and choosing the one you will go with.

You'll see this in action when we look at risk management in Chapter 11.

Reserve Analysis

You need to set aside some money for cost overruns. If you know that your project has a risk of something expensive happening, better to have some cash laying around to deal with it. Reserve analysis means putting some cash away just in case.

Since the next chapter is all about quality, you'll be learning a lot about this in Chapter 8.

Cost of Quality

You will need to figure the cost of all of your quality-related activities into the overall budget, too. Since it's cheaper to find bugs earlier in the project than later, there are always quality costs associated with everything your project produces. Cost of Quality is just a way of tracking the cost of those activities.

Cost of quality is how much money it takes to do the project right.

Let's talk numbers

There are a few numbers that will appear on the test as definitions. You won't need to calculate these, but you should know what each term means.

You'll get exam questions asking you to use BCR or NPV to compare two projects. The higher these numbers are, the better!

Benefit cost ratio (BCR)

This is the amount of money a project is going to make versus how much it will cost to build it. Generally, if the benefit is higher than the cost, the project is a good investment.

Net present value (NPV)

This is the actual value at a given time of the project minus all of the costs associated with it. This includes the time it takes to build it and labor as well as materials. People calculate this number to see if it's worth doing a project.

Opportunity cost

When an organization has to choose between two projects, they are always giving up the money they would have made on the one they don't do. That's called opportunity cost. It's the money you don't get because you chose not to do a project.

Internal rate of return

This is the amount of money the project will return to the company that is funding it. It's how much money a project is making the company. It's usually expressed as a percentage of the funding that has been allocated to it.

Depreciation

This is the rate at which your project loses value over time. So, if you are building a project that will only be marketable at a high price for a short period of time, the product loses value as time goes on.

Lifecycle Costing

Before you get started on a project, it's really useful to figure out how much you expect it to cost—not just to develop, but to support the product once it's in place and being used by the customer.

Now Alice knows how much the Lounge will cost

Once you apply all of the tools in this process, you get an estimate for how much your project will cost. It's always important to keep all of your supporting estimate information, too. That way, you know the assumptions you made when you were coming up with your numbers.

Outputs

Activity cost estimates

This is the cost estimate for all of the activities in your activity list. It takes into account resource rates and estimated duration of the activities.

Activity Cost Estimates

Activity cost estimate supporting detail

Just like the WBS has a WBS Dictionary, and the Activity List has Activity Attributes, the cost estimate has supporting detail. Here is where you list out all of the rates and reasoning you have used to come to the numbers you are presenting in your estimates.

Cost Estimate Supporting Detail

Updates to the cost management plan

Along the way, you might find that you need to change the way you measure and manage cost. These updates allow you to make changes to the Project Management Plan to deal with those improvements.

Cost Management Plan Updates

Requested changes

As you figure out which activities will need to be done, you may realize that the scope or schedule or risk register or anything else you have baselined needs to change. When that happens, you need to create a change request and send it through the change control system.

Change Request

Once Alice has an estimate of the project's cost, what should she do with that information?

The Cost Budgeting process

The next process in Cost Management is **Cost Budgeting**. Here's where you take the estimates that you came up with and build a budget out of them. You'll build on the Activity Cost Estimates and Cost Estimate Supporting Detail that you came up with in Cost Estimating.

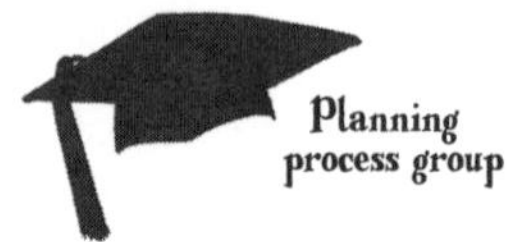

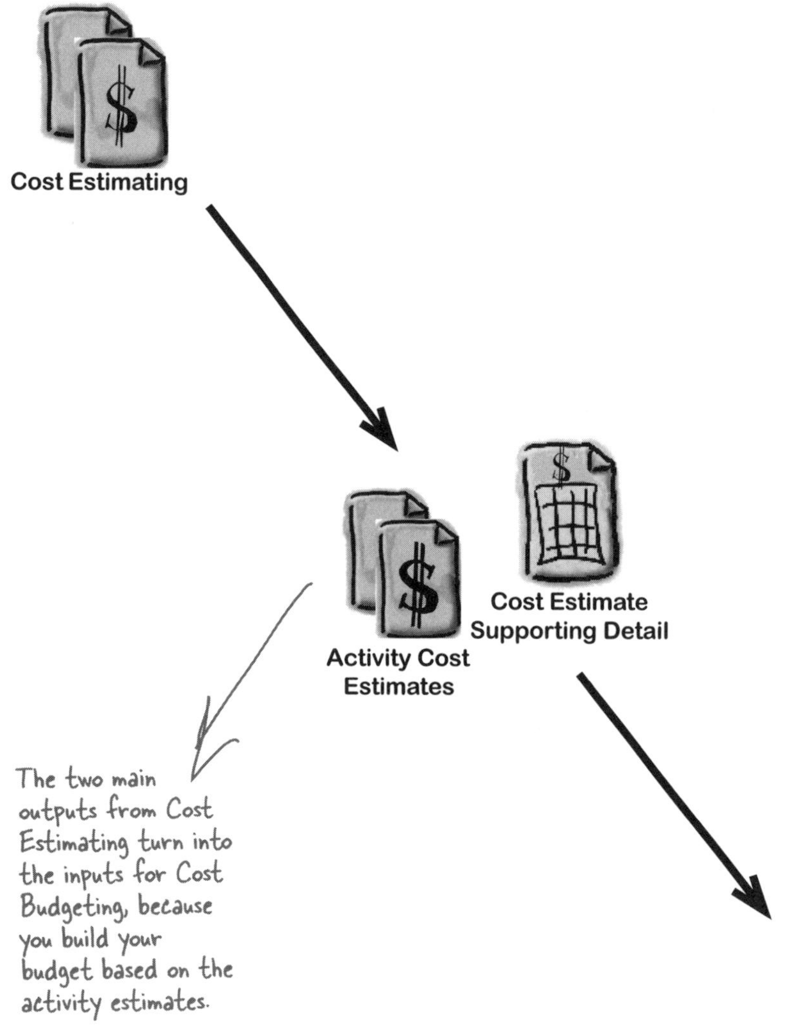

You use the outputs from the last process where you created estimates as inputs to this one. Now you can build your budget.

What you need to build your budget

Aside from Activity Cost Estimates and Cost Estimate Supporting Detail, the **inputs** to Cost Budgeting are the same ones that you saw in Cost Estimating.

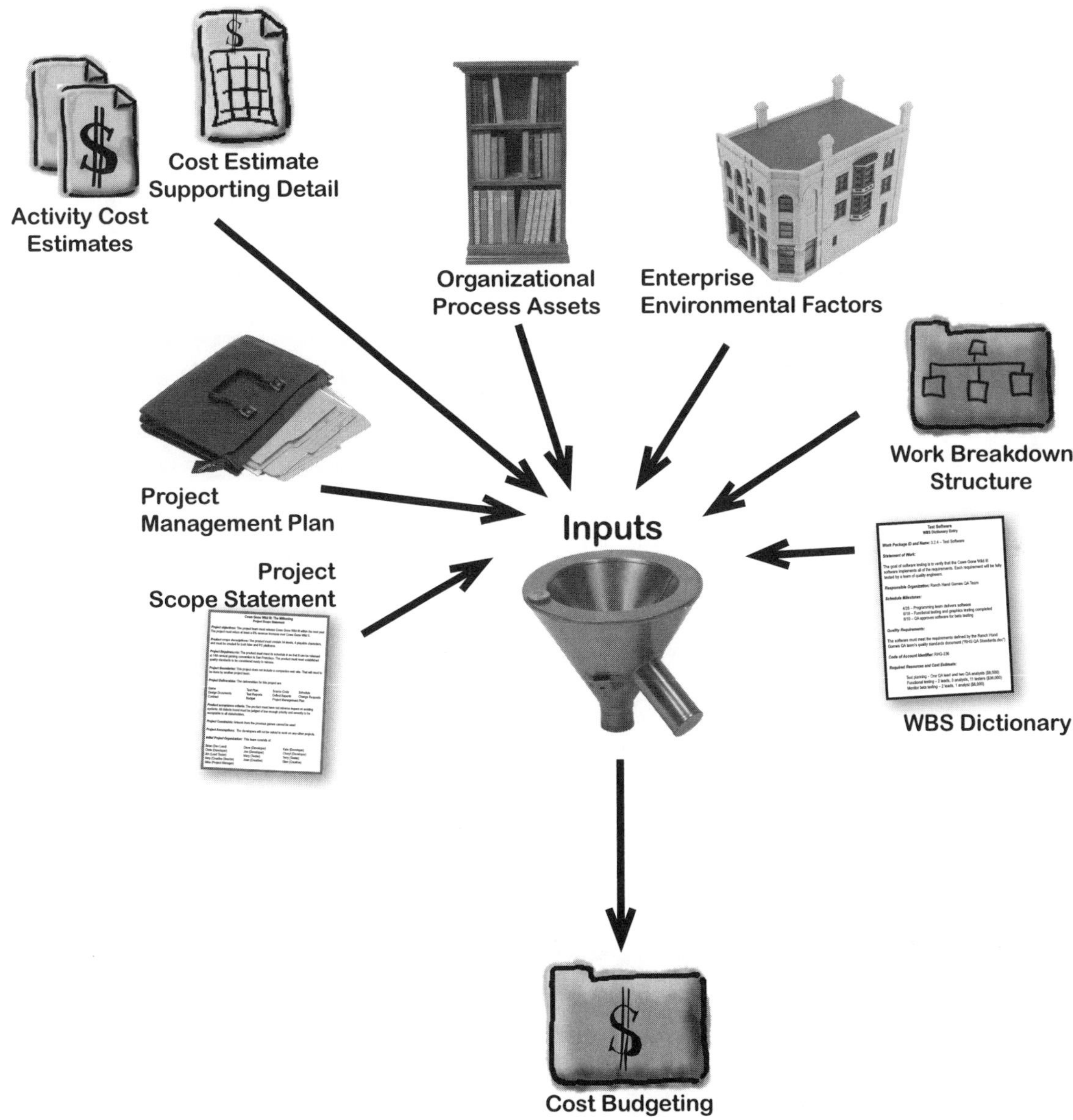

Cost budgeting: How to build a budget

1 Roll up your estimates into control accounts

This tool is called **cost aggregation**. You take your activity estimates and roll them up into control accounts on your Work Breakdown Structure. That makes it easy for you to know what each work package in your project is going to cost.

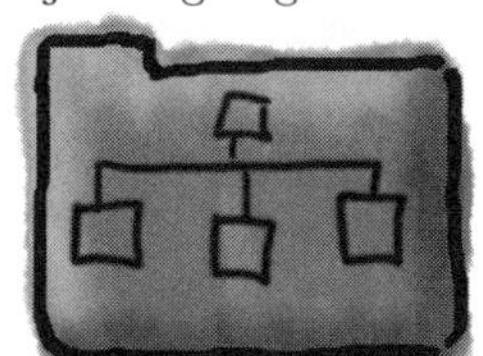

2 Come up with your reserves

When you evaluate the risks to your project, you will set aside some cash reserves to deal with any issues that might come your way.

Outputs

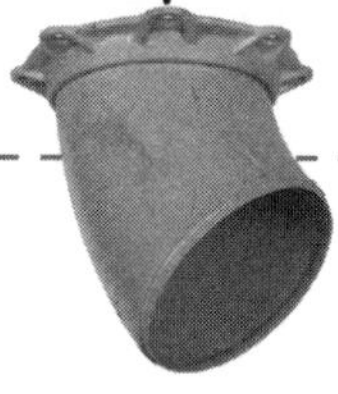

5 Build a baseline

Just like your scope and schedule baselines, a cost baseline is a snapshot of the planned budget. You compare your actual performance against the baseline so you always know how you are doing versus what you planned.

3 Use parametric estimation

Here's where you compare your project to historical data that has been collected on other projects to give your budget some grounding in real-world experience.

It's true that not everybody has access to historical data to do a check like this. But, for the purposes of the test, you need to know that it's a tool for making your budget accurate.

4 Make sure you haven't blown your limits

This tool is **Funding Limit Reconciliation**. Since most people work in companies that aren't willing to throw unlimited money at a project, you need to be sure that you can do the project within the amount that your company is willing to spend.

If you blow your limit, you need to replan or go to your sponsor to figure out what to do. It could be that a scope change is necessary. Or the funding limit can be increased.

---

6 Figure out funding requirements

It's not enough to have an overall number that everyone can agree to. You need to plan out how and when you will spend it. This output is about figuring out how you will make sure your project has money when it's needed, and that you have enough to cover unexpected risks as well as known cost increases that change with time.

7 Update your cost plan

Once you have estimated and produced your baseline and funding requirements, you need to update your cost management plan with anything you learned along the way.

Lounge conversation

Jeff: OK, how do we start? There are a lot of things to buy here.

Alice: We already have your savings, and the rest will come in July at the year end. The Lounge is having another great year, so the profits are pretty good. Your savings are around $4,000 and the profits will probably be closer to $6,000. That's definitely enough money to work with.

Charles: Well the furniture I want isn't back in stock until June.

Alice: OK, so we have to time our costs so that they're in line with our cash flow.

Jeff: Oh! I see. So we can start building now, but we'll still have money in June and July when the furniture comes in. Perfect.

What tool or technique is Alice using to build the budget?

1. Alice reads a newspaper article that says that there has been a sharp increase in lumber costs recently. She knows this wasn't in her contractor's original plan and decides to put a few hundred dollars aside to deal with the price hike if it should happen.

☐ Parametric estimating ☐ Reserve Analysis ☐ Cost aggregation ☐ Funding Limit Reconciliation

2. Jeff helps Alice add up all of the estimates they have done into control accounts so that they can figure out how much the stereo installation is going to cost versus the entertainment center building.

☐ Parametric estimating ☐ Reserve Analysis ☐ Cost aggregation ☐ Funding Limit Reconciliation

3. Once the budget is close to done, Alice looks over their financial plans for the year to be sure that they can afford everything at the time that it is needed.

☐ Parametric estimating ☐ Reserve Analysis ☐ Cost aggregation ☐ Funding Limit Reconciliation

Answers: 1. Reserve Analysis 2. Cost aggregation 3. Funding Limit Reconciliation

BULLET POINTS: AIMING FOR THE EXAM

- **Parametric estimation** is used in cost estimating and cost budgeting.
- **Cost Aggregation** is rolling up costs from the work package level to the control account level so that the numbers can be followed down through the WBS hierarchy.
- **Control accounts** are high-level WBS items that are used to track cost estimates. They do not represent activities or work packages. They represent the cost of the work packages and activities that appear under them in the WBS.
- **Cash flow** is how much money you have at a given time to apply to your project.
- The main output of Cost Estimating is the Activity Cost Estimate and the Activity Cost Estimate Supporting Detail. The main output of Cost Budgeting is the Cost Baseline and Project Funding Requirements.
- You will get questions on the exam asking you to select between projects using **Net Present Value** (NPV) or **Benefit Cost Ratio** (BCR). Always choose the project with the biggest NPV or BCR!
- **Lifecycle costing** means estimating the money it will take to support your product or service when it has been released.
- **Rough order of magnitude estimation** is estimating with very little accuracy at the beginning of a project and then refining the estimate over time. It's got a range of –50% to +100%.

there are no Dumb Questions

Q: Isn't it enough to know my project's scope and schedule, and then trust the budget to come out alright?

A: Even if you don't have a strict budget to work within, it makes sense to estimate your costs. Knowing your costs means that you have a good idea of the value of your project all the time. That means you will always know the impact (in dollars) of the decisions you make along the way. Sometimes understanding the value of your project will help you to make decisions that will keep your project healthier.

Many of us do have to work within a set of cost expectations from our project sponsors. The only way to know if you are meeting those expectations is to track your project against the original estimates.

It might seem like fluff. But knowing how much you are spending will help you relate to your sponsor's expectations much better as well.

Q: In my job I am just handed a budget. How does estimating help me?

A: In the course of estimating, you might find that the budget you have been given is not realistic. Better to know that before you get too far into the project work than later. You can present your findings to the sponsor and take corrective action right away if your estimate comes in pretty far off target. Your sponsor and your project team will thank you for it.

Q: What if I don't have all of this information and I am supposed to give a ballpark estimate?

A: This is where those rough order of magnitude estimates come in. That's just a fancy way of saying you take your best guess knowing that it's probably inaccurate and you let everybody know that you will be revising your estimates as you know more and more about the project.

Q: My company needs to handle maintenance of projects after we release them. How do you estimate for that?

A: That's called lifecycle costing. The way you handle it is just like you handle every other estimate. You sit down and try to think of all of the activities and resources involved in maintenance and project the cost. Once you have an estimate, you present it along with the estimate for initially building the product or service.

Q: I still don't get Net Present Value. What do I use it for?

A: The whole idea behind net present value is that you can figure out which of two projects is more valuable to you. Every project has a value—if your sponsor's spending money on it, then you'd better deliver something worth at least that much to him! That's why NPV is figured out by coming up with how much a project will be worth, and then subtracting how much it will cost. But for the exam, all you really need to remember are two things: net present value has the cost of the project built into it, and if you need to use NPV to select one of several projects, always choose the one with the biggest NPV. That's not hard to remember, because you're just choosing the one with the most value!

Cost estimating is just like activity estimating. You get the estimate and the supporting detail, updates to the plan and requested changes when you are done.

Match each scenario to the cost numbers that Alice is using in each one.

1. Alice does such a good job planning out her entertainment center remodeling that the Smiths down the street ask if they can have her help with their home theater upgrade. Since she is too busy doing the work on the lounge, she has to say no. Rob Smith says, "That's a shame, we were willing to pay $1,000 to someone to help us out with this."

2. The minute the TV gets installed, Alice starts inviting all of her friends over to the lounge to watch the games on the weekend. She charges a $2 cover charge for her football Saturdays and has been clearing about $20 per week even though the room isn't finished.

3. Even though the system she is currently installing is state of the art, Alice knows that within a year or so it will be on sale for half as much as she is paying now.

4. Alice wants to figure out how much the project is worth so far. So she adds up the value of all of the materials she has used and subtracts the labor and any depreciation that needs to be accounted for. The number she ends up with gives the value of the overall project right now.

5. Before Jeff and Charles decided to do the remodeling, they compared how much the project was going to cost to how much good they thought it would do for them.

A. Opportunity cost

B. Benefit cost ratio

C. Internal rate of return

D. Depreciation

E. Net Present Value

Answers: 1-A, 2-C, 3-D, 4-E, 5-B

The Cost Control process is a lot like schedule control

When a something unexpected comes up, you need to understand its impact on your budget and make sure that you react in the best way for your project. Just like changes can cause delays in the schedule, they can also cause cost overruns. The **Cost Control process** is all about knowing how you are doing as compared to your plan and making adjustments when you need to.

I just talked to our accountant. She says we need to put a third of our profits away for taxes.

Time for cost control!

Given what you already know about scope control and schedule control, how would you handle this problem?

Sharpen your pencil

Using what you already know about scope and schedule control, annotate what each of these inputs will be used for.

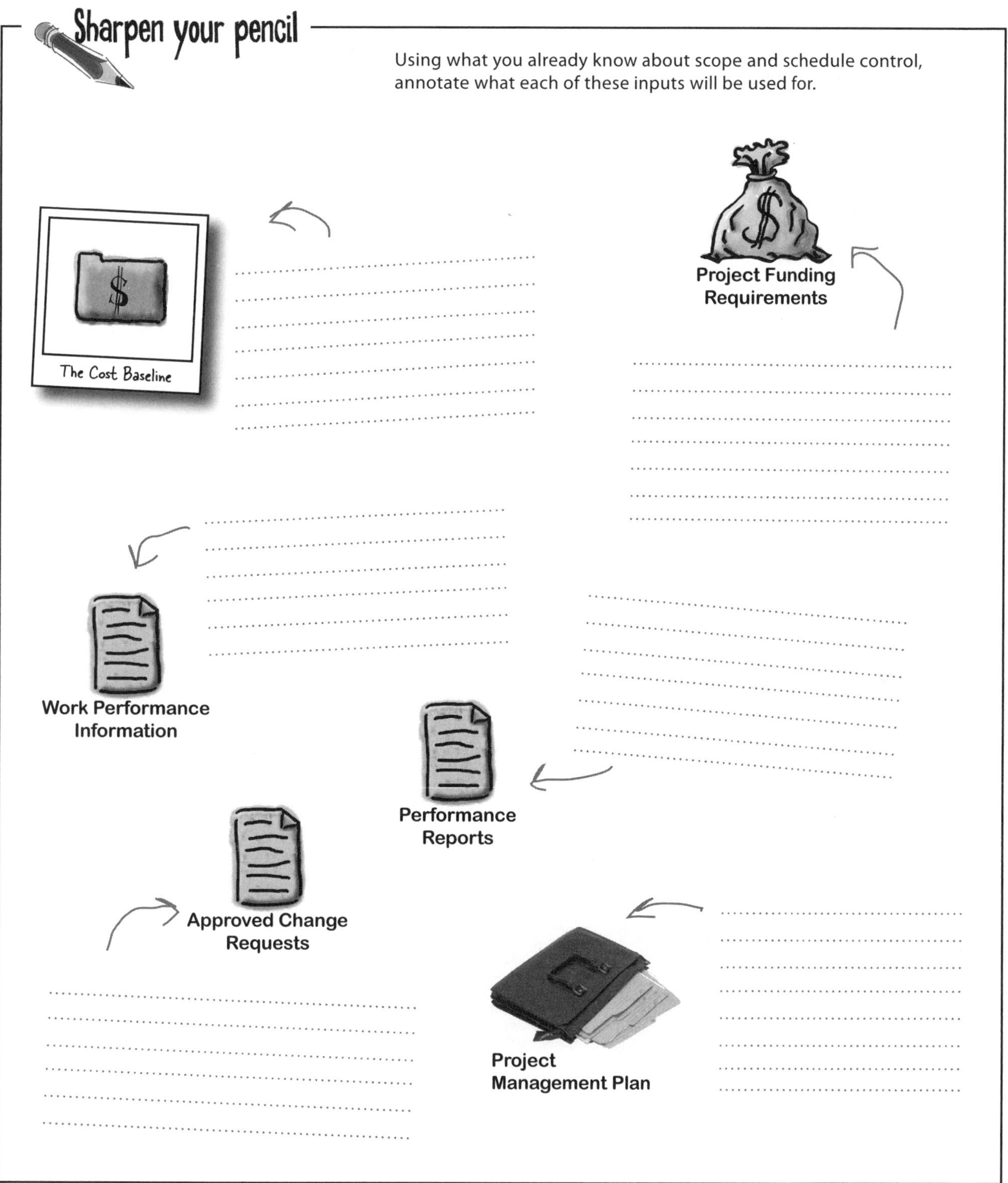

Sharpen your pencil Solution

Using what you already know about scope and schedule control, annotate what each of these inputs will be used for.

The cost baseline is what you compare all of your actual performance information to. This is the amount you budgeted for. Any changes that need to be made to the budget need to be made to this baseline.

Project funding requirements

On top of the baseline cost, you have added some reserves in to deal with known risks. You've also spread your budget out, so that you always have money when you need it. Changes to your project might also mean changes to your funding requirements.

This is the actual data being generated by your project. It tells how are you spending your budget right now. You'll need this information to figure out if you need to make any changes to stay on track.

Work Performance Information

Like the work performance information, performance reports give actual information on how your project is doing. You will use them to figure out whether or not you need to change your budget to deal with issues that have come up.

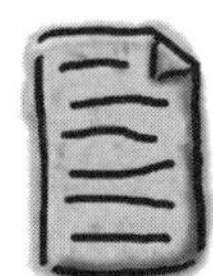

Performance reports

Approved Change Requests

Sometimes you've got to make changes to the cost baseline or funding requirements—that's what these approved change requests are all about. They come out of the Integrated Change Control as an input to cost control.

Project Management Plan

You may find that you need to change the PM Plan and its cost management plan as a result of information coming from your project. So, you'll need to evaluate your work performance information in relation to it.

A few new tools and techniques

The tools in cost control are all about helping you figure out where to make changes so you don't overrun your budget.

Cost change control system

Controlling changes to your budget is just like any other change control system we've studied. It defines the procedures you need to follow to change your cost baseline.

Performance measurement analysis

Here's where you measure how your project is doing compared to the plan. The main technique to know for this is the Earned Value technique.

Project performance reviews

Reviews are meetings where the project team reviews performance data to examine the variance between actual performance and the baseline. Earned value management is used to calculate and track the variance. Over time, these meetings are a good place to look into trends in the data.

Forecasting

Use the information you have about the project right now to predict how close it will come to its goals if it keeps going the way it has been. Forecasting uses some earned value numbers to help you come up with preventative and corrective actions that can keep your project on the right track.

Project management software

You can use software packages to track your budget and make it easier to know where you might run into trouble.

Variance analysis

Throughout your project, you are looking at how you are doing as compared to your plan. The variance between planned and actual performance needs to be carefully analyzed so you can head off problems before they make your project go over budget.

Forecasting and performance measurement are very important! You use them to find the changes you need to make in your project.

Question Clinic: The Red Herring

Sometimes a question will give you a lot of extra information that you don't need. It'll include a rambling story or a bunch of extra numbers that are irrelevant.

104. You are managing a highway construction project. You have to build a three-mile interchange at a cost of $75,000 per quarter-mile. Your project team consists of a road planner, an architect, an engineer, a foreman and sixteen highway workers. The workers are will not be available until week 10 of the project. Your preliminary scope statement is complete, and you have met with your stakeholders and sponsor. Your senior managers are now asking you to come up with an estimate. Your company has done four other highway projects very similar to this one, and you have decided to make your estimate by looking at the costs of those previous projects.

What kind of estimate involves comparing your project to a previous one?

A. Parametric

B. Analogous

C. Bottom-Up

D. Rough Order of Magnitude

Did you read that whole paragraph, only to find out the question had nothing to do with it?

You only needed to read this sentence to get the answer right.

When you see a Red Herring question, your job is to figure out what part of it is relevant and what's included just to distract you. It seems tricky, but it's actually pretty easy once you get the hang of it.

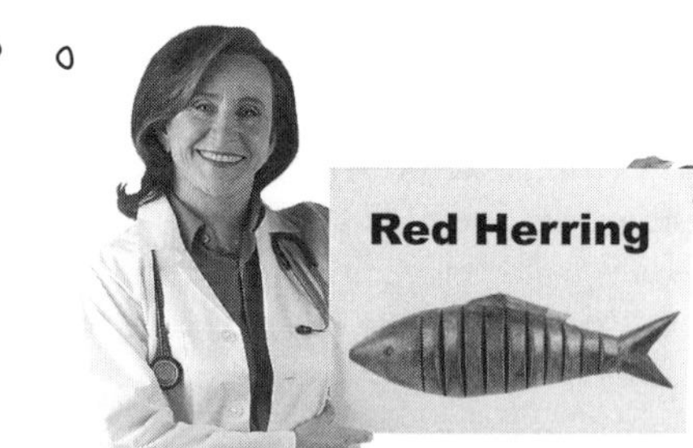

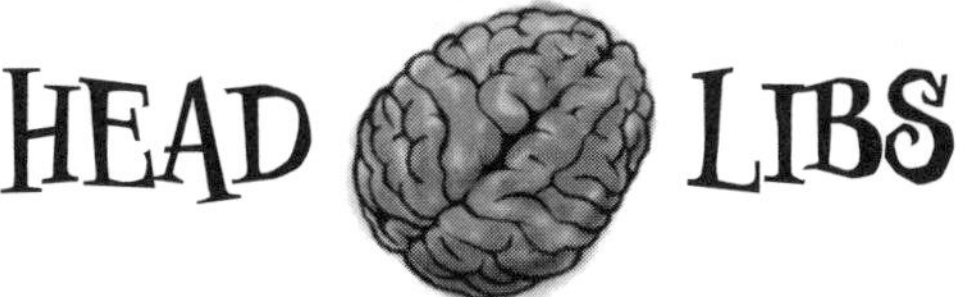

Fill in the blanks to come up with your own Red Herring question!

You are managing a ______________________ project.
(kind of project)

You have ______________________ at your disposal, with ______________________. Your
(describe a resource) (how that resource is restricted)

______________________ contains ______________________. The ______________________
(a project document) (something that document would contain) (a team member)

alerts you that ______________________, and suggests ______________________.
(a problem that affected your project) (a suggested solution)

____?
(a question vaguely related to one of the things in the paragraph above)

A. ____
(wrong answer)

B. ____
(trickily wrong answer)

C. ____
(correct answer)

D. ____
(ridiculously wrong answer)

Join the Head First PMP community at **http://www.headfirstlabs.com/PMP**
You can add your Head Libs answer, and see what Head Libs other project managers came up with!

Look at the schedule to figure out your budget

The tools in cost control are all about helping you figure out where to make changes so you don't overrun your budget.

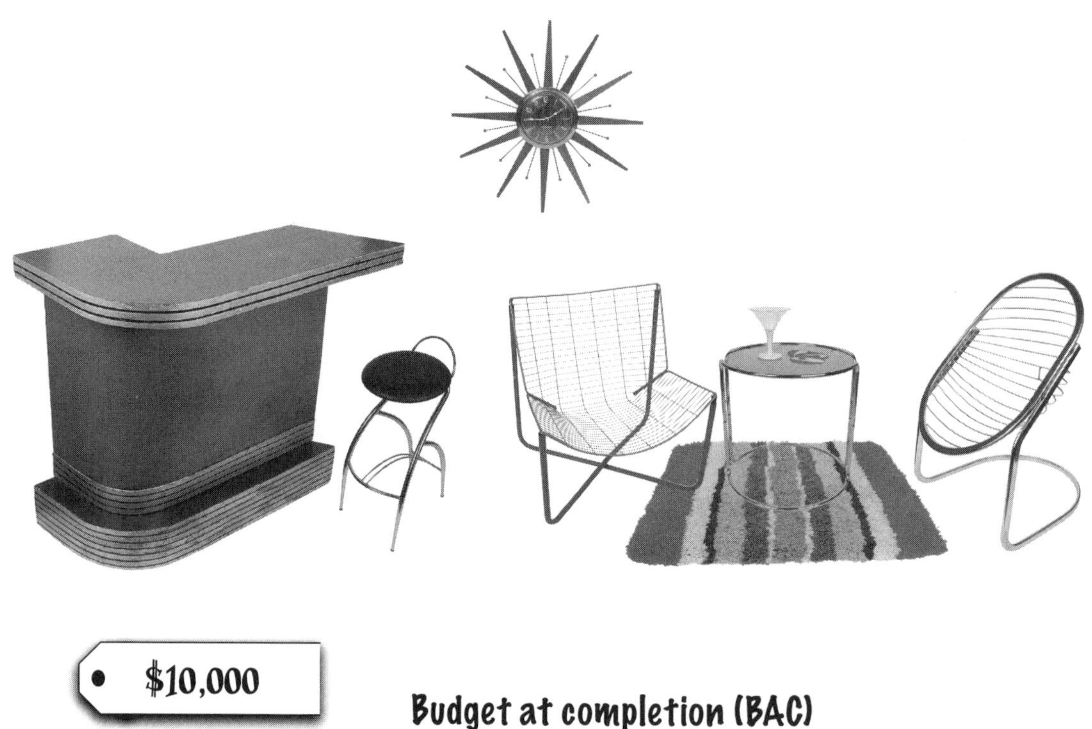

Budget at completion (BAC)

How much money are you planning on spending on your project? One you add up all of the costs for every activity and resource, you'll get a final number... and that's the total project budget. If you only have a certain amount of money to spend, you'd better make sure that you haven't gone over!

How to calculate planned value

Once you figure this out, you can figure out your project's planned value.

If you look at your schedule and see that you're **supposed to have done** a certain percentage of the work, then that's the percent of the total budget that you've "earned" so far. This value is known as Planned Value. Here's how you calculate it.

1. First, write down your

BAC—Budget At Completion

This is the ***first number you think of*** when you work on your project costs. It's the **total budget** that you have for your project—how much you plan to spend on your project.

BAC x

The name "BAC" should make sense—it's the budget of your project when it's complete!

2. Then multiply that by your

Planned % Complete

If the schedule says that your team should have done 300 hours of work so far, and they will work a total of 1,000 hours on the project, then your Planned % Complete is 30%.

BAC x Planned % Complete

Planned % Complete is easy to work out, as it's just the calculation Given amount ÷ Total amount.

3. The resulting number is your

PV—Planned Value

This is how much of your budget you planned on using so far. If the BAC is $200,000, and the schedule says your planned % complete is 30%, then the Earned Value is $200,000 × 30% = $60,000.

BAC x Planned % Complete = PV

BAC x Planned % Complete = PV

PV = BAC x Planned % Complete

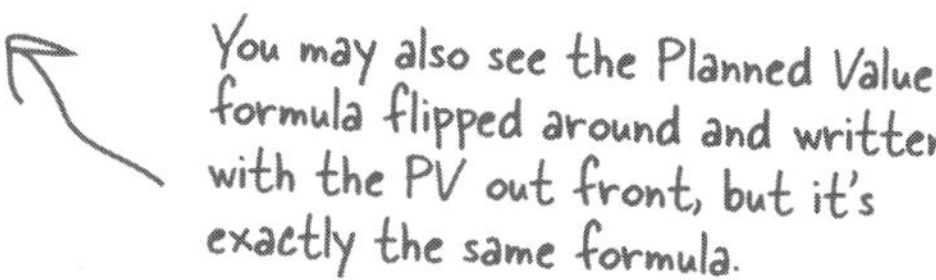

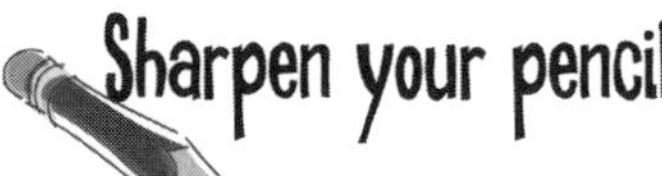

Now it's your turn! See if you can figure out BAC and PV for a typical project.

1. You're managing a project to install 200 windows in a new skyscraper and need to figure out your budget. Each week of the project costs the same: your team members are paid a total of $4,000 every week, and you need $1,000 worth of parts each week to do the work. If the project is scheduled to last 16 weeks, what's the BAC for the project?

   BAC = ...

2. What will the Planned % Complete be four weeks into the project?

   Planned % Complete = ...

This is the part that takes some thinking. How do you know what % you are through the project?

Even though we are at the beginning of the project now, we can still figure out what the PV will be in four weeks.

3. What should the PV be four weeks into the project?

   PV = ... x .... = ...

Answers on page 348.

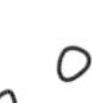

Hmm. Okay, but that doesn't tell me much about my budget, does it?

Not yet it doesn't.

But wouldn't be nice if, when your schedule said you were supposed to be 37.5% complete with the work, then you knew that you'd actually spent 37.5% of your budget?

Well, in the real world things don't always work like that, but there are ways to work out—approximately—how far on budget (or offtrack) your budget actually is.

Earned value tells you how you're doing

When Alice wants to track how her project is doing versus the budget, she uses **Earned Value**. This is a technique where you figure out how much of your project's value has been delivered to the customer so far. You can do this by comparing the value of **what your schedule says** you should have delivered against the value of what you **actually** delivered.

Your schedule tells you a lot about where you are supposed to be right now.

The actual cost of this project on May 14th is $1,650. The planned value was $2,200.

How to calculate earned value

If you could estimate each activity exactly, every single time, you wouldn't need earned value. Your schedule would always be perfectly accurate, and you would always be exactly on budget.

But you know that real projects don't really work that way! That's why Earned Value is so useful—it helps you put a number on how far offtrack your project actually is. And that can be a really powerful tool for evaluating your progress and reporting your results. Here's how you calculate it.

When you do work, you convert the money your sponsor invests in your project into value. So, **earned value** is about ***how much work you have been able to accomplish with the money you've been given***. When you calculate earned value, you're showing your sponsor how much value that investment has earned.

1. First, write down your

BAC—Budget At Completion

Remember, this is the **total budget** that you have for your project.

BAC x

2. Then multiply that by your

Actual % Complete

Say the schedule says that your team should have done 300 hours of work so far out of a total of 1000. But you talk to your team and find out they actually completed 35% of the work. That means the actual % complete is 35%.

BAC x Actual % Complete

If your team actually got 35% of the work done when the schedule says they should only have gotten 30% done, that means they're more efficient than you planned!

3. The resulting number is your

EV—Earned Value

This figure tells you how much your project *actually* earned. Every hour that each team member works adds value to the project. You can figure it out by taking the percentage of the hours that the team has actually worked and multiplying it by the BAC. If the total cost of the project is \$200,000, then the Earned Value is \$200,000 × 35% = \$70,000.

BAC x Actual % Complete = EV

Again, you might see the Earned Value formula flipped around and written with the EV out front, but remember, it's exactly the same formula.

EV = BAC x Actual % Complete

What's the difference between Actual Cost and Planned Value? What does it mean if your AC is bigger than your PV? What if it's smaller?

Put yourself in someone else's shoes

Earned value is one of the most difficult concepts that you need to understand for the PMP exam. The reason it's so confusing for so many people is that these calculations seem a little weird and arbitrary to a lot of project managers.

But ***they make a lot more sense*** if you **think about your project the way your sponsor thinks about it**. If you put yourself into the sponsor's shoes, you'll see that this stuff actually makes sense!

Think about earned value from the sponsor's perspective. It all makes a lot more sense then.

Let's say you're an executive:
You're making a decision to spend $300,000 of your company's money on a project. To a project manager, that's a project's budget. But to you, the sponsor, that's $300,000 of value you expect to get!

That's the total budget, or the BAC.

So how much value is the project delivering?
If you're the sponsor, you're thinking about the bottom line. And that bottom line is whether or not you're getting your money's worth from the project. If the team's done 50% of the work, then you've gotten $150,000 of value so far.

If you put the value in dollar terms your sponsor knows what return he's getting for his investment.

That's earned value—it's based on how much work the team actually did.

But if the schedule says that they should have done 60% of the work by now, then you're getting less value than you were promised!

The sponsor doesn't care as much about how you spend the budget. He just wants to get the most value for his money!

Look at the schedule to figure out how much value you planned to deliver to your sponsor.

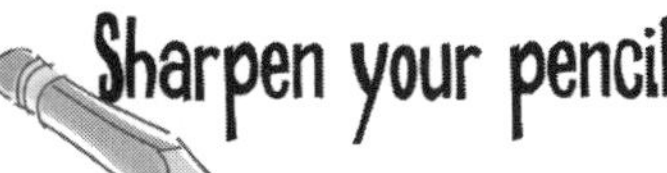

Let's get back to that 16-week project from page 326.
In the last exercise you figured out what the project should look like by using planned value. Now you can use earned value to figure out if your project is really going the way you planned.

1. Fast forward four weeks into the project installing those 200 skyscraper windows. Fill in the BAC and PV you figured out before. (Check your answer at the top of page 348 to make sure you got it right!)

BAC = ... PV = ...

Figure out the actual % complete by dividing the actual work done into the total amount you're planning on

2. You've checked with your team, but they have bad news. The schedule says they were supposed to have installed 50 windows by now, but they only installed 40. Can you figure out the actual % complete?

Actual % Complete = ... / .... = ...

Fill in the number of windows the team's actually installed

Fill in the total number of windows that will be installed over the course of the project.

3. What should the Earned Value be right now?

EV = ... x .... = ...

Fill in the BAC

Fill in the Actual % Complete

4. Look at the planned value, and then look at the earned value. Are you delivering all the value you planned on delivering?

☐ Yes ☐ No

Answers on page 348.

Neat. I think I can use these formulas to track my schedule and my budget!

You can definitely use them to track the schedule and budget on smaller projects.

But once your projects start getting more complex, your formulas are going to need to take into account that you've got several people all doing different activities, and that could make it harder to track whether you're ahead of schedule or over budget.

So now that you know how to calculate PV and EV, they're all you need to stay on top of everything... What are you waiting for? Flip the page to find out how!

Is your project behind or ahead of schedule?

Figuring out if you're on track in a small project with just a few people is easy. But what if you have dozens or hundreds of people doing lots of different activities? And what if some of them are on track, some are ahead of schedule, and some of them are behind? It starts to get hard to even figure out whether you're meeting your goals.

Wouldn't it be great if there were an easy way to figure out if you're ahead or behind schedule? Well, good news: that's exactly what earned value is used for!

Schedule Performance Index (SPI)

If you want to know whether you're ahead of or behind schedule, use SPIs. The key to using this is that when you're ***ahead of schedule***, you've ***earned more value*** than planned! So **EV will be bigger than PV**.

To work out your SPI, you just divide your EV by your PV.

$$SPI = \frac{EV}{PV}$$

If SPI is greater than one, that means EV is bigger than PV, so you're ahead of schedule!

If SPI is less than one, then you're behind schedule because the amount you've actually worked (EV) is less than what you'd planned (PV).

Schedule Variance (SV)

It's easy to see how variance works. The **bigger the difference** between ***what you planned*** and ***what you actually earned***, the **bigger the variance**.

So, if you want to know how much ahead or behind schedule you are, just subtract PV from EV.

Remember, for the sponsor's benefit, we measure this in dollars...

$$SV = EV - PV$$

... So if the variance is positive, it tells you exactly how many dollars you're ahead. If it's negative, it tells you how many dollars you're behind.

Don't get freaked out by the thought of all these formulas.

They're really not very complex. All you need to remember is that they all use EV and PV in different ways. Once you've learned how EV and PV interact in each one, you're golden!

Meanwhile back in the Lounge, Alice is working out if the project's coming in on schedule and on budget. Here are the steps she's taking and her notes. She was called away, so it's up to you to work out whether the guys need to push the schedule.

1. **Start with the schedule and budget.** Figure out how much work you planned, how much the team has done, and the total budget (BAC).

   BAC= ________

   Jeff and Charles have a total budget of $10,000, and they're currently halfway through the schedule.

   Planned % complete = ________

2. **Figure out PV.** Multiply the BAC by the percentage of the work that your schedule says the team should have worked so far to get the planned value.

   So their planned value is?

   PV = 50% x $10,000 = $5,000

   PV = BAC x Planned % Complete

3. **Figure out EV.** This is the part that actually takes some thinking! You need to figure out what percentage of work the team has actually done. Once you have that, multiply it with the BAC to find the earned value.

   Uh-oh! On a closer look, it seems they've really only gotten 40% of the work done.

   EV = 40% x $10,000 = $4,000

   EV = BAC x Actual % Complete

4. **Now you can calculate SPI and SV.** Once you've figured out EV and PV, you can do the calculations.

   Now that you have the EV and PV, you can tell Jeff and Charles if they're getting their money's worth!

   SPI = $5,000 ÷ $4,000 = 0.8

   SV = $5,000 - $4,000 = $1,000

5. **How's the schedule looking?** What do all these figures tell us?

   So are we ahead of schedule or behind it?

Answers on page 349.

Are you over budget?

You can do the same thing for your budget that you can do for schedule. The calculations are almost exactly the same, except instead of using Planned Value—which tells you how much work the schedule says you should have done so far—you use **Actual Cost** (AC). That's the amount of money that you've spent so far on the project.

Remember, EV measures the work that's been done, while AC tells you how much you've spent so far.

Relax

Measuring your cost difference in dollars is easy, but what if your schedule variance is –$5,000?

A lot of people worry about that, but it's actually not bad. Planned Value just means that you planned on delivering a certain amount of value to your sponsor at a certain time. An SV of –$5,000 just tells you that you haven't delivered all the value you promised.

Cost Performance Index (CPI)

$$CPI = \frac{EV}{AC}$$

If you want to know whether you're over or under budget, use CPI.

Cost Variance (CV)

$$CV = EV - AC$$

Remember what CV means to the sponsor: EV says how much of the total value of the project has been earned back so far. If CV is negative, then he's not getting good value for his money.

This tells you the difference between what you planned on spending and what you actually spent.

So, if you want to know how much under or over budget you are, just take AC away from EV.

You're within your budget if...

CPI is greater than 1 and CV is positive. When this happens, your actual costs are less than earned value, which means the project is delivering more value than it costs.

You've blown your budget if...

CPI is less than 1 and CV is negative. When your actual costs are more than earned value, that means that your sponsor is not getting his money's worth of value from the project.

Now Alice can take a look at the Lounge's checkbook. She figures out that she spent $5,750 on the project so far.

CPI = $5,000 ÷ $5,750 = 0.869

Since CPI is less than 1, it means that Jeff and Charles have blown their budget.

CV = 5,000 – $5,750 = –$750

And that's how much they've gone over! Jeff, Charles, and Alice had better figure out how to contain those runaway costs, or they'll have a nasty surprise later.

The Performance Measurement Analysis formulas

Performance Measurement Analysis is just one of the tools and techniques in the Cost Control process, but it's a big part of PMP exam preparation. When you use these formulas, you're using the **Earned Value technique (EVT)**, which is the way that you measure and analyze how far off your project is from your plan. Remember, think of everything in terms of how much value you're delivering to your sponsor! Take a look at the formulas one more time:

Remember, your sponsor always cares most about what the project is worth to him. BAC says how much value he's getting for the whole project, and EV tells him how much of that value he's gotten so far.

Name	Formula	What it says	Why you use it
BAC—Budget at Completion	No formula – it's the project budget	How much money you'll spend on the project	To tell the sponsor the total amount of value that he's getting for the project
PV—Planned Value	PV = BAC x Planned % Complete	What your schedule says you should have spent	To figure out what value your plan says you should have delivered so far
EV—Earned Value	EV = BAC x Actual % Complete	How much of the project's value you've really earned	EV lets you translate how much work the team's finished into a dollar value
AC—Actual Cost	What you've actually spent on the project	How much you've actually spent so far	The amount of money you spend doesn't always match the value you get!
SPI—Schedule Performance Index	$SPI = \frac{EV}{PV}$	Whether you're behind or ahead of schedule	To figure out whether you've delivered the value your schedule said you would
SV—Schedule Variance	SV = EV - PV	How much ahead or behind schedule you are	This puts a dollar value on exactly how far ahead or behind schedule you are
CPI—Cost Performance Index	$CPI = \frac{EV}{AC}$	Whether you're within your budget or not	Your sponsor is always most interested in the bottom line!
CV—Cost Variance	CV = EV - AC	How much above or below your budget you are	Your sponsor needs to know how much it costs to get him the value you deliver

Interpret CPI and SPI numbers to gauge your project

The whole idea behind the Earned Value Technique is that you can use it to easily put a number on how your project is doing. That's why there will be exam questions that test you on your ability to interpret these numbers! Luckily, it's pretty easy to evaluate a project based on the Earned Value formulas.

If the SPI is below 1, then your project is behind schedule. But if you see a CPI under 1, your project is over budget!

If your project is on track, that means you're delivering the value you promised.

You can tell that your project is on track because the two index numbers—CPI and SPI—are both very close to 1, and the variance numbers—CV and SV—are very close to zero dollars. It's very rare that you'll get exactly to a CPI of 1 or a SV of $0, but a SPI of 1.02 means you're very close to on time, and a CV of –$26 means you're very close to on budget.

A lot of PMOs have a rule where a CPI or SPI between 0.95 and 1.10 is absolutely fine!

Sometimes you'll see negative values written in parentheses—in this case, ($26)

Ahead of schedule or under budget

You can tell if your project is ahead of schedule or under budget by looking for larger numbers.

If the **CPI** is much **bigger than 1**, it means you're ***under budget***. And you can tell how much under by looking at the CV—that's what variance is for! It helps you see just how much the actual cost **varies** from the value you were supposed to earn by now.

Being a long way under budget isn't always a good thing. It means you asked for and were given resources that you didn't need—and which your company could have used elsewhere.

Behind schedule or over budget

A project that's behind schedule or over budget will have lower numbers.

When you see a **SPI** that's **between 0 and 1**, that tells you that the project is ***behind schedule***... and that means you're not delivering enough value to the sponsor! That's when you check the SV to see how much less value you're delivering. And the same goes for cost—a **low CPI** means that your project is ***over budget***, and CV will tell you how much more value you promised to deliver to the sponsor.

CPI and SPI can't be below zero, because they're ratios!

Oh, I get it: SPI and CPI are just ratios! If SPI is really close to 1, then SV will be really close to zero—and it means that my project is going as planned!

Exactly! And when your CPI is really close to 1, it means that every dollar your sponsor's spending on the project is earning just about a dollar in value.

The biggest thing to remember about all of these numbers is that **the lower they are, the worse your project is doing**. If you've got a SPI of 1.1 and a CPI of 1.15, then you're within your budget and ahead of schedule. But if you calculate a SPI of 0.9 and a CPI of 0.95, then you're behind schedule and you've blown your budget. And when these ratios are below 1, then you'll see a negative variance!

EV = BAC × Actual % Complete

wash the dog

LOWER = LOSER

Make it Stick

Remember:

Lower = Loser

If CPI or SPI is below 1, or if CV or SV is negative, then you've got trouble!

You'll definitely need to be able to calculate Earned Value numbers for the exam! But remember, like planning that trip way back in Chapter 3, the best way to do that is with practice.

Your project has a total budget of $300,000. You check your records and find that you've spent $175,000 so far. The team has completed 40% of the project work, but when you check the schedule it says that they should have completed 50% of the work. **Calculate the following:**

BAC = $ ....

AC = $ ....

There were two dollar values given in the problem. Which is AC, and which is BAC?

PV = $ .... x .... % = $ ....

EV = $ .... x .... % = $ ....

The trick is figuring out which percentage you need to put here!

SV = $ .... – $ .... = $ ....

CV = $ .... – $ .... = $ ....

Now you just need to figure out which numbers that you've already calculated are being divided into one another!

SPI = $ .... / $ .... = ...

CPI = $ .... / $ .... = ...

You're managing a highway construction project. Your total budget is $650,000, and there are a total of 7,500 hours of work scheduled on the project. You check with your accounting department, and they tell you that you've spent a total of $400,000. According to the schedule, your crew should have worked 4,500 hours, but your foreman says that the crew was allowed to work some overtime, and they've actually put in 5,100 hours of work. **Calculate these Earned Value numbers:**

BAC = ...

PV = ...

AC = ...

EV = ...

SV = ...

CV = ...

SPI = ...

CPI = ...

Answers on page 350.

You are the project manager at an industrial design firm. You expect to spend a total of $55,000 on your current project. Your plan calls for six people working on the project eight hours a day, five days a week for four weeks. According to the schedule, your team should have just finished the third week of the project. When review what the team has done so far, you find that they have completed 50% of the work, at a cost of $25,000. **Based on this information, calculate the Earned Value numbers:**

BAC = ...

PV = ...

AC = ...

EV = ...

SV = ...

CV = ...

SPI = ...

CPI = ...

Check all of the following that apply:

.... The project is ahead of schedule

.... The project is behind schedule

.... You should consider crashing the schedule

.... The project is over budget

.... The project is under budget

.... You should find a way to cut costs

Your current project is an $800,000 software development effort, with two teams of programmers that will work for six months, at a total of 10,000 hours. According to the project schedule, your team should be done with 38% of the work. You find that the project is currently 40% complete. You've spent 50% of the budget so far. **Calculate these numbers:**

BAC = ...

PV = ...

AC = ...

EV = ...

SV = ...

CV = ...

SPI = ...

CPI = ...

Check all of the following that apply:

.... The project is ahead of schedule

.... The project is behind schedule

.... You should consider crashing the schedule

.... The project is over budget

.... The project is under budget

.... You should find a way to cut costs

Answers on page 351.

Forecast what your project will look like when it's done

There's another piece of the Earned Value Technique, and it's part of the last tool and technique in Cost Management: **forecasting**. The idea behind forecasting is that you can use Earned Value to come up with a pretty accurate prediction of what your project will look like when it's at completion.

If you know your CPI now, you can use it to predict what your project will actually cost when it's complete. Let's say that you're managing a project with a CPI of 0.8 today. If you assume that the CPI will be 0.8 for the rest of the project—and that's not an unreasonable assumption when you're far along in the project work—then you can predict your total costs when the project is complete. We call that **Estimate at Completion** (EAC).

If your CPI is below 1, that means you're running over budget—which will give you an EAC that's larger than your current budget

If your CPI is above 1, you're running under budget, so the estimate will end up smaller than your BAC

> There are a bunch of different ways to calculate EAC, but this one is sufficient for the PMP exam.

Meanwhile, back in the Lounge

Alice is forecasting how the new Lounge project will look like when it's done.

If Jeff and Charles have a CPI of 0.869 and a total budget of $10,000, then they can forecast their final costs: EAC = BAC ÷ CPI...

$$\frac{\$10{,}000}{0.869} = \$11{,}507$$

Here's what Alice wrote down first...

... now Alice can take a look at the Lounge's checkbook. She figures out that she spent $5,750 on the project so far...

Once you've got an estimate, you can calculate a variance!

There are two useful numbers that you can compute with the EAC. One of them is called **Estimate to Complete** (ETC), which tells you how much more money you'll probably spend on your project. And the other one, **Variance at Completion** (VAC), predicts what your variance will be when the project is done.

You can use EAC, ETC and VAC to predict what your Earned Value numbers will look like when your project is complete.

ETC = EAC - AC

Since EAC predicts how much money you'll spend, if you subtract the AC, you'll find out how much money the rest of the project will end up costing.

VAC = BAC - EAC

If you end up spending more than your budget, the VAC will be negative... just like CV and SV!

If the EAC is $11,507, and the AC is $5,750, then I can figure out what Jeff and Charles have left to spend. ETC = EAC - AC.

So, we're over budget. But what will the damage be? At least now I can figure out the final variance. VAC = BAC - EAC.

$11,507 - $5750 = $5,757

... and now she knows how much money the rest of the project is likely to cost...

$10,000 - $11,507 = -$1,507

... but will the guys be able to come up with the extra money?

You're a project manager working on a large project scheduled to last for two years. You've got six different teams working on five major functional areas. Some teams are ahead of schedule, and others are falling behind. That means that you have cost overruns in some areas, but you've saved costs in others—and that's making it very hard to get an intuitive grasp on whether your project is over or under budget!

It's nine months into your project. The total budget for your project is $4,200,000. You've spent $1,650,000 so far, and you've got a CPI of .875. Use the Earned Value Technique formulas from Forecasting to figure out where things stand.

EAC = $ .... / .... = $ ....

ETC = $ .... – $ .... = $ ....

VAC = $ .... – $ .... = $ ....

Will the project be over or under budget when it's complete? (check one)

.... The project will be over budget .... The project will be within its budget

How much will the project be over or under budget? $ ....

Now it's six months later, and your project looks very different. You need to work out a new forecast for what your budget situation will be like at project completion. You've now spent a total of $2,625,000. You look at all of the activities done by the team, and you find that the project is 70% complete. Can you come up with a new forecast for your project?

BAC = $ ....

AC = $ ....

EV = ...

CPI = ...

EAC = ...

ETC = ...

VAC = ...

Your project will be **over / under** budget at completion. (circle one)

How much will the project be over or under budget?

$..................

Answers on page 352.

Finding missing information

Most of the Earned Value questions on the exam will be pretty straightforward: you'll be given the numbers that you need to plug into a formula, and when you do it you'll get the answer. But once in a while, you'll get a question that isn't quite so straightforward.

Let's say you're given...

... the CPI and Earned Value, and you want to figure out the actual costs. Why would you ever see this? Sometimes it's hard to figure out how important a project is unless you know how much it's really spending—if a project is more expensive, people in your company probably care more about it. If you're told that **a project's CPI is 1.14 and its EV is $350,000**, how do you figure out the actual costs?

Here's the formula for CPI. But what do you do if you're given CPI and EV, and need to figure out AC?

$$CPI = \frac{EV}{AC}$$

Let's fill in the numbers that we know!

$$1.14 = \frac{\$350{,}000}{AC}$$

You're going to have to use a little basic algebra here... but it's really easy!

$$AC = \frac{\$350{,}000}{1.14}$$

Now you know everything you need to calculate the final numbers.

$$AC = \$307{,}017$$

... the Earned Value and actual percent complete, and you want to figure out the project's budget. This can be really helpful when you need to "read between the lines" when you need to make a decision about a project when someone doesn't want to give you all the information you need. When you have **a project's EV of $438,750 and its actual % complete of 32.5%**, how do you figure out the total budget (BAC)?

Start with the formula that includes all the numbers you're looking for.

$$EV = BAC \times \text{Actual \% Complete}$$

$$\$438{,}750 = BAC \times 32.5\%$$

Don't forget that a 32.5% is the same as 0.325.

$$BAC = \frac{\$438{,}750}{0.325}$$

$$BAC = \$1{,}350{,}000$$

There are some times when you'll need to flip the formulas upside-down! Sometimes you're going to be on the receiving end of Earned Value numbers. If you're working at a company with a bunch of project managers, then sometimes you'll get a report from one of them that only gives you part of the picture!

You'll probably get a question or two where you'll need to flip your formulas over to figure out one of the values you'd normally be given. **Don't worry if you're math-phobic!** This is really easy—you'll definitely get it with a little practice.

If EV is $93,406 and SPI is 0.91, what is the planned value?

Write down the formula for SPI.

SPI = ... / .... = ... / .... = $ .... / ....

Fill in the numbers that you have.

Now flip around the formula so PV is on the left.

PV = ... / .... PV = ...

And now you can solve for PV!

If PV is $252,000 and BAC is $350,000, what is the scheduled percent complete?

Fill in the numbers that you have.

Start with the formula for PV.

PV = ... x .... = $ .... = $ .... x ....

Now flip around the formula so % complete is on the left.

% Complete = $............ / $............ % Complete = ...

And now you can solve it!

Now try one on your own. If BAC is $126,500 and EAC is $115,000, what is the CPI?

1. First write out the formula that has EAC, CPI and BAC

   ....

2. Next fill in the numbers that you know

   ....

3. Now flip around the formula so the number you're looking for is on the left.

   ....

4. Now you can solve the problem!

   ....

Answers on page 353.

there are no Dumb Questions

Q: What does CPI really mean, and why can it predict your final budget?

A: Doesn't it seem a little weird that you can come up with a pretty accurate forecast of what you'll actually spend on your project just by dividing CPI into your BAC, or the total amount that you're planning to spend on the project? How can there be one "magic" number that does that for you?

But when you think about it, it actually makes sense. Let's say that you're running 15% over budget today. If your budget is $100,000, then your CPI will be $100.000 ÷ $115,000 = .87. One good way to predict what your final budget will look like is to assume that you'll keep running 15% over budget. Let's say your total budget is $250,000. If you're still 15% over at the end of the budget, your final CPI will still be $250,000 ÷ $287,500 = .87! Your CPI will always be .87 if you're 15% over budget.

That's why we call that forecast EAC—it's an ESTIMATE of what your budget will look like AT COMPLETION. By dividing CPI into BAC, all you're doing is calculating what your final budget will be if your final budget overrun or underrun is exactly the same as it is today.

Q: Is that really the best way to estimate costs? What if things change between now and the end of the project?

A: EAC is a good way to estimate costs, because it's easy to calculate and relatively accurate—assuming that nothing on the project changes too much. But you're right, if a whole lot of unexpected costs happen or your team members figure out a cheaper and better way to get the job done, then an EAC forecast could be way off!

It turns out that there are over 25 different ways to calculate EAC, and the one in this chapter is just one of them. Some of those other formulas take risks and predictions into account. But for the PMP exam, you just need to know EAC = BAC ÷ CPI.

Q: Wow, there are a lot of Earned Value formulas! Is there an easy way to remember them?

A: Yes, there are a few ways that help you remember the Earned Value formulas. One way is to notice that the Performance Reporting formulas all have something either being divided into or subtracted from EV. This should make sense—the whole point of the Earned Value technique is that you're trying to figure out how much of the value you're delivering to your sponsor has been earned so far. Also, remember that a variance is always subtraction, and an index is always division. The schedule formulas SV and SPI both involve PV numbers you got from your schedule, while the cost formulas CV and CPI both involve AC numbers from your budget.

And remember, the lower the index or variance, the worse your project is doing! A negative variance or an index that's below 1 is bad, while a positive variance or an index that's above 1 is good!

Q: Aren't Net Present Value and Benefit Cost Ratios really about project selection methods?

A: Yes, NPV and BCR are definitely good project selection numbers, and you'll see questions on the exam about them. Luckily, they're easy to use. Given the choice between a project with a low NPV and a high NPV, always choose the high one because it's the one with the most value! (Makes sense, right?) And given the choice between a project with a low BCR and a high BCR, you want the one with the highest one, because that's the one that delivers the most benefit for the least cost.

The Earned Value formulas have numbers divided into or subtracted from EV. SV and SPI use PV, while CV and CPI use AC.

Party time!

Jeff and Charles finished the new Lounge! It looks great, and they're really happy about it… because Alice managed their costs well. She used Earned Value to correct their budget problems, and they managed to cut a few costs while they still had time. And they had just enough money left over at the end to throw a great party for her!

Sharpen your pencil Solution

Now it's your turn! See if you can figure out BAC and PV for a typical project.

1. You're managing a project to install 200 windows in a new skyscraper and need to figure out your budget. Each week of the project costs the same: your team members are paid a total of $4,000 every week, and you need $1,000 worth of parts each week to do the work. If the project is scheduled to last 16 weeks, what's the BAC for the project?

BAC = $5000 x 16 = $80,000

The project's 16 weeks long. Multiply that by the costs per week to get the total budget for the project.

Each week costs $4,000 for labor and $1,000 for parts.

2. What will the Planned % Complete be four weeks into the project?

Planned % Complete = 25%

You're 4 weeks into a 16-week project. That means you're 25% of the way through.

3. What should the PV be four weeks into the project?

Fill in the BAC from question 1.

PV = $80,000 x 25% = $20,000

Fill in the Planned % Complete from question 2. Now multiply them to get the PV.

Sharpen your pencil Solution

Let's get back to that 16-week project from page 326. Can you figure out how to use EV?

1. Fast-forward four weeks into the project installing those 200 skyscraper windows. Fill in the BAC and PV you figured out above. (Check your answer above to make sure you got it right!)

BAC = $80,000 PV = $20,000

2. You've checked with your team, but they have bad news. The schedule says they were supposed to have installed 50 windows by now, but they only installed 40. Can you figure out the actual % complete?

Actual % Complete = $\frac{40}{200}$ = 20%

The team installed 40 windows out of a total of 200. That means they're 20% of the way done with the work.

3. What should the Earned Value be right now?

EV = $80,000 x 20% = $16,000

4. Look at the planned value, and then look at the earned value. Are you delivering all the value you planned on delivering?

☐ Yes ☑ No

You planned on delivering $20,000 worth of value, but you've only delivered $16,000 worth. That means the customer isn't getting all the value he's paying for!

Meanwhile back in the Lounge, Alice is working out if the project's coming in on schedule and on budget. Here are the steps she's taking and her notes. She was called away, so it's up to you to work out whether the guys need to push the schedule.

1. **Start with the schedule and budget.** Figure out how much work you planned, how much the team has done, and the total budget (BAC).

   BAC= $10,000

   Jeff and Charles have a total budget of $10,000, and they're currently halfway through the schedule.

   Planned % complete = ________

2. **Figure out PV.** Multiply the BAC by the percentage of the work that your schedule says the team should have worked so far to get the planned value.

   So their planned value is?

   PV = 50% x $10,000 = $5,000

   PV = BAC x Planned % Complete

3. **Figure out EV.** This is the part that actually takes some thinking! You need to figure out what percentage of work the team has actually done. Once you have that, multiply it with the BAC to find the earned value.

   Uh-oh! On a closer look, it seems they've really only gotten 40% of the work done.

   EV = 40% x $10,000 = $4,000

   EV = BAC x Actual % Complete

4. **Now you can calculate SPI and SV.** Once you've figured out EV and PV, you can do the calculations.

   Now that you have the EV and PV, you can tell Jeff and Charles if they're getting their money's worth!

   SPI = $5,000 ÷ $4,000 = 0.8

   SV = $5,000 - $4,000 = -$1,000

5. **How's the schedule looking?** What do all these figures tell us?

   So are we ahead of schedule or behind it?

   The Lounge project is behind schedule.

You'll definitely need to be able to calculate Earned Value numbers for the exam! But remember, like planning that trip way back in Chapter 3, the best way to do that is with practice.

Your project has a total budget of $300,000. You check your records and find that you've spent $175,000 so far. The team has completed 40% of the project work, but when you check the schedule it says that they should have completed 50% of the work. **Calculate the following:**

BAC = $ **300,000**

PV = $ **300,000** x **50** % = $ **150,000**

Planned value uses what's on the schedule, earned value is uses what actually happened.

AC = $ **175000**

EV = $ **300,000** x **40** % = $ **120,000**

Did you notice how the formulas for SV and SPI use the same numbers? You subtract for one, and divide for the other!

SV = $ **120,000** – $ **150,000** = $ **-30,000**

CV = $ **120,000** – $ **175000** = $ **-55000**

You may have to round the CPI and SPI numbers. Don't worry – since PMP is multiple choice, you'll see a match!

SPI = $\frac{\$120,000}{\$150,000}$ = **0.8**

The formulas for CV and CPI use the same numbers, too.

CPI = $\frac{\$120,000}{\$175000}$ = **0.68**

You're managing a highway construction project. Your total budget is $650,000, and there are a total of 7,500 hours of work scheduled on the project. You check with your accounting department, and they tell you that you've spent a total of $400,000. According to the schedule, your crew should have worked 4,500 hours, but your foreman says that the crew was allowed to work some overtime, and they've actually put in 5,100 hours of work. **Calculate these Earned Value numbers:**

BAC = **$ 650,000**

4,500 out of a total of 7,500 hours you planned to work: 4,500 ÷ 7,500 = 60%

PV = **$ 650,000 x 60% = $ 390,000**

AC = **$ 400,000**

Do the same for actual hours: 5,100 ÷ 7,500 = 68%

EV = **$ 650,000 x 68% = $ 442,000**

SV = **$ 442,000 – $ 390,000 = $ 52,000**

CV = **$ 442,000 – $ 400,000 = $ 42,000**

SPI = $\frac{\$442,000}{\$390,000}$ = **1.13**

CPI = $\frac{\$442,000}{\$400,000}$ = **1.11**

You are the project manager at an industrial design firm. You expect to spend a total of $55,000 on your current project. You plan calls for six people working on the project eight hours a day, five days a week for four weeks. According to the schedule, your team should have just finished the third week of the project. When you review what the team has done so far, you find that they have completed 50% of the work, at a cost of $25,000. **Based on this information, calculate the Earned Value numbers:**

BAC = $55,000

AC = $25,000

PV = $55,000 x 75% = $41,250

The team should have just finished the third week of a four-week project, so the planned % complete is 75%

EV = $55,000 x 50% = $27,500

SV = $27,500 - $41,250 = ($13,750)

CV = $27,500 - $25,000 = $2,500

Get used to seeing negative numbers in parentheses instead of using a minus sign.

SPI = $27,500 / $41,250 = 0.67

CPI = $27,500 / $25,000 = 1.1

Check all of the following that apply:

- [ ] The project is ahead of schedule
- [x] The project is behind schedule
- [x] You should consider crashing the schedule

An SPI below 1 means your project's behind schedule. It's time to think about schedule compression!

- [ ] The project is over budget
- [x] The project is under budget
- [ ] You should find a way to cut costs

Your current project is an $800,000 software development effort, with two teams of programmers that will work for six months, at a total of 10,000 hours. According to the project schedule, your team should be done with 38% of the work. You find that the project is currently 40% complete. You've spent 50% of the budget so far. **Calculate these numbers:**

BAC = $800,000

AC = $400,000

PV = $800,000 x 38% = $304,000

EV = $800,000 x 40% = $320,000

SV = $320,000 - $304,000 = $16,000

CV = $320,000 - $400,000 = ($80,000)

SPI = $320,000 / $304,000 = 1.05

This SPI means that the project is ahead of schedule, but it's very close to 1, which means the schedule is pretty accurate.

CPI = $320,000 / $400,000 = 0.8

Since CPI is below 1 and CV is negative, the project is over budget. Cost-cutting is definitely a good idea!

Check all of the following that apply:

- [x] The project is ahead of schedule
- [ ] The project is behind schedule
- [ ] You should consider crashing the schedule
- [x] The project is over budget
- [ ] The project is under budget
- [x] You should find a way to cut costs

You're a project manager working on a large project scheduled to last for two years. You've got six different teams working on five major functional areas. Some teams are ahead of schedule, and others are falling behind. That means that you have cost overruns in some areas, but you've saved costs in others—and that's making it very hard to get an intuitive grasp on whether your project is over or under budget!

It's nine months into your project. The total budget for your project is $4,200,000. You've spent $1,650,000 so far, and you've got a CPI of .875. Use the Earned Value Technique formulas from forecasting to figure out where things stand.

EAC = $4,200,000 / 0.875 = $4,800,000

You're starting to get the hang of this stuff! These formulas look a little intimidating at first, but they're really not that bad once you get used to them.

ETC = $4,800,000 – $1,650,000 = $3,150,000

VAC = $4,200,000 – $4,800,000 = ($600,000)

Since VAC is negative, it means that you'll be $600,000 over budget at the end of the project.

Will the project be over or under budget when it's complete? (check one)

✓ The project will be over budget .... The project will be within its budget

How much will the project be over or under budget? $600,000

Now it's six months later, and your project looks very different. You need to work out a new forecast for what your budget situation will be like at project completion. You've now spent a total of $2,625,000. You look at all of the activities done by the team, and you find that the project is 70% complete. Can you come up with a new forecast for your project?

BAC = $4,200,000

AC = $2,625,000

EV = $4,200,000 x 70% = $2,940,000

CPI = $2,940,000 / $2,625,000 = 1.12

EAC = $4,200,000 / 1.12 = $3,750,000

ETC = $3,750,000 – $2,625,000 = $1,125,000

VAC = $4,200,000 – $3,750,000 = $450,000

Your project will be over / **under** budget at completion. (circle one)

How much will the project be over or under budget? $450,000

Take a second and think about what these numbers really mean. Are you delivering good value to the sponsor?

This VAC means your project is $450,000 under budget.

You'll probably get a question or two where you'll need to flip your formulas over to figure out one of the values you'd normally be given. **Don't worry if you're math-phobic!** This is really easy—you'll definitely get it with a little practice.

If EV is $93,406 and SPI is 0.91, what is the planned value?

$$SPI = \frac{EV}{PV} = 0.91 = \frac{\$93406}{PV}$$

When you're dividing, you just need to swap these two numbers.

$$PV = \frac{\$93406}{0.91} \qquad PV = \$102,644$$

Sometimes your answers aren't nice, round numbers. That doesn't mean that they're wrong!

If PV is $252,000 and BAC is $350,000, what is the scheduled percent complete?

$$PV = BAC \times \text{Scheduled \% Complete} \qquad \$252{,}000 = \$350{,}000 \times \text{Scheduled \% Complete}$$

$$\text{\% Complete} = \frac{\$252{,}000}{\$350{,}000} \qquad PV = 72\%$$

Don't forget that when you're calculating a percentage, 72% is the same as 0.72.

Now try one on your own. If BAC is $126,500 and EAC is $115,000, what is the CPI?

1. First write out the formula that has EAC, CPI and BAC

$$EAC = \frac{BAC}{CPI}$$

If you're still stumped here, don't worry! You'll only see one or two questions like this on the exam.

2. Next fill in the numbers that you know

$$\$115{,}000 = \frac{\$126{,}500}{CPI}$$

3. Now flip around the formula so the number you're looking for is on the left.

$$CPI = \frac{\$126{,}500}{\$115{,}000}$$

4. Now you can solve the problem!

$$CPI = 1.1$$

Exam Questions

Some of the Earned Value numbers have alternate 4-letter abbreviations. This one stands for "Budgeted Cost of Work Performed." Don't worry—you don't need to memorize them!

1. You are creating your cost baseline. What process are you in?

A. Cost Budgeting

B. Cost Control

C. Cost Estimating

D. Cost Baselining

2. You're working on a project that has an EV of $7362 and a PV (BCWP) of $8232. What's your SV?

A. –$870

B. $870

C. 0.89

D. Not enough information to tell

3. You are managing a project for a company that has previously done three projects that were similar to it. You consult with the cost baselines, lessons learned, and project managers from those projects, and use that information to come up with your cost estimate. What technique are you using?

A. Parametric Estimating

B. Net Present Value

C. Rough Order of Magnitude Estimation

D. Analogous Estimating

4. You are working on a project with a PV of $56,733 and an SPI of 1.2. What's the Earned Value of your project?

A. $68,079.60

B. $47,277.50

C. $68,733

D. .72

5. Your company has 2 projects to choose from. Project A is a billing software project for the Accounts payable department; in the end it will make the company around $400,000 when it has been rolled out to all of the employees in that department. Project B is a payroll application that will make the company around $388,000 when it has been put to use throughout the company. After a long deliberation, your board chooses to go ahead with Project B. What is the opportunity cost for choosing Project B over Project A?

A. $388,000

B. $400,000

C. $12,000

D. 1.2

Exam Questions

6. Your company has asked you to provide a cost estimate that includes maintenance, installation, support, and upkeep costs for as long as the product will be used. What is that kind of estimate called?

A. Benefit Cost Ratio

B. Depreciation

C. Net Present Value

D. Lifecycle Costing

7. You are working on a project with an SPI of .72 and a CPI of 1.1. Which of the following BEST describes your project?

A. Your project is ahead of schedule and under budget

B. Your project is behind schedule and over budget

C. Your project is behind schedule and under budget

D. Your project is ahead of schedule and over budget

8. Your project has a BAC of $4,522 and is 13% complete. What is the earned value (EV)?

A. $3934.14

B. There is not enough information to answer

C. $587.86

D. $4522

9. You are starting to write your preliminary scope statement with your project sponsor when the senior managers ask for a time and cost estimate for the project. You have not yet gathered many of the project details. What kind of estimate can you give?

A. Analogous Estimate

B. Rough Order of Magnitude Estimate

C. Parametric Estimate

D. Bottom-up Estimate

10. You are managing a project laying underwater fiber optic cable. The total cost of the project is $52/meter to lay 4 km of cable across a lake. It's scheduled to take 8 weeks to complete, with an equal amount of cable laid in each week. It's currently week 5, and your team has laid 1,800 meters of cable so far. What is the SPI of your project?

A. 1.16

B. 1.08

C. .92

D. .72

Exam Questions

11. During the execution of a software project, one of your programmers informs you that she discovered a design flaw that will require the team to go back and make a large change. What is the BEST way to handle this situation?

A. Ask the programmer to consult with the rest of the team and get back to you with a recommendation.

B. Determine how the change will impact the cost, scope, and schedule of the software.

C. Stop all work and call a meeting with the sponsor.

D. Update the cost baseline to reflect the change.

12. If AC (ACWP) is greater than your EV (BCWP), what does this mean?

A. The project is under budget.

B. The project is over budget.

C. The project is ahead of schedule.

D. The project is behind schedule.

13. A junior project manager is studying for her PMP exam, and asks you for advice. She's learning about Earned Value Management, and wants to know which of the variables represents the difference between what you expect to spend on the project and what you actually spent. What should you tell her?

A. Actual Cost (AC)

B. Cost Performance Index (CPI)

C. Earned Value (EV)

D. Cost Variance (CV)

14. You are managing an industrial architecture project. You've spent $26,410 so far to survey the site, draw up preliminary plans, and run engineering simulations. You are preparing to meet with your sponsor, when you discover that there a new local zoning law will cause you to have to spend an additional estimated $15,000 to revise your plans. You contact the sponsor and initiate a change request to update the cost baseline.

What variable would you use to represent the $26,410 in an Earned Value calculation?

A. PV

B. BAC

C. AC

D. EV

Exam Questions

15. You are working on the project plan for a software project. Your company has a standard spreadsheet that you use to generate estimates. To use the spreadsheet, you meet with the team to estimate the number of functional requirements, use cases and design wireframes for the project. Then you categorize them into high, medium or low complexity. You enter all of those numbers into the spreadsheet, which uses a data table derived from past projects' actual costs and durations, performs a set of calculations, and generates a final estimate. What kind of estimation is being done?

A. Parametric

B. Rough order of magnitude

C. Bottom-up

D. Analogous

16. Project A has a NPV of $75,000, with an internal rate of return of 1.5% and an initial investment of $15,000. Project B has a NPV of $60,000 with a BCR of 2:1. Project C has a NPV of $80,000, which includes an opportunity cost of $35,000. Based on these projects, which is the BEST one to select:

A. Project A

B. Project B

C. Project C

D. There is not enough information to select a project

17. What is the range of a Rough Order of Magnitude Estimate?

A. –5% to +10%

B. –25% to +75%

C. –50% to +100%

D. –100% to +200%

18. You are managing a software project, when one of your stakeholders needs to make a change that will affect the budget. What defines the processes that you must follow in order to implement the change?

A. Cost change control system

B. Monitoring & Controlling process group

C. Change control board

D. Cost baseline

Exam Questions

19. You are managing a software project, when one of your stakeholders needs to make a change that will affect the budget. You follow the procedures to implement the change. Which of the following must get updated to reflect the change?

A. Project management plan

B. Project cost baseline

C. Cost change control system

D. Project performance reviews

20. You are managing a project with a BAC of $93,000, EV (BCWP) of $51,840, PV (BCWS) of $64,800 and AC (ACWP) of $43,200. What is the CPI?

A. 1.5

B. 0.8

C. 1.2

D. $9,000

Again, don't panic if you see these four-letter abbreviations. You'll always be given the ones you're used to on the exam!

Exam Questions

1. Answer: A

This is really a question about the order of the processes. Cost Budgeting and Cost Control both use the cost baseline, so it has to be created before you get to them. Cost Baselining isn't a process at all, so you should exclude that from the choices right away. The main output of Cost Estimating is the cost baseline and supporting detail, so that's the right choice here.

D. Cost Baselining ← Watch out for fake processes! This isn't a real process name.

2. Answer: A

This one is just testing whether or not you know the formula for schedule variance. Just plug the values into the SV formula: SV = EV – PV and you get answer A. Watch out for negative numbers, though! Answer B is a trap because it's a positive value. Also, the test will have answers like C that check if you're using the right formula. If you use the SPI formula, that's the answer you'll get! You can throw out D right away—you don't need to do any calculation to know that you have enough information to figure out SV!

2. You're working on a project that has an EV of $7362 and a PV (BCWP) of $8232. What's your SV?

Don't get thrown off by four-letter abbreviations like BCWP—some people have different abbreviations for PV, EV, and AC. The PMP exam will always give you the abbreviations you're familiar with.

3. Answer: D

When you're using the past performance of previous projects to help come up with an estimate, that's called Analogous Estimation. This is the second time you saw this particular technique—it was also in the Time Management chapter. So there's a good chance that you'll get an exam question on it.

4. Answer: A

The formula for SPI is: SPI = EV ÷ PV. So you just have to fill in the numbers that you know, which gets you

1.2 = EV ÷ $56,733. Now flip it around. You end up with EV = 1.2 x $56,733, which multiplies out to $68,079.60.

Did you notice the red herring in the question? It didn't matter what the projects were about, only how much they cost!

5. Answer: B

If you see a question about opportunity cost of selecting one project over another, the answer is the value of the project that was not selected! So even though the answers were all numbers, there's no math at all in this question.

Exam ~~Questions~~ Answers

6. Answer: D

This is one of those questions that gives you a definition and asks you to pick the term that's being defined. So which one is it?

Try using the process of elimination to find the right answer! It can't be Benefit Cost Ratio, because you aren't being asked to compare the overall cost of the project to anything to figure out what its benefit will be. Depreciation isn't right—that's about how your project loses value over time, not about its costs. And it's not Net Present Value, because the question didn't ask you about how much value your project is delivering today. That leaves Lifecycle Costing.

If you don't know the answer to a question, try to eliminate all the answers you know are wrong.

Don't forget: Lower = Loser!

7. Answer: C

When you see an SPI that's lower than one, that means your project is behind schedule. But your CPI is above one, which means that you're ahead on your budget!

8. Answer: C

Use the formula: EV=BAC x Actual % Complete. When you plug the numbers into the formula, the right answer pops out!

I love these calculation questions because when I see that the answer on my calculator matches one of the choices, I know I got it right!

9. Answer: B

If you are just starting to work on your preliminary scope statement, it means you're just starting the project and you don't have enough information yet to do analogous, parametric, or bottom-up estimates.

The only estimation technique that you can use that early in the project is the Rough Order of Magnitude estimate. That kind of estimate is not nearly as accurate as the other kinds of estimate and is used just to give a rough idea of how much time and cost will be involved in doing a project.

Exam Questions

10. Answer: D

Some of these calculation questions can get a little complicated—but that doesn't mean they're difficult! Just relax—you can do them!

The formula you need to use is: SPI = EV ÷ PV. But what do you use for EV and PV? If you look at the question again, you'll find everything you need to calculate them. First, figure out earned value: EV = BAC x Actual % Complete. But wait! You weren't given these in the question!

OK, no problem—you just need to think your way through it. The project will cost $52/meter to lay 4 km (or 4,000 meters) of cable, which means the total cost of the project will be $52 x 4,000 = $208,000. And you can figure out Actual % Complete too! You've laid 1,800 meters so far out of the 4,000 meters you'll lay in total… so that's 1,800 ÷ 4,000 = 45% complete. All right! Now you know your earned value: EV = $208,000 x 45% = $93,600.

So what's next? You've got half of what you need for SPI—now you have to figure out PV. The formula for it is: PV = BAC x Scheduled % Complete. So how much of the project were you supposed to complete by now? You're 5 weeks into an 8 week project, so 5 ÷ 8 = 62.5%. Your PV is $208,000 x 62.5% = $130,000. Now you've got everything you need to calculate SPI!
EV ÷ PV = $93,600 ÷ $130,000 = .72

So that question was really about whether I could figure out how to calculate EV and PV from what I was given.

Did you think that this was a red herring? It wasn't—you needed all the numbers you were given.

11. Answer: B

You'll run into a lot of questions like this where a problem happens, a person has an issue or the project runs into trouble. When this happens, the first thing you do is stop and gather information. An that should make sense to you, since you don't know if this change will really impact cost or not. It may seem like a huge change to the programmer, but may not actually cost the project anything. Or it may really be huge. So the first thing to do is figure out the impact of the change, and that's what answer B says!

Exam ~~Questions~~ Answers

12. Answer: B

What formula do you know that has AC and EV? Right, the CPI formula does! Take a look at it: CPI = EV ÷ AC. So what happens if AC is bigger than EV? Make up two numbers and plug them in! You get CPI that's below 1, and you know what that means… it means that you've blown your budget!

12. If AC (ACWP) is greater than your EV (BCWP), what does this mean?

Here are more of those four-letter abbreviations. Don't worry—you don't need to memorize these

13. Answer: D

This question gave you a definition and is checking to see if you know what it refers to. You should take a minute to look at each of the four possible answers and see if you can think of the definition for each of them. It's definitely worth taking the time to understand what each of these formulas and variables represents in real life! It will make the whole exam a lot easier.

14. Answer: C

This is a classic red herring question! The money you've spent so far is the actual cost. It's a simple definition question, wrapped up in a whole bunch of fluff!

14. You are managing an industrial architecture project. You've spent $26,410 so far to survey…

This is the only part of the question that matters—the rest is a red herring.

15. Answer: A

When you plug a bunch of values into a formula or computer program, and it generates an estimate, that's called parametric estimation. Parametric estimation often uses some historical data, but that doesn't mean it's the same as analogous estimation!

16. Answer: C

You've been given a net present value (NPV) for each project. NPV means the total value that this project is worth to your company! It's got the costs—including opportunity costs—built in already. So all you need to do is select the project with the biggest NPV.

17. Answer: C

The Rough Order of Magnitude estimate is a very preliminary estimate that everyone knows is only within an order of magnitude of the actual cost. That means it can be anywhere from half the actual cost to twice the actual cost! That's what order of magnitude means.

18. Answer: A

You should definitely have a pretty good idea of how change control works by now! The change control system defines the procedures that you use to carry out the changes. And cost control has its own set of procedures, called the cost change control system.

19. Answer: B

You use the project cost baseline to measure and monitor your project's cost performance. The idea behind a baseline is that when a change is approved and implemented, the baseline gets updated.

I recognize this—a change is requested, approved and implemented, and then the baseline is updated. So I'm using the cost baseline just like I used the scope baseline back in the Scope Management chapter!

20. Answer: C

You should have the hang of this by now! Plug the numbers into the formula (CPI = EV ÷ AC), and it spits out the answer. Sometimes the question will give you more numbers than you actually need to use—just ignore them like any other red herring and only use the ones you need!

8 Quality Management

Getting it right

It's not enough to make sure you get it done on time and under budget. You need to be sure you make the right product to suit your stakeholders' needs. Quality means making sure that you build what you said you would and that you do it as efficiently as you can. That means trying not to make too many mistakes and always keeping your project working toward the goal of creating the right product!

What is quality?

Everybody "knows" what **quality** is. But the way the word is used in everyday life is a little different than how it is used in project management. Just like the triple constraint—scope, cost and schedule—you manage quality on your project by setting goals and taking measurements. That's why you need to understand the quality levels your stakeholders believe are acceptable, and that your project meets those targets... just like it needs to meet their budget and schedule goals.

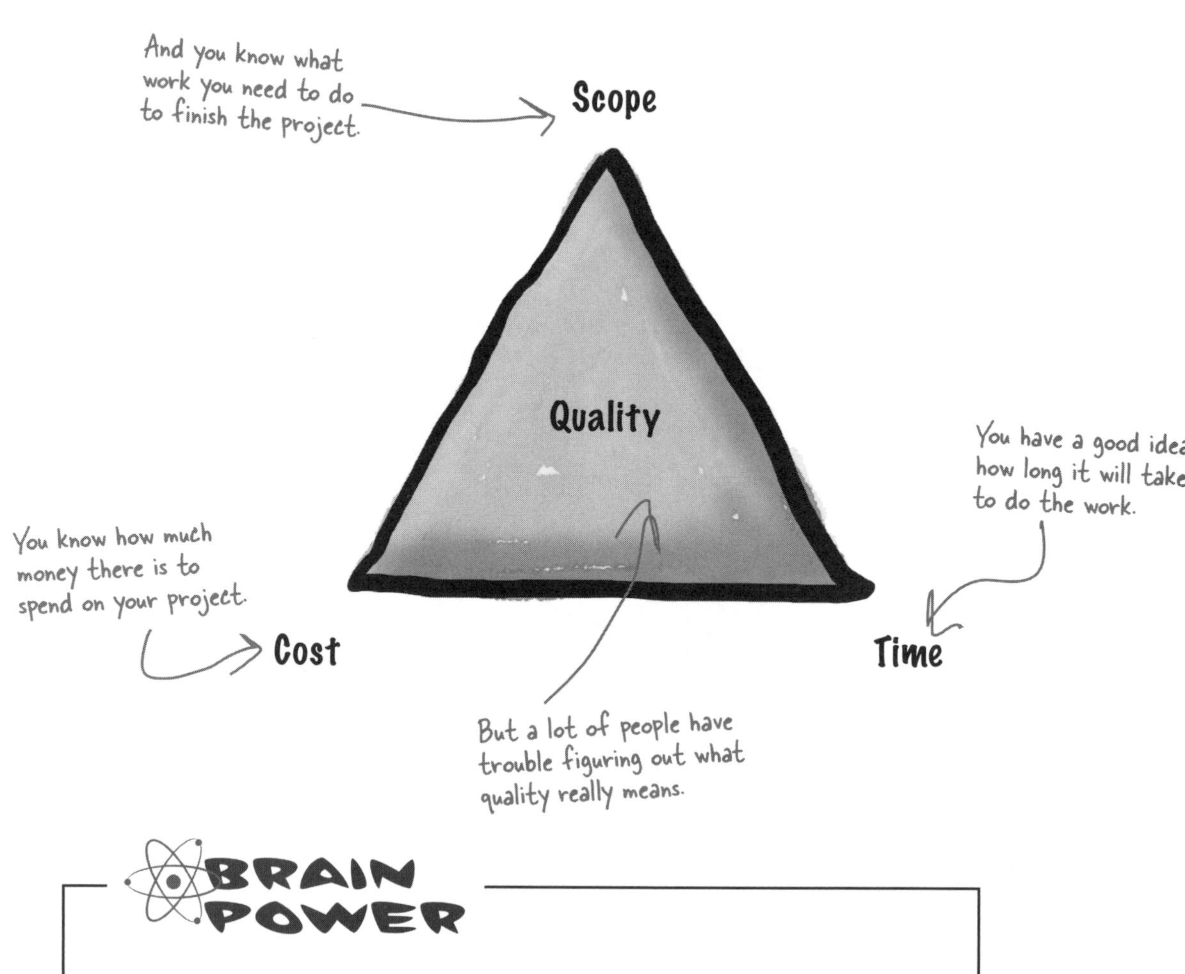

BRAIN POWER

How can you tell a high quality product from a low quality one?

You need more than just tests to figure out quality

A lot of people confuse quality with testing. When projects run into quality problems, some project managers will respond by adding more testers to the project to try to find more bugs. But testing is only one part of the story. To know your product's quality, you need to do more than test it:

The Black Box 3000™.

Scenario 1

Lisa presses the button, but nothing happens.

Scenario 2

Lisa presses the button and a voice comes out of the box that says, "You pressed the button incorrectly."

Scenario 3

Lisa presses the button and the box heats up to 628°F. Lisa drops the box and it shatters into hundreds of pieces.

Lisa, our tester, isn't sure what she's supposed to be testing for.

Once you know what the product is supposed to do, it's easy to tell which tests pass and which fail

Testing is all about checking to be sure that the product does what it is supposed to do. That means that you need to have a good idea of what it is supposed to do to judge its quality. That's why the most important concept in defining quality for the PMP exam is **conformance to requirements**. It just means that your product is only as good as the requirements you have written for it. To say that it is a high quality product means that it fulfils the requirements your team agreed to when you started the work.

Quality is the measurement of how closely your product meets its requirements.

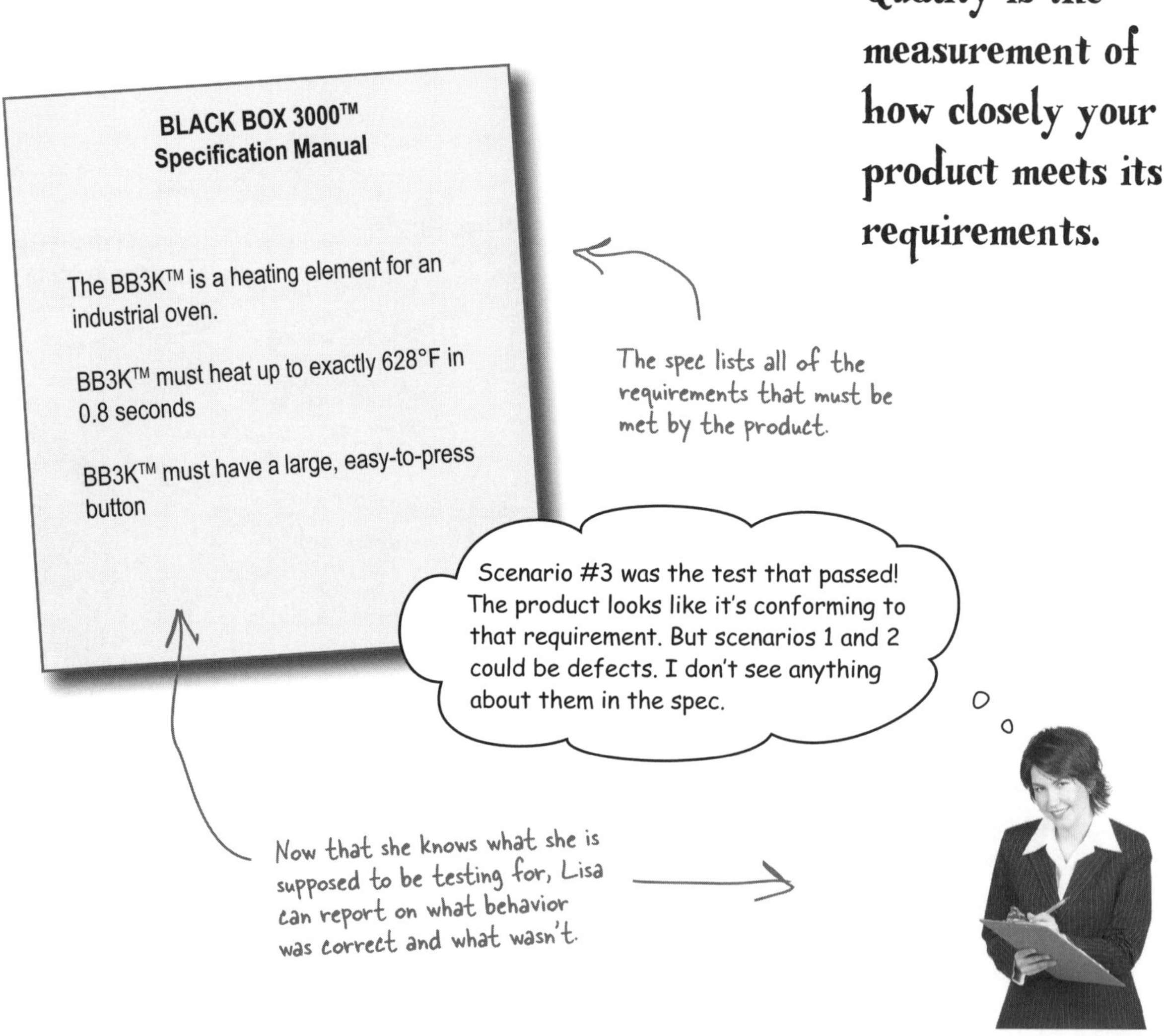

Quality up close

There are a few general ideas about quality that will help you understand a little better where the PMP exam is coming from. A lot of work has been done on quality engineering in the past 50 years or so that was originally focused on manufacturing. Those ideas have been applied to product quality over lots of different industries. Here are a few concepts that are important for the exam.

Customer needs should be written down as requirements before you start to build your product. That way, you can always plan on building the right thing.

Customer satisfaction is about making sure that the people who are paying for the end product are happy with what they get. When the team gathers requirements for the specification, they try to write down all of the things that the customers want in the product so that you know how to make them happy.

Some requirements can be left **unstated**, too. Those are the ones that are implied by the customer's explicit needs. In the end, if you fulfill all of your requirements, your customers should be really satisfied.

Some requirements are just common sense—like a product that people hold can't be made from toxic stuff that kills you. It might not be stated, but it's definitely a requirement.

Fitness to use is about making sure that the product you build has the best design possible to fit the customer's needs. Which would you choose: a product that's beautifully designed, well constructed, solidly built and all-around pleasant to look at but does not do what you need, or a product that does what you want despite being really ugly to look at and a pain in the butt to work with?

You'll always choose the product that fits your needs, even if it's seriously limited. That's why it's important that the product both does what it is supposed to do and does it well.

You could pound in a nail with a screwdriver, but a hammer is more fit for the job.

This idea came from a quality theorist named Joseph Juran.

Conformance to requirements is the core of both customer satisfaction and fitness to use. Above all, your product needs to do what you wrote down in your requirements specification. Your requirements should take into account what will satisfy your customer and the best design possible for the job.

Phillip Crosby made this idea popular in the early 1980s. It's been really important to quality engineering ever since.

In the end, your product's quality is judged by whether you built what you said you would build.

That means conforming to both stated and implied requirements.

Quality is a measure of how well your product does what you intend.

It's easy to mistake a low grade product for a low quality one.

When people talk about the quality of their car or their meal, they are often talking about its **grade**. You can judge something's *grade* without knowing too much about its requirements. But that's a lot different than knowing its *quality*.

Quality vs. grade

Quality means that something does what you needed it to do. Grade describes how much people value it.

You can eat a lobster platter for dinner, or you can eat a hot dog. They are both types of food, right? But they have very different tastes, looks, feels, and most importantly, cost. If you order the lobster in a restaurant, you'll be charged a lot more than if you order a hot dog. But that doesn't mean the lobster is a higher-quality meal. If you'd ordered a salad and got lobster or a hot dog instead, you wouldn't be satisfied.

Higher-grade stuff typically costs more, but just because you pay more for something doesn't mean it does what you need it to do.

The lobster is a high-grade meal; the hot dog is a low-grade one. But they're both low quality if you actually wanted a salad.

Sharpen your pencil

Take a look at each of these situations and figure out if they're talking about quality or grade.

1. You ordered mushrooms on your pizza, but you got onions.

☐ Quality ☐ Grade

2. You called the pizza parlor to complain and the guy yelled at you.

☐ Quality ☐ Grade

3. The pizza arrived, but it had canned mushrooms.

☐ Quality ☐ Grade

4. The pizza was cold.

☐ Quality ☐ Grade

---

5. You just got a brand new luxury car that cost a whole lot of money.

☐ Quality ☐ Grade

6. But it's in the shop every two weeks.

☐ Quality ☐ Grade

You probably didn't tell the salesman you needed the car to work, but you expected it to. That's an unstated requirement.

7. Your neighbors make fun of you because your chrome hubcaps aren't very classy…

☐ Quality ☐ Grade

8. … even though they do a great job of protecting the wheels from dirt, which is why you bought them in the first place.

☐ Quality ☐ Grade

Answers on page 404.

We've talked about how you can't just test the product to figure out its quality. Can you think of ways that you can make a product's quality higher?

"An ounce of prevention..."

It's not enough to go to the dentist to get your cavities filled. You need to brush your teeth every day. The same goes with product quality. If you focus on preventing mistakes on your project before they happen, you are more likely to get the product done on time and without spending too much money.

When it comes to defects, prevention is always better than inspection!

10% of the black boxes have buttons that stick when you press them.

We could hire a lot more inspectors to check to see if each of the products has a sticky button and send it for repair…

Or we could change the design to make the button a millimeter smaller and eliminate the problem altogether.

And that's why you need the three Quality Management processes!

There are **three processes** in the Quality Management knowledge area, and they're all designed to make sure that you and your team deliver the highest quality product that you can.

Quality Planning is like the other planning processes you've learned about—you create a Quality Management Plan to help guide you and your team through quality activities.

Perform Quality Control is the Monitoring & Controlling process where you look at each deliverable and inspect it for defects.

Perform Quality Assurance is where you take a step back and look at how well your project fits in with your company's overall quality standards and guidelines.

Which of these activities are prevention, and which are inspection?

1. You find that 40% of the sneakers your factory makes have the left foot insole put into the right shoe and the right insole put into the left shoe. So, you print an L on the underside of the left insole so that factory workers can tell them apart more easily.

   ☐ Prevention ☐ Inspection

2. The applications being built by your programming team have lots of bugs. So you add extra test cycles and make them longer and more intensive to try to find more problems before you ship.

   ☐ Prevention ☐ Inspection

3. The applications being built by your programming team have lots of bugs. So you write up coding standards that will guide everyone in building the product with more attention to quality.

   ☐ Prevention ☐ Inspection

4. Some of the black boxes being built at the factory are only heating up to 500 degrees when the button is pushed. So you set up an automated button presser to press each one and measure its temperature as it comes off of the assembly line.

   ☐ Prevention ☐ Inspection

5. You set up code reviews at important milestones in your project to catch defects as early as you can.

   ☐ Prevention ☐ Inspection

6. The programmers on your team write unit tests before they write the code for the application they're writing. That helps them to think of ways that the application's design might go wrong and avoid major pitfalls.

   ☐ Prevention ☐ Inspection

Which of these activities are prevention, and which are inspection?

1. You find that 40% of the sneakers your factory makes have the left foot insole put into the right shoe and the right insole put into the left shoe. So, you print an L on the underside of the left insole so that factory workers can tell them apart more easily.

   ☑ Prevention ☐ Inspection

   The focus here is on making sure that no more defects happen, rather than on finding them..

2. The applications being built by your programming team have lots of bugs. So you add extra test cycles and make them longer and more intensive to try to find more problems before you ship.

   ☐ Prevention ☑ Inspection

   Catching the bugs after they've been put in the product is not the most efficient way to deal with this problem. It will cost more money and take longer.

3. The applications being built by your programming team have lots of bugs. So, you write up coding standards that will guide everyone in building the product with more attention to quality.

   ☑ Prevention ☐ Inspection

   This is a much better way of dealing with the same problem. It focuses on making sure the bugs never make it into the software rather than finding them and fixing them.

4. Some of the black boxes being built at the factory are only heating up to 500 degrees when the button is pushed. So you set up an automated button presser to press each one and measure its temperature as it comes off of the assembly line.

   ☐ Prevention ☑ Inspection

   This one is also focused on finding the problems once they're in the product.

5. You set up code reviews at important milestones in your project to catch defects as early as you can.

   ☐ Prevention ☑ Inspection

6. The programmers on your team write unit tests before they write the code for the application they're writing. That helps them to think of ways that the application's design might go wrong and avoid major pitfalls.

   ☑ Prevention ☐ Inspection

Quality planning is how you prevent defects

Since prevention is the best way to deal with defects, you need to do a lot of planning to make sure that your product is made with as few defects as possible. The **Quality Planning process** focuses on taking all of the information available to you at the beginning of your project and figuring out how you will measure your quality and prevent defects.

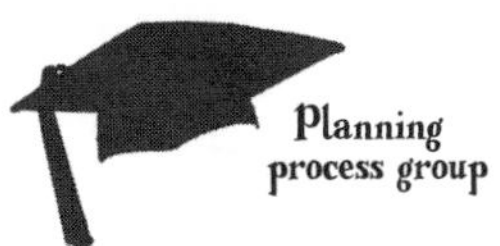

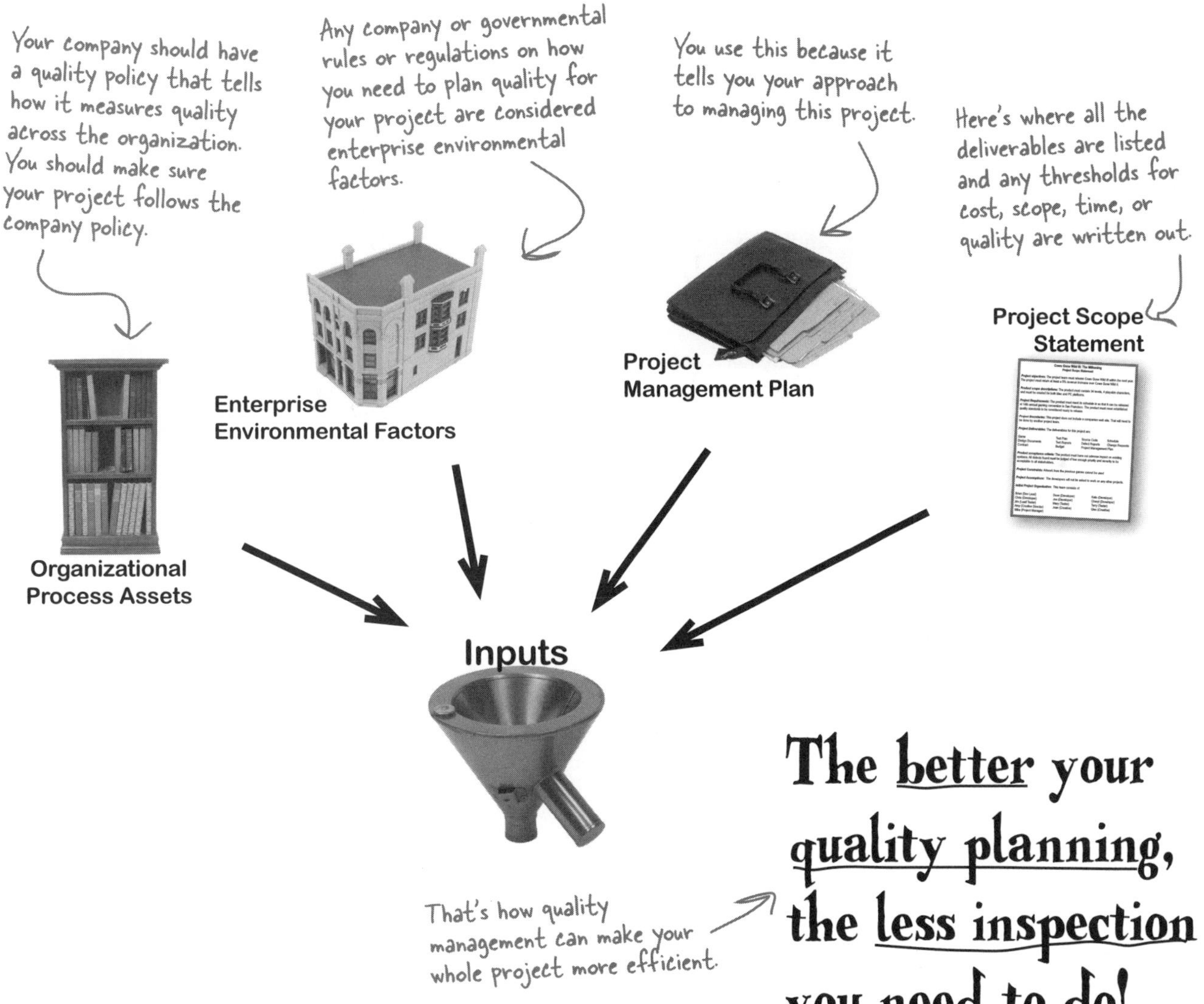

Your company should have a quality policy that tells how it measures quality across the organization. You should make sure your project follows the company policy.

Organizational Process Assets

Any company or governmental rules or regulations on how you need to plan quality for your project are considered enterprise environmental factors.

Enterprise Environmental Factors

You use this because it tells you your approach to managing this project.

Project Management Plan

Here's where all the deliverables are listed and any thresholds for cost, scope, time, or quality are written out.

Project Scope Statement

Inputs

That's how quality management can make your whole project more efficient.

The better your quality planning, the less inspection you need to do!

How to plan for quality

You need to plan out which activities you're going to use to measure the quality of the product of your project. And you need to be sure that the activities you plan are going to pay off in the end. So you'll need to think about the cost of all of the quality-related activities you want to do. Then you'll need to set some guidelines for what you're going to measure against. Finally, you'll need to design the tests you're going to run when the product is ready to be tested.

Cost benefit analysis is looking at how much your quality activities will cost versus how much you will gain from doing them. The costs are easy to measure; the effort and resources it takes to do them are just like any other task on your schedule. Since quality activities don't actually produce a product, though, it is harder for people to measure the benefits sometimes. The main benefits are less rework, higher productivity and efficiency and more satisfaction from both the team and the customer.

That makes sense. A team that is making a high quality product will be really proud of their work.

Benchmarking means using the results of quality planning on other projects to set goals for your own. You might find that the last project your company did had 20% fewer defects than the one before it. You would want to learn from a project like that and put in practice any of the ideas they used to make such a great improvement. Benchmarks can give you some reference points for judging your own project before you even get started with the work.

Design of experiments is the list of all the kinds of tests you are going to run on your product. It might list all of the kinds of test procedures you'll do, the approaches you'll take, and even the tests themselves.

In the software world, this is usually called test planning.

Cost of quality is what you get when you add up the cost of all of the prevention and inspection activities you are going to do on your project. It doesn't just include the testing. It includes any time spent writing standards, reviewing documents, meeting to analyze the root causes of defects, rework to fix the defects once they're found by the team—absolutely everything you do to ensure quality on the project.

Cost of quality can be a good number to check whether your project is doing well or having trouble. Say your company tracks cost of quality on all of its projects. Then you could tell if you were spending more or less than they are to get your project up to snuff.

Read each of these scenarios and identify which tool or technique is being used.

1. You look through your company's asset library and find that a recent project was able to reduce defects by 20% by inserting defect prevention meetings early in the construction phase. You put the same process in your quality plan and set the target for shipped defects to be 20% lower than the company average for your project.

   Tool/technique: ....

2. You add up all of the costs projected for quality activities and track that number in your quality plan. You use this number to gauge the health of your project compared to other projects in your company.

   Tool/technique: ....

3. You write up a list of all of the tests you are going to run on the Black Box 3000™ when it rolls off the assembly line. You determine what kinds of failures might cause you to stop testing, what it would take for you to resume test activities, and requirements that the product would need to fulfill to be considered accepted into test.

   Tool/technique: ....

Answers on page 405.

The quality management plan gives you what you need to manage quality

Once you have your quality management plan, you know your guidelines for managing quality on your project. Your strategies for monitoring your project quality should be included in the plan, as well as the reasons for all of the steps you are taking. It's important that everyone on the team understand the rationale behind the metrics being used to judge success or failure of the project.

The Quality management plan is the main tool for preventing defects on your project.

Outputs

A metric is just a number you use to measure your product's quality.

Even though this number is part of Time Management, you'll often measure it in your quality plan because it's part of customer satisfaction on the project.

BLACK BOX 3000™
Quality Management Plan

Project Background:

The project goal is to create as many industrial heating elements as possible with no defects. Past problems included sticky buttons and difficulty testing the product. This was corrected when a specification was given to the test team.

Goals for Project Metrics:

Metric	Goal	Rationale	How we'll do it
Schedule Variance	<5%	Because shipments of black boxes are planned with clients in advance very few delays are acceptable.	Track any activities that might cause delays. Use extra resources if necessary to meet the deadline.
Defect Density	0 High Priority 2 Medium Priority 5 Low Priority (defects per thousand black boxes)	Defect repair is extremely costly. We need to get as many products shipped as possible on the first try.	Set up defect prevention activities early in the process. Monitor the results of inspections and adjust if necessary.

Defect Prevention Plan:

Outputs

Checklists are there to help people head off mistakes that might cause defects. You can create checklists to avoid common errors as part of your quality planning process and then put them to use throughout your project as a defect prevention technique. Checklists can also be used for inspecting products to be sure that they display specific characteristics.

This means you need to think about more than just building the product of the project. You also need to think about how your company does all of its projects.

Process Improvement Plan is a plan for improving the process you are using to do the work. In it, you come up with strategies for finding inefficiencies and places where the way you work might be slowing you down or creating a low quality product. You set goals for how you can monitor the process during your project and make recommendations to make it better.

Quality Baseline is your starting point for measuring your project's quality goals. It's the way you expect your project to perform when you are measuring your quality metrics. When you compare your actuals to your plan, you're comparing your measurements to this baseline. You create the baseline by taking a snapshot of the quality management plan and your initial measurements.

Quality Metrics are the kinds of measurements you'll take throughout your project to figure out its quality. If you're running a project to install windows in a skyscraper, and 15% of them have to be reinstalled because they were broken, that's an important metric. You'll probably want to work with your company to bring that number down.

Here's where you document how you'll be figuring out the product's quality. You need to write down the formulas you'll use, when you will do the measurements, why you are taking them, and how you will interpret them.

Project Management Plan Updates

Project Management Plan Updates might need to be made because you have found new information in the course of planning your quality activities that affects one of the other plans you've already made. That's why this process includes an output for making those kinds of changes.

Match each Quality Planning output to its description.

Quality Management Plan	Helps you to make sure that each deliverable it up to company standards.
Process Improvement Plan	Helps you to plan out all of your quality activities
Checklists	Gives you something to compare your work performance information to.
Quality Baseline	Helps you change the way you work for the better.

Answers on page 405.

there are no Dumb Questions

Q: Why do you need to track the cost of testing?

A: You mean Cost of Quality, right? Cost of Quality isn't just the cost of testing. It's the cost of all of your quality activities. Even preventive activities like spending time writing checklists and standards are part of it. The reason you track Cost of Quality is that it can tell you a lot about the health of your project as a whole.

Say you find you're spending twice as much on quality activities as you are on building your product. You need to use that number to start asking some questions about the way the work is being done.

Are people not doing enough up front to prevent defects and adding a lot of expensive test activities at the end of the project to compensate? Is the design not clear, so your team needs to do a lot of re-work trying to get what the customer needs? There are many reasons that could be causing a high cost of quality number, but you wouldn't even know to ask about them if you didn't track it.

Q: How do you know your benchmarks before you start building?

A: That's what your Organizational Process Assets are for. Since your company keeps a record of all of the projects that have been done over the years, those projects' quality measurements can help you get a gauge on how your project will perform too. If your company knows that all of the projects in your division had a cost of quality that was 40% of the cost of the overall cost of development, you might set 40% cost of quality as a benchmark for your project as well. Your company might have stated a goal of having a schedule variance of plus or minus 10% on all projects for this calendar year. In that case, the schedule variance is a benchmark for your project.

Q: I don't really have good requirements for my projects because everyone on the team starts out with just a good idea of what we're building. How do I handle quality?

A: You should never do that. Remember how requirements were an input to the Initiating processes? Well, this is why you needed them. And it's why it's **your** responsibility to make sure that the project starts out with good, well-defined, and **correct** requirements. If you don't have them, you can't measure quality—and quality is an important part of project management.

Without requirements, you have no idea what the product is supposed to do, and that means you can't judge its quality. You can learn a lot about a product by testing it, but without knowing its requirements, a product could pass all of its tests and still not do what the customer expects it to do. So having good requirements really is the only way to know whether or not your product is high quality.

Inspect your deliverables

It's not enough to inspect the final product. All of the things that you make throughout a project should be looked at to find bugs. In fact, the earlier you find them, the easier they are to fix. The **Perform Quality Control process** is all about inspecting work products to find defects.

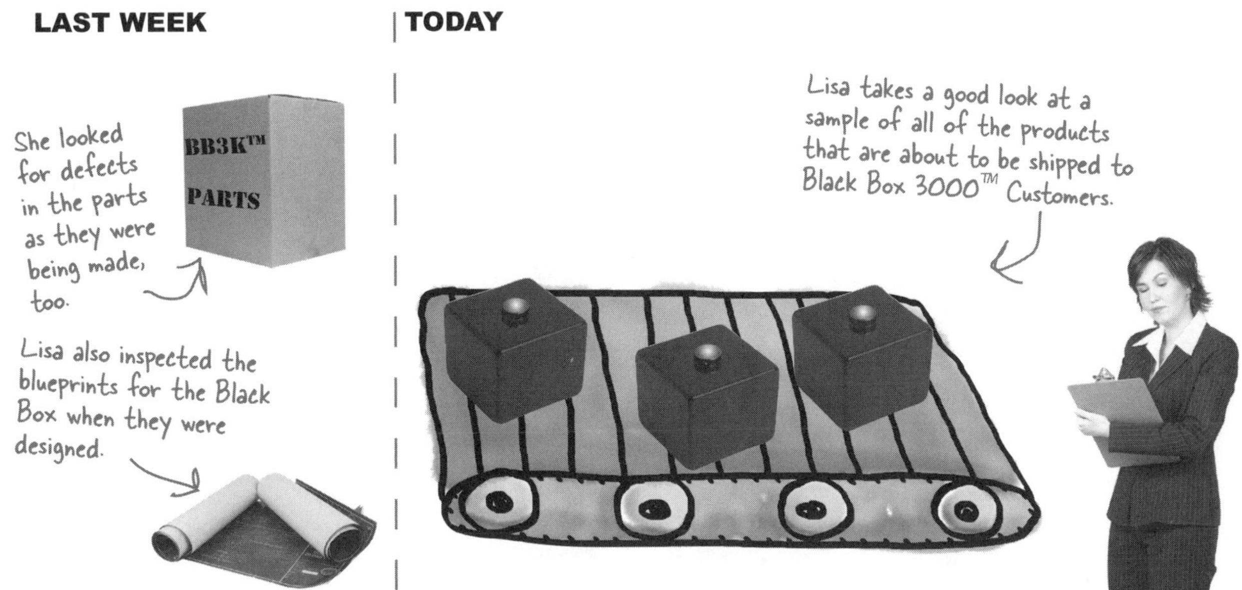

Quality control is in the Monitoring & Controlling process group. Like Scope Control and Cost Control, you look at the work performance information that is coming from your project and compare it to your plan. ***If there are problems, you recommend corrective or preventative action.***

How would you use your checklists and metrics to inspect all of the deliverables and find defects?

Use the planning outputs for Perform Quality Control

You've come up with a plan to make sure each deliverable is right. Now it's time to monitor the work that's being done to the requirements—and that's just a matter of following your plan! You'll need to look at everything that is being produced and make sure that it stands up to all of the requirements that have been gathered. And you'll need nearly everything you produced in Quality Planning in order to get a handle on your product's quality.

Metrics make it easy for you to check how well your product meets expectations.

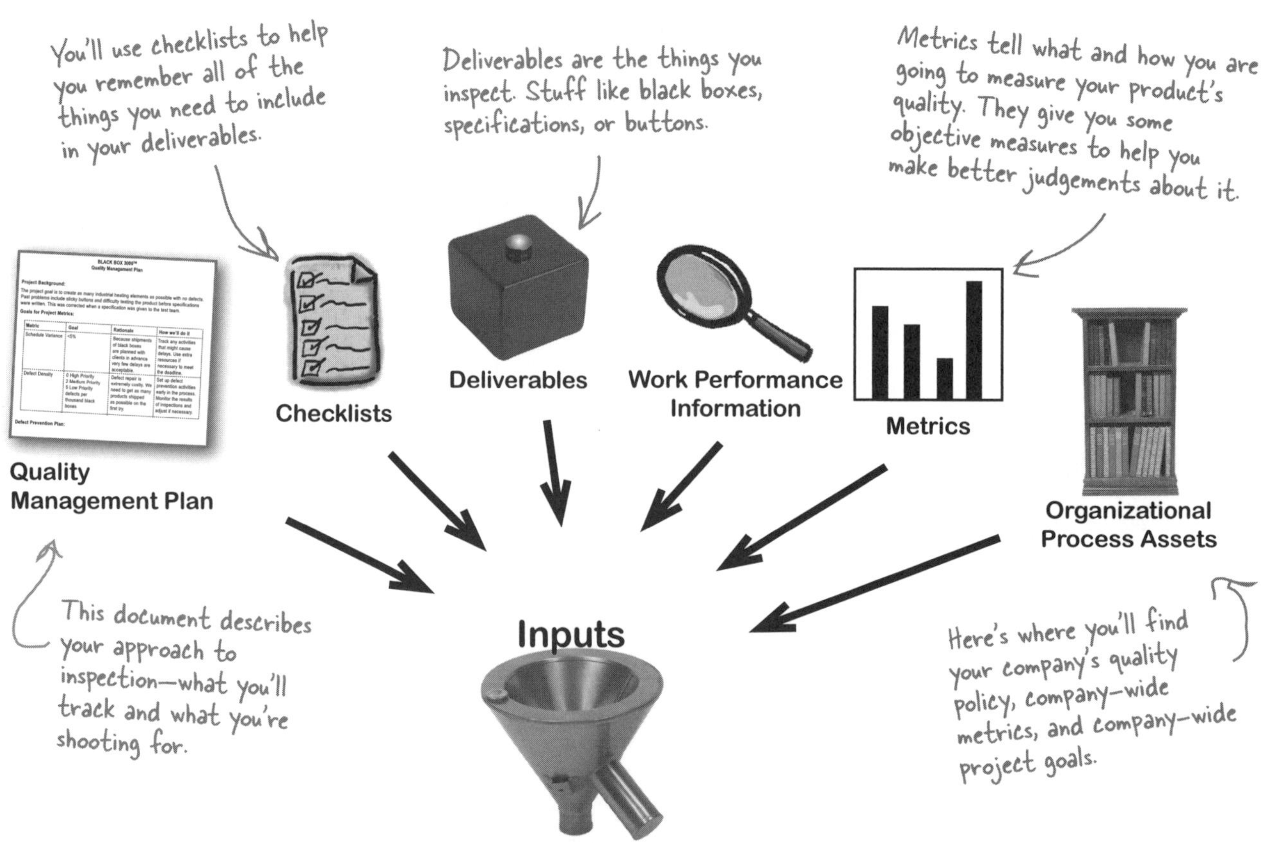

The seven basic tools of quality

These charts and tools are so common in quality control that they have a name. They're called the **seven basic tools of quality**. Expect a bunch of questions on these in the exam.

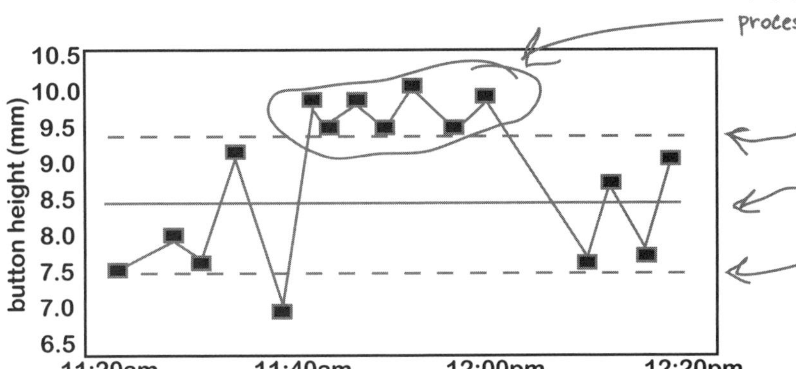

These points are showing the Rule of Seven AND that this process is out of control.

There are three lines on a control chart. The first one is the upper control limit.

Mean—the average height in your sample of buttons.

The lower control limit is the last line. This one represents the shortest that you want the buttons to be.

Control Charts are a way of visualizing how processes are doing over time. Let's say that the button on each black box needs to be between 7.5 and 9.5 millimeters tall, and the chart above represents sample height measurements of boxes being made. We want the boxes to all be between 7.5mm and 9.5mm. The **lower control limit** of the chart is 7.5mm, and the **upper control limit** is 9.5mm. The chart above shows control limits as dashed lines. The **mean** is the solid line in the middle, and it shows the average height of all of the buttons in the sample. By looking at the chart above, you can see that there are a lot of buttons that were taller than 9.5mm manufactured and only one that was shorter than 7.5mm. When a data point falls outside of the control limits, we say that data point is **out of control**; and when this happens we say that the **entire process is out of control**.

It's pretty normal to have your data fluctuate from sample to sample. But when seven data points in a row fall **on one side of the mean**, that's an uncommon enough occurrence that it means your process might have a problem. So when you see this, you need to look into it and try to figure out what's going on. That's called the **rule of seven**, and *you'll definitely see questions about it on the PMP exam.*

When you're looking at the whole process, that's called Quality Assurance—and it's coming up next.

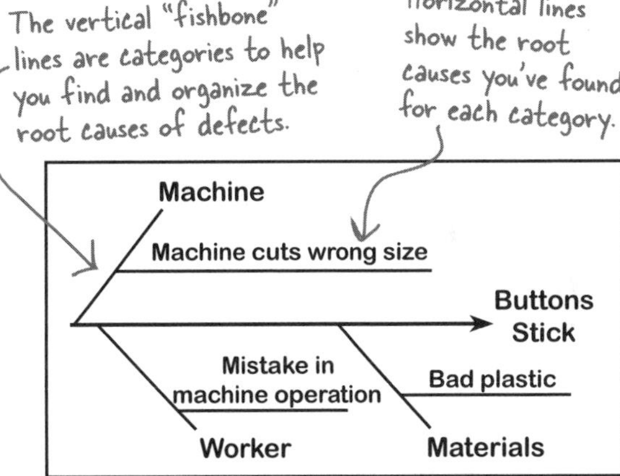

Fishbone or Ishikawa Diagram

Cause and effect diagrams are also called **Fishbone** and **Ishikawa** diagrams. They are used to figure out what caused a defect. You list all of the categories of the defects that you have identified and then write the possible causes of the defect you are analyzing from each category.

Fishbone diagrams help you **see all of the possible causes** in one place so you can think of how you might prevent the defect in the future.

Pareto charts, Flowcharts, and Histograms

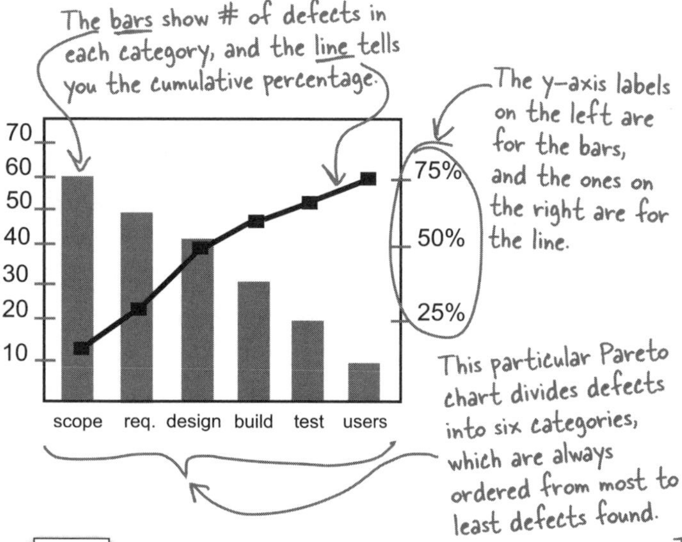

Pareto charts help you to figure out which problems need your attention right away. They're based on the idea that a large number of problems are caused by a small number of causes. In fact, that's called the **80/20 rule**—80% of the defects are usually caused by 20% of the causes. Pareto charts plot out the frequency of defects and sort them in descending order. The right axis on the chart shows the cumulative percentage. For the example here, the most defects are caused by scope issues. So, improving the way projects are scoped would be the best way to prevent defects in upcoming projects.

Scope
Req
Design
pass review ? — No
Build
pass unit tests? — No
Test
pass tests? — No
Release

Flowcharts let you show how processes work visually. You can use a flowchart to show how the tasks in your project interrelate and what they depend on. They are also good for showing decision-making processes.

The example on the left shows a high-level view of a software development process. First the high level scope is decided, then the requirements, and then the design. After design there is a decision to be made: Does the design pass a review? If yes, then move on to the build phase; if no, there's still some design work to do. After the build process, the product needs to pass its unit tests to make it into the test phase.

The flowchart helps you to see how all of the phases relate to each other. Sometimes the way you are working is responsible for defects in your product. Flowcharts help you get a handle on the way you are working by showing you a picture of the whole process.

This product probably isn't ready to ship—it still has a lot of bugs But at least you know that the bugs aren't all critical!

60
50
40
30
20
10
Critical High Med Low

Don't call this a "bar chart"! In the PMP world, a bar chart is another name for a Gantt chart, which is a kind of project schedule.

Histograms give you a good idea of how your data breaks down. If you heard that your product had 158 defects, you might think that they were all critical. So looking at a chart like the one above would help you to get some perspective on the data. A lot of the bugs are low priority. It looks like only 28 or so are critical. Histograms are great for helping you to compare characteristics of data and make more informed decisions.

Run charts and Scatter charts

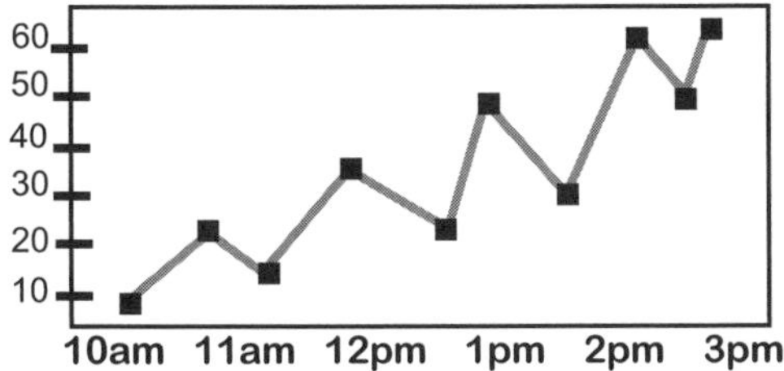

Run charts tell you about **trends** in your project by showing you what your data looks like as a line chart. If the line in the chart were the number of defects found in your product through each quality activity, that would tell you that things were getting worse as your project progressed. In a run chart, you are looking for trends in the data over time. Does it seem to be going up or down as the project progresses? Is there a steady climb or a spike when a particular activity occurs?

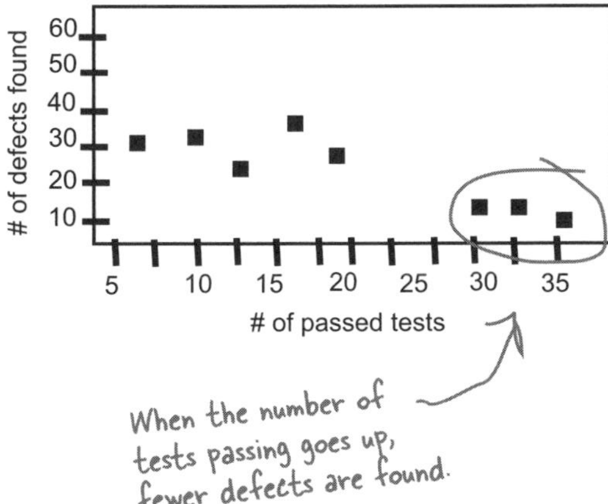

Scatter charts show how two different types of data relate to each other. If you worked with your test team to create a bunch of new tests, you might use a scatter chart to see if the new test cases had any impact on the number of defects you found. The chart here shows that as more test cases pass, fewer defects are found.

The seven basic tools are all about charting defects. Why do you think that would be useful in Quality Control?

More quality control tools

Inspection is what you're doing when you look at the deliverables and see if they conform to requirements. It's important to remember that you don't just inspect the final product. You also look at all of the deliverables that are made along the way.

Defect repair review is when you inspect a repaired defect to be sure that it is actually fixed.

It's not enough to fix defects. You need to be sure that they don't cause more damage once they're fixed.

Statistical sampling helps you make decisions about your product without looking at each and every thing you make. Lisa is responsible for the quality of the Black Box 3000™, but there's no way she can inspect each one as it comes off the assembly line. It makes sense for her to take a sample of the products and inspect those. From that sample she can learn enough about the project to make good judgments.

Answer the questions about the Black Box 3000™ using the Quality Control Charts below.

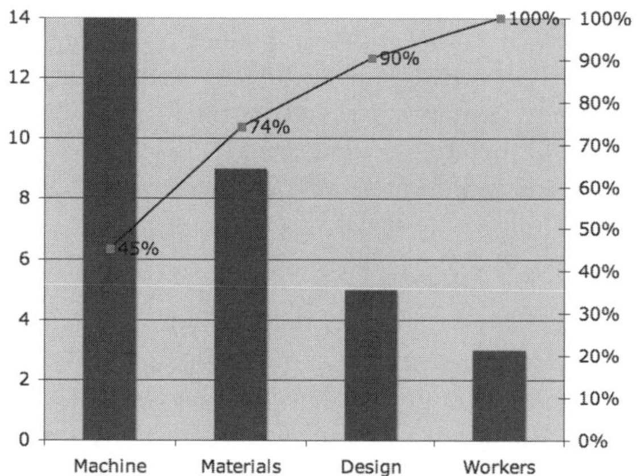

Which root cause is responsible for the most defects in the project?

....

What is the lowest priority area for defect prevention?

....

What is the cumulative percentage of design defects?

....

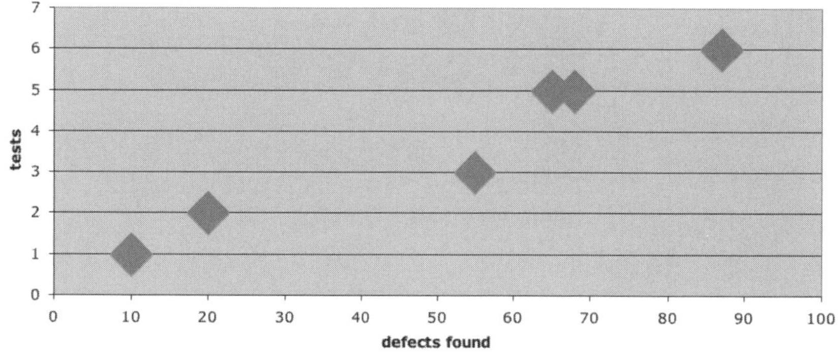

Hint: Look for a gap in the chart that shows you how adding an extra test caught a lot more defects.

Did adding more tests find more bugs?

....

Where did you see the biggest increase in defect detection?

....

Looking at this chart, should you continue to add more tests to the project?

In other words, did adding extra tests help you find more defects?

....

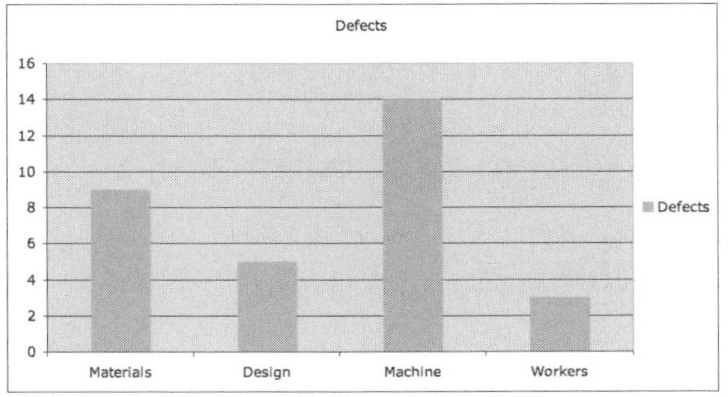

How many machine defects were found?

....

How many defects were caused by workers?

....

How many total defects are shown on this chart?

....

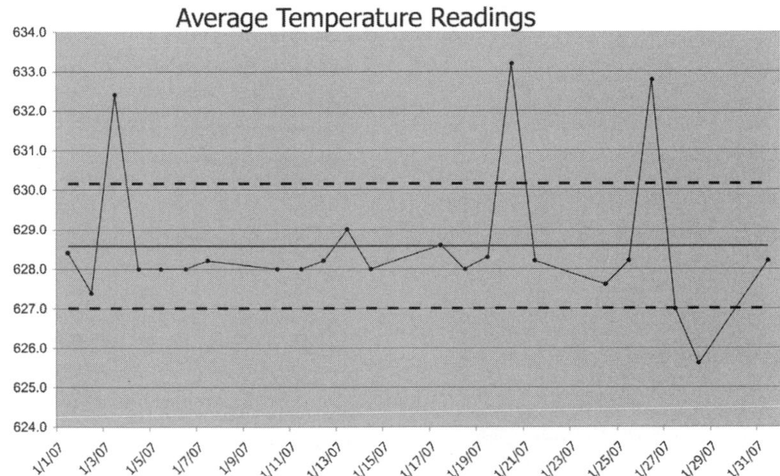

Circle the data points that make up the rule of seven.

Is this process in control?

....

What's the upper control limit?

....

What's the mean temperature reading?

....

What's the lower control limit?

....

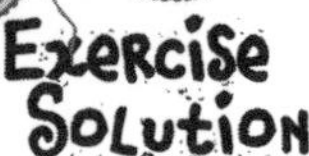

Answer the questions about the Black Box 3000™ using the Quality Control Charts below.

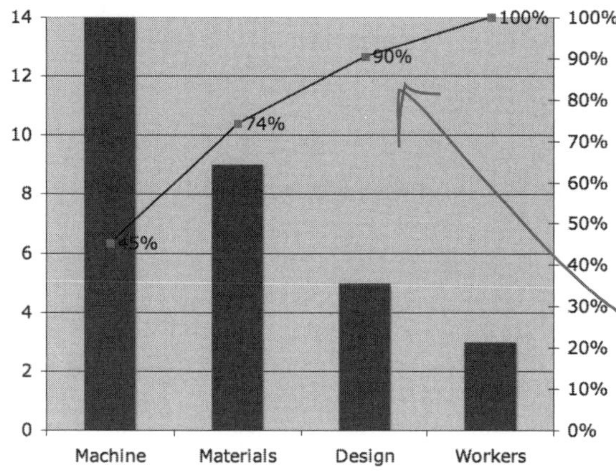

You have the most Machine defects. So, that's the root cause you should tackle first.

Which root cause is responsible for the most defects in the project?

Machine

What is the lowest priority area for defect prevention?

Workers

What is the cumulative percentage of Design Defects?

90%

Since you don't have very many worker-related defects, they're the lowest priority for improvement tasks.

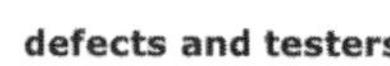

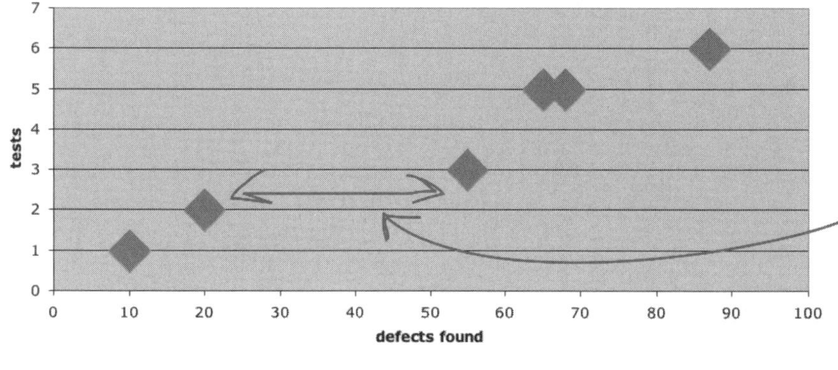

The gap between 2 and 3 was the largest, so that's where we had the biggest jump in defect detection.

Did adding more tests find more bugs?

Yes

Looks like the number of defects found kept increasing as you added more tests.

Looking at this chart, should you continue to add more tests to the project?

Yes

Where did you see the biggest increase in defect detection?

3 tests

Defects

16
14
12
10
8
6
4
2
0

Materials Design Machine Workers

Defects

How many machine defects were found?

14

How many defects were caused by workers?

3

How many total defects are shown on this chart?

31

Adding up all of the numbers in the chart tells you how big the dataset is.

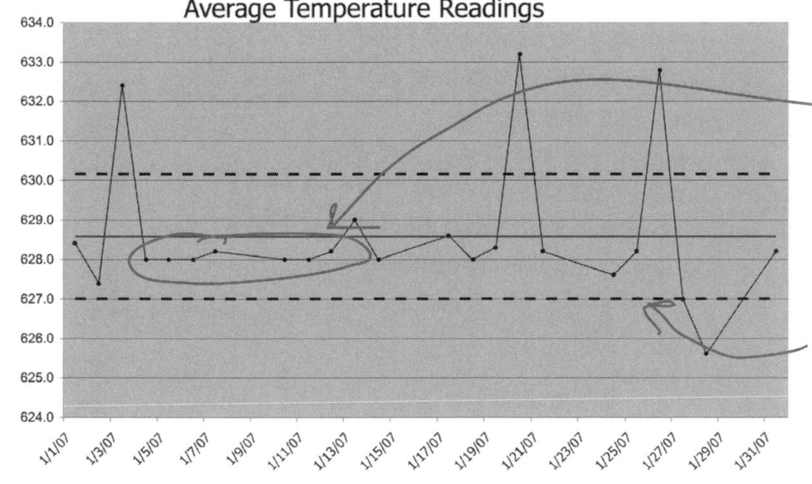

Looks like there's something worth investigating here. There are seven data points in a row that are on the lower side of the mean.

The lower limit is the bottom line and the mean is in the middle

Circle the data points that make up the rule of seven.

Is this process in control?

No

The points both above and below the control limits tell us that the process is out of control.

What's the upper control limit?

630.2

What's the mean temperature reading?

628.6

What's the lower control limit?

627

Question Clinic: The "Which-One" Question

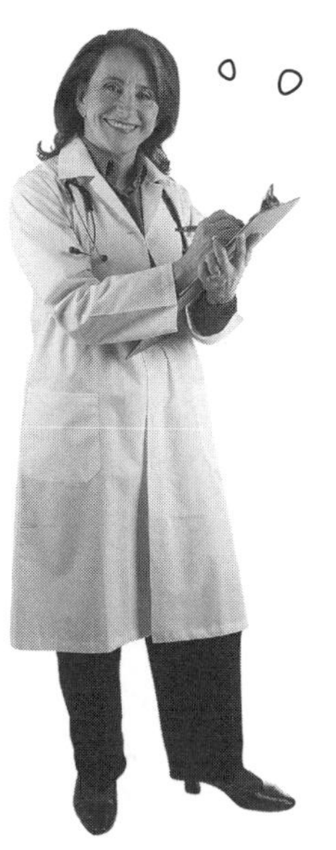

You'll see a lot of questions on the exam that describe a situation, and ask you to identify the tool, technique or process that's being used or is most appropriate. Luckily, process of elimination is really useful when you see a "Which-One" question.

83. You're managing a project to install 13,000 light switches in a new strip mall. You hire a team of inspectors to help your lead electrician find any defective light switches. They check a sample of 650 light switches, and find that 15% of them are defective. You ask your lead electrician to produce a chart that shows you these defects, broken down by category, and shown in order of importance. Which quality control tool will show this information?

A. Rule of Seven

B. Run chart

C. Histogram

D. Pareto chart

This can't be right—it's not even a tool! It's just a rule.

The run chart just tells you trends, and that's not what you're looking for.

Getting closer... the histogram will show you categories, but not importance.

Aha! This is what a Pareto chart is for. It shows you categories of defects, and which category is the most important because it has the most defects.

When you think about it, **all** questions are "Which-One" questions... but when the question asks to choose one item from a list of four really similar or related things, then that's when you really get to work your way backwards and start eliminating them one at a time.

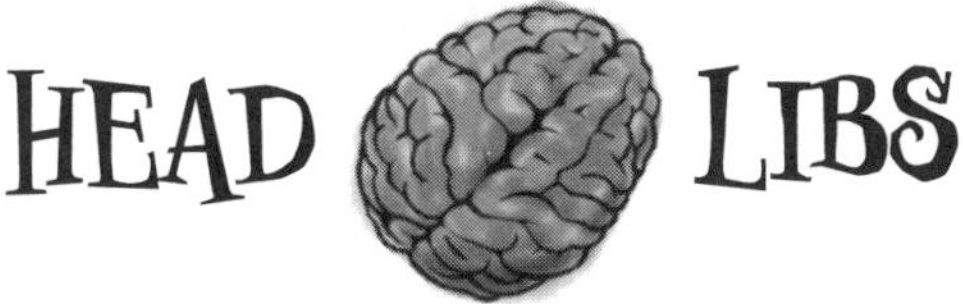

Fill in the blanks to come up with your own "Which-One" question! Start by thinking of the correct tool and then figure out three really similar answers that sound right, but can't be because the question gives more specific details allowing you to eliminate the wrong ones.

You're working on a ______________________ project, and you want to
(kind of project)

measure ______________________ .Which of the seven basic tools of
(something you'd measure on a project)

quality is best for doing that?

A. ______________________
(an obviously wrong tool)

B. ______________________
(something that isn't a tool at all)

C. ______________________
(another incorrect tool)

D. ______________________
(the right answer)

Join the Head First PMP community at **http://www.headfirstlabs.com/PMP** You can add your Head Libs answer, and see what Head Libs other project managers came up with!

Quality control means finding and correcting defects

When you look for bugs in your deliverables, you produce two kinds of things: outputs from the inspections and outputs from the repairs you've made. All of the **outputs of the Perform Quality Control process** fall into those two categories.

Outputs

Quality control measurements are all of the results of your inspections: the numbers of defects you've found, numbers of tests that passed or failed—stuff like that. You'll use them when you look at the overall process you are using in your company to see if there are trends across projects.

That's coming up in the Quality Assurance process. That's next!

Recommended corrective actions are what you get from evaluating all of your inspection data and figuring out where things are going wrong. If you find that most of your problems have been caused by machine errors, you recommend that a repair service be brought in to look at the machine and find out if it's broken.

Recommended preventative actions are your suggestions for heading off problems before they happen. If you were to find that the majority of defects were caused by poor materials in your project, you might recommend that you switch suppliers to prevent more defective material being used.

Recommended defect repairs are corrective actions for specific defects you find in your project. Say you find that 10% of the black boxes have buttons that stick because they are too big. You might recommend that those black boxes be sent back for repair so that they could eventually be sold.

Validated deliverables and validated defect repair are two of the most important outputs of Perform Quality Control. Every single deliverable on the project needs to be inspected to make sure it meets your quality standards. If you find defects, the team needs to fix them—and then those repairs need to be checked, to make sure the defects are now gone.

First the team inspects every deliverable to find defects that need to be fixed.

Deliverables

When you've finished inspecting your product, you know whether or not your fixes worked.

Validated Defect Repair

Quality baseline updates are like any other baseline updates that happen through control processes. As the project goes on, you might find that metrics are coming out differently than you had planned. Maybe your original goals weren't aggressive enough, or maybe they were just off the mark. When you adjust your overall goals for quality, you will need to update your baseline, too.

Whenever a change to your quality goals is approved, you need to update the baseline to include it.

Requested changes are recommended or preventative actions that also require changes to the way you are doing your project. Those kinds of changes will need to be **put through change control**, and the appropriate baselines and plans will need to be updated if they are approved.

You might need to update templates for Quality metrics or checklists.

Organizational Process Assets Updates

Project Management Plan Updates

there are no Dumb Questions

Q: What exactly are Pareto charts for?

A: Pareto charts go together with the 80/20 rule. It says that 80 percent of the problems you'll encounter in your project are caused by 20 percent of the root causes you can find. So if you find that most of your problems come from misunderstanding requirements, changing the way you gather requirements and making sure that everybody understands them earlier in the process will have a big impact on your project's quality

To get the data for your Pareto chart, first you have to categorize all of the defects that have been found in your project by their root causes. Then you can graph them in a Pareto chart to show the frequency of bugs found with each root cause and the percentage of the cumulative defects that are caused by each root cause. The one with the highest frequency is the root cause that you should work on first.

Q: If I am trying to prevent quality problems, why can't I just test more?

A: You can find a lot of problems by testing. If you find them during testing, then you have to go back and fix them. The later you find them, the more expensive they are to fix. It's much better for everybody if you never put the bugs in the product in the first place. It's much easier to fix a problem in a specification document than it is to fix it in a finished product. That's why most quality planning is centered around setting standards and doing reviews to be sure that bugs are never put into your product and, if they are, they're caught as early as possible.

Q: I still don't get that thing where a control chart can show you defects that are out of control, but also show you that your process is out of control.

A: The reason that's a little confusing to some people is that you use the same tool to look at defects that you do when you're looking at the whole process.

A lot of the time, you'll use charts to measure processes, not just projects. They're used to look at sample data from processes and make sure that they operate within limits over time. But they *are* considered quality control tools because those data samples come from inspecting deliverables as they are produced. Yes, it's a little confusing, but if you think of control charts as the product of inspection, you'll remember that they are Perform Quality Control tools for the test.

BULLET POINTS: AIMING FOR THE EXAM

- **Inspection** means **checking each deliverable** for defects. That means checking your specs and your documentation, as well as your product, for bugs.
- The better your quality planning, the **less inspection** you need.
- Ishikawa diagrams help you to **pinpoint the causes** of defects.
- The **rule of seven means** that any time you have seven data points in a row that fall on the same side of the mean on a control chart, you need to figure out why.
- When data points fall above the upper limit or below the lower limit on a control chart, the process is out of control.
- For the test, using any of the seven basic quality tools is **usually** a good indication that you are in the Quality Control process.
- **Ishikawa**, **fishbone**, and **cause-and-effect** diagrams are all the same thing.
- **Scatter charts** help you look at the **relationship** between two different kinds of data.
- **Flowcharts** help you get a handle on how processes work by showing all of the decision points graphically.
- **Grade** refers to the **value** of a product, but not its quality. So, a product can be low-grade by design, and that's fine. But if it's a low-quality product, that's a big problem.

Trouble at the Black Box 3000™ factory

It's not enough to inspect your deliverables. Sometimes it's the way you work that's causing your problems. That's why you need to spend some time thinking about how you will make sure you are doing the work efficiently and with as few defects as possible. The **Perform Quality Assurance process** is about tracking the way you work and improving it all of the time.

These boxes are full of parts that the company uses to build the Black Box 3000™ They were ordered from suppliers who delivered them to the BB3K™ warehouse, but they've been sitting around for weeks taking up valuable space.

What do you do if the quality is good but you aren't satisfied with the speed or efficiency of the work?

Introducing Quality Assurance

In the **Perform Quality Assurance process**, you take all of the outputs of from Quality Planning and Perform Quality Control and look at them to see if you can find ways to improve your process. If you find improvements, you recommend changes to your process and your individual project plan to implement them.

This is in the Executing group because you need to make sure your project is done in a way that complies with your company's quality standards.

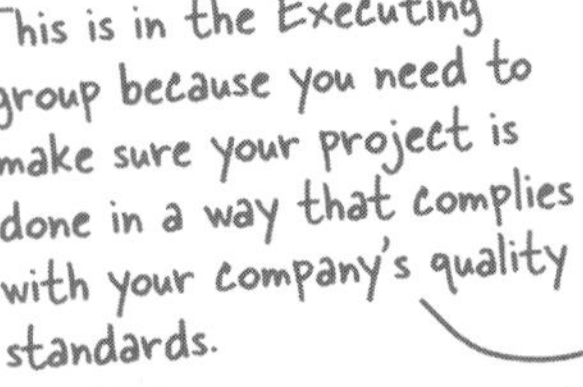

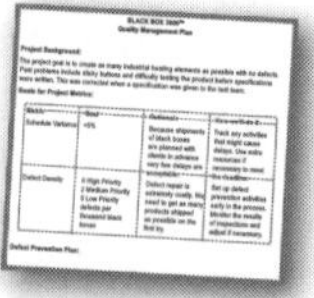

Quality Management Plan

Organizational Process Assets

Process Improvement Plan

Quality Metrics

Quality Control Measurements

Work Performance Information

Implemented Change Requests

Inputs

The inputs are ALL of the outputs from all of the other quality processes.

Implemented Corrective Actions

Implemented Defect Repair

Implemented Preventative Actions

Tools

Quality Planning tools and techniques are all of the tools you used in Quality Planning. They come in handy when reviewing your process, too.

Quality Control tools and techniques are all of the tools from Perform Quality Control. You can use histograms, control charts, and flowcharts—all of them can be used to help you figure out how your process is

Quality Audits are reviews of your project by your company. They figure out whether or not you are following the company's process.

Process Analysis is when you look at your process to find out how to make it better. You use your process improvement plan to do this one.

Outputs

Project Management Plan Updates

Requested Changes

Recommended Corrective Actions

Organizational Process Assets Updates

A closer look at some tools and techniques

Fixing the bugs in your project solves the problems that give you trouble. But fixing bugs in your **process** means that other projects can learn from the problems you've faced and avoid your project's bugs altogether. The tools that are used in quality assurance are the same as the ones in quality control, but they're used to examine the process rather than the project.

Even if your company has the best process in the world, it doesn't do your project any good if you don't follow it!

Quality Audits are when your company reviews your project to see if you are following its processes. The point is to figure out if there are ways to help you be more effective by finding the stuff you are doing on your project that is inefficient or that causes defects. When you find those problem areas, you recommend corrective actions to fix them.

A lot of companies have Quality Assurance departments whose job is to perform these audits and report findings from projects to a process group.

Process Analysis means following your process improvement plan to compare your project's process data to goals that have been set for your company. If you find that the process itself needs to change, you recommend those changes to the company and sometimes update Organizations Process assets as well as your own project management plan to include your recommendations.

When Lisa noticed that the warehouse was full of black box parts that weren't needed yet, she was really noticing a problem with the process. Why spend money on overstocked inventory?

Quality Control tools and techniques are the same ones you already know about from earlier in this chapter. But instead of using them to look for problems with specific defects, you'll use them to look at your overall process. A good example of this is using a control chart to see if your whole process is in control. If it's not, then you'll want to make a change to the whole way you do your work in order to bring it under control.

Here's another example. If you created a Pareto chart that showed all of the defects in all of your projects, you could find the one or two categories of defects that caused problems for the whole company. Then you could get all of the PMs together to figure out an improvement that they could all make that would help the whole company.

How would **you** use these tools to manage your project?

More ideas behind quality assurance

There are a couple more things you need to know about quality assurance. These are some of the most important ideas behind modern quality and process improvement.

Kaizen means continuous improvement. It's all about constantly looking at the way you do your work and trying to make it better. *Kaizen* is a Japanese word that means ***improvement***. It focuses on making small improvements and measuring their impact. Kaizen is a philosophy that guides management, rather than a particular way of doing quality assurance.

Just In Time means *keeping only the inventory you need on hand when you need it*. So, instead of keeping a big inventory of parts sitting around, the Black Box company might have only the parts they need for that day. Some companies have done away with warehouses all together and had production lines take the parts directly off the trucks to do the work. If you're working in a Just In Time shop, quality is really important because ***there isn't any extra inventory to deal with mistakes***.

Plan-Do-Check-Act is one way to go about improving your process, and it's used by a lot of Kaizen practitioners. It comes from a well known quality theorist named W. Edwards Deming and is also known as The Deming Cycle. Plan-Do-Check-Act is about *making small improvements*, and *measuring* how much *benefit* they make ***before*** *you change your process* to include them. Here's how it works:

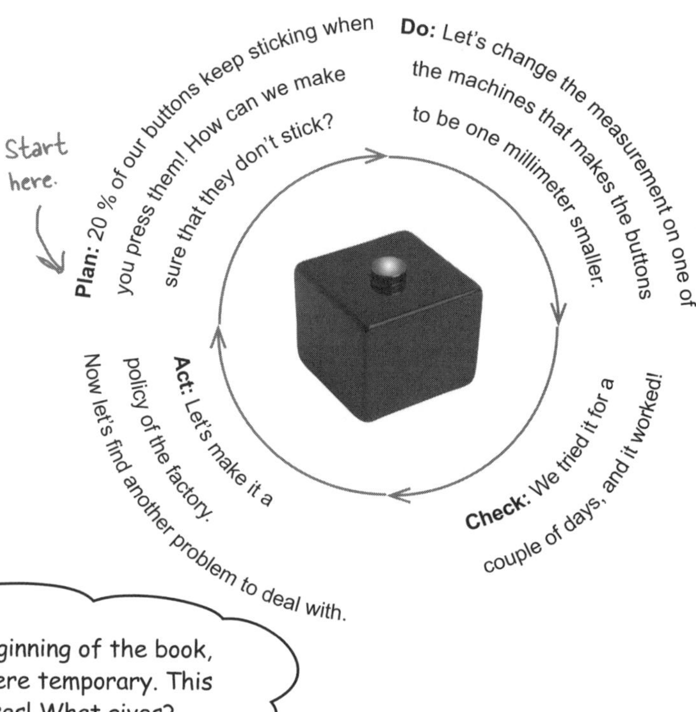

You're right. The Perform Quality Assurance process is all about improving the process and that isn't what most of project management is about. But, your project is really affected by the process you are working in, so you should really understand it and help to make it better wherever you can. The bottom line is that your project has a better chance of succeeding if you stay involved with process improvement and keep your eye on how your project stacks up to your company's expectations of quality and process.

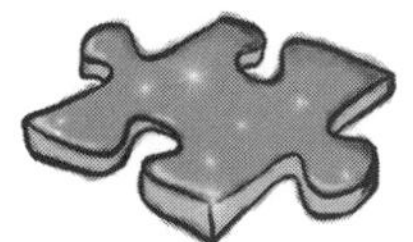

Qualitycross

Take some time to sit back and give your right brain something to do. It's your standard crossword; all of the solution words are from this chapter.

Across

3. When a process has data points above the upper limit or below the lower limit. those data points are out of _________.

5. The middle line on a control chart.

7. The theorist who came up with Plan-Do-Check-Act.

9. ______________ is more important than inspection in Quality Management.

11. An important definition of quality is ________________ to requirements.

12. Tool used to make sure your project is following the company's process.

13. What you compare your work performance information to.

14. Tool for finding the 20% of root causes responsible for 80% of defects.

15. Tool for comparing two kinds of data to see if they are related.

16. Tool used in quality planning to set numeric goals for your project.

Down

1. Quality theorist who came up with the idea of Fitness For Use

2. Tool for finding the root cause of a defect.

4. Synonym for continuous improvement.

6. Process where you inspect deliverables to look for defects.

8. Tool that helps you visualize processes and all of their decision points.

10. Heuristic that says that seven data points on one side of the mean requires investigation.

Answers on page 406.

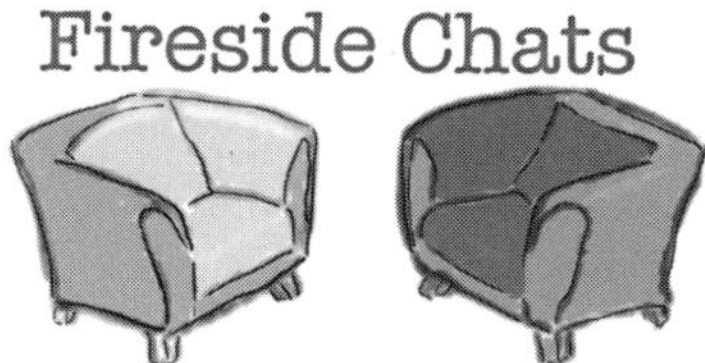

Tonight's talk: **Two quality processes discuss the best ways to correct problems on your project.**

Perform Quality Control:

I'd like to go first, because I'm what most people think of as quality. Whenever you see one of those "Inspected by #8" stickers on the inside of your sneaker, that's me!

Perform Quality Assurance:

You're right—most people do think that quality begins and ends with inspection. Which is funny, because we wouldn't even need you if people paid attention to me.

Perform Quality Control:

Whoa, there, buddy. That's a strong statement!

Perform Quality Assurance:

Now don't get me wrong. Nobody's ever felt comfortable enough with me that they've eliminated inspection entirely. You always need someone at the end of the line to look at what's been produced and make sure that we delivered what we meant to.

Perform Quality Control:

That's right. And don't forget, I'm everywhere. Any time you call for customer service, I'm there to tell you that your call will be recorded for quality purposes. I'm always warning you to make sure package contents haven't shifted, and to check your car's emissions once a year.

Perform Quality Assurance:

Right, but don't you get tired of doing all of that tedious work? An ounce of prevention is worth a pound of cure, after all.

Perform Quality Control:

I guess I don't really understand exactly how you do your job, then, because I'm having a hard time figuring out how I would ever be able to take a long weekend.

Perform Quality Assurance:

Let's take a look at those sneakers you mentioned. What's the most common reason you throw a pair back to the factory floor to be restitched?

Perform Quality Control:

Well, last week it was because the company logo came out upside down on a bunch of the shoes. It turned out that the logo was being stitched into the leather and then put on another assembly line, and once in a while it was placed on the belt upside-down.

Perform Quality Control:

Perform Quality Assurance:

That seems like an honest mistake. How much did it cost?

We had to throw out about 10% of our sneakers last week. Let's just say that the boss wasn't happy. You could see the little veins in his forehead throbbing. It was kind of gross.

Wow, that sounds expensive. What's keeping it from happening again?

The boss yelled at everyone, and we'll check even more carefully to make sure we don't ship it.

So next week your inspection costs will be even higher, and you'll probably still have to throw out just as many shoes, or more!

Wow, I never thought of that.

What if you painted a little arrow on the inside of the leather showing which direction it should be placed on the belt?

We'd have to pay someone else to paint that on. This is no time to be *increasing* our costs!

But a small increase in the cost of painting the leather will cause you to throw out a whole lot fewer sneakers.

I call that ***cost of quality***. You have to pay more to put quality in at the beginning, but you can reduce the number of inspectors and scrap a lot less product. In the end, I save you far more money that I cost. Can you say the same about yourself?

Huh. Um. No.

Choose whether the tools are being used for Perform Quality Control or Perform Quality Assurance.

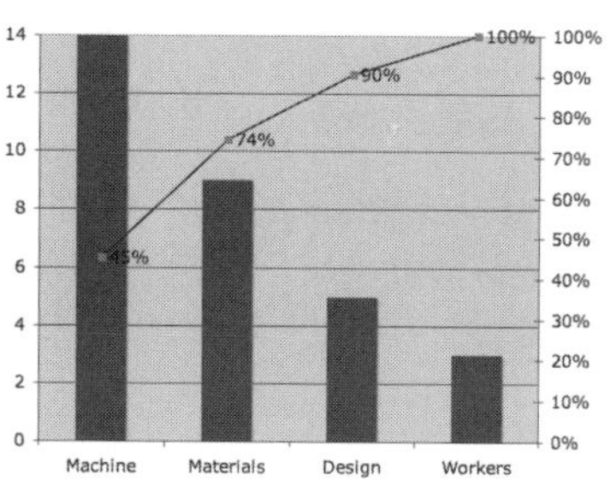

1. You use a Pareto chart to figure out which root causes are responsible for the most defects in the current batch of Black Boxes. It looks like most of them are coming from a Machine Calibration problem. So you run them back through the machine after recalibrating it.

☐ Perform Quality Control ☐ Perform Quality Assurance

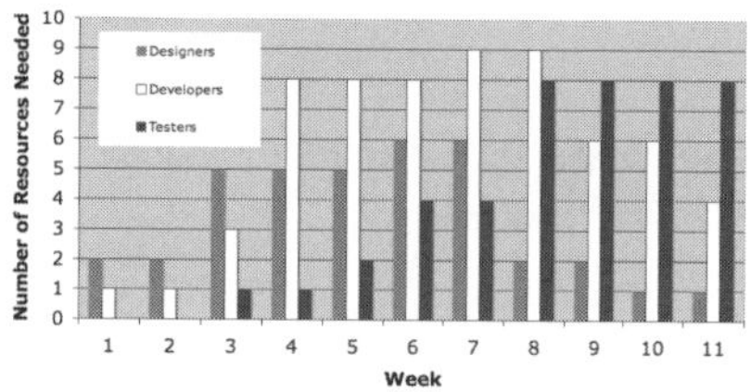

2. You use a histogram to look at the root cause category for all defects that have been found over the past year. You find that Machine errors are habitually responsible for the largest number of errors across all batches of Black Boxes. You schedule Machine calibration checks at the start of every shift to be sure that the machine is always set properly.

☐ Perform Quality Control ☐ Perform Quality Assurance

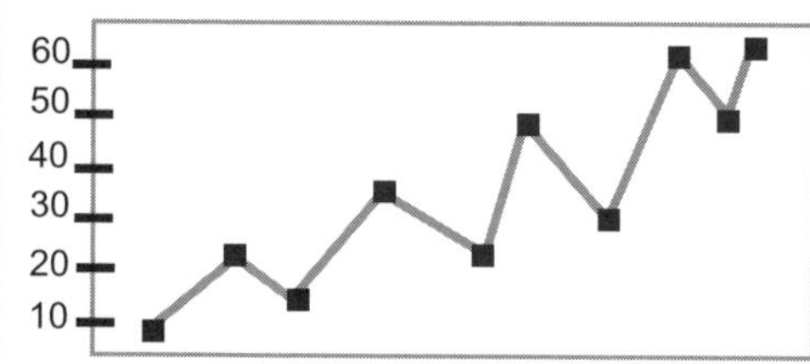

3. You look at defects in all of the inspection runs for the past year and notice that you seem to be finding more and more defects per inspection as time goes on. You create a quality task force to try to figure out what is causing these defects.

☐ Perform Quality Control ☐ Perform Quality Assurance

Answers on page 407.

The Black Box 3000™ makes record profits!

People who bought the product were thrilled with it. They were happy that the Black Box company always kept its promises and the products were always high quality. The company managed to save a lot of money by implementing process improvement measures that caught defects before they cost too much money to fix. And Lisa got a big promotion—now she's in charge of quality assurance for the whole company. Great job, Lisa!

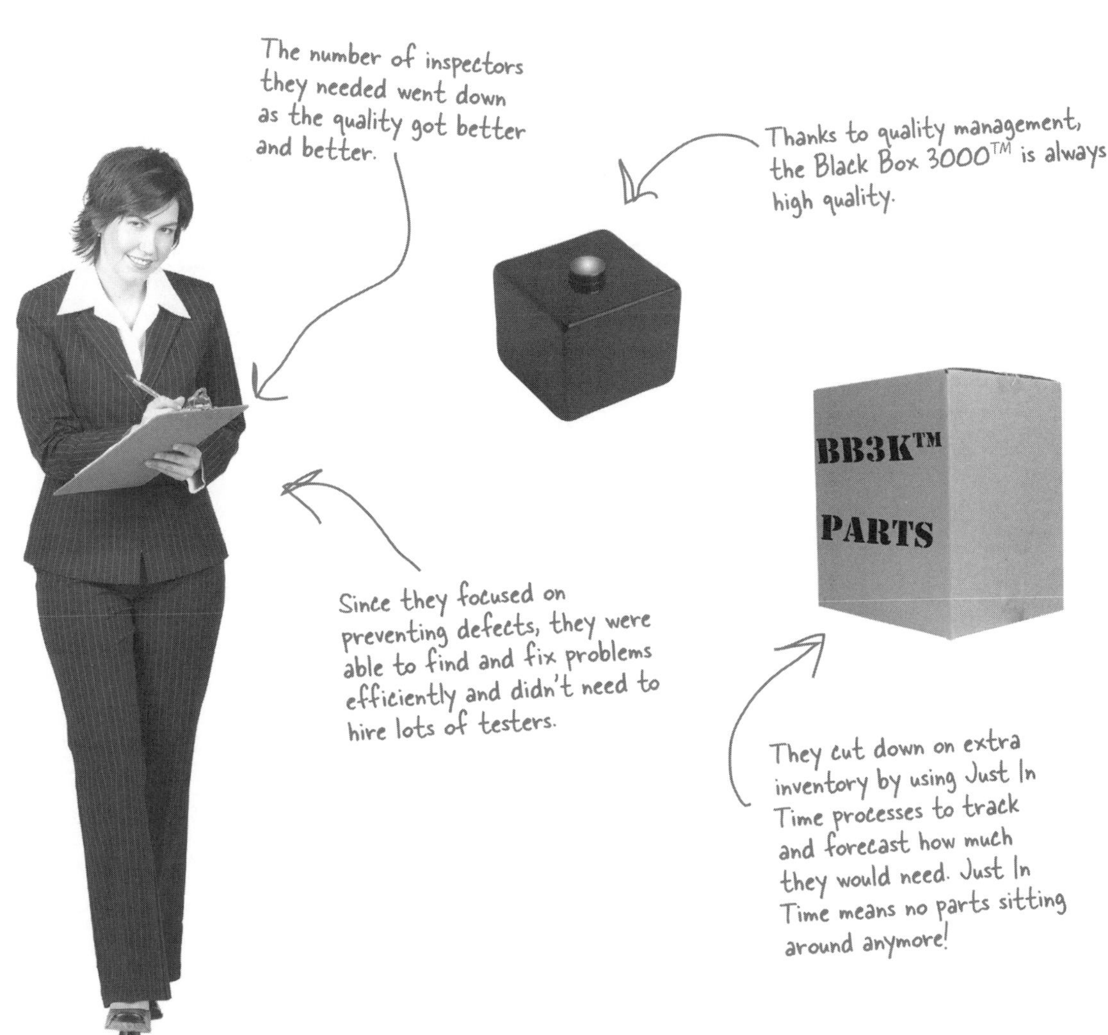

Sharpen your pencil Solution

Take a look at each of these situations and figure out if they're talking about quality or grade.

1. You ordered mushrooms on your pizza, but you got onions.

   ☑ Quality ☐ Grade

2. You called the pizza parlor to complain and the guy yelled at you.

   ☑ Quality ☐ Grade

3. The pizza arrived but it had canned mushrooms.

   ☐ Quality ☑ Grade

4. The pizza was cold.

   ☑ Quality ☐ Grade

---

5. You just got a brand new luxury car that cost a whole lot of money.

   ☐ Quality ☑ Grade

6. But it's in the shop every two weeks.

   ☑ Quality ☐ Grade

7. Your neighbors make fun of you because your chrome hubcaps aren't very classy…

   ☐ Quality ☑ Grade

8. … even though they do a great job of protecting the wheels from dirt, which is why you bought them in the first place.

   ☑ Quality ☐ Grade

Read each of these scenarios and identify which tool or technique is being used.

1. You look through your company's asset library and find that a recent project was able to reduce defects by 20% by inserting defect prevention meetings early in the construction phase. You put the same process in your quality plan and set the target for shipped defects to be 20% lower than the company average for your project.

   Tool/technique: **Benchmarking**

2. You add up all of the costs projected for quality activities and track that number in your quality plan. You use this number to gauge the health of your project compared to other projects in your company.

   Tool/technique: **Cost of quality**

3. You write up a list of all of the tests you are going to run on the Black Box 3000™ when it rolls off the assembly line. You determine what kinds of failures might cause you to stop testing, what it would take for you to resume test activities, and requirements that the product would need to fulfill to be considered accepted into test.

   Tool/technique: **Design of experiments**

Match each Quality Planning output to its description.

Quality Management Plan	Helps you to make sure that each deliverable it up to company standards.
Process Improvement Plan	Helps you to plan out all of your quality activities
Checklists	Gives you something to compare your work performance information to.
Quality Baseline	Helps you change the way you work for the better.

(Lines drawn: Quality Management Plan → Helps you to plan out all of your quality activities; Process Improvement Plan → Helps you change the way you work for the better; Checklists → Helps you to make sure that each deliverable it up to company standards; Quality Baseline → Gives you something to compare your work performance information to.)

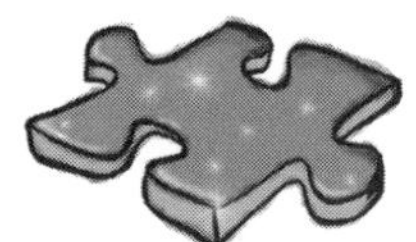

Qualitycross

Take some time to sit back and give your right brain something to do. It's your standard crossword; all of the solution words are from this chapter.

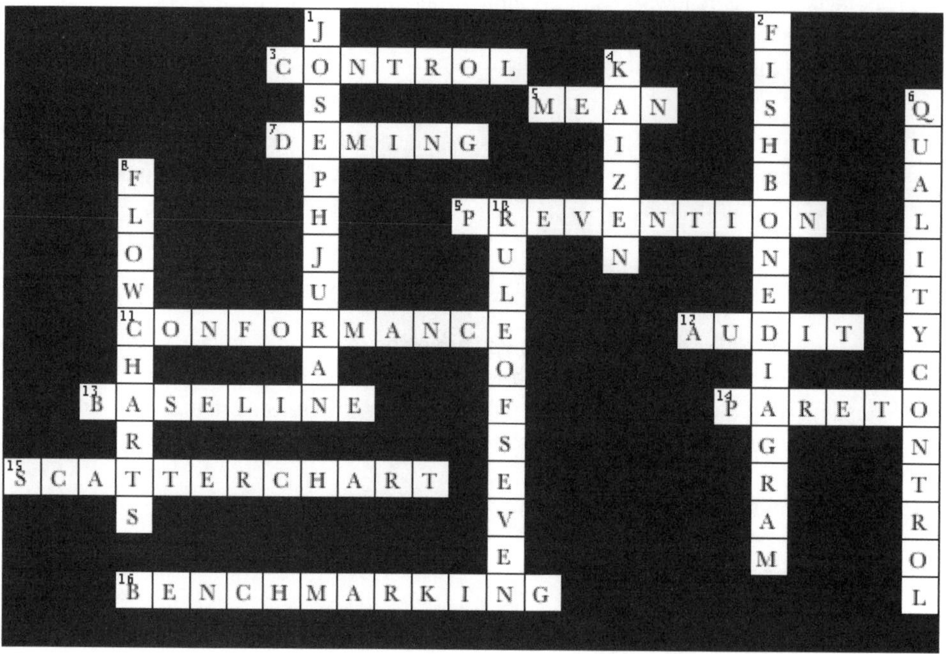

Across

3. When a process has data points above the upper limit or below the lower limit, those data points are out of _________.

5. The middle line on a control chart.

7. The theorist who came up with Plan-Do-Check-Act.

9. _______________ is more important than inspection in Quality Management.

11. An important definition of quality is ________________ to requirements.

12. Tool used to make sure your project is following the company's process.

13. What you compare your work performance information to.

14. Tool for finding the 20% of root causes responsible for 80% of defects.

15. Tool for comparing two kinds of data to see if they are related.

16. Tool used in quality planning to set numeric goals for your project.

Down

1. Quality theorist who came up with the idea of Fitness For Use

2. Tool for finding the root cause of a defect.

4. Synonym for continuous improvement.

6. Process where you inspect deliverables to look for defects.

8. Tool that helps you visualize processes and all of their decision points.

10. Heuristic that says that seven data points on one side of the mean requires investigation.

Choose whether the tools are being used for Perform Quality Control or Perform Quality Assurance.

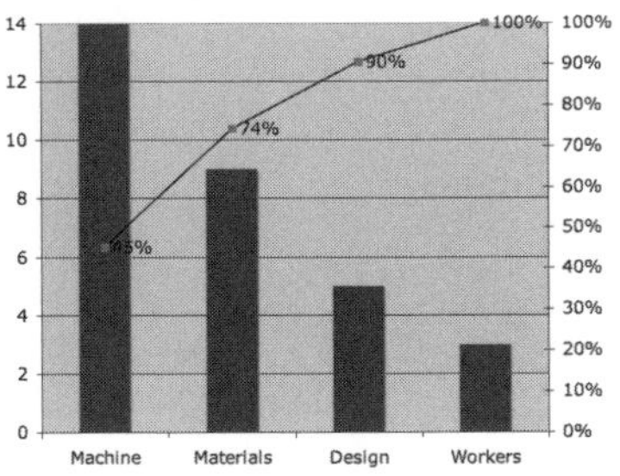

1. You use a Pareto chart to figure out which root causes are responsible for the most defects in the current batch of black boxes. It looks like most of them are coming from a Machine Calibration problem. So you run them back through the machine after re-calibrating it.

   ☑ Perform Quality Control ☐ Perform Quality Assurance

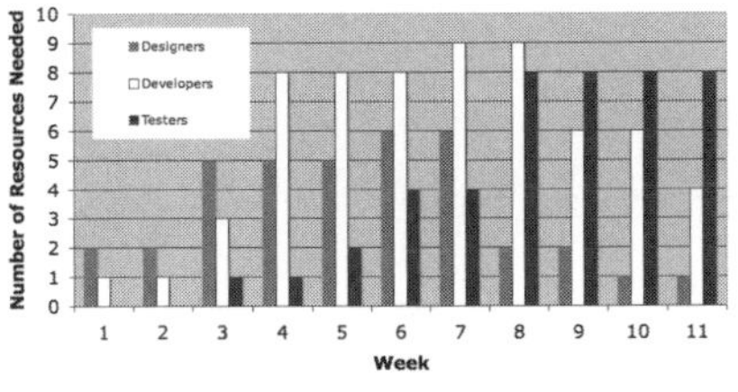

2. You use a histogram to look at the root cause category for all defects that have been found over the past year. You find that Machine errors are habitually responsible for the largest number of errors across all batches of Black boxes. You schedule Machine calibration checks at the start of every shift to be sure that the machine is always set properly.

   ☐ Perform Quality Control ☑ Perform Quality Assurance

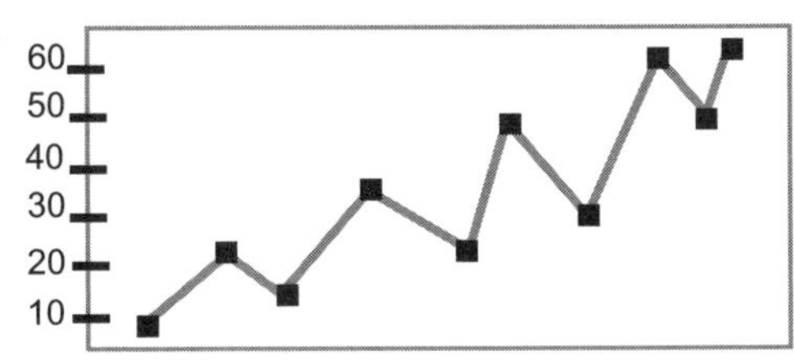

3. You look at defects in all of the inspection runs for the past year and notice that you seem to be finding more and more defects per inspection as time goes on. You create a quality task force to try to figure out what is causing these defects.

   ☐ Perform Quality Control ☑ Perform Quality Assurance

Exam Questions

1. Which of the following is NOT a part of quality?

A. Fitness to use
B. Conformance to requirements
C. Value to the sponsor
D. Customer satisfaction

2. A project manager is using a histogram to analyze defects found by the team during inspection activities. What process is being performed?

A. Quality Planning
B. Perform Quality Control
C. Perform Quality Assurance
D. Scope Verification

3. Which of the following is NOT an example of Cost of Quality?

A. Having team members spend extra time reviewing requirements with the stakeholders
B. Paying extra programmers to help meet a deadline
C. Hiring extra inspectors to look for defects
D. Sending a crew to repair a defective product that was delivered to the client

4. You're working with an audit team to check that your company's projects all meet the same quality standards. What process is being performed?

A. Quality Planning
B. Perform Quality Control
C. Perform Quality Assurance
D. Perform Quality Management

5. You're managing a project to deliver 10,000 units of custom parts to a manufacturer that uses Just In Time management. Which of the following constraints is most important to your client?

A. The parts must be delivered on time
B. The parts must be delivered in a specific order
C. The parts must conform to ISO specifications
D. The parts must be packaged separately

Exam Questions

6. Which of the following is NOT part of the quality management plan?

A. Strategies for handling defects and other quality problems

B. Guidance on how the project team will implement the company's quality policy

C. Metrics for measuring your project's quality

D. A description of which deliverables don't have to be inspected

7. Which of the following tools and techniques is used to show which categories of defects are most common?

A. Control charts

B. Pareto charts

C. Run charts

D. Flow charts

8. You're managing a highway construction project. The foreman of your building team alerts you to a problem that the inspection team found with one of the pylons, so you use an Ishikawa diagram to try to figure out the root cause of the defect. What process is being performed?

A. Quality Management

B. Quality Planning

C. Perform Quality Control

D. Perform Quality Assurance

9. Which tool or technique is used to analyze trends?

A. Scatter chart

B. Run chart

C. Checklist

D. Flow chart

10. When is inspection performed?

A. At the beginning of the project

B. Any time a project deliverable is produced

C. Just before the final product is delivered

D. At the end of the project

Exam Questions

11. What's the difference between Quality Control and Scope Verification?

A. Quality Control is done at the end of the project, while Scope Verification is done throughout the project

B. Quality Control is performed by the project manager, while Scope Verification is done by the sponsor

C. Quality Control is performed by the sponsor, while Scope Verification is done by the project manager

D. Quality Control means looking for defects in deliverables, while Scope Verification means verifying that the product is acceptable to the stakeholders

12. You're a project manager at a wedding planning company. You're working on a large wedding for a wealthy client, and your company has done several weddings in the past that were very similar to the one you're working on. You want to use the results of those weddings as a guideline to make sure that your current project's quality is up to your company's standards. Which tool or technique are you using?

A. Checklists

B. Benchmarking

C. Design of Experiments

D. Cost-Benefit Analysis

13. You are using a control chart to analyze defects, when something on the chart causes you to realize that you have a serious quality problem. What is the MOST likely reason for this?

A. The rule of seven

B. Upper control limits

C. Lower control limits

D. Plan-Do-Check-Act

14. Which of the following BEST describes defect repair review?

A. Reviewing the repaired defect with the stakeholder to make sure it's acceptable

B. Reviewing the repaired defect with the team to make sure they document lessons learned

C. Reviewing the repaired defect to make sure it was fixed properly

D. Reviewing the repaired defect to make sure it's within the control limits.

15. The project team working on a project printing 3,500 technical manuals for a hardware manufacturer can't inspect every single manual, so they take a random sample and verify that they have been printed correctly. This is an example of:

A. Root cause analysis

B. Cost benefit analysis

C. Benchmarking

D. Statistical sampling

Exam Questions

16. What's the difference between Perform Quality Control and Perform Quality Assurance?

A. Perform Quality Control involves charts like histograms and control charts, while Perform Quality Assurance doesn't use those charts

B. Perform Quality Control and Perform Quality Assurance mean the same thing

C. Perform Quality Control means inspecting for defects in deliverables, while Perform Quality Assurance means auditing a project to check the overall process

D. Perform Quality Assurance means looking for defects in deliverables, while Perform Quality Control means auditing a project to check the overall process

17. Which Quality Control tool is used to analyze processes by visualizing them graphically?

A. Checklists

B. Flowcharts

C. Pareto charts

D. Histograms

18. You are looking at a control chart to figure out if the way you are doing your project is fitting into your company's standards. Which process are you using ?

A. Quality Planning

B. Quality Assurance

C. Quality Control

D. Quality Management

19. Which of the following is associated with the 80/20 rule ?

A. Scatter chart

B. Histogram

C. Control chart

D. Pareto chart

20. Validated defect repair is an output of which process ?

A. Integrated Change Control

B. Quality Planning

C. Perform Quality Control

D. Perform Quality Assurance

Exam ~~Questions~~ Answers

1. Answer: C

It's important for projects to produce a valuable product, but value isn't really a part of quality. That's why earned value is part of Cost Management, not Quality Management.

2. Answer: B

In the Perform Quality Control process, the team inspects the product for defects and uses the seven basic tools to analyze them. Since the defects came from inspection, you know it's Perform Quality Control.

3. Answer: B

Cost of Quality is the time and money that you spend to prevent, find, or repair defects.

4. Answer: C

The Perform Quality Assurance process is all about how well your company meets its overall quality goals.

Keep an eye out for fake process names like Perform Quality Management.

5. Answer: A

A manufacturer that uses Just In Time management is relying on its suppliers to deliver parts exactly when they're needed. This saves costs, because they don't have to warehouse a lot of spare parts.

But those parts had better not have a lot of defects, because there aren't a lot of spare parts lying around to do repairs!

6. Answer: D

Your project team needs to inspect ALL of the deliverables! That means every single thing that gets produced needs to be reviewed by team members, so they can find and repair defects.

7. Answer: B

A Pareto chart divides your defects into categories, and shows you the percentage of the total defects each of those categories represents. It's really useful when you have limited budget for quality planning and want to spend it where it's most effective!

Don't forget that ALL deliverables need to be inspected, including the stuff you create—like the schedule, WBS, and project management plan. So you'll get defects for them, too!

Exam ~~Questions~~ Answers

8. Answer: C

Keep your eye out for questions asking you about Ishikawa or fishbone diagrams. When you use those tools to analyze defects, you're in quality control.

Watch it!

Don't assume that just because you're using a fishbone diagram, you're always doing quality control! *It's also used in Risk Management; you'll see that in Chapter 11. The key thing to watch for here is that the fishbone diagram is being used to find the root cause of a DEFECT, not a risk or something else.*

9. Answer: B

A run chart is one of the seven basic tools of quality. It's a long line graph that shows you the total number of defects that were found over time.

OK, so I can use a run chart to figure out whether quality is getting better or worse over the course of my project.

10. Answer: B

Inspection is when your team examines something that they produced for defects… and every single deliverable needs to be inspected! That's what "prevention over inspection" means: if you produce a deliverable that's needed later in the project today, it's a lot cheaper to fix defects in it now than it will be when that deliverable is used later on in the project.

11. Answer: D

A lot of people get Quality Control and Scope Verification confused because they seem really similar. Both of them involve looking closely at deliverables to make sure that they meet requirements. But they serve really different purposes! You use Quality Control to find defects that you're going to repair. Scope Verification happens at the very end of the Executing phase; it's when you work with the stakeholder to get their formal acceptance for the deliverables.

You'd better have found all the defects before you take the product to the customer!

12. Answer: B

Benchmarking is when you use previous projects to set quality guidelines for your current project. You can always find the results of the past projects in the Organizational Process Assets.

Exam ~~Questions~~ Answers

13. Answer: A

The rule of seven tells you that when seven consecutive data points on your control chart come out on the same side of the mean, you've got a process problem. That sounds a little complicated, but it's actually pretty straightforward. Defects tend to be scattered around pretty randomly; in any project that makes a lot of parts, even if they're all within the specification, you'll get a couple of parts that are a little bigger, and a couple that are a little smaller. But if you have a bunch of them in a row that all run a little big, that's a good indication that something's gone wrong on your assembly line!

14. Answer: C

Going back and repairing defects can be a pretty risky activity, because it's really easy to introduce new defects or not fully understand why the defect happened in the first place. Answer C says exactly that: you go back and review the defects to make sure they're fixed.

15. Answer: D

A lot of times it's impractical to check every single product that rolls off of your assembly line. Statistical sampling is a great tool for that; that's when you pull out a small, random sample of the products and inspect each of them. If they're all correct, then there's a very good chance that your whole product is acceptable!

16. Answer: C

A lot of people get confused about the difference between Perform Quality Control and Perform Quality Assurance. Quality Control is where you inspect deliverables for defects, while Quality Assurance is where you audit the project to make sure the quality activities were performed properly.

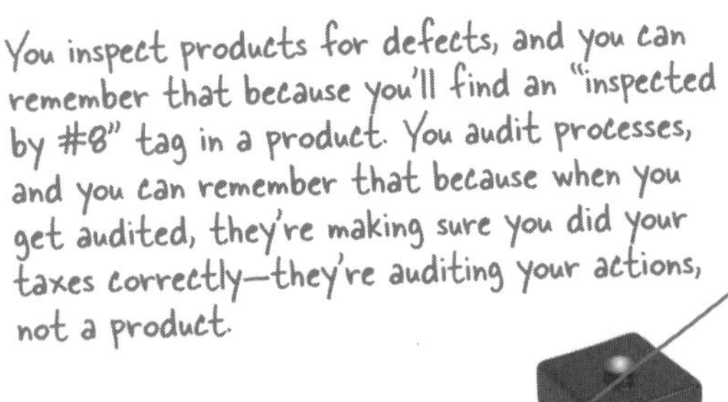

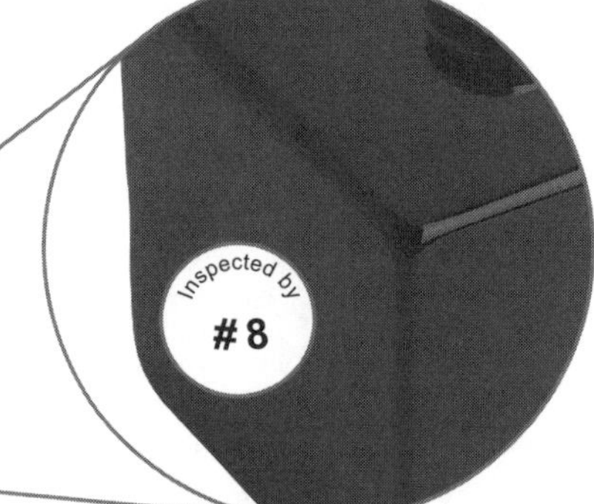

Exam ~~Questions~~ Answers

17. Answer: B

A flowchart is one of the seven basic tools of quality. You use it to analyze processes that are part of your project in order to look for quality problems and inefficiencies.

18. Answer: B

You're analyzing the process, so you are using Perform Quality Assurance.

Just because you see a Perform Quality Control tool, that doesn't mean you're in the Perform Quality Control process... because they're also tools used in Perform Quality Assurance! You always need to figure out what you're using them for.

19. Answer: D

Pareto charts are based on the 80/20 rule. They sort your defects in descending order by root cause. So you always know which 20% of root causes are responsible for 80% of defects on your project.

20. Answer: C

Perform Quality Control is where you inspect your work, including your repairs!

Getting the team together

Behind every successful project is a great team. So how do you make sure that you get—and keep—the best possible team for your project? You need to **plan carefully**, set up a good **working environment**, and negotiate for the **best people** you can find. But it's not enough to put a good team together... If you want your project to go well, you've got to keep the team motivated and deal with any conflicts that happen along the way. **Human resource management** gives you the tools you need to get the best team for the job and lead them through a successful project.

Mike needs a new team

Cows Gone Wild III was a huge success! But now the Ranch Hand Games team is gearing up for their next big hit. How are things shaping up?

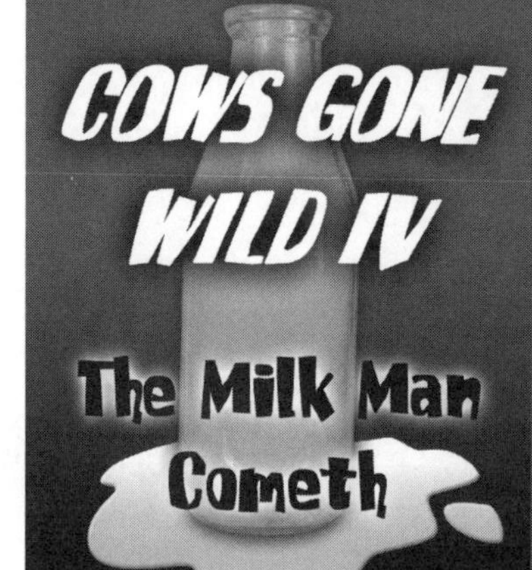

The box is done, but Brian, Mike and Amy are just getting started on the game.

Mike, the project manager

Uh-oh! Looks like Mike's going to need to put together a new team.

Brian, the development team manager

Cubicle conversation

Hey, we're all on the same team here. Look, why don't we have people from our teams just help out whenever you need someone.

Amy, the creative director

Brian: Yeah, there's no reason you need our resources dedicated to your project. We can get **multiple** projects done that way.

Mike: Come on, guys. You don't really think that's gonna work, do you?

Amy: Sure, why not?

Mike: We can't just staff up as we go; that's going to cause huge problems.

Brian: You're overreacting, Mike. Look, I'm a team player, and I want to get the project done. You just tell me when you need someone off my team, and I'll make sure you've got the developers and testers you need. What's wrong with that?

Mike: Okay, so what if I need three developers starting tomorrow for the next two weeks. Can you do that?

Brian: Well, no, I've got a deadline on Friday. It'll have to wait until next Monday. But that's just a couple of days.

Mike: See, that's what I'm talking about! A few days here, a few days there... if we have to wait a few days every time the team needs someone, we'll totally blow the schedule.

How can Mike solve his problem? What can he do to make sure that he gets the team members he needs when he needs them?

Get your team together and keep them moving

You want to stay in control of your project team, right? But when you work in a matrixed organization, your team members don't directly report to you. So how do you make sure you get the best people, and keep them motivated and productive? That's what the four processes in **Human Resource Management** are for: guiding you through all the things you need to do to make sure you get everyone for your project when you need them.

A lot of the stuff in this chapter applies mostly to matrixed organizations... but you'll still find it really useful, even if you don't work in a matrixed company!

This shouldn't be a surprise—almost every knowledge area has its planning process, and Human Resource Planning is no exception.

Planning process group

In the Human Resource Planning process, you plan out exactly which resources you'll need, and how you'll train your team and make sure they stay motivated.

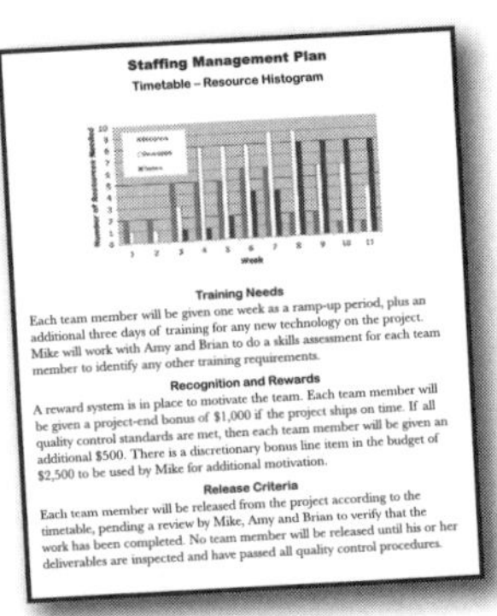

Staffing Management Plan

Timetable – Resource Histogram

Training Needs

Each team member will be given one week as a ramp-up period, plus an additional three days of training for any new technology on the project. Mike will work with Amy and Brian to do a skills assessment for each team member to identify any other training requirements.

Recognition and Rewards

A reward system is in place to motivate the team. Each team member will be given a project-end bonus of $1,000 if the project ships on time. If all quality control standards are met, then each team member will be given an additional $500. There is a discretionary bonus line item in the budget of $2,500 to be used by Mike for additional motivation.

Release Criteria

Each team member will be released from the project according to the timetable, pending a review by Mike, Amy and Brian to verify that the work has been completed. No team member will be released until his or her deliverables are inspected and have passed all quality control procedures.

Human Resource Planning

This is where you plan out the staffing needs for your project, and how you'll manage and reward the team.

It makes sense that Acquire Project Team and Develop Project Team are in the Executing group—you only put the team together AFTER the project has started.

Executing process group

You'll need to train your team, and keep them motivated with rewards in order to get the project done.

No project goes perfectly. People have conflicts, and it's up to you to make sure they get resolved.

CEO

Brian

Mike

Amy

Dev. Team

Test Team

Design Team

Acquire Project Team

1st

Develop Project Team

Manage Project Team

Once the project gets started, you need to put together your team. This means you may need to negotiate for some of the resources.

This is a Monitoring & Controlling process—you need to constantly monitor the team and look for conflicts.

Monitoring & Controlling process group

What can you do to make sure that you get the right people for your team exactly when you need them? What can you do before the project starts to make sure they stay motivated?

Figure out who you need on your team

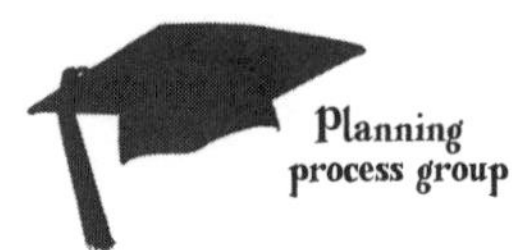

Project teams don't just assemble themselves spontaneously! It takes a lot of planning and guidance to get a team together, and that's the idea behind the **Human Resource Planning** process. Remember, in a matrixed organization your team doesn't report directly to the project manager. You need to work with the functional managers to get you the team members that you need for your project… which means there's a lot of information that you need to give to everyone so they know exactly who you need for your team.

You've seen these three inputs a whole bunch of times now!

Inputs

Project Management Plan

Enterprise Environmental Factors

Organizational Process Assets

Tools

Organization charts tell everyone how your team is structured.

Networking means informally interacting with other people in your company and industry to stay on top of everything.

Organizational theory is where you use proven principles to guide your decisions.

This is a lot like the other planning processes you've seen already! You start with your project plan and what you know about your company, and you come up with a plan.

The staffing management plan tells everyone on the project who you'll need on your team, when you need them, and what skills they'll need.

Outputs

These are the three outputs of Human Resources Planning

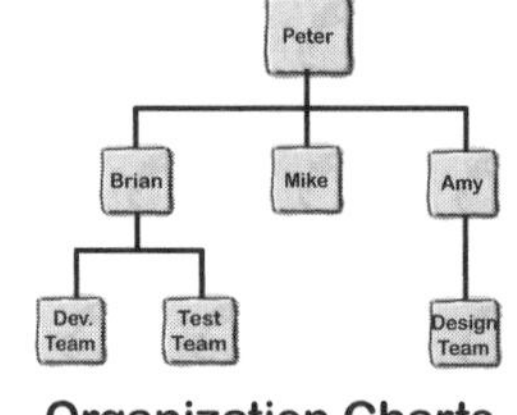

Organization Charts

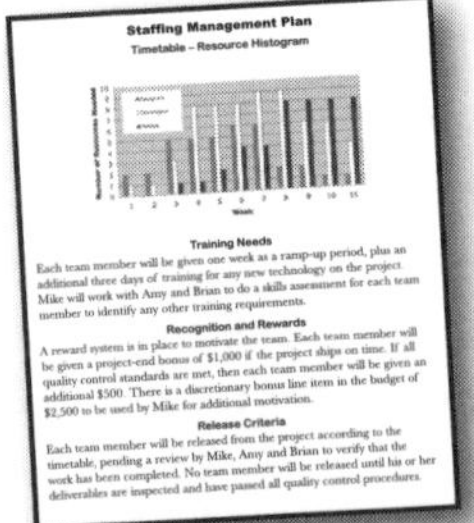

Staffing Management Plan

Timetable – Resource Histogram

Training Needs

Each team member will be given one week as a ramp-up period, plus an additional three days of training for any new technology on the project. Mike will work with Amy and Brian to do a skills assessment for each team member to identify any other training requirements.

Recognition and Rewards

A reward system is in place to motivate the team. Each team member will be given a project-end bonus of $1,000 if the project ships on time. If all quality control standards are met, then each team member will be given an additional $500. There is a discretionary bonus line item in the budget of $2,500 to be used by Mike for additional motivation.

Release Criteria

Each team member will be released from the project according to the timetable, pending a review by Mike, Amy and Brian to verify that the work has been completed. No team member will be released until his or her deliverables are inspected and have passed all quality control procedures.

Staffing Management Plan

RACI Matrix		Role			
		Mike	Amy	Brian	Peter
Work Package	Project Management	R	I	I	I
	Design	C	R	C	I
	Construction	C	C	R	I
	Testing	C	C	R	I
R = Responsible A = Accountable C = Consult I = Inform					

Roles and Responsibilities

The inputs, tools & techniques, and outputs of **Human Resource Planning** should seem pretty familiar! Write down what you think you'd use each of them for. Notice that there are a few that you haven't seen before—take an educated guess at those.

INPUTS

Enterprise Environmental Factors

Organizational Process Assets

Project Management Plan

TOOLS AND TECHNIQUES

Organization Charts

There are a couple of other tools & techniques—this isn't the only one!

OUTPUTS

Staffing Management Plan

Roles and Responsibilities

Project Organization Charts

Think about how this is different than the "Organization Charts" listed under Tools & Techniques.

Sharpen your pencil Solution

The inputs, tools & techniques, and outputs of **Human Resource Planning** should seem pretty familiar! Write down what you think you'd use each of them for. Notice that there are a few that you haven't seen before—take an educated guess at those.

INPUTS

Enterprise Environmental Factors

This is information about the company's culture and structure

Your company's culture is really important—stuff like common languages, technical disciplines, and how people normally relate to each other.

Organizational Process Assets

Templates and lessons learned from past projects

You've already seen lots of way we use templates and checklists. They're just as important in Human Resource Planning.

Project Management Plan

The PM Plan has the resource requirements for each activity

Remember when we created this in Time Management? Well, this is where you use that information!

TOOLS AND TECHNIQUES

Organization Charts

It's easy to lose track of who reports to who, and what different people do in your company. You need to know that stuff if you want to staff your project!

Shows the relationships between managers, team members and other people inside and outside the company who will work on the project.

OUTPUTS

Staffing Management Plan

Your Staffing Management Plan describes who will be on your project, when they'll do the work and for how long, and describes the reward system you'll use to keep the team motivated.

Describes how you'll manage and control your resources

Roles and Responsibilities

Every role on the project needs to be defined—it has a title, has authority to do certain things, and is responsible for specific deliverables.

Lists each role on the project that needs to be filled

Project Organization Charts

Shows the reporting structure of the resources assigned to the project team

This is a lot like the org chart for your whole company, except that it only lists the specific people on the project.

Hold on—how can organization charts be both tools & techniques *and* outputs?

You need two charts because you have two "organizations."

One organization is the whole company—along with any subcontractors or consultants you've got access to for your project team. The other organization is just the people who are on the team. The team might have people from different groups in your company, and they need to know how they interact. That's why you create a chart just for the team.

Some people will bring in a consultant or expert to manage or lead part of the team. Make sure the project's org chart shows that relationship, even if it's not part of the company!

The Project Organization Chart shows how your team members relate with each other.

This might include people or relationships that may not necessarily show up on a company organization chart. If you've got a team built from multiple consultants and subcontractors, this chart will be the only place where everyone is listed at once.

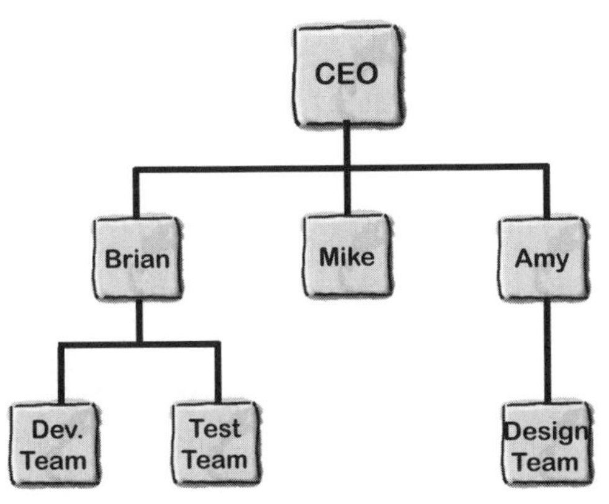

Roles and Responsibilities show who's responsible for what.

It's really common to see the roles and responsibilities for a project written out as a **RACI matrix**, which is just a table that lists the role or people on the top; the specific activities, work, or responsibilities down the side; and indicates the level of responsibility that each person or role has for each of the activities or responsibilities. (RACI stands for "Responsible, Accountable, Consult and Inform.")

This could also list roles, like "Project Manager," "Creative Director" or "Development Manager"

RACI Matrix		People			
		Mike	Amy	Brian	CEO
Work Package	Project Management	R	I	I	I
	Design	C	R	C	I
	Construction	C	C	R	I
	Testing	C	C	R	I
R = Responsible A = Accountable C = Consult I = Inform					

The staffing management plan

The most important output of Human Resource Planning is the **Staffing Management Plan**. It tells you everything that you need in order to build your team, keep them motivated, and manage them to resolve conflicts and get the work done.

Everything you do with your team—acquiring them, developing them, and managing them—depends on a good Staffing Management Plan.

A common way of showing the timetable—or when people will work on what—is to use a resource histogram.

This is really important for telling the functional managers exactly who you'll need on your team, so they can provide the staff that you need to get the job done.

Staffing Management Plan

The resource histogram tells you the type and number of resources you need at any time.

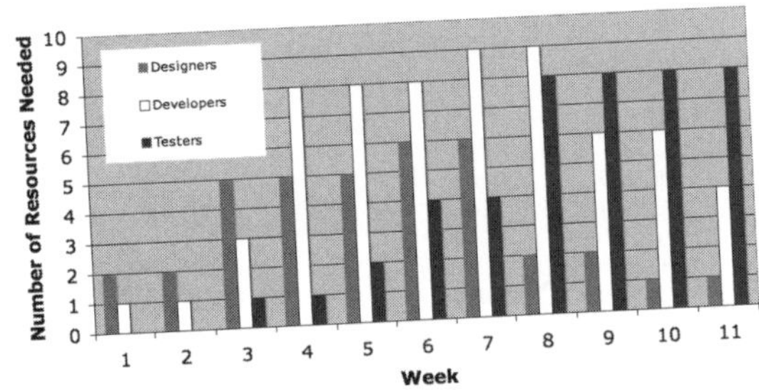

You need to make sure everyone on the team has the skills he or she needs to do the job.

Training Needs

Each team member will be given one week as a ramp-up period, plus an additional three days of training for any new technology on the project. Mike will work with Amy and Brian to do a skills assessment for each team member to identify any other training requirements.

A really important part of human resource management is keeping your team motivated, and rewards tied to goals are a great way to do that.

Recognition and Rewards

A reward system is in place to motivate the team. Each team member will be given a project-end bonus of $1,000 if the project ships on time. If all quality control standards are met, then each team member will be given an additional $500. There is a discretionary bonus line item in the budget of $2,500 to be used by Mike for additional motivation.

You'll need to plan out exactly how your team members will roll off of your project so functional managers and other project managers will know if they're available for other projects.

Release Criteria

Each team member will be released from the project according to the timetable, pending a review by Mike, Amy and Brian to verify that the work has been completed. No team member will be released until his or her deliverables are inspected and have passed all quality control procedures.

Read the **Staffing Management Plan** on the facing page and answer these questions about the project.

1. How many designers, developers and testers are needed in week #7 of the project?

   .... designers .... developers .... testers

2. Who is responsible for verifying that each team member has the skills appropriate to the project?

   ....

3. Rewards should always be tied to performance goals in order to motivate the team. What performance goal has been set for the team, and what reward will each team member receive if it's achieved?

   ....

   ....

Answers on page 450.

there are no Dumb Questions

Q: I still don't get the resource histogram. Am I supposed to make this myself, or does it come from somewhere?

A: You need to come up with the histogram yourself when you put together the staffing management plan. Since you're managing the project, you're the only one who knows when each person is needed on the project. Remember all of the activities that you came up with, back when you were building the schedule in the Time Management chapter? Well, each of those activities had resource requirements, right? That means you know exactly what resources you'll need at any time in your project!.That's why the Project Management Plan is an input to Human Resource Planning—you need the schedule and the activities in order to figure out the timetable. The histogram is the easiest way to show that information.

Q: Is that RACI chart really necessary?

A: Yes, definitely! Sometimes people split up responsibilities in ways that aren't immediately obvious just from people's titles or the names of their roles on the project—that's one of the big advantages of a matrixed organization. RACI charts help everyone figure out their assignments. Mike might have Brian's senior developers sit in on Amy's design meetings, even though they don't usually do that. He'd put that in the RACI matrix to show everyone that's now part of their jobs for the project.

Q: Can the "halo effect" really affect my projects?

A: The halo effect is something that happens when you've got a team member who's very good at a job—especially a technical job, like computer programmer or engineer. It's easy to forget that just because someone is very good at one job, it doesn't mean he or she has the skills to do another, equally hard job. This happens a lot with functional managers: the top programmer will often get promoted to a management position... but if she doesn't have management or leadership skills, then the company just lost their best programmer and gained a lousy manager.

Q: Once I know what roles need to be filled on my project, how do I actually get the team on board?

A: That's what the next process is all about! It's called **Acquire Project Team**, and it's where you actually staff up your project. Of course, you don't staff it up during the planning phase. You have to wait until the project work begins, which is why it's in the *Executing* process group.

The hardest part about staffing up your project is negotiating with the functional managers. The best resources are the ones that are in demand, which means your negotiating skills will be very important when it comes time to staff up your project team.

Get the team together

Your staffing management plan is in place, your project is ready to roll, and now it's time to begin the actual project work! You need your team, and the way you bring them on board is the **Acquire Project Team** process.

This is where you negotiate with functional managers for your project team members. You need the right people for the project, and you've done all the prep work to figure out who you need and when you need them. So now it's time to go get your team!

Watch it!

Beware of the halo effect!

That's when you put someone in a position they can't handle, just because they're good at another job.

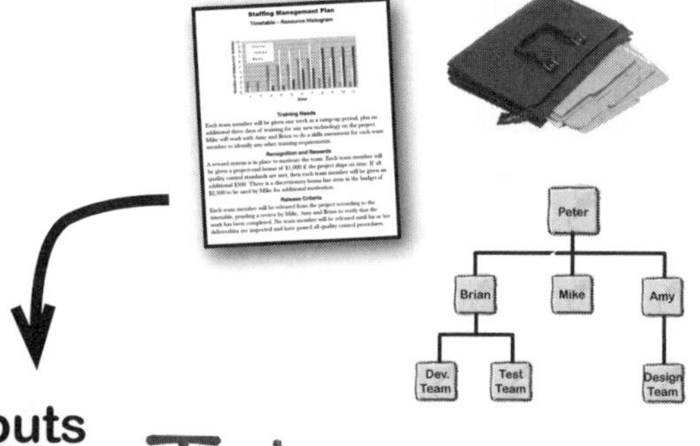

RACI Matrix		People			
		Mike	Amy	Brian	Peter
Work Package	Project Management	R	I	I	I
	Design	C	R	C	I
	Construction	C	C	R	I
	Testing	C	C	R	I
R = Responsible A = Accountable C = Consult I = Inform					

Take a minute and think about why you need each of these inputs.

Inputs

Tools

Negotiation is the most important tool in this process. There are resources that you need for your project, but they don't report to you. So you need to negotiate with the functional managers—and maybe even other project managers—for their time.

Pre-Assignment is when you can actually build the assignments into your staffing management plan. Sometimes you have resources who are guaranteed to you when you start the project, so you don't need to negotiate for them.

There aren't any surprises here—if you've staffed up a project team, you've done all of these things.

Virtual Teams are when your team members don't all work in the same location. This is really useful when you're relying on consultants and contractors for outsourced work. Instead of meeting in person, they'll use phone, email, instant messaging, and online collaboration tools to work together.

Acquisition means going outside of your company to contractors and consultants to staff up your team.

Don't be thrown by the word "acquisition"—even though this is the Acquire Project Team process, this particular technique only refers to acquiring resources from outside.

Hey Brian! Don't forget about the two developers I need for the racing simulator level. We talked about this a few weeks ago, right?

Yeah, I remember. You can take Joe and Sue, who are freed up right now.

Mike needs to negotiate for resources...

...but the negotiation isn't going so well

Hold on! Weren't those guys the ones who kept coming in late on all their deadlines in our last project? I need top performers.

How about if I give you Sue, but I also send along a more senior engineer to help mentor her?

That doesn't sound like such a great compromise. What's Mike going to do? What would *you* do?

Outputs

Resource Availability

Resource Availability tells the company exactly when the team members will be available once they're done.

If you need a team member for a few weeks at the beginning, and then again for another week later, make sure the resource availability reflects this!

Staffing Assignments

Staffing Assignments are the whole point of the process! They're what you get when you secure a team member and assign him or her to a specific role on the project.

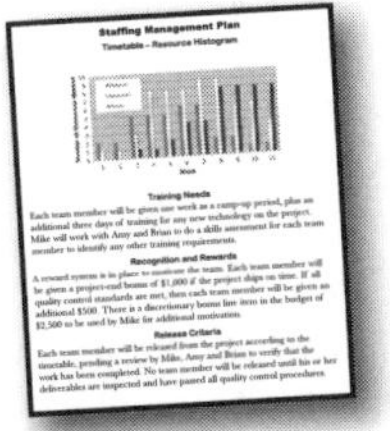

Staffing Management Plan (updates)

Update the Staffing Management Plan. During Human Resource Planning, you might not have all the information. You might discover a better team structure, or find out that certain resources simply aren't available. Keep the plan up to date with this new information.

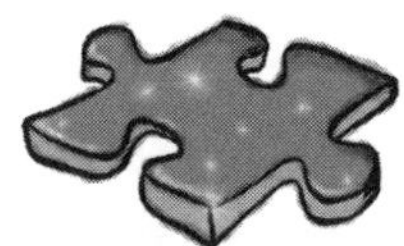

Human Resourcecross

Take some time to sit back and give your right brain something to do. It's your standard crossword; all of the solution words are from this chapter.

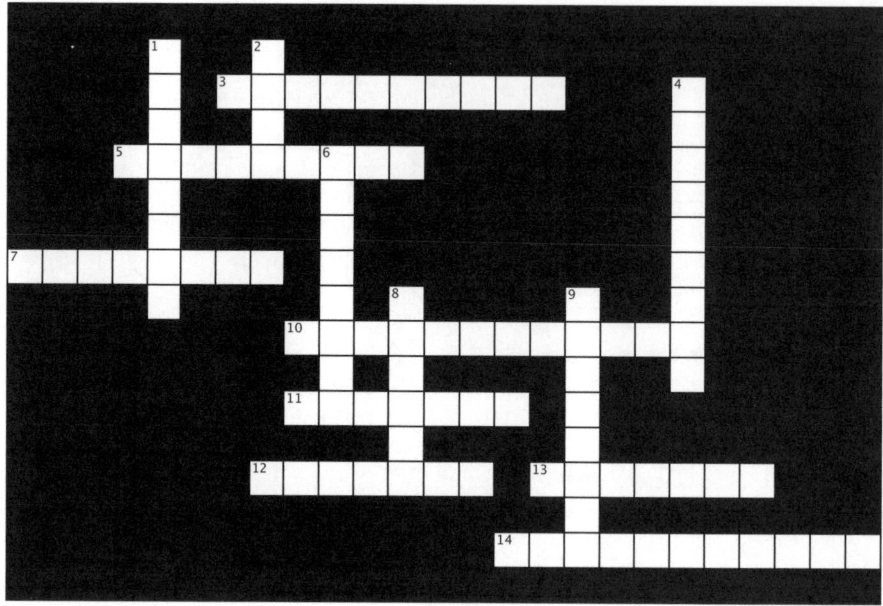

Answers on page 451.

Across

3. This is a great tool for communicating roles and responsibilities
5. Chart in the staaffing management plan that tells you the type and number of resources you need
7. Human Resource Planning is part of the ___________ process group
10. This kind of chart tells you how team members relate to each other
11. A great way to motivate your team
12. The ______________ Organization Chart shows only the people assigned to your team, including consultants and subcontractors
13. You use _____ teams when your team members don't all work in the same location
14. The most important tool in Acquire Project Team

Down

1. What you provide for a resource in order to ensure they have the skills necessary to do the project
2. The _____ effect causes people with technical expertise to be put in positions for which they're unqualified
4. Acquire Project Team and Develop Project Team are part of the _________ process group
6. _________ availability is an output that describes when each team member will be available
8. The Human Resource Management process in the Monitoring & Controlling process group is __________ Project Team
9. The main output of Acquire Project Team is ___________ assignments

Cubicle conversation

Looks like Mike's negotiation went well in the end! So now he's got his team... but can he get them motivated?

Amy: I haven't noticed anything. What's up?

Mike: Well, maybe it's nothing, but a couple of the design team members have been missing some deadlines. Nothing major, but it's starting to concern me.

Amy: Well, okay. I can keep an eye on them.

Mike: That's not all. One of them hasn't been replying to emails at all, and another scheduled a vacation right in the middle of a huge deadline week. I think we may have a real motivation problem.

Amy: You're right, that sounds pretty bad. What can I do about it?

Mike: Well, I built a discretionary bonus budget into the plan.

Amy: Right, that $2,500. But should we really be talking about giving bonuses? I thought these were underperformers. Shouldn't we only reward good behavior?

Mike: Well, right, but if we tie the bonus to meeting an aggressive deadline or high quality standards, it might help get them energized again.

Amy: We can give it a shot, but I'm skeptical.

Do you think Mike's idea will work? Why is it a good idea to make the bonus contingent on meeting specific goals? Can this plan backfire?

Develop your project team

The **Develop Project Team** process is the most important one in Human Resource Planning. It's the one where you make sure your team is motivated and well-managed—and those are some of the most important things that project managers do! You do it throughout the *entire* Executing phase of the project, because you need to keep your team moving towards the goal.

Get the team involved in planning—the more they feel like they're in control, the better they feel about the project!

General Management Skills is one of the tools & techniques for this process—and there's a good reason for that: your management skills are what you rely on to keep your team working.

This makes it more challenging to stay on top of the team and make sure the work is getting done.

Motivation

- [ ] One of your most important jobs as project manager is keeping the team motivated and constantly monitoring them to make sure they stay motivated.
- [ ] A really effective way to motivate your team is to set up a reward system. But make sure that they understand exactly what they're being rewarded for—and it MUST be fair, or it could backfire!
- [ ] Training is another great way to keep a team motivated. When people feel that they're growing professionally, they stay more involved and get more excited by their work.

Management

- [ ] When the project is being planned, you're directing everything—but by the time it's executing, the project manager is more of a coach and a facilitator.
- [ ] That's why it's really important for a project manager to have "soft skills"—you need to really understand what makes your team members tick, and help with their problems.
- [ ] A really good way to make sure that your project team sticks together is to establish **ground rules** for your project, which set a standard for how everyone works together.

This is one of the tools & techniques for Develop Project Team.

You develop your project team by keeping them motivated, and you do this all the way through your entire project.

Develop the team with your management skills

How do you keep your team motivated and up and running? With the tools and techniques for **Develop Project Team**, that's how. When you're working with your team, you need to be a leader. That means setting the rules for how people interact with each other, making sure they have the skills they need, setting up a good working environment, and keeping them motivated.

The inputs to Develop Project Team are the outputs you just created.

Staffing Assignments

Resource Availability

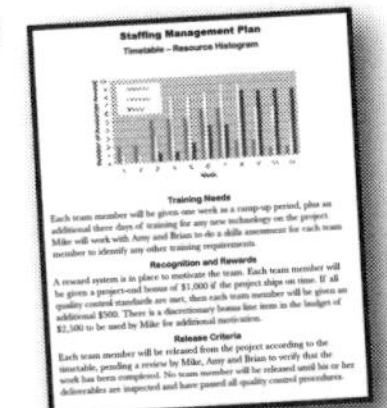

Staffing Management Plan (updates)

Inputs

Tools

Recognition and rewards are the best way to keep your team motivated!

It's also a good way to motivate your team! People always want to feel like they're growing professionally.

Training is a really important part of developing your team. If you've got a team member who doesn't have the skills to do the job, you need to get them trained… and it's up to you to plan enough of the project's time and budget to make sure it happens!

Discussing ground rules with the team can be really valuable, because it helps everyone see what's important to their teammates!

Ground rules help you prevent problems between team members, and let you establish working conditions that everyone on the team can live with.

For example, you might have a rule where everyone always emails the team when they take a day off.

Co-location is the opposite of virtual teams. When you have all of your team located in the same room, you can increase communication and help them build a sense of community. Sometimes that room is called a **war room**.

Team-building activities are important throughout your entire project. You're responsible for keeping the team together!

These tools and techniques do a lot to help you manage your team. But do they really establish you as a leader? What's the difference between management and leadership?

Lead the team with your management skills

You've seen tools and techniques that help you set up a great environment for your team to succeed, but you need more than that to get them through a tough project. You need **leadership skills**, those "soft skills" you use to influence your team and keep them directed toward the project's goals.

Wait a second! How can a multiple-choice test quiz me on my leadership skills?

You use leadership skills throughout the entire project! But they're most important in Develop Project Team because that's where you lead your team through their work.

You're right, it can't. What the PMP exam *can* quiz you on is your ***knowledge*** of leadership skills. There's been a lot of research on how people wield power in companies. The PMP exam concentrates on research done by two social psychology researchers named French and Raven who came up with five different kinds of power that people use to influence others.

The five kinds of power

There are five kinds of power that a project manager typically uses on a project. The first is called **legitimate power**, which is what you use when you assign work to someone who reports to you.

When you work in a matrixed organization, you don't have direct reports! So you'll need to use the other kinds of power to influence your team.

Reward power is what you have when you can award a bonus or another kind of reward in order to motivate team members. Always make sure that rewards are **fair**—you don't want to single out one person who is eligible for a reward without giving others a chance at it! And rewards work best when they're tied to specific goals or project priorities.

Making everyone compete for one single reward isn't fair—it's actually demotivating to force people to compete for an arbitrary prize.

Expert power means that the team respects you for your expertise in a specific area, and gives you credibility because of that. Think about it: a team of programmers is more likely to respect you and do what you ask them to do if they know that you're an accomplished software engineer!

Everyone on the team will get an extra $500 bonus if we meet all of the quality standards in the spec!

Reward and expert power are the most effective kinds of power that a project manager can use

I spent a few years leading a game design team, and I got the best results when we held joint design meetings with the programmers.

Referent power means you're standing in for someone who has more position or power in the company. You'll usually use this if you've been given specific power or authority by the CEO or another senior manager. But sometimes a project manager will have a close—but unofficial—relationship with that person, and will still be able to wield referent power.

This might get the job done, but the team could start to resent you if you abuse it.

The CEO's really counting on us... and he put me in charge of this project, so I need you to finish this job.

Punishment power is exactly what it sounds like—you correct a team member for poor behavior. **Always remember to do this one-on-one and in private!** Punishing someone in front of peers or superiors is extremely embarrassing, and will be really counterproductive.

Match each form of power to the scenario where it's being used.

Legitimate Power	"We're not meeting our quality standards, and until we do we're going to have to work weekends."
Reward Power	A project manager sets up an "Accolade Wall" and posts awards for team members who come in ahead of schedule.
Expert Power	Everyone always does what Shelly says because a senior director assigned her personally.
Referent Power	A functional manager assigns a tester to work on the project manager's team.
Punishment Power	The programmers always listen to the team lead because he's a really good software architect.

Answers on page 450.

Motivate your team

This stuff is all part of Recognition and Rewards—one of the tools and techniques for Develop Project Team.

No matter how good your "soft skills" are, if your team has a lousy work environment they're going to have a hard time getting the project done. Luckily, there's been more research over the years to figure out exactly what makes for a good working environment. For the PMP exam, you'll be expected to be familiar with the most popular theories of motivation and organization.

You might see this in a question about "Maslow's theory", or it might show on the exam as "Hierarchy of Needs" or "Maslow's Hierarchy".

Maslow's hierarchy of needs says that people have needs, and until the lower ones are satisfied they won't even begin to think about the higher ones.

Maslow says you can't achieve the higher needs until you're comfortable with the lower ones...

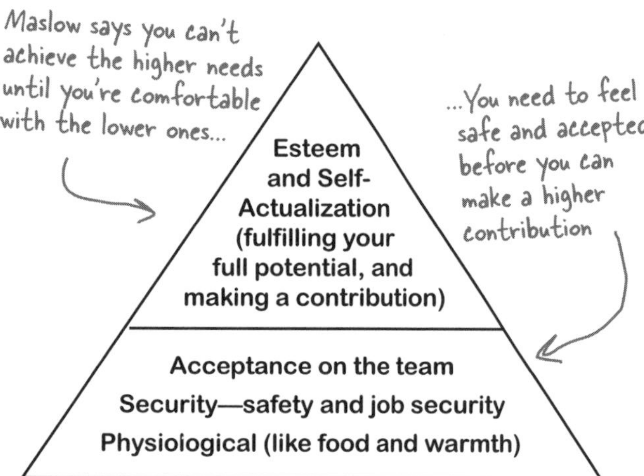

...You need to feel safe and accepted before you can make a higher contribution

A "hygiene factor" is something like a paycheck or status—stuff that people need in order to do the job. If people don't have this stuff, it's really hard to motivate them!

Herzberg's Motivation-Hygiene Theory

Sure, you love being a project manager. But would you do the job if you weren't getting a paycheck? Of course not!

What Herzberg figured out was that you need things like good working conditions, a satisfying personal life, and good relations with your boss and coworkers—stuff he called "hygiene factors." Until you have them, you don't really care about "motivation factors" like achievement, recognition, personal growth, or career advancement.

Herzberg says that people need the stuff they normally expect out of a job—like hot coffee—before you can get them motivated about achievement and personal growth.

McGregor's Theory X and Theory Y

McGregor tells us that there are two kinds of managers: ones who assume that everyone on the team is selfish and unmotivated, and ones who trust their team to do a good job. He calls the kind of manager who distrusts the team a "Theory X" manager, and the kind who trusts them a "Theory Y" manager. **You could get exam questions where the answer could be "Theory X" or "Theory Y"—or both!**

A Theory X manager will micromanage the team, looking over everyone's shoulder all the time and making them feel like they aren't trusted.

It's much better—and easier—to be a Theory Y manager. If you trust the team to do their jobs, they won't let you down!

Two more theories that might appear on the PMP exam—although they're not nearly as common as the others.

Expectancy Theory says that you need to give people an expectation of a reward in order to motivate them—but this only works if that award is achievable. If everyone knows the award is either worthless or impossible to achieve, it will actually demotivate them!

McLelland's Achievement Theory says that people need **achievement, power, and affiliation** to be motivated. Achievement is when someone performs well and is recognized for it. Power means he or she has a lot of control or influence in the company. And someone feels a strong sense of affiliation from being a part of a working team and having good relationships with coworkers.

Each of the following scenarios demonstrates one of the motivational theories at work. Write down which theory each scenario describes.

1. Bob is a programmer on the team, but he doesn't really feel like he's "one of the guys." He doesn't really have a lot of control over the work he's assigned. Recently, Bob put in a long weekend to get his work done, but nobody really seemed to take notice.

   ....

2. There was a break-in in the office, and now people are really jittery. Plus, the heating system has been broken for weeks, and it's freezing! No wonder nobody's getting any work done.

   ....

3. Eric's a functional manager, but his team seems to move really slowly. It turns out that everyone who reports to him has to hand him their work first, before they can give it to anyone else. He goes through it line by line, which sometimes takes hours! He doesn't trust his team to release anything he hasn't seen.

   ....

4. Joe's a functional manager, and his team is very efficient. He spot-checks their work, but for the most part he sets realistic performance goals and trusts them to meet it—he only pulls people aside if he finds that there's a specific problem that has to be corrected.

   ....

5. A project manager is having a lot of trouble motivating the team. He tries setting up rewards and a good working environment. But the team remains difficult to motivate—mostly because their paychecks all bounced last week, and everyone is angry at the CEO because they didn't get bonuses..

   ....

Answers on page 452.

How's the team doing?

There's only one output of Develop Project Team, and it's the **Team Performance Assessment**. Developing the project team means working with them to keep everyone motivated, and training them to improve their skills.

You'll need to keep track of how well the team is performing, because when the team has problems you'll have a good baseline to compare against.

The project manager should look at how the team's skill set has improved, and make sure it's documented here.

Has the team performance improved? Are the motivational techniques working? If so, that goes here!

You can measure how motivated and happy the team is by keeping an eye on the turnover rate.

Cows Gone Wild IV
Team Performance Assessment

Competencies / Skills improvements
Developers: attended three-day training course on new vector graphics coding techniques. Designers: brought in industrial design professor from Ivy College to hold seminar on design techniques.

Team Performance
There's been a marked improvement in team cohesion, and it's resulted in a lower defect rate. We've awarded 50% of our $2,500 bonus budget.

Turnover Rate
Two designers and one developer have left the team, which is an improvement from CGW III.

BULLET POINTS: AIMING FOR THE EXAM

- Project managers use their **general management skills** ("soft skills") to motivate and lead the team.
- In a matrixed organization, the project manager doesn't have **legitimate** power, because the team doesn't directly report to the project manager.
- The most effective forms of power are **reward power**, where the project manager sets up rewards and recognition for the team, and **expert power**, which means the team respects the project manager's technical expertise.
- **Referent power** means influence that comes from being a proxy for or friendly with someone else who has legitimate power.
- **Punishment power** is the least effective form of power. The project manager should never punish a team member in front of peers or managers!
- Project managers should be familiar with modern **theories of motivation and management**.
- **McGregor's Theories X and Y** state that there are poor Theory X managers who don't trust their teams, and good Theory Y managers who do.
- **Maslow's Hierarchy of Needs** is the theory that says that people can't achieve "self-actualization" (full potential) or esteem (feeling good and important) until lower needs like safety and security are met.
- **Herzberg's Theory** says that it's difficult to motivate people unless hygiene factors like a paycheck and job security are already in place.
- **Expectancy Theory** holds that people only respond to rewards that are tied to goals they feel they have a realistic chance of achieving.

Cubicle conversation

Amy: Look, we've been over this, Brian. My team is working on level design, and that's the priority right now

Brian: Mike, is that true?

Mike: I checked the schedule, and all three of those things are part of the current activity. It's not really clear which one of them is the priority.

Brian: Look, my team will be halted if we don't get those models and textures.

Amy: Come on, Brian. You guys have a whole bunch of unit tests that you can write, and I know you're a week behind on code reviews. Can't you just work on those in the meantime?

Brian: My team's been reviewing code for two weeks now. They need a break!

Amy: Aha! So it's not really that you're going to fall behind if you don't get the textures immediately.

Brian: Well, no, but I'll be dealing with a team that has motivation problems. And I'm the one who has to clean up that mess!

Mike: OK, hold on, guys. Let's see if we can work this out.

Amy: I don't see what there is to work out. He's being unreasonable.

It looks like Brian and Amy are having a serious conflict, and it could have a big impact on the project if Mike doesn't get it under control! What usually causes conflicts in projects, and what can the project manager do about it when those conflicts happen?

Managing your team means solving problems

Wouldn't it be great if your team members never had any conflicts? Well, we all know that conflicts are a fact of life in any project. A good project manager knows how to handle conflicts so they don't delay or damage the project. And that's what the **Manage Project Team** process is about.

Monitoring & Controlling process group

This is a Monitoring and Controlling process—where you deal with changes.

You already know what these inputs are, and what they're for.

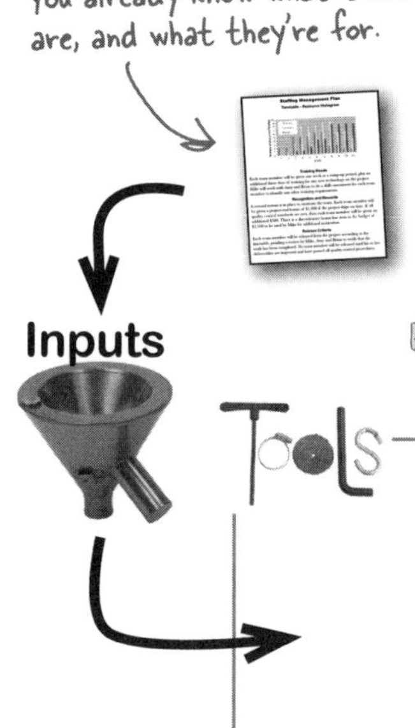

Inputs

This comes from Direct and Manage Execution, and tells you how the work's been done.

Work Performance Information

Performance Reports

We'll see these in the next chapter! They tell you if the project's deviated from the plan.

Tools

Conflict management is the most important tool in Manage Project Team, because it's where you resolve conflicts between people.

Issue logs are really useful for keeping track of any issue, problem or conflict that happens throughout the project. As each issue is resolved, write down the resolution.

Performance appraisals means looking at each person's work and assessing his or her performance.

A lot of project managers use a "360 degree" review, in which they assess someone's performance by getting feedback from everyone that person works with.

Outputs

Sharpen your pencil

You should have a really good feel for what the outputs are from any process in the Monitoring & Controlling process group. Write them in here.

....

....

....

....

....

....

....

Answers on page 451.

Conflict management up close

It's probably no surprise that over half of conflicts come from priorities, schedules and people. That's why so many of the processes you're learning about are focused on preventing conflicts. Ground rules, good planning practices, and pretty much anything that has to do with communication are all there to prevent the most common reasons that conflicts happen.

Some of the common reasons that conflicts happen

These three things are the source of 50% of all conflicts!

Resources are scarce—that's why you have to negotiate for them. Have you ever been in a situation where there's a "good" conference room, or top-performing team member, or even that photocopy machine that always seems to be in use? Well, that's a scarce resource. No wonder resources cause so many conflicts.

Priorities mean one project or person is more important than another, and gets more budget, resources, time, prestige or other perks. If the company's priorities aren't crystal clear, then conflicts are definitely going to happen.

Schedules decide who gets what, when. Have you ever had a client, sponsor or stakeholder get upset because your project won't come in as early as he or she wanted it to? Then you've had a conflict over schedules.

Over half of all conflicts are caused by resources, priorities and schedules.

Some more sources of conflict

Personalities are always clashing. Sometimes two people just don't get along, and you're going to have to find a way to make them work together in order to get your project done.

Cost disagreements seem to come up a lot, especially where contracts are involved. Even when the price is agreed upon up front, buyer's remorse will set in, and it will lead to issues.

Technical opinions are definitely a reason that conflicts happen, because it's really hard to get an expert to change his mind… so when two of them disagree, watch out!

What's the best way to deal with a conflict between two people on your project team?

How to resolve a conflict

When you're managing a project, you depend on people to get the work done. But when they have any sort of conflict, your project can grind to a halt… and you're the one who has to face the music when it causes delays and costs money! Since you're on the hook when a conflict threatens your project, **you're the one who has to resolve it**. Luckily, there are some techniques for getting your conflicts resolved.

The best way to resolve a conflict is to confront the problem: do your research, figure out what's behind it, and fix the root cause.

Confronting—or problem-solving—is the most effective way to resolve a conflict. When you confront the source of the conflict head-on and work with everyone to find a solution that actually fixes the reason that conflicts happen, then the problem is most likely to go away and never come back!

Compromise sounds good, doesn't it? But hold on a second—when two people compromise, it means that each person gives up something. That's why a lot of people call a compromise a "lose-lose" solution.

You should always try to confront the problem first—you should only forge a compromise after you've tried every possible way to solve the real problem.

Smoothing is what you're doing when you try to play down the problem and make it seem like it's not so bad. It's a temporary solution, but sometimes you need to do it to keep tempers from flaring and give people some space to step back and really figure out what's going on.

Forcing means putting your foot down and making a decision. One person wins, one person loses, and that's the end of that.

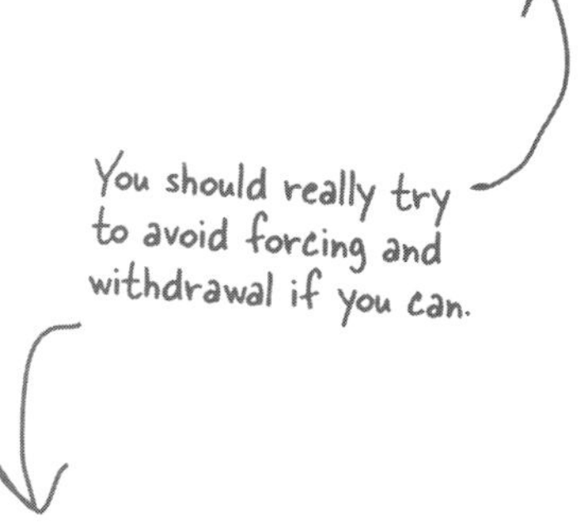

Withdrawal doesn't do much good for anyone. It's when one person gets so frustrated, angry or disgusted that they just walk away from the argument. It's almost always counterproductive. If someone withdraws from a problem before it's resolved, it won't go away—and your project will suffer.

No! Confrontation is just another name for problem-solving, because you solve a problem by confronting it head-on, doing your research, and fixing whatever is causing it. If you always remember to:

Confront the problem

"Confronting" is another way of saying "problem-solving." Any time two people have a conflict, you need to step back and figure out what's actually causing the problem. That's how you "confront" it—by finding and fixing the underlying issue!

It will really help you through a bunch of questions on the exam!

Make it Stick

Fix the root cause

Confront the Problem

Wash the dog

Take a look at each of these attempts to resolve a conflict and figure out which conflict resolution technique is being used.

1. "I don't really have time for this–let's just do it your way and forget I ever brought up the problem."

   ....

2. "Look Sue, Joe's already filled me in on your issue. I've considered his position, and I've decided that he's right, so I don't need to hear anymore about it."

   ....

3. "Hold on a second, let's all sit down and figure out what the real problem is."

   ....

4. "Joe, you've got a solid case, but Sue really brings up some good points. If you just make two little concessions, and Sue gives up one of her points, we'll all be good."

   ....

5. "You guys are almost entirely in agreement—you just differ on one little point! I'll bet we'll be laughing about this next week."

   ....

6. "I don't really have time to deal with this right now. Just figure it out and get back to me."

   ....

7. "I know this problem seems really big, but I'll bet if we take a long, hard look at it, we can figure out how to fix it permanently."

   ....

Answers on page 453.

there are no Dumb Questions

Q: How do I know what form of power to use?

A: You should always try to use expert power or reward power if you can. Expert power is effective because people naturally follow leadership from someone who they respect. And reward power is also good because rewards help people motivate themselves.

When you use referent power, you're really riding someone else's coattails—people will often resent it because it can feel like you're wielding power that isn't really yours. And when you use punishment, you have to be very careful because it can be highly demotivating to the team. When you use it, always be careful not to punish someone in front of the team or other managers in your company. That can be embarrassing for them, and just makes you look vindictive. Remember, you goal is to get your project back on track, not to put someone in his or her place!

Q: It sounds like compromise is a bad thing. But I've always been told that when people are fighting, I should always look for a middle ground!

A: Yes, as little kids a lot of us were told that we should always look for a compromise. And that probably is the right thing to do on the playground. But when you're managing a project, you're judged by the success of your final product, not by how happy your team is. When you forge a compromise instead of really figuring out what's causing the problem, you're usually taking the easy way out.

Q: I was looking through the PMBOK® Guide, but I couldn't find anything about conflict resolution, motivational theories, or different kinds of power. Do I really need to know this stuff?

A: Yes, you do! The PMP exam is there to make sure you're familiar with the state of the art in project management, not how much of the PMBOK® Guide you can memorize. Remember, the PMBOK® Guide is the **Guide** to the Project Management Body of Knowledge. It's not a complete reference for all project management information; in a lot of cases, it tells you what kind of information you need to know. In other words, the PMBOK® Guide is a reference, not a training manual! It's up to you to educate yourself. What you see in this chapter is an overview of the most widely held theories on organizational theory, motivation, conflict resolutions and organizational influence.

Try to avoid using punishment. When you do have to punish someone, make sure to do it in private, and not in front of peers or other managers.

BULLET POINTS: AIMING FOR THE EXAM

- 50% of project problems and conflicts are caused by **resources, schedules and priorities**.
- The best way to solve a problem is to **confront** it, which means doing your research, figuring out what's causing the problem, and fixing it.
- Don't be fooled by questions that make it sound like "confronting" is a bad thing. **Confronting is just another word for problem-solving**.
- **Smoothing** is minimizing the problem, and it can help cool people off while you figure out how to solve it.
- You should **only compromise if you can't confront** the problem.
- **Forcing** means making a decision without considering the facts. It's a really ineffective way to solve problems.
- **Withdrawal** happens when someone gives up and walks away from the problem, usually because they're frustrated or disgusted. If you see a team member doing this, it's a warning sign that something's wrong.

The Cows Gone Wild IV team ROCKS!

The odds were against Mike—he had to fight for a whole new team, keep them motivated, and solve some pretty serious problems. But he followed his plan, got a great team together, kept them on track, and got the product out the door!

Mike made sure everyone had a great working environment...

...he set up rewards that kept the team motivated...

...there were conflicts and arguments, but he confronted each of them and got the project back on track...

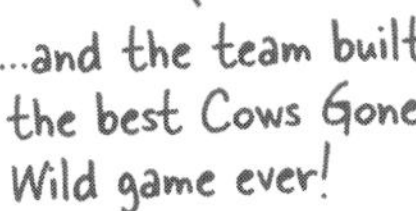

...and the team built the best Cows Gone Wild game ever!

Question Clinic: The "Have-A-Meeting" Question

There are a whole lot of questions on the exam that give you a situation where there's a conflict, an issue, or even a crisis, and ask you what to do first. The trick is that *in all of these cases*, one of the options is to have a meeting. Sounds odd, right? But this is actually really important for a project manager to know! That's because you need to gather information from other people before you make a decision.

Don't be fooled—even though this asks about conflict, that doesn't mean it's asking you for a conflict resolution technique.

It's not always team members who have conflicts. You could have an unhappy client who has a complaint about you or your team members... and that client could be right.

Sounds like these guys are right, and the other person is wrong... right? Well, maybe not.

198. Three people on your project team are having conflicts about priorities. A junior team member wants to do the activities out of order, while two senior members want to follow the schedule that you had originally put together. What's the first step in resolving this conflict?

A. Tell everyone to work out the problem among themselves.

B. Tell the junior member that you should always follow the schedule.

C. Tell them to keep to the original schedule

D. Meet with all three people and get all the information

Never push off your management responsibilities on the team.

That's not true! What if the schedule has a problem and needs change control? The junior team member could be right.

You shouldn't make a unilateral decision without understanding the conflict.

This is the right answer. Get all the facts <u>before</u> you make any move.

Remember how you always look at the impact of a change before you decide whether or not to make it? Well, this is the same idea! You always want to look at all the facts *before* you make a move.

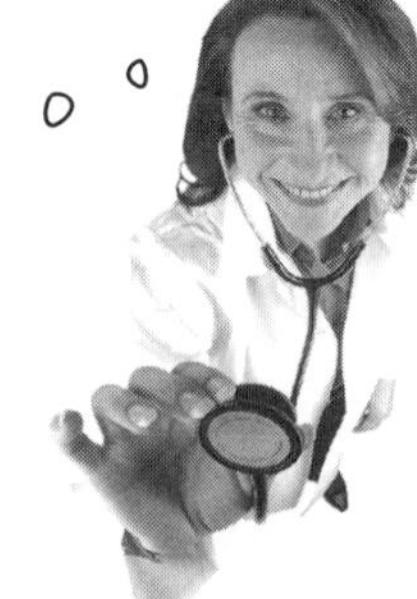

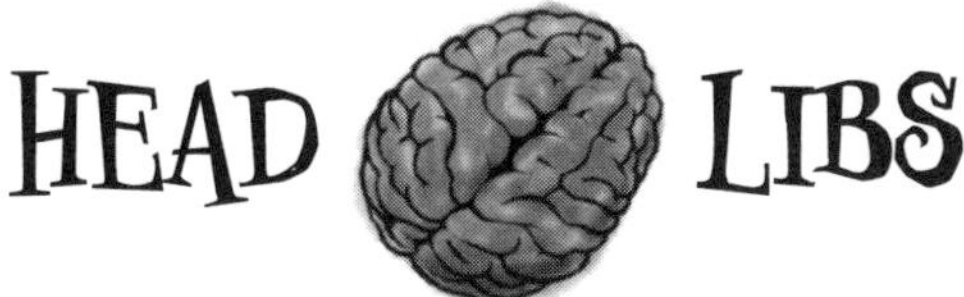

Fill in the blanks to come up with your own "Have-A-Meeting" question!

You're managing ____________ (description of a project), when ____________ (two people with a conflict) come to you with a disagreement about ____________ (source of disagreement). One team member says ____________ (one idea about how to resolve it), while the other says ____________ (a different idea about how to solve it). What's the first thing that you do?

A. ____________ (make a unilateral decision)

B. ____________ (side with one person)

C. ____________ (side with the other person)

D. ____________ (have a meeting)

Here's an additional "Have-A-Meeting" exercise to help get you used to this kind of question.

How many different ways can you say "Have a meeting"?

Fill in a few more.

Gather information from everyone involved ____________

Talk to the people involved directly ____________

Make sure you know everything you need about the situation ____________

Don't make a move until you've got all the information ____________

Join the Head First PMP community at http://www.headfirstlabs.com/PMP
You can add your Head Libs answer, and see what Head Libs other project managers came up with!

Read the **staffing management plan** on the facing page and answer these questions about the project.

1. How many designers, developers and testers are needed in week #7 of the project?

   6 designers 9 developers 4 testers

2. Who is responsible for verifying that each team member has the skills appropriate to the project?

   Mike, Amy and Brian

3. Rewards should always be tied to performance goals in order to motivate the team. What performance goal has been set for the team, and what reward will each team member receive if it's achieved?

   Each team member will receive $1,000 if the schedule is met, and $500 more if all quality control standards are met.

Match each form of power to the scenario where it's being used.

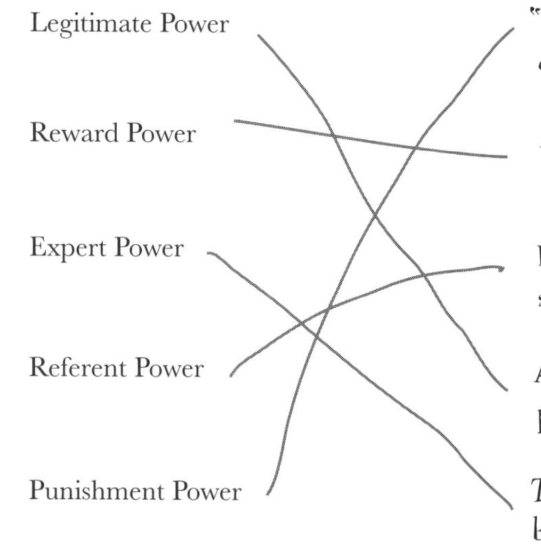

Legitimate Power → A functional manager assigns a tester to work on the project manager's team.

Reward Power → A project manager sets up an "Accolade Wall" and posts awards for team members who come in ahead of schedule.

Expert Power → The programmers always listen to the team lead because he's a really good software architect.

Referent Power → Everyone always does what Shelly says because a senior director assigned her personally.

Punishment Power → "We're not meeting our quality standards, and until we do we're going to have to work weekends."

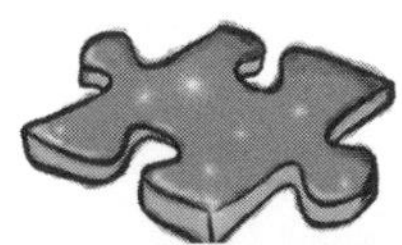

Human Resourcecross Solution

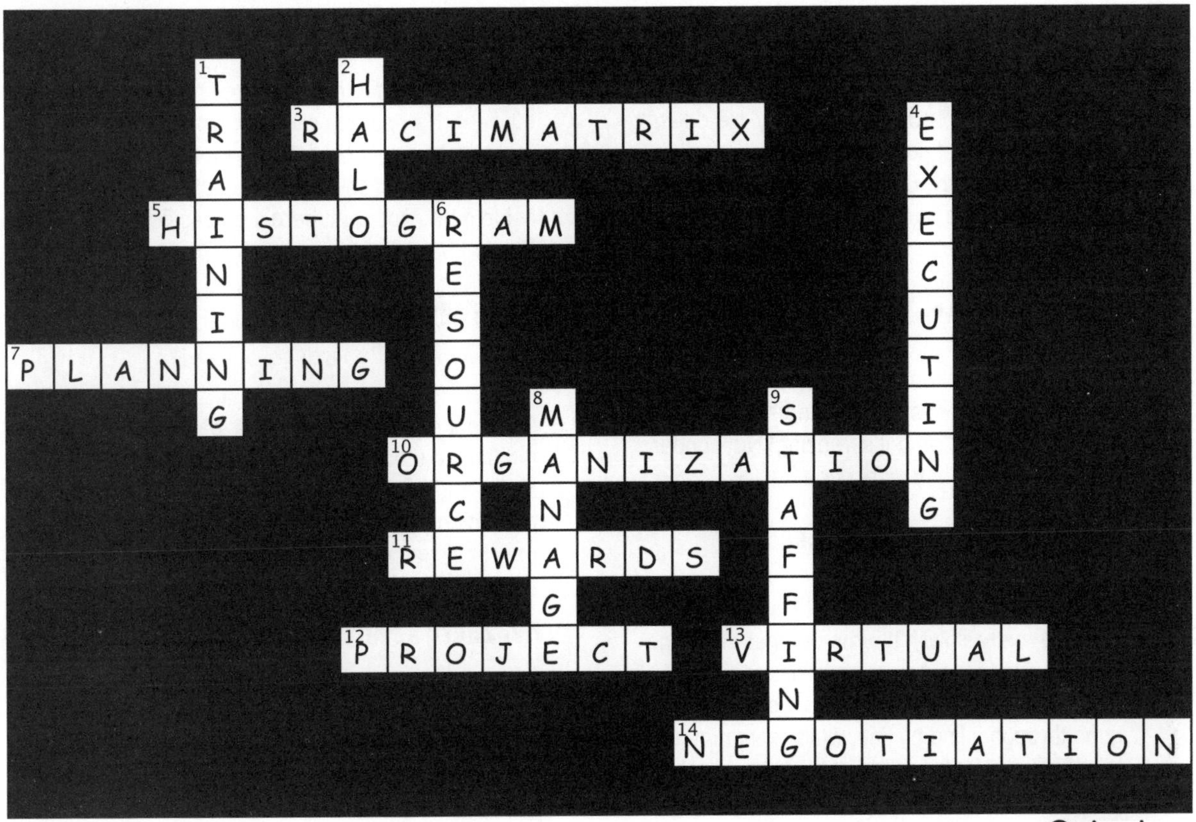

3 RACIMATRIX
5 HISTOGRAM
7 PLANNING
10 ORGANIZATION
11 REWARDS
12 PROJECT
13 VIRTUAL
14 NEGOTIATION

1 TRAINING
2 HALO
4 EXECUTING
6 RESOURCE
8 MANAGE
9 STAFFING

Outputs

Sharpen your pencil Solution

You should have a really good feel for what the outputs are from any process in the Monitoring & Controlling process group. Write them in here.

Requested changes

Recommended corrective actions

Recommended preventive actions

Updates to the organizational process assets

Updates to the project management plan

Each of the following scenarios demonstrates one of the motivational theories at work. Write down which theory each scenario describes.

1. Bob is a programmer on the team, but he doesn't really feel like he's "one of the guys." He doesn't really have a lot of control over the work he's assigned. Recently, Bob put in a long weekend to get his work done, but nobody really seemed to take notice.

   McLelland's Achievement Theory

2. There was a break-in in the office, and now people are really jittery. Plus, the heating system has been broken for weeks, and it's freezing! No wonder nobody's getting any work done.

   Maslow's Hierarchy of Needs

3. Eric's a functional manager, but his team seems to move really slowly. It turns out that everyone who reports to him has to hand him their work first, before they can give it to anyone else. He goes through it line by line, which sometimes takes hours! He doesn't trust his team to release anything he hasn't seen.

   McGregor's Theory X

4. Joe's a functional manager, and his team is very efficient. He spot-checks their work, but for the most part he sets realistic performance goals and trusts them to meet them—he only pulls people aside if he finds that there's a specific problem that has to be corrected.

   McGregor's Theory Y

5. A project manager is having a lot of trouble motivating the team. He tries setting up rewards and a good working environment. But the team remains difficult to motivate—mostly because their paychecks all bounced last week, and everyone is angry at the CEO because they didn't get bonuses.

   Herzberg's Motivation-Hygiene Theory

Take a look at each of these attempts to resolve a conflict and figure out which conflict resolution technique is being used.

1. "I don't really have time for this–let's just do it your way and forget I ever brought up the problem."

   Withdrawal

2. "Look Sue, Joe's already filled me in on your issue. I've considered his position, and I've decided that he's right, so I don't need to hear any more about it."

   Forcing

3. "Hold on a second, let's all sit down and figure out what the real problem is."

   Confronting (or problem-solving)

4. "Joe, you've got a solid case, but Sue really brings up some good points. If you just make two little concessions, and Sue gives up one of her points, we'll all be good."

   Compromise

5. "You guys are almost entirely in agreement—you just differ on one little point! I'll bet we'll be laughing about this next week."

   Smoothing

6. "I don't really have time to deal with this right now. Just figure it out and get back to me."

   Withdrawal

7. "I know this problem seems really big, but I'll bet if we take a long, hard look at it, we can figure out how to fix it permanently."

   Confronting (or problem solving)

Exam Questions

1. A RACI Matrix is one way to show roles and responsibilities on your project. What does RACI stand for?

A. Responsible, Approve, Consult, Identify

B. Responsible, Accountable, Consult, Inform

C. Retain, Approve, Confirm, Inform

D. Responsible, Accountable, Confirm, Inform

2. Everybody does what Tom says because he and president of the company are golfing buddies. What kind of power does he hold over the team?

A. Legitimate

B. Reward

C. Punishment

D. Referent

3. What's the most effective approach to conflict resolution?

A. Smoothing

B. Confronting

C. Compromise

D. Withdrawal

4. Two of your team members are having a disagreement over which technical solution to use. What's the first thing that you should do in this situation?

A. Consult the technical documents

B. Tell the team members to work out the problem themselves

C. Ask the team members to write up a change request

D. Meet with the team members and figure out what's causing the disagreement

5. Joe is a project manager on a large software project. Very late in his project, the customer asked for a huge change and wouldn't give him any more time to complete the project. At a weekly status meeting, the client demanded that the project be finished on time. Joe told the client that he wasn't going to do any more status meetings until the client was ready to be reasonable about the situation. Which conflict resolution technique was he using?

A. Forcing

B. Compromise

C. Withdrawal

D. Confronting

Exam Questions

6. You've just completed your resource histogram. What process are you in?

A. Acquire Project Team
B. Develop Project Team
C. Human Resource Planning
D. Manage Project Team

7. Which of the following describes Maslow's Hierarchy of Needs?

A. You can't be good at your job if you don't have a nice office
B. You need to feel safe and accepted to want to be good at your job
C. Your boss's needs are more important than yours
D. The company's needs are most important, then the boss's, then the employee's

8. Jim and Sue are arguing about which approach to take with the project. Sue makes some good points, but Jim gets frustrated and storms out of the room. What conflict resolution technique did Jim demonstrate?

A. Withdrawal
B. Confronting
C. Forcing
D. Smoothing

9. Tina is a project manager who micromanages her team. She reviews every document they produce and watches when they come and go from the office. Which kind of manager is she?

A. Theory X
B. Theory Y
C. Theory Z
D. McGregor Manager

10. Which of the following is NOT one of the top sources of conflict on projects?

A. Resources
B. Technical opinions
C. Salaries
D. Priorities

11. What is the "halo effect"?

A. When a project manager is good, the team is good, too.
B. The tendency to promote people who are good at technical jobs into managerial positions
C. When a project manager picks a star on the team and always rewards that person
D. When a technical person does such a good job that no one can find fault with them

Exam Questions

12. You are working on a construction project that is running slightly behind schedule. You ask the team to put in a few extra hours on their shifts over the next few weeks to make up the time. To make sure everyone feels motivated to do the extra work, you set up a $1,500 bonus for everyone on the team who works the extra hours if the deadline is met. What kind of power are you using?

A. Legitimate

B. Reward

C. Expert

D. Referent

13. Two team members are having an argument over priorities in your project. One thinks that you should write everything down before you start doing any work, the other thinks you can do the work while you finish the documentation. You sit both of them down and listen to their argument. Then you decide that you will write most of it down first but will start doing the work when you are 80% done with the documentation. What conflict resolution technique are you using?

A. Forcing

B. Confronting

C. Smoothing

D. Compromise

14. What is a war room?

A. A place where managers make decisions

B. A room set aside for conflict management

C. A room where a team can sit together and get closer communication

D. A conflict resolution technique

15. You are writing a Performance Assessment for your team. Which process are you in?

A. Develop Project Team

B. Acquire Project Team

C. Manage Project Team

D. Human Resource Planning

16. You are working in a matrix organization. You don't have legitimate power over your team. Why?

A. They don't report to you

B. They don't trust you

C. They don't know whether or not they will succeed

D. You haven't set up a good bonus system

Exam Questions

17. Tom is using an organization chart to figure out how he'll staff his project. What process is he performing?

A. Human Resource Planning

B. Acquire Project Team

C. Develop Project Team

D. Manage Project Team

18. You're a project manager on an industrial design project. You've set up a reward system, but you're surprised to find out that the team is actually less motivated than before. You realize that it's because your rewards are impossible to achieve, so the team doesn't expect to ever get them. What motivational theory does this demonstrate?

A. Herzberg's Hygiene Theory

B. Maslow's Hierarchy of Needs

C. MacGregor's Theory of X and Y

D. Expectancy Theory

19. You're managing a software project, when two of your programmers come to you with a disagreement over which feature to work on next. You listen to the first programmer, but rather than thinking through the situation and gathering all the information, you decide to go with his idea. Which conflict resolution technique did you use?

A. Compromise

B. Forcing

C. Confronting

D. Smoothing

20. Your client comes to you with a serious problem in one of the deliverables that will cause the final product to be unacceptable. Your team members look at his complaint and feel that it's not justifiable, and that the product really does meet its requirements. What's the first thing that you do?

A. Confront the situation by making the change that needs to be made in order to satisfy the client

B. Explain to the client that the solution really is acceptable

C. Work with the client and team members to fully understand the problem before making a decision

D. Write up a change request and send it to the change control board

Exam ~~Questions~~ Answers

1. Answer: B

Think about how you organize the work on your project and the RACI chart makes sense. Being **responsible** for a specific task or area of work means you're the one who's on the hook if it doesn't get done. Being **accountable** means you might not be doing it directly but you have influence over it. Some people need to be **consulted** but don't get involved in the work, while others should just be kept **informed** of status.

2. Answer: D

Did you choose punishment? People might be afraid of punishment from the president of the company if they don't agree with Tom. But since Tom isn't the one who would punish them, it's referent power.

The power is here is referent. People are reacting to Tom's relationship to the president of the company, not his own authority.

3. Answer: B

Confronting does sound like it would be negative, but it just means solving the problem. If you actually solve the problem, there's no more reason for people to fight at all. That's always the best way to deal with a conflict. Any of the other options could lead to more problems later.

4. Answer: D

This is a classic "Have a Meeting" question! You should always gather the information you need before you make any kind of decision.

5. Answer: C

Joe decided that the best tactic was to refuse to talk to the client anymore—that's withdrawing. It's also probably not going to solve the problem.

6. Answer: C

You create the Histogram as part of the Staffing Management Plan. It's the main output of the Human Resource Planning process.

7. Answer: B

Maslow's Hierarchy of Needs says that your safety and acceptance are a prerequisite for you being able to do your best.

Exam Questions

8. Answer: A

Jim took his ball and went home. That's withdrawal.

It seems like Jim and Sue had a confrontation, right? But that's not what "confronting" means here! It really means "problem-solving".

9. Answer: A

A micromanager is a Theory X manager. They believe that all employees need to be watched very closely, or they will make mistakes.

10. Answer: C

You definitely need to know what causes conflicts on projects. Resources, technical opinions, priorities, and personalities all cause people to conflict with each other, and there's a good chance you'll get a question on that!

11. Answer: B

Just because someone is good at a technical job, it doesn't mean they will be good at management. The jobs require very different skills.

12. Answer: B

You are motivating the work by offering a reward for it. People might be motivated by the bonus to put in the extra time even if they would not have been motivated by the deadline alone.

13. Answer: D

Both of them had to give something up, so that's a compromise.

14. Answer: C

War rooms are part of co-location. It's a way to keep your entire team in one room so they don't have any communication gaps.

Exam ~~Questions~~ Answers

15. Answer: A

Developing the team is where you evaluate performance and set up motivational factors. Manage Project Team is where you solve conflicts.

16. Answer: A

In matrix organizations, team members usually report to their functional managers. A project manager never has legitimate power over the team in those situations.

17. Answer: A

Don't forget that there are two org charts—one for the company, and one for the project.

Tom's project is at the very beginning—he's using the organization chart as a tool to figure out who's going to be assigned to his team.

18. Answer: D

Expectancy Theory says that people only get motivated by rewards that they can achieve, and that are fair. If you set up a reward system that selects people who don't deserve rewards, or that has rewards that are unattainable, then it will backfire and cause people to resent their jobs.

19. Answer: B

Whenever you choose one side over another without thinking or actually finding the root cause of the problem, you're forcing a solution on it. This is NOT a good way to solve problems!

20. Answer: C

Any time there's any sort of conflict, the first thing you need to do is gather all the information. And that's especially true when there's a disagreement between the client and the team! You'd better have your facts straight in such a charged situation.

He should have sat down with both programmers and figured out what the real problem was. Even if the solution isn't perfect, at least it's more fair.

10 Communications Management

Getting the word out

Communications management is about keeping everybody in the loop. Have you ever tried talking to someone in a really loud, crowded room? That's what running a project is like if you don't get a handle on communications. Luckily, there's **Communications Management**, which is how to get everyone talking about the work that's being done, so that they all **stay on the same page**. That way everyone has the information they need to **resolve any issues** and keep the project **moving forward**.

Party at the Head First Lounge!

Jeff and Charles want to launch their new Head First Lounge, so they're going to have a party for the grand opening. They're thinking of all of the things they need to do: the DJ, the hors d'oeuvres, the drinks, hula dancing. They need to start contacting caterers, DJs, and suppliers to make sure it all goes off without a hitch.

But something's not right

When Jeff called the caterer and the DJ to request everything he wanted for the party, his old staticky phone made it hard for everybody to understand what he was asking. Sometimes their taste for retro furniture can make things a little difficult.

BRAIN POWER

What can Jeff and Charles do to get a handle on their communication problems?

Anatomy of communication

When you communicate with your team, you need to **encode** your message into a phone call, a document, an IM chat, or sometimes even a different language for them to understand. Your team then **decodes** that message so they can get its content. If something happens to your message along the way (static on the phone line, your printer inserts garbage characters, your Internet connection is spotty, or your translation isn't very good), then your team might not get the intended message. The kind of interference that can alter your message is called **noise**.

Match each communication element to what it does.

Sender	The thing used to transmit the message
Receiver	The person who gets the message
Medium	Something that interferes with the message
Feedback	Modifying a message that has been sent so that it can be understood
Noise	A response to a message
Encode	Modifying a message so that it can be sent
Decode	The person who needs to initiate the communication

Answers on page 496.

Get a handle on communication

Any kind of communication can have interference. The wrong person can get the message; noise can garble the transmission; you can make mistakes decoding or encoding the message. It turns out that 90% of a project manager's job is communication, which is why there's a whole knowledge area devoted to it. The **Communications Management** processes are here to help you avoid these common kinds of errors, through planning and careful tracking of stakeholder communications on your project. Just like every other knowledge group we've covered so far, it all starts with a plan.

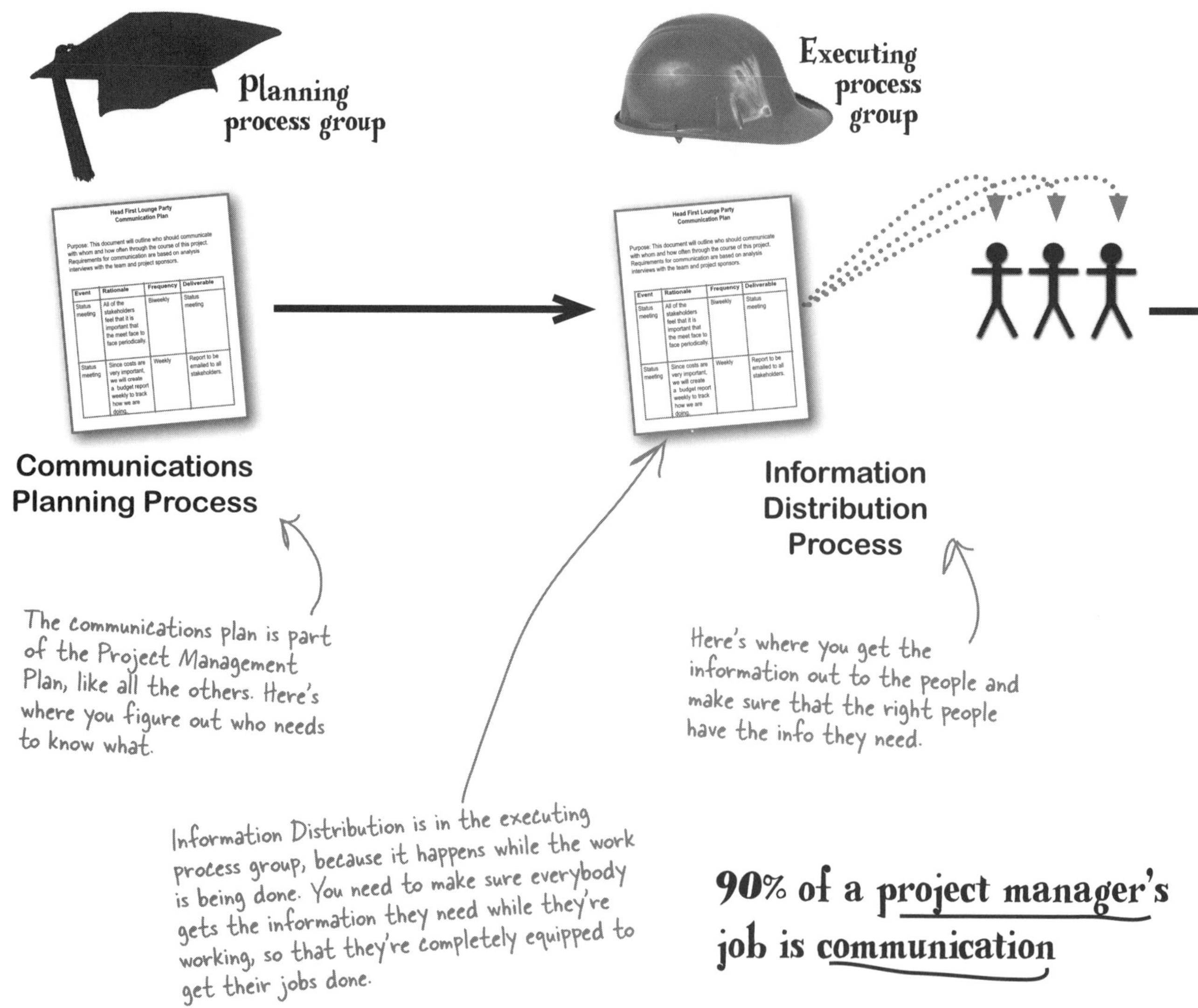

90% of a project manager's job is communication

Communications Management makes sure everybody gets the right message at the right time.

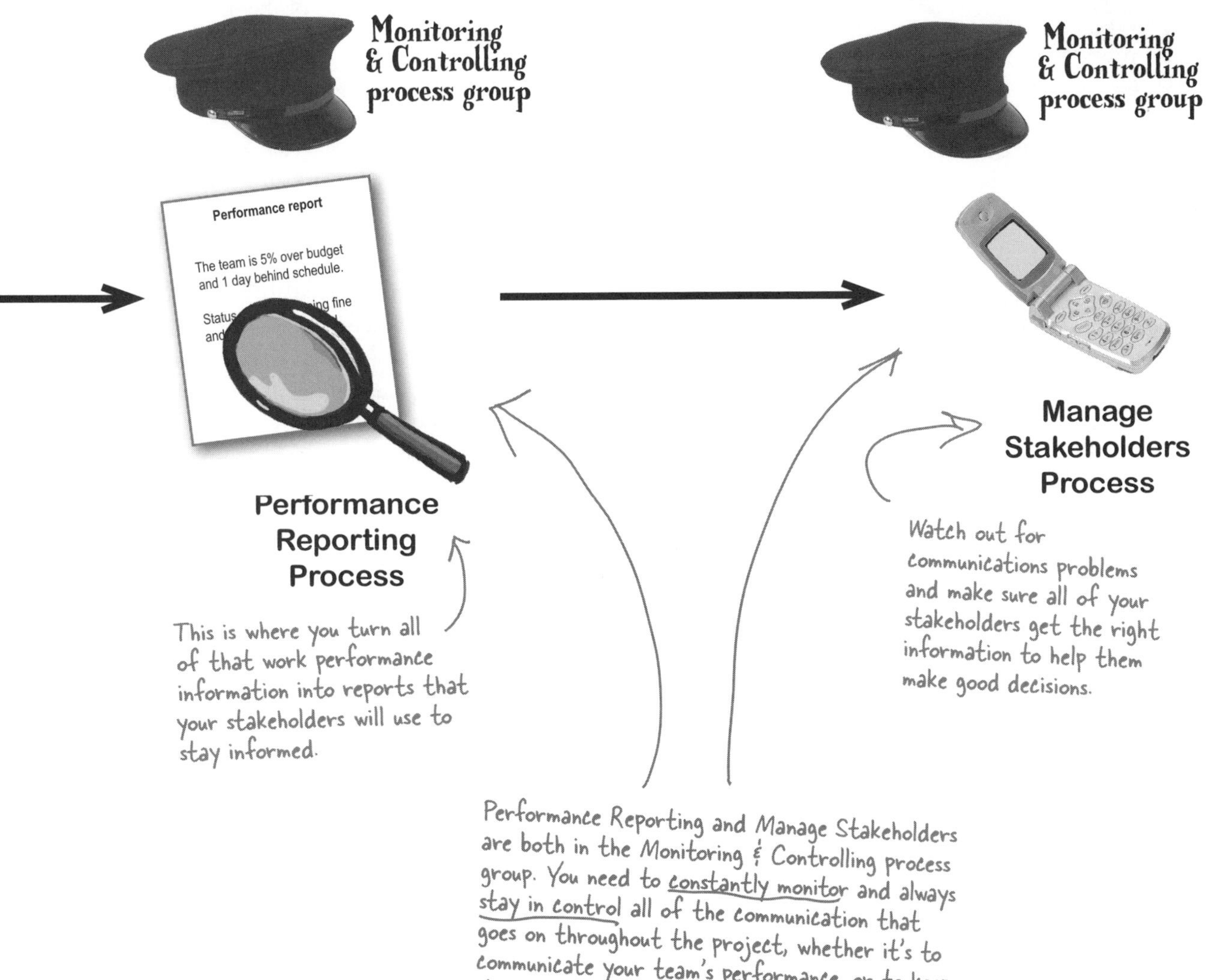

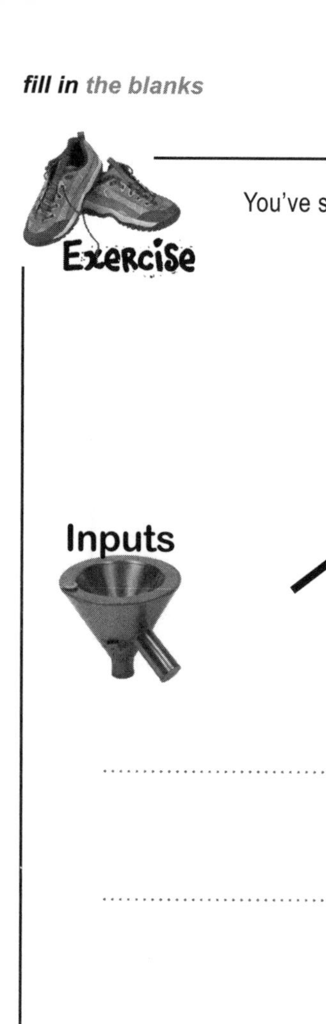

You've seen a lot of planning processes now. Can you fill in the Inputs and Outputs for this one?

Tools

Communications Requirements Analysis means figuring out what kind of communication your stakeholders need from the project so that they can make good decisions. Your project will produce a lot of information; you don't want to overwhelm every member of your project team with all of it. Your job here is to figure out what all of them feel they need to stay informed and to be able to do their jobs properly.

Here's an example: Jeff and Charles will definitely care about the cost of the overall catering contract, but they don't need to talk to the caterer's butcher, liquor supplier, grocer, or other companies they work with.

....

This one is your company's culture and policies toward project communication.

....

Here's where your company keeps all of its templates and lessons learned.

....

You need to know what your project is going to accomplish to do a communications plan.

....

This is where you'll find all of your other plans that might affect this one.

These four inputs show up in most of the planning processes.

Communications Technology has a major impact on how you can keep people in the loop. It's a lot easier for people to get information on their projects if it's all accessible through a web site than it is if all of your information is passed around by paper memos. The technologies available to you will definitely figure into your plan of how you will keep everyone notified of project status and issues.

Outputs

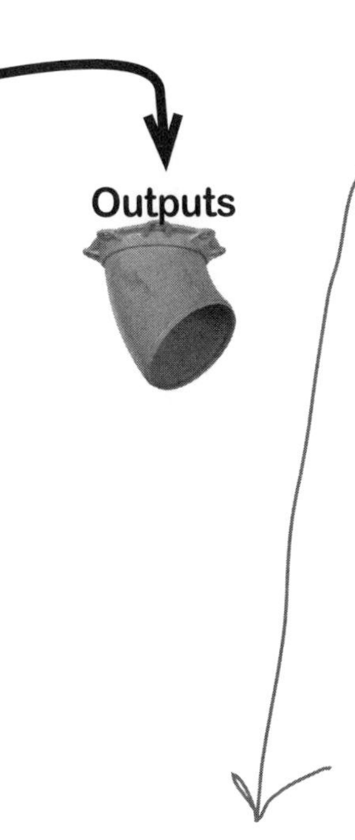

Are you surprised at how much of this process you can fill in? Looks like you're getting the hang of this stuff!

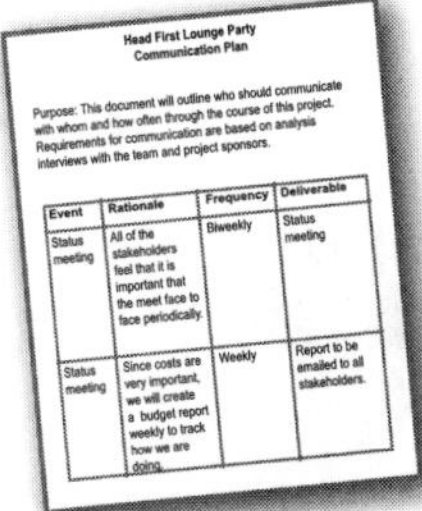

Head First Lounge Party
Communication Plan

Purpose: This document will outline who should communicate with whom and how often through the course of this project. Requirements for communication are based on analysis interviews with the team and project sponsors.

Event	Rationale	Frequency	Deliverable
Status meeting	All of the stakeholders feel that it is important that the meet face to face periodically.	Biweekly	Status meeting
Status meeting	Since costs are very important, we will create a budget report weekly to track how we are doing.	Weekly	Report to be emailed to all stakeholders.

Communications Planning Process

....

There's only one output. Can you guess what it is?

You've seen a lot of planning processes now. Can you fill in the Inputs and Outputs for this one?

Communications Requirements Analysis means figuring out what kind of communication your stakeholders need from the project so that they can make good decisions. Your project will produce a lot of information; you don't want to overwhelm every member of your project team with all of it. Your job here is to figure out what all of them feel they need to stay informed and to be able to do their jobs properly.

Here's an example: Jeff and Charles will definitely care about the cost of the overall catering contract, but they don't need to talk to the caterer's butcher, liquor supplier, grocer or other companies they work with.

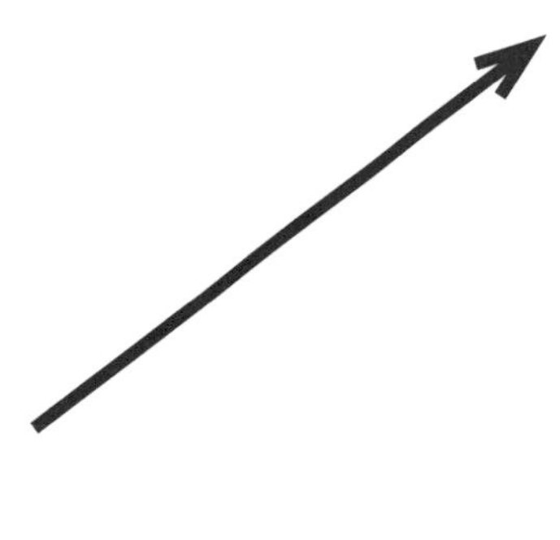

Inputs

Enterprise Environmental Factors

Organizational Process Assets

Project Scope Statement

Project Management Plan

You use all that you know about the project so far to figure out what will be the most important things to communicate.

Then you go and interview the stakeholders to see what they think they need and the best way to get it to them.

Communications Technology has a major impact on how you can keep people in the loop. It's a lot easier for people to get information on their projects if it's all accessible through a web site than it is if all of your information is passed around by paper memos. The technologies available to you will definitely figure into your plan of how you will keep everyone notified of project status and issues.

Outputs

Planning process group

This is the only output of the Communications Planning process.

Head First Lounge Party Communication Plan

Purpose: This document will outline who should communicate with whom and how often through the course of this project. Requirements for communication are based on analysis of interviews with the team and project sponsors.

Event	Rationale	Frequency	Deliverable
Status meeting	All of the stakeholders feel that it is important that they meet face to face periodically.	Biweekly	Meeting minutes to be emailed to all stakeholders. Archived in the document repository.
Budget report	Since costs are very important, we will create a budget report weekly to track how we are doing.	Weekly	Report to be emailed to all stakeholders.

It's important that everyone involved understand why you are doing the meetings and reports you create.

The plan tells how you will distribute the information, to whom, and how often.

The PM's not always responsible for every communication. The plan makes it clear who communicates what on the project.

Tell everyone what's going on

Executing process group

Once you have the communication plan completed, it's time to start making sure that everybody is getting the information that they need to help your project succeed. The **Information Distribution** process is all about making sure that the right information makes it to the right people.

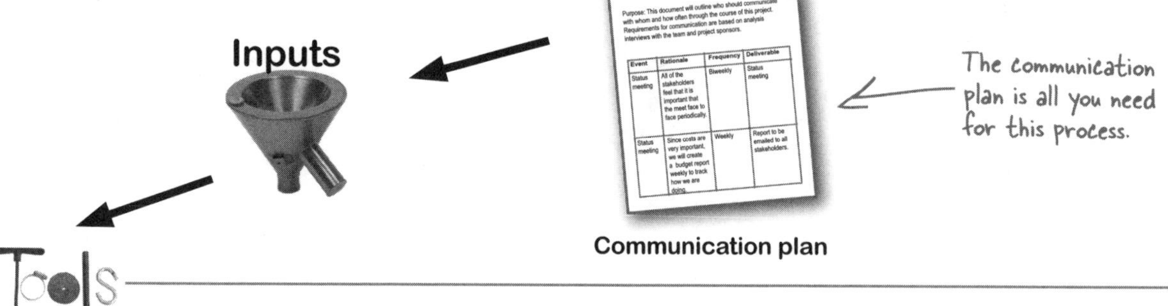

Head First Lounge Party
Communication Plan

Purpose: This document will outline who should communicate with whom and how often through the course of this project. Requirements for communication are based on analysis interviews with the team and project sponsors.

Event	Rationale	Frequency	Deliverable
Status meeting	All of the stakeholders feel that it is important that the meet face to face periodically.	Biweekly	Status meeting
Status meeting	Since costs are very important, we will create a budget report weekly to track how we are doing.	Weekly	Report to be emailed to all stakeholders.

Communication plan

The communication plan is all you need for this process.

Tools

Communication skills There are a lot of different ways to get a message across. For the test you will need to know four different kinds of communication and when to use them.

1 Formal written

Anytime you're signing a legal document or preparing formal documentation for your project, that's formal written communication.

Any time you see anything that has to do with a contract, you should always use formal written communication.

Blueprints, specifications and all other project documents are examples of formal written communication.

2 Informal written

If you drop someone a quick email or leave them a memo or a sticky note, that's informal written communication.

3 Formal verbal

If you ever have to give a presentation to update people on your project, that's formal verbal communication.

4 Informal verbal

Speeches and prepared talks are formal. Meetings, hallway chats, and planning sessions are informal.

Just calling somebody up to chat about your project is informal verbal communication.

Choose which kind of communication is being used in each situation.

1. You and your business analysts write a requirements specification for your project.

☐ Formal verbal ☐ Informal verbal
☐ Formal written ☐ Informal written

2. You call up the executive who is backing your project to let him or her know that you are on schedule and expect to deliver under budget.

☐ Formal verbal ☐ Informal verbal
☐ Formal written ☐ Informal written

3. You present your project's status to your company's executive committee.

☐ Formal verbal ☐ Informal verbal
☐ Formal written ☐ Informal written

4. You send an email to some of your team members to get more information about an issue that has been identified on your project.

☐ Formal verbal ☐ Informal verbal
☐ Formal written ☐ Informal written

5. You leave a voicemail message for your test team lead following up on an issue he or she found.

☐ Formal verbal ☐ Informal verbal
☐ Formal written ☐ Informal written

6. You IM with your team members.

☐ Formal verbal ☐ Informal verbal
☐ Formal written ☐ Informal written

7. You prepare an RFP (request for proposals) for vendors to determine which of them will get a chance to contract a new project with your company.

☐ Formal verbal ☐ Informal verbal
☐ Formal written ☐ Informal written

Hint: We haven't talked about RFPs yet, but you don't need to know what they are to answer this question.

Answers on page 497.

Be careful about when you use different kinds of communication. *Any time you need to get a message to a client or sponsor, you use* ***formal*** *communication. Meetings are always* ***informal verbal****, even if the meeting is to say something really important. And any project document—like a project management plan, a requirements specification or especially a contract—is always* ***formal written****.*

Get the message?

Tools

Communication is about more than just what you write and say. Your facial expressions, gestures, tone of voice, and the context you are in have a lot to do with whether or not people will understand you. **Effective communication** takes the way you act and sound into account, and it's the first of the tools and techniques in the Information Distribution process because most project communication takes place in this process. It's got a few important pieces:

Nonverbal communication means your gestures, facial expressions, and physical appearance while you are communicating your message. Imagine what Jeff and Charles would think of the caterer if he negotiated the contract for their party while wearing a chicken suit. They probably wouldn't take him very seriously. You don't always think about it, but the way you behave can say more than your words when you are trying to get your message across.

When you're communicating with other people, you actually do more nonverbal communication than verbal!

Paralingual communication is the tone and pitch of your voice when you are telling people what's going on with your project. If you sound anxious or upset, that will have an impact on the way people take the news you are giving. You use paralingual communication all the time—it's a really important part of how you communicate. When your tone of voice makes it clear you're really excited about something, or if you're speaking sarcastically, that's paralingual communication.

If someone has dread in his voice when he tells you about a promotion, you get a much different impression than if he'd emailed you about it.

Feedback is when you respond to communication. The best way to be sure people know you are listening to them is to give lots of feedback. Some ways of giving feedback are to summarize their main points back to them, letting them know that you agree with them, or asking questions for clarification. When you give a lot of feedback to someone who is speaking, that's called **active listening**.

Like effective communication, EFFECTIVE LISTENING is about taking everything the speaker says and does in to consideration and asking questions when you don't understand.

So it's not enough to say the right thing. You need to say it the right way, too.

You do most of the project communication when you're performing the Information Distribution process.

Jeff and Charles are interviewing new bartenders to help with the expanded space. Choose which kind of communication is being used in each situation.

1. One applicant came in 30 minutes late and was dressed unprofessionally. The guys knew that he would not be a good fit for the position.

   ☐ Paralingual ☐ Nonverbal
   ☐ Feedback

2. Charles asked an applicant about her background. Her tone of voice was really sarcastic, and he got the impression she didn't take the job seriously. Charles and Jeff decided to pass on her, too.

   ☐ Paralingual ☐ Nonverbal
   ☐ Feedback

3. Charles asked the next applicant if he knew how to make a sidecar. He said "A sidecar? Sure. It's one part brandy or cognac, one part Cointreau, and one part lemon juice."

   ☐ Paralingual ☐ Nonverbal
   ☐ Feedback

4. Then the applicant told them about his background as a bartender for other retro clubs. As he spoke, he made eye contact with them and made sure to confirm agreement with them.

   ☐ Paralingual ☐ Nonverbal
   ☐ Feedback

Answers on page 496.

We found a bartender for the new space!

This new guy will be great. He has awesome communication skills.

More information distribution tools

Tools

The tools in this process area are all about getting information from your team and making sure that it makes it to the people who need it. As you learn more about your project, you write down decisions you make and everything you learn on the project as lessons learned, and update your process assets to include them.

Information gathering and retrieval systems are how you get the information your team needs to do the job. You might have an inbox where everyone puts their status information. You could also have a software application that gathers information about your project and saves it to a database so that you can make your reports. Your company might have a time sheet system for tracking hours spent on a project or a budgeting system for tracking expenditures. All of those are information gathering and retrieval systems because the data they produce will be used to make decisions about your project.

Three more tools & techniques in Information Distribution

Information distribution methods are all about getting the information you have gathered to the right people. You might be emailing it to people, printing it out and putting it under people's doors, updating people in presentations or status meetings, calling people to let them know what's up—all of those are information distribution methods.

Lessons learned are all of the corrective and preventative actions that you have had to take on your project, and anything you have learned along the way.

Head First Lounge
Party Project

Lessons Learned:

1. Don't use 70s phones for calling external vendors.
2. Be sure to hire people with effective communication skills.

Next time they plan a party, Jeff and Charles won't run into the misunderstandings that they had on this one.

It's important to write down the good things you learned on the project, too. That way, you can be sure to repeat your successes next time.

Organizational Process Asset updates
You've used lessons learned from all of the other projects your company has done as you planned out your work. Here's where you get a chance to give your project's experience back to the company and help future project managers to learn from what's happened on your project.

Requested changes
As you're gathering and distributing information, you might find that you need to make changes to the way work is being done. You handle that like you would handle any other change request—through change control.

there are no Dumb Questions

Q: What do I do with lessons learned after I write them?

A: The great thing about lessons learned is that you get to help other project managers with them. You add them to your company's process asset library, and other project managers then use them for planning their projects.

Since Jeff and Charles learned that they shouldn't use their retro phones for planning parties, no one should ever have to deal with that problem when planning a party for Jeff and Charles again. They wrote down the lesson they learned and filed it away for future planning efforts.

Q: I still don't get the different types of communication.

A: When you think about it, they are pretty easy to remember. You have formal and informal communication and verbal and written communication types. The four different ways you can mix those up are all of the communication types. Think of informal verbal as phone calls between different team members. Formal verbal is giving a presentation. Informal written is sending out notes, emails, or memos. Formal written is when you have to write specifications or other formal project documentation.

For the test, you need to be able to identify which is which. If you just think of these examples, it should be a snap for you.

Q: Now, who's decoding, who's encoding, and where does feedback come from?

A: Think of encoding as making your message ready for other people to hear or read. If you write a book, you are encoding your message into a book. The person who buys the book needs to read it to decode it. The same is true for a presentation. When you present, you encode your thoughts into presentation images and text. The people who are listening to your presentation need to read the text, hear your voice, and see the visuals to decode it.

Feedback is all about the person who decodes the message letting the person who encoded it know that they received it. In the case of a book, this could be a reader sending a question or a note to the author or writing a review of it on a web site. In a presentation, it could be as simple as nodding your head that you understand what's being said.

Q: Do I have to know everything that will be communicated to build a plan?

A: No. As you learn more about the project you can always update the plan to include new information as you learn it. Pretty much all of the planning processes allow for progressive elaboration. You plan as much as you can up front and then put all changes through change control from then on. So, if you find something new, put in a change request and update the plan when it's approved.

There are only four communication types; formal written, informal written, formal verbal, and informal verbal. For the test, you need to be able to tell which is which.

Let everyone know how the project's going

You spend a lot of time collecting valuable information about how your projects are doing. So what do you do with it? You *communicate* it. And that's what the **Performance Reporting** process is for: taking the information you gathered about how work is being done and distributing it to the stakeholders who need to make decisions about the project.

Remember, the team members are all stakeholders, too—and this information is especially important to them!

You created this when you were executing the project – it was where you reported how the project work was going. Now you're using it to report the performance of the team to the stakeholders and the rest of the company.

It all starts with Work Performance Information

You create one of the most important outputs of your entire project when the team is doing the project work in Direct and Manage Execution. **Work Performance Information** tells you the status of each deliverable in the project, what the team's accomplished, and all of the information you need to know in order to figure out how your project's going. But you're not the only one who needs this—your team members and stakeholders need to know what's going on, so they can adjust their work and correct problems early on.

Work Performance Information

Whenever you hear back from a team member about how the job is going, that's work performance information.

Take a close look at the work being done

Work performance information isn't the only information you need to figure out how the project is going. There are a whole lot of outputs from the Executing processes that you need to look at if you really want to get a clear picture of your project.

Performance Reporting takes the outputs from the Executing process in Information Distribution and turns them into Performance Reports and Forecasts

Remember how you used Earned Value to see how your project is performing? Well, now you use that information to get a handle on your project's progress.

...and you used that Earned Value information to come up with forecasts of when the project would be completed.

Don't forget to look at the stuff the team's produced so far.

Forecasted Completion

If you want a complete picture of your project, you'll need to take a look at the quality of the deliverables.

You already know what these are for! Can you think of why they're important for performance reporting?

Performance Measurements

Deliverables

Quality Control Measurements

Approved Change Requests

Work Performance Information

Inputs

Project Management Plan

This tells you how the project execution is going...

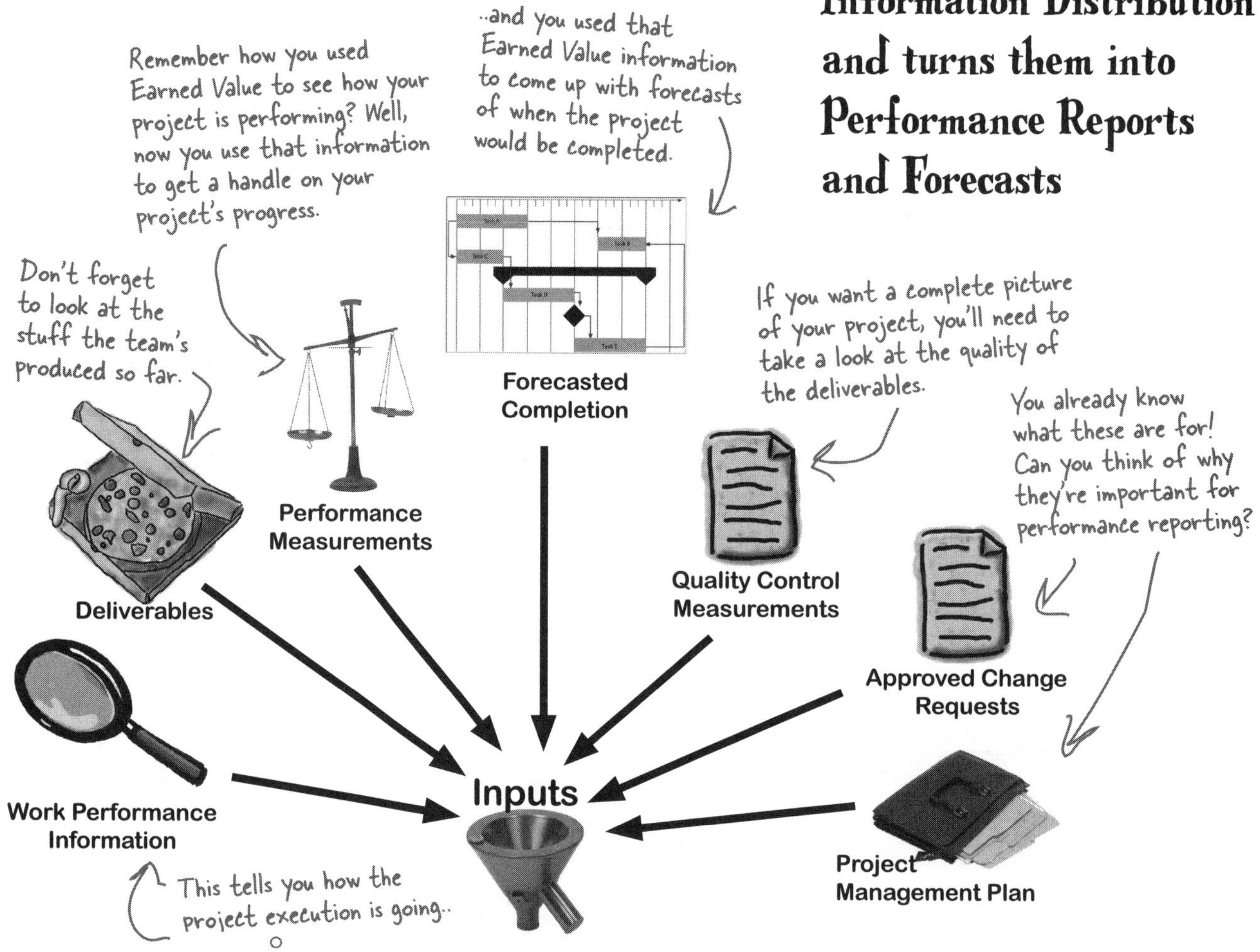

Relax

Performance reports and forecasts are a lot easier than they look—because you already know all about them!

Take a minute and flip back to Cost Control in Chapter 7. You learned how to use CPI and SPI to measure your project's performance, and you used EAC and ETC to forecast when the project would be complete. Now you're just taking that information and communicating it!

Performance Reporting is one of those PMBOK® Guide processes that's really familiar to a lot of project managers. Can you figure out what each of its **tools and techniques** is for just from the name?

Tools

Information Presentation Tools

Performance Information Gathering and Compilation

Status Review Meetings

Time Reporting Systems

Cost Reporting Systems

Performance Reporting is one of those PMBOK® Guide processes that's really familiar to a lot of project managers. Can you figure out what each of its **tools and techniques** is for just from the name?

Information Presentation Tools

Reports, slide presentations, spreadsheets, charts

Have you ever used a PowerPoint presentation to tell the team or your boss how the project is going? Then you were doing Performance Reporting. Take a minute and think about how you'd use each of these to spread the information that you gathered for your project.

Performance Information Gathering and Compilation

Finding all the important information and putting it all together

There's a whole lot of information floating around on a project, and it's your job to get a good handle on all of it. You need to talk to people, take measurements, make forecasts, go through deliverables, and generally get your nose in everything in order to really figure out where the project is. And once you get all of that information, you need to put it together so it makes sense and is easy to work with.

Status Review Meetings

Meetings with the team to go over how the project is doing

There's no better way to gather information than to sit down with the team and talk about the status of the project. You should do this regularly.

Time Reporting Systems

A system to keep track of how much time people spend doing work

Cost Reporting Systems

A system to keep track of how much money is being spent

A lot of people use specialized computer systems to keep track of time and cost. But sometimes all you need is a couple of spreadsheets to get the job done. The important thing is that you've got an organized way of keeping track of the time people are putting into the project and how much money is being spent.

Now you can get the word out

Now that you've gathered up all the information about how the project's being done, it's time to get it out to the people who need it. The **outputs from Performance Reporting** shouldn't be particularly surprising… you're just packaging up the information you collected and turning it all into stuff that's easy to distribute to all the stakeholders.

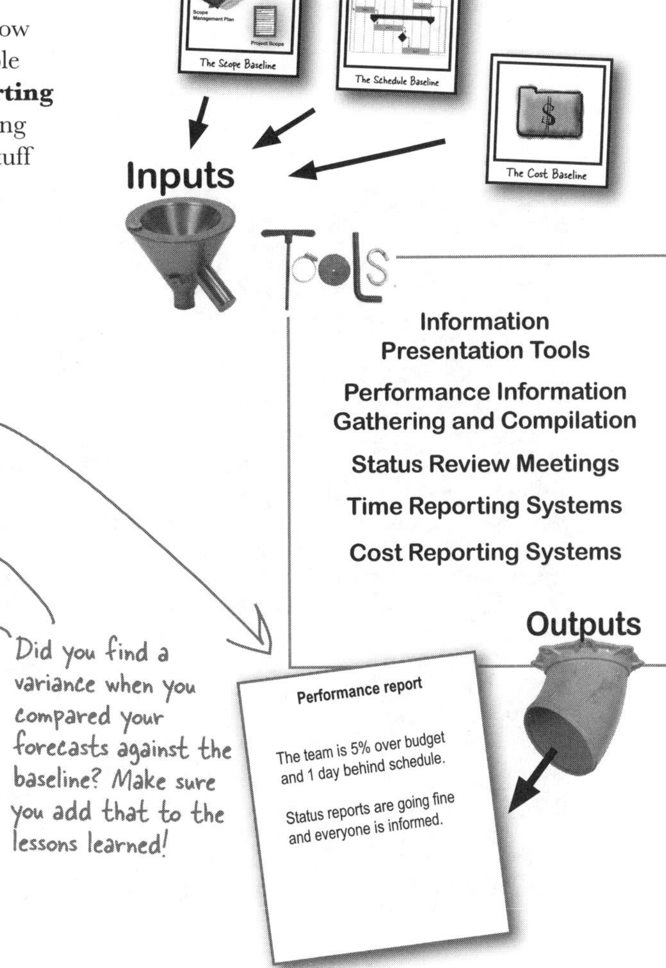

Performance Reports are the most important output of the process—which shouldn't be a surprise, since the process is called Performance Reporting. Your performance reports tell everyone exactly how the project is doing, and how far off it is from its time, cost and scope baselines.

Forecasts are what you turn your EAC and ETC numbers into, so everyone has a good idea of when the project is going to finish.

Lessons learned go into your **Organizational Process Assets**—there are always a lot of lessons to be learned when you're gathering this kind of project information.

Changes happen when you do performance reporting. What do you do if you find out that your forecasts have your project coming in too late or over budget? You put the **change request** in as soon as possible. And if you need the project to change course, you'll need to **recommend corrective actions** to the team.

You've seen these change control outputs several times now. Get ready for change control.

Performance Reporting is about more than just telling people how the project is doing. It's also about finding problems. What kind of problems are you likely to uncover when you sit down with stakeholders and put together your performance reports and forecasts?

Communicationcross

Take some time to sit back and give your right brain something to do. It's your standard crossword; all of the solution words are from this chapter.

Across

3. A contract is always _______ written communication.
4. Information should be distributed to all ___________.
6. When a message is received, the receiver needs to _______ the message before it can be understood.
7. _______ percent of project management is communication.
9. _______ is when a listener uses both verbal and nonverbal clues, like nodding and repeating the listener's words to make sure the message is received.
10. A discussion in a hallway is an example of _________ verbal communication.
11. Most communication on a project takes place in the Information ___________ process.

Down

1. When building the performance reports, it's important to compare the current project performance against the scope, time, cost and _______.
2. This kind of communication includes vocal but nonverbal signals, such as changing the pitch and tone of voice.
5. You can use the ETC and EAC calculations from Cost Management to create _________.
8. This interferes with a message sent from a sender to a receiver.

Answers on page 498.

People aren't talking!

There's so much information floating around on any project, and if you're not careful it won't get to the people who need it. That's why so much of your job is communication—if you don't stay on top of all of it, your project can run into some serious trouble!

The forecast looked good, and everyone was on top of their jobs. We thought we were on track for Friday night. Then all these problems came up...

Problems

- The caterer's serving food that doesn't go with the drinks or theme.
- The DJ and the band want to set up in the same place.
- All the guests are telling us they like different food.
- Has anyone even talked to the neighbors about the noise.
- Three people are bringing friends, but nobody told the caterer.

... How are we gonna get a handle on this?

What's causing all of these problems? Will better communication help?

The **Manage Stakeholders** process is a typical Monitoring & Controlling process. You already know the inputs, tools & techniques, and outputs. See if you can figure out what the inputs, outputs and tools & techniques do from their names, and write down a description for each of them.

Inputs

Communications Management Plan

....

....

....

....

Organizational Process Assets

....

....

....

....

Try to think of ways that these inputs can be used to help resolve communications issues with stakeholders.

Tools

The Communications Methods tool has two pieces: face-to-face communication and holding kickoff meetings. Take an educated guess and write down what you think you do for each of them.

Communications Methods

Face-to-face communication

....

....

....

....

Holding kickoff meetings

....

....

....

....

Manage Stakeholders process

Monitoring & Controlling process group

Since the Manage Stakeholders process is all about resolving communications issues that the stakeholders experience, the tools are focused on communicating with the stakeholders about those issues.

Issue Logs

....

....

....

....

The other tool is Issue Logs. Write down what you think you'd use an issue log for.

Outputs

Resolved Issues

....

....

....

....

Approved Change Requests

....

....

....

....

Approved Corrective Actions

....

....

....

....

Organizational Process Asset Updates

....

....

....

....

Project Management Plan Updates

....

....

....

....

How will the outputs be used to communicate with stakeholders? Don't forget that every team member is a stakeholder!

The **Manage Stakeholders** process is a typical Monitoring & Controlling process. You already know the inputs, tools & techniques, and outputs! See if you can figure out what the inputs, outputs and tools & techniques do from their names, and write down a description for each of them.

Inputs

Communications Management Plan

Tells you how the communication with stakeholders should be handled on the project.

Organizational Process Assets

Stores historical information, lessons learned, and how past projects handled communications problems.

Tools

Communications Methods

Face-to-face communication

This means talking to stakeholders directly in order to resolve any communications problems.

Holding kickoff meetings

Brings all stakeholders together at the beginning of the project to get communications started properly.

Kickoff meetings are really important for any project. You should bring everyone together, go over lessons learned from previous projects, and make sure that each stakeholder knows how communication is supposed to happen. This can help prevent problems down the line.

Manage Stakeholders process

Monitoring & Controlling process group

When you resolve a stakeholder issue, it usually means that you need to make a substantive change to the project—like if you decide the resolution requires staff changes, financial changes, contract changes or other kinds of changes.

Issue Logs
Keeps a running log of all problems and events that happen over the course of the project to make sure they're all addressed.

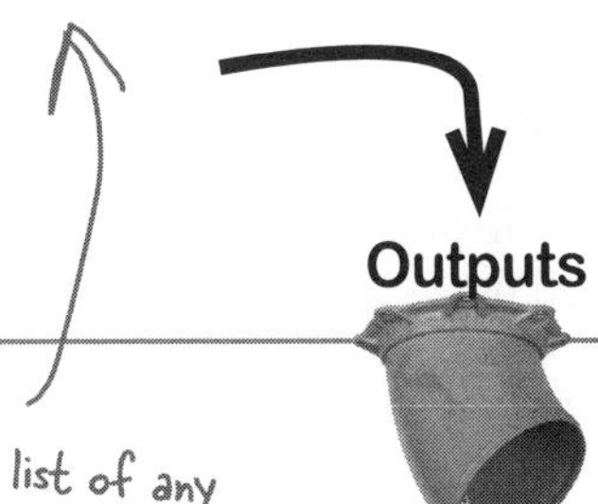

Outputs

An issue log is a running list of any issues that happen during the project. You can use it to monitor the issues and make sure none of them slip through the cracks.

Resolved Issues
The goal of managing stakeholders is to resolve issues, so these are the resolutions that the PM, team and other stakeholders reach.

Approved Change Requests
These are any changes to the project plan or other documents that involve stakeholder communication.

Approved Corrective Actions
These are any corrections to the way the project work is done that involve communication.

Organizational Process Asset Updates
Any lessons learned from talking to stakeholders are added to the Organizational Process Assets.

Project Management Plan Updates
Approved changes actually need to be made to the project plan.

Count the lines of communication

How many people need to talk to each other? Well, Jeff and Charles need to talk. But what about the DJ and the band? They wanted to set up their equipment in the same place—it looks like they need to talk, too. And the bartender needs to coordinate with the caterer… Wow, this is starting to get complicated. A good project manager needs to get a handle on all this communication, because it's really easy to lose track of it. That's why you need to know how to **count the lines of communication** on any project.

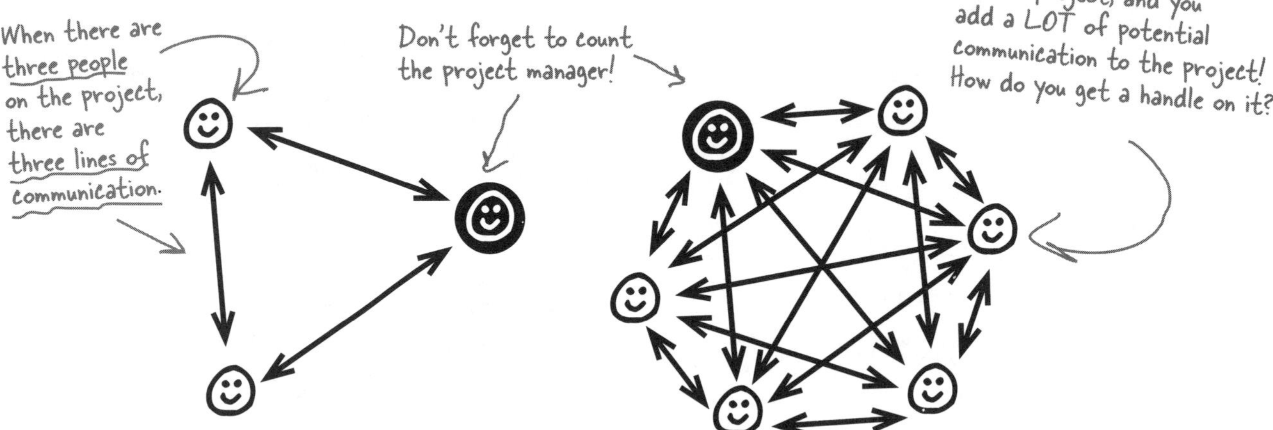

Counting communication lines the easy way

It would be really easy to get overwhelmed if you tried to count all the lines of communication by hand. Luckily, there's a really easy way to do it by using a simple formula. Take the total number of people on the project—including the project manager—and call that number **n**. Then all you need to do is plug that number into this simple formula:

$$\#\text{ lines for n people} = \frac{n \times (n - 1)}{2}$$

You'll need to know this formula on the PMP exam. Just keep using it, though, and you'll get it down in no time.

So, how many more lines of communication were added when three more people joined the three-person project above? You know there were **three lines** to start with. So now just figure out ***how many lines*** there are ***for 6 people***:

$$\#\text{ lines for 6 people} = \frac{6 \times (6 - 1)}{2} = (6 \times 5) \div 2 = 15$$

When you added three more people to the three-person project—that had three lines of communication—the new team has 15 lines. So you **added 12 lines**.

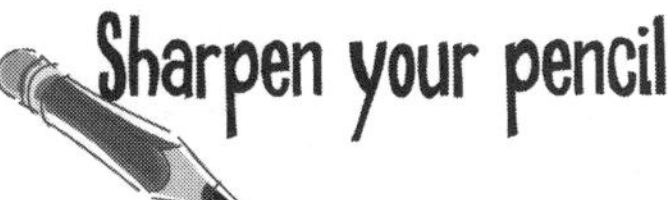

You'll need to know how to calculate the number of lines of communication for the exam… but don't worry, It's really easy, once you get a little practice.

1. You're managing project with five people on the team, plus one additional stakeholder—the sponsor. Draw in all the lines of communication on this picture.

Don't forget the project manager. There are six people on the team, but the total number of people who need to communicate is seven people, because the PM needs to communicate with the team members and sponsor.

2. Wow, that was a lot of work. Luckily, you won't need to do that again. Now do it the easy way: use the formula to figure out how many lines of communication there are for seven people.

$$\text{\# lines for} \ldots \text{ people} = \frac{\ldots \times (\ldots - 1)}{2} = (\ldots \times \ldots) \div 2 = \ldots$$

3. Okay, now let's say that you've added two team members and two more stakeholders, so there are now 11 people on the project who need to communicate with one other. How many lines did you add?

First figure out how many lines there are for 11 people:

$$\text{\# lines for} \ldots \text{ people} = \frac{\ldots \times (\ldots - 1)}{2} = (\ldots \times \ldots) \div 2 = \ldots$$

So how many lines were added when four people joined the seven-person project?

 # lines added = # lines for 11 people - # lines for 7 people

$$= \ldots - \ldots = \ldots$$

Answers on page 499.

there are no Dumb Questions

Q: Some of those communication skills seem like the same thing. What's the difference between active and effective listening?

A: Some of the communications ideas do have names that are a little confusing. But don't worry, they're really easy concepts for you to understand.

Active listening just means when you're listening to something, you keep alert and take specific actions that help make sure you understand. It includes both effective listening and feedback. Effective listening is a way that you do active listening—it means paying attention to both verbal and nonverbal communication. Feedback means doing things like repeating back the words that you were told in order to make sure you understood them, and giving your own nonverbal cues to show the speaker that you got the message.

Q: Okay, so what about nonverbal and paralingual communication? Aren't those the same thing?

A: They *are* very similar, but they're not exactly the same. Nonverbal communication is any kind of communication that doesn't use words. That includes things like changing your body language, making eye contact, and using gestures. Paralingual communication is a kind of nonverbal communication—it's changing your tone of voice or intonation, finding ways to communicate things above and beyond just the words that you're saying. For example, the same words mean very different things if you say them sarcastically than if you say them in a normal tone of voice.

Q: Why is all that stuff about different kinds of communication important?

A: It's important because 90% of project management is communication, so if you want to be the best project manager that you can be, you need to constantly work to improve your communication skills!

Q: Should I always have a kickoff meeting?

A: Yes, absolutely! You should always have a kickoff meeting for every project. Not only that, but if you're running the kind of project with several phases, and you go through all of the process groups for each phase, then you should have a separate kickoff meeting for each new phase. Kickoff meetings also help you define who's responsible for various communications. Kickoff meetings are really important, because they give the team a chance to meet face-to-face, and give you the opportunity to make sure that everyone really understands all of the ways they can communicate with each other. That's a great way to head off a lot of potential project problems!

Q: Why do I need to be able to calculate the number of lines of communication?

A: It may seem like the lines of communication formula is something arbitrary that you just need to memorize for the exam, but it's actually pretty useful.

Let's say that you have a project with a whole lot of people on it. You set up a good communication system in your communication management plan, but you want to make sure that you really included every line in it, because if you missed one then you could run into communications problems down the line. So what do you do? Well, one thing you can do to check your work is to calculate the total number of lines of communication in your project, and then make sure that every one of those lines is represented somewhere in your communications plan. It's a little more work up front, but it could really save you a lot of effort down the line!

Q: I spent all that time working on performance reports. What do I do with them once I'm done with them?

A: The same thing you do with any information that you generate on your project. You add them to your Organizational Process Assets!

Think back to how you came up with your estimates in Time Management and Cost Management. You spent a lot of time doing Analogous Estimation, right? That's where you use performance from past projects to come up with a rough, top-down estimate for your new project. Well, where do you think the performance information from those past projects came from? You got them from your Organizational Process Assets. And how did they end up there? Project managers from those past projects took their performance reports and added them. So you should add your performance reports, too. That way, project managers on future projects can use your project when they need to look up historical data.

You should add all of your performance reports to the Organizational Process Assets so that project managers on future projects can use them as historical information.

It's party time!

The Head First Lounge party is a big hit! Everything came together beautifully, and Jeff and Charles are the new downtown sensation!

Head First
Lounge Two:
Underground

Man! We are ***SO*** going to have to open another one of these Lounges!

Question Clinic: The Calculation Question

You'll run across a bunch of questions on the exam asking you to use some of the formulas that you learned. Luckily, these are some of the easiest questions that you can answer.

This is the wrong answer you'd get if you calculate the the number of lines of communication BEFORE include the team and two sponsors, but forget to include the project manager.

12. You're managing a project with two client sponsors, and you have a 10-person team reporting to you. You've been given a budget increase, which allowed you to increase your team size by 30%. How many lines of communication were added?

A. 66

B. 78

C. 120

D. 42

This wrong answer is the number of lines of communication BEFORE the team size was increased. You have 13 people (10 team members, 2 client sponsors and you), so the number of lines is $13 \times 12 \div 2 = 78$

This wrong answer is the number of lines of communication AFTER the team size was increased by 30%. You have 16 people (13 team members, 2 client sponsors and you), so the number of lines is $16 \times 15 \div 2 = 120$

Aha! Here's the right answer. Take the number of lines for 16 people and subtract the number of lines for 13 people: $120 - 78 = 42$

When you sit down to take an exam at a computer testing center, you'll be given scratch paper. You'll also have 15 minutes to go through a tutorial that shows you how use the exam system. Before you finish the tutorial, take a minute and write down all of the formulas. Write down the earned value formulas and the formula to calculate the lines of communication on the scratch paper. That will make any calculation question easy.

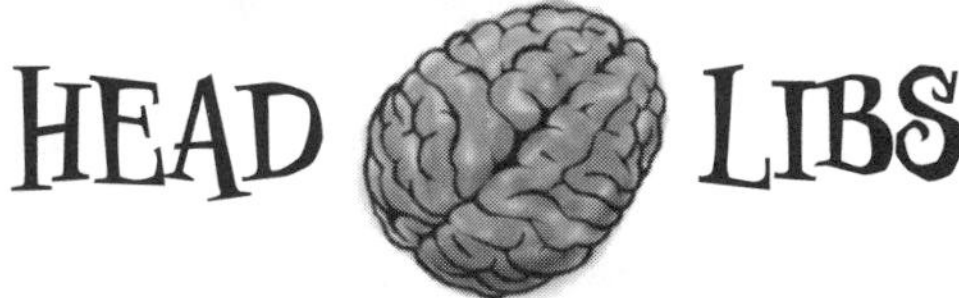

Try coming up with your own calculation question! But this time, try using one of the Earned Value formulas from Chapter 7.

You are managing a ______________________ project.
(kind of project)

You have ______________________, ______________________,
(a value needed for the calculation) (another value needed for the calculation)

and ______________________.
(an irrelevant value that is NOT needed for the calculation)

Calculate ______________________ for your project.
(name of a formula)

A. ______________________
(the answer you'd get if you plug the wrong value into the formula)

B. ______________________
(the answer you'd get if you used the wrong formula)

C. ______________________
(the correct answer)

D. ______________________
(a totally bizarre answer that comes out of nowhere)

Join the Head First PMP community at **http://www.headfirstlabs.com/PMP**
You can add your Head Libs answer, and see what Head Libs other project managers came up with!

WHAT'S MY PURPOSE

Match each communication element to what it does

- Sender → The person who needs to initiate the communication
- Receiver → The person who gets the message
- Medium → The thing used to transmit the message
- Feedback → A response to a message
- Noise → Something that interferes with the message
- Encode → Modifying a message so that it can be sent
- Decode → Modifying a message that has been sent so that it can be understood

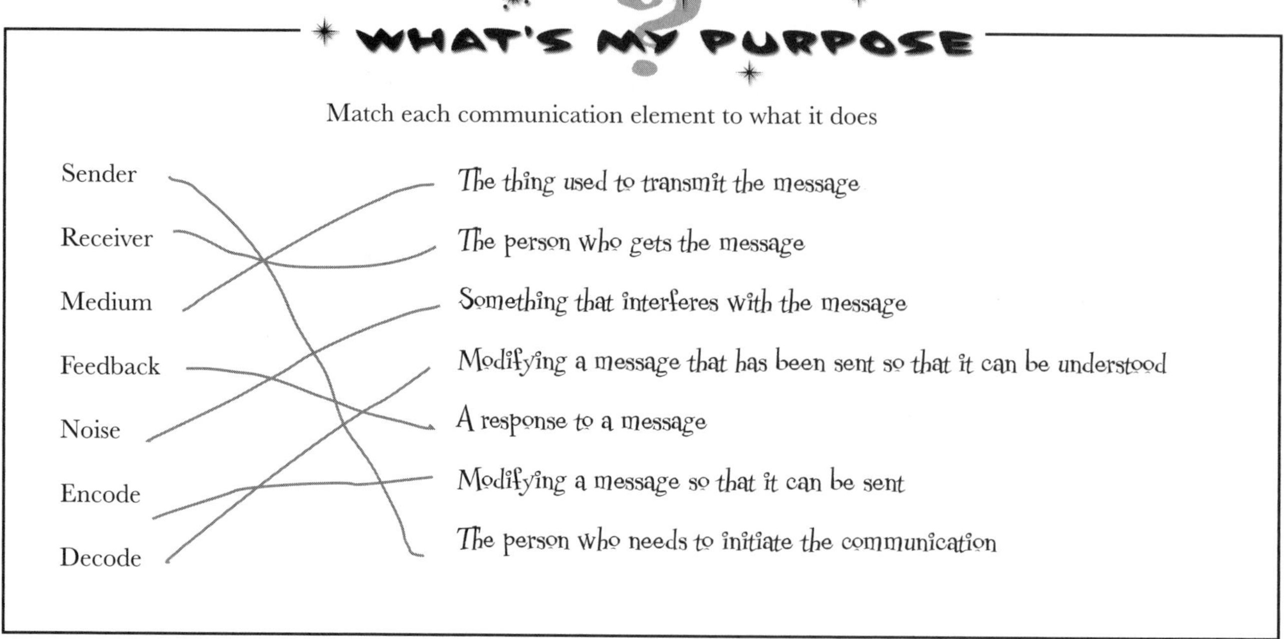

Exercise Solution

Jeff and Charles are interviewing new bartenders to help with the expanded space. Choose which kind of communication is being used in each situation.

1. One applicant came in 30 minutes late, and was dressed unprofessionally. The guys knew that he would not be a good fit for the position.

   [X] Paralingual [ ] Nonverbal [ ] Feedback

2. Charles asked an applicant about her background. Her tone of voice was really sarcastic, and he got the impression she didn't take the job seriously. Charles and Jeff decided to pass on her too.

   [ ] Paralingual [X] Nonverbal [ ] Feedback

3. Charles asked the next applicant if he knew how to make a sidecar. He said "A sidecar? Sure. It's one part brandy or cognac, one part Cointreau, and one part lemon juice."

   [ ] Paralingual [ ] Nonverbal [X] Feedback

4. Then the applicant told them about his background as a bartender for other retro clubs. As he spoke, he made eye contact with them and made sure to confirm agreement with them.

   [ ] Paralingual [X] Nonverbal [ ] Feedback

The candidate repeated the question. That's a great example of feedback.

Choose which kind of communication is being used in each situation.

1. You and your business analysts write a requirements specification for your project.

- [ ] Formal verbal
- [ ] Informal verbal
- [x] Formal written
- [ ] Informal written

2. You call up the executive who is backing your project to let him or her know that you are on schedule and expect to deliver under budget.

- [ ] Formal verbal
- [x] Informal verbal
- [ ] Formal written
- [ ] Informal written

3. You present your project's status to your company's executive committee.

- [x] Formal verbal
- [ ] Informal verbal
- [ ] Formal written
- [ ] Informal written

4. You send an email to some of your team members to get more information about an issue that has been identified on your project.

- [ ] Formal verbal
- [ ] Informal verbal
- [ ] Formal written
- [x] Informal written

5. You leave a voicemail message for your test team lead following up on an issue he or she found.

- [ ] Formal verbal
- [x] Informal verbal
- [ ] Formal written
- [ ] Informal written

6. You IM with your team members.

- [ ] Formal verbal
- [ ] Informal verbal
- [ ] Formal written
- [x] Informal written

7. You prepare an RFP (request for proposals) for vendors to determine which of them will get a chance to contract a new project with your company.

- [ ] Formal verbal
- [ ] Informal verbal
- [x] Formal written
- [ ] Informal written

Anything that has to do with a contract is always formal written.

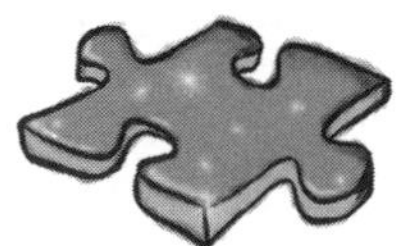

Communicationcross

Take some time to sit back and give your right brain something to do. It's your standard crossword; all of the solution words are from this chapter.

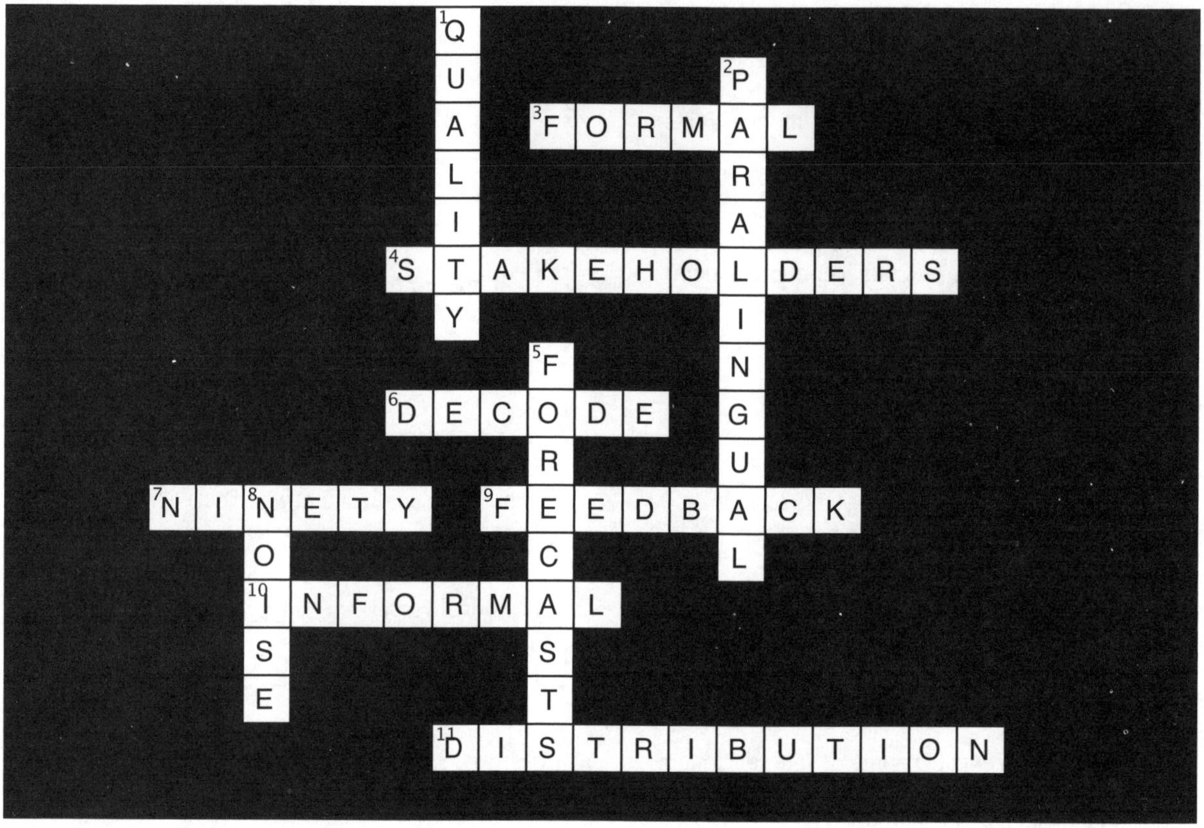

Across

3. FORMAL
4. STAKEHOLDERS
6. DECODE
7. NINETY
9. FEEDBACK
10. INFORMAL
11. DISTRIBUTION

Down

1. QUALITY
2. PARALINGUAL
5. FORECAST
8. NOISE

You'll need to know how to calculate the number of lines of communication for the exam... but don't worry, It's really easy, once you get a little practice.

1. You're managing a project with five people on the team, plus one additional stakeholder—the sponsor. Draw in all the lines of communication on this picture.

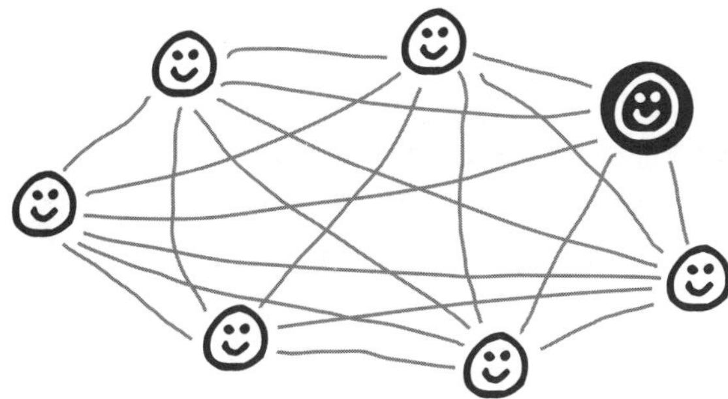

2. Wow, that was a lot of work. Luckily, you won't need to do that again. Now do it the easy way: use the formula to figure out how many lines of communication there are for seven people.

$$\text{\# lines for } 7 \text{ people} = \frac{7 \times (7 - 1)}{2} = (7 \times 6) \div 2 = 21$$

3. Okay, now let's say that you've added two team members and two more stakeholders, so there are now 11 people on the project who need to communicate with one other. How many lines did you add?

First figure out how many lines there are for 11 people:

$$\text{\# lines for } 11 \text{ people} = \frac{11 \times (11 - 1)}{2} = (11 \times 10) \div 2 = 55$$

So how many lines were added when four people joined the seven-person project?

 # lines added = # lines for 11 people - # lines for 7 people

$$= 55 - 21 = 34$$

Exam Questions

1. Keith, the project manager of a large publishing project, sends an invoice to his client. Which communication type is he using?

A. Formal verbal

B. Formal written

C. Informal written

D. Informal verbal

2. Which of the following is NOT an input to the Communications Planning process?

A. Enterprise environmental factors

B. Organizational process assets

C. Information gathering techniques

D. Project scope statement

3. You take over for a project manager who has left the company and realize that team is talking directly to the customer and only having status meetings when there are problems. The programming team has one idea about the goals of the project, and the testing team has another. Which document is the FIRST one that you should create to solve this problem?

A. Communication plan

B. Status report

C. Meeting agenda

D. Performance report

4. You ask one of your stakeholders how things are going on her part of the project and she says "things are *fine*" in a sarcastic tone. Which is the BEST way to describe the kind of communication that she used?

A. Feedback

B. Active listening

C. Nonverbal

D. Paralingual

5. You're managing an industrial design project. You created a communication plan, and now the team is working on the project. You've been communicating with your team, and now you're looking at the work performance information to evaluate the performance of the project. Which of the following BEST describes the next thing you should do?

A. Use formal written communication to inform the client of the project status

B. Compare the work performance information against the time, cost and scope baselines and look for deviations

C. Update the organizational process assets with your lessons learned

D. Hold a status meeting

Exam Questions

6. You have five people working on your team, a sponsor within your company, and a client, all of whom need to be kept informed of your project's progress. How many lines of communication are there?

A. 28

B. 21

C. 19

D. 31

7. Which of the following is NOT an example of active listening?

A. Nodding your head in agreement while someone is talking

B. Restating what has been said to be sure you understand it

C. Asking questions for clarification

D. Multitasking by checking your email during a conversation

8. Sue sent a message to Jim using the company's voicemail system. When he received it, Jim called her back. Which of the following is true?

A. Sue encoded the voicemail, Jim decoded it, and then encoded his feedback message.

B. Sue decoded her voicemail message; Jim encoded his phone call and decoded the feedback.

C. Jim sent feedback to Sue, who encoded it.

D. Sue decoded her voicemail message and Jim encoded his feedback.

9. You're managing a construction project. Suddenly the customer asks for some major changes to the blueprints. You need to talk to him about this. What's the BEST form of communication to use?

A. Informal written

B. Informal verbal

C. Formal written

D. Formal verbal

10. Kyle is the project manager of a project that has teams distributed in many different places. In order to make sure that they all get the right message, he needs to make sure that his project plan is translated into Spanish, Hindi, French, and German. What is Kyle doing when he has his communications translated?

A. Encoding

B. Decoding

C. Active listening

D. Effective listening

Exam Questions

11. There are 15 people on a project (including the project manager). How many lines of communication are there?

A. 105

B. 112

C. 113

D. 52

12. Which communication processes are in the Monitoring & Controlling process group?

A. Information Distribution, Performance Reporting

B. Manage Stakeholders, Information Distribution

C. Communication Planning, Performance Reporting

D. Performance Reporting, Manage Stakeholders

13. You're working at a major conglomerate. You have a 24-person team working for you on a project with five major sponsors. The company announces layoffs, and your team is reduced to half its size. How many lines of communication are on your new, smaller team?

A. 66

B. 153

C. 276

D. 406

14. You've consulted your Earned Value calculations to find out the EAC and ETC of your project. Which of the following is the BEST place to put that information?

A. Work performance information

B. Forecasts

C. Quality control measurements

D. Lessons learned

15. Which of the following is an example of noise?

A. An email that's sent to the wrong person

B. A project manager who doesn't notice an important clause in a contract

C. Garbled text and smudges that make a fax of a photocopy hard to read

D. When the team is not paying attention during a status meeting

Exam Questions

1. Answer: B

Any communication that can be used for legal purposes is considered formal written communication. An invoice is a formal document.

See the word, "technique"? That's a good indication that it's a tool and not an input.

2. Answer: C

Information gathering techniques are part of Information Distribution but not part of Communications Planning.

3. Answer: A

The Communication Plan is the first thing you need to create in this situation. It will help you organize the meetings that are taking place and get everyone on the same page. The communication plan will help you to streamline communications so that the customer can use you as a single point of contact, too.

I get it! You can't do any communications unless you've got a good communication plan.

4. Answer: D

Paralingual communication happens when additional information is conveyed by the tone or pitch of your voice. It's when you use more than just words to communicate.

5. Answer: B

When you look at work performance information, you're in the Performance Reporting process. And what do you do with the work performance information? You compare it against the baselines to see if your project is on track! If it isn't, that's when you want to get the word out as quickly as possible.

A lot of people choose B here. Don't forget to include yourself! Look out for questions like this on the exam too.

6. Answer: A

The formula for lines of communication is n x (n-1) ÷ 2. In this problem there were seven people named, plus you. (8x7) ÷ 2 = 28.

Exam ~~Questions~~ Answers

7. Answer: D

All of the other options show the speaker that you understand what they are saying. That's active listening.

Active listening is saying things like "I agree," or "can you explain that a little further?"

8. Answer: A

This question is just asking if you know the definitions of encode, decode, and feedback. Encoding is making a message ready for other people to understand, while decoding it involves receiving the message and understanding it. Feedback means letting the sender know that you got the message.

Anytime you see anything about a formal document in communication with a client, it's Formal written.

9. Answer: C

Anytime you are communicating with the customer about the scope of your project, it's a good idea to use Formal Written communication.

10. Answer: A

He has to encode his message so that others will understand it.

11. Answer: A

(15 x 14) ÷ 2 = 105 This one is just asking if you know the formula n x (n-1) ÷ 2.

12. Answer: D

Performance Reporting and Manage Stakeholders are the two Monitoring & Controlling processes.

Exam ~~Questions~~

13. Answer: B

There are now 12 team members, five sponsors and a project manager. That gives you 18 people. Use the formula: n x (n – 1) ÷ 2 to calculate this: 18 x 17 ÷ 2 = 153.

Did you get one of the other answers? Make sure you included the five sponsors and the project manager!

14. Answer: B

The idea behind forecasts is that you are using the Earned Value calculations that forecast the completion of the project to set everyone's expectations. That's why you use EAC (which tells you how much you're expecting to spend) and ETC (which gives you a good idea of how long it will take).

Oh, I get it. I already came up with good cost and time forecasts using EAC and ETC. Now I can package them up as forecasts and tell them to the team.

15. Answer: C

There are plenty of ways that communication can go wrong. When you send email to the wrong person, your communication had trouble—but that's **not** noise. Noise is the specific thing that interferes with the communication. In this case, the garbled text is a great example of noise.

11 Project Risk Management

Planning for the Unknown

Even the most carefully planned project can run into trouble. No matter how well you plan, your project can always run into **unexpected problems**. Team members get sick or quit, resources that you were depending on turn out to be unavailable—even the weather can throw you for a loop. So does that mean that you're helpless against unknown problems? No! You can use ***risk planning*** to identify potential problems that could cause trouble for your project, **analyze** how likely they'll be to occur, take action to **prevent** the risks you can avoid, and **minimize** the ones that you can't.

What's a risk?

There are no guarantees on any project! Even the simplest activity can run into unexpected problems. Any time there's anything that ***might*** occur on your project and change the outcome of a project activity, we call that a **risk**. A risk can be an event (like a fire), or it can be a condition (like an important part being unavailable). Either way, it's something that may or may not happen... but if it does, then it will force you to change the way you and your team will work on the project.

A risk is any uncertain event or condition that might affect your project. Not all risks are negative.

Not all risks are negative

Some events (like finding an easier way to do an activity) or conditions (like lower prices for certain materials) can help your project! When this happens, we call it an **opportunity**… but it's still handled just like a risk.

How you deal with risk

When you're planning your project, risks are still uncertain: they haven't happened yet. But eventually, some of the risks that you plan for *do* happen. And that's when you have to deal with them. There are four basic ways to handle a risk:

1 Avoid

The best thing that you can do with a risk is avoid it—if you can prevent it from happening, it definitely won't hurt your project.

2 Mitigate

If you can't avoid the risk, you can mitigate it. This means taking some sort of action that will cause it to do as little damage to your project as possible.

3 Transfer

One effective way to deal with a risk is to pay someone else to accept it for you. The most common way to do this is to buy insurance.

4 Accept

When you can't avoid, mitigate, or transfer a risk, then you have to accept it. But even when you accept a risk, at least you've looked at the alternatives and you know what will happen if it occurs.

Risk Management Planning

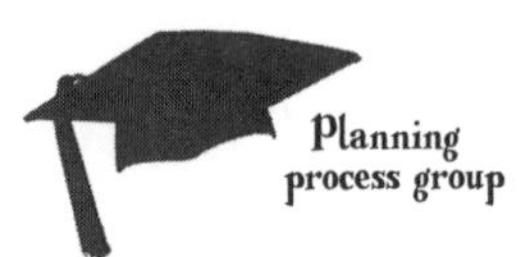

By now, you should have a pretty good feel for how each of the planning processes work. The past few knowledge areas started out with their own planning process, and Risk Management is no different. You start with the **Risk Management Planning** process, which should look very familiar to you.

By the time a risk actually occurs on your project, it's too late to do anything about it. That's why you need to plan for risks from the beginning and keep coming back to do more planning throughout the project.

Inputs

You'll need to see if there are standard templates, roles and responsibilities, or risk categories that your company uses.

Organizational Process Assets

Enterprise Environmental Factors

Are people at your company risk takers? Do they play it safe? Every company has people with different attitudes about risk.

Project Scope Statement

Project Management Plan

You should be able to figure out why you need the project management plan and the scope statement. Take a minute to think it through.

Watch it!

Are you starting to see a pattern here?

You may get a question on the exam that asks which processes use Organizational Process Assets! Think about why you need them for Risk Management Planning and the other planning processes. That should help you remember which processes need 'em.

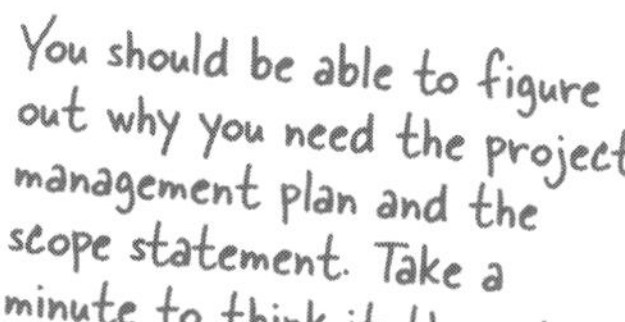

The Risk Management Plan is the only output

It tells you how you're going to handle risk on your project—which you probably guessed, since that's what management plans do. It says how you'll assess risk on the project, who's responsible for doing it, and how often you'll do risk planning (since you'll have to meet about risk planning with your team throughout the project).

The plan has parts that are really useful for managing risk:

- ❑ It has a bunch of categories that you'll use to classify your risks. Some risks are technical, like a component that might turn out to be difficult to use. Others are external, like changes in the market or even problems with the weather.
- ❑ You might find a Risk Breakdown Structure (RBS) here. It's a great tool for managing your risk categories. It looks like a WBS, except instead of tasks it shows how the risks break down into categories.
- ❑ It's important to come up with guidelines to help you figure out how big a risk's impact is. The impact tells you how much damage the risk will cause to your project. A lot of projects classify impact on a scale from minimal to severe, or from very low to very high.
- ❑ The plan should also give you a scale to help figure out the probability of the risk. Some risks are very likely; others aren't.

The risk management plan is your guide to identifying and analyzing risks on your project.

Risk Management Plan

It tells you who identifies and analyzes the risks, how they do it, and how often it happens.

Use a risk breakdown structure to categorize risks

You should build guidelines for risk categories into your risk management plan, and the easiest way to do that is to use a **risk breakdown structure** (RBS). Notice how it looks a lot like a WBS? It's a similar idea—you come up with major risk categories, and then decompose them into more detailed ones.

This is what an RBS looks like. The idea here is that you want to come up with a way to take each risk and give it a category.

When you sit down with the team to come up with a list of risks, the RBS will be really useful. The categories are a great reminder when you're brainstorming.

The RBS is just one way to categorize risks. It's not a tool or technique by itself; you'll include it as part of the Risk Management Plan.

- **Project Risks**
  - **Technical Risks**
    - Quality Issues
    - Part Compatibility
  - **External Risks**
    - Weather Problems
    - Customer Issues
    - New Government Regulations
  - **Organizational Risks**
    - Staff Attrition
    - Project Priority Changes
    - Funding Cuts

Once you come up with a list of risks, you'll label each one of them with one of these categories. That will make it easier to figure out how to deal with the risks later.

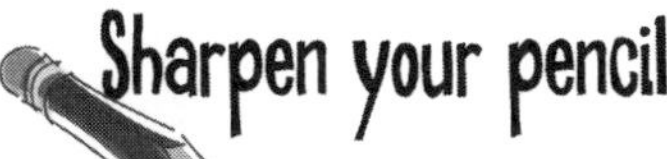

Take a look at how each of these project risks is handled and figure out if the risk is being avoided, mitigated, transferred, or accepted.

1. Stormy weather and high winds could cause very slippery conditions, so you put up a tent and wear slip-resistant footwear to keep from losing your footing.

   ☐ Avoided ☐ Mitigated
   ☐ Transferred ☐ Accepted

2. You buy a surge protector to make sure a lightning strike won't blow out all of your equipment.

   ☐ Avoided ☐ Mitigated
   ☐ Transferred ☐ Accepted

3. Flooding could cause serious damage to your equipment, so you buy an insurance policy that covers flood damage.

   ☐ Avoided ☐ Mitigated
   ☐ Transferred ☐ Accepted

4. The manufacturer issues a warning that the safety equipment you are using has a small but nonzero probability of failure under the conditions that you'll be facing. You replace it with more appropriate equipment.

   ☐ Avoided ☐ Mitigated
   ☐ Transferred ☐ Accepted

5. A mud slide would be very damaging to your project, but there's nothing you can do about it.

   ☐ Avoided ☐ Mitigated
   ☐ Transferred ☐ Accepted

6. A team member discovers that the location you planned on using is in a county that is considering regulations that could be expensive to comply with. You work with a surveying team to find a new location.

   ☐ Avoided ☐ Mitigated
   ☐ Transferred ☐ Accepted

7. Surrounding geological features could interfere with your communications equipment, so you bring a flare gun and rescue beacon in case it fails.

   ☐ Avoided ☐ Mitigated
   ☐ Transferred ☐ Accepted

Answers: 1 - mitigated 2 - mitigated 3 - transferred 4 - avoided 5 - accepted 6 - avoided 7 - mitigated

Anatomy of a Risk

Once you're done with Risk Planning, there are four more risk management processes that will help you and your team come up with the list of risks for your project, analyze how they could affect your project, and plan how you and your team will respond if any of the risks materialize when you're executing the project.

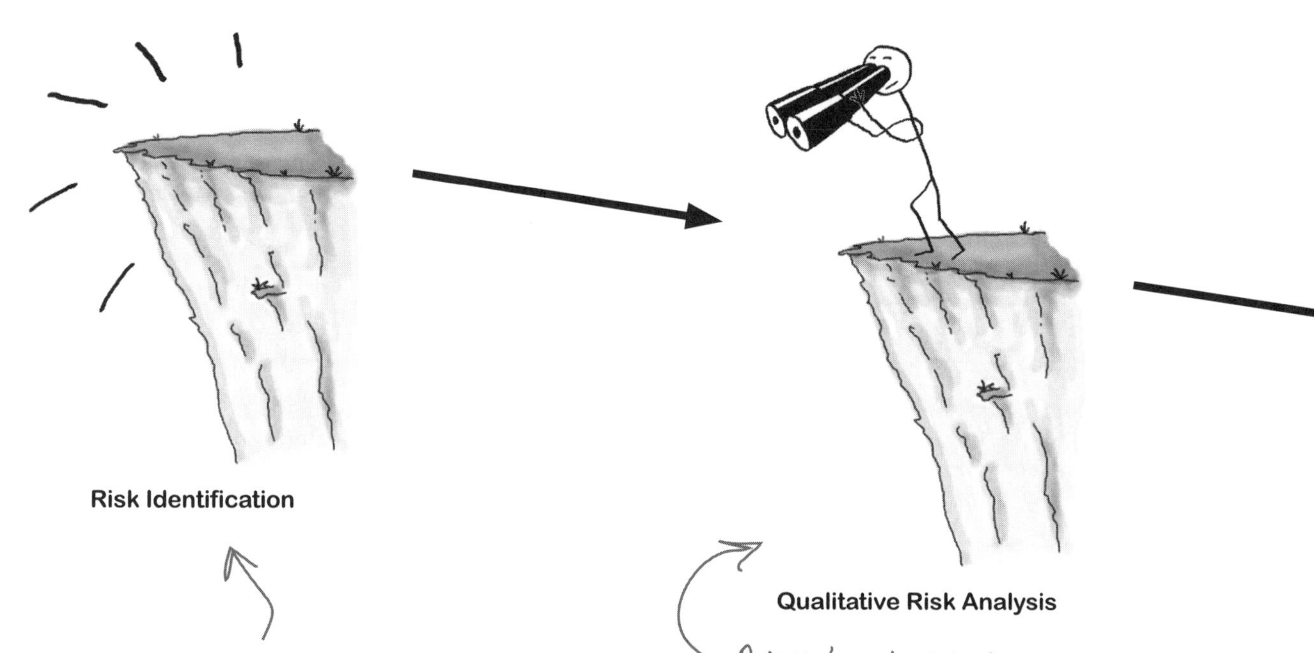

The first thing you need to do when planning for risks is to gather the team together and come up with a list of every possible risk you can think of.

The RBS you created during Risk Management Planning will make it a lot easier to do this.

Once you've got a list of risks, you'll need to get a good idea of the probability and impact of each risk.

Remember the probability and impact guidelines in the risk management plan? This is where you use them to assign a probability and impact to each risk!

By the time you get here, you've got a list of risks, with a probability and impact assigned to each risk. That's a great starting point, but sometimes you need more information if you want to make good decisions...

All four of these Risk Management processes are in the Planning process group—you need to plan for your project's risks before you start executing the project.

Quantitative Risk Analysis

...You can make better decisions with more precise information. That's what this process is about—assigning numerical values for the probability and impact of each risk.

All that's left now is to plan responses to each risk! This is where you decide whether to avoid, mitigate, transfer, or accept... and how you'll do it!

Risk Response Planning

Why do you need to do qualitative risk analysis first and quantitative risk analysis second?

What could happen to your project?

Planning process group

You can't plan for risks until you've figured out which ones you're likely to run into. That's why the first risk management process is **Risk Identification**. The idea is that you want to figure out every possible risk that might affect your project. Don't worry about how unlikely the risk is, or how bad the impact would be—you'll figure that stuff out later.

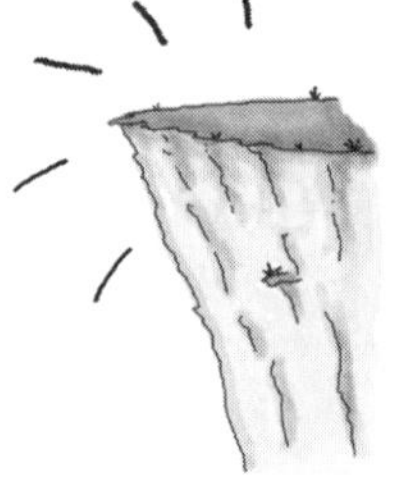

Risk Identification

Remember the assumptions you put in here? Those are all risks—if you assume something that's not true, it will change the project.

You should look at lessons learned from past projects to see what went wrong.

Risk Management Plan

Project Management Plan

Organizational Process Assets

Project Scope Statement

Enterprise Environmental Factors

Inputs

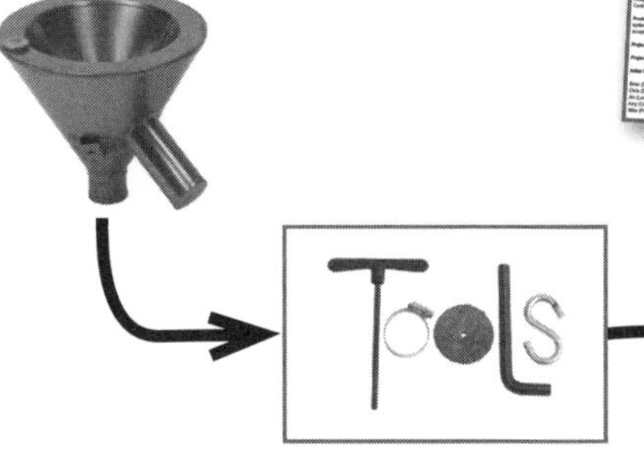

The tools and techniques—especially Risk Identification—are all about gathering information from people and making sure it's right.

The goal of all of the risk planning processes is to produce the risk register. That's your main weapon against risk.

Identified Risks	Potential Responses	Root Causes
Landslide caused by loose gravel and dirt on the nearby mountain	Put up barrier or dig trench	Geological data review found loose topsoil nearby
High winds can lead to cliff disaster	Reinforce tent stakes; obtain weatherproof equipment	National weather service predicts 35% chance of high winds
Truck rental is unavailable	Pay to reserve equipment at a second company	Higher than expected demand for equipment in the area this season
Equipment failure during project	No responses were found by the team	Recent industry report cites higher-than-expected failure rates for critical equipment

Risk Register

The risk register is the only output—and it's the most important part of risk management. It's a list of all of the risks and some initial ideas about how you'd respond to them.

Information gathering techniques for Risk Identification

You probably already guessed that the goal of risk identification is to identify risks—seems pretty obvious, right? And the most important way to identify those risks is to gather information from the team. That's why the first—and most important—technique in Risk Identification is called **Information Gathering Techniques**. These are time-tested and effective ways to get information from your team, stakeholders, and anyone else that might have information on risks.

Five useful information gathering techniques

There are a lot of different ways that you can find risks on your project. But there are only a few that you're most likely to use—and those are the ones that you will run across on the exam.

Brainstorming is the first thing you should do with your team. Get them all together in a room, and start pumping out ideas. Brainstorming sessions always have a **facilitator** to lead the team and help turn their ideas into a list of risks.

The facilitator is really important—without her, it's just a disorderly meeting with no clear goal.

The team usually comes up with risks that have to do with building the product, while the sponsor or someone who would use the product will think about how it could end up being difficult to use.

Interviews are a really important part of identifying risk. Try to find everyone who might have an opinion and ask them about what could cause trouble on the project. The sponsor or client will think about the project in a very different way than the project team.

The Delphi technique is a way to get opinions and ideas from experts. This is another technique that uses a facilitator, but instead of gathering team members in a room, they send questionnaires to experts asking about important project risks. They take those answers and circulates them all to the experts—but each expert is kept **anonymous** so that they can give honest feedback.

The Delphi technique is always anonymous. People will give more honest opinions if they know their names won't be attached to them.

SWOT analysis lets you analyze strengths, weaknesses, opportunities, and threats.

Root cause identification is analyzing each risk and figuring out what's actually behind it. Even though falling off of the cliff and having your tent blow away are two separate risks, when you take a closer look you might find that they're both caused by the **same thing**: high winds, which is the root cause for both of them. So you know that if you get high winds, you need to be on the lookout for *both* risks!

What's the big difference between Brainstorming and the Delphi Technique? Can you think of a situation where one would be more useful than the other?

More risk identification techniques

Even though gathering information is the biggest part of risk identification, it's not the only part of it. There are other tools and techniques that you'll use to make sure that the risk register you put together has as many risks as possible. The more you know about risk going into the project, the better you'll handle surprises when they happen. And that's what these tools and techniques are for—looking far and wide to get every risk possible.

Documentation reviews are when you look at plans, requirements, documents from your organizational process assets, and any other relevant documents that you can find to squeeze every possible risk out of them.

The RBS you created in Risk Planning is a good place to start for this. You can use all the risks you categorized in it as a jumping-off point.

Assumptions analysis is what you're doing when you look over your project's assumptions. Remember how important assumptions were when you were estimating the project? Well, now it's time to look back at the assumptions you made and make sure that they really are things you can assume about the project. Wrong assumptions are definitely a risk.

The team made assumptions during planning to deal with incomplete information... and there's a risk that each assumption could turn out to be wrong.

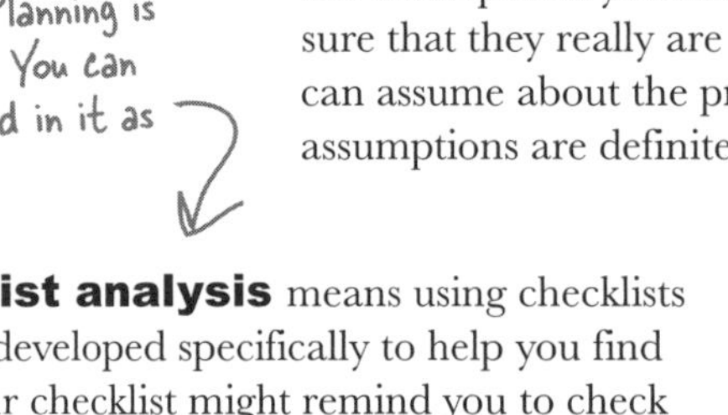

Checklist analysis means using checklists that you developed specifically to help you find risks. Your checklist might remind you to check certain assumptions, talk to certain people, or review documents you might have overlooked.

Diagramming techniques should be pretty familiar to you already. You can use the Ishikawa or Fishbone diagrams from Quality Management to help you find the root cause of a risk, just like you did for a defect. You can also use flowcharts to see how parts of your system interact—any place where they get complex or uncertain is a good source of risks.

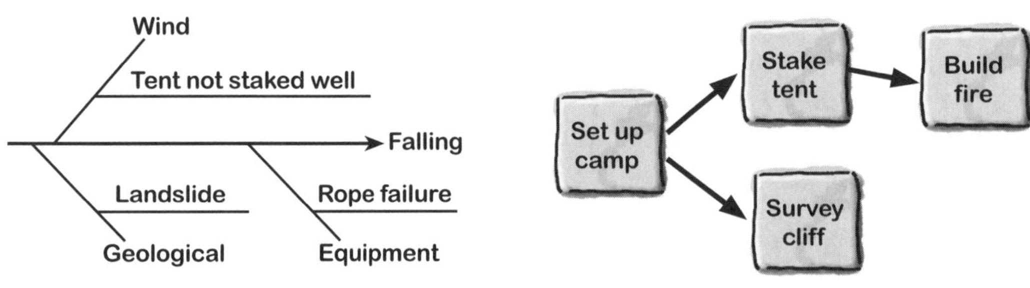

Fishbone or Ishikawa Diagram

Flowchart

Read each of these scenarios and identify which tool or technique is being used. If a scenario uses an information gathering technique, specify which one.

1. Your project requires that you set up a campsite on the edge of a cliff. You gather your team members, including a geologist, a meteorologist, a tracker, and three campsite workers, and lead them in a directed discussion where they identify as many risks as possible.

2. You look through your company's asset library and discover that two previous projects involved setting up camp in this area. You look through the lessons learned to figure out what went wrong, and what could have been avoided through better planning.

3. You've sent a questionnaire to a park ranger and engineers at tent and hiking equipment companies to gather their opinions on the risk of falling off of a cliff. You remove their names from their responses, copy them, and send them back to everyone to get their feedback.

4. You've identified a risk that is very complex, so you identify the root cause. You use the Ishikawa technique to gain insight into it.

5. You've reviewed your estimates and find that you had assumed that seasonal weather patterns would hold. If they change, then it could cause serious problems with the project.

6. You meet individually with many different people: the sponsor, stakeholders, team members, and experts. You ask each of them detailed questions about what they think could go wrong on the project.

1. Information gathering techniques – Brainstorming 2. Documentation reviews
3. Information gathering techniques – Delphi technique 4. Diagramming techniques
5. Assumptions analysis 6. Information gathering techniques – Interviews

Where to look for risks

A good way to understand risks for the exam is to know where they come from. If you start thinking about how you find risks on your project, it will help you figure out how to handle them.

Here are a few things to keep in mind when you're looking for risks:

1. **You can't always depend on all the resources you were promised.**
Have you ever been promised a person, equipment, conference room, or some other resource, only to be told at the last minute that the resource you were depending on wasn't available? What about having a critical team member get sick or leave the company at the worst possible time? Check your list of resources. If a resource might not be available to you when you need it, then that's a risk.

2. **The critical path is full of risks.**
Remember the critical path method from the Time Management chapter? Well, an activity on the critical path is a lot riskier than an activity with plenty of float, because any delay in that activity will delay the project.

If an activity that's not on the critical path has a really small float, that means a small problem could easily cause it to become critical—which could lead to big delays in your project.

3. **"When you assume..."**
Have you ever heard that old saying about what happens when you assume? At the beginning of the project, your team had to make a bunch of assumptions in order to do your estimates. But some of those assumptions may not actually be true, even though you needed to make them for the sake of the estimate. It's a good thing you wrote them down—now it's time to go back and look at that list. If you find that some of them that are likely to be false, then you've found a risk.

4. **Look outside your project.**
Is there a new rule, regulation or law being passed that might affect your project? A new union contract being negotiated? Could the price of a critical component suddenly jump? There are plenty of things outside of your project that are risks—and if you identify them now, you can plan for them and not be caught off guard.

Finding risks means talking to your team and being creative. Risks can be anywhere.

These areas are a good start, but there are plenty of other places on your project where you can find risks. Can you think of some of them?

Now put it in the risk register

Outputs

The point of the Risk Identification process is to… well, identify risks. But what does that really give you? You need to know enough about each risk to analyze it and make good decisions about how to handle it. So when you're doing interviews, leading brainstorming sessions, analyzing assumptions, gathering expert opinions with the Delphi technique, and using the other Risk Identification tools and techniques, you're gathering exactly the things you need to add to the risk register.

Each risk that you and the team come up with should go here.

Your Risk Identification meetings should always include a discussion of how to respond to the risks.

This is where the results of your root cause analysis go.

Identified Risks	Potential Responses	Root Causes
Landslide caused by loose gravel and dirt on the nearby mountain	Put up barrier or dig trench	Geological data review found loose topsoil nearby
High winds can lead to cliff disaster	Reinforce tent stakes; obtain weatherproof equipment	National weather service predicts 35% chance of high winds
Truck rental is unavailable	Pay to reserve equipment at a second company	Higher than expected demand for equipment in the area this season
Equipment failure during project	No responses were found by the team	Recent industry report cites higher-than-expected failure rates for critical equipment

Risk Register

You might discover new risk categories, like "Equipment". If you do, you'll go back to the RBS and add them.

You'll get a chance to come up with more complete responses later.

Some risks do not have an obvious response.

You already created the Risk Management Plan in the last process. Now you're going back and updating it by adding the risk register.

The Risk Register is built into the Risk Management Plan. It's the only output of the Risk Identification process.

Rank your risks

Planning process group

It's not enough to know that risks are out there. You can identify risks all day long, and there's really no limit to the number of risks you can think of. But some of them are likely to occur, while others are very improbable. It's the ones that have much better odds of happening that you really want to plan for.

Besides, some risks will cause a whole lot of damage to your project if they happen, while others will barely make a scratch… and you care much more about the risks that will have a big impact. That's why you need the next risk management process, **Qualitative Risk Analysis**—so you can look at each risk and figure out how likely it is and how big its impact will be.

Qualitative Risk Analysis

Remember all the stuff you put in here about risk categories and definitions? Those will come in handy.

If you didn't put that stuff in the plan, then you should go ahead and do it now.

You need to know what risks you've identified in order to analyze them.

Identified Risks	Potential Responses	Root Causes
Landslide caused by loose gravel and dirt on the nearby mountain	Put up barrier or dig trench	Geological data review found loose topsoil nearby
High winds can lead to cliff disaster	Reinforce tent stakes; obtain weatherproof equipment	National weather service predicts 35% chance of high winds
Truck rental is unavailable **New risk category: Equipment**	Pay to reserve equipment at a second company	Higher than expected demand for equipment in the area this season
Equipment failure during project	No responses were found by the team	Recent industry report cites higher-than-expected failure rates for critical equipment

Risk Register

Organizational Process Assets

Risk Management Plan

Project Scope Statement

Inputs

A good way to figure out whether a risk is likely is to look at lessons learned and see if it happened before.

Does the project use new technology for the first time? Is it very complex? Then it will be more risky.

Why do you think Enterprise Environmental Factors are NOT an input to the Qualitative Risk Analysis process?

Examine each risk in the register

Not all risks are created equal. Some of them are really likely to happen, while others are almost impossible. One risk will cause a catastrophe on your project if it happens; another will just waste a few minutes of someone's time.

Risk data quality assessment means making sure that the information you're using in your risk assessment is accurate. Sometimes it makes sense to bring in outside experts to check out the validity of your risk assessment data. Sometimes you can even confirm the quality of the data on your own, by checking some sample of it against other data sources.

Risk categorization is all about grouping your risks so that you can come up with a better strategy for dealing with them. You might group them by the phase of the project where you'll see them or by the source of the risk. Or you could come up with a bunch of additional categories that would help you to organize your response better and be ready for the risk if it should happen.

Creating risk categories can help you deal with whole groups of risks in one response plan.

Risk urgency assessment is checking out how soon you're going to need to take care of a particular risk. If a risk is going to happen soon, you'd better have a plan for how to deal with it soon, too.

If a risk is going to occur early in the project, it's a good idea to think of a response strategy early, too.

Qualitative Risk Analysis helps you <u>prioritize</u> each risk and figure out its <u>probability</u> and <u>impact.</u>

Risk probability and impact assessment One of the best ways to be sure that you're handling your risks properly is to examine how likely they are to happen, and how bad (or good) it will be if they do. This process helps you assign a probability to the likelihood of a risk occurring, and then figure out the actual cost (or impact) if it does happen. You can use these values to figure out which of your risks need a pretty solid mitigation plan, and which can monitored as the project goes on.

Sometimes you'll find that some risks have obviously low probability and impact, so you won't put them in your register. Instead, you can add them to a <u>watchlist</u>, which is just a list of risks, like those you don't want to forget about, but you don't need to track as closely. You'll check your watchlist from time to time to keep an eye on things.

Probability and impact matrix is a table where all of your risks are plotted out according to the values you assign. It's a good way of looking at the data so you can more easily make judgments about which risks require response. The ones with the higher numbers are more likely to happen and will have a bigger impact on your project if they do. So you'd better figure out how to handle those.

Probability	P&I				
.9	.09	.27	.45	.63	.89
.7	.07	.21	.35	.49	.63
.5	.05	.15	.25	.35	.45
.3	.03	.09	.15	.21	.27
.1	.01	.03	.05	.07	.09
Impact	**.1**	**.3**	**.5**	**.7**	**.9**

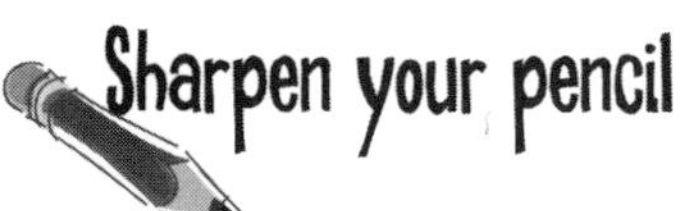

Here are some facts about the cliff project that were uncovered during qualitative analysis. Update the risk register on the facing page with the appropriate information.

Risk	Probability	Impact
1. Landslide	.1	.9
2. Winds	.7	.9
3. No truck	.3	.7
4. Storms	.5	.3
5. Supplies	.1	.5
6. Illness	.1	.7

During the qualitative risk analysis sessions, the team assigned a probability and impact number to each of the risks on the facing page.

Prob. & Impact Matrix

Probability					
.9	.09	.27	.45	.63	.89
.7	.07	.21	.35	.49	.63
.5	.05	.15	.25	.35	.45
.3	.03	.09	.15	.21	.27
.1	.01	.03	.05	.07	.09
	.1	.3	.5	.7	.9

Impact

This gives you a good picture of the threshold the company has set for evaluating risks.

You can figure out the priority of each risk based on its probability and impact. Low priority risks have no shading, medium ones are light gray, and high ones are dark gray.

1. The organizational process assets at your company set a high-priority risk as any risk with a Probability and Impact score higher than 0.20. Medium-priority risks are those between 0.10 and 0.19, and low-priority are those between 0–0.09. Low-priority risks can be monitored on a watchlist, but High and Medium ones must have a response strategy.
   Fill in the missing values in the Priority and Probability columns in the risk register on the right, using the Probability and Impact matrix to figure out which ones are low, medium or high. For example, we filled in "High" under Priority for row #3 by looking up risk ("No truck") in the first table, finding the probability and impact values, and then using the Probability & Impact Matrix. The probability is .3 and the impact is .7, so you can find the corresponding box in the matrix. Since it's dark gray, its priority is "High."

2. After analyzing your data, you came up with three risk categories for the project: natural, equipment, and human.
   Fill in the missing values in the "Category" column of the risk register with either "Natural," "Equipment," or "Human." We started you out by filling in a few of them.

3. For this particular project, you'll need the equipment at the start of the project, so any equipment risks are considered high urgency. Natural and human risks are all medium urgency, except for ones that have to do with storms, which you consider low urgency for this project because of limited mitigation potential.
   Figure out the whether the urgency for each risk is "Low," "Medium," or "High" and fill in the "Urgency" column in the risk register.

It's okay for some responses to be blank—you'll fill them in later during the Risk Response Planning process.

	Identified Risks	Potential Response	Root Cause	Category	Priority	Urgency
1.	Landslide caused by loose gravel and dirt on the nearby mountain	Put up barrier or dig trench	Geological data review found loose topsoil nearby			
2.	High winds can lead to cliff disaster	Reinforce tent stakes; obtain weatherproof equipment	National weather service predicts 35% chance of high winds	Natural		Medium
3.	Truck rental is unavailable		Higher than expected demand for equipment this season	Equipment	High	
4.	Storms predicted through the first two weeks of project schedule time	Create reserves to account for time lost due to storms	El Niño weather pattern		Medium	Low
5.	Supply shortage if we don't accurately predict food needs		Nearest store is 30 miles away	Equipment		
6.	If someone gets sick, it could be a problem getting medical care	Bring a doctor with us on the project	Nearest hospital is 50 miles away			

Outputs

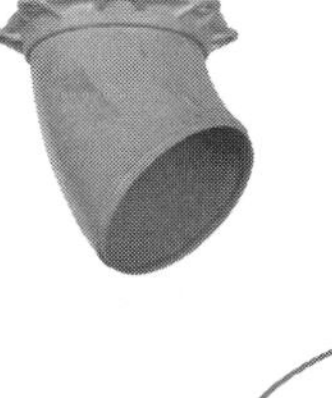

Qualitative analysis helps you figure out which risks are most important to your project's success. When you've finished your analysis, you should have a risk register that tells you a lot more about what could go wrong.

The only output of qualitative risk analysis is the updated risk register.

	Identified Risks	Potential Response	Root Cause	Category	Priority	Urgency
1.	Landslide caused by loose gravel and dirt on the nearby mountain	Put up barrier or dig trench	Geological data review found loose topsoil nearby	Natural	Low	Medium
2.	High winds can lead to cliff disaster	Reinforce tent stakes; obtain weatherproof equipment	National weather service predicts 35% chance of high winds	Natural	High	Medium
3.	Truck rental is unavailable		Higher than expected demand for equipment this season	Equipment	High	High
4.	Storms predicted through the first two weeks of project schedule time	Create reserves to account for time lost due to storms	El Niño weather pattern	Natural	Medium	Low
5.	Supply shortage if we don't accurately predict food needs		Nearest store is 30 miles away	Equipment	Low	High
6.	If someone gets sick it could be a problem getting medical care	Bring a doctor with us on the project	Nearest hospital is 50 miles away	Human	Low	Medium

there are no Dumb Questions

Q: Who does qualitative risk analysis?

A: The whole team needs to work on it together. The more of your team members who are helping to think of possible risks, the better off your plan will be. Everybody can work together to think of different risks to their particular part of the work, and that should give an accurate picture of what could happen on the project.

Q: What if people disagree on how to rank risks?

A: There are a lot of ways to think about risks. If a risk has a large impact on your part of the project or your goals, you can bet that it will seem more important to you than the stuff that affects other people in the group. The best way to keep the right perspective is to keep everybody on the team evaluating risks based on how they affect the overall project goals. If everyone focuses on the effect each risk will have on the cost, quality, and scope of your project, risks will get ranked in the order that is best for everybody.

Q: Where do the categories come from?

A: You can create categories however you want. Usually, people categorize risks in ways that help them come up with response strategies. Some people use project phase. That way, they can come up with a risk mitigation plan for each phase of a project, and they can cut down on the information they need to manage throughout. Some people like to use the source of the risk as a category. If you do that, you can find mitigation plans that can help you deal with each source separately. That might come in handy if you are dealing with a bunch of different contractors or suppliers and you want to manage the risks associated with each separately.

Q: How do I know if I've got all the risks?

A: Unfortunately, you never know the answer to that one. That's why it's important to keep monitoring your risk register throughout the project. It's important that you are constantly updating it and that you never let it sit and collect dust. You should be looking for risks throughout all phases of your project, not just when you're starting out.

Q: I'm still not clear on the difference between Delphi and brainstorming.

A: It's easy to get those two confused because both are about people sitting and thinking of risks. Delphi is a technique where you ask experts to give their opinion anonymously, and then you evaluate those opinions. Brainstorming is just you and your team sitting in a room thinking of risks.

Q: What's the point in even tracking low-priority risks? Why have a watchlist at all?

A: Actually, watchlists are just a list of all of the risks that you want to monitor as the project goes on. You might be watching them to see if conditions change and make them more likely to happen. By keeping a watchlist, you make sure that all of the risks that seem low priority when you are doing your analysis get caught before they cause serious damage if they become more likely later in the project.

The conditions that cause a risk are called triggers. So, say you have a plan set up to deal with storms, and you know that you might track a trigger for lightning damage, such as a thunderstorm. If there's no thunderstorm, it's really unlikely that you will see lightning damage, but once the storm has started, the chance for the risk to occur skyrockets.

Q: I still don't get the difference between priority and urgency.

A: Priority tells you how important a risk is, while urgency tells you when you need to deal with it. Some risks could be high priority but low urgency, which means that they're really important, but not time-critical. For example, you might know that a certain supplier that provides critical equipment will go out of business in six months, and you absolutely need to find a new supplier. But you have six months to do it. Finding a new supplier is a high priority, because your project will fail if it's not taken care of. But it's not urgent—even if it takes you four months to find a new supplier, nothing bad will happen.

Qualitative vs. quantitative analysis

Let's say you're a fitness trainer, and your specialty is helping millionaires get ready for major endurance trials. You get paid the same for each job, but the catch is that you only get paid if they succeed. Which of these clients would you take on?

Running a Marathon **vs.** **Climbing Mount Everest**

One client wants you to help him train so that he can finish a marathon. He doesn't have to win, just get to the finish line.

Another client wants you to help him get to the top of Mount Everest. He won't be satisfied unless he gets to the summit.

It's much more likely that you can get even an out-of-shape millionaire to finish a marathon than it is that you can get him to climb Mount Everest successfully.

In fact, since the 1950s, 10,000 people have attempted to climb Mount Everest, and only 1,200 have succeeded. 200 have died. Your qualitative analysis probably told you that the climbing project would be the *riskier* of the two. But having the numbers to back up that judgment is what quantitative analysis is all about.

Quantitative risk analysis

Once you've identified risks and ranked them according to the team's assessment, you need to take your analysis a little further and make sure that the numbers back you up. Sometimes you'll find that your initial assessment needs to be updated when you look into it further.

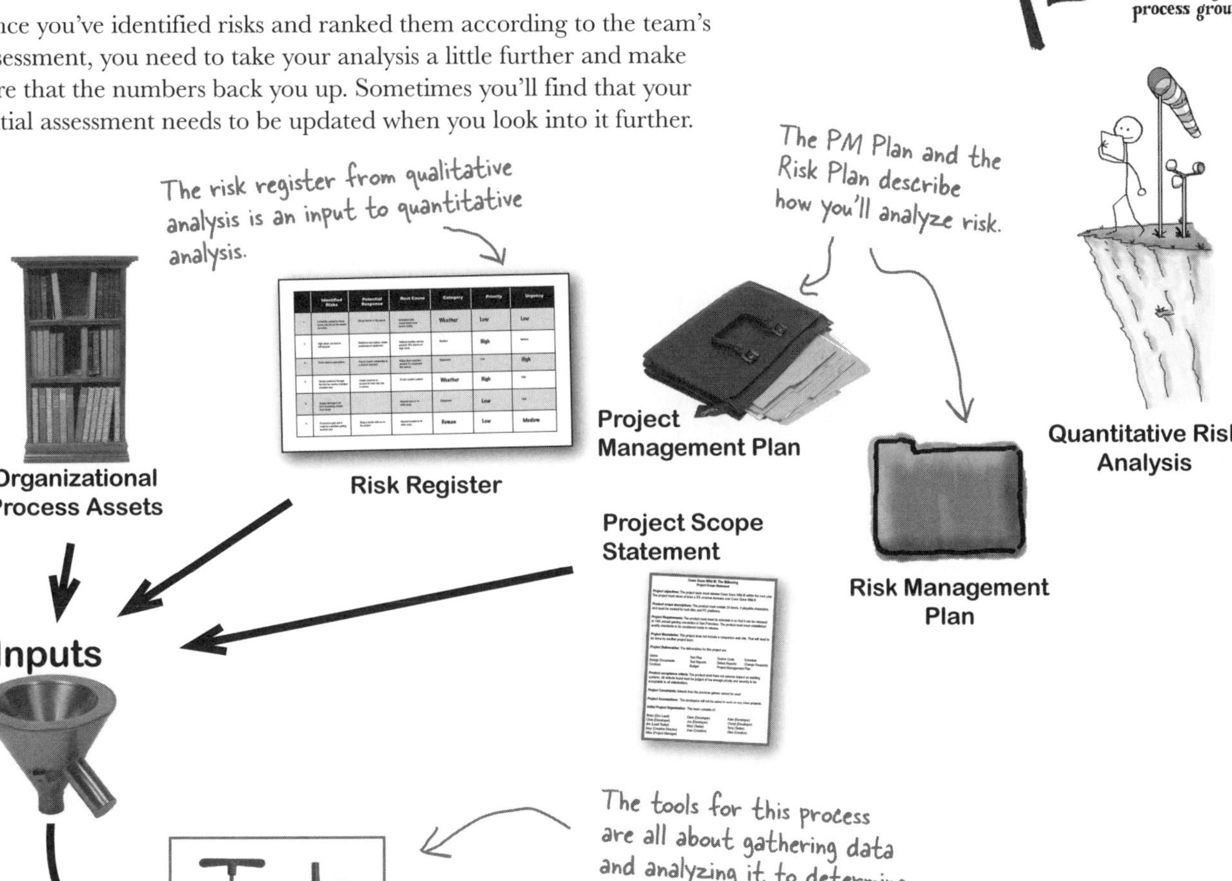

	Identified Risks	Potential Response	Root Cause	Category	Priority	Urgency
1.	Landslide caused by loose gravel and dirt on the nearby mountain	Put up barrier or dig trench	Geological data review found loose topsoil nearby	Weather	Low	Low
2.	High winds can lead to cliff disaster	Reinforce tent stakes; obtain weatherproof equipment	National weather service predicts 35% chance of high winds	Weather	High	Medium
3.	Truck rental is unavailable	Pay to reserve equipment at a second company	Higher than expected demand for equipment this season	Equipment	Low	High
4.	Storms predicted through the first two weeks of project schedule time	Create reserves to account for time lost due to storms	El niño weather pattern	Weather	High	High
5.	Supply shortage if we don't accurately predict food needs		Nearest store is 30 miles away	Equipment	Low	High
6.	If someone gets sick it could be a problem getting medical care	Bring a doctor with us on the project	Nearest hospital is 50 miles away	Human	Low	Medium

Risk Register

Once you're done analyzing, you update the risk register with the data you've gathered.

First gather the data...

Quantitative tools are broken down into two categories: the ones that help you get more information about risks and the ones that help you to analyze the information you have. The tools for gathering data focus on gathering numbers about the risks you have already identified and ranked.

Interviewing

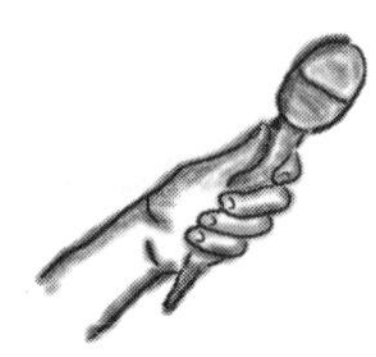

Sometimes the best way to get hard data about your risks is to interview people who understand them. In a risk interview, you might focus on getting three-point cost estimates so that you can come up with a budget range that will help you mitigate risks later. Another good reason to interview is to establish ranges of probability and impact, and document the reasons for the estimates on both sides of the range.

Probability distribution

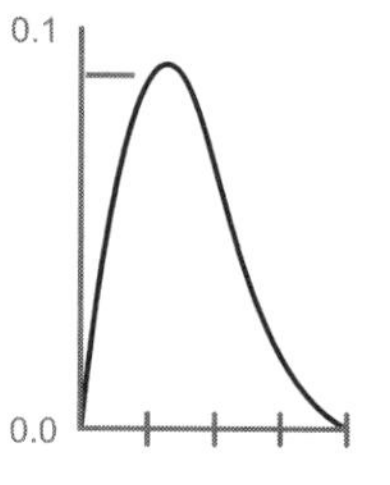

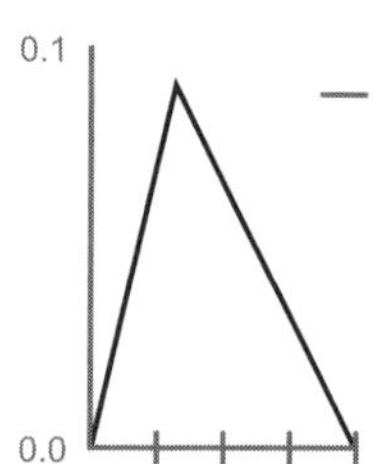

Sometimes taking a look at your time and cost estimate ranges in terms of their distribution will help you generate more data about them. You probably remember these distribution curves from your probability and statistics classes in school. Don't worry, you won't be asked to remember the formal definition of probability distributions or even to be able to create them. You just need to know that they are another way of gathering data for quantitative analysis.

Expert judgment

It's always a good idea to contact the experts if you have access to them. People who have a good handle on statistics or risk analysis in general are always helpful when you are doing quantitative analysis. Also, it's great to hear from anybody who has a lot of experience with the kind of project you are creating, too.

... then analyze it

Now that you have all the data you can get about your risk register, it's time to analyze that information. Most of the tools for analyzing risk data are about figuring out how much the risk will end up costing you.

Sensitivity analysis is all about looking at the effect one variable might have if you could completely isolate it. You might look at the cost of a windstorm on human safety, equipment loss, and tent stability without taking into account other issues that might accompany the windstorm (like rain damage or possible debris from nearby campsites). People generally use tornado diagrams to look at a project's sensitivity to just one risk factor.

Tornado Diagram

Human safety costs

equipment costs

Variable Cost

0 100 200 300 400 500 600

The tornado diagram lets you look at just one uncertain factor while assuming that all other data will stay where you expect it to.

Expected monetary value analysis lets you examine costs of all of the paths you might take through the project depending on which risks occur and assign a monetary value to each decision. So, if it costs $100 to survey the cliff and $20 to stake your tent, choosing to stake your tent *after* you've looked at the cliff has an expected monetary value of $120.

The main method of Expected Monetary value analysis you need to know for the test is **Decision Tree Analysis.** For decision tree analysis, you just diagram out all of the decisions you think you will need to make to deal with risks. Then you add up all that you would need to spend to make each decision.

We'll talk about this on page 534..

The wind's blowing at 31 mph SE. I weigh 153 lbs. According to my simulations, I have a 28.3% chance of falling off the cliff in these conditions.

Quantitative analysis means taking measurements and coming up with exact numbers to describe your risks.

Modeling and distribution. It's also a good idea to run your project risks through modeling programs if you can. Monte Carlo analysis is one such tool that can randomize the outcomes of your risks and the probabilities of them occurring to help you get a better sense of how to handle the risks you have identified.

This is the same technique you learned in Chapter 6 for cost estimation.

Monte Carlo analysis lets you run a lot of simulations to come up with data about what could happen on your project.

Calculate the Expected Monetary Value of your risks

Okay, so you know the probability and impact of each risk. How does that really help you plan? Well, it turns out that if you have good numbers for those things, you can actually figure out how much those risks are going to cost your project. You can do that by calculating the **Expected Monetary Value** (or EMV) of each risk:

1. Start with the probability and impact of each risk.

You can find these in your risk register.

Risk	Probability	Impact
High winds	35%	cost $48 to replace equipment
Mudslide	5%	lose $750 in damage costs
Wind generator is usable	15%	save $800 in battery costs
Truck rental unavailable	10%	cost $350 for last-minute rental

2. Take the first risk and multiply the probability by the impact. For opportunities, use a positive cost. For threats, use a negative one. Then do the same for the rest of the risks.

High winds: 35% x -$48 = -$16.80

Mudslide: 5% x -$750 = -$37.50

Wind generator: 15% x $800 = $120.00

Truck rental: 10% x -$350 = -$35.00

Even though the impact of a mud slide is big, the probability is low so the EMV is small.

The wind generator risk is an opportunity because you'll save money if it happens. So when you do the EMV calculation, you use a positive number for the impact.

3. Now that you've calculated the EMV for each of the risks, you can add them up to find the total EMV for all of them.

EMV = -$16.80 + -$37.50 + $120.00 + -$35.00 = -$30.70

If you add $30.70 to the budget, then it should be enough to account for these risks.

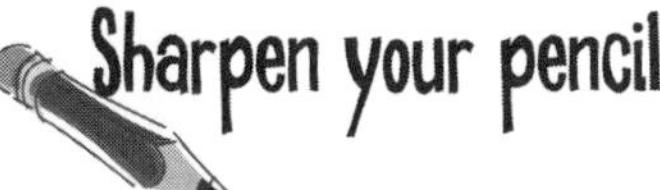

You'll need to know how to do EMV calculations for the test. Give them a shot now—they're pretty easy once you get the hang of them.

Take a look at this table of risks.

Risk	Probability	Impact
Navigation equipment failure	15%	costs $300 due to getting lost
Unseasonably warm weather	8%	saves $500 in excavation costs
Wild animals eat rations	10%	costs $100 for replacement run

1. Calculate the EMV for each of these three risks.

2. If these are the only risks on the project, calculate the total EMV.

3. The latest weather report came out, and there is now a 20% chance of unseasonably warm weather. What's the new EMV for the project?

4. Now the cost of replacement rations goes up to $150. What's the new EMV for the project?

Answers on page 554.

Decision tree analysis uses EMV to help you make choices

There's another way to do EMV—you can do it visually using something called a **decision tree**. This decision tree shows the hidden costs of whether or not you buy a heavier tent. The tent is more expensive—it costs $350, while the lighter tent costs $130. But the heavier tent has better protection against the wind, so if there are high winds, your equipment isn't damaged.

If you buy a heavy tent, then it protects your equipment better, but it'll cost more. You figure that if there are high winds, you'll lose $953 worth of equipment with a light tent, but only $48 worth if you have a heavy one. If there are low winds, then you'll only lose $15 worth with a light tent and $10 worth with a heavy tent.

The national weather service says there's a 35% chance of high winds, which means there's a 65% chance of low winds.

Is it worth spending $350 on a heavier tent, rather than $130 on the lighter one?

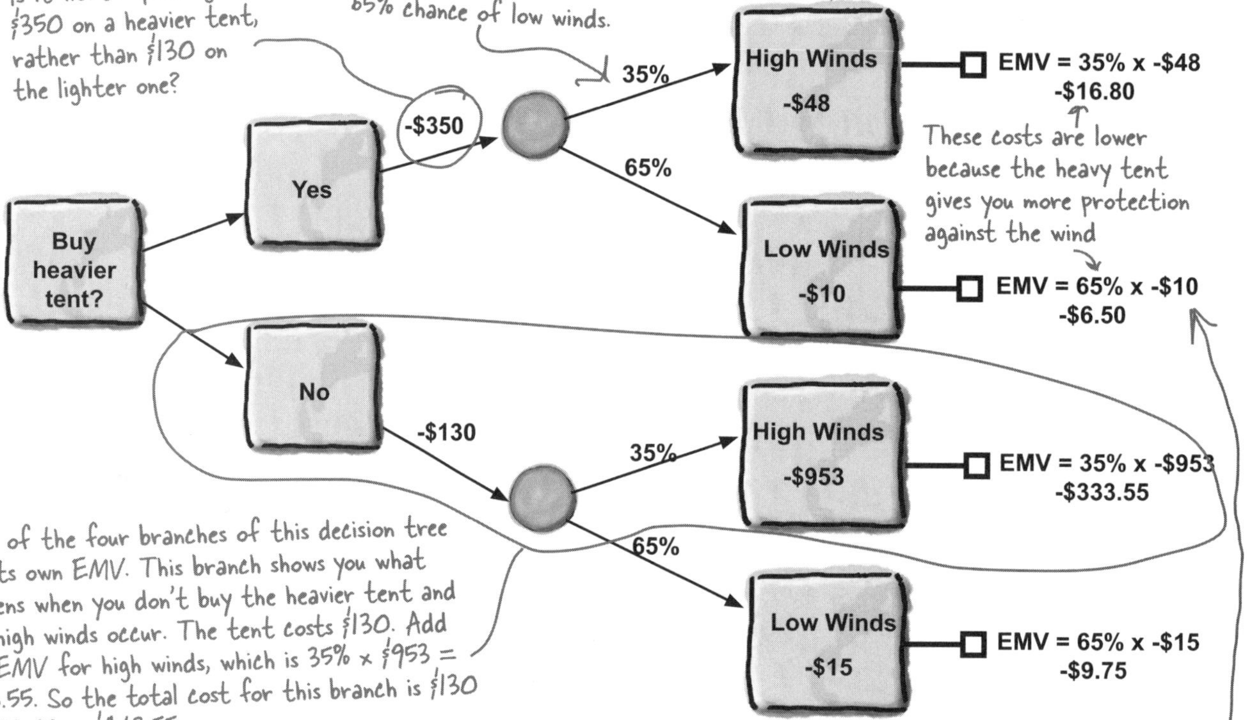

Buy heavier tent?
Yes → -$350 → 35% High Winds -$48 → EMV = 35% x -$48 -$16.80
65% Low Winds -$10 → EMV = 65% x -$10 -$6.50
No → -$130 → 35% High Winds -$953 → EMV = 35% x -$953 -$333.55
65% Low Winds -$15 → EMV = 65% x -$15 -$9.75

These costs are lower because the heavy tent gives you more protection against the wind

Each of the four branches of this decision tree has its own EMV. This branch shows you what happens when you don't buy the heavier tent and the high winds occur. The tent costs $130. Add the EMV for high winds, which is 35% x $953 = $333.55. So the total cost for this branch is $130 + $333.55 = $463.55

What's the EMV – or how much it's likely to cost you – of choosing the heavier tent?

If we add the EMV for high winds plus the EMV for low winds to the cost of the tent, we'll figure out the "real" cost of choosing the heavier tent. So that's -$16.80 + -$6.50 + -$350 = -$373.30.

This is just the EMV of the low winds if you buy the heavier tent. The probability of low winds is 65%, and the cost is $10. So it's just like the other EMV calculations: 65% x -$10 = -$6.50.

Compare that with the EMV of choosing the lighter tent. Which decision makes sense?

We can do the same thing for the bottom two branches of the tree. The "cheaper" tent costs -$130 + -$333.55 + -$9.75 = $473.30. So it's actually more expensive!

Exercise

Looking at the decision tree on the facing page, see if you can figure out the expected monetary value depending on the decisions the team makes.

Hint: Figure out the new EMV for each branch—that will tell you if the decision makes sense.

1. You hear a weather report that says there's now a 45% chance of high winds. Does it still make sense to buy the heavier tent?

2. If you don't buy the heavier tent, then you have room to take along a wind generator that can power your equipment, and that will save you $1,100 in portable batteries if there's a heavy wind. If there's still a 45% chance of high winds, does it still make sense to buy the heavier tent?

Answers on page 555.

This is an opportunity. So it should have a POSITIVE value when you do the EMV calculation.

there are no Dumb Questions

Q: I still don't get this Monte Carlo stuff. What's the deal?

A: All you really need to know about Monte Carlo analysis for the test is that it's a way that you can model out random data using software. In real life, though, it's a really cool way of trying to see what could happen on your project if risks do occur. Sometimes modeling out the data you already have about your project helps you to see better the real impact of a risk if it did happen.

Q: I can figure out how much the risk costs using EMV, or I can do it with Decision Tree Analysis. Why do I need two ways to do this?

A: That's a good question. If you take a really careful look at how you do Decision Tree Analysis, you might notice something... it's actually doing exactly the same thing as EMV. It turns out that those two techniques are really similar, except that EMV does it using numbers and Decision Tree Analysis spells out the same calculation using a picture.

Q: I understand that EMV and decision trees are related, but I still don't exactly see how.

A: It turns out that there are a lot of EMV techniques, and decision tree analysis is just one of them. But it's the one you need to know for the test, because it's the one that helps you make decisions by figuring out the EMV for each option. You can bet that you'll see a question or two that asks you to calculate the EMV for a project based on decision tree like the one on the facing page. As long as you remember that risks are negative numbers and that opportunities are positive ones, you should do fine.

Q: So are both quantitative analysis and qualitative analysis really just concerned with figuring out the impact of risks?

A: That's right. Qualitative analysis focuses on the impact as the team judges it in planning. Quantitative analysis focuses on getting the hard numbers to back up those judgments.

Update the risk register based on your quantitative analysis results

When you've finished gathering data about the risks, you change your priorities, urgency ratings and categories if necessary and update your risk register. Sometimes modeling out your potential responses to risk helps you to find a more effective way to deal with them.

Analysis showed us that this would be the most expensive risk if it were to occur. So it got upgraded to a high priority.

	Identified Risks	Potential Response	Root Cause	Category	Priority	Urgency
1.	Landslide caused by loose gravel and dirt on the nearby mountain	Put up barrier or dig trench	Geological data review found loose topsoil nearby	Natural	**High**	Medium
2.	High winds can lead to cliff disaster	Reinforce tent stakes; obtain weatherproof equipment	National weather service predicts 35% chance of high winds	Natural	High	Medium
3.	Truck rental is unavailable	Pay to reserve equipment at a second company	Higher than expected demand for equipment this season	Equipment	High	High
4.	Storms predicted through the first two weeks of project schedule time	Create reserves to account for time lost due to storms	El Niño weather pattern	Natural	Medium	Low
5.	Supply shortage if we don't accurately predict food needs		Nearest store is 30 miles away	Equipment	Low	**High**
6.	If someone gets sick, it could be a problem getting medical care	Bring a doctor with us on the project	Nearest hospital is 50 miles away	Human	Low	**Low**

This one got downgraded when quantitative analysis showed that it was not very likely to happen on such a short-term project.

BULLET POINTS: AIMING FOR THE EXAM

- The main output of all of the risk management **planning** processes is an **updated risk register**.
- The first step in risk management is **Risk Identification**, where you work with the whole team to figure out what risks could affect your project.
- Qualitative and quantitative analysis are all about **ranking risks** based on their probability and impact.
- Qualitative analysis is where you take the **categories** in your risk plan and **assign** them to each of the risks that you've identified.
- Quantitative analysis focuses on **gathering numbers** to help evaluate risks and **make the best decisions** about how to handle them.
- **Decision Tree Analysis** is one kind of **Expected Monetary Value** analysis. It focuses on adding up all of the costs of a decisions being made on a project so that you can see the overall value of risk responses.
- To calculate EMV, be sure to **treat all negative risks as negative numbers** and all **opportunities as positive ones**. Then add up all of the numbers on your decision tree.
- Don't forget **watchlists**. They let you monitor lower-priority risks so that you can see if triggers for those risks occur and you need to treat them as higher priorities.
- All of the processes in Risk Management are **planning or control processes**. There are **no executing** processes here. Since the goal is to plan for risks, there is no need to focus on actually doing the work. By then, it's too late to plan for risks.

Your risk register should include both threats and opportunities. Opportunities have positive impact values, while threats have negative ones. Don't forget the plus or minus sign when you're calculating EMV.

How would you handle the risks listed in the risk register so far?

How do you respond to a risk?

After all that analysis, it's time to figure out what you're going to do if a risk occurs. Maybe you'll be able to keep a reserve of money to handle the cost of the most likely risks. Maybe there's some planning you can do from the beginning to be sure that you avoid it. You might even find a way to transfer some of the risk with an insurance policy.

However you decide to deal with each individual risk, you'll update your risk responses in the risk register to show your decisions when you're done. When you're done with **Risk Response planning**, you should be able to tell your change control board what your response plans are and who will be in charge of them so they can use them to evaluate changes.

Risk Response Planning

Risk response planning is figuring out what you'll do if risks happen.

The risk register is the output of all of your analysis so far. It should contain everything you know about the risks facing your project, and even some preliminary responses you might have thought of along the way.

You might consult the risk management plan to figure out who is responsible for what in risk response planning or even guidelines for risk priorities.

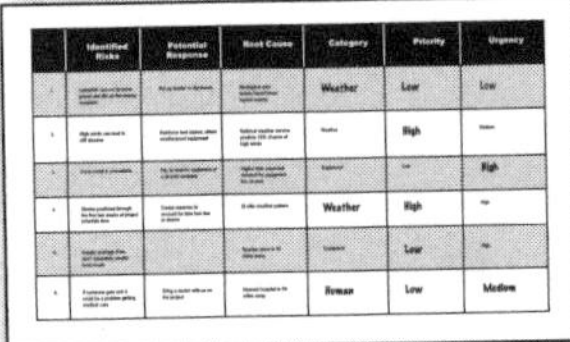

Risk Register

Risk Management Plan

Notice that organizational process assets aren't here. You can't use a template for this one. It's all about figuring out the responses that make sense for your project's SPECIFIC risks.

Inputs

It isn't always so bad

Remember the strategies for handling negative risks—avoid, mitigate, transfer, and accept—from earlier? Well, there are strategies for handling positive risks, too. The difference is that **strategies for positive risks** are all about how you can try to get the most out of them. The strategies for handling negative and positive risks are the tools and techniques for the Risk Response Planning process.

The strategies for negative risks are also tools & techniques for this process. They're the ones you already learned: avoid, mitigate, transfer and accept. Acceptance is a technique for both negative and positive risks.

1. **Exploit**

   This is when you do everything you can to make sure that you take advantage of an opportunity. You could assign your best resources to it. Or you could allocate more than enough funds to be sure that you get the most out of it.

2. **Share**

   Sometimes it's harder to take advantage of an opportunity on your own. Then you might call in another company to share in it with you.

3. **Enhance**

   This is when you try to make the opportunity more probable by influencing its triggers. If getting a picture of a rare bird is important, then you might bring more food that it's attracted to.

4. **Accept**

   Just like accepting a negative risk, sometimes an opportunity just falls in your lap. The best thing to do in that case is to just accept it!

Response planning can even find more risks

Secondary risks are risks that come from a response you have to another risk. If you dig a trench to stop landslides from taking out your camp, it's always possible for someone to fall into the trench and get hurt.

Residual Risks are those that remain after your risk responses have been implemented. So even though you reinforce your tent stakes and get weatherproof gear, there's still a chance that winds could destroy your camp if they are strong enough.

Which risk response technique is being used in these situations? Match each technique to its scenario.

Mitigate	If the weather's good, then there's a chance you could see a meteor shower. If the team gets a photo that wins the meteor photo contest, you can get extra funding. You have your team stay up all night with their telescopes and cameras ready.
Avoid	You hear that it's going to rain for the first three days of your trip, so you bring waterproof tents and indoor projects for the team to work on in the meantime.
Accept	You read that there's a major bear problem in the spring on the cliff where you are planning to work. You change your project start date to happen in the fall.
Transfer	On your way up the cliff, you meet another team that is looking to survey the area. You offer to do half of the surveying work while they do the other half and then trade your findings with one another.
Exploit	There's a high probability of water damage to some of your equipment, so you buy insurance to avoid losses.
Share	There's always the chance that someone could make a mistake and fall off the cliff. No matter how much you plan for the unexpected, sometimes mistakes happen.
Enhance	About 10 years ago a really rare bird, the black-throated blue warbler, was seen on this cliff. If you could get a picture of it, it would be worth a lot of money. So, you bring special seeds that you have read are really attractive to this bird, and you set up lookout points around the cliff with cameras ready to get the shot.

→ **Answers on page 556.**

Add risk responses to the register

You guessed it— more updates to the risk register. All of your risk responses will be tracked through change control. Changes that you need to make to the plan will get evaluated based on your risk responses, too. It's even possible that some of your risk responses will need to be added into your contract.

Every risk needs to have one person who owns the response plan.

	Identified Risks	Potential Response	Root Cause	Risk Owner	Cat	Priority	Urgency
1.	Landslide caused by loose gravel and dirt on the nearby mountain	Put up barrier or dig trench	Geological data review found loose topsoil nearby	Joe S.	Natural	High	Medium
2.	High winds can lead to cliff disaster	Reinforce tent stakes; obtain weatherproof equipment	National weather service predicts 35% chance of high winds	Tanya T.	Natural	High	Medium
3.	Truck rental is unavailable	Pay to reserve equipment at a second company	Higher than expected demand for equipment this season	Joe S.	Equipment	High	High
4.	Storms predicted through the first two weeks of project schedule time	**Buy storm insurance in case the equipment is damaged**	El niño weather pattern	Michael R.	Natural	Medium	Low
5.	Supply shortage if we don't accurately predict food needs		Nearest store is 30 miles away	James S.	Equipment	Low	High
6.	If someone gets sick, it could be a problem getting medical care	Bring a doctor with us on the project	Nearest hospital is 50 miles away	Tanya T.	Human	Low	Low
7.	Someone could fall in the landslide trench	Set up a trench patrol to make sure no one gets hurt	Dig trench for landslides	Joe S.	Human	Low	Low

During risk response planning, the team agreed to buy insurance for this one.

This is a secondary risk that is caused by the response to risk #1.

Sometimes you'll need to change the contract to account for risks.

Project Management Plan Updates

The PM plan needs to be updated so that Integrated Change Control can include the risk responses.

Contract updates

This week's interview:
Stick figure who hangs out on cliffs

Head First: We've seen you hanging out on cliffs for a while now. Apparently, you've been paying people to stand on the cliff for you or getting a friend to hold a trampoline at the foot of the cliff; we've even seen you jump off of it. So now that I've finally got a chance to interview you, I want to ask the question at the top of everyone's mind: "Are you insane? Why do you spend so much time up there?"

Stick Figure: First off, let me dispel a few myths that are flying around out there about me. I'm not crazy, and I'm not trying to get myself killed! Before Risk Management entered my life I, like you, would never have dreamed of doing this kind of thing.

Head First: Okay, but I'm a little skeptical about your so-called "Risk Management." Are you trying to say that because of Risk Management you don't have to worry about the obvious dangers of being up there?

Stick Figure: No. Of course not! That's not the point at all. Risk Management means you sit down and make a list of all of the things that could go wrong. (And even all the things that could go right.) Then you really try to think of the best way to deal with anything unexpected.

Head First: So you're doing this Risk Management stuff to make it less dangerous for you?

Stick Figure: Yes, exactly! By the time I'm standing up there on that cliff, I've really thought my way through pretty much everything that might happen up there. I've thought through it both qualitatively and quantitatively.

Head First: Quantitatively?

Stick Figure: Yes. You don't think I'd go up there without knowing the wind speed, do you? Chance of landslides? Storms? The weight of everything I'm carrying? How likely I am to fall in weather conditions? I think about all of that and I measure it. Then I sit down and come up with risk response strategies.

Head First: OK, so you have strategies. Then what?

Stick Figure: Then I constantly monitor my risks while I'm on the cliff. If anything changes, I check to see if it might trigger any of the risks I've come up with. Sometimes I even discover new risks while I'm up there. When I do, I just add them to the list and work on coming up with responses for them.

Head First: I see. So you're constantly updating your list of risks.

Stick Figure: Yes! We call it a **Risk Register**. Whenever I have new information, I put it there. It means that I can actually hang out on these cliffs with a lot of confidence. Because, while you can't guarantee that nothing will go wrong, you can be prepared for whatever comes your way.

Head First: That's a lot of work. Does it really make a difference?

Stick Figure: Absolutely! I'd never be able to sleep at night knowing that I could fall off the cliff at any time. But I've planned for the risks, and I've taken steps to stay safe… and I sleep like a baby.

You can't plan for every risk at the start of the project

Even the best planning can't predict everything—there's always a chance that a new risk could crop up that you hadn't thought about. That's why you need to constantly monitor how your project is doing compared to your risk register. If a new risk happens, you have a good chance of catching it before it causes serious trouble. When it comes to risk, the earlier you can react, the better for everybody. And that's what the **Risk Monitoring and Control process** is all about.

The park ranger's come by to let you know about some recent bear sightings on this cliff.

	Identified Risks	Potential Response	Root Cause	Risk Owner	Cat	Priority	Urgency
1.	Landslide caused by loose gravel and dirt on the nearby mountain	Put up barrier or dig trench	Geological data review found loose topsoil nearby	Joe S	Weather	High	Low
2.	High winds can lead to cliff disaster	Reinforce tent stakes; obtain weatherproof equipment	National weather service predicts 35% chance of high winds	Tanya T	Weather	High	Medium
3.	Truck rental is unavailable	Pay to reserve equipment at a second company	Higher than expected demand for equipment this season	Joe S	Equipment	Low	High
4.	Storms predicted through the first two weeks of project schedule time	**Buy storm insurance in case the equipment is damaged.**	El niño weather pattern	Michael K	Weather	High	High
5.	Supply shortage if we don't accurately predict food needs		Nearest store is 30 miles away	James S.	Equipment	Low	High
6.	If someone gets sick it could be a problem getting medical care	Bring a doctor with us on the project	Nearest hospital is 50 miles away	Tanya T	Human	Low	Low
7.	Someone could fall in the landslide trench	Set up a trench patrol to make sure no one gets hurt	Dig trench for landslides	Joe S.	Human	Low	Low

The risk register doesn't say anything about handling bears. Looks like this is a new risk altogether...

Risk monitoring and control is another change control process

Risks responses are treated just like changes. You monitor the project in every status meeting to see how the risks in the risk register are affecting it. If you need to implement a risk response, you take it to your change control board because it amounts to a change that will affect cost, quality, or schedule.

How to control your risks

Controlling risks means keeping your finger on the pulse of the project. If you are constantly reviewing all of the data your project is producing, you will be able to react quickly if a new risk is uncovered or if it looks like one of your response strategies needs to spring into action. Without careful monitoring, even your best plans won't get implemented in time to save your project if a risk happens.

Risk reassessment

You should have some regularly scheduled reassessment meetings to go over all of the information you have to date and see if your risk register still holds true. In a reassessment, your main goal is to find any new risks that have come up. That's why it's important to re-assess your risk register every so often and be sure that all of the risks in it are still the right ones.

Variance and trend analysis

Comparing the actual project performance to the plan is a great way to tell if a risk might be happening. If you find that you're significantly over budget or behind schedule, a risk could have cropped up that you didn't take into account. Looking for trends in your defects or schedule variance, for example, might show patterns that indicate that risks have occurred before you would have found that out on your own.

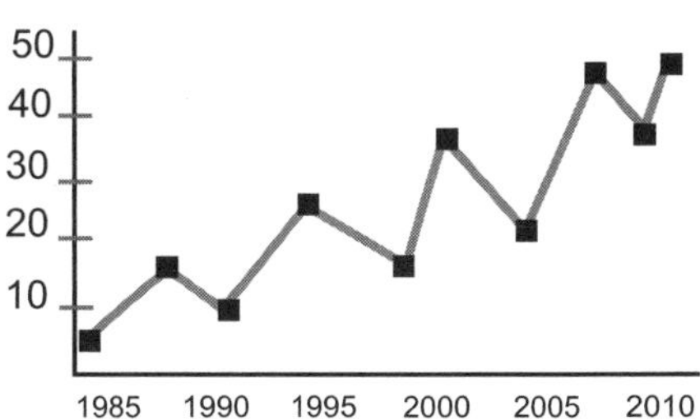

Reserve analysis

Just like you keep running tabs on your budget, you should always know how much money you have set aside for risk response. As you spend it, you should be sure to subtract it so you know if you have enough to cover all of your remaining risks. If you start to see that your reserves are running low and there are still a lot of risks being identified, you might be in trouble. Keeping tabs on your reserve means that you will always know if you need to reserve more funds or make different choices about how to handle risks as they come up.

Sometimes this kind of reserve is called a "contingency"—because its use is contingent on a certain risk happening.

More risk monitoring and control techniques

There are just a few more tools in the **Risk Monitoring and Controlling** process. They're all focused on finding new risks if they crop up, dealing with changes to the risks you've already planned for, and responding quickly to risks you know how to handle.

Never stop looking for new risks and adapting your strategies for dealing with them.

Risk audits are when you have an outside party come in and take a look at your risk response strategies to judge how effective they are. Sometimes risk audits will point out better ways of handling a specific risk so that you can change your response strategy going forward.

Auditors will also look at how effective your overall processes for risk planning are.

Technical performance measurement means comparing the performance of your project with its planned performance. So if you expected to hit a specific milestone, you could check performance information on your product at that time to see if it measured up to the plan. If not, that might indicate that there are risks you didn't plan for.

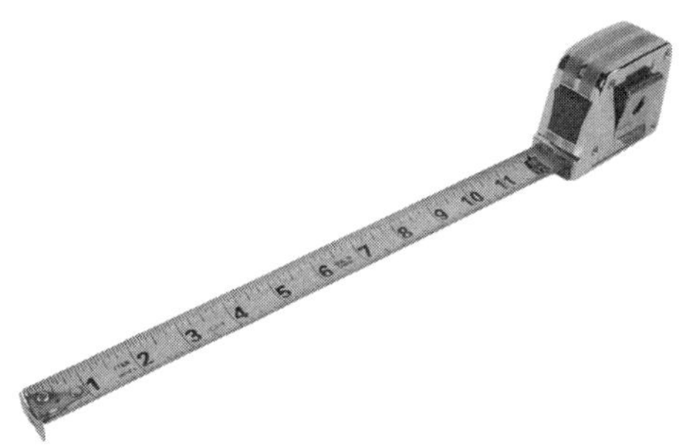

Status meetings are the most important way to keep the team up to date on risk planning—so important that **they should happen throughout the entire project**. The more you talk about risks with the team, the better. Every single status meeting should have risk review on the agenda. Status meetings are a really important way of noticing when things might go wrong, and of making sure that you implement your response strategy in time. It's also possible that you could come across a new opportunity by talking to the team.

Here are some risk monitoring and control activities. Can you determine which of the tools is being used in each one?

1. At every milestone, you do a new round of risk identification and make sure that the risks in your risk register still apply to the project.

- [ ] Reassessment
- [ ] Audit
- [ ] Technical Performance Measurement
- [ ] Trend Analysis
- [ ] Reserve Analysis

2. You check to make sure that you have all of the features developed in your project that you had planned when you reach the "feature complete" milestone. When you find that you are missing one of the planned features, you realize that a new risk has shown up—you missed one of the required features in your functional specification.

- [ ] Reassessment
- [ ] Audit
- [ ] Technical Performance Measurement
- [ ] Trend Analysis
- [ ] Reserve Analysis

3. You take a look at the number of defects you have found in your project per phase and find that it is higher in your project than it has been in most other projects that the company is doing. You dig a little deeper and find some previously unplanned risks that have been causing trouble on your project.

- [ ] Reassessment
- [ ] Audit
- [ ] Technical Performance Measurement
- [ ] Trend Analysis
- [ ] Reserve Analysis

4. Your company sends a risk expert in to take a look at your risk response strategies. She finds that you are missing a few secondary risks that might be caused by the responses you have planned. So you update your risk register to include the secondary risks.

- [ ] Reassessment
- [ ] Audit
- [ ] Technical Performance Measurement
- [ ] Trend Analysis
- [ ] Reserve Analysis

5 You decide to implement a risk response that costs $4,000. You check to make sure that you have enough money to cover the rest of the risks that might happen from here on out in the project.

- [ ] Reassessment
- [ ] Audit
- [ ] Technical Performance Measurement
- [ ] Trend Analysis
- [ ] Reserve Analysis

Answers:
1 - Reassessment
2 - Technical Performance Measurement
3 - Trend Analysis
4 - Audit
5 - Reserve Analysis

there are no Dumb Questions

Q: Why do I need to ask about risks at every status meeting?

A: Because a risk could crop up at any time, and you need to be prepared. The better you prepare for risks, the more secure your project is against the unknown. That's also why the triggers and watchlists are really important. When you meet with your team, you should figure out if a trigger for a risk response has happened. And you should check your watchlist to make sure none of your low-priority risks have materialized.

For the test, you need to know that status meetings aren't just a place for you to sit and ask each member of your team to tell you their status. Instead, you use them to figure out decisions that need to be made to keep the project on track or to head off any problems that might be coming up. In your status meetings, you need to discuss all of the issues that involve the whole team and come up with solutions to any new problems you encounter. So, it makes sense that you would use your status meetings to talk about your risk register and make sure that it is always up to date with the latest information.

Q: I still don't get trend analysis. How does it help me find risks?

A: It's easy to miss risks in your project—sometimes all the meetings in the world won't help your team see some of them. That's why a tool like trend analysis can be really useful. Remember the control chart from the Quality Management chapter? This is really similar, and it's just as valuable. It's just a way to see if things are happening that you did not plan for.

Q: Hey, didn't you talk about risks back in the Time Management chapter too?

A: Wow—it's great that you remembered that! The main thing to remember about risks from the Time Management chapter is that having multiple critical paths means you have a riskier project. The riskiest is when all of the activities are on the critical path. That means that a delay to even one activity can derail your whole project.

Q: Shouldn't I ask the sponsor about risks to the project?

A: Actually the best people to ask about risks is the project team itself. The sponsor knows why the project is needed and how much money is available for it, but from there, it's really up to the team to manage risks. Since you are the ones doing the work, it makes sense that you would have a better idea of what has gone wrong on similar projects and what might go wrong on this one. Risk Identification, analysis, and response planning are some of the most valuable contributions the team makes to the project. They can be the difference between making the sponsor happy and having to do a lot of apologizing.

Q: Why do we do risk audits?

A: Risk audits are when you have someone from outside your project come in and review your risk register—your risks and your risk responses—to make sure you got it right. The reason we do it is because risks are so important that getting a new set of eyes on them is worth the time.

Q: Hold on, didn't we already talk about reserves way back in Cost Control? Why is it coming up here?

A: That's right, back in Chapter 7 we talked about a **management reserve**, which is money set aside to handle any unknown costs that come up on the project. That's a different kind of reserve than the one for controlling risks. The kind of reserve used for risks is called a **contingency reserve**, because its use is *contingent* on a risk actually materializing.

Project managers sometimes talk about both kinds of reserves together, because they both have to show up on the same budget. When they do, you'll sometimes hear talk of "known unknowns" and "unknown unknowns." The management reserve is for unknown unknowns—things that you haven't planned for but could impact your project. The contingency reserve is for known unknowns, or risks that you know about and explicitly planned for and put in your risk register.

The better you prepare for risks, the more secure your project is against the unknown.

Sharpen your pencil

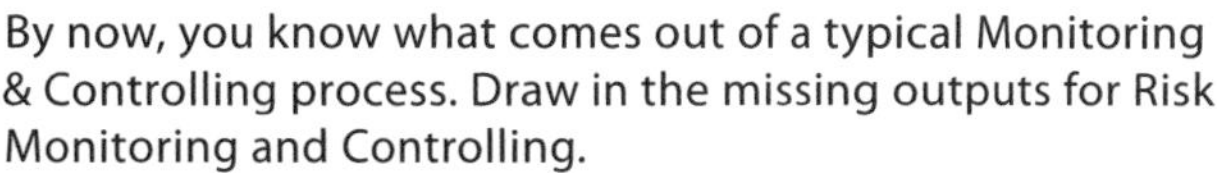

By now, you know what comes out of a typical Monitoring & Controlling process. Draw in the missing outputs for Risk Monitoring and Controlling.

Outputs

You'll find all sorts of things that need to be fixed. But you can't just go update the plan—you need this as an input to kick off change control.

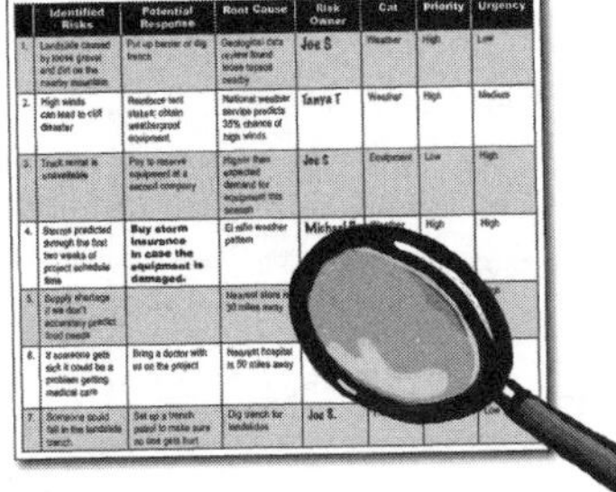

Risk Monitoring and Controlling

This one's all about helping others to learn from what's happened on your project

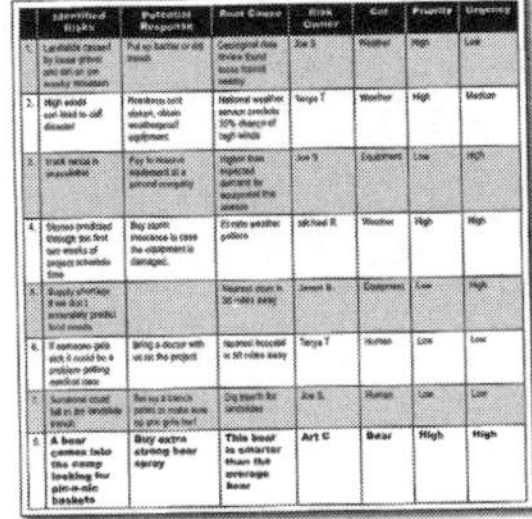

Risk Register Updates

Project Management Plan Updates

For these two, think about what you do once you have evaluated work performance information and found that something needs to happen.

Sharpen your pencil Solution

By now, you know what comes out of a typical Monitoring & Controlling process. Draw in the missing outputs for Risk Monitoring and Controlling.

Outputs

Risk monitoring and control is exactly like the other change control processes.

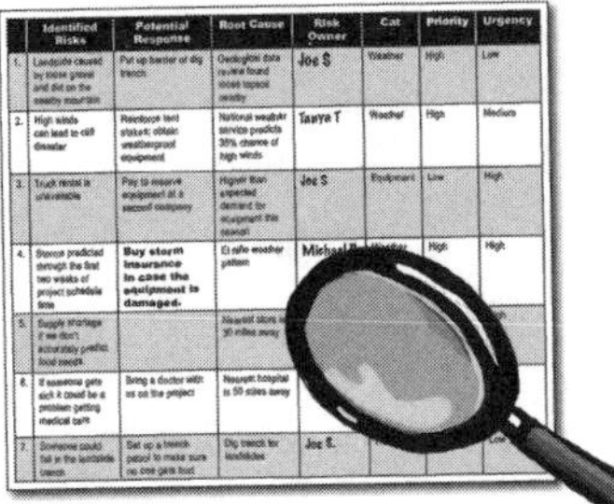

Risk Monitoring and Controlling

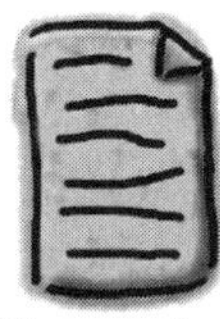

Requested Changes

Organizational Process Assets

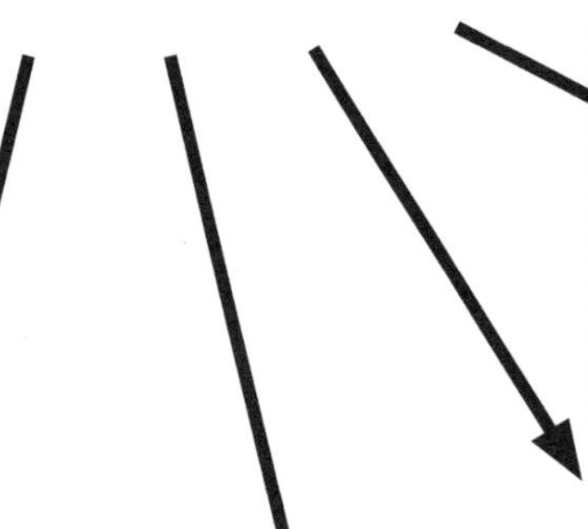

Project Management Plan Updates

Risk Register Updates

We added a risk to the register to account for a bear coming into the camp.

Recommended Corrective Actions

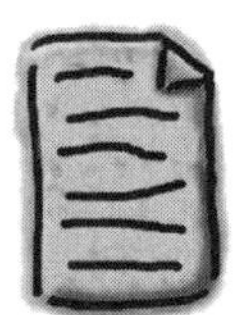

Recommended Preventative Actions

Recommended corrective and preventative actions are always outputs from a Monitoring & Controlling process.

* Note from the authors: We're not exactly sure why he feels his mission was accomplished after spraying a bear in the face and then jumping off of a cliff. But it seems to work!

Question Clinic: The "Which-is-NOT" Question

You'll see some questions on the exam that list inputs, outputs, tools, or concepts and ask you to determine which one of them is not part of the group. Usually, you can figure them out by going through the answer choices one by one and eliminating the one that doesn't belong.

117. Which of the following is not a Quantitative Analysis technique?

A. Sensitivity analysis

B. Expected monetary value

C. Reserve analysis

D. Monte Carlo analysis

This is the one with tornado diagrams. It's got to be part of the Group.

This one is definitely a quantitative analysis technique. Multiplying probability with the value of positive and negative outcomes of the project is all about putting numbers to risk.

Hmm. This one doesn't look quite right. It's about numbers. But it isn't concerned with assigning numbers to the risk. It's about assigning numbers to the contingency reserve. This might be the right answer.

D has to be the answer! This one is about using random numbers to model out possible risks on the project. It's definitely a part of quantitative analysis.

Take your time and think your way through it. All of them will have something in common but one. As long as you remember the group you're fitting them into, you won't have any trouble.

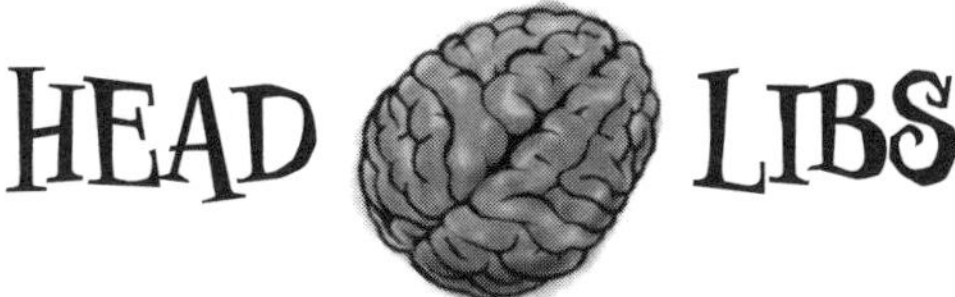

Fill in the blanks to come up with your own "Which-is-Not" question!

Which of the following is NOT a ______________________________ ?
(input, output, tool, process, or concept)

A. ______________________________
(input, output, tool, or process that is in the group)

B. ______________________________
(input, output, tool, or process that is in the group)

C. ______________________________
(input, output, tool, or process that is in the group)

D. ______________________________
(the right answer)

Join the Head First PMP community at **http://www.headfirstlabs.com/PMP** You can add your Head Libs answer, and see what Head Libs other project managers came up with!

Sharpen instructions go here. Careful not to get too close to the logo. Click on it and you'll see little blue lines that show the area you should avoid.

Take a look at this table of risks.

Risk	Probability	Impact
Navigation equipment failure	15%	costs $300 due to getting lost
Unseasonably warm weather	8%	save $500 in excavation costs
Wild animals eat rations	10%	costs $100 for replacement run

1. Calculate the EMV for each of these three risks.

Navigation equipment failure: 15% x -$300 = -$45.00

Unseasonably warm weather: 8% x $500 = $40.00

Wild animals eat rations: 10% x -$100 = -$10.00

Don't forget to use a positive value here because it's an opportunity, not a threat.

2. If these are the only risks on the project, calculate the total EMV.

Total EMV = -$45.00 + $40.00 + -$10.00 = -$15.00

You get the total EMV by adding up the EMV for each risk.

3. The latest weather report came out, and there is now a 20% chance of unseasonably warm weather. What's the new EMV for the project?

Unseasonably warm weather: 20% x $500 = $100.00

The new total EMV = -$45.00 + $100.00 + -$10.00 = $45.00

The EMV is now positive, which means the project should cost less than you originally budgeted.

4. Now the cost of replacement rations goes up to $150. What's the new EMV for the project?

Wild animals eat rations: 10% x -$150 = -$15.00

The new total EMV = -$45.00 + $100.00 + -$15.00 = $40.00

When the probability of high winds changed to 45%, then the probability of low winds also changed: to 55%.

Exercise Solution

Looking at the decision tree on the facing page, see if you can figure out the expected monetary value depending on the decisions the team makes.

1. You hear a weather report that says there's now a 45% chance of high winds. Does it still make sense to buy the heavier tent?

   EMV of choosing the heavier tent: -$350 plus (45% x -$48) plus (55% x -$10) = -$377.10

   EMV of choosing the lighter tent: -$130 plus (45% x -$953) plus (55% x -$15) = -$567.10

   It still makes sense to choose the heavier tent.

2. If you don't buy the heavier tent, then you have room to take along a wind generator that can power your equipment, and that will save you $1100 in portable batteries if there's a heavy wind. If there's still a 45% chance of high winds, does it still make sense to buy the heavier tent?

   EMV of choosing the heavier tent: -$350 plus (45% x -$48) plus (55% x -$10) = -$377.10

   EMV of choosing the lighter tent: -$130 plus (45% x $147) plus (55% x -$15) = -$72.10

   Now it makes sense to choose the lighter tent.

So where did this $147 come from? Well, if there's a heavy wind, then the generator turns this into an opportunity. You'll still see $953 in equipment damage, but that's offset by the $1,100 in savings for portable batteries. That puts you ahead by $147—but only if there's a

Which risk response technique is being used in these situations? Match each technique to its scenario.

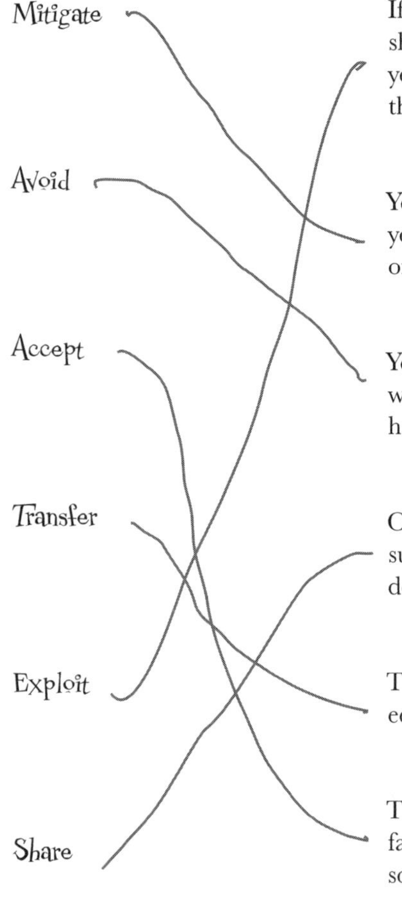

If the weather's good, then there's a chance you could see a meteor shower. If the team gets a photo that wins the meteor photo contest, you can get extra funding. You have your team stay up all night with their telescopes and cameras ready.

You hear that it's going to rain for the first three days of your trip, so you bring waterproof tents and indoor projects for the team to work on in the meantime.

You read that there's a major bear problem in the spring on the cliff where you are planning to work. You change your project start date to happen in the fall.

On your way up the cliff, you meet another team that is looking to survey the area. You offer to do half of the surveying work while they do the other half and then trade your findings with one another.

There's a high probability of water damage to some of your equipment, so you buy insurance to avoid losses.

There's always the chance that someone could make a mistake and fall off the cliff. No matter how much you plan for the unexpected, sometimes mistakes happen.

About 10 years ago a really rare bird, the black-throated blue warbler, was seen on this cliff. If you could get a picture of it, it would be worth a lot of money. So, you bring special seeds that you have read are really attractive to this bird, and you set up lookout points around the cliff with cameras ready to get the shot.

Exam Questions

1. The project manager for a construction project discovers that the local city council may change the building code to allow adjoining properties to combine their sewage systems. She knows that a competitor is about to break ground in the adjacent lot and contacts him to discuss the possibility of having both projects save costs by building a sewage system for the two projects.

This is an example of which strategy?

A. Mitigate

B. Share

C. Accept

D. Exploit

2. Which of the following is NOT a risk response technique?

A. Exploit

B. Transfer

C. Mitigate

D. Confront

3. You are using an RBS to manage your risk categories. What process are you performing?

A. Risk Planning

B. Risk Identification

C. Qualitative Analysis

D. Quantitative Analysis

4. Which of the following is used to monitor low priority risks?

A. Triggers

B. Watchlists

C. Probability and Impact Matrix

D. Monte Carlo analysis

Exam Questions

5. You're managing a construction project. There's a 30% chance that weather will cause a three-day delay, costing $12,000. There's also a 20% chance that the price of your building materials will drop, which will save $5,000. What's the total EMV for both of these?

A. –$3,600

B. $1,000

C. –$2,600

D. $4,600

6. Joe is the project manager of a large software project. When it's time to identify risks on his project, he contacts a team of experts and has them all come up with a list and send it in anonymously. What technique is Joe using?

A. SWOT

B. Ishikawa diagramming

C. Delphi

D. Brainstorming

7. Susan is project manager on a construction project. When she hears that her project has run into a snag due to weeks of bad weather on the job site, she says "No problem, we have insurance that covers cost overruns due to weather." What risk response strategy did she use?

A. Exploit

B. Transfer

C. Mitigate

D. Avoid

8. You're performing risk identification on a software project. Two of your team members have spent half of the meeting arguing about whether or not a particular risk is likely to happen on the project. You decide to table the discussion, but you're concerned that your team's motivation is at risk. The next item on the agenda is an discussion of a potential opportunity on the project in which you may be able to purchase a component for much less than it would cost to build.

Which of the following is NOT a valid way to respond to an opportunity?

A. Exploit

B. Transfer

C. Share

D. Enhance

Exam Questions

9. Risks that are caused by the response to another risk are called

A. Residual risks
B. Secondary risks
C. Cumulative risks
D. Mitigated risks

10. What's the main output of the Risk Management processes?

A. The Risk Management Plan
B. The Risk Breakdown Structure
C. Work Performance Information
D. The Risk Register

11. Tom is a project manager for an accounting project. His company wants to streamline its payroll system. The project is intended to reduce errors in the accounts payable system and has a 70% chance of saving the company $200,000 over the next year. It has a 30% chance of costing the company $100,000.

What's the project's EMV?

A. $170,000
B. $110,000
C. $200,000
D. $100,000

12. What's the difference between management reserves and contingency reserves?

A. Management reserves are used to handle known unknowns, while contingency reserves are used to handle unknown unknowns.
B. Management reserves are used to handle unknown unknowns, while contingency reserves are used to handle known unknowns.
C. Management reserves are used to handle high-priority risks, while contingency reserves are used to handle low-priority risks.
D. Management reserves are used to handle low-priority risks, while contingency reserves are used to handle high-priority risks.

Exam Questions

13. How often should a project manager discuss risks with the team?

A. At every milestone
B. Every day
C. Twice
D. At every status meeting

14. Which of the following should NOT be in the risk register?

A. Watchlists of low-priority risks
B. Relative ranking of project risks
C. Root causes of each risk
D. Probability and impact matrix

15. Which of the following is NOT true about risk management?

A. The project manager is the only person responsible for identifying risks
B. All known risks should be added to the risk register
C. Risks should be discussed at every team meeting
D. Risks should be analyzed for impact and priority

16. You're managing a project to remodel a kitchen. You find out from your supplier that there's a 50% chance that the model of oven that you planned to use may be discontinued, and you'll have to go with one that costs $650 more. What's the EMV of that risk?

A. $650
B. –$650
C. $325
D. –$325

17. Which risk analysis tool is used to model your risks by running simulations that calculate random outcomes and probabilities?

A. Monte Carlo analysis
B. Sensitivity analysis
C. EMV analysis
D. Delphi technique

Exam Questions

18. A construction project manager has a meeting with the team foreman, who tells him that there's a good chance that a general strike will delay the project. They brainstorm to try to find a way to handle it, but in the end decide that if there's a strike, there is no useful way to minimize the impact to the project. This is an example of which risk response strategy?

A. Mitigate

B. Avoid

C. Transfer

D. Accept

19. You're managing a project to fulfill a military contract. Your project team is assembled, and work has begun. Your government project officer informs you that a supplier that you depend on has lost the contract to supply a critical part. You consult your risk register and discover that you did not plan for this. What's the BEST way to handle this situation?

A. Consult the probability and impact matrix

B. Perform quantitative and qualitative risk analysis

C. Recommend preventive actions

D. Look for a new supplier for the part

20. Which of the following BEST describes risk audits?

A. The project manager reviews each risk on the risk register with the team

B. A senior manager audits your work and decides whether you're doing a good job

C. An external auditor reviews the risk response strategies for each risk

D. An external auditor reviews the project work to make sure the team isn't introducing new risk

Exam ~~Questions~~ Answers

1. Answer: B

Sharing is when a project manager figures out a way to use an opportunity to help not just her project but another project or person as well.

It's okay to share an opportunity with a competitor—that's a win-win situation.

2. Answer: D

Confronting is a conflict resolution technique.

2. Which of the following is NOT a risk response technique?

A. Exploit

You can exploit opportunities if they come up. Even positive risks have risk response techniques.

3. Answer: A

You use an RBS to figure out and organize your risk categories even before you start to identify them. Then you decompose the categories into individual risks as part of risk identification.

4. Answer: B

Your risk register should include watchlists of low priority risks, and you should review those risks at every status meeting to make sure that none of them have occurred.

5. Answer: C

The expected monetary value (or EMV) of the weather risk is the probability (30%) times the cost ($12,000), but don't forget that since it's a risk, that number should be negative. So its EMV is 30% x -$12,000 = -$3,600. The building materials opportunity has an EMV of 20% x $5,000 = $1,000. Add them up and you get -$3,600 + $1,000 = -$2,600.

When you're calculating EMV, negative risks give you negative numbers.

6. Answer: C

Using the Delphi technique, experts supply their opinions of risks for your project anonymously so that they each get a chance to think about the project without influencing each other.

6. Joe is the project manager of a large software project. When it's time to identify risks on his project, he contacts a team of experts and has them all come up with a list and send it in anonymously. What technique is Joe using?

D. Brainstorming

Common sense would tell you that this is the answer. But brainstorming doesn't have to be anonymous. So, it's got to be Delphi.

7. Answer: B

Susan bought an insurance policy to cover cost overruns due to weather. She transferred the risk from her company to the insurance company.

Wow, did you see that huge red herring?

8. Answer: B

You wouldn't want to transfer an opportunity to someone else! You always want to find a way to use that opportunity for the good of the project. That's why the response strategies for opportunities are all about figuring out ways to use the opportunity to improve your project (or another, in the case of sharing).

9. Answer: B

A secondary risk is a risk that could happen because of your response to another risk.

10. Answer: D

Most of the processes of Risk Management are about creating or updating the Risk Register.

The key to this one is to remember that the money the project makes is positive, and the money it will cost is negative.

11. Answer: B

$200,000 x 0.70 = $140,000 savings, and $100,000 x 0.30 = -$30,000 expenses. Add them together and you get $110,000.

Exam ~~Questions~~

12. Answer: B

Contingency reserves are a way to do risk response planning. You can think of a risk as a "known unknown"—an uncertain event that you know about, but which may not happen—and you can add contingency reserves to your budget in order to handle them. Management reserves are part of Cost Management – you use them to build a reserve into your budget for any unknown events that happen.

That's why it's useful to figure out the EMV for a risk—so you know how big your contingency reserve should be.

13. Answer: D

Risk monitoring and response is so important that you should go through your risk register at every status meeting!

14. Answer: D

The probability and impact matrix is a tool that you use to analyze risks. You might find it in your project management plan, but it's not included in the risk register.

15. Answer: A

It's really important that you get the entire team involved in risk response planning. The more people who look for risks, the more likely it is that you'll find the ones that will actually occur on your project.

16. Answer: D

Even though this looks a little wordy, it's just another EMV question. The probability of the risk is 50%, and the cost is -$650, so multiply the two and you get -$325.

17. Answer: A

This is just the definition of Monte Carlo analysis. That's where you use a computer simulation to see what different random probability and impact values do to your project.

Exam Questions

18. Answer: D

There are some risks that you just can't do anything about. When that happens, you have to accept them. But at least you can warn your stakeholders about the risk, so nobody is caught off guard.

19. Answer: D

You've got an unplanned event that's happened on your project. Is that a risk? No. It's a project problem, and you need to solve that problem. Your probability and impact matrix won't help, because the probability of this happening is 100%—it's already happened. No amount of risk planning will prevent or mitigate the risk. And there's no sense in trying to take preventive actions, because there's no way you can prevent it. So the best you can do is start looking for a new part supplier.

I see—this wasn't a risk at all, it was just a problem that came up during the project. I bet better risk planning might have helped the team prepare for this!

20. Answer: C

It's a good idea to bring in someone from outside of your project to review your risks. The auditor can make sure that each risk response is appropriate and really addresses the root causes of each risk.

12 Procurement Management

Getting Some Help

Some jobs are just too big for your company to do on its own. Even when the job isn't too big, it may just be that you don't have the expertise or equipment to do it. When that happens, you need to use **Procurement Management** to find another company to **do the work for you**. If you find the **right seller**, choose the **right kind of relationship**, and make sure that the **goals of the contract are met**, you'll get the job done, and your project will be a success.

Victim of her own success

Kate's last project went really well. In fact, maybe a little too well. The company's customer base grew so much that now the IT department's technical support staff is overwhelmed. Customers who call up looking for technical support have to spend a long time on hold, and that's not good for the company.

Calling in the cavalry

Kate: No problem. The hard part will be figuring out how to manage the transition. Are we going to try to expand the team immediately, or call in a supplier to help us out?

Ben: Whoa, hold on there! Is going outside the company even an option?

Kate: Look, our tech support team is already at full capacity, and it'll take months to upgrade the facilities to handle more people... not to mention hire and train up the staff. We may be able to handle it ourselves, but there's a good chance that the easiest way to get the job done is to go outside our company to find a vendor to do the work.

Ben: But isn't it kind of risky thinking about working with another company? I mean, what if they go out of business during our project? Or what if they cost too much?

Kate: Well, we'll need to make sure that we answer those questions. But this isn't the first time our company's brought on a contractor like this. The legal department has done this kind of thing before. I'll set up a meeting with somebody over there and see if they can help us out.

Ben: Okay, you can follow up on that. But I'm still not sure about this.

Sometimes you need to hire an outside company to do some of your project work. That's called procurement, and the outside company is called the seller.

Wait a minute. I'm not a lawyer. Why should I have to know a bunch of details about contracting?

You need to be involved because it's your project, and you're responsible for it.

One of the most common mistakes people make on the exam (and in real life) is to assume that if another company is selling products or services for your project and they don't deliver, it's not your problem. After all, you've got a contract with the company, right? So if they don't deliver, they won't get paid.

Well, it's not that simple. Yes, there are plenty of sellers who fail to deliver on their contracts. But for each seller that doesn't deliver, there's a frustrated project manager whose project ran into trouble because of it. That's why a lot of the Procurement Management tools and techniques are focused on selecting the *right* seller and communicating exactly what you'll need to the people doing the work.

Watch it!

The PMP exam is based on contracting laws and customs in the United States.

Are you used to working in a country that ISN'T the U.S.? Then you should be especially careful about these processes. You may be used to working with contracts in a way that isn't exactly the same as how they'll work on the exam questions. Luckily, the U.S. government publishes a lot of information on contracting at http://www.acquisition.gov/ Take a look at the site if you want a little more background.

Contract Process Magnets

There are six Procurement Management processes. They're pretty easy to understand—you can probably guess which ones are which from their descriptions. Connect the description of each process with its name, and then try to guess which process group it's in.

Descriptions of each process	Process names	Process groups
Plan out what you'll purchase, and how and when you will need the contracts to be negotiated for your project.	....	....
Come up with a plan for each contract you need to have. Figure out how you will evaluate different sellers, how you will make sure that all interested sellers are given a fair shot at the contract, and what you need to do to make sure that it runs smoothly.	....	....
Get information about your project out to sellers who want to do the work. Figure out who is qualified to help you and who isn't.	....	....
Decide on the seller (or sellers) you are going to work with, and finalize and sign the contract.	....	....
Keep tabs on the contract. Make sure your company is getting what you paid for.	....	....
Confirm that the work was done right and that all obligations are fulfilled on both sides.	....	....

Plan Purchases & Acquisitions

Closing

Request Seller Responses

Monitoring & Controlling

Contract Administration

Planning

Planning

Executing

Select Sellers

Executing

Contract Closure

Plan Contracting

Contract Process Magnets Solutions

There are six Procurement Management processes. They're pretty easy to understand—you can probably guess which ones are which from their descriptions. Connect the description of each process with its name, and then try to guess which process group it's in.

Descriptions of each process	Process names	Process groups
Plan out what you'll purchase, and how and when you will need the contracts to be negotiated for your project.	Plan Purchases & Acquisitions	Planning
Come up with a plan for each contract you need to have. Figure out how you will evaluate different sellers, how you will make sure that all interested sellers are given a fair shot at the contract, and what you need to do to make sure that it runs smoothly.	Plan Contracting	Planning
Get information about your project out to sellers who want to do the work. Figure out who is qualified to help you and who isn't.	Request Seller Responses	Executing
Decide on the seller (or sellers) you are going to work with, and finalize and sign the contract.	Select Sellers	Executing
Keep tabs on the contract. Make sure your company is getting what you paid for.	Contract Administration	Monitoring & Controlling
Confirm that the work was done right and that all obligations are fulfilled on both sides.	Contract Closure	Closing

The first planning process is for planning everything you're doing for procurement. The second process is for planning each individual contract.

You'll see the word "seller" used to refer to any person or company selling a service. It means the same thing as "consultant," "vendor," "contractor," etc.

The "buyer" is the person or company that hires the seller.

This process is for making changes to the contract, and correcting any problems with the seller's work.

There are only two Closing processes, and this is one of them.

Ask the legal expert

Kate: Thanks for coming by, Steve. We're looking for a contractor to handle tech support while we bring on more people in our call center. How do we normally handle this stuff?

Steve: Here's how it usually works. I'll actually write the contract and do the negotiation. But before I do that, I'll need to sit down with you to understand what the contract has to accomplish.

Kate: So I'm not involved at all?

Steve: Oh, you're definitely involved. You need to help with the negotiations, because you're the only person who really understands what we're trying to accomplish with the contract.

Kate: Okay, that makes sense. So when do we get started?

Steve: Well, not so fast. We need to be really sure that the way we pick our vendors is absolutely fair. We've got some company guidelines that you'll need to follow. And once we've got the contract signed and the work is underway, we'll need to meet to make sure the contract is really being followed. And if there's a problem and we need to negotiate a change to the contract, you'll need me to do it.

Kate: Okay, I can handle that. So should I start working on something to send out to sellers?

Steve: Not quite. Before we even get started with all of that, are you sure we really need to contract this work?

What should Kate do to figure out if it's really a good idea to contract the work?

Anatomy of a contract

Procurement is pretty intuitive, and the **six Procurement Management processes** follow a really sensible order. First you plan what you need to contract; then you plan how you'll do it. Next, you send out your contract requirements to sellers. They bid for the chance to work with you. You pick the best one, and then you sign the contract with them. Once the work begins, you monitor it to make sure the contract is being followed. When the work is done, you close out the contract and fill out all the paperwork.

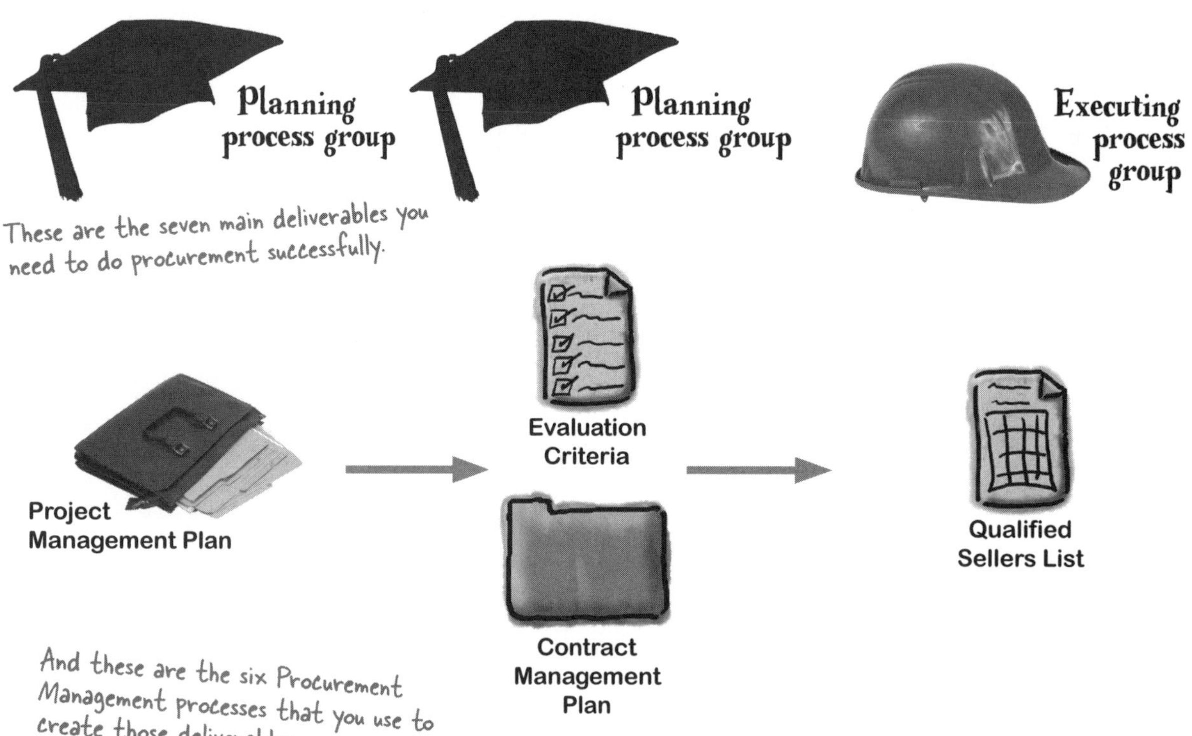

Plan Purchases and Acquisitions process

Here's where you take a close look at your needs, to be sure that you really need to create a contract. You figure out what kinds of contracts make sense for your project, and you try to define all of the parts of your project that will be contracted out.

Plan Contracting process

Here's where you plan out each individual contract for the project work. You work out how you manage the contract, what metrics it will need to meet to be considered successful, how you'll pick a seller, and how you'll administer the contract once the work is happening.

Request Seller Responses process

This process is all about getting the word out to potential contract partners about the project and how they can help you. You hold bidders conferences and find qualified sellers that can do the work.

You can have several contracts for a single project

The first Procurement Management process is **Plan Purchases and Acquisitions**. It's a familiar planning process, and you use it to plan out all of your procurement activities for the project. The other five processes are done for every contract. Here's an example. Say you're managing a construction project, and you've got one contract with an electrician and another one with a plumber. That means you'll go through those five processes two separate times, once for each contractor.

Executing process group

Monitoring & Controlling process group

Closing process group

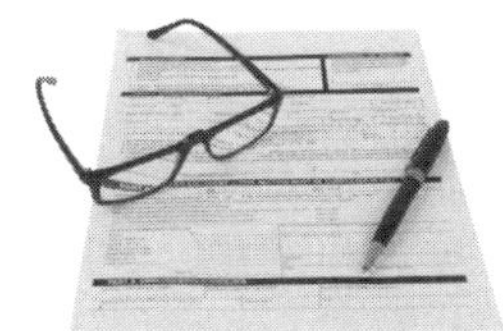

Contract

Contract Management Plan

Closed Contracts

The Contract Management Plan tells you how to handle changes to your contract—just like any other Monitoring & Controlling process.

Select Sellers process

Next, you evaluate all of the responses to your procurement documents and find the seller that suits your needs the best. When you find them, you sign the contract and then the work can begin.

Contract Administration process

When the contract is underway, you stay on top of the work and make sure the contract is adhered to. You monitor what the contractor is producing and make sure everything is running smoothly. Occasionally, you'll need to make changes to the contract. Here's where you'll find and request those changes.

Close Contract process

When the work is done, you'll close your contract out. You'll make sure that the product that is produced meets the criteria for the contract and that the contractor gets paid.

Start with a plan for the whole project

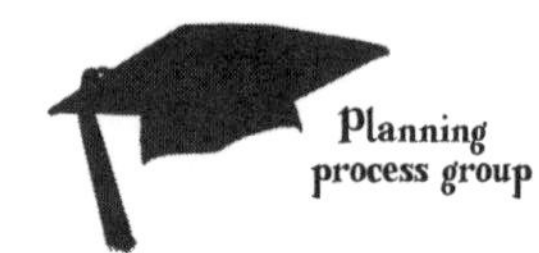

You need to think about all of the work that you will contract out for your project before you do anything else. The **Plan Purchases and Acquisitions process** is all about figuring that out and writing up a plan for how you'll do it.

Inputs

Here's where you'll find a good description of the work you're going to contract.

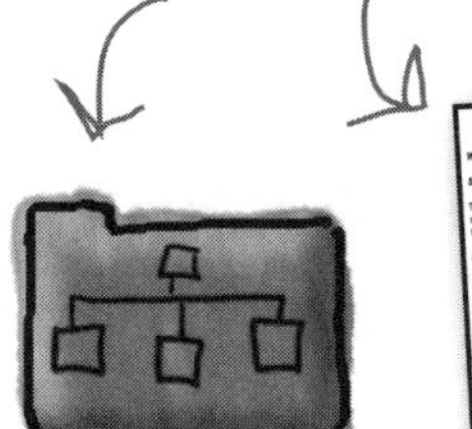

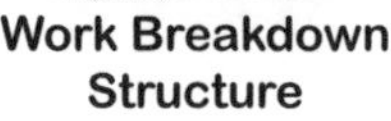

Work Breakdown Structure

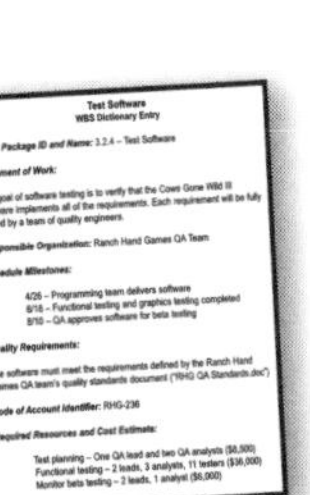

WBS Dictionary

Your scope and PM Plan tell you a lot about the work you need to do and how this contract will fit into it.

Project Scope Statement

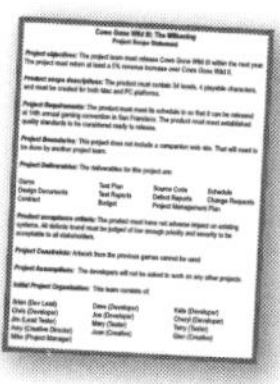

Project Management Plan

You need to consider the level of expertise your company has with the product or work you're thinking of contracting, as well as the job and contracting markets you operate in.

Enterprise Environmental Factors

Organizational Process Assets

Here's where your company's procurement policies and templates are kept.

Tools

Make or buy analysis means figuring out whether or not you should be contracting the work or doing it yourself. It could also mean deciding whether to build your own solution to your problem or buy one that is already available. Most of the same factors that help you make every other major project decision will help you with this one. How much does it cost to build it versus buy it? How will this decision affect the scope of your project? How about your project schedule? Do you have time to do the work and still meet your commitments? As you plan out what you will and won't contract, you need to have thought through your reasoning pretty carefully.

There are some resources (like heavy equipment) that your company can buy, rent, or lease depending on the situation. You'll need to examine leasing versus buying costs and determine the best way to go forward.

This plan will have:

- the planned delivery dates for the work or products you are contracting
- the company's standard documents you will use
- the contract types you plan to use, and any metrics that will be used to measure the contractor's performance
- any constraints or assumptions you need to know about all of the contracts you plan to create for your project

Procurement Management Plan

Expert Judgment means asking someone who's made the same kind of decision before to help you look at all the information you have for your project and make the right decision. Experts can be really helpful in evaluating technology, or providing insight into how your work might be done in different sourcing scenarios.

Contract types: You should know a little bit about the major kinds of contracts available to you so that you choose the one that creates the most fair and workable deal for you and the contractor. Some contracts are **Fixed Price**: no matter how much time or effort goes into them, you always pay the same. Some are **Cost Reimbursable**—sometimes called **Cost Plus**—where the seller charges you for the cost of doing the work plus some fee or rate. The third major kind of contract is **Time and Materials**. That's where the buyer pays a rate for the time spent working on the project and also pays for all of the materials used to do the work.

These contract types will show up on the PMP exam. But don't worry if you don't feel like you get them yet. We'll spend plenty of time on them a little later in this chapter.

Outputs

This is just a list of the work that will be contracted. This statement of work will be given to potential contracting partners later.

Contract Statement of Work

After doing your make or buy analysis, you write down what you learned so that other people understand your rationale.

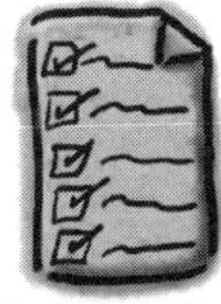

Make or Buy Decisions

While you're doing procurement planning, you might find some changes that need to be made to other plans.

Requested Changes

Because sometimes it's not worth having your team do part of the job.

If your company needed to renovate your office, would you hire the carpenter, electrician, and builders? Would you buy the power tools, cement mixer, trucks, and ladders? Of course not. You'd hire a contractor to do the work, because it would cost too much to buy all that stuff for one job, and you wouldn't want to hire people just for the job and then fire them when it was done. Well, the same goes for a lot of jobs on your projects. You don't always want to have your company build everything. There are a lot of jobs where you want to hire a ***seller***.

There are a lot of words for the company you're hiring: contractor, consultant, external company... but for the PMP exam, you'll always see the term "seller."

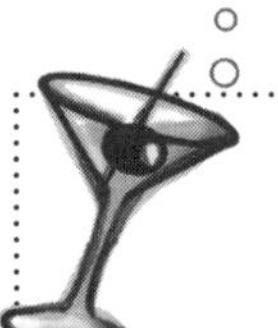

It's natural to feel a little nervous about this contracting stuff.

A lot of project managers have only ever worked with teams inside their own companies. All this talk of contracts, lawyers, proposals, bids, and conferences can be intimidating if you've never seen it before. But don't worry. Managing a project with a contractor is really similar to managing one that uses your company's employees. There are just a few new tools and techniques that you need to learn… but they're not hard, and you'll definitely get the hang of them really quickly.

Make or Buy Magnets

Figure out whether or not Kate and Ben should contract out the tech support work by organizing these facts about the project into make or buy columns. The first few have been done for you.

This really is how a lot of people handle make or buy decisions—looking at all of the information you have for the project and using it to determine whether the facts line up under "Make" or "Buy."

Make	Buy
Training the contractor's employees will be less valuable because we won't be able to use their knowledge when the contract is up.	The next big product release is 6 months away.
	We think the procurement process will take around 3 months, and ramping up staff in the call center will take 8 months.

It might be hard to control quality of the contractor's work.

Our estimate is that it will cost around $30,000 per month to hire an additional 10 people and reduce wait time to 10 minutes per call. The cheapest contract for this is around $40,000 per month.

The contract team can have a staff trained and ready within a month from the signed contract.

The cost for equipment and training for a 10-person team is around $50,000. Contracts could be drawn up to cut that cost down a lot.

Contracting companies who specialize in tech support have access to a lot of information and best practices that could make the project go more smoothly.

Make or Buy Magnets Solutions

Figure out whether or not Kate and Ben should contract out the tech support work by organizing these facts about the project into make or buy columns. The first few have been done for you.

There's no way they are going to be able to support even more customers with a new product in 6 months if they don't have the staff then.

Make

It might be hard to control quality of the contractor's work.

Our estimate is that it will cost around $30,000 per month to hire an additional 10 people and reduce wait time to 10 minutes per call. The cheapest contract for this is around $40,000 per month.

Training the contractor's employees will be less valuable because we won't be able to use their knowledge when the contract is up.

Buy

The next big product release is 6 months away.

We think the procurement process will take around 3 months and ramping up staff in the call center will take 8 months.

The cost for equipment and training for a 10-person team is around $50,000. Contracts could be drawn up to cut that cost down a lot.

The contract team can have a staff trained and ready within a month from the signed contract.

Contracting companies who specialize in tech support have access to a lot of information and best practices that could make the project go more smoothly.

Even though the staff costs will be higher with the contractor, not having to pay for equipment and training could offset the higher labor cost.

Sometimes contractors can bring their expertise from running lots of similar projects and make everything run more smoothly than it would if you do it yourself.

The decision is made

Doing make or buy analysis just means understanding the reasons for the contract and deciding whether or not to contract out the work. Once you've done that, if you still think contracting is an option, then you should have a good idea of what you need to get out of the contracting process.

Types of contracts

If you want to see a really thorough overview of the different types of contracts, check out the U.S. Federal Acquisition Regulation web site:

http://www.acquisition.gov/far/

It's a good idea to know a little bit about the most commonly used contract types. They can help you come up with a contract that will give both you and the seller the best chance of success.

Fixed price contracts

Some PMP exam questions might just refer to a contract type by its acronym (FP, CPFF, etc.).

Fixed price (FP) means that you are going to pay one amount regardless of how much it costs the contractor to do the work. A fixed price contract only makes sense in cases where the scope is very well known. If there are any changes to the amount of work to be done, the seller doesn't get paid any more to do it.

Fixed price plus incentive fee (FPIF) means that you are going to pay a fixed price for the contract and give a bonus based on some performance goal. You might set up a contract where the team gets a $50,000 bonus if they manage to deliver an acceptable product before the contracted date.

Don't worry about trying to cram these into your head right now—you'll get a lot of practice with them throughout the chapter.

Cost-reimbursable contracts

Costs plus fixed fee (CPFF) means what it says. You pay the seller back for the costs involved in doing the work, plus you agree to an amount that you will pay on top of that.

Costs plus percentage of costs (CPPC) is similar to the CPFF contract, except that instead of paying a fee on top of the costs, you agree to pay a percentage of the total costs of the project.

Costs plus incentive fee (CPIF) means you'll reimburse costs on the project and pay a fee if some performance goals are met. Kate could set up her project using this contract type by suggesting that the team will get a $50,000 bonus if they keep the average wait time for the calls down to seven minutes per customer for over a month. If she were on a CPIF contract, she would pay the team their costs for doing the work, and also the a $50,000 bonus when they met that goal.

A lot of people say that the T&M contract is a lot like a combination of a cost-plus and fixed price contract, because you pay a fixed price per hour for labor, but on top of that you pay for costs like in a cost-plus contract.

Time and Materials

Time and Materials (T&M) is used in labor contracts. It means that you will pay a rate for each of the people working on your project plus their materials costs. The "Time" part means that the buyer pays a fixed rate for labor – usually a certain number of dollars per hour. And the "Materials" part means that the buyer also pays for materials, equipment, office space, administrative overhead costs, and anything else that has to be paid for. The seller typically purchases those things and bills the buyer for them. This is a really good contract to use if you don't know exactly how long your contract will last, because it protects both the buyer and seller.

Even if your project has several contracts, they don't all have to be the same type. That's why you need to administer each one separately.

Sharpen your pencil

This is a tough one—take your time and think about each kind of contract.

There are advantages and disadvantages to every kind of contract. Different kinds of contracts carry different risks to both the buyer and seller. Can you think of some of them?

Here's a hint: FP contracts don't have much risk for the buyer.

Fixed price (FP)

Risks to the buyer ....

Risks to the seller ....

Fixed price plus incentive fee (FPIF)

Risks to the buyer ....

Risks to the seller ....

Cost plus fixed fee (CPFF)

Risks to the buyer ....

Risks to the seller ....

CPPC contracts are really risky for the buyer, not the seller. Can you figure out why?

Cost plus percentage of costs (CPPC)

Risks to the buyer ....

Risks to the seller ....

Cost plus incentive fee (CPIF)

Risks to the buyer ....

Risks to the seller ....

Time and Materials (T&M)

Risks to the buyer ....

Risks to the seller ....

Sharpen your pencil Solution

There are advantages and disadvantages to every kind of contract. Different kinds of contracts carry different risks to both the buyer and seller. Can you think of some of them?

There are a lot of right answers—even if yours aren't here, it doesn't mean that they're wrong.

A fixed-price contract has a lot more risk for the seller than the buyer.

Fixed price (FP)

Risks to the buyer: **The only risk is if the seller doesn't deliver because of costs**

Risks to the seller: **Unexpected costs could be bigger than the contract itself**

Fixed price plus incentive fee (FPIF)

Risks to the buyer: **There's still not much risk to the seller in fixed price contracts**

Risks to the seller: **The seller still has the same risks as FP, but may make more**

Cost plus fixed fee (CPFF)

CPFF contracts have risks for both the buyer and the seller.

Risks to the buyer: **If the costs are too high, the buyer will have to pay a lot more**

Risks to the seller: **A fixed fee on top of costs might not be worth it for the seller**

Cost plus percentage of costs (CPPC)

CPPC contracts are the most risky ones for the buyer, because if costs get really high then they end up paying a whole lot of money for it

Risks to the buyer: **If costs get high, then this is REALLY expensive for the buyer**

Risks to the seller: **The seller doesn't have much risk in this kind of contract**

Cost plus incentive fee (CPIF)

Incentive fees are a really good way to reduce the risk to the buyer on a cost-plus contract.

Risks to the buyer: **There's still a risk of cost overruns, but it's not as bad**

Risks to the seller: **The incentive fee isn't guaranteed, so it might not be paid**

Time and Materials (T&M)

A lot of T&M contracts include a "cost-not-to-exceed" clause to make sure this doesn't happen. If the contract doesn't have this, it can get really risky for the buyer!

Risks to the buyer: **If costs are too high, the contract could get expensive**

Risks to the seller: **The contract might not cover high overhead costs**

Take a minute and try to figure out *why* the T&M contract is a really good choice if you don't know how long the job will last.

More about contracts

There are just a few more things you need to know about any contract to do procurement work.

Every contract needs to outline the work to be done and the payment for that work.

- You might see an exam question that mentions "consideration"—that's just another word for the payment.
- Remember in Risk Management how you used insurance to transfer risk to another company? You did that using a special kind of contract called an insurance policy.
- You might get a question that asks about ***force majeure***. This is a kind of clause that you'll see in a contract. It says that if something like a war, riot, or natural disaster happens, you're excused from the terms of the contract.

Always pay attention to the point of total assumption.

- The **point of total assumption** is the point at which the seller assumes the costs. In a fixed price contract, this is the point where the costs have gotten so large that the seller basically runs out of money from the contract and has to start paying the costs.

You should always make sure both the buyer and seller are satisfied.

- When you negotiate a contract, you should make sure that the buyer and the seller **both** feel comfortable with the terms of the contract. You don't want the people at the seller's company to feel like they got a raw deal—after all, you're depending on them to do good work for your project.

You might see this kind of question about whether to make or buy. Here's a chance to get a little more practice with making contract decisions.

Kate has **18 months** to build up the capacity her company needs to handle all the technical support calls. See if you can figure out whether it's a better deal for Kate to make or buy.

1. If they handle the extra work within the company instead of finding a seller, it will cost an extra $35,000 in overtime and $11,000 in training costs in total, on top of the $4,400 per person per month for the five-person team needed to do the extra support work. What's the total cost of for keeping the work within the company?

2. Kate and Ben talked to a few companies and estimate that it will cost $20,000 per month to hire another company to do the work, but they'll also need to spend $44,000 in setup costs. What will contracting the work cost?

3. So does it make more sense to make or buy? Why?

Answers on page 608.

Build a separate plan for each contract

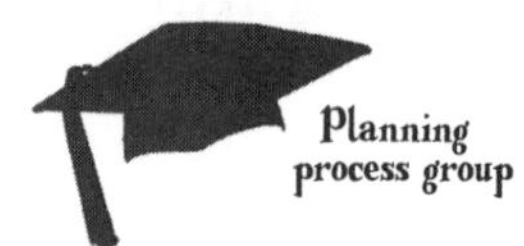

If you've got a good relationship with a single seller, you can call someone up at the seller and easily make a deal. But most procurement doesn't really work like that—especially if you want to contact multiple sellers and ask them to submit bids, so you can compare them and hire the one that's the best fit. There's a lot of homework you need to do before you start getting in touch with sellers, and that's what the **Plan Contracting process** is for.

Inputs

The first three inputs are ones that came right out of the Plan Purchases and Acquisitions process.

Procurement Management Plan

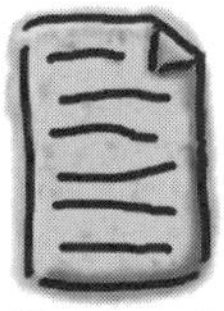

Contract Statement of Work

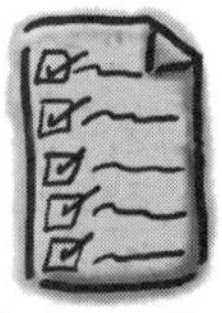

Make or Buy Decisions

Organizational Process Assets

Can you think what organizational process assets you'd need to plan out each contract?

Tools

Standard Forms

One of the most common ways that you find sellers for a job is by putting together a **Request for Proposals**, or **RFP**. This is when you prepare a description of the job to send to potential sellers to let them know what kind of work you need done. If you work in a company that hires a lot of sellers, then it usually has a "fill-in-the-blanks" style template or other kind of form that makes it a lot easier for you to create the documents you need to send out to the potential sellers.

It would be really hard to start putting together some of the documents you need to send out to sellers by opening up a blank document in a word processor. That's why standard forms are really helpful.

Here's what the Plan Contracting process looks like. It's pretty straightforward, with just two tools.

Any time you need to write a contract or other documents you'll send to a seller, you'll need to bring in legal experts.

Expert Judgment

Just like in the last process, you'll almost always need to rely on **experts** from outside your project team to help with the legal stuff. For example, you'll send out to potential sellers, because they usually have legal stuff in them.

Outputs

You'll use this output to help you find the sellers that will do the work.

Procurement Documents

And you'll use this one to help you figure out which seller you want to hire.

Evaluation Criteria

While you're planning each contract, you'll usually figure out that there's additional stuff you want the seller to do, so you'll go back and update the SOW.

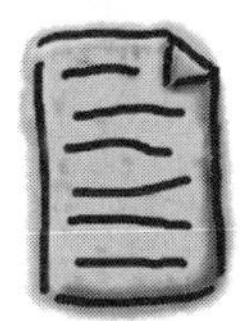

Contract Statement of Work Updates

What's the difference between the Plan Purchases and Acquisitions process and the Plan Contracting process? What do you think you'd use the outputs of Plan Contracting for?

Figure out how you'll sort out potential sellers

The two big outputs of Plan Contracting are the **procurement documents** and **evaluation criteria.** The procurement documents are what you'll use to find potential sellers who want your business. The evaluation criteria are what you'll use to figure out which sellers you want to use.

Procurement Documents

A big part of Procurement Management is making sure that both the buyers and sellers are treated fairly. Writing out evaluation criteria beforehand is a good way to make sure each seller gets a fair shake.

Evaluation Criteria

You'd be amazed at how many sellers respond to bids that they have no business responding to. You definitely need to make sure the seller has the skill and capacity to do the work you need.

There are a bunch of different documents you might want to send to sellers who want to bid on your work.

You'll usually include the **contract statement of work (SOW)** so that sellers know exactly what work is involved.

An **invitation for bid (IFB)** is a document that tells sellers that you want them to submit proposals. This is the **same thing as the RFP**.

There's another kind of invitation—an **invitation for quote (IFQ)**. This is a way to tell sellers that you want them to give you a quote on a fixed-price contract to do the work.

A **purchase order** is something you'll send out to a seller who you know that you want to work with. It's an agreement to pay for certain goods or services.

In some cases you'll want to allow for more flexibility in your contract. If you're hiring a seller to build something for you that you've never built before, you'll often encourage them to help you set the scope instead of locking it down.

Decide in advance on how you want to evaluate whether or not to hire sellers.

There are a lot of ways you can evaluate a potential seller. Figuring out if a seller is appropriate for your work is something that takes a lot of talking and thinking—and there's no single, one-size-fits-all way of evaluating sellers. But there are some things that you should definitely look for in any seller:

- Can the seller actually do the work you need done?
- How much will the seller charge?
- Can the seller cover any costs and expenses necessary to do the job?
- Are there subcontractors involved that you need to know about?
- Does the seller really understand everything in the SOW and contract?
- Is the seller's project management capability up to the task?

You always put together procurement documents and evaluation criteria <u>before</u> you start talking to individual sellers who want your business.

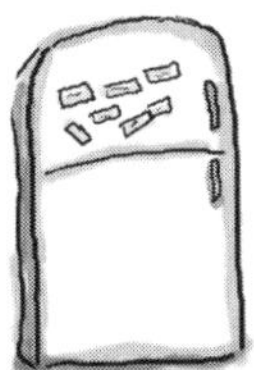

Contract Magnets

Which of the magnets are part of the procurement documents, and which of them are part of the evaluation criteria?

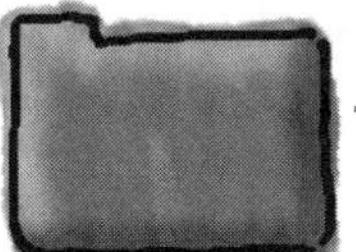

Procurement Documents

Get a financial statement or credit report and verify that the seller is insured.

Contract statement of work.

Meet with the project manager and review project processes

Notification to sellers requesting a quotation for fixed price work

Sample contract for review

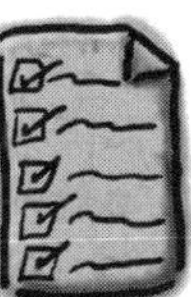

Evaluation Criteria

Go over final pricing plan and contract terms

Request for proposals

Review the SOW with the seller to make sure it's understood

Answers on page 609.

Get in touch with potential sellers

The next step in procurement is pretty straightforward. You use the **Request Seller Responses process** to, well, get the word out to sellers and see what kind of responses you get.

If your company has a list of preferred sellers, you'll find it here.

Inputs

You're using the procurement documents from the last process as an input to this one.

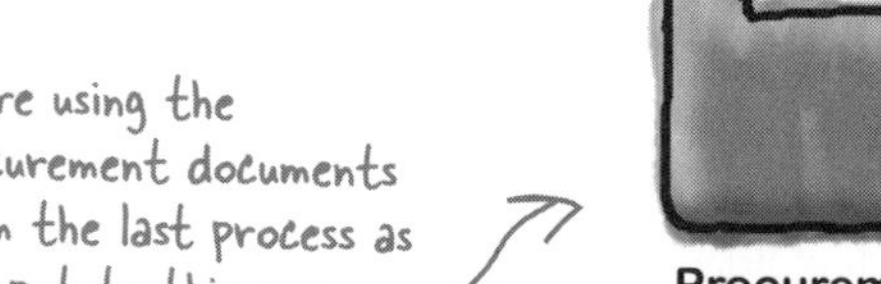

Procurement Documents

Procurement Management Plan

Organizational Process Assets

Tools

Bidder Conferences

It's really important that you make sure all of the bidders can compete in a fair, unbiased way. And the best way to do that is to get them all in a room together, so that they can ask questions about your contract. That way you don't give any one seller an advantage by providing inside information that the other sellers don't have access to.

A qualified seller is any potential seller who you or your company thinks is capable of doing the work for the contract.

Advertising

Sometimes the best way to get in touch with sellers is to place an ad. Also, sometimes you are **required** to take out an ad (like for some government-funded projects) in order to give all sellers full notice.

Develop Qualified Sellers List

Some companies have a qualified seller list that every project manager uses. This is just a list of all of the sellers that the company knows about and does business with. It's always a good idea to have a list of sellers, though, so if there isn't one for your company, you should put one together specifically for the project. That way you can keep track of all the sellers.

Outputs

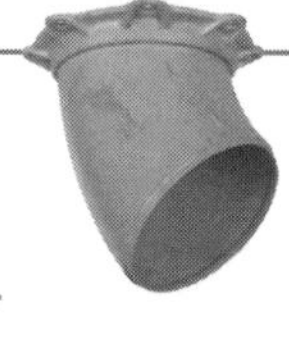

This is just the procurement documents all packaged up so that they're easy to deliver to a seller.

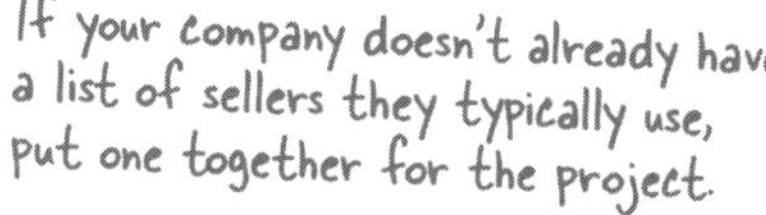

If your company doesn't already have a list of sellers they typically use, put one together for the project.

Procurement Document Package

Qualified Sellers List

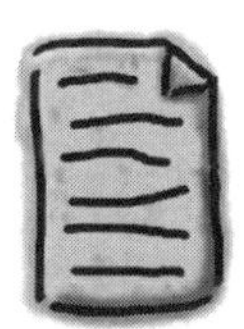

Proposals

The seller puts together a proposal and sends it to the buyer. This is the seller's answer to everything you asked for. If you asked for bids or quotes, you'll find them here.

Kate is putting out an RFP to find a seller to provide technical support for her company. Can you figure out which Request Seller Responses tool she's using?

1. Kate checks her company's organizational process asset library to see if there are any standard sellers it typically uses. She can't find one, so she creates it herself.

   ....

2. Kate's contacts an IT trade journal and places a classified ad to try to find sellers.

   ....

3. The CEO's brother-in-law runs a company that's bidding on the contract. Kate needs to make sure he gets fair—not preferential—treatment. She doesn't want to give him an unfair advantage, but she also doesn't want to exclude him from the bidding process. So she gathers representatives from all sellers into a room where they can ask questions about the contract out in the open and hear the responses to each question.

   ....

4. Kate's company takes part in an equal-opportunity program in which seller companies owned by minorities must be given notice of any RFPs. She uses a web site approved by the program to make sure she gives them notice.

   ....

Answers on page 608.

there are no Dumb Questions

Q: Do I always need to hold a bidder conference whenever I do procurement?

A: No, you don't always need a bidder conference. Sometimes your company has a preferred supplier who you always deal with, so you don't have to advertise for sellers. And sometimes there's a **sole source** for a particular service or part—there may only be one company that provides it. In that case, advertising and bidder conferences would be pointless.

The bidder conference has two goals. The first is to make sure that you answer all of the questions from potential sellers. But the other is to make sure that all potential sellers are treated equally and have access to the same information.

Q: I'm still not clear on why I'd want to use a "cost plus" contract.

A: One of the best reasons to use a cost plus contract is to make sure that the seller you're working with doesn't end up getting a raw deal. A fixed price contract can be pretty risky for a seller. When the seller uses a cost plus contract—like a cost plus incentive fee, or cost plus fixed fee—it means that there's a built-in guarantee that the seller won't have to swallow cost overruns. If you're reasonably certain that the costs can be contained, or if you set up a good incentive system, then a cost plus contract can be a really good one for making sure that both the buyer and seller are treated fairly.

Q: Why all this talk about treating the seller fairly? I'm trying to get the best deal I can. Doesn't that mean I should try to get as many concessions from sellers as possible?

A: One of the most important parts of procurement is that both the buyer and seller should feel like they're getting a good deal. You should never expect a seller to have to take on a bad contract. After all, you're depending on the seller to deliver a necessary piece of your project. That's why the goal in any procurement should always be for the buyer and seller to both feel like they were treated fairly.

Pick a partner

You've figured out what services you want to procure, and you've gone out and found a list of potential sellers. Now it's time to choose one of them to do the project work—and that's exactly what you do in the **Select Sellers process**.

Inputs

Procurement Document Package

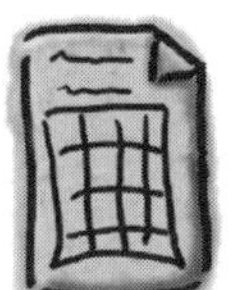

Qualified Sellers List

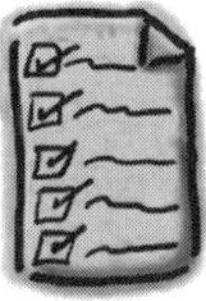

Evaluation Criteria

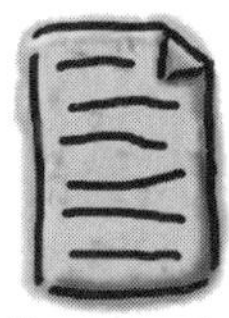

Proposals

Organizational Process Assets

Procurement Management Plan

Remember how the Procurement Management processes all come one after another? That's why all the inputs to Select Sellers are exactly what you put together in the last two processes.

Tools

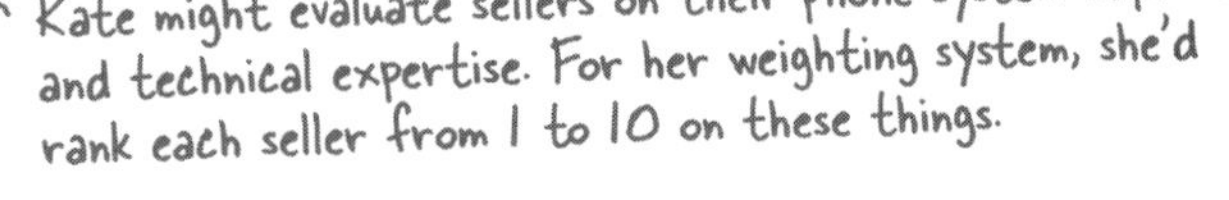

Weighting System

A really effective way to make sure you're evaluating sellers fairly is to figure out how to assign a number to each of the evaluation criteria. This gives you an objective measurement for each potential partner.

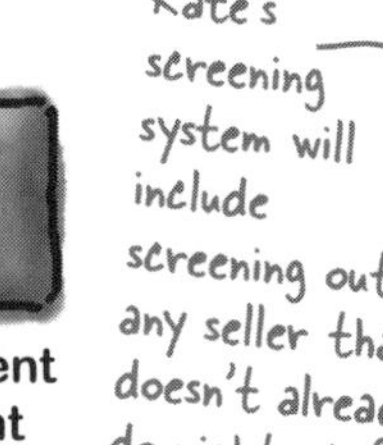

Screening System

This tool works well with the weighting system, and it's very good for working with long lists of potential sellers. You publish a list of criteria that each seller must meet and don't even accept bids from any sellers who don't meet the criteria.

Independent Estimates

A lot of the time, you don't have the expertise in your company to figure out whether or not a seller is quoting you a fair price. That's why you'll often turn to a third party to come up with an estimate of what the work should cost.

Seller Rating System

A lot of companies will have a separate rating system already set up to help you choose a seller. They keep track of how well the sellers' work has gone in the past and rate each seller on their performance so you can easily evaluate them.

Expert Judgment

Here's another case where it's really good to bring in someone from outside your project to help evaluate each proposal. You should bring in someone with a lot of specific expertise in the work being done to make sure the seller is up to the job.

The whole point of the Select Sellers process is, well, to select sellers... and here they are. Along with the contract, this is the most important output of the process.

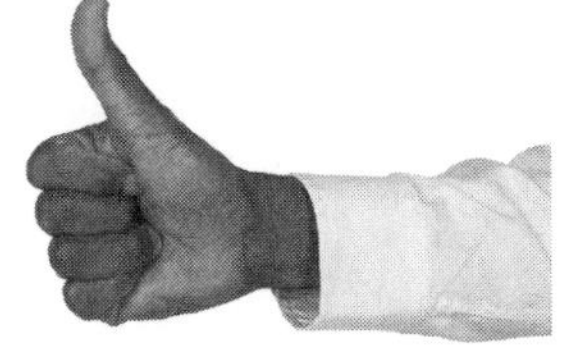

Selected Sellers

Contract

Finally! Everyone's signed on the dotted line, and you've got your contract.

Contract Negotiation

When you send out a package of procurement documents to a potential seller, it usually has some information about the contract you want to sign: the type of contract, some of the terms, maybe some rough calculations and estimates of the total costs and other numbers. But not all sellers will want to sign that particular contract, even ones who you'll eventually want to work with. That's why you need to negotiate the terms of the contract.

This is one of those times where your company's lawyers will probably do most of the talking—but that doesn't mean you're not a critical part of the process. Your job is to provide the expertise and in-depth understanding. After all, you're the one who understands your project and your project's needs better than anyone else.

Proposal Evaluation Techniques

You're going to have to work closely with the seller to figure out if their proposal really is appropriate for the work. You need to be very careful before you choose someone to do the work. That's what this tool is for—it's a kind of "catch-all" that's there to remind you that there's no single way to evaluate a proposal. You need to look at the whole picture—the seller, your needs, and the job.

This is a plan that tells you exactly how you'll handle contract changes and any issues that come up. There's one for each contract.

Contract Management Plan

If your contract makes some of the seller's resources available to you, you'll need this in order to update your Staffing Management Plan.

Resource Availability

Any time you do negotiations, you usually end up making some adjustments to your plans—so you'll need to use these for change control.

Outputs

Requested Changes

Procurement Management Plan Updates

When Kate selects a seller, she'll need to help her company's legal team negotiate the terms of the contract. Which type of contract do you think is right for Kate's project?

The Select Sellers process is where you finally sign a contract with a seller. Here are some proposals that Kate is evaluating. Match each one up to the contract type that's most appropriate for the proposal.

Proposal	Contract type
The buyer will pay for the cost of phone service, rent on the facilities, and employees, plus an additional $2,500 per month.	Fixed price
The buyer will pay the seller a total of $285,000 for 18 months of technical support services.	Fixed price incentive fee
The buyer will pay for the cost of phone service and rent on the facilities, plus $4,500 per month for employees' time. Costs will not exceed $14,500 per month.	Cost plus fixed fee
The buyer will pay for the cost of phone service, rent on the facilities, and employees. An additional $2,750 will be awarded each month that the seller provides an average of 10 issues resolved per person per day and an average wait time of under 3 minutes.	Cost plus incentive fee
The buyer will pay for the cost of phone service, rent on the facilities, and employees. An additional 10% over costs will be paid each month.	Cost plus percentage of cost
The buyer will pay the seller a total of $285,000 for 18 months of technical support services. An additional $2,750 will be awarded each month that the seller provides an average of 10 issues resolved per person per day and an average wait time of under 3 minutes.	Time and materials

Answers on page 596.

Kate needs to use all of the tools and techniques in Select Sellers. Which technique is Kate using in each of these scenarios?

1. This is the first time that Kate's company has contracted out technical support services, so she hires a consultant to help her and the legal team estimate a fair price for the contract.

....

2. Kate sets up criteria for each seller. Before they can submit a bid, they must show that they have handled technical support contracts before and have facilities that can handle over 150 simultaneous calls.

....

3. The CIO and the director of the IT department at Kate's company spent a lot of time setting up the company's existing technical support department, so Kate meets with them to get their technical opinions.

....

4. When Kate looked in the organizational process asset library for her company's qualified seller list, she found a spreadsheet that listed every seller the company has worked with, along with scores from past project managers that graded the sellers on technical performance, management processes, and deliverable quality.

....

5. Kate puts together her own spreadsheet that lets her rank the sellers herself by giving each one of them a score from 1 to 10 for technical skill, communications, project management, financial capability, and facilities quality.

....

6. Kate and her company's legal team sit down with the sellers and work out the terms of the contract. There's a lot of back and forth, but they settle on an agreement that everyone is comfortable with.

....

The Select Sellers process is where you finally sign a contract with a seller. Here are some proposals that Kate is evaluating. Match each one up to the contract type that's most appropriate for the proposal.

The buyer will pay for the cost of phone service, rent on the facilities, and employees, plus an additional $2,500 per month.

The contract lays out the costs, and then adds a dollar amount fee on top of that. That's a fixed fee, so it's a CPFF contract.

The buyer will pay the seller a total of $285,000 for 18 months of technical support services.

Since a preset price will be paid, this is a fixed price (or lump sum) contract

The buyer will pay for the cost of phone service and rent on the facilities, plus $4,500 per month for employees' time. Costs will not exceed $14,500 per month.

A lot of T&M contracts will have a "not-to-exceed" clause to limit risk for the buyer

The buyer will pay for the cost of phone service, rent on the facilities, and employees. An additional $2,750 will be awarded each month that the seller provides an average of 10 issues resolved per person per day and an average wait time of under 3 minutes.

Notice how the incentive fee was tied to specific quality measurements. That's a great way to motivate the seller to do a good job.

The buyer will pay for the cost of phone service, rent on the facilities, and employees. An additional 10% over costs will be paid each month.

This is the same agreement from the fixed price contract, but it's got the incentive fee from the CPIF contract. So it's fixed price incentive fee.

The buyer will pay the seller a total of $285,000 for 18 months of technical support services. An additional $2,750 will be awarded each month that the seller provides an average of 10 issues resolved per person per day and an average wait time of under 3 minutes.

Fixed price

Fixed price incentive fee

Cost plus fixed fee

Cost plus incentive fee

Cost plus percentage of cost

Time and materials

Kate needs to use all of the tools and techniques in Select Sellers. Which technique is Kate using in each of these scenarios?

1. This is the first time that Kate's company has contracted out technical support services, so she hires a consultant to help her and the legal team estimate a fair price for the contract.

Independent estimates

It's often hard to come up with a fair price yourself, because the skills you need to do that are usually the same skills that you need to do the job. Sometimes you don't have those skills in your company, which could be why you looked for a seller in the first place.

2. Kate sets up criteria for each seller. Before they can submit a bid, they must show that they have handled technical support contracts before and have facilities that can handle over 150 simultaneous calls.

Screening system

When you screen out potential sellers, it makes the job of selecting a seller a lot easier.

3. The CIO and the director of the IT department at Kate's company spent a lot of time setting up the company's existing technical support department, so Kate meets with them to get their technical opinions.

Expert judgment

You've seen a whole lot of other processes that have this same technique. Expert judgment always means getting an opinion from someone outside your project.

4. When Kate looked in the organizational process asset library for her company's qualified seller list, she found a spreadsheet that listed every seller the company has worked with, along with scores from past project managers that graded the sellers on technical performance, management processes, and deliverable quality.

Seller rating system

The difference between this tool and the weighting system is that this one is used by your company to rate ALL sellers it deals with, and all PMs in the company will contribute to it.

5. Kate puts together her own spreadsheet that lets her rank the sellers herself by giving each one of them a score from 1 to 10 for technical skill, communications, project management, financial capability, and facilities quality.

Weighting system

The weighting system is something you do just for your project to help you sort through a whole bunch of proposals. If you only have one or two potential sellers, you probably don't need to use it.

6. Kate and her company's legal team sit down with the sellers and work out the terms of the contract. There's a lot of back and forth, but they settle on an agreement that everyone is comfortable with.

Contract negotiation

Project managers don't usually do the negotiation themselves. They'll get involved and provide expertise and knowledge, but usually rely on a lawyer or legal department to work out the actual terms of the contract.

Two months later...

Kate's procurement project had been going really well… or so she thought. But it turns out there's a problem.

Keep an eye out for questions that ask about unions, even when they don't have to do with contracts or procurement management.

When you work with a union, even if it's through a seller, then the union contract (also called a ***collective bargaining agreement****) can have an impact on your project. That means you need to consider the union itself a stakeholder, and when you do your planning you need to make sure any union rules and agreements are considered as constraints.*

What could Kate have done to prevent this problem? Could she have detected it sooner? What should she do now?

Keep an eye on the contract

You wouldn't just start off a project and then assume everything would go perfectly, would you? Well, you can't do that with a contract either. That's why you use the **Contract Administration process**.

The idea behind the Contract Administration process is that staying on top of the work that the seller is doing is more difficult than working with your own project. That's because when you hire a seller to take over part of your project, the team who's doing the work doesn't report to you. That's why **the first three inputs are especially important**. The approved change requests are the way that you change the terms of the contract if something goes wrong, and the work performance information and performance reports are how the seller tells you how the project is going.

The tools and techniques for the Contract Administration process are on the next page.

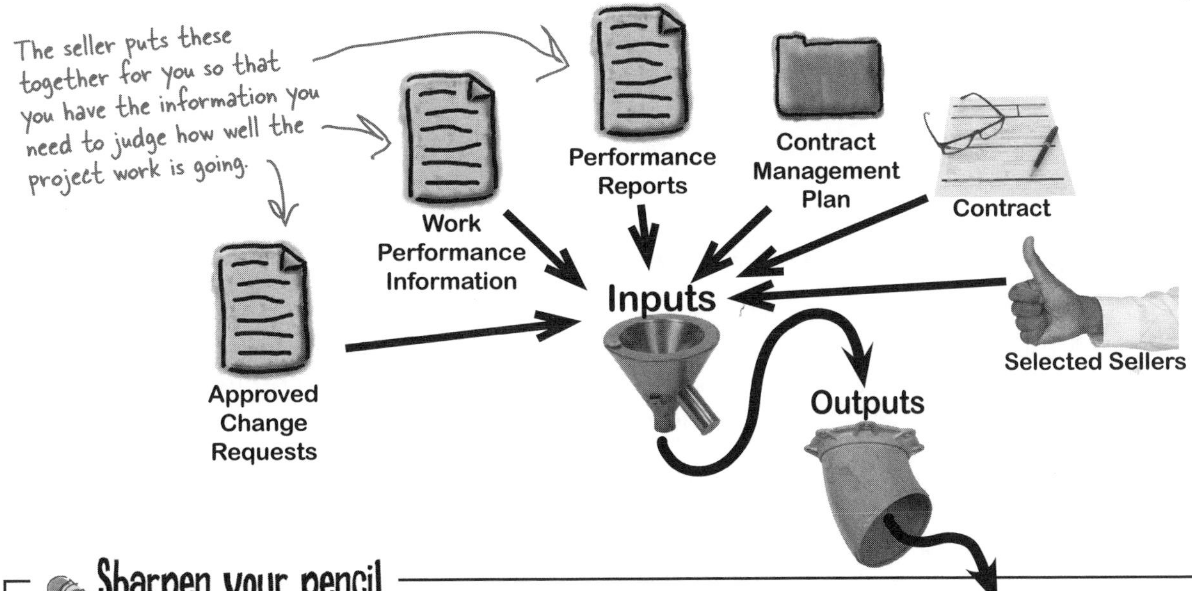

The seller puts these together for you so that you have the information you need to judge how well the project work is going.

Performance Reports

Contract Management Plan

Contract

Work Performance Information

Inputs

Selected Sellers

Approved Change Requests

Outputs

Sharpen your pencil

Contract Administration is a typical Monitoring & Controlling process, which means you should be able to figure out most of the outputs. The first one's filled in—can you fill in the others?

1. **Contract documentation** ....

This means the contract, any supporting documents, and information from the seller.

2. ....

3. Updates to ....

4. ....

5. Updates to ....

→ Answers on page 610.

Stay on top of the seller

The **tools and techniques for Contract Administration** are all there to help you work with the seller. Some of them help you look for any potential problems with the seller and make changes to correct them. Others help you with the day-to-day administration work that you need to do in order to keep your project running.

There are eight tools & techniques for the Contract Administration process

Tools and techniques to keep your project running

Payment System

Your partner won't be very happy if you don't pay. The payment system is how your company pays its sellers. It's usually established by an Accounting or Accounts Receivable department.

Records Management System

There are a lot of records produced by a typical contract: invoices, receipts, communications, memos, emails, instructions, clarifications, etc. You'll need to put a system in place to manage them.

Information Technology

Fifty years ago, project managers managed procurement and contracts with file cabinets and paper. Luckily, we've got computers to help us keep track of everything, and that's why you need IT.

Tools and techniques to find and fix problems

You can conduct a performance review to get the data you need for your performance report.

Claims Administration

When there's a dispute between a buyer and a seller, that's called a **claim**. Most contracts have some language that explains exactly how claims should be resolved—and since it's in the contract, it's legally binding, and both the buyer and seller need to follow it.

Performance Reporting

The easiest way for you to keep track of the contract work being done is to write up performance reports. These are exactly like the performance reports that you saw earlier in the book—you'll use them to monitor the project work and report on the progress to your company's management.

Buyer-Conducted Performance Review

Most contracts lay out certain standards for how well the seller should do the job. Is the seller doing all the work that was agreed to? Is the work being done on time? The buyer has the right to make sure this is happening, and the way to do this is to go over the performance of the seller's team.

Inspections and Audits

This tool is how the buyer makes sure that the product that the seller produces is up to snuff. This is where you'll check up on the actual product or service that the project is producing to make sure that it meets your needs and the terms of the contract.

Contract Change Control System

This is just like all of the other change control systems that you've seen already. It's a set of procedures that are set up to handle changes in the contract. You might have a different one for every contract in your project.

Buyer-conducted performance reviews let buyers check all of the work that the sellers are doing.

Which of the tools and techniques from Contract Administration should Kate use for each problem?

1. An important client calls technical support, but ends up spending two hours waiting on hold.

....

2. The CEO's mother calls technical support, but spends two hours waiting for them to answer. Kate needs to make sure the seller is delivering the quality they promised.

....

3. Kate gets a call from the accounting department about a duplicate invoice that was accidentally paid twice.

....

4. According to the statement of work, the seller is supposed to have weekly training sessions with technical support staff, but Kate isn't sure they're being conducted as often as they should be.

....

5. A manager at the seller says that they're not responsible for training sessions, but Kate thinks they are.

....

Which of the tools and techniques from Contract Administration should Kate use for each problem?

1. An important client calls technical support, but ends up spending two hours waiting on hold.

Records management system

A records management system can help Kate by giving her a place to store all the reports from the seller.

2. The CEO's mother calls technical support, but spends two hours waiting for them to answer. Kate needs to make sure the seller is delivering the quality they promised.

Inspections and audits

You use inspections and audits when you want to review the quality of the product or service being produced.

3. Kate gets a call from the accounting department about a duplicate invoice that was accidentally paid twice.

Payment system

4. According to the statement of work, the seller is supposed to have weekly training sessions with technical support staff, but Kate isn't sure they're being conducted as often as they should be.

Buyer-conducted performance review

If you need to check whether work is being done well, you can use a buyer-conducted performance review.

5. A manager at the seller says that they're not responsible for training sessions, but Kate thinks they are.

Claims administration

there are no Dumb Questions

Q: Should I only care about unions when I'm working with contracts?

A: Unions come up in procurement and contracts whenever a seller has an existing contract with a union. That contract is called a **collective bargaining agreement**, and if that agreement impacts the work that the seller is going to do for you, then you need to make sure that your legal department considers it when they work out the terms of the contract.

But unions are also important when you're doing Human Resource Management. If your company has a collective bargaining agreement with a union, then you need to consider the terms of that contract as **external constraints** to your project plan. Here's an example: Let's say you're managing a construction project, and your workers are all union members. Then you need to make sure that you consider any overtime rules and other restrictions on resource availability when you put together your team, your budget, and your plan.

Whenever you see "inspection" or "audit" it means that you're looking at the products that the seller delivered to see if they meet your standards.

Q: Once a contract is signed, does that mean it's never allowed to change?

A: No. This confuses some people, because when you sign a contract, it's legally binding—which means you must abide by the terms of the contract. But that doesn't mean those terms can't change. If both the buyer and the seller agree to make a change to the contract, then they have every right to do so. That's why you have a contract change control system—so you can make sure these changes are made properly.

But you can't always assume that you have the ability to change a contract that you're not happy with. Once your company has agreed to a contract, then you're absolutely required to meet its terms and complete your side of it. If you want to make a change to it, you need to negotiate that change, and it's possible that the seller won't agree to it—just like you have every right to refuse an unreasonable change that the seller requests.

Q: Does the type of contract make a difference in how changes are handled?

A: No, it doesn't. While the type of contract definitely affects a lot of things, changes are always handled the same way. You always use the contract change control system to handle the changes.

That's why the contract change control system is so important. It tells you the exact rules that you need to go through in order to make a change to a contract. No contract is perfect, and most of the time there are little tweaks that both the buyer and seller want to make. This gives them the tools they need to make only the changes that they need, without anyone agreeing to a change that they don't want included in the contract.

Q: I still don't get the difference between a performance review and an audit.

A: The difference is that performance reviews are about the **work**, while inspections and audits are about the **deliverables and products**.

You'll use a performance review when you want to make sure that the team at the seller is doing every activity that they should. For example, if you have a contract that requires the seller to perform certain quality control or project management tasks, you might conduct a performance review where you observe the team and verify that they do those tasks. On the other hand, if you want to make sure that the products that the team is producing meet your requirements and standards, you'll send out an auditor to inspect the products that the seller is making to verify that they meet the requirements.

Q: So do project managers usually get involved in contract negotiations?

A: Project managers don't usually do the negotiating themselves, but they do often get involved in contract negotiations. Remember, nobody knows more about the project than the project manager—you know what work needs to be done, what requirements the product must meet, and what kind of budget you need to stay within. So even though a lawyer or legal department will do the actual negotiation, they won't know if the seller is capable of doing the job without the project manager's help.

Close the contract when the work is done

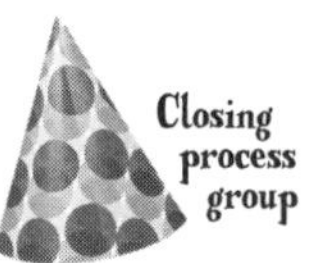

When the seller's work is done, it's time to close the contract, and that's when you use the **Contract Closure** process. Even if your contract ends disastrously (or in court), you still need to close out the contract so that you can make sure all of your company's responsibilities are taken care of—and that you learn from the experience.

There's only one other process in the Closing group. Take a minute and flip back to page 116 to refresh your memory.

Contract Management Plan

This tells you what steps you need to take—like who to pay, and which records to save—in order to settle the contract.

Inputs

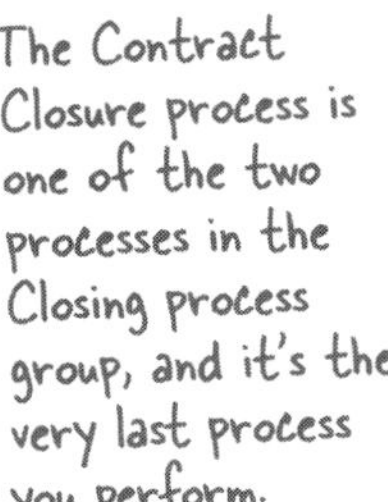

Procurement Management Plan

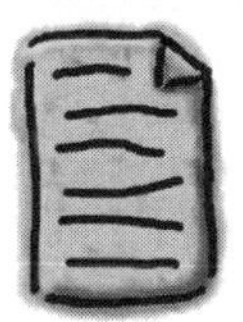

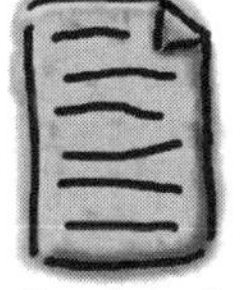

Contract Documentation

Contract Closure Procedure

The contract is complete when all of its terms are met... even if the buyer or seller is not completely satisfied with the work.

Tools

The Contract Closure process is one of the two processes in the Closing process group, and it's the very last process you perform.

Procurement audits

Once you've closed out the contract, you go over everything that happened on the project to figure out the lessons learned and look for anything that went right or wrong.

Records management system

When you were working with the legal team to put the contract together, you looked at information about past contracts. So where did it come from? Past project managers stored their contracts and other documents in the records management system.

Outputs

The way you close out a contract is to give a notice—a formal written one—that the contract is complete... and instructions for doing that should be part of the contract terms.

Closed Contracts

Organizational Process Assets

Any lessons you learned from the procurement audits should be added here, along with any documentation and a copy of the formal acceptance that you gave to the seller.

Contractcross

Give your right brain something to do. It's your standard crossword; all of the solution words are from this chapter.

Across

4. The contract closure __________ tells you exactly what steps you must follow in order to close out the contract

5. The contract-related process in the Monitoring and Controlling group is Contract ______________

6. The _______ management system stores all of the documents, communications and information related to the contract

8. The buyer creates the __________ criteria before contacting potential sellers to help determine how to select the winning bid

10. The company or organization that's performing services for the contract

12. Some organizations maintain a __________ sellers list, which has all sellers that project managers are allowed to work with

15. The contract __________ of work describes all of the work that the seller wants the buyer to perform

16. This kind of analysis is used to determine whether to procure a product or service, or whether to stay within the company

17. You can use a _________ system in which you require all sellers to meet certain standards before you even consider them for the contract

Down

1. The potential seller submits a _________ to the buyer that explains how the contract would be fulfilled

2. You can use a _________ system to assign a number to various seller attributes in order to objectively compare them

3. ___________ documents contain all the information the seller wants to communicate to potential buyers

7. The kind of contract where the buyer pays a lump sum

9. The point of total ___________ is the point at which the seller is responsible for all remaining costs

11. Even if the buyer fails to deliver on the contract and it has to be terminated early, you still need to perform the Contract ________ process.

13. A disagreement between the buyer and seller is called a ______

14. The company or organization that's procuring services

Answers on page 610.

Kate closes the contract

The 18-month contract's ready to close! The seller did a great job handling technical support, and that gave Kate and Ben the time they needed to ramp up their own company's team and facilities.

Question Clinic: BYO Questions

See if you can come up with questions on your own! Give it a shot:

Write a Which-is-BEST question about Qualitative Risk Analysis

See page 162

See page 322

Write a Red Herring question about Select Sellers

Write a Calculation question about CPI

See page 246

See page 494

Write a Which-Comes-Next question about the Scope Management processes

Here's a great study tool. Any time you get a practice question wrong, or don't understand a particular concept, write a question about it! That's a great way to help you remember stuff for the exam.

Did you come up with a good question? Join the Head First PMP community and upload your question at **http://www.headfirstlabs.com/PMP**

Kate has **18 months** to build up the capacity her company needs to handle all the technical support calls. See if you can figure out whether it's a better deal for Kate to make or buy.

1. If they handle the extra work within the company instead of finding a seller, it will cost an extra $35,000 in overtime and $11,000 in training costs in total, on top of the $4,400 per person per month for the five-person team needed to do the extra support work. What's the total cost of for keeping the work within the company?

   The total cost for keeping the work is the monthly cost ($4,400 per person × 5 people × 18 months = $396,000) plus the extra costs ($35,000 overtime and $11,000 training costs). $396,000 + $35,000 + $11,000 = $442,000 total costs for keeping the work inside the company ("making")

2. Kate and Ben talked to a few companies and estimate that it will cost $20,000 per month to hire another company to do the work, but they'll also need to spend $44,000 in setup costs. What will contracting the work cost?

   The cost for hiring another company to do the work is $20,000 per month × 18 months plus the $44,000 in setup costs. ($20,000 × 18) + $44,000 = $404,000 total costs for contracting out the work ("buying")

3. So does it make more sense to make or buy? Why?

   In this case, it makes more sense to buy because the costs of making ($442,000) are greater than the costs of buying ($404,000).

Sharpen your pencil Solution

Kate is putting out an RFP to find a seller to provide technical support for her company. Can you figure out which Request Seller Responses tool she's using?

1. Kate checks her company's organizational process asset library to see if there are any standard sellers it typically uses. She can't find one, so she creates it herself.

   Develop qualified seller list

2. Kate's contacts an IT trade journal and places a classified ad to try to find sellers.

   Advertising

3. The CEO's brother-in-law runs a company that's bidding on the contract. Kate needs to make sure he gets fair—not preferential—treatment. She doesn't want to give him an unfair advantage, but she also doesn't want to exclude him from the bidding process. So she gathers representatives from all sellers into a room where they can ask questions about the contract out in the open and hear the responses to each question.

   Bidder conference

4. Kate's company takes part in an equal-opportunity program in which seller companies owned by minorities must be given notice of any RFPs. She uses a web site approved by the program to make sure she gives them notice.

   Advertising

Contract Magnets Solution

Which of the magnets are part of the procurement documents, and which of them are part of the evaluation criteria?

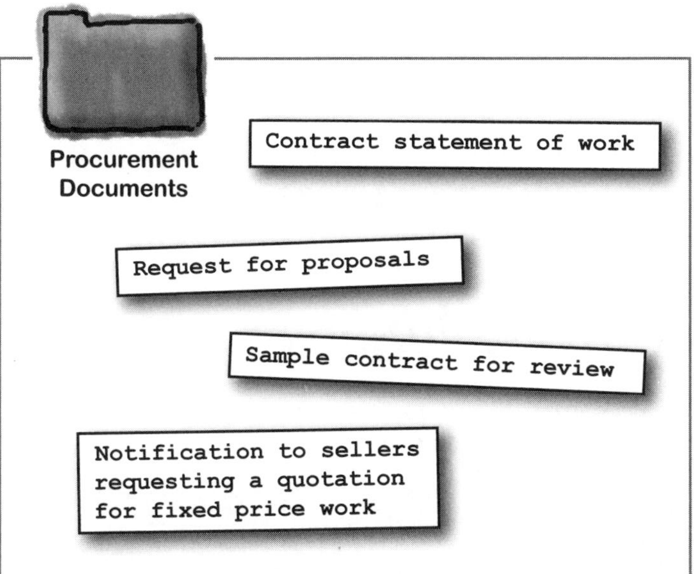

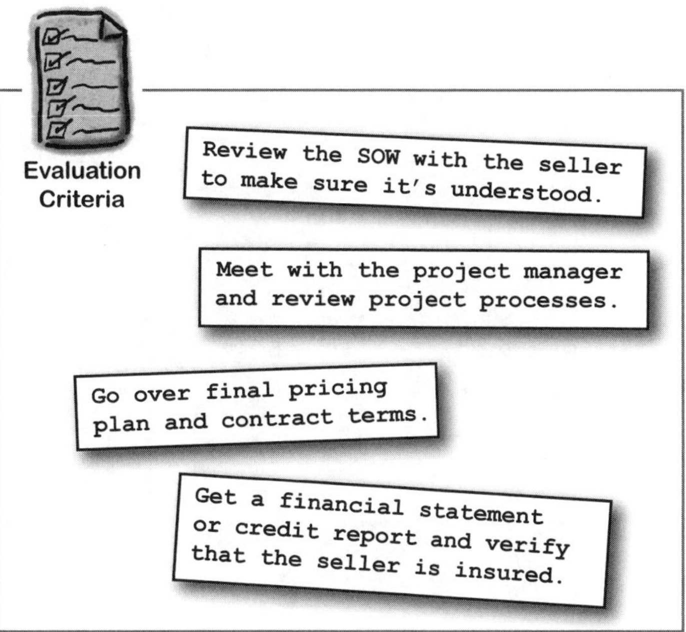

Sharpen your pencil Solution

Contract Administration is a typical Monitoring & Controlling process, which means you should be able to figure out most of the outputs. The first one's filled in—can you fill in the others?

1. **Contract documentation**

2. **Requested changes**

If you have to make a change because of poor performance problems with the seller, you'll definitely want to keep track of that here.

Either the buyer OR the seller could find other things in the project that need to change.

3. Updates to **Organizational process assets**

4. **Recommended corrective actions**

5. Updates to **Project management plan**

Contractcross Solutions

Give your right brain something to do. It's your standard crossword; all of the solution words are from this chapter.

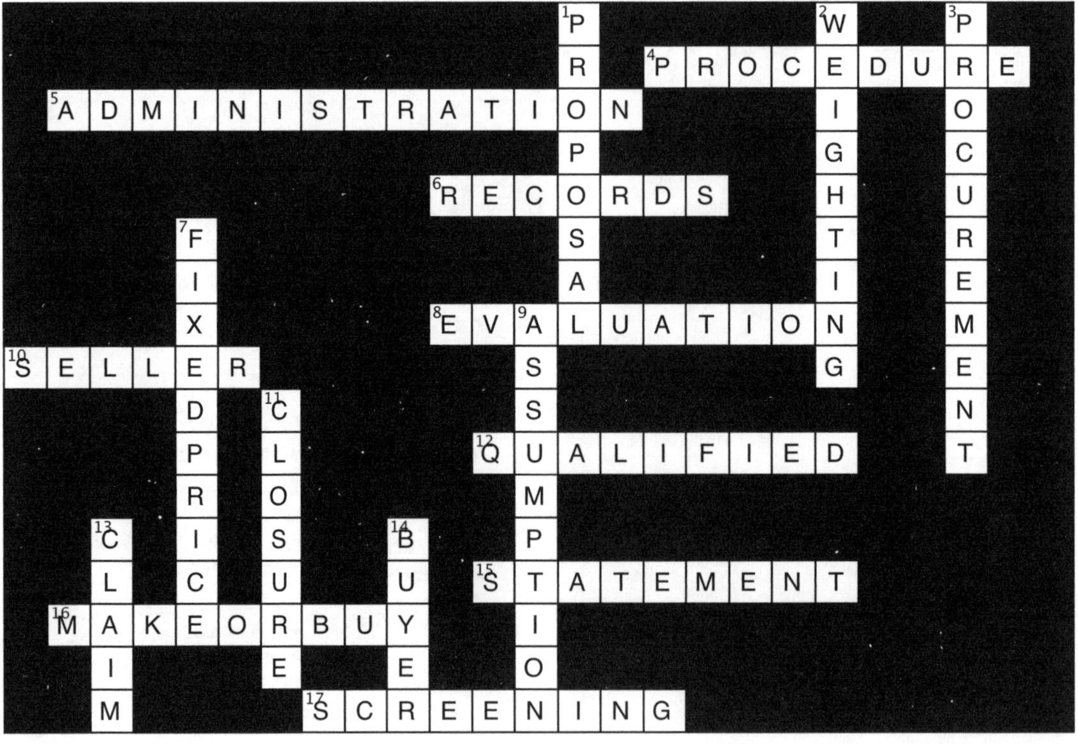

Exam Questions

1. Tom is a project manager for a software company. He is contracting a long-term software project with an external company. That company charges him $20/hour per employee and $300 overhead per month. What kind of contract is he using?

A. FP

B. CPPC

C. CR

D. T&M

2. Which of the following is NOT true about bidder conferences?

A. All potential sellers should meet separately with the buyer

B. Potential sellers should ask questions in an open forum so other sellers can hear the answers

C. Bidder conferences are a good way to make sure sellers are treated fairly

D. All sellers are given the same procurement documents

3. You work for a seller that is bidding on a contract. Which type of contract has the MOST risk for your company?

A. CPIF

B. T&M

C. FP

D. CPPC

4. Which of the following BEST describes the "point of total assumption" for a contract?

A. The point in a cost-plus contract where the buyer assumes that the seller will need to be paid

B. The total cost of a T&M contract

C. The point in a fixed price contract where the seller has to assume all costs going forward

D. The total number of resources required for a contract

5. You're trying to decide whether or not to contract out a construction job. To do it within your company, you will have to hire an engineer for $35,000 and pay a construction team $15,000 per week. A contractor quotes you a price of $19,000 per week, and your expert agrees that you won't find a lower price than that. The job will take 16 weeks. What's the BEST way to proceed?

A. Pay the contractor to do the job.

B. Select a T&M contract.

C. Don't contract out the work. Hire the engineer and pay the construction team to do the work.

D. Make sure the contract has a force majeure clause.

Exam Questions

6. You're managing a project that might have to contract out work, and you're comparing the relative advantages and disadvantages of finding a seller versus having your company do the work itself. Which process are you in?

A. Plan Purchases and Acquisitions

B. Plan Contracting

C. Select Sellers

D. Request Seller Responses

7. You're working on creating a qualified sellers list. Which process are you in?

A. Plan Purchases and Acquisitions

B. Plan Contracting

C. Select Sellers

D. Request Seller Responses

8. You've been contracted by an industrial design firm to manage their contracting. Your client asks you to take over the negotiations for an important contract to design a new lighting remote control system. You've narrowed it down to one seller, and now you're working with the legal department at the buyer to negotiate the terms of the contract. Which of the following BEST describes your goal?

A. You want to get the best deal for your client by making sure the seller's price is as low as possible, no matter what it costs them

B. You want to get a fair deal for both the buyer and the seller

C. You want to make sure that the seller gets as much money as possible

D. You want to prolong the negotiation so that you earn a higher fee

9. You've been contracted by a construction company to manage their contracting. They have a choice of either buying an excavator or renting it. To buy it, the company would have to pay $105,000, but owning it will require approximately $10,000 in maintenance costs per year. The price to rent the excavator is $5,000 per month, with a one-time service charge of $2,000. What's the minimum number of months the company needs to use the excavator in order for it to make sense to buy it rather than rent?

A. 8 months

B. 16 months

C. 21 months

D. 25 months

10. Which of the following contracts has the MOST risk for the buyer?

A. FP

B. CPPC

C. CPIF

D. T&M

Exam Questions

11. You're managing a project that is difficult to estimate, so you don't have a good idea of when the project will end. Which of the following contracts is BEST?

A. FP

B. CPPC

C. CPIF

D. T&M

12. You're looking for a seller to do work for your project. When do you send out an RFP?

A. After you create the procurement documents, but before you select the seller

B. Before you plan contracting, but after you plan purchases and acquisitions

C. After the bidder conference, but before you select the seller

D. During contract administration

13. You're creating evaluation criteria for your contract. What process are you in?

A. Plan Procurement and Acquisitions

B. Plan Contracting

C. Request Seller Responses

D. Select Sellers

14. You're managing a project, when you and the seller both agree that you need to have the seller add more resources to the project in order to finish on time. The number of resources is written into the contract. What's the BEST way to proceed?

A. Your project will be late because you can't change the contract once it's signed

B. You need to convince the buyer to sign a new contract

C. You need to use the contract change control system to make the change to the contract

D. You need to use claims administration to resolve the issue

15. Which of the following BEST explains the difference between a seller audit during Contract Administration and a procurement audit during Contract Closure?

A. The seller audit reviews the products being created, while the procurement audit reviews how well the seller is doing the job

B. The procurement audit reviews the products being created, while the seller audit reviews how well the seller is doing the job

C. The seller audit reviews the products being created, while the procurement audit is used to examine successes and failures and gather lessons learned

D. The procurement audit reviews the products being created, while the seller audit is used to examine successes and failures and gather lessons learned

Exam ~~Questions~~ Answers

1. Answer: D

This contract is a Time and Materials contract. It's charging a rate for labor and overhead for materials.

Eliminating the wrongs answers works really well with questions like this.

2. Answer: A

One of the most important things about a bidder conference is that no one seller is given better access to the buyer. They should all have the same opportunity to gather information, so that no single seller is given preferential treatment.

Sellers should meet in the same room, and any time one of them asks the question, everyone else should hear the answer.

3. Answer: C

A fixed price contract is the riskiest sort of contract for the seller. That's because there's one price for the whole contract, no matter what happens. So if it turns out that there's a lot more work than expected, or the price of parts or materials goes up, then the seller has to eat the costs.

4. Answer: C

This is just the definition of the point of total assumption.

5. Answer: C

This is a simple make-or-buy decision, so you can work out the math. The contractor's quote of $19,000 per week for a 16-week job means that buying will cost you $19,000 x 16 = $304,000. On the other hand, if you decide to keep the work in-house, then it will cost you $35,000 for the engineer, plus $15,000 per week for 16 weeks: $35,000 + (16 x $15,000) = $275,000. It will be cheaper to make it rather than buy it!

Exam ~~Questions~~ Answers

6. Answer: A

This question describes Make or Buy Analysis, which is part of the Plan Purchases and Acquisitions process.

That makes sense. You can't start contracting until you figure out whether or not you should.

7. Answer: D

One of the important things that you do when you're looking for seller responses is to come up with a list of sellers to solicit bids from. You need to know where to send those procurement documents! That's why you need to put together a qualified sellers list.

8. Answer: B

One of the most important parts of Procurement Management is that both the buyer and the seller want to feel like they're getting a good deal. Every procurement should be a win-win situation for both parties!

9. Answer: D

This may look like a tough problem, but it's actually pretty easy. Just figure out how much the rental would cost you for each of the answers:

A.	8 months	8 months x $5,000 per month + $2,000 service charge = $42,000
B.	16 months	16 months x $5,000 per month + $2,000 service charge = $82,000
C.	21 months	21 months x $5,000 per month + $2,000 service charge = $107,000
D.	25 months	25 months x $5,000 per month + $2,000 service charge = $127,000

Now look at what the excavator would cost for 25 months. It would cost $105,000 plus $20,000 for the maintenance costs, for a total of $125,000. So at 25 months, the excavator is worth buying, but before that it makes more sense to rent.

If this seems a little out of place, remember that renting equipment is a kind of contract, and the same kind of make-or-buy decision is necessary.

10. Answer: B

The cost plus percentage of cost (CPPC) contract is the riskiest one for the buyer, because there's no incentive for the seller to control the costs. In fact, the opposite is true—the higher the costs, the more money the buyer makes.

Exam ~~Questions~~ Answers

11. Answer: D

Both cost-plus and fixed price contracts are based on the idea that you know how long the contact is going to last. A seller would only agree to a fixed price contract if there's a good idea of how much it's going to cost. And a cost-plus contract will hurt the buyer if it goes over. Only the time and materials contract will give both the buyer and seller a fair deal if neither has a good idea of how long the work will take.

That's the only time you really should use a T&M contract.

12. Answer: A

Contracting is a pretty linear process—first you plan the contract, then you put together a package of procurement documents to send to potential sellers, and then you select a seller and start the work. So you send out a request for proposals after you've put together the procurement document package so that you can select a seller for the job.

13. Answer: B

You put together the evaluation criteria as part of the Plan Contracting process. That way you can use the criteria when you're looking at the responses you get from sellers.

14. Answer: C

You can always change a contract, as long as both the buyer and the seller agree to it. When you do that, you need to use the contract change control system—just like with any other change.

This is not what claims administration is for. Since the buyer and seller agree, there is no claim.

15. Answer: C

It's easy to get mixed up with all of these audits, but if you think about how they're used, it gets less confusing. When you're performing Contract Administration, the most important part of your job is to figure out if the products that the seller is producing meet your requirements. By the time closure happens, the products have all been done—if there was a problem, you should have caught it during Contract Administration. All you can do now is come up with any lessons learned so that you can avoid mistakes in the future.

13 Professional Responsibility

Making Good Choices

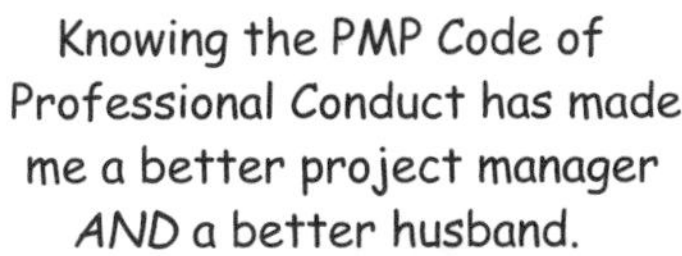

It's not enough to just know your stuff. You need to make good choices to be good at your job. Everyone who has the PMP credential agrees to follow the **PMP Code of Professional Conduct**, too. The Code helps you with **ethical decisions** that aren't really covered in the body of knowledge—and it's a big part of the PMP exam. Most of what you need to know is **really straightforward**, and with a little review, you'll do well.

Doing the right thing

You'll get some questions on the exam that give you situations that you might run into in running your projects and then ask you what to do. Usually, there's a clear answer to these questions: ***it's the one where you stick to your principles.*** Questions will make the decisions tougher by offering rewards for doing the wrong thing (like money for taking a project shortcut), or they will make the infraction seem really small (like photocopying a copyrighted article out of a magazine). If you stick to the principles in the PMP Code of Professional Conduct regardless of the consequences, you'll **always** get the questions right.

The main ideas

In general, there are a few kinds of problems that the code of ethics prepares you to deal with.

1. **Follow all laws and company policies.**
2. **Treat everybody fairly and respectfully.**
3. **Have respect for the environment and the community you're working in.**
4. **Give back to the project management community by writing, speaking, and sharing your experience with other project managers.**
5. **Keep learning and getting better and better at your job.**
6. **Respect other people's cultures.**
7. **Respect copyright laws.**
8. **Always be honest with everyone on the project.**
9. **If you find that another person has done something to damage the PMP credential in any way, you must report them to PMI.**

So if you find out that someone has stolen questions from the PMP exam, cheated on the PMP exam, falsely claimed to have a PMP certification, or lied about anything related to the PMP certification process, then you MUST report them to PMI.

Ethics and professional responsibility questions make up 10% of the exam. That's good news because these questions are really easy if you understand the ideas behind the PMP Code of Professional Conduct.

Being a PMP-certified project manager means that you know how to do your job and that you will do it with integrity.

It might seem like it doesn't really matter how you will handle these situations, but think about it from an employer's perspective for a minute. Because of the code of conduct, they know that when they hire a PMP-certified project manager, they are hiring someone who will follow company policies and do everything aboveboard and by the book. That means that you'll help to protect their company from litigation and deliver on what you promise, which is actually pretty important.

BRAIN POWER

Can you think of some situations where you might need to make decisions using these principles in your own projects?

Keep the cash?

A lot of ethics questions on the PMP exam concern bribery. It is never, under any circumstances, okay to accept a bribe—even if your company and customer might benefit from it somehow. And bribes aren't always cash. They can be anything ranging from free trips to tickets to a ball game. Any time you're offered anything to change your opinion or the way you work, you must decline the offer and disclose it to your company.

In some countries, even though you may be "expected" to pay a bribe, it's not okay to do it—even if it's customary or culturally acceptable.

Awesome. I've been wanting to go shopping for a while. And what about that vacation? Acapulco, here we come!

I would never accept a gift like that. Doing a good job is its own reward!

The right way

The easy way

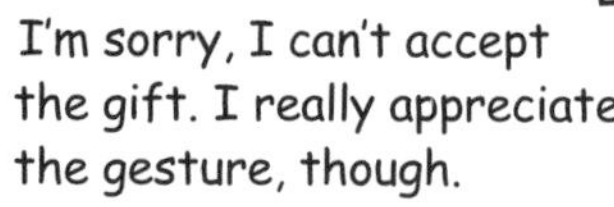

Fly business class?

Any time there's a policy in your company, you need to follow it. Even if it seems like no harm will be done if you don't follow the policy, and even if you will be able to get away with it, you should not do it. And that goes double for laws—under no circumstances are you ever allowed to break a law, no matter how much good it "seems" to do you or your project.

And if you ever see someone in your company breaking the law, you need to report it to the authorities.

We've got some extra money in the budget and you're really doing a great job. I know the travel policy says we always fly coach. But we can afford to splurge a bit. Why don't you buy a business ticket this time?

Did you know that those chairs go into totally flat beds? This is so cool. You've worked so hard, you've totally earned it!

There's no excuse for not following the rules. The travel policy says fly coach. No exceptions!

Wow, Ben. That's really nice of you. But the economy fare will be fine.

New software

When it comes to copyright, it's never OK to use anything without permission. Books, articles, music, software... you always need to ask before using it. For example, if you want to use some copyrighted music in a company presentation, you should write to the copyright owner and ask for permission.

Hey Kate, I just got a copy of that scheduling software you wanted. You can borrow my copy and install it.

Absolutely! This will totally make your job about 100 times faster, and it's **free**? It's your lucky day.

That software was created by a company that deserves to be paid for their work. It's just wrong not to buy a licensed copy.

Thanks for letting me know it's available. I'll go buy a copy.

Shortcuts

You might see a question or two that asks if you really need to follow all of the processes. Or you might be asked by your boss to keep certain facts about your project hidden from stakeholders or sponsors. You have a responsibility to make sure your projects are run properly, and to never withhold information from people who need it.

We don't have time for all of this documentation. Let's cut out a couple of these plans to keep our project on schedule.

All right. Less work for you—let's face it, it's not like you have all the time in the world for writing plans!

I would never do a project without fallowing ALL of the 44 processes outlined in The PMBOK® Guide.

I know we don't have much time, but taking this shortcut could actually cost us more time than it saves in the end.

A good price or a clean river?

Being responsible to the community is even more important than running a successful project. But it's more than being environmentally aware—you should also respect the cultures of everyone else in your community, and the community where your project work will be done.

That means even though languages, customs, holidays and vacation policies might be different from country to country, you need to treat people the way they are accustomed to being treated.

The earth is our home and is so much more important than this project. We have to do what's right...

We're not all angels

We know that the choices you make on your project are not always black and white. Remember that the questions on the exam are designed to test your knowledge of the PMP Code of Professional Conduct and how to apply it. A lot of situations you will run into in real life will have a hundred circumstances around them that make these decisions a little tougher to make than the ones you see here. But if you know what the code would have you do, you're in a good position to evaluate those scenarios as well.

Seriously, it's a quick read—and it'll help you on the exam.

Now, go read the PMP Code of Professional Conduct before you take these exam questions. Go to this URL and click on the "Code of Conduct" link.

http://www.headfirstlabs.com/hfpmp

I may not be the life of the party, but think like me, and you'll nail the ethics part of the exam.

Exam Questions

1. You read a great article over the weekend, and you think your team could really benefit from it. What should you do?

A. Photocopy the article and give it to the team members

B. Type up parts of the article and email it to the team

C. Tell everyone that you thought of the ideas in the article yourself

D. Buy a copy of the magazine for everyone

2. You find out that a contractor that you're working with discriminates against women. The contractor is in another country, and it's normal in that country. What should you do?

A. Respect the contractor's culture and allow the discrimination to continue

B. Refuse to work with the contractor, and find a new seller

C. Submit a written request that the contractor no longer discriminates

D. Meet with your boss and explain the situation

3. You're a project manager at a construction company that's selling services to a client. You are working on a schedule and a budget, when the CEO at the client demands that you do not produce those things. Instead, he wants you to begin work immediately. What the BEST thing that you can do?

A. Meet with the CEO to explain why the budget and schedule are necessary.

B. Stop work immediately and go into claims administration.

C. Don't produce the schedule and budget.

D. Ask the buyer to find another company to work with.

4. You're working on a project, when the client demands that you take him out to lunch every week if you want to keep his business. What's the BEST thing to do?

A. Take the client out to lunch and charge it to your company

B. Refuse to take the client out to lunch because it's a bribe

C. Take the client out to lunch, but report him to his manager

D. Report the incident to PMI

5. You are working on one of the first financial projects your company has attempted, and you have learned a lot about how to manage the project along the way. Your company is targeting financial companies for new projects next year. What's the BEST thing for you to do:

A. Talk to your company about setting up some training sessions so that you can teach others what you have learned on your project.

B. Keep the information you've learned to yourself so that you'll be more valuable to the company in the next year.

C. Decide to specialize in financial contracts.

D. Focus on your work with the project and don't worry about the helping other people to learn from the experience.

Exam Questions

6. You find out that you could save money by contracting with a seller in a country that has lax environmental protection rules. What should you do?

A. Continue to pay higher rates for a environmentally safe solution.

B. Take advantage of the cost savings.

C. Ask your boss to make the decision for you.

D. Demand that your current contractor match the price.

7. You overhear someone on your team using a racial slur. This person is a critical team member and you are worried that if they leave your company it will cause project problems. What should you do?

A. Pretend you didn't hear it so that you don't cause problems.

B. Report the team member to his boss.

C. Bring it up at the next team meeting.

D. Meet in private with the team member and explain that racial slurs are unacceptable.

8. You've given a presentation for your local PMI chapter meeting. This is an example of what?

A. A PDU

B. Contributing to the project management body of knowledge

C. Donating to charity

D. Volunteering

9. You are about to hold a bidder conference, and a potential seller offers you great tickets to a baseball game for your favorite team. What should you do?

A. Go to the game with the seller but avoid talking about the contract.

B. Go to the game with seller and discuss the contract.

C. Go to the game, but make sure not to let him buy you anything because that would be a bribe.

D. Politely refuse the tickets.

10. Your company has sent out an RFP, and your brother wants to bid on it. What's the BEST thing for you to do?

A. Give your brother inside information to make sure that he has the best chance at getting the project.

B. Publicly disclose your relationship with him and excuse yourself from the selection process.

C. Recommend your brother but don't inform anyone of your relationship.

D. Don't tell anyone about your relationship but be careful not to give your brother any advantage when evaluating all of the potential sellers.

Exam ~~Questions~~ Answers

1. Answer: D

You should never copy anything that's copyrighted. Make sure you always respect other people's intellectual property!

2. Answer: B

It's never okay to discriminate against women, minorities, or others. You should avoid doing business with anyone who does.

3. Answer: A

This is a difficult situation for any project manager. But you can't cut corners on the project management processes, and you certainly can't tell the client that you're refusing their business. The best thing you can do is meet with the CEO to explain why you need to follow the rules.

4. Answer: B

The client is demanding a bribe, and paying bribes is unethical. You should not do it. If your project requires you to bribe someone, then you shouldn't do business with that person.

5. Answer: A

This is called contributing to the project management body of knowledge.

You should always try to help other people learn about managing projects.

6. Answer: A

You should never contract work to a seller who pollutes the environment. Even though it costs more to use machinery that doesn't damage the environment, it's the right thing to do.

Exam ~~Questions~~

7. Answer: D

You should make sure that your team always respects other people.

8. Answer: B

Any time you help share your knowledge with others, you are contributing to the project management body of knowledge, and that's something you should do as a certified project manager!

9. Answer: D

You have to refuse the tickets even if the game sounds like a lot of fun. The tickets amount to a bribe, and you shouldn't do anything that might influence your decision in awarding your contract.

10. Answer: B

You have to disclose the relationship. It's important to be up front and honest about any conflict of interest that could occur on your projects.

14 A little last-minute review

Check Your Knowledge

Wow, you sure covered a lot of ground in the last 13 chapters! Now it's time to take a look back and drill in some of the most important concepts that you learned. That'll keep it all fresh and give your brain a final workout for exam day!

Process Magnets

Can you put all of the processes in the right knowledge areas? Give it a shot—and while you're at it, see if you can put them inside each knowledge area in the order that they're typically performed on a project.

Integration	Scope	Time	Cost
1	1	1	1
2	2	2	2
3	3	3	3
4	4	4	**Quality**
5	5	5	1
6		6	2
7			3

Risk Monitoring and Control

Activity Duration Estimating

Integrated Change Control

Cost Budgeting

Scope Control

Cost Estimating

Develop Project Team

Select Sellers

Risk Management Planning

Scope Definition

Develop Project Management Plan

Schedule Development

Acquire Project Team

Quantitative Risk Analysis

Communications Planning

Quality Planning

Plan Contracting

Human Resources	Communications	Risk	Procurement
1	1	1	1
2	2	2	2
3	3	3	3
4	4	4	4
		5	5
		6	6

Contract Closure

Plan Purchases and Acquisitions

Develop Project Charter

Manage Project Team

Human Resource Planning

Request Seller Responses

Perform Quality Assurance

Manage Stakeholders

Contract Administration

Scope Verification

Information Distribution

Activity Resource Estimating

Monitor and Control Project Work

Activity Sequencing

Direct and Manage Project Execution

Scope Planning

Close Project

Cost Control

Schedule Control

Create WBS

Performance Reporting

Risk Identification

Risk Response Planning

Qualitative Risk Analysis

Develop Preliminary Project Scope Statement

Activity Definition

Perform Quality Control

Answers on page 640.

Processcross

How well do you know the 44 processes in the PMBOK® Guide? Let's find out!

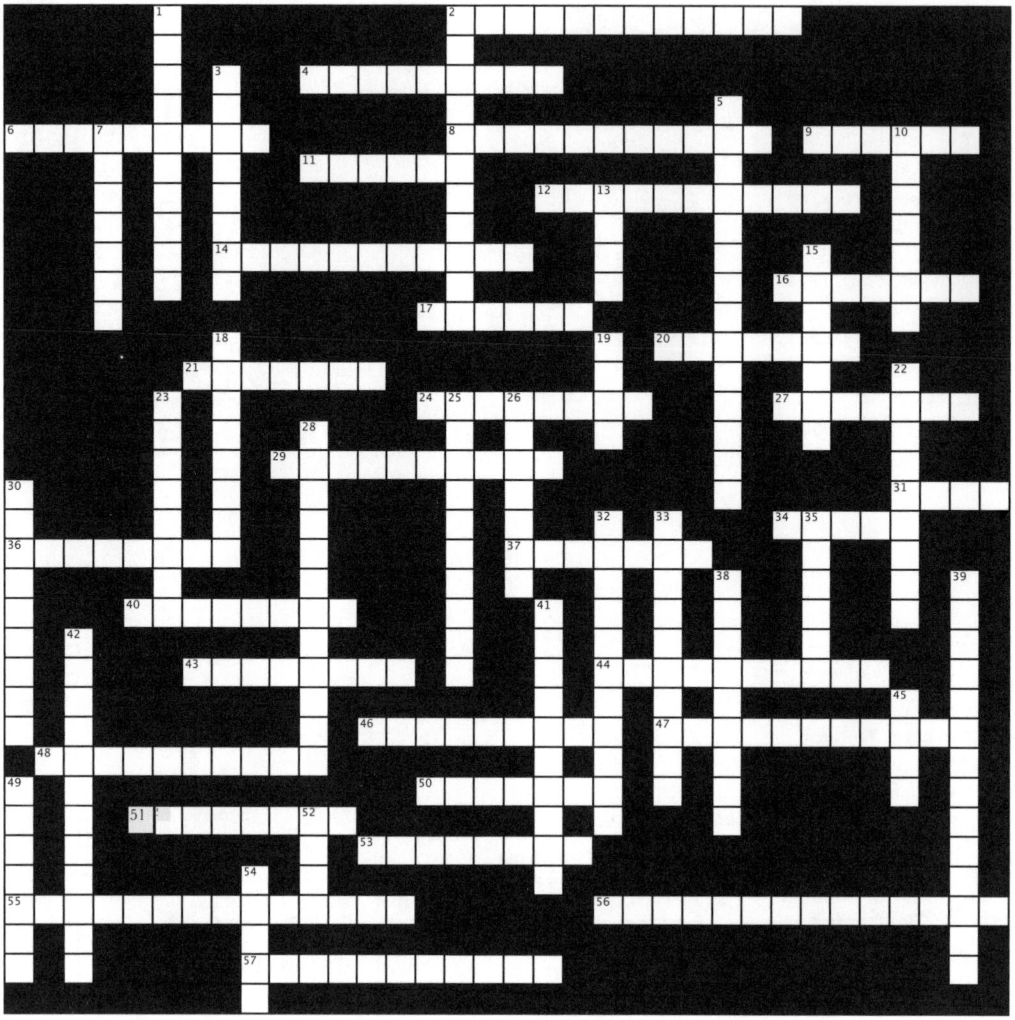

Answers on page 642.

Across

2. In the ___________ Risk Analysis process, you assign numerical values to your risks in order to more accurately assess them.

4. In the Plan _________ and Acquisitions process, you decide what work you'll want to contract out to a seller.

6. The ___________ process group is where the team does the project work.

8. _____________ Distribution means making sure the right people get the right message. It's where most of the communication on the project happens.

9. The ___________ Project Team process is the Monitoring & Controlling process for Human Resources.

11. The ____________ Sellers process is where you determine which sellers will do the work.

12. ______________ Reporting is where you figure out how your project is doing, and let everyone else know.

14. In the Plan __________ process, you plan out each individual contract for your project, and create procurement documents.

16. In the Perform Quality ___________ process, your team looks for defects in deliverables.

17. The Request __________ Responses process involves bidder conferences.

20. The _____________ Planning process is where you create a plan to ensure that your product conforms to its requirements and is fit for use.

Across

21. The ___________ Project Team process is where you keep your team motivated, and set goals and rewards for them.
24. The Risk _______________ Planning process is where you decide how you will react to each risk, should it occur.
27. The Scope _______________ process is where you look for changes to the scope, and only make those changes that are necessary.
29. The Scope __________ process is where you write down exactly what the team will do to produce the product.
31. In the ______________ Management knowledge area, you determine how long the work will take.
34. In the _______ Planning process, you figure out how you'll come up with all of your work packages and control any changes to them.
36. The ___________________ Control process is where you look for changes to your activities and schedule, and make sure you only make those changes that are necessary.
37. The document that authorizes you to do the project is built in the Develop Project __________process.
40. The Activity __________ Estimating process is where you figure out what people, equipment and other things you need for the project, and when you'll need them.
43. In the Activity _____________ Estimating process, you generate an estimate of how long each activity will take.
44. You create a document that defines how you'll handle everything on the project in the Develop Project _________________ Plan process.
46. The deliverables and work performance information are created in the Direct and Manage Project _________ process.
47. ______________ Management is the knowledge area where you bring all of the project work and plans together.
48. In the Activity _________ process, you decompose each work package into a complete list of activities for the project.
50. In the ________ and Control Project Work process, you constantly look for any changes or problems that occur.
51. The Human ______________ Management knowledge area is where you put together and manage your team.
53. The ____________ process group is where you do the most work. It's where you build a document to guide you through each of the knowledge areas.
55. The Risk _____________ process is where you create the risk register that contains a list of risks that might affect your project.
56. The Contract ___________ process is the Monitoring & Controlling process for Procurement, and it's where you look for changes in your contracts.
57. In the ______________ Management knowledge area, you contract with sellers to do project work.

Down

1. The __________ and Controlling process group is concerned with finding and dealing with changes.
2. The _____________ Risk Analysis process is where you categorize each risk.
3. The Close __________ process is where you make sure all your procurement activities are finished.
5. _________________ Planning is the process where you figure out how you will handle messages, lines of communication, meetings, and reporting.
7. The __________ process group is where you shut down the project.
10. In the ______________ Project Team process, you assign your team to the project.
13. The _______ Management Planning process is where you create a plan that tells you how you'll manage unexpected events.
15. The Cost ________________ process means tracking your work closely and watching for any changes in cost.
18. The Human ____________ Planning process is where you create a plan for how you will assign and manage your staff.
19. In the ________ Monitoring and Control process, you look for any new risks, or changes to your risk register.
22. The ___________ process is where you create a graphical, hierarchical document that describes all work packages.
23. The ___________ Development process is when you build a bar chart, calendar, or other document out of all of your estimates.
25. The Cost ________ process is where you figure out how much money you'll spend on each activity in the schedule.
26. The Close ___________ process is where you make sure that the project is finished and all of your lessons learned are documented.
28. The Scope ____________ process is where you make sure that all of the work has been done and get formal approval from the stakeholders.
30. In the Perform Quality ___________ process, you make sure your entire project and quality processes meet your company's quality standards.
32. The Develop _____________ Project Scope Statement process is where you create an initial document that describes your best idea of the work that you're going to do.
33. The Activity __________ process is the one where you put the list of activities in order and create network diagrams.
35. The Integrated _____________ Control process is where you work with stakeholders and sponsors to decide whether or not to make changes.
38. In the Cost ______________ Process, you add up all of your estimated costs and figure out how much money your project will spend in total.
39. ______________ Management is the knowledge area where you figure out who's talking to who, and how.
41. The _____________ process group is where you make sure the project starts out right.
42. In the Manage _______________ process, you manage all communication with the people who are affected by your project.
45. ______________ Management is the knowledge area where you plan for the unknown.
49. In the ______________ Management knowledge area, you make sure your deliverables conform to their requirements.
52. The ______________ Management knowledge area is all about figuring out your budget.
54. ______________ Management is the knowledge area in which you figure out the work that needs to be done for the project.

These questions are all about specific things that you're likely to see on the exam. They're drawn from many different knowledge areas. Take some time and try to answer all of them—remember, these are a little harder than questions you'll see on the exam, since they're not multiple choice!

1. What's it called when you bring your stakeholders together at the beginning of the project in order to figure out how everyone will communicate throughout the project?

2. What do you call the point in a fixed-price contract where the seller assumes the rest of the cost?

3. Which conflict resolution technique is most effective?

4. What's the range for a Rough Order of Magnitude estimate?

5. Which contract type is best when you don't know the scope of the work?

6. What are you doing when you add resources to the critical path in order to shorten the schedule?

7. Which management theory states that employees can't be trusted and need to be constantly monitored?

8. What are the top three causes of conflict on projects?

9. Customer satisfaction is part of which knowledge area?

10. Which type of power is typically unavailable to project managers in a matrixed organization?

Answers on page 643.

11. Which form of communication is *always* necessary whenever you are performing Procurement processes?

12. What's it called when you add up the costs of inspection, test planning, testing, rework (to repair defects discovered), and retesting?

13. What are the three characteristics of a project that differentiate it from a process?

14. Where would you find out details about a specific work package, such as an initial estimate or information about what account it should be billed against?

15. What do you do when you and your team can't identify a useful response to a risk that you've identified?

16. What do you decompose work packages into before you can build your schedule?

17. What's the float for any activity on the critical path?

18. What percentage of a project manager's time is spent communicating?

19. What should you do with the factors that cause change?

20. Which two types of estimate require historical information?

You'll definitely get a bunch of calculation questions on the exam. Luckily, you've got a handle on them! Here's your chance to get a little more practice.

1. How many lines of communication are there on a project with nine people (including the project manager)?

2. Your project has a budget at completion of $250,000. You've completed half of the work, but your schedule says you should have completed 60% of the work. Calculate PV and EV.

3. Your project has a BAC of $7,500. Your scheduled % complete is 35%, but your actual % complete is 30%. Calculate the SPI. What does that SPI tell you about your project?

4. You were managing a project with a team of eight people, plus you (as the project manager), when you added an additional four team members. How many additional lines of communication were added?

5. You've got a project with a budget of $500,000. Your project is 75% complete, and you have spent $400,000 so far. Calculate the EAC and ETC. What does that tell you about the project?

6. You've identified two risks and an opportunity for your project. Risk A has a probability of 35% and a cost of $500. Risk B has a probability of 60% and a cost of $750. Opportunity C has a probability of 10% and a value of $1,000. What's the total EMV of Risk A, Risk B, and Opportunity C?

7. Your project has a CPI of 1.2 and an EV of $150,000. Calculate the actual cost of the project so far.

Answers on page 644.

Great job! It looks like you're almost ready

If you've read all the chapters, done all the exercises and taken all of the practice questions, then you have a solid grasp on the material for the PMP exam. You're *almost ready* to get certified! By the way, don't worry if you didn't get some of the questions on the past few pages. This was really hard stuff—some of it was even harder than the PMP exam. Remember, a great way to prepare is to write your own Question Clinic–style questions for anything that's giving you trouble.

So if you did get them, you should feel very proud of yourself!

Here are some final tips to help you on the day of the exam.

1. ***Make sure to get a good night's sleep before you take the PMP exam. And make sure you eat something!*** It can take up to **four hours** to complete the exam. That's longer than you expect, and you don't get a snack break.

2. The first thing you see when you sit down to take the computerized version is a fifteen minute tutorial on how to use the software. You won't need much time to go through it, because the software is very intuitive. ***Use this time to relax.***

3. ***Seriously. Relax. Everyone taking the exam gets jittery.*** A good thing to do is look at the fifteen minute countdown timer for the tutorial and breathe. Take a whole minute and use it to breathe. If your heart is still pounding, take another minute. You'll be glad you did.

4. ***Don't click away from that tutorial yet!*** You'll get some sheets of scratch paper to use. Write down **every** formula **before** you click the button to start the exam. That way they'll be there for the questions that need them—and you won't be nervous about forgetting them.

5. The exam software lets you mark a question for review. ***If you're at all unsure of a question, mark it.*** Sometimes a later question will help trigger your memory, so when you come back to it, the answer will suddenly "come" to you. This really works!

6. ***Don't get too stuck on a question*** as you're going through—better to take your best guess, mark it for review, and move on. You can go back to it as many times as you need.

Pretty soon, this will be YOU!

Finish up your PMP exam preparation by visiting the Head First PMP website:
http://www.headfirstlabs.com/PMP
You can find more practice questions, and join the Head First PMP community.

Process Magnets Solutions

Can you put all of the processes in the right knowledge areas?
Give it a shot—and while you're at it, see if you can put them inside each knowledge area in the order that they're typically performed on a project.

Integration

1. Develop Project Charter
2. Develop Project Management Plan
3. Develop Preliminary Project Scope Statement
4. Direct and Manage Project Execution
5. Monitor and Control Project Work
6. Integrated Change Control
7. Close Project

Scope

1. Scope Planning
2. Scope Definition
3. Create WBS
4. Scope Control
5. Scope Verification

Time

1. Activity Definition
2. Activity Sequencing
3. Activity Resource Estimating
4. Activity Duration Estimating
5. Schedule Development
6. Schedule Control

Cost

1. Cost Estimating
2. Cost Budgeting
3. Cost Control

Quality

1. Quality Planning
2. Perform Quality Control
3. Perform Quality Assurance

Human Resources	Communications	Risk	Procurement
1 Human Resource Planning	1 Communications Planning	1 Risk Management Planning	1 Plan Purchases and Acquisitions
2 Acquire Project Team	2 Information Distribution	2 Risk Identification	2 Plan Contracting
3 Develop Project Team	3 Performance Reporting	3 Qualitative Risk Analysis	3 Request Seller Responses
4 Manage Project Team	4 Manage Stakeholders	4 Quantitative Risk Analysis	4 Select Sellers
		5 Risk Response Planning	5 Contract Administration
		6 Risk Monitoring and Control	6 Contract Closure

Processcross Solutions

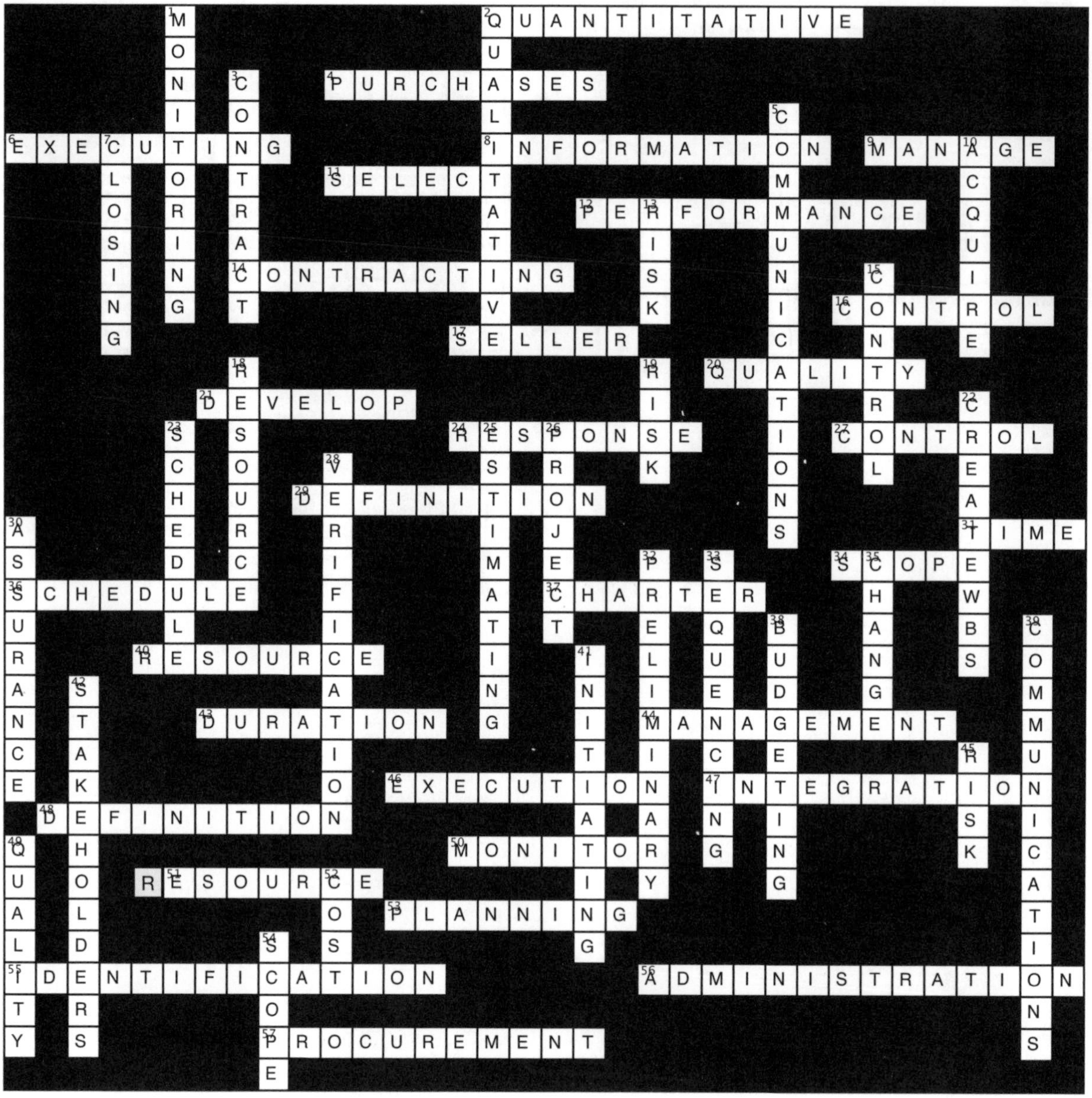

1 MONITORING
2 QUANTITATIVE / QUALITATIVE
3 CONTRACT
4 PURCHASES
5 COMMUNICATIONS
6 EXECUTING
7 CLOSING
8 INFORMATION
9 MANAGE
10 ACQUIRE
11 SELECT
12 PERFORMANCE
13 RISK
14 CONTRACTING
15 CONTROL
16 CONTROL
17 SELLER
18 RESOURCE
19 RISK
20 QUALITY
21 DEVELOP
22 CREATEWBS
23 SCHEDULE
24 RESPONSE
25 ESTIMATING
26 PROJECT
27 CONTROL
28 VERIFICATION
29 DEFINITION
30 ASSURANCE
31 TIME
32 PRELIMINARY
33 SEQUENCING
34 SCOPE
35 CHANGE
36 SCHEDULE
37 CHARTER
38 BUDGETING
39 COMMUNICATIONS
40 RESOURCE
41 INITIATING
42 STAKEHOLDERS
43 DURATION
44 MANAGEMENT
45 RISK
46 EXECUTION
47 INTEGRATION
48 DEFINITION
49 QUALITY
50 MONITOR
51 RESOURCE
52 COST
53 PLANNING
54 SCOPE
55 IDENTIFICATION
56 ADMINISTRATION
57 PROCUREMENT

These questions are all about specific things that you're likely to see on the exam. They're drawn from many different knowledge areas. Take some time and try to answer all of them—remember, these are a little harder than questions you'll see on the exam, since they're not multiple choice!

1. What's it called when you bring your stakeholders together at the beginning of the project in order to figure out how everyone will communicate throughout the project?

   kickoff meeting

2. What do you call the point in a fixed-price contract where the seller assumes the rest of the cost?

   point of total assumption

3. Which conflict resolution technique is most effective?

   problem-solving or confronting

4. What's the range for a Rough Order of Magnitude estimate?

   -50% to +100% (or half to double)

5. Which contract type is best when you don't know the scope of the work?

   time & materials

6. What are you doing when you add resources to the critical path in order to shorten the schedule?

   crashing the schedule

7. Which management theory states that employees can't be trusted and need to be constantly monitored?

   McGregor's Theory X

8. What are the top three causes of conflict on projects?

   resources, priorities, and schedules

9. Customer satisfaction is part of which knowledge area?

   quality management

10. Which type of power is typically unavailable to project managers in a matrixed organization?

    legitimate power

11. Which form of communication is *always* necessary whenever you are performing Procurement processes?

    formal written

12. What's it called when you add up the costs of inspection, test planning, testing, rework (to repair defects discovered), and retesting?

    cost of quality

13. What are the three characteristics of a project that differentiate it from a process?

    temporary, unique, and progressively elaborated

14. Where would you find out details about a specific work package, such as an initial estimate or information about what account it should be billed against?

    WBS dictionary

15. What do you do when you and your team can't identify a useful response to a risk that you've identified?

    accept it

16. What do you decompose work packages into before you can build your schedule?

    activities

17. What's the float for any activity on the critical path?

    zero

18. What percentage of a project manager's time is spent communicating?

    90%

19. What should you do with the factors that cause change?

    try to influence them

20. Which two types of estimate require historical information?

    analogous and parametric

You'll definitely get a bunch of calculation questions on the exam. Luckily, you've got a handle on them! Here's your chance to get a little more practice.

1. How many lines of communication are there on a project with nine people (including the project manager)?

   The formula for # lines of communication is: # lines = n x (n – 1) ÷ 2

   So # lines = 9 x (9 – 1) ÷ 2 = 9 x 8 ÷ 2 = 36 lines of communication

2. Your project has a budget at completion of $250,000. You've completed half of the work, but your schedule says you should have completed 60% of the work. Calculate PV and EV.

   The formulas are: PV = BAC x Scheduled % Complete EV = BAC x Actual % Complete

   So the answers are: PV = $250,000 x 60% = $150,000 EV = $250,000 x 50% = $125,000

3. Your project has a BAC of $7,500. Your scheduled % complete is 35%, but your actual % complete is 30%. Calculate the SPI. What does that SPI tell you about your project?

   The formula is: SPI = EV ÷ PV. So first calculate EV and PV: EV = $7,500 x 30% = $2,250
   PV = $7,500 x 35% = $2,265

   Now calculate SPI: SPI = $2,250 ÷ $2,265 = .86 Since SPI is lower than 1, your project is behind schedule.

4. You're managing a project with a team of eight people, plus you (as the project manager), when you added an additional four team members. How many additional lines of communication were added?

   We already figured out the team of 9 people in question 1—you have 36 lines of communication. The new team has four more team members, or a total of 13, So # lines = 13 x (13 – 1) ÷ 2 = 13 x 12 ÷ 2 = 78 lines
   So the number of lines added are 78 lines – 36 lines = 42 lines of communication

5. You've got a project with a budget of $500,000. Your project is 75% complete, and you have spent $400,000 so far. Calculate the EAC and ETC. What does that tell you about the project?

   The formulas are: EV = BAC x % complete CPI = EV ÷ AC EAC = BAC ÷ CPI and ETC = EAC – AC
   First calculate EV = $500,000 x 75% = $375,000 then calculate CPI = $375,000 ÷ $400,000 = .94

   Now you can calculate EAC = $500,000 ÷ .94 = $531,915 and ETC = $531,915 – $400,000 = $131,915
   This means that you should expect to spend about $131,915 before the project ends.

6. You've identified two risks and an opportunity for your project. Risk A has a probability of 35% and a cost of $500. Risk B has a probability of 60% and a cost of $750. Opportunity C has a probability of 10% and a value of $1,000. What's the total EMV of Risk A, Risk B, and Opportunity C?

   To calculate EMV, add up the individual probabilities multiplied by costs (negative) or values (positive).

   EMV = .35 x –$500 + .60 x –$750 + .10 x $1,000 = –$525

7. Your project has a CPI of 1.2 and an EV of $150,000. Calculate the actual cost of the project so far.

   The formula is: CPI = EV ÷ AC. First fill in what we know: 1.2 = $150,000 ÷ AC

   Now flip it around: AC = $150,000 ÷ 1.2 = $125,000

The End.

Index

Numbers

44 PMBOK Guide processes 48–50, 49, 50

80/20 rule 384, 394, 411, 415

A

AC (see actual cost)

acquire project team process 421, 427–430, 455–457, 632, 641

acquisition 428

active listening 474, 492, 501, 504

activity-on-arrow (AOA) (see arrow diagramming method)

activity-on-node (see precedence diagramming method)

activity attributes 223–225, 225, 231, 235, 238–245, 271, 276, 287

  updates 233, 271

activity cost estimates 309–311

activity definition process 215–216, 219, 235, 245–246, 256, 291, 294, 633, 640

  outputs 223

activity duration estimating 215, 216, 238–242, 245, 256, 283, 291, 294–296, 298, 632, 640

activity estimating 316

activity list 216, 219, 223, 225, 235, 238–240, 244–246, 276, 287

  updates 233

activity resource estimating process 215, 216, 236, 238, 245, 291, 294, 633, 640

activity sequencing 215–216, 225, 245–246, 256, 265, 289, 291, 294, 633, 640

actual cost (AC) 307, 327, 329, 334–346, 336, 351, 352, 356–359, 362, 363

administrative closure 117

advertising 590, 608

alternatives analysis 236, 283

alternatives identification 157

Analogous Estimating 241, 305, 306, 643

AOA (see arrow diagramming method)

AON (see precedence diagramming method)

Approved Change Requests 102, 154, 165, 480, 487, 489

Approved Corrective Actions 487, 489

areas of responsibility 6–14

  neglected 13–14

arrow diagramming method (ADM) 227–233, 251, 265, 284, 286, 291

assumptions 84–93, 240, 309, 516–521, 577

Assumptions analysis 518, 519

audits 603, 613

authorization 80, 94

B

BAC (see budget at completion)

backward pass 259–265

balanced matrix organizations 24

bar chart 278, 384, 635

Benchmarking 376, 405, 410, 413

benchmarks 380

Benefit Cost Ratio (BCR) 308, 315, 317

benefit measurement models 82

best practices 7

Bidder Conferences 590

bottom-up estimating 236, 283, 305, 306

brainstorming 517, 519, 527, 558, 563

bribery 620

budget at completion (BAC) 324–352, 637, 644

budgets 23–28, 34–36, 38, 41
- building 311
- over 334

buffer 220, 241, 242, 290

buyer-conducted performance review 600, 602

C

calendar constraints 269

cash flow 315

cause and effect diagrams 383, 394

certification 16
- exams 15
- why get certified? 1–18

change control board (CCB) 107, 113, 115

change control process 110, 138, 544

change control system 101, 112–115, 131–136, 183, 186

change requests 108, 112–113, 128–136, 184, 189, 190, 201, 207, 223, 225, 233, 477, 478, 483

changes
- anatomy of 184

changing plans 107

checklist 22, 40, 518

checklist analysis 518

claim 15, 600, 616

Claims Administration 600, 602

clients (see customers)

Close Contract process 575

Close Project process 116, 117, 136, 633, 640

closing process group 571, 572, 575, 604

co-located teams 433

Code of Conduct URL 625

code of ethics (see PMP Code of Professional Conduct)

collective bargaining agreement 603

communications 10, 18, 55
- counting lines of 490–492

Communication Skills 472

Communications Management 97, 99, 461–506

Communications Management Plan 486, 488

Communications Planning process 466, 469, 632, 641

Communications Requirements Analysis 468, 470

Communications Technology 469, 471

communication types 478

comparative approach 82

Configuration Management System 183, 187, 188

conflict management 440, 636, 643
- common reasons 441
- compromising 442
- confronting 442
- forcing 443
- resolving conflicts 442–443
- smoothing 443
- withdrawal 443

conformance to requirements 368, 369, 408

constrained optimization 82

constraints 34–37, 84–86

contingency reserve 241, 290, 293, 295, 548, 552, 564

Contract Administration process 571, 572, 575, 599–602, 610, 613, 616, 633, 641

Contract Change Control System 600

Contract Closure process 571, 572, 604, 613, 633, 641

contracting 570, 578

Contract Management Plan 574, 575, 593, 599, 604

contract negotiations 573, 597, 603, 612

contracts 599, 603
- build separate plans for 586
- more about 585

contract statement of work (SOW) 577, 586–589, 609

contract types 577, 582, 636

Control Account 219

Control Charts 383, 387, 389

control limits 383, 387, 389

copyright issues 622

corrective action 104, 110, 137

cost 10, 12, 14, 18, 55
- constraints 36
- managing 34

cost-reimbursable contracts (see cost plus contracts)

cost aggregation 312

cost baseline 312, 320, 321, 354–359, 363

cost benefit analysis 376, 410

Cost Budgeting process 303, 310–315, 354, 632, 640

Cost change control system 321, 357, 358

Cost Control process 303, 318, 335, 633, 640

Cost Estimate Supporting Detail 309–311, 315

Cost Estimating 632, 640

Cost Estimation process 303, 304

cost management 97, 99, 111, 113, 299–364
- processes 303

Cost Management Plan updates 309

Cost of Quality 307, 377, 405, 643

Cost Performance Index (CPI) 334–363, 637, 644

cost plus contracts 577, 582

Cost Reporting Systems 481–483

costs plus fixed fee (CPFF) contract 582–584, 596

costs plus incentive fee (CPIF) contract 582–584, 596, 611–613

costs plus percentage of costs (CPPC) contract 582–584, 611–615

Cost Variance (CV) 334, 356

CPFF (see costs plus fixed fee contract)

CPI (see Cost Performance Index)

CPIF (see costs plus incentive fee contract)

CPPC (see costs plus percentage of cost contract)

crashing schedules 266, 273, 289, 294, 643

Create WBS process 149, 164, 174, 178, 633, 640
- outputs 178
- (see also Work Breakdown Structure (WBS))

Create WBS tool 169

Critical chain method 269, 273, 290, 295

critical path 636, 643

Critical Path method 249–251, 284
- critical path calculations 261–263
- finding critical path 250

Crosby, Philip 369

customers
- PMP exam 89
- unhappy 72
- unrealistic requests 2

customer satisfaction 369, 636

D

data points, out of control 383

Decision Tree Analysis 531, 534, 535, 537

decode 464, 478, 504

decomposition 168–170, 202, 219

defect density 378

defect repair 102, 108, 109

defect repair review 385

defects 103–105, 110, 128, 130, 133, 135

deliverables 73, 89, 93, 96, 102–107, 110, 116, 126, 131, 134
- decomposing 168
- inspecting 381
- inspecting every one 193
- matching requirements and project management plan 192
- validated 393
- work breakdown by 171

delivery dates, problems 2

Delphi technique 517, 519, 521, 560, 563

Deming, W. Edwards 398

dependencies 230

depreciation 308, 317, 355, 360

design of experiments 376, 405

Develop Preliminary Project Scope Statement 633, 640

Develop Preliminary Scope Statement Process 77, 91, 92, 94
(see also scope, preliminary statement)
develop Project Charter process 77, 80, 81, 84, 633, 640
(see also project charter)
Develop Project Management Plan process 96, 97, 632, 640
Develop Project Team process 421, 432–438, 455–457, 632, 641
diagramming techniques (see network diagram)
Direct and Manage Project Execution process 102–104, 633, 640
discretionary dependencies 230
documentation 623
documentation reviews 518, 519

E

EAC (see Estimate At Completion)
early start and early finish 257
Earned Value (EV) 321, 325, 327, 331, 335–351, 354, 356, 637, 644
calculating 328
formulas 346
sponsor's perspective 330
Earned Value Management 108, 356
Earned Value technique (EVT) 335
effective communication 474
effective listening 492
EMV (see expected monetary value)
encoding 464, 466, 478, 504
Enterprise Environmental Factors 80, 87, 91, 96, 101, 129, 137, 151, 218, 235, 238, 423, 424, 470
environmental awareness 624
Estimate at Completion (EAC) 340, 637, 644
Estimate to Complete (ETC) 341, 637, 644
ethics, code of 618–630
evaluation criteria 574, 587–589, 592, 609, 613, 616
executing process group 65, 427, 466, 571–575
Expectancy Theory 437, 438, 457, 460
expected monetary value (EMV) 531, 532–537, 554–555
calculating 532
Decision Tree Analysis 534
Expert Judgment 81, 92, 96, 108, 109, 119, 120, 138, 152, 157, 219, 236, 241, 283, 530, 577, 587, 592
Expert Power 434, 435, 450
External Dependencies 230

F

face-to-face communication 486, 488
fast tracking schedules 267, 273, 285, 289, 296
Feedback 465, 474, 475, 478, 492, 496, 500, 504
FF (see finish-to-finish (FF))
finish to finish (FF) 230
finish to start (FS) 230
fishbone diagram 383, 394, 409, 413
fitness to use 369, 408
Fixed Price (FP) contracts 577, 582, 582–584, 611–613
fixed price plus incentive fee (FPIF) contracts 582–584
float 252–254, 636, 643
finding 254
flowcharts 384, 409
force majeure 585, 611
forecasting 321, 340, 342, 352
forecasts 114, 115, 480, 483, 502
formal acceptance 192
formal acceptance documentation 116
formal verbal communication 472, 478
formal written communication 472, 473, 478, 497, 500, 503, 643
formulas 15
forward pass 259–265

functional managers 26

functional organizations 23, 26, 41
  versus projectized 26, 41

Funding Limit Reconciliation 313, 315

funding requirements 313, 319, 320

G

Gannt chart (see bar chart)

gold plating 181, 182

grade 370, 371, 394, 404
  versus quality 370, 371, 404

ground rules 432, 433

H

Herzberg's Motivation-Hygiene Theory 436, 452

histograms 384, 411

historical information 116, 137

Human Resource Management 97, 417–460

Human Resource Planning process 420–429, 432, 455–458, 633, 641

human resources 10, 18, 55

I

Implemented Change Request 102

implemented defect repair 104

independent estimates 592

informal verbal communication 472, 473, 478

informal written communication 472, 478

information distribution methods 476

information distribution process 466, 472, 474, 476, 480, 502, 503, 633, 641

information distribution tools 476

information gathering and retrieval systems 476

information gathering techniques 517

information presentation tools 481–483

information technology 600

inputs 51–54, 62, 116
  same on multiple processes 53

inspection 372–377, 382, 392, 394, 399–402, 406–413

inspections and audits 600, 602

Integrated Change Control process 75, 76, 79, 107, 107–109, 111, 123, 135, 149, 165, 184, 207, 632, 640

integration 10, 18, 55

integration management 69–138

interference 464, 466

internal rate of return 308, 317

interviewing 530

interviews 517

invitation for bid (IFB) 588

invitation for quote (IFQ) 588

Ishikawa diagram (see fishbone diagram)

issue logs 440, 487, 489

J

Juran, Joseph 369

Just in Time management 398, 403, 408, 412

K

Kaizen 398

kickoff meetings 486, 488, 492, 643

knowledge areas 10–15, 18, 43, 53, 55, 60
  matching to descriptions 56–59
  versus process groups 60

L

late start (LS) and late finish (LF) 258

leadership skills 427, 434

leads and lags 231, 248, 293
  adjusting 269

legitimate power 434, 435, 450

lessons learned 80, 87, 116, 117, 128, 131, 137, 476, 483, 502

LF (see late start and late finish)

Lifecycle Costing 308, 355, 360

LS (see late start and late finish)

M

maintenance 29, 32, 33, 38

management reserve 548

Manage Project Team process 440, 455–457, 460, 633, 641

Manage Stakeholders process 467, 487, 489, 633, 641

Mandatory Dependencies 230

Maslow's Hierarchy of Needs 436, 438, 452, 455–458

mathematical models 82, 83, 124

matrix organizations 24, 26, 636, 643

McGregor's Theory X and Theory Y 436

McLelland's Achievement Theory 437, 452

mean 383

medium 464, 465, 496

Microsoft Project 81, 98, 236, 250, 264, 278, 279

Milestone lists 223, 270

milestones, schedule 94

Modeling and distribution 531

Monitor and Control Project Work process 107–109, 135, 633, 640

Monitoring & Controlling process group 186, 467, 487, 489, 502, 571, 572, 599, 610

Monster.com 21

Monte Carlo Analysis 268, 273, 535

Motivation 432, 436, 452

murder boards 82

N

needs 46
- satisfying 12, 14

Negotiation 428

Net Present Value (NPV) 308, 315, 317

network diagram 216, 226–233, 246, 249–261, 265, 273, 284, 286, 289–292, 295–298, 518, 519
- forward pass and backward pass 259, 260

Networking 422

next-longest path 253

noise 464, 466, 485, 502, 505

nonverbal communication 474, 492

objectives, establishing 12, 14

OpenWorkbench 81

opportunity cost 308, 317, 354, 357, 359

optimistic estimate 241

organizational process assets 80, 87, 91, 96, 116, 119, 120, 137, 151, 154, 165, 169, 218, 235, 238, 244, 276, 423, 424, 470, 477, 483, 486, 487, 488, 489, 492, 500
- Risk Management Planning and 510

organizational theory 422

organizations, types of 24, 27, 28

out-of-control process 383

outputs 51–54, 62

P

paralingual communication 474, 492, 503

parametric estimation 241, 256, 305, 313, 354, 362, 643

Pareto charts 384, 394, 409, 411, 415

Payment system 600, 602

PDM (see precedence diagramming method)

performance
- measuring and reporting 277
- reports and forecasts 480, 483

performance appraisals 440

Performance Information Gathering and Compilation 481–483

performance measurement analysis 321, 335

Performance Reporting process 467, 479, 503, 600, 633, 641

performance reports 279, 319, 320, 480, 483

performance reviews 602, 603

Perform Quality Assurance process 372, 395, 396, 400–402, 407–415, 633, 640

Perform Quality Control process 372, 381, 392–396, 400–402, 407, 408, 411–415, 633, 640
- outputs 392
- planning outputs for 382
- versus Perform Quality Assurance 402

pessimistic estimate 241

phase (see project phase)

Plan-Do-Check-Act 398, 399, 406, 410

Plan Contracting process 571–574, 586–588, 612, 613, 616, 632, 641

Planned % Complete 325, 326, 333, 335, 348, 349

planned value (PV) 327–329, 331–335, 345, 348, 349–351, 353
- calculating 325

Planning Component 219

Planning Package 219

planning process group 97, 466, 571–574

Plan Purchases and Acquisitions process 571–576, 586, 587, 612, 615, 633, 641

PMBOK® Guide 4–15
- knowledge areas
- nine elements of 55

PMIS (see project management information system)

PMP-certified project manager 17, 619

PMP Code of Professional Conduct 617, 618–630, 625

point of total assumption 585, 611, 614, 643

policies at work, following 621

power, knowing what form to use 446

preassignment 428

precedence diagramming method (PDM) 226–228, 231, 233, 251, 255, 265, 284, 286, 291, 297

preliminary scope statement (see scope, preliminary statement)

preventative or corrective action 102

prevention of defects 372–379, 386, 388, 400, 405, 413
- versus inspection 373, 374

preventive action 114, 115

principles, sticking to 618

printing problems, typos 3

priorities, conflicts and 441

priority versus urgency 527

probability and impact matrix 523, 560

probability distribution 530

problems, correcting problems on projects 400–401

process analysis 396, 397

processes
- anatomy of 51
- breaking down 48
- combining 54
- partially managing 53
- same input on multiple 53
- within process groups 53, 60

processes versus projects 31, 42

process framework 43–68
- exam questions 64–67

process groups 7–11, 18, 43, 46, 55, 60, 65
- closing 47
- executing 47
- initiating 46
- initiating versus planning 60
- Integration Management and 78
- Monitoring and Controlling 47
- planning 46
- processes within 53, 60
- versus knowledge areas 60

Process Improvement Plan 379, 380, 396, 405

procurement 10, 18, 55, 88, 89, 97, 99

procurement audits 604

procurement documents 575, 588–590, 593, 609–616

Procurement Management 567–616
- processes 571, 574–575

procurement processes 636, 643

product analysis 156–158

product scope 145, 155, 158

professional responsibility 617–630

programming manager 27–29

progressive elaboration 478

progress reporting 278, 280, 287

project boundaries 93

project calendar 271, 279
  updates 271

project charter 74–78, 80, 84–92, 123, 128–132, 135, 136, 138, 151, 154, 167, 196
  necessity of 88

Project Closure Documents 116

project coordinators 26

project execution 75, 76, 79, 107, 123

project expeditors 21, 26
  versus project coordinator 26

project files 116

project funding requirements 319, 320

project integration management (see integration management)

projectized organizations 23, 24, 41
  versus functional 26, 41

project management, benefits of successful 61

project management information system (PMIS) 81, 92, 96, 102, 108, 109, 113, 116, 119, 120

Project Management Methodology 81, 92, 94, 96, 102, 108, 109

project management plan 69, 74–78, 97, 98, 101–105, 109, 112–118, 123, 126–131, 134–136, 304, 309, 311, 319, 320, 423, 424, 427, 466, 470, 487, 489
  updates 271

Project Management Plan Updates 379, 487, 489

project management software 236, 278, 279, 287, 305, 306, 321

project managers 26

Project Organization Charts 422–424

Project performance reviews 321, 358

project phase 170, 199, 527

projects
  closing 75
  defined 30
  figuring out how long it will take 238
  steps to follow 44–47
  versus processes 31, 42
  work, monitoring and directing 75, 76, 79, 89, 96, 104, 107, 123, 131, 134, 137, 138

project schedule 98, 130

project scope 145, 149, 153–156, 159, 161, 188, 194, 200–204

Project Scope Statement 158–161, 185, 191, 192, 218, 238–240, 470

project selection methods 81–84, 94, 124

published estimating data 236, 283

punishment power 435, 450

purchase order 588

PV (see planned value)

Q

Qualified Sellers List 574, 590, 592

qualitative risk analysis 514, 522–527, 561, 633, 641
  output 526
  versus quantitative risk analysis 528, 535

quality 10, 18, 55
  correcting problems on projects 400–401
  defined 368
  managing 34
  planning for 376–377
  seven basic tools of 383–386
  tracking cost of testing 380
  versus grade 370, 371, 404
  versus testing 367
  what is 366

quality assurance
  introduction to 396
  more ideas behind 398

Quality Audits 396, 397

Quality Baseline 379, 380, 405

quality baseline updates 393

quality control measurements 392, 396

Quality Control tools and techniques 396, 397

Quality Management 365–416
- three processes 372

quality management 97, 99

Quality Management Plan 104, 372, 378, 380, 405

quality metrics 379, 396

quality plan 377, 378, 405
- checklists 379, 380

quality planning 632, 640

Quality Planning process 372, 375, 380, 382, 396, 405, 408, 411

Quality Planning tools and techniques 396

quantitative risk analysis 515, 529–531, 552, 632, 641
- versus qualitative risk analysis 528

R

RACI matrix 425, 427

RBS (see risk breakdown structure)

realistic estimate 241

Receiver 465, 496

Recommended Corrective Actions 392, 396

Recommended Defect Repairs 392

Recommended Preventative Actions 392

Records Management System 600, 602, 604

referent power 435, 450

regulations 375, 513

replanning 183, 187

requested changes 223, 275, 393, 396, 477

request for proposals (RFP) 586

Request Seller Responses process 571–574, 590, 591, 608, 612, 613, 633, 641

requirements
- identifying 12, 14
- unstated 369

reserve analysis 241, 307, 315, 545, 552

Residual Risks 539

Resolved Issues 487, 489

resolving conflicts 636, 643

Resource Availability 235, 429, 433, 593

resource calendar 298

resource cost rates 307

resource histogram 426, 427, 455

resource leveling 269

Resource Requirements, updates 271

resources
- conflicts and 441
- estimating 235, 236
- problems 234

reward power 434, 435, 450

RFP (see request for proposals)

risk audits 546, 548

risk breakdown structure (RBS) 511–514, 518, 521, 557, 562

risk category 523

risk data quality assessment 523

Risk Identification 514–518, 537, 548, 557, 633, 641
- output 521

risk management 97, 99, 507–566

Risk Management Plan 511, 512, 516, 521, 522, 529, 538, 559

risk management planning process 510, 514, 632, 641

risk management processes 514–515

Risk Monitoring and Control process 543–546, 549, 550, 632, 641
- activities 547

risk planning 507–566
- processes 514, 516

risk probability and impact assessment 523

risk reassessment 545

risk register 516, 521, 522, 529, 538, 544, 549, 550, 559, 563
- adding risk responses 541
- updating 536

risk response planning process 515, 525, 538, 539, 633, 641

risks 10, 18, 55
- accepting 513
- anatomy of 514–515
- avoid 513, 519
- categorizing 512
- controlling 545
- dealing with 509
- defined 508
- examining 523
- mitigating 513
- opportunity 508
- ranking 522, 527
- residual 539
- responding to 538
- secondary 539
- strategies for positive risks 539
- transferring 513, 563
- where to look for 520

Risk urgency assessment 523

Roles and Responsibilities 422–425

rolling wave planning 220

root cause identification 517

Rough Order of Magnitude estimate 307, 360, 363, 636, 643

rule of seven 383, 387, 389, 394, 410, 414

Run charts 385, 409

S

Scatter charts 385, 394

schedule, constraints 36

Schedule Baseline 271, 272, 275, 276, 287

Schedule Change Control System 278, 287

Schedule Comparison Bar Charts 278

schedule compression 267, 285, 298

schedule control process 215, 217, 246, 275–280, 287, 633, 640
- tools 278

schedule development process 215, 217, 244–246, 279, 290, 291, 294, 295, 632, 640
- outputs 270

schedule management plan 99

schedule milestones 93, 99

Schedule Model 268, 276, 287

schedule model data 279

Schedule Performance Index (SPI) 278, 332–339, 345–355, 359–361

schedules
- conflicts and 441
- managing 34

Schedule Variance (SV) 278, 332–341, 346, 349–351, 354, 359, 378

scope 10, 12, 14, 18, 34, 55
- changes 181
- constraints 36
- creep 145, 181
- defining 154, 156
- management 139–210
- power of 148
- planning processes 147
- preliminary statement 74, 76, 90–93, 123, 128–131, 134, 137
- problem 145
- product (see product scope)
- project (see project scope)
- what is included 146

scope baseline 166, 167, 176–178, 183–187, 190, 199, 202, 204, 207

Scope Control process 149, 158, 183, 187, 187–190, 189, 190, 199–209, 202, 632, 640

Scope Definition process 149, 154, 156, 164, 199–203, 208, 632, 640

Scope Management Plan 147–155, 149, 152–154, 158–161, 176, 177, 178, 186, 191, 192, 194, 200, 204, 206, 207, 208
- updates 158

Scope Management process 97, 99, 149

Scope Planning process 149–156, 164, 170–173, 178, 183, 199, 202, 203, 208, 633, 640

scope statement 149, 151, 153, 154–161, 155, 158, 165, 178, 183–187, 191, 192, 196, 203–208

Scope Verification process 149, 190–194, 199–206, 633, 640

screening system 592, 597

secondary risks 539

Select Sellers process 571, 572, 575, 592–597, 607, 612, 613, 632, 641

seller
- sorting out potential 588
- staying on top of 600

Seller Rating System 592, 597

Sender 465, 496

sensitivity analysis 531, 552, 560

shortcuts 623

SOW (see statement of work)

sponsor 74, 84, 86, 88, 89, 104, 107, 115, 129, 130, 132

SS (see start to start)

staffing assignments 429, 433

Staffing Management Plan 99, 422–430, 433, 450, 458
- updating 429

stakeholder analysis 156

stakeholders 35–38, 63

start to start (SS) 230

statement of work (SOW) 80, 91, 96

Statistical sampling 385, 410, 414

status meetings 546, 548

status review meetings 481–483

storyboards 156

strategies for positive risks 539

strong matrix organizations 25

sub-projects 73

subsidiary plans 97–99

SWOT analysis 517

T

T&M (see time and materials contract)

team-building activities 433

Team Performance Assessment 438

teams
- co-located 433
- cost disagreements 441
- expert power 434
- figuring out who you need on your team 422
- getting team together 428
- ground rules 433
- leadership skills 434
- legitimate power 434
- motivating 436
- personalities 441
- punishment power 435
- recognition and rewards 433
- referent power 435
- reward power 434
- solving problems 440
- training 433

technical opinions and conflicts 441

technical performance measurement 546

templates 152, 154, 165, 169, 203, 207, 219

testing, tracking cost of 380

Three-Point Estimates 241

time 10, 12, 14, 18, 55

time and materials (T&M) contract 577, 582–584, 596, 611–613, 614, 616

time management 97, 211–298

time reporting systems 481–483

tips, exam 638

tools and techniques 51, 60, 62, 116

trend analysis 548

triple constraint 34, 34–36, 37

VAC (see variance at completion)

validated defect repair 393

validated deliverables 393

variance analysis 183, 187, 278, 287, 321

variance and trend analysis 545

variance at completion (VAC) 341

vendor bid analysis 307

virtual teams 428

watchlists 527, 537, 548, 562

WBS (see work breakdown structure)

WBS Dictionary 167, 174–178, 183–187, 191, 192, 199–208, 218

weak matrix organizations 24

weighting system 592, 597

work authorization system 87, 96, 101, 129–131, 135, 137

work breakdown structure (WBS) 149, 164–210, 218
- breaking down the work 166
- by deliverables 171, 173
- by project or phase 167, 170, 172
- Cows Gone Wild III project 182

work performance information 102, 103, 108, 119, 120, 137, 319, 320, 479, 480

wrapping objects. *See* Adapter Pattern, Decorator Pattern, Facade Pattern

written confirmation 192

Better than e-books

Buy *Head First PMP* and access the digital edition FREE on Safari for 45 days.

Go to www.oreilly.com/go/safarienabled
and type in coupon code QGRKIXA

Search
thousands of top tech books

Download
whole chapters

Cut and Paste
code examples

Find
answers fast

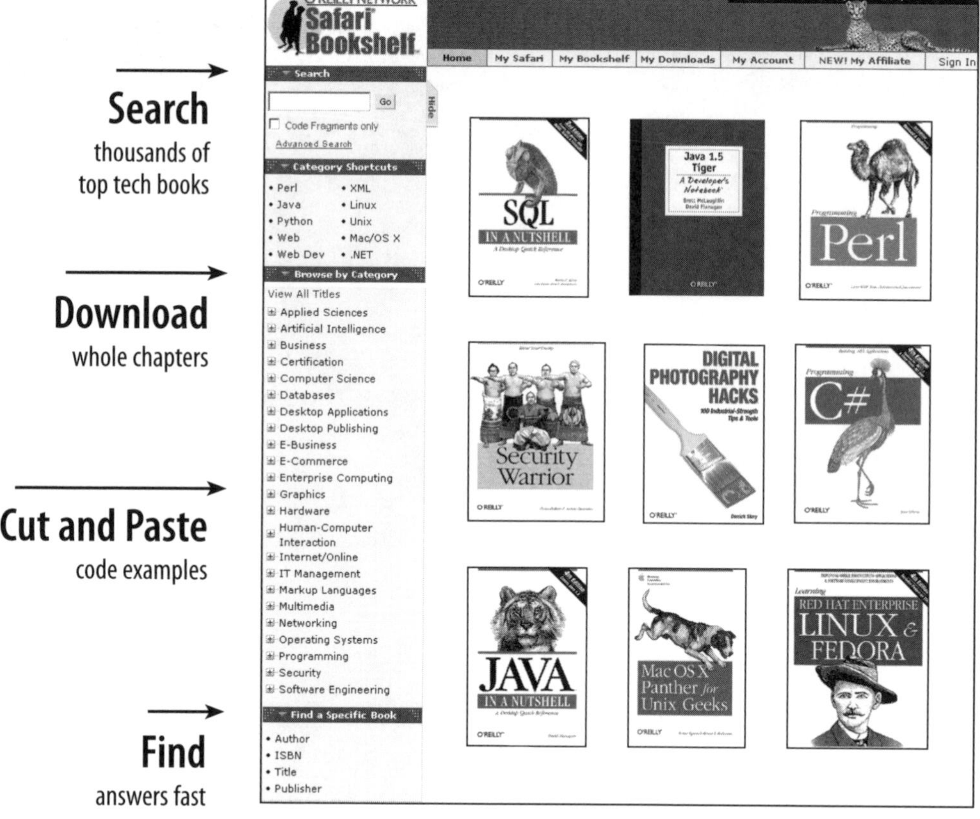

Search Safari! The premier electronic reference library for programmers and IT professionals.

PRENTICE HALL PTR

O'REILLY®

Related Titles from O'Reilly

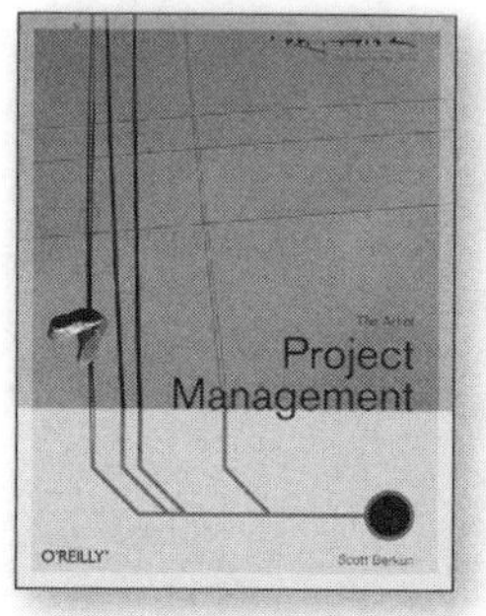

Software Development

Applied Software Project Management

Designing Interfaces

Essential Business Process Modeling

Enterprise Service Bus

Head First Design Patterns

Head First Design Patterns Poster

Head First Object-Oriented Analysis and Design

Head First PMP

Head First Software Development

Learning UML 2.0

Practical Development Environments

Prefactoring

Process Improvement Essentials

The Art of Project Management

UML 2.0 in a Nutshell

UML 2.0 Pocket Reference